PUBLICATIONS

OF THE

NAVY RECORDS SOCIETY

VOL. 147

THE MILNE PAPERS, VOLUME I

The Navy Records Society was established in 1893 for the purpose of printing unpublished manuscripts and rare works of naval interest. The Society is open to all who are interested in naval history, and any person wishing to become a member should apply to the Hon. Secretary, Department of War Studies, King's College London, Strand, London WC2R 3LS. The annual subscription is £30, which entitles the member to receive one free copy of each work issued by the Society in that year, and to buy earlier issues at much reduced prices.

Subscriptions and orders for back volumes should be sent to the Membership Secretary, 1 Avon Close, Petersfield, Hants GU31 4LG.

THE MILNE PAPERS

The papers of Admiral of the Fleet
Sir Alexander Milne, Bt., K.C.B.
(1806–1896)

VOLUME I

1820–1859

Edited by

JOHN BEELER
Professor of History, University of Alabama

PUBLISHED BY ASHGATE
FOR THE NAVY RECORDS SOCIETY
2004

Published by

Ashgate Publishing Limited
Gower House
Croft Road
Aldershot
Hants GU11 3HR
England

Ashgate Publishing Company
Suite 420
101 Cherry Street
Burlington, VT 05401-4405
USA

Ashgate website: http://www.ashgate.com

British Library Cataloguing in Publication Data

Milne, Alexander
The Milne papers : the papers of Admiral of the Fleet Sir Alexander Milne, Bt., K.C.B. (1806–1896)
Vol. 1: 1820–1859. – (Publications of the Navy Records Society ; no. 147)
1.Milne, Alexander – Archives 2.Great Britain. Royal Navy – History – 19th century – Sources 3. Admirals – Great Britain – Archives 4.Great Britain – History, Naval – 19th century – Sources 5. Great Britain – Military policy – Sources
I.Title II.Beeler, John F. (John Francis), 1956– III.Navy Records Society
359'.0092

Library of Congress Cataloging-in-Publication Data

Milne, Alexander, 1806–1896.
The Milne papers : the papers of Admiral of the Fleet Sir Alexander Milne, Bt., K.C.B. (1806–1896) / edited by John Beeler.
p. cm. – (Navy Records Society Publications ; v. 147) Includes bibliographical references and index.
ISBN 0-7546-5063-4 (v. 1 : alk. paper)
1. Milne, Alexander, 1806–1896. 2. Admirals – Great Britain – Biography – Sources. 3. Great Britain – History, Naval – 19th century – Sources. 4. Great Britain. Royal Navy – History – 19th century – Sources. I. Beeler, John. II. Title. III. Series: Publications of the Navy Records Society ; vol. 147.

DA70.A1 vol. 147
[DA88.1.M]
359'.0092–dc22

2003025119

ISBN 0 7546 5063 4

Printed on acid-free paper

Typeset in Times by Manton Typesetters, Louth, Lincolnshire, UK.
Printed and bound in Great Britain by MPG Books Ltd, Bodmin, Cornwall.

CONTENTS

INTRODUCTION

Not once during 60 years of naval service did Admiral of the Fleet Sir Alexander Milne, Bt., K.C.B. hear British guns fired in anger, yet, on the basis of talents and abilities ideally suited to the century of the *Pax Britannica*, he numbers among the greatest officers of the post-Napoleonic-era Royal Navy. Milne was the pre-eminent naval administrator in the Victorian period, perhaps of the years 1815–1900 – although both Sir Thomas Byam Martin[1] and Sir George Cockburn[2] compete for this distinction – serving as a Junior Lord for almost twelve straight years during the late 1840s and 1850s, as First Naval Lord from 1866 to 1868, and again from 1872 to 1876, when he retired from active service.[3] During his break from the Admiralty in the early 1860s he served in an equally critical capacity as Commander-in-Chief of the North America and West Indies Station, where he played a principal role in Anglo-American relations during the US Civil War.[4] Here too, Milne's administrative strengths, to say nothing of his diplomatic skills, were much needed. Later, between his stints as First Naval Lord, he commanded the Mediterranean Squadron (1869–70) and served on a committee appointed to help resolve the *Alabama* claims. Even following his retirement from the Navy, Milne's services remained in demand; Benjamin Disraeli's second Ministry appointed him to chair a Colonial Office Committee on Colonial Defence during the Eastern Crisis in 1878, and when that body was

[1]Sir Thomas Byam Martin, Kt., K.C.B., G.C.B. (1773–1854). Entered, 1785; Lt, 1790; Cmdr, 1793; Capt., 1793; Rear-Adm., 1811; Vice-Adm., 1819; Adm., 1830; Adm. of the Fleet, 1849; M.P., 1818–32; Deputy-Comptroller of the Navy, 1815–16; Comptroller of the Navy, 1816–31.

[2]Sir George Cockburn, Bt., K.C.B., C.C.B., F.R.S. (1772–1853). Entered, 1786; Lt, 1793; Cmdr, 1793; Capt., 1794; Rear-Adm., 1812; Vice-Adm., 1819; Adm., 1837; Adm. of the Fleet, 1851; M.P., 1818–32, 1841–47; Lord of the Admiralty, 1818–30; First Naval Lord, 1834–35, 1841–46.

[3]For Byam Martin, see the Navy Records Society vols. 12, 19, and 24, *Journals and Letters of Admiral of the Fleet Sir Thomas Byam Martin, 1773–1853*. For Cockburn, see Roger Morriss, *Cockburn and the British Navy in Transition: Admiral Sir George Cockburn 1772–1853* (Columbia, SC, 1997).

[4]For Milne's activities 1860–64, see Regis Courtmanche, *No Need of Glory* (Annapolis, MD, 1977).

replaced by Lord Carnarvon's Commission on Imperial Defence the following year, Milne was selected as its naval member. It may be said, with little exaggeration, that Milne played an important role in almost every step of the Navy's transformation from wood to iron and in the accompanying processes of devising a modern system of recruiting and training enlisted personnel and evolving a coherent strategy suitable for a steam-powered fleet.

Ironically, his name is almost unknown today, save perhaps as Sir Archibald Berkeley Milne's father. In an era when many senior officers felt no compunctions about inflicting their memoirs – usually of the 'sport and service' variety – on the public, Milne remained notably shy of publicity. Nor was he deemed worthy of that fixture of the Victorian literary landscape, the 'tombstone biography', although close contemporary Admiral Sir Astley Cooper Key's life and career received exemplary treatment at the hands of fellow-officer Sir Philip Colomb.[1] Other naval luminaries of the period have been memorialised in less scholarly (albeit more readable) fashion. Admiral Sir Geoffrey Phipps Hornby's attainments received unsurprisingly sympathetic and surprisingly candid coverage by his daughter; even ill-fated Vice-Admiral Sir George Tryon was the subject of a contemporary biography.[2] Yet when it came to Milne, Tryon's biographer – Rear-Admiral Charles Cooper Penrose Fitzgerald – had little to say beyond praising his tact and diplomacy while in command of the North American and West Indies Station: he was 'that able and hard-headed Scotchman', and that was that.[3] This neglect is all the more perplexing owing to the abundance of material from which a biography could be fashioned.

Milne was born into a naval family, albeit one of comparatively recent origin. His paternal grandfather, David Milne Esq., of Campie House, Musselburgh, was a silk merchant.[4] Alexander's father – also named David – established the family's service tradition.[5] The younger

[1]Philip Colomb, *Memoir of the Right Honble Sir Astley Cooper Key, G.C.B., D.C.L., F.R.S., etc.* (London, 1898).

[2]Mary Augusta Egerton, *Admiral of the Fleet Sir Geoffrey Phipps Hornby, G.C.B., A Biography* (Edinburgh, 1896); Charles Cooper Penrose Fitzgerald, *Life of Vice-Admiral Sir George Tryon, K.C.B.* (Edinburgh, 1897).

[3]Charles Cooper Penrose Fitzgerald, *Memories of the Sea* (London, 1913), p. 187.

[4]Milne's paternal great-grandfather was also named David, although he spelled the family name Mylne. His grandfather was born in 1735 and, in 1761, married Susan, daughter of Robert Vernor, Esq., of Musselburgh.

[5]A portrait of Sir David can be found facing p. 224 in vol. 6 of William Laird Clowes' *The Royal Navy* (London, 1901), or following p. 550 in the 1997 Chatham reprint edition. My thanks to Alan Pearsall for stressing to me the extent to which Lowland and Border Scots gentry were represented in the officer corps of the nineteenth century.

David Milne, also born and raised in Musselburgh, entered the Navy in 1779 and served throughout the French Revolutionary and Napoleonic Wars, during which he distinguished himself as a bold and enterprising frigate captain, capturing the French frigates *Seine* in June 1798 and *Vengeance* in August 1800.[1] Milne received his flag in June 1814, and was appointed two years later to command the North America and West Indies Squadron. He was, however, allowed to delay taking up his command in order to accompany Lord Exmouth's punitive expedition against the Dey of Algiers. During the Anglo-Dutch assault on the Dey's capital (27 August 1816), Milne's flagship, HMS *Impregnable*, was in the thick of the action, suffering 50 killed and 160 wounded, the heaviest casualties in the fleet. For his part in the attack Milne was awarded the K.C.B.

The Mediterranean campaign concluded, Sir David sailed for his new command in March 1817, reaching Bermuda in late April. He remained in American waters until June 1819, when he was relieved by Rear-Admiral Edward Griffith.[2] Despite promotion to Vice-Admiral (27 May 1825) and Admiral (23 November 1841), Milne saw no further active service until appointed to the Plymouth command in April 1842, a position for which he applied at the urging of his son Alexander.[3]

As was true of many of his contemporaries, Sir David Milne owed his success to the opportunities afforded by the prolonged contest with France and to his Tory sympathies and connections, as well as to his own combativeness.[4] He was both magistrate and Deputy-Lieutenant for the county of Berwickshire – where lay his family seat, Milne Graden[5] – and was, in 1820, elected M.P. for Berwick-upon-

[1]*Dictionary of National Biography* (reprint edn, London: Oxford University Press, 1967–68), vol. 13, pp. 453–4.

[2]Edward Griffith Colpoys (*né* Edward Griffith), K.C.B. (*c*.1766–1832). Entered, 1778; Lt, 1783; Cmdr, 1794; Capt., 1794; Rear-Adm., 1812; Vice-Adm., 1821.

[3]See below, Milne to David Milne, 1 and 6 December 1841 [**109**, **110**]. His second marriage offers an explanation for Sir David's not seeking employment during the 1820s. The Tories' fall from power in 1830 probably accounts for his lack of appointments during the subsequent decade.

[4]*Impregnable*'s heavy losses and damage – she was struck in the hull some 233 times during the engagement – suggest dogged determination rather than tactical subtlety.

[5]Sir David purchased Milne Graden in 1821. Prior to that date his seat had been Inveresk, in Musselburgh, where his son David (1805–90), and probably Alexander too, was born. Upon Sir David's death in 1845, David Milne the younger inherited Milne Graden: Alexander got Inveresk, which he shared with his stepmother until her death. Alexander's letters of May and June 1824 [**21**, **22**] and the reference in note 7 on p. 36 suggest that his father carried out extensive alterations to the Milne Graden property after its purchase. See Marjory Roy, 'David Milne-Home a Biographical Sketch', *The Edinburgh Geologist*, 34 (Spring 2000): http://www.edinburghgeolsoc.org/z_34_02.html

Tweed in the Tory interest, although he subsequently lost the seat on petition.[1]

Alexander, the second son of Sir David and his first wife, Grace, was in at least two vital respects very different from his father.[2] First, as his lengthy administrative career suggests, Alexander, rather than inheriting Sir David's fiery temperament, possessed in abundance both patience and discretion.[3] Second, and of equal importance for his career, the younger Milne was ideologically non-partisan. Thus, in political and professional worlds still dominated by patronage and connections, he was able to win appointment to command the brig/sloop HMS *Snake* from a Whig Admiralty in 1836 and, of even greater significance, be invited to join the Board in late 1847 by Whig First Lord Auckland (with whom Sir David also corresponded) despite his own lack of party antecedents. As can easily be discerned from letters in this collection, the latter appointment was at least in part dependent on patronage, but it was patronage based on Milne's perceived merit, rather than on his family or his political affiliations. As he himself remarked many years later, 'When I joined the Admiralty in December 1847, it was under the distinct understanding with Lord Russell, then Prime Minister, and Lord Auckland, the First Lord of the Admiralty, that I was to be entirely free from all political matters.'[4]

[1]William Richard O'Byrne, *A Naval Biographical Dictionary* (London, 1849), vol. 2, pp. 763–4; biographical sketch of Sir David Milne reprinted from the *Edinburgh Post and Record* (Scottish National Library Manuscripts collection, Acc. 7467, box 1, no. xxiii). The sketch also states that Sir David later stood for the Leith District of Edinburgh but was defeated. In a letter of 8 June 1827 to his brother David [**32**], Alexander referred to the 1826 General Election in a manner suggesting that Sir David stood and lost.

[2]Sir David Milne married twice; first (1804) to Grace, daughter of Sir Alexander Purves, and, in 1819, Agnes, daughter of George Stephen of Grenada. Grace Milne died of consumption in Bordeaux in 1814. David Milne the younger married Jean Foreman Home of Paxton House, Berwickshire in 1832. In 1852 Jean and David inherited the properties of Wedderburn, Billie, and Paxton from her father. At that point David altered his surname to Milne-Home.

[3]MLN/174: David Milne to Milne, 15 January 1843. A single letter from David Milne to Alexander has been preserved among the latter's papers in the National Maritime Museum, and from it a one can get a glimpse of Sir David's personality and devotion to the service. David's wife Jean invited Alexander to join them in Edinburgh while the latter was serving as Sir David's Flag Captain at Devonport (1842–45). When this idea was vetted with Sir David, however, he replied: 'It would no doubt be useful, and I may add very agreeable for me to be at home, to see how matters are proceeding at M. Graden. But that is out of the question, at present: – and I suspect I may have enough to do here in the Spring. As for Alex getting my leave of absence, I cannot have the least objection, if he has any proper object in view. But as to his going, in order to attend Balls, gaieties &c[,] as Jean wrote, that is entirely out of the question. He might be useful in Berwickshire, and see that the works there were going on in a proper manner. However this rests with himself.'

[4]MLN/145/5: 'Measures brought forward by Captain Milne when a Member of the Board of Admiralty, from December 1847,' nd.

His non-partisanship notwithstanding, Milne's early naval career owed much to the service's traditional means of advancement: family connections and patronage. His first berth, as a First-class Volunteer was, unsurprisingly, in HMS *Leander*, his father's flagship on the North America and West Indies Station. As Alexander's letters to his brother also reveal, Sir David was on good terms with important figures in the Tory political establishment, among them long-time First Lord Melville[1] – another lowland Scot – and Cockburn,[2] Tory M.P. for several constituencies 1818–46, Junior Lord of the Admiralty 1818–30 and 1834–35, and First Naval Lord 1841–46, and with several of Alexander's early captains, in particular Basil Hall[3] (see [**20**]).

The bare facts of Milne's career are as follows. He entered the Navy as a Volunteer aboard *Leander* on 8 February 1817. That vessel was paid off on 27 July 1819, and Milne did not join another ship until 30 June 1820, when he was appointed to HMS *Conway*, bound for the Brazil (South America) Station. *Conway* returned to England in 1823, and Milne was paid off on 24 March. The following day he joined HMS *Ramillies*, a harbour-service ship at Portsmouth which, among other things, housed midshipmen between sea-going berths. On 25 June 1823 he was transferred to HMS *Ganges*, which carried troops to Barbados that autumn. Milne contracted a tropical fever while in the Caribbean and was invalided home in March 1824. He spent several months at his father's estate before reporting to HMS *Albion* in July 1824, although he had been officially assigned to that vessel on 6 May. He remained on board *Albion* – another harbour ship – until 10 February the following year, when he returned to HMS *Ganges*, then serving as a port vessel, in which he was to remain until June 1827. Fortunately, in September 1826 *Ganges* was ordered to fit out as Flagship on the Brazil Station, thus sparing Milne from the tedium of harbour service. On 7 December 1825 he passed his examination for Lieutenant, but actual promotion had to wait until 27 June 1827, when Rear-Admiral Robert Waller Otway[4] appointed him Acting Lieutenant of HM Brig *Cadmus*. This promotion was confirmed by the Admiralty on 8 September 1827.

Milne remained with *Cadmus* until that vessel paid off on 7 May 1830, serving as Acting First Lieutenant from April 1828 onward. The

[1]Robert Saunders Dundas, second Viscount Melville (1771–1851). President of the Board of Control, 1807–12; First Lord of the Admiralty, 1812–27, 1828–30.

[2]Cockburn's father, Sir James Cockburn, owned estates at Ayton and Eyemouth in Berwickshire.

[3]Basil Hall, F.R.S. (1761–1844). Entered, 1802; Lt, 1808; Cmdr, 1814; Capt., 1817.

[4]Sir Robert Waller Otway, Bt., K.C.B., G.C.B. (1770–1846). Entered, 1784; Lt, 1793; Cmdr, 1795; Capt., 1795, Rear-Adm., 1814; Vice-Adm., 1830; Adm., 1841.

following November (25) he was promoted to Commander by Cockburn who bestowed a 'haul-down' promotion on his good friend Sir David's son.[1] Nonetheless, Milne spent the entire period from May 1830 to 26 December 1836 ashore on half-pay. On the latter date he was appointed to command HM Brig/Sloop *Snake*, fitting out at Sheerness for the North America and West Indies Station. Milne was in *Snake* for more than two years before being transferred to the frigate *Crocodile* as Acting Captain on 16 April 1839. His promotion to post rank was subsequently confirmed by the Admiralty, which backdated his commission to 30 January 1839. Milne remained with *Crocodile* until 30 October 1840, when he was assigned to another, larger, frigate, HMS *Cleopatra*. This appointment was temporary, however; he returned to *Crocodile* on 17 February 1841, for a final summer in American waters (his fifth consecutive) before finally returning to Plymouth in November, where the ship and crew were paid off on the 25th.

The following April Milne was appointed Flag Captain to his father, who had been selected Commander-in-Chief at Plymouth. Milne accordingly took command of HMS *Caledonia*, the 120-gun, three-decked Port Admiral's flagship. For the next three years Milne remained in *Caledonia*, usually in Hamoaze or Plymouth Sound. At times, however, she was ordered to sea: in September–October 1843 to cruise with the Channel Squadron; in November of that year to Cork, where she remained until the following January; from July through early October 1844 first to Tangier, then Lisbon; and, finally, in October and November 1844 in the Bay of Biscay. In the first instance Milne was temporarily placed under the orders of Admiral Sir Charles Rowley,[2] in the second, Rear-Admiral Sir William Bowles,[3] in the third, Vice-Admiral Sir Edward Owen,[4] and in the last, Bowles again. For the final six months of this commission, however, Milne and *Caledonia* were back at Plymouth, under Sir David's command, until both were paid off on 28 April 1845.

Milne remained ashore slightly more than a year after decommissioning *Caledonia*. In September 1846 Admiral Sir Charles Ogle[5] offered

[1]Cockburn to Sir David Milne, 25 November 1830, Scottish National Library Manuscripts collection, Acc. 7467, Box 1, no. ii.

[2]Sir Charles Rowley, Bt., G.C.H., G.C.B. (1770–1845). Entered, 1785; Lt, 1789; Cmdr, 1795; Capt., 1795; Rear-Adm., 1814; Vice-Adm., 1825; Adm., 1841.

[3]Sir William Bowles, C.B., K.C.B. (1780–1869). Entered, 1796; Lt, 1803; Cmdr, 1806; Capt., 1807; Rear-Adm., 1841; Vice-Adm., 1852; Adm., 1860; Adm. of the Fleet, 1869.

[4]Sir Edward William Campbell Rich Owen, K.C.B., G.C.H., G.C.B. (1771–1849). Entered *c.*1786; Lt, 1793; Cmdr, 1796; Capt., 1798; Rear-Adm., 1825; Vice-Adm. 1837; Adm., 1846, M.P., 1826–27.

[5]Sir Charles Ogle, Bt. (1775–1858). Entered, *c.*1786; Lt, 1793; Cmdr, 1794; Capt., 1796; Rear-Adm., 1816; Vice-Adm., 1830; Adm., 1841; Adm. of the Fleet, 1851.

him the Flag-Captaincy of HMS *St Vincent*, Port Admiral's Flagship at Portsmouth. Milne assumed command of *St Vincent* on 17 October, and remained with her until December the following year. On 17 May 1847, however, Ogle's flag was replaced by that of Rear-Admiral Sir Charles Napier,[1] and *St Vincent* dispatched to the Tagus.

Milne left Napier and *St Vincent* at Lisbon on 8 December 1847 and, upon reaching Portsmouth, was transferred to the books of HMS *Victory*, the Port Flagship. This assignment lasted only a few days, however; on 18 December he was appointed a Naval Lord of the Admiralty. There he was to remain for the next eleven and a half years, serving, successively, the Ministries of Lord John Russell[2] (Whig, 1846–52), Lord Derby[3] (Conservative, 1852), Lord Aberdeen[4] (Whig/Peelite coalition, 1852–55), Lord Palmerston[5] (Whig, 1855–58), and Lord Derby again (1858–59). In 1855 he was granted a Good Service Pension (GSP), on 20 January 1858 was promoted to Rear-Admiral, and on 20 December of that year was gazetted with the civil K.C.B. in recognition of his lengthy service at Whitehall, in particular his labours during the Russian War.

He left the Admiralty with the change of government on 27 June 1859, and applied that autumn for the North America and West Indies Command. His application was approved, he was given the temporary rank of Vice-Admiral, and in December he hoisted his flag on board HMS *Emerald*. Early the following year he made the voyage to Bermuda, arriving there in March. His term as Commander-in-Chief, due to end in 1863, was extended a year in consequence of his valuable services during the American Civil War, and on 25 February 1864 he received the military K.C.B., with dispensation to wear both orders.

Upon his return from the North American and West Indies Station in mid-1864, Milne spent over two years on half-pay, although he was

[1]Sir Charles Napier, C.B., K.C.B. (1786–1860). Entered, 1799; Lt, 1794; Cmdr, 1807; Capt., 1809; Rear-Adm., 1846; Vice-Adm., 1853; Adm., 1858; M.P., 1841–47, 1855–60.

[2]Lord John, First Earl Russell (1792–1878). Paymaster of the Forces, 1830–34; Home Secretary, 1835–39; Colonial Secretary, 1839–41; Foreign Secretary, 1852–55, 1859–65; Prime Minister, 1846–51, 1865–66.

[3]Edward George Geoffrey Smith Stanley, Fourteenth Earl of Derby (1799–1869). Undersecretary of Colonies, 1827–28; Chief Secretary for Ireland, 1830–33; Colonial Secretary, 1833–34, 1841–45; Prime Minister, 1852, 1858–59, 1866–68.

[4]George Gordon, Fourth Earl of Aberdeen (1784–1860). Chancellor of the Duchy of Lancaster, 1828; Foreign Secretary, 1828–30, 1841–46; Colonial Secretary, 1834–35; Prime Minister, 1852–55.

[5]Henry John Temple, Third Viscount Palmerston (1784–1865). Lord of the Admiralty, 1807–09; Secretary at War, 1809–28; Foreign Secretary, 1830–34, 1835–41, 1846–51; Home Secretary, 1852–55; Prime Minister, 1855–58, 1859–65.

promoted to Vice-Admiral during this interval (13 April 1865). In June 1866, Lord Derby, embarking on his third Premiership, invited Milne to return to the Admiralty as Senior Naval Lord, a post that he held for the next two years and five months, leaving office with the Conservatives in December 1868.

The following April the Liberals appointed Milne Commander-in-Chief of the Mediterranean Squadron, the most prestigious of the Navy's overseas commands. He served in that capacity to September 1870, also exercising command of the Channel Squadron during August and September 1870, when the two forces cruised in company. During his tenure as Commander-in-Chief, Mediterranean, Milne was promoted to full Admiral (1 April 1870). After relinquishing that command he was appointed to a committee charged with examining and responding to claims put forward by the United States Government for compensation owing to the depredations of the British-built commerce raider *Alabama*.

On 24 May 1871 Milne was awarded the G.C.B., and the following year the Liberals offered him another opportunity to serve as First Naval Lord. Milne accepted and spent the next four years at the Admiralty, again being retained by another Ministry, following the Conservative triumph in the General Election of 1874. Only in 1876 did he step down, having reached the mandatory retirement age of 70. In recognition of his six decades of service, he was created a Baronet upon his retirement (1 November).

Retirement or no, his services were still highly valued. For much of the rest of his life Milne was called upon to serve on committees and commissions. As late as 1887 he chaired a committee of Naval officers delegated to present a 'jubilee offering' to Queen Victoria as part of her Golden Jubilee celebration. As noted above, he also made vital contributions to two bodies investigating the state of Britain's Colonial and Imperial defences during the late 1870s and early 1880s.[1] Indeed, even prior to his retirement Milne had been an active participant in civic affairs, serving as one of the commissioners for the Great Exhibition (Crystal Palace) of 1851, and the subsequent 1867 Paris Exhibition.

Milne did not marry until 1850, to his first cousin, Euphemia Cochran.[2] The Milnes had four children, one of whom, Alexander David, died in September 1860, a few months shy of his ninth birthday. The remaining children were Archibald Berkeley (1855–1938), Margaret Agnes (b.

[1]For his activities as Chair of the Colonial Office Committee on Colonial Defence (1878–79) and the Carnarvon Commission on Imperial Defence (1879–82), see Donald M. Schurman, *Imperial Defence, 1868–1887*, ed. John Beeler (London, 2000).

[2]Euphemia's mother, Margaret Purves Cochran, was the sister of Alexander's mother.

1854), and Grace Alice. Archibald Berkeley, of course, followed his father's and grandfather's profession, rising to flag rank by the outbreak of World War I.

More detailed synopses of Milne's career and service activities will be found at the opening of each section of this collection.

***

This collection is drawn principally from two sources: the Milne Papers deposited in the National Maritime Museum at Greenwich, and the Admiralty Papers in the Public Record Office.[1] The former collection, although voluminous, is not comprehensive. Milne composed thousands of letters, memoranda, and reports during his lengthy career. Some of these have been systematically preserved in the form of official letter, log, and signal books, particularly from his service afloat. The survival of many others though, including his private correspondence and Admiralty memoranda, has been dependent more upon chance than intent. While Milne himself kept much of his correspondence and drafts of many of his papers, there are clear gaps amongst those housed in the National Maritime Museum. The situation with regard to the Admiralty's Secretariat papers – interdepartmental and intra-Board correspondence – is, especially for the 1840s and 1850s, similarly fragmentary, thanks to draconian 'weeding' of the ADM1 (Secretariat) files, the most pertinent for tracing the Board's activities. The documentary record, therefore, is not complete, although enough has survived in the two principal collections and other archives containing letters and papers by or related to Milne – the papers of Henry Pelham Fiennes Pelham-Clinton, fifth Duke of Newcastle-under-Lyme;[2] Sir Charles Wood, first Viscount Halifax;[3] Sir Charles Napier;[4] Sir William Fanshawe Martin;[5] Sir John Pakington, first Baron Hampton;[6] Sir Geoffrey Phipps Hornby;[7] William Ewart Gladstone;[8] Henry Molyneaux Herbert, fourth Earl of Carnarvon;[9] and Benjamin Disraeli, first Earl of Beaconsfield[10] – to compile a detailed picture of

[1]The Scottish National Library houses a large collection of Milne's personal and family papers.

[2]In the University of Nottingham Library.

[3]In the British Library's Manuscript Collection.

[4]In the British Library's Manuscript Collection.

[5]In the British Library's Manuscript Collection.

[6]In the Worcester Record Office.

[7]In the National Maritime Museum

[8]In the British Library's Manuscript Collection.

[9]In the Public Record Office.

[10]The Hughenden Papers, in the Bodleian Library, Oxford University.

many important aspects of peacetime service afloat during the early nineteenth century, and of the nature and workings of naval administration during a period of dramatic technological and social change.

PART I

SERVICE AFLOAT, 1817–30

Alexander Milne first went to sea in February 1817 as a First-class Volunteer on board HMS *Leander* (58 guns), Captain Edward Chetham,[1] flagship of his father, Rear-Admiral Sir David Milne. He spent slightly more than two years on the North America and West Indies Station, returning to England in late summer 1819. The only information surviving from the younger Milne's first cruise is the series of logbooks he was required to keep.[2]

The principal source of information regarding Milne's early service are letters from him to his elder brother David. What could be found of this correspondence was compiled by David's daughter Grace Milne Home in the early 1890s, after her father's death in 1890, and copied into four letter books, to which both she and Sir Alexander added annotation. Through these letters, one gets a vivid picture of life on foreign stations in peacetime, Milne's powers of observation and scientific curiosity, and the range of duties undertaken by the Royal Navy as *de facto* police of the seas.

One characteristic of these letters, and indeed all of his correspondence, both official and unofficial, is worthy of note, that being Milne's quaint grammar and oft-times unorthodox spelling. These traits were simultaneously the product of the early end of his formal schooling and of the period in which he grew up; grammatical standardization was, as of the Regency era, still on the horizon. Indeed, many of Milne's stylistic quirks remained to the end of his life: 'show' was almost always rendered as 'shew', and 'superintendent' as 'superintendant', for instance. He also appears never to have learned the rules for employing apostrophes, often failing to use them in contractions ('dont')

[1]Sir Edward Chetham Strode, C.B., K.C.B. (1775–1862). Entered, 1786; Lt, 1794; Cmdr, 1800; Capt., 1807; Rear-Adm., 1841; Vice-Adm., 1852; Adm., 1857. Chetham was First Lt to David Milne in HMS *La Seine*, 1798. He adopted the surname Strode in 1845.

[2]Unlike his later cruises, Milne evidently sent few letters home while on board *Leander*. The reasons, aside from his youth, are not far to seek. His father was a widower (indeed, he remarried while on the North America and West Indies Station), and Alexander's elder brother also accompanied his father overseas. See Roy, 'David Milne-Home', p. 1.

and for indicating the possessive, and frequently inserting them in inappropriate places ('your's truly' is a common example). By modern standards, too, his approach to upper- and lower-case was eccentric; nouns are often, although not consistently, capitalized, as are, owing to his penmanship, almost all words beginning with the letter 'e'. His punctuation – and that of many of those with whom he corresponded – is similarly erratic; for the sake of comprehensibility, the documents in this volume have had punctuation added in brackets: [,], [.], and so on.

In June 1820 Alexander was assigned to HMS *Conway*, a frigate of 26 guns, Captain Basil Hall,[1] which spent the following three years in South American waters. Alas, apart from the ubiquitous logbooks, we have only the handful of surviving letters to his brother recounting his activities. Four relate to his journey to Plymouth, where *Conway* was fitting out. He went first to London, accompanying his father [**1**, **2**], where the latter introduced Alexander to several political and society figures and showed him some of the more famous sights of the capital. Once on board the *Conway* his letters [**3**, **4**] convey the excitement and activity that accompanied putting to sea. *Conway* sailed for South America on 10 August 1820, touching at Tenerife en route [**6**]. Milne wrote his brother from Rio de Janeiro in October 1820 [**7**], after which *Conway* sailed for Valparaiso by way of Buenos Aires, arriving at the former port on 19 December 1820 and remaining there until 27 January 1821.[2] During this lengthy sojourn Milne was able to explore the countryside around Valparaiso [**8**]. Here his scientific curiosity was much in evidence; he collected mineral specimens and furnished his brother with descriptions of the fauna he observed while hunting or fishing.

From Valparaiso *Conway* sailed for Callao, at which she arrived on 5 February 1821, returning to the former place on 18 March, where she remained until 26 May [**9**].[3] Her next destination was Arica, just south of the modern-day boundary between Chile and Peru, which was reached on 7 June 1821. Three days later *Conway* headed north along the coast, to Ilo (12 June) and Mollendo (13 June), where she remained until the

[1]Hall was a noted author of scientific and travel works, and during *Conway*'s cruise carried out a series of pendulum observations, an account of which was subsequently published in *Philosophical Transactions* (1823, pp. 211–88). After his return to England he also published an account of the voyage, *Extracts from a Journal written on the Coasts of Chili, Peru, and Mexico in the years 1820–1821–2* (Edinburgh, 1824), which enjoyed considerable commercial success. See *Dictionary of National Biography* (*DNB*), vol. 8, pp. 942–3.

[2]Hall's *Extracts from a Journal* provides a narrative of *Conway*'s travels in the Pacific; a track chart of the ship's movements makes up the frontispiece. All citations of Hall's work in this volume refer to the third edition.

[3]See Hall, *Extracts from a Journal*, vol. 2, appendix 1, pp. 9–26.

20th, when Hall pointed her towards Callao. This cruise, which including witnessing a minor naval skirmish in the Peruvian War for Independence, is described by Milne in his letter to David of 6 September 1821 [**10**].

The next surviving letter was written more than a year later. During this interval *Conway* briefly visited Ancón, 20 miles up the coast from Callao (17 July 1821, also described in [**10**]) and, later, Huacho (2 August), before returning to Valparaiso (10 August). Hall next took his ship to Concepcion, 220 miles south of Valparaiso (1 October), returned to Valparaiso (26 October), and was sent again to Callao. On the way *Conway* stopped at Coquimbo (16 November) and Guasco (26 November), reaching Callao on 9 December and remaining there until the 17th. On the latter date she sailed for Guayaquil, in modern-day Ecuador, where she arrived on the 25th. On 30 December Hall pointed her toward the Galapagos Islands, arriving on 5 January 1822 and departing for Panama on the 16th. She anchored briefly in Panama Roads on 2 February before pushing on to Taboga (4 February), Acapulco (7 March), and, finally, San Blas,[1] Mexico (28 March), where more than half-a-million dollars was loaded aboard for transport to London.[2] While there Milne evidently contracted a tropical fever, described in a letter to his father not in this collection (see note 5 on p. 15). *Conway* left San Blas on 15 June, bound for Cape Horn, Rio de Janeiro, and ultimately England.[3]

Milne wrote again to David in late November 1822, by which time *Conway* had returned to Rio de Janeiro and was in preparation for the voyage to England. Milne himself was again taken ill with a serious tropical fever late in *Conway*'s commission, described in Hall's letter to Sir David Milne [**12**], and spent some time on shore convalescing before being assigned to HMS *Ramillies* (74 guns), Captain Edward Brace,[4] of the Home Squadron [**13**]. When *Ramillies* was sent to the dockyard for refitting (June 1823), Brace and his crew transferred to the hulk HMS *Ganges* in Portsmouth Harbour, where Milne joined her in August following a stretch ashore on leave [**14**]. In late August 1823, the *Ganges* was sent to the dockyard to fit out for sea and her crew temporarily transferred to another hulk [**15**]. In October orders were

[1]A small port near the regional capital of Tepic, in 21.33N latitude, 105.13W longitude.

[2]Brian Vale's *A Frigate of King George: Life and Duty on a British Man-of-War* (London, 2001) describes *Conway*'s specie-carrying voyage (p. 84), but mistakenly states that the treasure was loaded in Ecuador.

[3]Hall, *Extracts from a Journal*, vol. 2, appendix 1, pp. 27–57.

[4]Sir Edward Brace, C.B. (*c*.1770–1841). Entered 1781; Lt, 1792; Cmdr, 1797; Capt., 1800; Rear-Adm., 1830; Vice-Adm., 1838.

issued for the *Ganges* to proceed to sea, carrying troops for Barbados, where a slave uprising appeared imminent [**16–19**]. While in the tropics, Milne again fell seriously ill, and was invalided home in early 1824 [**20**; note 2 on p. 23].

He spent the spring and early summer of 1824 at his father's house, Milne Graden, in Berwickshire [**21–22**] before reporting to HMS *Albion* (84 guns), Captain Sir William Hoste[1] in July [**23**]. He remained on board her – confined to Portsmouth Harbour – until the following February [**24–26**]. After a brief leave of absence he rejoined the *Ganges*, (April 1825), now back from the West Indies, under the command of Captain Patrick Campbell.[2]

In December Milne took and passed an examination on board HMS *Victory* for Lieutenant and, the following month, took and passed another such examination at the Naval College [**26**, note 3 on p. 27], although actual promotion required action by a flag officer and confirmation by the Admiralty. Following these successes he was stricken with Scarlet Fever and spent some time ashore in the care of family friend, Dr Quarrier.[3]

In March 1826 he secured two months' leave, and when he rejoined the *Ganges* in May she was under the command of Captain Samuel Hood Inglefield[4] and bearing the flag of Rear-Admiral Robert Waller Otway – another friend of Sir David's – the newly appointed Commander-in-Chief of the Brazil Station. In August *Ganges* left England; Milne was to remain away from home for the next three years and nine months. He served in the *Ganges* until June 1827, during which the ship spent much time at Rio de Janeiro, where, among other things, he recorded his impression of the slave market [**28**] and at Montevideo, observing the conflict between Brazil and Argentina over what is now Uruguay [**29–32**].[5]

In late June 1827, Milne was promoted to Acting Lieutenant by Otway (subsequently confirmed by the Admiralty, 8 September 1827) and assigned to the Brig *Cadmus* (14 guns) [**33**], Captain Charles

[1]Sir William Hoste, Bart., K.C.B. (1780–1828). Entered, 1793; Lt, 1798; Cmdr, 1798; Capt., 1802.

[2]Sir Patrick Campbell, C.B., K.C.B. (1773–1841). Entered, *c.*1785; Lt, 1794; Cmdr, 1797; Capt., 1800; Rear-Adm., 1830; Vice-Adm., 1838.

[3]Dr Daniel Quarrier, originally from Musselburgh, Midlothian, later dwelt at Alverstoke, Hampshire. Quarrier was Surgeon aboard HMS *Leander*, when Sir David Milne's flagship on the North America and West Indies Station.

[4]Samuel Hood Inglefield, C.B. (1783–1848). Entered, 1791; Lt, 1798; Cmdr, 1802; Capt., 1807; Rear-Adm., 1841.

[5]For coverage of this conflict, see Brian Vale, *A War Betwixt Englishmen: Brazil versus Argentina in the River Plate, 1825–30* (London, 1995).

Gordon,[1] yet another acquaintance of Sir David Milne. For the next two years and eleven months Milne served on board *Cadmus* in South American waters, first under Gordon, and then Captain Sir Thomas Thompson,[2] with whom Milne had served in *Conway*. The brig's chief task was monitoring the situation between Brazil and Argentina, a duty that took her from Rio to Montevideo in July 1827 [**33**], suffering through a serious gale in passage. From Montevideo, *Cadmus* cruised down the Argentinean coast during the autumn of 1827 [**36**], running aground at the mouth of the Rio Negro, before returning to Rio de Janeiro in early 1828 [**36**]. In April 1828, Milne was promoted to Acting First Lieutenant [**36**], in which capacity he remained until *Cadmus* was paid off in May 1830. Early in 1830, Milne and his shipmates finally sailed for England, arriving at Portsmouth at the beginning of May [**42**]. Milne evidently suffered a return of the fever, perhaps malaria, he had contracted during one of his previous tours in South American waters, and spent several days recuperating at Dr Quarrier's [**43**] before meeting his father in London and waiting on First Lord Melville and Sir George Cockburn [**44**]. Finally, after four years away from home, Milne reached Berwickshire at the end of May 1830 [**45**]. He hoped that he would be back at sea in a few months' time. Instead, he was to remain ashore for the next six and a half years.

[1]Charles Gordon (*c*.1798–1849). Entered, 1810; Lt, 1818; Cmdr, 1826; Capt., 1828.

[2]Sir Thomas Raikes Trigge Thompson, Bt. (1804–65). Entered, 1818; Lt, 1825; Cmdr, 1828; Capt., 1837; Rear-Adm. (Res.) 1857; Vice-Adm. (Res.), 1863. Milne and Thompson were fellow midshipmen in *Conway*.

[1] *Milne to David Milne*

[London]
4 July 1820

My dear Brother

I have taken this opportunity of writing to you as Papa has gone to call for Lord Melville. Tell Lady Milne she might have come up with me in the Smack, as we met the *Ocean* and *Delight* at the mouth of the Thames[.] Papa took me to call for Capt Hall but he was not at home[.] We met Mr Steel[,] the Mayor of Berwick[,] who was going to call for Lord Ossulston[1]

July 10th

I received your kind letter this morning & was glad to hear you were all well. Papa took me on the 7th to Covent Garden, & on the 8th to see the Picture of the shipwreck of the *Medusa* French Frigate[2] and in the evening to Drury Lane Theatre. We always went at 9 o'clock and I got in [at] half price. Papa took me to see Richmond. It is a most beautiful place. All the people of London come up the river in the Steamboat in the morning and dine under the trees on the islands. We dined there yesterday. The people go down in the Steamboat in the evening. Papa & I dine with Sir James Cockburn[3] to morrow. I saw Major Cooper two days ago. Lord [?Lindsay][4] & James are coming home. We go down to Portsmouth on the 18th or thereabout.

July 16th

We go to Portsmouth to morrow. I have bought a tool chest for you, which Papa will take to you. The *Conway* is to be ready for sea on the 15th[.] Capt Elliot[5] goes out with us[.] Papa saw the King two days

[1]Charles Augustus Bennet, fifth Earl of Tankerville (1776–1859). At this date Bennet had not yet succeeded to the Earldom, and was thus given the courtesy title Lord Ossulston.

[2]Théodore Géricault's famed 'Raft of the Medusa', which had first been exhibited at the 1819 Paris Salon.

[3]Sir James Cockburn, Bt., G.C.H. (1770–1852). Cockburn, a Major General, was the elder brother of Sir David Milne's friend Sir George Cockburn. Sir James was Under-secretary of State in 1806, C-in-C of Curaçoa, 1807–11, and Governor of Bermuda in 1811.

[4]Probably James Lindsay, twenty-fourth Earl of Crawford and seventh Earl of Balcarres (1783–1869). As of 1820 Lindsay's father Alexander was still alive, and thus he would have been styled Lord Lindsay. He also had a young son named James. Alexander Lindsay, sixth Earl of Balcarres, was governor of Jamaica 1793–1801; Sir David Milne was stationed in the Caribbean from 1793 to 1796 and again from 1799 to 1802.

[5]Robert Elliot (1767–1854). Entered, 1781; Lt, 1793; Cmdr, 1801; Capt., 1808; Rear-Adm., 1846; Vice-Adm., 1853. See also below, note 2 on p. 11.

ago, riding in Hyde Park[.] Papa took me to Sadlers Wells last night. It was very pretty.

[2] *Milne to David Milne*

[Plymouth]
23 July 1820

My dear David

I received your letter of the 15th a few days ago. I have just been at church with Miss Meek, but we had a very bad Minister, who could not read one word. I have not been on board the *Conway* yet, but I am going to morrow & I have got my uniform[.] We dined with Dr. Quarrier yesterday & I had a ride on his pony[.] We dine with Admiral Walker[1] to day. he [*sic*] lives in the country. Capt Hall is going with us. The Duke of Gloucester[2] went away two days ago. I have not seen Dr Scott since I left the Smack. He was not very well on the voyage up. I am getting a great many books & among them a Spanish grammar & dictionary.

[3] *Milne to David Milne*

HMS *Conway*, Plymouth Sound
6 August 1820

My dear Brother

I have taken this opportunity of writing you[,] as all are asleep in their berths except myself, but I am very tired, for I had the middle watch last night and had only about two hours sleep[.] We sail on Tuesday the 8th if the wind is fair[.] I hope you have had a good trip to the Highlands. You must excuse me for my bad writing, as there is no place for writing here except upon chests & trunks[.] We are most dreadfully full of [?stores] and other things going out to South America[,] and all our berth is full of ropes & barrels. Give my love to all my friends and [*sic*: 'at'] Sinkfield & Inveresk . . .

[1]James Walker, C.B. (1764–1831). Entered, 1776; Lt, 1781; Cmdr, 1794; Capt., 1797; Rear-Adm., 1821. Walker was actually still a Captain in 1820.

[2]William Frederick, second Duke of Gloucester (1776–1834). William Frederick's father, William Henry, was the third son of Frederick Louis, Prince of Wales, the eldest son of George II.

[4] *Milne to David Milne*

HMS *Conway*, Plymouth Sound
10 August 1820

The Captain (Hall) has just come on board & we have made the signal for a pilot[.] We are now getting up the anchor & expect to be at Madeira next week & I shall write you all from there[.] I have begun navigation from the beginning of Norries' [*sic*] Navigation[1][.] I have been on duty for some time & had the middle watch last night, so have had no time to write[.] please tell Papa & Lady Milne with [*sic*] my love, & now I must go to my post in the Mizzen top. Adieu for the present my dear David[.]

[5] *Milne to David Milne*

HMS *Conway*, at sea
19 August 1820

My dear Brother

I am now writing you in case we fall in with any vessel, but I have had little time to write[.] We go to school at half past nine in the Morning & end at half past eleven & then we take to our Sextants[.] I have been made Aide de Camp to Mr Bentley[2] the Master & I work his sights, when I have the forenoon watch. There are two besides myself.[3] We go to school again at one o'clock & leave off at 3. I do not think we are going to Madeira, but will make the Island and pass it[.] Capt Hall teaches us navigation[,] and also Mr Bentley[,] who is very attentive to us[.] We have always very good dinner & have a very good cook, a black fellow. I am learning navigation & the way to work the Azimuth Compass. I had very little sleep last night[,] as I had the middle watch & we are all roused up at six o'clock now for not having had our hammocks up at half past seven[.] We muster our logs [*sic*] every Sunday at two o'clock. I am going to get a check jacket to wear below, as it is getting very warm. The thermometer stands at 72° in the shade & it is the same with the sea.

[1]John William Norie's *A Complete Epitome of Practical Navigation* (London, 1805, and many subsequent editions).

[2]F.P. Bentley, *Conway*'s Sailing Master.

[3]It is unclear whether Milne meant that there were two other midshipmen, two others on the forenoon watch, or two other aides-de-camp.

[**6**] *Milne to David Milne*

HMS *Conway*, Tenerife
24 August 1820

My dear Brother

I have not had an opportunity to writing more to you [*sic*], I have been to[o] much on duty with the boats. The Captain has been up at the very top of the Peaks of Tenerife, and Mr Robertson[1] whom I have this minute brought on board.[2] I am very tired because I have been away the whole day with the boats & it is now about 8 o'clock at night. I have taken a view of the Peak, which we have seen for the first time. we [*sic*] can scarcely ever see it for the clouds & high land. We have not been at Madeira[,] as the wind was foul we passed it. This is a most beautiful place altogether. It is curiously formed[.] All the hills are very high & are almost perpendicular[.] I asked leave to go on shore yesterday & Mr Darby[3] gave me leave, & I went with other two of the midshipmen [*sic*], and we got plenty of figs & grapes, pears & bananas. I managed to speak with the people very well[.] All of the midshipmen go to an Inn & Coffee house, & there they drink wine & most of them come off drunk, but I always take a boat & G—— who hates me & calls me all kinds of names is quite drunk to night. I believe we will sail to morrow at 8 A.M. The Captain is coming on board to morrow morning. He arrives from the Peak at daylight[.] I have no more time to write to you now, as we are going to supper & I have not a moment to spare, for they are making up the Letterbag. Tell Papa and Lady Milne I have not had time to write them[.] Give them my love & my Aunts & Cousins . . .

[1]William Robertson (*c.*1791–1861). Entered, 1803; Lt, 1810; Cmdr, 1827; Capt., 1837; Rear-Adm. (Ret.), 1857. One of *Conway*'s Lieutenants.

[2]Milne himself wrote on the back of this page: 'There is mentioned in these my original letters of 1820–26 a Captain Robert Elliot[;] he was a friend and companion of Captain Basil Hall and shared his Cabin. He was very kind to me and taught me navigation[.] He however left the ship (*Conway*) and returned to England. He settled at Tower Hill and he was the first man who estab[lishe]d Sailors Home[.] This must have been about the year 1824[.]' The *DNB* contains a brief entry for Elliot, describing him as a 'captain in the Royal Navy and topographical draughtsman' (*DNB* 6: 680). Elliot is mentioned in [**1**] and [**7**].

[3]Horatio D'E. Darby, *Conway*'s First Lt. In *A Frigate of King George*, Brian Vale claims that Darby 'deserted in Callao, guilt-ridden at the detection of his homosexuality' (p. 121), but fails to provide the source of this information. Darby's name vanished from the *Navy List* in mid-1823.

[7] *Milne to David Milne*

HMS *Conway*, Rio de Janeiro
1 October 1820

My dear Brother

I have taken this opportunity of writing you[,] as a packet sails for England to morrow [*sic*] morning. We have had a very pleasant time of it and have been all [*sic*] very happy. We found no English men of war lying here, but there are plenty of Spanish & Portuguese ships of war & also an American frigate called the *Constellation*[.] She is going exactly the same way as we are. Her Captain came on board to see this ship and instruments. The midshipman that was with him, as he was coming up the side, tumbled overboard and got a complete wetting. He came down and had some dinner with us. We arrived here yesterday afternoon. This is a most beautiful place. We were hailed from a fort called Santa Cruz as we sailed into the harbour, which is very large. I have not been on shore yet[.] Capt Hall has got a house on shore for an Observatory & has taken all of his instruments with him[.] He is going to get me introduced to some of the people, as I have got no letters to anybody. I have taken several views of this place, and I mean to take more. Capt Elliot has given me a few lessons. He caught a shark on our passage out, but a very small one. The people are always setting up [*sic*: off] rockets, they send up their prayers with them, because they think the rockets go to heaven.

We have got very good fruit here, viz. Oranges, bananas, Cocoanuts [*sic*], limes, guavas & other things & they have also very good cheese and bread[.] Capt Hall has made me Mate of the first watch, & Mr [?Beeston][1] officer of it[.] The midshipmen have been drawing Bills for twenty pounds but I have drawn nothing[.] I got two doubloons to pay the Mess Money, & two months advance, as we are going to lay in a stock of things to serve us round Cape Horn and back again[.] We expect the *Creole* every day & I expect a box from Papa by her. We are to sail in about a week or more[.] We are going to the River Plate & then to Cape Horn. There was a Lieutenant killed by the Spaniards belonging to one of the ships as he was out shooting [*sic*].

I must now close my letter, My [*sic*] dear brother, but I will write you again in a few days, as a packet is expected every day from England . . .

[1]A. Beeston was Second Lt of Marines.

[**8**] *Milne to David Milne*

HMS *Conway*, Valparaiso
3 January 1821

My dear Brother

I take the opportunity of writing to you by a [?Merchant] Brig, which I expect will sail in a few hours[.] We arrived here Dec 28th from Buenos Ayres [*sic*] & had a very good passage round the Horn.[1] We went a long way to the southard [*sic*] to lat 61 and long 82. I make the latitude every day at 12 o'clock & have to shew it to the first Lieutenant. I have got a drawing of Cape Horn & Christmas[.]

We expect to be here some time. It is a very pleasant place & very beautiful houses [*sic*][.] I have been on shore three or four times & have had a ride 15 or 16 Miles into the country, but it is very dangerous. There was a man stabbed two nights ago & he is now dead & the man who stabbed him is to be shot. I have collected a great number of minerals for you, which are very curious. I have numbered them all & put them into a box[.] There is very good shooting here[.] I mean to go out shooting some day soon, if I can get the gunner to give me some powder. I have not seen any humming birds as yet. There are plenty of fish & I caught about 4 dozen[.] There are plenty of seals. I fired at one yesterday with ball, but did not hit him[.] I mean to bring some seal skins home, they are very cheap here[.]

We can see the Andes from here very plainly sometimes . . .

[**9**] *Milne to David Milne*

HMS *Conway*, Valparaiso
20 May 1821

My dear Brother

I take the opportunity of writing you by the *Recovery*, a whaler, which has been on the coast of California for two years, but she has got no curiosities save Penguins nests which are very pretty[.] I have got four & also a cap made of them which is a regular fool's cap! I was up at [?Quintero][2] which is a great shooting place & I got the loan of a gun & shot three ducks which are very beautiful and heavy.

[1]See Hall, *Extracts from a Journal*, vol. 1, pp. 1–6, for his description of *Conway*'s voyage around the Horn.

[2]A village about 25 miles north of Valparaiso, the site of Lord Cochrane's estate while he was in Chilean service.

There are a number of swans there and flamingoes which are also very beautiful. I mean to bring one home if I can get one[.] The people at Quintero ensnared all the partridges here two days ago, they caught five & twenty in nets[.] The river of course is very beautiful and extensive & covered with ducks. There are also a number of [?Parrots]. I should like very much to have a double barrelled gun with the detonating powder,[1] which is [*sic*] very useful here[,] particularly for shooting penguins and [?doves] which are very plentiful[.] I have been living ashore with Capt Hall at the Observatory, as my name was the best in the list which went in to Capt Hall, at least I had done the most in the last week.

Mr. Bentley our Master is invalided & is going home in the *Recovery*. The Commodore[2] arrived here a few days ago from Callao[.] Lima has not fallen yet.[3] There is a great noise at Rio [de] Janeiro, where the *Superb* is obliged to guard the —— —— —— & another ship is detained. We are going to Panama in a week's time, where we are going to get a freight —— —— ——[4] to the river Plate & give our freight to the *Fairy*[,] when I expect to get a line from home.

[**10**] *Milne to David Milne*

HMS *Conway*, Valparaiso
6 September 1821

My dear Brother

I am now writing to you by the *Owen Glendower* frigate that has been out here for nearly three years. We expected to have gone round the Horn but the *Owen Glendower* has gone round instead of us & we will remain here for some time longer as we will be the only ship here. Sir Thomas Hardy is at present at Callao in the *Superb*[.] The *Creole* has gone in search of a brig that has taken an English whaler & killed all the men. When we sailed from Valparaiso in May we went to Arica

[1]Milne presumably meant percussion caps.

[2]Sir Thomas Masterman Hardy, Bt., K.C.B., G.C.B. (1769–1839). Entered, 1781, Lt, 1793; Cmdr, 1797; Capt., 1798; Rear-Adm., 1825; Vice-Adm., 1837; First Naval Lord, 1830–34. C-in-C, Brazil (South America) Station, 1819–23.

[3]That is, to the rebels struggling for independence. See Hall, *Extracts from a Journal*, vol. 1, pp. 56–85 for his account of the war.

[4]Probably a freight of specie, either from British merchants anxious to have it safely conveyed to English banks, or from native merchants and residents anxious to purchase English goods. See Hall, *Extracts from a Journal*, vol. 2, p. 275. Milne was evidently mistaken about the voyage itself; Hall records no such trip to Panama. *Conway* did, however, touch at several intermediate ports en route from Valparaiso to Lima between 24 May and 24 June 1821.

& then to Ylo[1] and from thence to Malindo.[2] We stayed there some days & when we arrived there was a loyalist Boat there with a Lieut and a party of men & also a good companion – a great gun & also several muskets – to lay wait for a brig that had been getting loaded with wheat for Lima. The *San Martin* came in there one day while the Brig was there. She cut her cables & made off but [*sic*] the *San Martin* could not catch her as she sailed much better, the brig being a French Man of war & the *San Martin* an old East Indiaman, & she had made a number of voyages to India. We sailed from Malindo when we had been there 2 or 3 days, & the day we sailed, when we were getting the buoy's anchor up, the *San Martin* came in & told us we must get out of the way, as she would have to fire on the town. It is a beautiful town indeed – only 3 or 4 straw huts! and [*sic*] as soon as the inhabitants saw the *San Martin* coming they took their mules & made the best of their way off to Arequipa, a large town about 40 miles from Malindo.[3] When we arrived at Callao, almost all the fleet were away. There was a new passage – called the Boqueron passage[,] between San Lorenzo and the Mainland, which seem once to have been joined. This passage is very narrow & we were the first English man of war, that ever went through, being a ship of science. We have surveyed the Bay & the passage & sounded all of the passage. When we used to come off in boats from Callao, there was a boom across the harbour & it was close to the shore, between which you had to pass[,] & when an English boat used to pass, they used to be pelted & some of the men were hurt.

I have got a few specimens for you & I am getting some furs for Lady Milne. I shall get as many as I can, but I think I will get them cheaper at Buenos Ayres.

From Callao we went down to Anson[4] where we stayed some time and exercised great guns at a mark. They fired beautifully & so did the Mids. Lieut Darby knocked the target all to pieces at the first shot[.] The target was tied to a boathook stuck up on shore. Give my love to all at home[,] my Aunts & Friends & particularly to Lady Louisa[.] I am writing to Lady Milne . . . [5]

[1]Ilo.

[2]Mollendo.

[3]See Hall, *Extracts from a Journal*, vol. 1, pp. 189–208, for his description of this voyage.

[4]Ancón. See ibid., p. 251.

[5]Grace Milne Home added: '(Note I can find no letter after this till Nov 1822 . . . The *Conway* had been cruizing about for a long time and there was no opportunity of sending letters home. There seems however to have been one to Sir David in May or June of 1822[.] After that his son was laid up with fever at San Blas).'

[**11**] *Milne to David Milne*

HMS *Conway*, Rio de Janeiro
22 November 1822

My dear Brother

I am writing to you for the last time, until we arrive in England[.] We sail from this place to morrow [*sic*] or [the] next day for Bahia from which place we sail for Spithead. I expect we will be home by the end of January. We have a large freight of about 30000 dollars.[1] Capt Hall is quite well. The *Louis*[2] frigate arrived here from Valparaiso a few days ago. We are all very busy getting money on board, but it will all be on board to day [*sic*]. I received the gun my father sent me, for which I am very much obliged, but I have only been out once.

Lieut Rawdon[3] has [been] invalided & sailed this morning for London[.] He was the greatest friend I had on board[.]

Give my love to all at home . . .

[**12**] *Hall to Sir David Milne*

HMS *Conway*, Spithead
20 February 1823

My dear Sir

Sandy has been very ill[,] poor fellow[,] but he is now out of danger & doing well[,] though still confined to bed & incapable of writing even to you[.] I shall consider immediately about [*sic*] the best way of having him taken care of, but I am not sure if he can bear removal. At all events, he shall have the benefit of the best advice. He has had a return of the febrile attack which he had at San Blas, and again at Rio di [*sic*] Janeiro. I had fondly hoped that a return to a cold climate would have effectually re-established his health, & so I trust it will be by & by, but my disappointment was great indeed, when about 10 days ago, when he was apparently in full health, & certainly in the finest spirits, he suddenly fell ill again with violent fever & for a day or so gave me great apprehension[.] As soon as I can[,] I shall

[1]This was an understatement, *Conway* having loaded more than half-a-million at San Blas in May. See Hall, *Extracts from a Journal*, vol. 2, p. 275.

[2]There was no vessel of this name in the Royal Navy in 1822. Perhaps Milne was referring to a French warship.

[3]Charles Wyndam Rawdon (*c.*1800–1865). Entered, 1812; Lt, 1821; Lt (Res.), 1851; Cmdr (Ret.), 1864. *Conway*'s entire complement of Lieutenants was changed in the summer of 1822; Rawdon was one of the new arrivals.

get a medical opinion for you & by tomorrow's post or perhaps by to day's [*sic*] I may have it in my power to tell you exactly how he is, & you may take your steps accordingly, but I think you will be disposed to come to us at once[.] Your presence would cheer him & you could be more certain that nothing was omitted, that could conduce to his re-establishment[.]

He has grown greatly & in every respect has given me the most entire satisfaction[.] His talents, his industry, his spirit, his temper & his professional knowledge are all just such as your fondest hopes could suggest[.] We have had a passage of seven weeks from Bahia & although I date this Spithead[,] we are now off Portland Light at 2 A.M. Sandy tells me he will write a word or two in this letter[.]

[Milne:] P.S. Excuse me for this short letter, as I am in so weak a state of health, but I hope in a few days time I may be able to write you a longer one[.]
Love to all at home . . . [1]

[**13**] *Milne to David Milne*

17 Bury Street, London
14 March 1823

My dear Brother

We arrived here last evening from Portsmouth. I was discharged from the Hospital on the 12th which I was glad to leave[,] as they kept me on rather low diet. I go down to Chatham to morrow morning. If Capt Hall does not get another ship, I am to be put on the *Ramillies* books, & get leave from Capt Brace, who commands her. I received your letter when we arrived at Portsmouth but it was so long, & I was so very ill that I could not manage to read it . . .

[PS:] Five feet 11!

[1]On the reverse of the page Grace Milne Home wrote: 'Sir David did join his son at once & remained with him at Haslar Hospital.'

[**14**] *Milne to David Milne*

HMS *Ganges*, Portsmouth
1 August 1823

My dear Brother

I joined the *Ganges* on Tuesday last & saw Capt Brace that morning as he was starting for the Isle of Wight to see a boat race & he has not been on board for some days [*sic*]. I had to keep the 6 to 8 watch the very afternoon I got on board[.] The King was expected down to day, but he has not yet arrived. Tell Papa there is a schoolmaster on board, whom I should wish to attend if he has no objections [–] Mr. Bradley – who teaches navigation[.] He was formerly Professor at the Naval College on shore[.] I have got about 28 messmates at present[.] We shift into another Hulk next week[.]

[**15**] *Milne to David Milne*

HMS *Ganges*, Portsmouth
25 August 1823

My dear Brother

I received your extremely long letter yesterday, by which I was glad to hear that I was to join the *Alacrity*,[1] for here you have hardly anything to do in your watch[.] I went to see her this morning. She is in dock undergoing a complete repair – at least her Decks &c. I went to the Hospital this morning to see one of my messmates who is dangerously ill. Indeed the Doctors say he never will recover[.] He had a boil on his cheek, which swelled his face so, that it affected the brain[.] He is the son of a Mr. Waldron, a Purser in the Navy. I have heard nothing about the [?*Bellette*] going to the Mediterranean but I believe the *Alacrity* goes there. Capt Brace is quite well & was on board this forenoon. I called on Capt Yorke[2] a few days ago but he was absent at Southampton Races [*sic*]. I suppose Papa will write to him soon because I am

[1]Presumably this information came from Sir David Milne; it was incorrect, as subsequent letters reveal.

[2]Charles Philip Yorke, fourth Earl of Hardwicke (1799–1873). Entered, 1813; Lt, 1818; Cmdr, 1823; Capt., 1825; Rear-Adm. (Ret.), 1854; Vice-Adm. (Ret.), 1858; Adm. (Ret.), 1863. Yorke was *Alacrity*'s Captain. Previously, he had served in HMS *Leander*, while Sir David Milne's Flagship on the North America and West Indies Station; indeed, the elder Milne appointed Yorke Acting Lieutenant in HMS *Phaëton* in August 1819, a promotion subsequently confirmed by the Admiralty. Yorke succeeded to the Earldom in 1834, and subsequently served as Postmaster General in Lord Derby's brief 1852 Ministry.

afraid the vacancy will be filled up. The *Revenge* sailed the day before yesterday, bearing the flag of Sir Harry Niel[1] [*sic*] for the Mediterranean[.] My messmates are most of them very good fellows. There are only 19 now, some having joined seagoing ships[.] I like the first lieutenant very much.[2] He is very strict & a very gentlemany man, indeed so are all the officers[.] We all mess in the gunroom, which is very large but not so neat & clean as the *Ganges*.[3] The *Ganges* is 50 tons larger than the *Victory* & draws 3 feet more water forward. Her bowsprit weighs 30 tons[.] I saw it this forenoon. I never saw such a spar before! The hulk that we are in at present lies at the King's Stairs at the Dockyard, so that we lie a long way from the Hard[.]

The *Ganges* has a round stern & a balcony at the Capt's windows where he can walk about. I can stand upright on all the decks, which I am afraid I will not be able to do on the *Alacrity*. I am sorry I shall not be able to keep you company when you go out shooting in Scotland for some years[,] which I am very sorry for [*sic*]. Of course you have hooked a great many salmon, grilse[4] & whittings [*sic*] since I left & of course got them[,] as you always said I frightened them off the hook[.] But I hope I shall be home before I leave England to see you all again & also have the pleasure of seeing the new house (Milne Graden)[.] Portsmouth will be very gay to morrow & [the] next day, for the regatta is to take place & between every race of the large vessels, one squadron of boats belonging to the ships in ordinary are to sail . . . I intended to have gone to Littlegreen[5] on Sunday, but it rained all day[.] Yesterday made up 40 days of rain – at least there has always been a shower within the 24 hours . . . I have taken your broad hint & must begin to make a close. Give my love to Papa & Lady Milne & all at Paxton.[6] I shall write you soon[.]

[1]Sir Harry Burrard Neale (*né* Harry Burrard), Bt., K.C.B., G.C.B., G.C.M.G. (1765–1840). Entered, 1778; Lt, 1787; Cmdr, 1790; Capt., 1793; Rear-Adm., 1810; Vice-Adm., 1814; Adm., 1830; M.P., 1790–1802, 1806–07, 1812–23, 1823–34.

[2]Edward Reeves Philip Mainwaring (1788–1865). Entered, 1799; Lt, 1807; Cmdr, 1841; Capt. (Ret.), 1854; Rear-Adm. (Ret.), 1862.

[3]This passage and the following two sentences are unclear. Evidently the *Ganges*' crew was transferred to another hulk temporarily, perhaps to enable the former ship to visit the dockyard[,] preparatory to her fitting out.

[4]Young salmon.

[5]Dr Quarrier's estate.

[6]Paxton was the estate of William Foreman Home, near Milne Graden in Berwickshire.

[**16**] *Milne to David Milne*

HMS *Ganges*, Portsmouth
26 October 1823

My dear Brother

Orders came down Friday morning to say, we were to get ready for sea as soon as possible[.] Accordingly we are making all haste & have got our main and lower deck guns in, & to day we got our topgallant masts up[.] Our other guns will come on board to morrow[.] We expect to take troops out to Demerara[,] as the black fellows have been kicking up a noise. We shall remain at Spithead for some time & I do not expect that we shall be away for more than six months at the furthest. We received men from *Queen Charlotte* & the *Albion* – in all about 200[,] & 200 of our own men, but we are to have a complement of 700. The *Superb* at Plymouth is also fitting for sea, I believe also to take troops out[.] I am not certain whether I am to go or not, as Lady Milne was rather frightened about me going to that place, but I should wish to go, as it would look rather odd my leaving the ship, as it were[,] for that[.][1]

The *Carnatic* was launched on Tuesday last, amidst an immense concourse of people[.] Capt Brace had a large party & I was picked out as one to take them on board the *Melville*[,] 74 guns – fitted up on purpose to see the Launch[.]

I hope I shall be home next year to spend Christmas & New Year, a thing I have not done for 4 years. I saw the old house at [?Faccham][2] a few days ago. I walked up to Mrs. Newman's [&] stayed two days. I wish you every success in your classes . . .
I shall write you again soon & let you know our destination[.]

[**17**] *Milne to David Milne*

HMS *Ganges*, Spithead
9 November 1823

My dear Brother

Excuse me, but I am in a great hurry; I must go on deck for it is my watch[.] We came out here Friday – towed by the *Comet*[,] Steampacket[,]

[1]On the reverse of the page, Milne himself added 'note The *Superb* and *Ganges* were to take a Regiment to Barbadoes[.] A Milne Feb 92.'

[2]Grace Milne Home added: '(where he & his brother had been with their Mother 1813)'.

belonging to [the] government[.] We have had 6 or 7 lighters constantly along side since we came here. It looks very like a war.

Nov: 10th [1823]
I must now write you a longer letter. I wrote to Sir David yesterday, we were to sail to morrow which now I am certain is to be the case. We hoisted Blue Peter this morning, the signal for sea[.] But I think this is rather dry mast [*sic*] for you, reading letters which contain nothing, but about one going to sea! I was much disappointed at my not being able to get home this winter for the shooting, & also to see you all again before I went abroad, but people[,] when they entre [*sic*] the service[,] must obey orders & go on whatever service they are sent on[,] & such as are not so [willing] are generally not looked upon for any thing. Our first Lieut[,] Mr Mainwaring[,] seems to have a great regard for me, as he sends for me generally when he wants any thing done[.] Capt Brace has paid me every attention, & I shall do everything in my power to retain it. I hope I shall be home in August or September, but fear you will be [away] from home. I wish you every success in your studies & in the prizes [*sic*][.] I shall certainly get what specimens I can for you & any other things[.] It looks very much like a war. The *Cambridge* 80 & *Albion* 74 guns are ordered for sea, with war complement of men[.] We have about 30 messmates at present[.] Two of our Mids are to join the *Antelope* & take her to Bermuda & from thence to Barbadoes [*sic*] & there they will join us again. I will write you another letter to morrow, if we do not sail to day.

[**18**] *Milne to David Milne*

HMS *Ganges*, off the Lizard
12 November 1823

My dear Brother

I am sorry I did not write to you again before we sailed, but I was too busy[.] We are all well & I hope may remain so[.] We sailed before noon yesterday & got aground twice[,] which detained us. The *Phaeton* was keen to speak [to] us[.] She is just home from the West Indies[.] I have written Sir David by the same opportunity[.] I hope you are all in good health. Good bye for the present[.] in great haste . . .

[19] *Milne to David Milne*

HMS *Ganges*, Gibraltar
27 November 1823

My dear Brother

We arrived here on the 24th & would have much sooner had we not had to wait for the *Superb*. We sail very well & run the *Superb* out of sight in about 4 hours with our topgallant sails & she with every sail she could set. I went on shore yesterday & went up to St Michael's cave, & also to the top of the Rock of Gibraltar. I collected a few specimens from the cave, which appears to be the same as those at Bermuda [*sic*]. If possible[,] I will get some specimens of the Rock made into different things, but everything is scarce. The streets are filthy dirty & also the inhabitants[.] The *Tribune* Frigate is lying here. There is a report that she goes out to Barbadoes [*sic*]. There is also a report about a French war,[1] which I hope will turn out true, as I think we will be able to give some of them a licking.

The *Superb* and we [*sic*] take in troops to morrow [*sic*] & I suppose will sail next day, if the wind is easterly, but not unless, as it is impossible to beat through the gut. We do not yet know where we are going when we get to Barbadoes [*sic*] but I suppose we will find orders there for us[.] There is some shooting here, but you have some distance to go for it. I must hereafter give you an account of the place[,] as I have now no room left[.] I will write you again by the next opportunity[.] I am very tired after my walk yesterday, & at the same time getting wet through[.] I shall not go on shore again while I am here[.] Give my love to all my friends in George's Square & to John Wilkie[.]

[20] *Milne to David Milne*

HMS *Ganges*, Carlisle Bay, Barbados
7 February 1824

My dear Brother

I write you again by a merchant ship which will sail to morrow. The packets arrived from England the other day – one having had a rather long passage & the other a short one[,] so they came in together. I expected to have received a letter at least by one of them, but alas there

[1]This rumour almost certainly related to France's intervention in the Spanish uprising of 1823. See *The Times* (London) 15 October 1823, p. 2; and 25 December 1823, p. 2.

was not even one! I wrote you by the last packet[1] but I must not occupy your time with nonsense[.] You have something else to attend to, which will in course of a month [*sic*] be drawing to a close & for my own part & that of my affected brother, I must wish you every success. We are anxiously looking out for the *Hussar* Frigate, which we expect will bring our orders. We do not know where we are to go or what we are to do, or anything else[.] Reports are constantly flying about[,] especially about our going to S. America[,] which I thought would be the case when we left Portsmouth[.] In the Navy List they have got us down at Jamaica[.]

I am tired of this place already, though the climate here is very good, this being the healthy season[.] I have got some lemon grass for you already dried & some seeds for Lady Milne[.]

Capt Brace is quite well, but I still would rather be in the *Conway* again with Capt Hall, to whom you must kindly remember me, when you see him[.]

I shall soon know when he gets a ship[,] as some of our Mids know the first Clerk of the Admiralty & he always sends out a list of promotions & appointments[.][2] I see by the Navy List that Col: Drinkwater's son is made Flag[.][3] Capt Hall will have the *Laurel* Frigate in the Spring & & [*sic*] I should like to join him if possible[.] Everything is so dull in this ship. The Captain is always so very distant[.] The First Lieut: [Mainwaring] is the best in the ship & one of the best First Lieuts in the Service[.] This ship is like a palace, so clean & neat, but a great deal too large for me.

The *Hussar* has arrived but there are no orders for us, therefore we are completely left in suspense[.] Give my love to all &c. . . .

[1]'This letter is now not to be found,' Grace Milne Home wrote.

[2]On the reverse of the page Milne added 'I was sent Home to England invalided from the *Ganges* and arrived at Ports[mouth] in the *Vandalia* transport[,] I think[,] March 1824[.] A Milne Feb 92'.

[3]Grace Milne Home inserted a question mark after 'Flag'. The line refers to Charles Ramsay Drinkwater Bethune, formerly Drinkwater (1802–84). Entered, 1815; Lt, 1822; Cmdr, 1828; Capt., 1830; Rear-Adm., 1855; Vice-Adm., 1862; Adm., 1866; Retired, 1870. Drinkwater Bethune, the son of Lt Col. John Drinkwater, served on *Leander*, Sir David Milne's flagship 1817–19.

[**21**] *Milne to David Milne*

Milne Graden, Berwickshire
25 May 1824

My dear Brother

I intended to have written to you some days ago, but having no fish to send I delayed. Herewith I send you 4 grilses. The first day I fished I caught a dozen & a half very good trout – since then I have caught but a few. I have been busy about the Flag Staff & got it finished this morning & the Jack was hoisted[,] [it] being Sir David's Birthday[.]

I have got the boat repaired, launched & washed out for the Paxton party[.] They stay with us till next Thursday[.] Every thing is looking well, particularly the Bank which is beautiful.

[**22**] *Milne to David Milne*

Milne Graden, Berwickshire
8 June 1824

You have no idea how this place has altered – of course for the better[.] The bank behind the house is quite green & beautiful[.] Every one that [*sic*] comes here admires it very much[.] The Tweed has been so small [*sic*: low]. The back of the Island[,] at least at the top of it[,] is quite dry, so that there is no fishing there. I have only shot one rabbit since I came, though I have hit most I have fired at[.] The fishing at present is not good except in the evenings[.] as soon as I can get some fish I will send them to you[.]

June 21st
On Friday last I shot <u>6</u> rabbits & <u>3</u> woodpigeons [*sic*], & 1 rabbit on Saturday, so that you cannot brag of my only shooting 1 rabbit.[1]

[**23**] *Milne to David Milne*

HMS *Albion*, Portsmouth
12 July 1824

My dear Brother

Excuse me for not writing sooner, but there was no post on Saturday[.] We did not arrive at Blackwall until nearly 1/2 pas[t] 6 & I did

[1]Grace Milne Home added '(His brother had written about it in fun – declaring it must have been asleep)'.

not get to the Angel Inn till 1/4 to 8[,] & thence I went down in the mail the same night[.] The reason we did not reach Blackwall sooner was that we had a strong S.E. gale & heavy rain all Wednesday[,] & on Friday we had a thick fog at the Mouth of the Thames, so that we could not give her the full power of the Engines, & at one time Capt Bentson was going to anchor. I arrived here about 1/2 past six A.M. & went to Dr Quarrier's before I came on board. I assure you it is very hard & tiresome work here[.] There are only two mids besides myself who keep watch, & when any one goes ashore, we have to keep watch & watch[.][1] Yesterday I had the afternoon 4 to 6 port [watch], & part of the middle watch & I have just had the forenoon & will have an hour of the afternoon & also the 4 to 6! We are very badly off for mids, but I think we will be still worse off, as some of them are going to leave us[.]

Mrs Quarrier has been offering me some good shooting about 18 miles from this[.] She has also told the farmer of it, so if I can get leave, you must send me my guns[.]

There are a great many of my old acquaintances here – I mean Lieuts of the *Conway* & *Creole*[.] We lie close to the shore here at a place called Hardway about a mile above Portsmouth[.] There is a nice meadow which lines the beach, where we play cricket & Quoits in the evening[.] I went on Saturday & played & will go again this evening if possible. Give my love to &c & the Paxtons, if you are out there which I heartily wish. . . .

[**24**] *Milne to David Milne*

HMS *Albion*, [Portsmouth]
24 October 1824

My dear David

I am greatly disappointed that Sir David did not intend to ask for leave for me. I certainly expected to have seen you all again by this time[.] However it cannot be long now[.] I think it likely that you & I will be under the same roof this winter, but I suppose about the beginning of next year I shall have to start for a foreign station – probably the North American.

I think I might laugh more at you about shooting, than you do at me, for after all, I have shot nearly as much as you, though there is scarcely any thing here & you have a good dog & plenty of game[.] I was out yesterday but saw only one brace & did not get a shot! Fine shooting!

[1]That is, stand more than one watch.

Next week I am going with Dr Quarrier to his property for some pheasant shooting, at least if there are any!

[**25**] *Milne to David Milne*

HMS *Albion*, Portsmouth
10 November 1824

My dear Brother

I wanted to have written to you sooner, But [*sic*] I was not sure if you were still at Milne Graden.

I have just received Lady Milne's kind letter & now by the time you receive this, you will be busy at your profession, at least with the beginning of it. Lady Milne mentions you are going to study law. If so, I wish you every success[.] She does not say a word about my going to attend classes but I expect to hear from Sir David in a day or two[,] & he will of course let me know. Lady Milne tells me you are to have a grand party to day, being my birthday. I wish I could have been at the party, but I am in hopes of being down on your birthday[.] I have not been in Scotland on my birthday for five years, which have passed very quickly away[.] I was to have gone to a Ball at Gosport yesterday, but the 1st Lieut could not let me go, there being no [other] Midshipman to keep watch[.] Sir William Hoste is quite well[.] He was on board on Sunday[.]

Give my love to Sir David & Lady Milne & friends in Edinburgh. . . .

[**26**] *Milne to David Milne*

HMS *Albion*, Portsmouth
28 November 1824

My dear David

You must have been surprised at my long silence, but I received a letter from Lady Milne two days after I received yours & wrote to her on Thursday[,] & intended writing to you the same day, but had not time & yesterday I was away for [?land]. You must understand that it is now Saturday night, but I have dated my letter for to morrow [*sic*][.] We have had most terrible weather here[.] On Monday it blew most terribly hard & at 8 A.M. the *Wellesley* parted from her moorings & drove athwart the *Boyne*[,] 120 guns[,] & from her she drifted inside the *Seahorse*[,] which is moored close to the dockyard[,] & from thence gave the *Ganges* a very close shave, & ran foul of the *Bellerophon*[,] 74 guns[,] & along with her drove on the sand.[1] I had to go on board of her on Wednesday & lend a hand to get her off[.] There are five vessels about the mouth of the harbour on shore, and two vessels which ran into the harbour could not bring up, & they ran themselves on the mud close to us, where they are likely to remain for some time.

Sir David wrote me a postscript to Lady Milne's letter saying he would write me in a few days & I have waited every day expecting a letter, but to no purpose[.] I am anxiously waiting for the time when you & I are to be together. I have been cruelly disappointed several times in that way. I shall not in future expect long letters from you as I find you are so much engaged but I hope soon to be next door to you, when we will be able to converse on things that have passed, for you & I have been but little together for five years[.]

I shall not close this letter till to morrow[.] Sir William Hoste will be on board here to morrow, as there is to be a Court Martial on Monday morning to try a man for stabbing a Midshipman three times with a knife[.] We are all very comfortable here & we have a capital stove but the only thing I don't at all like is the Watchkeeping [*sic*] [in] this cold weather & it is now very cold here[.] I wrote this letter last night, but do not close till this afternoon (Sunday) as I may have a chance of getting a letter from Sir David[.]

I have just received a letter from Sir David & I am glad to say that this is the last letter you will receive from me[.] He has written to Sir W. Hoste for two months leave for me, but if he cannot give me it, he is to give me my discharge so you may expect me soon. He says I am to attend some Masters. I shall[2] . . . probably leave this place on Wednesday & spend a day in London[.][3]

[1]For information on the extent of shipping damage caused by this gale, see *The Times* (London), 25 November 1824, p. 3; 26 November 1824, p. 3; 27 November 1824, p. 3; 4 December 1824, p. 2.

[2]Here two pages are completely stuck together, making it impossible to read the second page.

[3]On the back of this page Milne himself wrote: 'I was app[oin]t[e]d to the *Ganges* May 1825. But in June or July 1826 was [?transferred] for [*sic*: to] the Flag of Sir Robt. Otway for the Brazil Commd[,] see further on[.] AM'. Grace Milne Home added: 'The two brothers had the joy of being together for the winter. They were boarded as well as some other young men with Dr. Anderson in George Square Edinburgh'[.] She also summarised the events which occurred between this letter and the next that she copied:

> In May 1825[,] Alexander was appointed to the *Ganges*, Captain Campbell[,] stationed for the time at Portsmouth. Sadly did his brother miss him, & he wrote he felt quite lonely, as there was no one to whom he could so converse & confide in, & his brother wrote in the same affectionate strain [*sic*] saying 'I think in my night watches what you are all about, & often wish I was at home', though he also says 'We have got a nice mess here – 31 members – 14 just come to sea & everything

[**27**] *Milne to David Milne*

HMS *Ganges*, Tenerife
9 September 1826

My dear David

We arrived here yesterday from Madeira, at which place we only remained one day. We sailed from Lisbon in the 31st. I was at a Bull fight at Lisbon of which at present I cannot give you a full account, but there were 4 bulls killed which were tormented by having spears driven into their necks by men on foot & on horseback – they also drove fireworks [*sic*] into them by means of sharp pointed instruments attached to them.

I think the Island of Madeira is the most beautiful place I ever beheld, at least from the ship for I could not get on shore. The hills[,] which rise at a very great angle to the height of 4000 feet[,] are completely covered with vines & other fruit trees particularly peaches, which are very common everywhere we have been. There are numerous villas scattered about the hills & neatly whitewashed. There is also half way up the hill a convent & Church[,] which forms a very picturesque appearance[.] Some of the trees are of very great dimensions, but they cannot be observed from the ship, owing to the great height of the hill, which takes off every appearance of that kind [*sic*][.] There is one tree 80 feet in circumference at the Trunk.

What are all the good folks of Edinburgh and Berwickshire about[?] I shall expect to hear from you every month, as I hate to be disappointed in a letter, especially when so few opportunities occur[.] We sail this afternoon for Rio [de] Janeiro[.] Excuse bad writing as I am in

appears very comfortable') There was not much of interest to relate from Portsmouth & the young midshipman got very weary of the monotonous life & wrote in the autumn 'When I go on shore, I have nothing to do, I wish I was in a seagoing ship', & again 'It is being inspired with love for my profession which makes me glow with ardent desire to be actively employed, when I may employ my abilities to obtain that fame which Sir David has before acquired. Can I employ them here? No! I am here in a most detestable idle life with which I will ever be disgusted!'

In December he passed an examination on board the *Victory*[,] & in January one at the College[,] for Lieut: with success – & in March 1825 [*sic*: 1826] got leave to go home for some weeks. After the examination in January he was laid up with Scarlet fever at Alverstoke – where I suppose there must have been a hospital ['Dr Quarrier's house', Milne himself wrote].

In May he again joined the *Ganges*[,] commanded by Capt Inglefield, of whom he wrote 'I saw Capt Inglefield yesterday morning[.] He appears to be a very pleasant man, but very particular[.] Directly he heard that we dined at two, he said it was not the custom of the service & that in future we should dine at 12' – and again 'Capt Inglefield is rather a Saint – He preaches every Sunday after the prayers are read['].
In August 1826 they left England for the South American Station.

a great hurry. Give my kindest love to Sir David[,] Lady Milne & the Paxton family. I shall take every opportunity of writing. I hope you will ever enjoy health & happiness. . . .

P.S. I have not been able to Mineralize [*sic*] as yet, as I have only been ashore at Lisbon, but I shall do all I can, therefore cannot do more. I grudge your shooting exceedingly!

[**28**] *Milne to David Milne*

HMS *Ganges*, Rio de Janeiro
26 October 1826

My dear Brother

We had a very pleasant passage from Tenerife – of 35 days[,] & arrived here on the 18th. I have not been ashore yet but I intend going some day soon. We seldom get leave & when we do we have to wear cocked hats &c which in a place so dreadfully hot as this is enough to deter one from going. I have made a few drawings since I left England, & I have on hand at present a Panorama of the harbour on an exceedingly small scale.

The slave market is well stocked at present. Not less than 3,000 arrived last week from Africa[.] It is a most horrible sight to see the poor wretches[.] The general number that arrive annually is 25,000.

The Emperor had a great Court some days ago[,] at which there was an immense assemblage of the nobility of Rio. He is a very haughty man & when he goes to the Opera, which is a very good one, should he happen to tire of the performance[,] he always orders it to finish & begin another part!

[**29**] *Milne to David Milne*

HMS *Ganges*, Rio de Janeiro
27 November 1826

I am making a collection of insects for you[,] which are in great number here[.] I have collected very few minerals yet. I hope to get more soon, but the intense heat makes it more a toil than a pleasure[.]

The Brazilians are getting fast on [*sic*][.] Yesterday the Emperor sailed in a Line of Battle Ship[,] having with him one frigate of 60 guns, [and] 1 corvette[,] besides transports with troops. He has gone down to the army & to join his fleet in the river Plate. The Frigate he has with him was built in America & brought here not more that 3 weeks ago. From what I have heard the gold mines have turned out badly, & many of the miners have returned to England without any riches whatever. You say this country must be full of incident and interest! I should like to know where either of them are to be found! We just find it as insipid & stupid here as staying at Portsmouth Harbour! I know no person on shore, nor does one hear anything that is going on[.] I have had no shooting and I expect none till we go to the River Plate, which it is said we shall do in a fortnight & remain there 3 or 4 months.

Your friend Charles St Clair[1] is quite well & very stout, but would be better in a smaller vessel. I have not heard anything of John Purvis[2] but shall make enquiries . . .

[**30**] *Milne to David Milne*

HMS *Ganges,* Montevideo
11 January 1827

My dear David

We arrived here about a fortnight ago, after rather a long passage from Rio & a good deal of bad weather. It is war here at present, & no one knows when it is likely to end. This place is in possession of the Brazilians & they have in the town between 3 & 4 thousand men. The Buenos Ayrian [*sic*] army, if it may be called such, is besieging this place. It is composed of the country people who are all mounted on their own horses and receive nothing from the Government except a Musket, Pistol or Sword, nor are they formed into any kind of regiment, but go about in hordes plundering everything in their way. They are in great want of money, but by letting provisions into the town, paying a certain duty on them, they obtain a good deal. This is besieging with a vengeance!

Our surgeon went out riding a day or two ago from the town &[,] having gone beyond the Brazilian lines[,] he entered those of the Buenos Ayrians[.] Some fellows came up to him & told him the horse did not belong to him & that he had stolen it, and accordingly they took it away from him and he was obliged to walk back to the town, besides having the pleasure of paying for the horse[.]

[1]Charles St. Clair (*c.*1812–63). Entered, 1824; Lt, 1837, Cmdr, 1842; Cmdr (Ret.), 1860. St Clair married Jean Milne Home's sister.

[2]Possibly Milne meant George Thomas Maitland Purvis (1802–83). Entered, 1815; Lt, 1823; Cmdr, 1842; Cmdr (Ret.), 1860; Capt. (Ret.), 1862. Purvis served on the South American Station during the late 1820s in a number of vessels, including HMS *Creole.*

I returned yesterday from a shooting expedition but kept out of the way of any of the warriors, who are not to be trusted[.] I shot only six brace & a half of Partridges[.] They are much smaller than our own[.]

The Empress of Brazil[1] died on the 11th of last month, much lamented through out the Brazils[.] She was of great service to the Empire in receiving assistance from Germany[.]

The Emperor is said to have used her very ill, & that the Commander in Chief of the German & Austrian troops applied some months ago to have her sent home to her father. The Emperor was absent when she died[.] I think he will soon fall in the estimation of those European soldiers & they will leave him[.] They are certainly the finest troops he has.

We are likely to remain here sometime longer. We lie a long way from the shore[.] The best port is Maldonado[2] about 70 miles from here, but the Brazilians for some reason or other do not wish us to go there.

Admiral Otway is well & is hardly ever out of the ship. Gladstone[3] goes round Cape Horn very soon. Lady Milne mentioned a Lieut Smith[4] having called. He was with me in the *Ganges* with Capts Brace & Campbell & was always a friend of mine.

This is a very fine climate from what we have lately been accustomed to, & it resembles England more than any foreign climate I was ever in.

I must conclude as the [mail] bag is making up. Give my kind love to &c &c[,] & wishing you & them all a Happy New Year . . . [5]

[**31**] *Milne to David Milne*

HMS *Ganges*, Rio de Janeiro
17 April 1827

My dear David

I am almost ashamed of not having answered your letter before this, but there has only been one opportunity since, & by that I wrote to Sir

[1]Leopoldina of Austria, wife of Emperor Pedro I.

[2]Now in Uruguay.

[3]John Neilson Gladstone (*c*.1808–63). Entered, 1820; Lt, 1827; Cmdr, 1842; Capt. (Ret.), 1860; M.P., 1841, 1842–47, 1852–57, 1859–63. Years later, Milne encountered Gladstone as one of his examiners on John A. Roebuck's Committee investigating conduct of the Crimean War.

[4]Charles Smith (*c*.1794–1875). Entered, 1806; Lt, 1813; Cmdr, 1830; Capt., 1841; Rear-Adm. (Ret.), 1862; Vice-Adm. (Ret.), 1867; Adm. (Ret.), 1875.

[5]Milne himself added to the bottom of the page: 'I was promoted by Sir Robt Otway to the Act Lieut of *Ganges* but transferred to the Brig *Cadmus*[,] I think 7 Sept [July] 1827. Confirmed by the Lord High Admiral the Duke of Clarence.'

David and Lady Milne. I was surprised to perceive 3 Great King Street at the head of your letter, but it was absolutely necessary you should live in town[,] & by a letter from Lady Milne I understand Sir David has offered £4000 to Mr McQueen for a house in York Place. It is a pleasant situation, at least a very quiet one, & if on the right side of the street, a view of the castle is attained.

I must commence a history of my career since I last wrote[.] On our arrival here from the River Plate the 9th of last month, we found everything as before – dull, insipid & hot. I find it quite impossible to do anything in this harbour. I tried fishing à la Banks of the Tweed, but found it a complete mockery. It was from an island in the harbour for Guard fish,[1] & I certainly caught a dozen, but the trouble getting out of the ship does away with all the expected pleasure[.] No more than 24 hours can be obtained [away] from the ship, & if you remain longer your name is sent to the Admiralty[.] This is an order from the Admiralty[.]

I have now collections from the different strata & also numbered them[,] which I hope may prove serviceable[.] This place has been very quiet for the last six months owing to the death of the Empress & all public places shut up, but they were re-opened yesterday. The last week has been a time of fasting for the Catholics & on Saturday they had Judas hung up all over the town & their ships with yards topped up had also one, but at 1/2 past 10 in the forenoon the town was complete confusion[.] The Judases were cut down, beaten with sticks, burnt and completely destroyed[.] Those on board the ships are beaten & the ships' crews jump overboard to drown them. I was on shore at the time & saw all the ceremony. I also went to the Emperor's Chapel. It is small but the Altar[,] Candlesticks &c are all solid silver & a great deal of gilt work[.] The singing is very fine[.]

We are making preparations for sea & will likely sail for Montevideo to morrow. Our Ambassador Mr Gordon[2] is in very bad health & has been obliged to go to sea in the [?*Forte*] Frigate[.] Gladstone has left us some time, but I expect he will be in the *Warspite* with Capt Dundas.[3]

I have not been able to get any information about the Catholics, but I know the Emperor abolished many of the Clergy & several convents[,]

[1]An alternative spelling of garfish.

[2]Sir Robert Gordon (1791–1847). Gordon was sent to Brazil as envoy extraordinary and minister plenipotentiary in July 1826.

[3]Richard Saunders Dundas, C.B., K.C.B. (1802–61). Entered, 1815; Lt, 1821; Cmdr, 1823; Capt., 1824; Rear-Adm., 1853; Vice-Adm., 1858; Lord of the Admiralty, 1853–55, 1856–59; First Naval Lord, 1859–61. Dundas was the second son of long-time First Lord of the Admiralty Robert Saunders Dundas, second Viscount Melville. Milne later worked closely with him at the Admiralty.

which he has turned into Barracks. I expect ere long to see a general turn up in this country[.][1] At the Emperor's levées he hurries every one on (except foreigners) and the friends of a particular class to whom he has a great dislike[.] He laughs at them & tries to make them [look] ridiculous. He had a row with the American Minister[,] who has gone home about a vessel he ordered to be seized on suspicion [*sic*]. He has got himself into a hobble – so much so, that he has sent a vessel to the United States to say that he will deliver up all vessels seized during the war.

This ship is not in good order, although we have a great deal of punishment, almost every 12 days on average & sometimes as many as 19 dozen [lashes] is [*sic*] given[.] I am almost certain the Admiralty will make some row about it. But it cannot be helped[.] Duty must be done & orders enforced[.] Some of you shore going fellows want to do away with it[.] But I don't think it can ever be done without.

You will have heard ere this that Maitland[2] is promoted. He is a clever steady fellow & a very good officer, judging only from what I have seen of him in this ship[,] & I don't think I am deceived in him[.]

I am exceedingly sorry I did not go to the West Indies. If I had I should have been a Lieutenant many weeks back; at present I have no advance [*sic*] but everything is being done that can be done, therefore I must let patience be my mottoe [*sic*]. I have a messmate here who with his brother started in life without any interest – one in the Army, the other in the Navy. The one in the Army is a Colonel, the other a Mid 11 years past & is now a messmate of mine.

I was very sorry at the death of poor Mrs Wauchope.[3] The whole family have gone off very suddenly. Poor Sir James Baird[4] must be in terrible affliction to see the last of his family go off.

Give my kindest love to Sir David & Lady Milne & my regards to all animals of the Paxton family creation [*sic*][.] I remain your most affectionate, mindful & serious brother
Alexander Milne
I must give myself a good character!

[1]Milne presumably meant an uprising. It duly occurred in 1831, when Pedro I was forced to abdicate.

[2]Thomas Maitland Eleventh Earl of Lauderdale, Kt., C.B., K.C.B., G.C.B. (1803–78). Entered, 1816; Lt, 1823; Cmdr, 1827; Capt., 1837; Rear-Adm., 1857; Vice-Adm., 1863; Adm., 1868; Adm. of the Fleet (Ret.), 1877. Maitland was appointed to *Ganges* on 1 March 1826. He subsequently served as Deputy Lord Lieutenant for Berwickshire.

[3]Henrietta Cecilia, wife of John Wauchope, Esq., of Edmonstone, Midlothian.

[4]Sir James Gardiner Baird, Bt., of Saughton Hall. Henrietta Cecilia was his daughter.

[32] *Milne to David Milne*

HMS *Ganges*, Rio de Janeiro
8 June 1827

My dear David

We have been at Montevideo but only remain there a fortnight[,] long enough however to enable me to have two days shooting. I have found out a place in the country where one can always sleep, most capital shooting all round, and the country people are very civil. They speak much of the termination of the war & of Montevideo to be delivered into the hands of the English, which they say will make up for the losses they have sustained & open the country for trade[.]

I received your letter from Paxton five days ago. I was much surprised at the changes going on in Berwick & am sorry Sir David did not succeed[,] but am glad that he did not thro[w] away money on such a worthless set[.] When Gladstone was in this ship, he mentioned the opposite party intended to appeal against the election, but at the same time stated they would not succeed[.]

You mention your two friends having left Scotland. It certainly is a very painful task to part with friends who have so long lived together & enjoyed each other's society[.] I know the feeling well, but am afraid it has seldom affected me when parting from shipmates. Indeed, on board one seldom finds friends sufficiently friendly to unburden one's mind to.

We have fallen in with the *Adventure* and *Beagle* surveying vessels[.] They have been surveying Magellan Straits. They have found deep water clear of rocks & shoals, but a very strong tide. They anchored in a Gale of wind, tide running six knots an hour. One of the ships went through the Straits into the Pacific[.] The Narrowest part is 3 miles across. They have not discovered any Patagonians of such enormous size as stated by former travellers[.] The tallest man seen measured 6 feet 2 – but in a sitting posture they have the appearance of being 7 or 8 feet, to which disception [*sic*] may have led to the history of some navigators [*sic*][.]

I am promised a collection of specimens from the North Pole from a clerk in this ship who has them on board & made them while on a voyage there[.]

I must conclude – with love . . .

[**33**] *Milne to David Milne*

HMB *Cadmus*, Montevideo
12 July 1827

My dear David

I write both to thank you for the pleasure of your letters arriving with great regularity every mail, & to give you an account of my proceedings. By this time you will have heard of my appointment as acting Lieut: of this Brig[.] I lay under the greatest obligations to Admiral Otway for it, being one which the Lord High Admiral's taking command did away with Lord Melville's list[1] [*sic*][,] & no one had arrived on the station, & was occasioned by one of the Lieuts of the *Ganges* invaliding [*sic*]. I hope I may be able to get my confirmation, as it would be [a] rather disagreeable change to go back to a Midshipman's berth. Capt Charles Gordon commands this brig, a very fine & at the same time gentlemany man[.] He does all in his power to make every one comfortable[.] I believe he is the son of the Marquis of Huntley[.][2] He was introduced to Sir David in London at a Mr Gardner's before he came out to S. America & he begs to offer his best regards to Sir David[.]

We left Rio on the 24th June & only arrived here this morning after a terrible passage. Two days after leaving Rio we met with a S.E. gale which drove us on a lee shore, but it luckily veered round to S.W. & blew for some days, as if the whole power of the heavens was opened against us. I expected to have seen our guns go overboard & indeed it was in contemplation. The gale continued for seven days – five of which it roared without ceasing. I was certainly well inducted into the manners & customs of a 10 gun brig, joining her at a few hours notice – at sea seven days in a gale, & my cabin – 6 feet by 4 [–] leaked so much that all my bedding got wet.

I hope now to see a little more of the country, for a Mid on the station [it] is a complete <u>blank</u>!

We sail this evening or in the morning of [*sic*: for] Buenos Ayres[,] having dispatches for our Ambassador[,] Lord Ponsonby.[3]

[1]William, Duke of Clarence, was appointed Lord High Admiral in 1827, and any promotions planned by Lord Melville were thus thrown into doubt. Milne, however, received his Acting Lieutenancy from Otway, on one of *Ganges*' Lieutenants invaliding home. Such appointments were the perquisites of C-in-C on overseas stations.

[2]George Gordon, Ninth Marquis of Huntly (1761–1853).

[3]John, Viscount Ponsonby (*c*.1770–1855). Diplomat; appointed envoy-extraordinary and minister-plenipotentiary at Buenos Aires, 28 February 1826; transferred to Rio de Janeiro in the same roles, 12 February 1828.

July 13th

Some dissention has arisen between Lord Ponsonby and the Buenos Ayrians. They say that had it not been for the English[,] that peace would have been declared[,] but at present war is still the signal [*sic*][,] although the Buenos Ayrian Ambassador had arrived from Rio [de] Janeiro. The *York*[1] has been at Buenos Ayres concerning the dispute[,] but as yet we have not heard the right [*sic*] story.

I am in very good health & in good spirits, but would be better if I had but the pleasure of being among you all, but this service is one where [*sic*] these feelings must not be given in to. This place & also the coast is infested with Privateers & they have plundered several English vessels. We are on the look out for them[.] Some of them mount 18 guns. I shall now try to supply Jamieson's[2] [*sic*] expectations as well as your own, but I have not got quite settled in my new abode, where I have about 2 inches to spare in length!

Nov: 10th

I have begun to collect for Jameson[3] & also to write a small account of the different formations &c which have fallen in my way, since on the station[,] & I hope it may prove of some utility. The Journal! O the Journal! is begun [*sic*], so far from your advice I shall continue it [*sic*], and hope to make it worthy of perusal to anyone who may so far honour me or take the trouble to do so.[4] We have just heard of the death of Mr Canning.[5] It will make a terrible change in the Ministerial assignments, & it will also be a great loss to the Country. He appears to have been universally adored abroad as well as in England.

I enclose a small memento of our former days in a small sketch [of] Milne Graden Mill – it is intended for a watch case. Make the ladies at Paxton make some also, & say also I have no purse and require their assistance. Tell Jean[6] to make one of blue & Maggie one of different colours[.][7]

[1]Grace Milne Home added a question mark after the ship's name.

[2]Robert Jameson (1774–1854); mineralogist, appointed Regius Professor of Natural History, Edinburgh University, 1804.

[3]Grace Milne Home added: '(Professor of Natural Philosophy in Edinburgh)'.

[4]The journal to which Milne refers was either not continued, not preserved, or not donated to the National Maritime Museum. Nor is it listed among the Milne papers held by the Scottish National Library.

[5]Prime Minister George Canning, who died 8 August 1827.

[6]David Milne's future wife.

[7]There is on the back of the page a small watercolour rendering, neatly done, of the Mill, with Milne's inscription underneath: 'The Old Mill at Milne Graden as it existed in 1820. It was pulled down but the water wheel was retained for providing water to the stables & House[.]'

I am half asleep through sending messages to such fair young ladies, but I am much [?homesick] & the vessel sails at Daylight. I think we may be sent to Rio & also to Bahia . . .

[**34**] *Milne to David Milne*

HMB *Cadmus*, Montevideo
1 February 1828

My dear David

You will be surprised at my long silence, but I have been so unfortunate as to miss the last packet & the previous one by being on a cruise at Rio Negro on the Coast of Patagonia, where we got aground on the bar & remained for several hours.[1] The current there is exceedingly strong & the rise & fall 14 feet[,] which left us nearly high & dry[,] & with the pleasant expectation of going to pieces should it begin to blow; but by landing our guns & starting all our water, we were enabled to float sooner than we expected, but it being dark at this time, we were obliged to light fires on shore for leading marks & we had the satisfaction of getting into deeper water, but the next morning the tide made so strong out of the river as to carry away all our stoppers – out went the cable & we were again grounded[,] remaining for some hours in a very unpleasant situation, but by continued perseverance in carrying out anchors[2] we were enabled to get safe inside the river, which we were very glad of. I shall say nothing more of Patagonia[,] having written a long letter to Sir David in which I have mentioned all. Capt Thompson who at present commands this Brig is[,] I think[,] likely to be superseded again by Capt Gordon[,] who was appointed by Admiral Otway to the *Menai*[,] but the Lord High Admiral has also sent a Captain from England for the ——[,] & thus the Admiral's appointment will be cancelled.

[1]On the page opposite is a neat small watercolour of the ship aground, with Milne's inscription: 'HMS *Cadmus* aground at [?Entrance] of the Rio Negro South of the River Plate Dec 10 1827[.] A Milne Actg Lieutenant'.

[2]Probably a reference to kedging.

[35] *Milne to David Milne*

[HMB *Cadmus*,] Rio de Janeiro
17 March 1828

My dear David

Every letter which I write makes the time fly fast & indeed the pleasure of communicating with a Brother from whom I am so far separated, although but several times a year, still makes the intervening period look but a few hours[.] I have now been separated from you two years, but it appears as if it were only so many months[.] Two years more are likely to pass ere we meet again & then the pleasure of meeting will be so much the more pleasant[.] The reflection of it &[,] at the same time[,] the thought of our both being so much advanced in age from the period of parting[,] bring sensations agreeable & attractive. I wish I could make a second in the house in York Place. I would be a companion to you in your dreariness.

I am sorry to hear that things go badly in the County[.] It is a great pity that unanimity cannot prevail.

Capt Maitland married here the other day a Miss Young, daughter of a Merchant of some note & I believe he has got some money by her.[1] I think from what I have heard she can & will hold her head very high[,] which will answer the Lauderdale family exceedingly well.

The Navarino[2] business appears to have created great rumours in England with regard to the power of Sir E. Codrington,[3] but whatever may have been his power, the action was soon settled & appears to have commenced in a short period of time [*sic*].

The Irish emigrants who arrived here some time since are kicking up fine rows. The black Negroes said on their arrival that the Emperor had imported White Negroes[.] This set the Irish blood up & they took such a dislike to the Blacks, that they have regularly hunted them and murdered several at the public watering place[.] In a row[,] a Black stabbed an Irishman[,] & when some Blacks were passing the Barracks the next morning[,] out sallied the Irish, & brought in a person who was supposed to have stabbed their comrade & without more ado, they cut his throat.

I have been hailed in the street by 'And is not that one of our own dear country men sure'? This morning St Patrick's Day I understand

[1]Thomas Maitland married Amelia Young of Rio de Janeiro on 7 February 1828.

[2]The Battle of Navarino took place on 20 October 1827.

[3]Edward Codrington, K.C.B., G.C.B., G.C.M.G. (1770–1851). Entered, 1783, Lt, 1793; Cmdr, 1794; Capt., 1795; Rear-Adm., 1819; Vice-Adm., 1825; Adm., 1841. Commander of the British squadron at Navarino.

they are playing the —— —— on shore. However the Emperor last week has divided them among several forts . . . A common saying among them is 'The Emperor had better mind what he's about or we will have to take his palace from him, he allows us to drill, but after drill our muskets are taken away from us, but we won't stand it sure'. These people were expecting to come out as emigrants & to have so much land allotted to them. Such was the promise made, but instead of that they have been made soldiers of!

I must now conclude as my fund of information is at an end . . .

[**36**] *Milne to David Milne*

HMB *Cadmus*, Rio de Janeiro
19 April 1828

My dear David

I can but write a few lines & those are written in a hurry as I am now First Lieutenant of this Brig & am busy fitting after being hove down. The former first Lieut: has joined the *Ganges* & an acting Lieut: appointed. It is seldom [that] a person of my age becomes so soon a candidate for such a situation. Our extent of damage when hove down was but trivial, amounting to 18 sheets of copper off & a little damage to the keel, which is now all repaired & I believe we shall be again at sea before many days, but where our destination is I know not. We have had little peace. Wherever we go 'hurry & confusion' should be our mottoe [*sic*] & no doubt it will continue so 'to the end of the chapter', as the saying is! Admiral Otway has been often on board lately. He always enquires kindly for Sir David & sends him his kind regards[.] Lieut: Paget[,][1] the Flag Lieut[,] has gone home to take his appointment as Capt[,] & a Lieut: Duntze[,][2] who bears the arms which are over Duntze Castle[,] is appointed Flag Lieut: by the Admiral & he will be promoted before the *Ganges* returns home, leaving another vacancy which may be filled up by his[3] nephew, but he is at present waiting for his promotion as Lieut.

[1]Charles Henry Paget (1806–45). Entered, 1818; Lt, 1826; Cmdr, 1828; Capt., 1829. Paget was the son of Vice-Admiral Sir Charles Paget, Kt., G.C.H., under whom Milne later served on the North America and West Indies Station.

[2]John Alexander Duntze (1806–82). Entered, 1818; Lt, 1825; Cmdr, 1828; Capt., 1829; Rear-Adm., 1855, Vice-Adm., 1862; Vice-Adm. (Ret.), 1866.

[3]Otway's.

April 23rd

Since writing [the] above[,] I have been so much engaged that I missed the packet. The year of the Brig's servitude is now broken in upon & should fortune favour my ardent wishes, it will be those [*sic*] of meeting all friends again ere a year has elapsed, but when I again consider the time I have to serve[,] I must put aside with a sigh the most pleasing reflections, I am capable of giving vent to & again say 'I wish it were to morrow'.

I have been using my rod here in the few spare moments & many a recollection it brought to mind of the Banks of the Tweed & Till[,] the Wishing Well &c[,] the streams where you & I have enjoyed so many days[.]

The Packet from England has arrived this afternoon April 25th & by her the sad news of Capt Thompson's father's death has arrived [*sic*][.] This will probably necessitate his return home & we will consequently have another Capt:. I expected a letter but none has arrived as yet[.] We hear that the King is exceedingly ill & is obliged to be carried out of his carriage. I am quite at a loss what more to say that would be in any way diverting or pleasing to you, as this horrible place yields no news.

I can but say the war still continues with all the ardour the two States are capable of employing, which is but trivial[.]

I send many kind loves [*sic*] to Sir David[,] Lady Milne & the Paxton family . . .

[**37**] *Milne to David Milne*

HMB *Cadmus*, Santos, Brazil
23 August 1828

It is some time my dear David since I wrote you, as we have been so much at sea of late that we have lost [i.e., missed] several packets. We have been here three days & remain a few more, when we proceed to Rio. Nothing like keeping young officers at sea & giving them plenty of fresh air! This is a very pleasant spot & one of much beauty[,] containing fine views of wood & water[,] hill & dale, but I am much afraid my pencil cannot do justice to the scene. Huge rocks of almost all the same description are cropping out from the side of the hills, and which I have been destroying with as much strength as my arms assisted by a heavy mallet will allow, but their degree of hardness overcomes my temper sometimes & their weight in carrying them still oftener! And then what becomes of them I won't say!

In two days time I shall find more easy access into the middle of a large rock, as we are going to exercise one great gun on one as a target, which will relieve me of a great deal of trouble[.]

It is with heartfelt satisfaction I congratulate you on your success of [*sic*] obtaining the Medal & £50 for your essay on Comets & I trust the zeal & determination of prosecuting your studies may raise you to the head of the Profession you have chosen[.]

Conceive not that time & distance are making any change in me with regard to those who are at home, or indeed to my love of Scotland. Nothing gives me greater delight than to hear of the changes & fireside news of home[.]

I conceive of a letter from you to be more as a day's or a forenoon's conversation than as a thing of course, as it is regarded by some people[.]

I suppose you know Capt Thompson is now a Baronet by the death of his father[.] He expects before many months to get his next step, & I think he will probably take the Brig home.

I think I must remain out, as I conceive it would be folly returning home when I have not served my time. Still[,] I would be glad the day had arrived when I should again meet you all[.] I can look round now & see no one that I can in any way call a friend[,] & I may look further & see none save those who are in Scotland.

Of my messmates – we all agree well, yet still I cannot convey to any of them the appellation of friend which contains so much[.]

I saw Lieut Smith[1] of the *Briton* some days back[.] He is a good upright man & has no nonsense about him. You will likely see him when he returns to Scotland[.] Be civil to him if it lies in your power – also to Capt Gordon – late of *Cadmus* who returned home some weeks ago having obtained his promotion[.]

Aug: 25

Since writing the above I have been up one of the rivers, to witness & partake in a hunting party. It in no way resembled the English mode. The dogs are turned out into the wood, & the sportsmen remain in any open spot where a shot may be had at the Deer on his passing, being driven by the dogs towards the spot, [*sic*] where the shooters are stationed. I did not see the Deer the whole day, although he passed very close[.] However[,] he was shot crossing the river[.] They are very small but very swift[.]

[1]The same Smith referred to in note 4 on p. 31. He served in the *Briton*, which was engaged on Particular Service, from 1827 to 1830.

[**38**] *Milne to David Milne*

HMB *Cadmus*, Montevideo
24 March 1829

My dearest David

I received a letter from you about six weeks ago dated 10th October. I had been anxiously expecting a letter[.] It indeed gives me great pleasure to hear from you often[,] although you may not hear from me in answer to every letter. Yet I write whenever opportunities offer . . .

There will be a great row at Rio [de] Janeiro ere long. Our government has demanded the restitution of all vessels captured during the late war, & should they refuse, the British Admiral has orders at the expiration of 30 days to blockade Rio & make reprisals on Brazilian vessels. I know this from Sir T. Thompson to whom Lord Strangford[1] gave the information.

[**39**] *Milne to David Milne*

HMB *Cadmus*, Rio de Janeiro
18 June 1829

I must give you an account of our proceedings since I last wrote to Lady Milne & I wrote you from Monte Video in March[.] Thence we went to Buenos Ayres & sailed again on May 31st for Monte Video – left [the] next day for Rio where we arrived June 11th but next day again sailed from Rio to join Admiral Otway off Cape Ferio[2] which we did on the 14th[,] returning to Rio the 15th[.] During our stay at Buenos Ayres we were much taken up with the war between the province of that name & the Monteneros or provinces of Santa Fé & others – which is a Civil War. We lay within a mile of the beach, which for some days was the scene of action[,] & to see the charges of cavalry, the dead & the wounded was an awful sight[.] To add to the scene, one night the boats of a French Frigate & Corvette cut out two Buenos Ayrian Men of war, one a Brig of 14 guns, the other a Schooner of six[,] & they burnt a third in the Harbour; – since which they have taken [an]other five vessels of various descriptions. They have done this to punish the Buenos Ayrian Gov: for their insult to the French Consul[,] & also for forcing the French merchants to take up

[1]Percy Clinton Smythe, Sixth Viscount Strangford and First Baron Penshurst (1780–1855). Diplomat; sent to Brazil in August 1828.

[2]Cape Frio.

arms for the defence of the town – & when we left they had come to no terms whatever[.]

I have at last made up a box for Jamieson [*sic*] & have sent duplicates in the box, so should you wish any of them no doubt you will be welcome[.] Lieut. Buckle[,][1] one of the Lieuts of the *Ganges* . . . whom you may remember at Taylor's School[,] Musselburgh[,] will take charge of the Box as far as Portsmouth[.]

I have also sent some drawings, some Cardinals for Lady Milne &c[.] The box will go home by the *Ganges*. As the *Cadmus* is to remain on the station[,] Admiral Otway has advised me to remain in her with Sir Thomas Thompson. Admiral Otway expects her to be out another 12 months[.]

We are in such a confusion, I have not a moment to myself & really cannot write any more[,] as we are ordered to sea with the greatest haste[.] Our destination again is the River Plate[,] owing to some thing having taken place with the French & one of our Frigates. I have managed to write a few lines to Sir David. Remember me to all friends & with my best wishes for your health and prosperity . . .

[**40**] *Milne to David Milne*

HMB *Cadmus*, Rio de Janeiro
10 July 1829

My dear David

Though I have nothing here with [which] to fill a letter, I cannot let the packet go without a few lines[.] We are likely to remain here for three weeks to refit – & I shall have little time[.] But plenty of employment drives away care & keeps the mind from melancholy thoughts, not that I am much given to such thoughts, but I cannot help thinking of you all at home & longing for the day of my return. Even when the *Ganges* sailed I had the same feeling as of leaving a home, as I have [*sic*] so long served in that ship[,] & having known many on board of her for the last three years[,] it was natural the parting should create this feeling[.] You will see St Clair when the *Ganges* is paid off, as I have requested him to call when he goes to Edinburgh, & I have also given your address to Claude Buckle. Should you see him, pray receive him as my friend. You will find him an excellent good fellow & a

[1]Claude Henry Mason Buckle (1803–94). Entered *c.*1820; Lt, 1827; Cmdr, 1836; Capt., 1845; Rear-Adm., 1863; Rear-Adm. (Ret.), 1870; Vice-Adm. (Ret.), 1870; Adm. (Ret.), 1877.

worthy friend. Gladstone is in the *Warspite*, & a great friend of mine[.] He always puts me much in mind of you, both in character & expression of countenance [*sic*][.] Should we be able to associate much, our friendship would no doubt be more lasting & our intercourse continual, but as we are in different ships, & our destinations on the station different, we may not meet for some months.

Aug: 10th

Admiral Baker[1] is a very kind & attentive person[.] He differs greatly from old Otway, for we have been in harbour two months, which is something strange to us, as Admiral Otway hardly ever let us remain as many days[,] & at present I see no prospect of our going to sea till we sail for England . . .

I hope soon to revisit the scenes of 1825 & find full & happy enjoyment on my return from this land of everlasting strife[.]

[**41**] *Milne to David Milne*

HMB *Cadmus*, Buenos Aires
4 December 1829

My dear David

With great joy and satisfaction I received your letter about five days ago dated Aug: 6th[,] having been so long in a state of anxious suspense[,] having received no letter or any tiding whatever since June 14th [*sic*]. When your letter was dated March 14th you say, you wonder at my long silence, but the passage of the packets to England is very variable, as they have to call at so many intermediate ports – but depend upon it, the fault, if such it can be called[,] does not lie with your humble servant, who ever anxious & thoughtful of those at home, never lets any means of conveyance pass, unless he has written but a few days before.

I trust I may join you in the pleasing month of May. How great indeed will the happiness be to mingle in the society of those from whom the long & heavy time of 4 years has now intervened[.] I certainly think a person after being out here for 3 years requires to rusticate & renew his health. You often hear people speaking of the fine climate of South America. Some places may certainly claim that appellation[,] but the changes even in those is [*sic*] very great[.] This river presents some days [a picture] of the utmost serenity, but these are of short duration & the

[1]Thomas Baker C.B., K.C.B. (*c*.1770–1845). Entered, 1781; Lt, 1792; Cmdr, 1795; Capt., 1797; Rear-Adm., 1821; Vice-Adm., 1837. Baker replaced Otway as Station C-in-C on 6 March 1829.

changes which soon follow amply compensate for the former pleasure. I have known the Ther: to vary 30° in 24 hours from heat to cold. A most curious circumstance is the fatality of sores in this river, which will never heal without much trouble, & persons with amputated limbs are generally obliged to be sent to sea or some other place.

We have heard that a vessel is fitting out to relieve the *Cadmus*[,] & expect she will be at Rio about the end of this month.

I lost a worthy & good messmate not long since. He died on board the *Warspite*. He & I had been together except for a few months, ever since 1823[.] He belonged to the *Ganges*, but remained out, if possible to obtain his promotion. He was as hardy & stout a fellow as ever was, but in 14 days he was lying on a grating, covered with a Union Jack[.] He had foolishly been out shooting in the Marshes & low ground of Rio & also got wet from hauling the Seine in the night, which brought on delirious fever, which made him raving mad for some days before his decease[.][1]

What with that & a serious quarrel which Sir Thomas Thompson has got into, I have been much annoyed. He has had to fight a duel[.] It originated in two Brazilian Naval Officers quarrelling & one called the other some name[,] & said something against his character, which he could not prove[,] & he gave Sir T. Thompson as his authority[.] The other therefore called Sir T. out – but he would not receive the person who brought the challenge[.] Upon this[,] Sir T's name was posted upon the customs house & all the public offices as a coward! Sir Thomas[,] of course[,] did not relish this[,] & when on shore was assaulted & abused by the person who gave him up as the author of the scandal, upon which Sir Thomas called him out, but he could not get him to meet him for some time and [not] until he was forced to by the person who had posted Sir Thomas[.]

Then he made a written apology, & this was posted on the Custom House. The affair is at last ended – but the person who met Sir Thomas would not meet the other man[.]

The Admiral wanted to make a Government affair of it, but he found, [*sic*] that if Sir Thomas had at first accepted the challenge & seen the person who brought it – the whole thing might have been settled. These very gentlemen were messmates of Sir Thomas & mine in the *Conway*[.]

We have heard that the Spaniards have affected a landing at Tampico, but I am doubtful whether they will ever again regain their former footing[.] This place is now quiet & they have formed a new Govern-

[1]Grace Milne Home marked the end of the sentence with an x and noted on the page opposite '(The young man's name was Wheatley)'.

ment a few days ago – on the same day as Governor Dorego [*sic*] died a twelvemonth ago. I find nothing here worth bringing home to you, the place is so deserted on account of the late revolution[.]

I wish you all the prosperity and happiness of the approaching New Year & many happy returns of the 22nd January[.][1]
Give my kindest love to Sir David and Lady Milne & the Paxton family . . .

[42] *Milne to David Milne*

HMB *Cadmus*, Portsmouth
2 May 1830

My dear Brother

Day after day I have been waiting with the utmost anxiety for a letter from home[.] Some mistake must have arisen or my letter not arrived. In my letter from Rio in February[2] I have mentioned our getting on shore[.] We were coming from Buenos Ayres Jan: 7th &[,] while beating along shore[,] saw the Buoy of the Pamella [*sic*] Rock, which ought to have been to the S.W. of the Rock, as the Master knew such was the direction. We passed to the S.W. of the Buoy, but alas! we [*sic*] did not pass it, but stuck on the Rock itself going 5 knots[.] An anchor was immediately laid out, & having shortened sail & got the boats & part of the guns out[,] we hove her off without having sustained any material damage[.]

An English ship was close to us at the time &[,] being bound for England[,] gave the tidings which you will have seen in the newspapers[.] It gave great annoyance to many. Our surgeon's wife[,] who saw the report with the addition that every one was lost, got quite melancholy & the news of our arrival has given her such a shock, she has gone raving mad.

Nearly four years have passed away since you & I have met, but I trust ere long to have the great blessing of meeting you under the parental roof. Many kind friends have been down to see me – Capt & Mrs Revans[3] [*sic*] &c but their attentions I cannot enjoy till I hear from

[1]David Milne's birthday.

[2]Which appears not to have survived.

[3]Thomas Revans (1781–1863). Entered, *c.*1794; Lt, 1806; Cmdr, 1816; Capt. (Res.), 1856. Revans served under Sir David Milne in HMS *Impetueux*, 1806, and HMS *Dublin*, *Venerable*, and *Bulwark* 1812–14. 'In May 1816 he became Flag Lieutenant, in the *Leander* 50, to his old commander, then Rear-Admiral Milne, under whom he fought in that capacity in the *Impregnable* 104, at the Battle of Algiers and was there intrusted with the command of a division of the flotilla' (O'Byrne, p. 967).

some of you, that you are all well[.] You may smile at my ideas[,] but when one has been banished from the [?company] of all friends & not seen the countenance of a relative, it is heartrending to wait for so long a period without any information.

I expect we shall be paid off on Wednesday & I will stay at Dr Quarrier's till I hear[.]

[**43**] *Milne to David Milne*

[Dr Daniel Quarrier's,] Alverstoke, Hampshire
12 May 1830

My dear David

At last I can put pen to paper to give you some information considering my present condition[.] My illness has nearly subsided & I am fast getting better[,] though some tendency to fever still remains & I hope ere long to be able to trudge my weary way north – but full of hope & a variety of happy feelings better known than expressed[.] I had a letter from Sir David this morning from London & he will be here to morrow. I have also received yours from Messrs Cook & Halford & yours from Milne Graden[.]

I know nothing of my future destiny[,] but I only trust to get clear of the sea for some months, as my long service in the *Cadmus* – alias Washing Tub – has given me a sort of Hydrophobia & in these cases water is generally shunned. In my case, which is a new variety of the disease[,] the effect is only confined to nasty salt water, and my head & shoulders have suffered so much from the lowness of the deck & the concussions against the beams, that I require somewhere to stand upright & expand both mentally and bodily[.] I shall get some flys [*sic*] to tempt the greedy Trouts & I have no doubt they will come to me with all the fondness of an old acquaintance and friend[.]

God bless you, my dear David . . .

[**44**] *Milne to David Milne*

89 Jermyn Street, London
21 May 1830

My dear David

At last I have arrived out of sight of salt water – but for what time I cannot at present say. We came up last evening by the Gosport Coach.

May 25th

We have just been to the Admiralty & Sir David introduced me to Sir George Cockburn & Lord Melville[.] The former was exceeding civil &[,] I think[,] will give me a ship in a few months time, if possible on the same station[.] Lord Melville said nothing, but I have no doubt if he can promote me he will do so, particularly if a general promotion takes place, if the Duke[1] should be called to the throne[.]

The accounts of the King last night were very bad. The Duke of Wellington conveyed a message to the Lords that the King could not sign papers & therefore they were to cause some measure to be formed for the purpose while His Majesty's indisposition continues[.] The Bulletins say but little yet their tone holds out little hopes [*sic*] of recovery[.][2]

We went to Greenwich on Saturday & returned here on Monday – yesterday[.]

We have taken our places for Wednesday on board the *United Kingdom*, if possible to be landed at Berwick . . . But I shall try hard to get to Edinburgh, as I will in that case have the pleasure of seeing you, which otherwise I would not be able to do for some time[.]

I have been unwell since yesterday[.] The long tramps here are very wearisome to me after being cramped up on board the Washing Tub for 3 years, I get quite tired & my ankles swollen which is very uncomfortable[.]

It is astonishing to see the improvements making here since you & I were in London four years ago[.] New Streets – & the absence of Carlton Palace[.] The new Club rooms are very handsome – also the Strand & Exeter Change [*sic*] – the narrow parts having been taken down.

[45] *Milne to David Milne*

Paxton House, Berwickshire
30 May 1830

My dear David

We arrived here last evening about 7:30 & took the party by surprise[.] We had a long passage[,] having carried away one of the bolts of the machinery & were obliged to put into the Humber, where we had to remain 14 hours. I am only sorry not to have the pleasure of seeing

[1]William, Duke of Clarence, the future William IV.
[2]George IV died on 26 June 1830.

you[,] & at what time it will be I have no idea, as I do not think Sir David will let me go to Edinburgh[,] & I am therefore much annoyed & distressed. I see great changes here in persons & places.

I believe we go to Milne Graden to morrow. If Sir David goes in himself to Edinburgh[,] I hope to obtain leave to accompany him[.] I want to hear from you about all & various proceedings between Milne Graden & Paxton people, in which perhaps you may be acting a principal part[.][1] No doubt every thing has changed since my departure 4 years ago & may now be fixed.

[1]Grace Milne Home added: '(Probably this refers to [the] engagement between his brother and Miss Home of Paxton)'. The two became engaged in 1829, although they did not marry for three years.

PART II

COMMANDER AND CAPTAIN, 1837–41

Milne was promoted to Commander on 25 November 1830, thanks to the good offices of Sir George Cockburn, who was given a 'haul-down' promotion on quitting the Admiralty. As Cockburn informed Sir David, 'Lord Melville has been kind enough in consideration of the long spell I have been here & as a Mark of his approbation to allow me on retiring from office to name a Lieutenant to be made a Commander and I have felt the greatest pleasure in availing myself of this last opportunity, to insure the advancement of your Son. . . . '[1] Yet despite the promotion, Milne spent a lengthy stretch on shore: from his return to England in May 1830 to December 1836, when he was appointed Captain of the brig/sloop HMS *Snake*. These years constituted the only significant period spent on half-pay during his whole career.

The Tories' departure from office was the cause of Milne's prolonged unemployment. For the next several years Sir David lobbied tirelessly on behalf of his son, both to the 1830–34 Whig government and to the brief 1834–35 Conservative ministry, but to no avail. In early 1835 he even applied for the North America and West Indies Station command '[o]n Alex's account'.[2] It would be, he admitted 'a great sacrifice for me to have gone abroad, but it was to serve my son'. Sir Peter Halkett[3] was selected for the command, however, leaving Sir David to lament that Alexander's chances for employment were 'quite uncertain'.

Uncertain they remained until late 1836, when Sir David's entreaties finally paid off. Curiously, while his approaches to the Conservative government had not borne fruit, those to their Whig successors did, Sir David's own political affinities notwithstanding. In this instance, however, the personal trumped the political. Although the Whigs were in office, First Lord Minto[4] was, like the elder Milne, a lowland Scots-

[1]Cockburn to Sir David Milne, 25 November 1830, Scottish National Library Manuscript collection, Acc. 7467, Box 1, no. ii.

[2]Sir David Milne to Agnes Milne, 9 March 1835, Scottish National Library Manuscripts collection, Acc. 7467, Box 6, no. iv.

[3]Sir Peter Halkett (*c.*1769–1839). Entered, *c.*1781; Lt, 1789; Cmdr, 1793; Capt., 1794; Rear-Adm., 1812; Vice-Adm., 1821; Adm., 1837.

[4]Gilbert Elliot, second Earl of Minto (1782–1859), First Lord of the Admiralty, 1835–41; Lord Privy Seal, 1846–52.

man. Indeed, the two were neighbours in Berwickshire; Minto, moreover, had married Mary, daughter of Patrick Brydone of Coldstream. In 1839 Sir David wrote a letter to Minto in which he forthrightly stated: 'I shall ever feel grateful for your former kindness in having appointed [Alexander] to the command of the *Snake*, when all my other applications for some years had failed.'[1]

While Sir David was making those repeated applications, his son appears to have made the best of his enforced professional idleness by pursuing studies in Edinburgh. Years later, when urging the Board of Admiralty to revise the curriculum at the Royal Naval College, he recalled 'when I was a young Commander on Half Pay, I attended the Edinburgh College for several winters and derived the greatest benefit from doing so. The lectures were on subjects more or less connected with General Service . . . '[2]

Upon receiving his commission, Milne lost no time in offering nomination of his First Lieutenant's post to Sir George Cockburn [**46**], demonstrating his continued solicitude for family friends. His efforts to prepare the *Snake* for sea were dogged by the greatest problem facing the peacetime Navy: securing crewmen [**48**, **49**]. As a consequence, the brig's sailing date, originally set for early February 1837, was delayed a full month [**50**]. The *Snake* sailed from Sheerness on 2 April 1837 and arrived at Barbados on 22 April, have stopped briefly at Madeira to adjust the rigging. From thence Milne sailed first for Bermuda, and then Halifax, bearing orders for station Commander-in-Chief Sir Charles Paget,[3] who assigned *Snake* to the Jamaica Division.

Once on station, *Snake*, her captain, and crew were quickly introduced to the multifarious activities of the peacetime Navy: anti-slavery patrol, carrying mail and specie, upholding British commercial interests, and myriad other duties. As an instance of such, in early October 1837 Milne was ordered by John Strutt Peyton,[4] senior officer at Jamaica, to carry out a sequence of tasks. First, he was to proceed in company with the tank vessel *Fountain* to Falmouth, Antigua, to land specie, then to head for the western part of Campeche Bay in the Gulf of Mexico in search of an uncharted shoal, on which HMS *Madagascar* had earlier grounded. Having located the shoal, Milne was directed to

[1]Sir David Milne to Minto (draft), 11 April 1839, Scottish National Library Manuscripts collection, Acc. 7467, Box 1, no. i.

[2]ADM1/5698: Milne note, holograph, 1858.

[3]Sir Charles Paget, M.P., K.C.H., G.C.H. (1778–1839). Entered, 1790; Lt, 1796; Cmdr, 1797; Capt., 1797; Rear-Adm., 1823; Vice-Adm., 1837.

[4]John Strutt Peyton, K.C.H. (1786–1838). Entered, 1797; Lt, 1805; Cmdr, 1807; Capt., 1811.

recover the anchors, guns, and chain cable which *Madagascar* had been forced to jettison, survey the shoal and, those tasks completed, to part company with the *Fountain* and head for Campeche, Mexico, to investigate reports of piratical activities by ships from the Texas Republic 'and take such steps in the affair as you may upon consideration deem the matter to require'. Once that operation was finished, Milne was to rendezvous with the *Fountain* and return 'with the least possible delay' to Port Royal for further orders.[1]

As luck would have it, on 23 November, while homeward bound to Jamaica, *Snake* spotted a strange vessel off Cape Antonio, Cuba, and pursued it, using sweeps when the wind died completely. Upon hauling in range of the vessel it was found to be *Arrogante*, a Portuguese-flagged ship with a cargo of 406 slaves, bound for Havana [**53**, **56**].[2] The following day, another slaver, the *Maria Therese*, was stopped [**56**], but her human cargo had already been unloaded and, being also under Portuguese colours, she could not be seized unless slaves were actually on board.[3] Following this piece of bad luck, Milne and his crew headed for Port Royal. Before reaching Jamaica, however, the *Snake* fell in with another slaving vessel on the afternoon of 4 December. This was the Spanish-flagged schooner *Matilda*, carrying 259 slaves [**54**, **56**]. A prize crew was appointed, with orders to take the captured vessel to Havana [**55**]. Milne had confided to his brother prior to leaving England his hopes for opportunities to chase slavers [**47**]. Less than a year into his commission his wish would seem to have been amply fulfilled, although in a subsequent letter to David [**57**] Milne expressed horror at the condition of the slaves on board *Arrogante*.

For the next sixteen months Milne and the *Snake* were engaged chiefly in the Carribbean, and generally on anti-slavery patrol [**62**, **66**], although there were voyages to Cuba [**59**, **60**, **62**, **63**, **67**] and Vera Cruz, Mexico [**68**]. As during his earlier commissions, Milne's activities were reported to his brother David [**62**, **67**, **68**].

On 30 January 1839, Sir Charles Paget died at Port Royal, before having chosen a successor to James Polkinghorne, captain of HMS *Crocodile*, who predeceased the Commander-in-Chief by three weeks. Promoting officers via such 'death vacancies' was one of the preroga-

[1]MLN/102/6: 10 October 1837. *The Times* (London) subsequently printed a letter from Paget to Admiralty Secretary Charles Wood, dated 22 December 1837, on the piratical activities of Texas vessels (*The Times*, 1 March 1838, p. 2).

[2]*The Times* (London; 26 January 1838, p. 6) made note of Milne's capture on stating that dysentery had broken out among the slaves aboard.

[3]Milne explained the different search and seizure regulations depending on slavers' nationalities in a letter to his brother of 31 January 1838 ([**57**] below).

tives of officers commanding overseas stations. Consequently, the empty spot was left to Commodore Peter John Douglas[1] to fill. As Milne remembered the episode later in life,

> Commodore Douglas was instructed to promote a Commdr to be Captain. He asked my opinion, I said 'as Capt Polkinghorne had died before the Admiral[,] I think you should give the vacancy promotion to Sir C. Paget's nominee.' Next morning[,] on going on board to wait on the Commodore[,] he met me at the Gangway & gave me my Commission as Captain[,] as he had no knowledge of Sir C. Paget's intentions. But Sir C[harles] P[aget's] Sec[retar]y wrote to the Admiralty to say what were the intentions of Sir C. P. The Admiralty [then] claimed the vacancy and confirmed the Commodore's promotion. So I got my Post rank and joined the *Crocodile* at Bermuda.[2]

Again, too, Sir David took advantage of his friendship with Minto to write, urging that Douglas's appointment be confirmed, a request to which the First Lord replied most cordially. 'Strictly speaking,' he informed Sir David, the vacancy caused by Polkinghorne's death 'did not devolve upon Commodore Douglas, and had lapsed to the Admiralty, but under the circumstances I thought the case one which might justify a special minute confirming the appointment . . . ' '[I]t has gratified me much,' he concluded, 'that one of the last acts of my administration should have been the advancement of an officer of Captain Milne's high professional merit.'[3] On 12 March 1839, before news of the appointment had even reached Sir David, Douglas ordered Milne to proceed from Vera Cruz to Barbados to join *Crocodile*,[4] after which he was 'immediately afterwards to proceed to Bermuda in that ship for further orders from me'.[5] On 16 April he noted in *Snake*'s logbook, 'Gave up Command of HMS *Snake* . . . '[6]

[1]Peter John Douglas (1787–1855). Entered 1779; Lt., 1804; Cmdr., 1807; Capt., 1811; Rear-Adm., 1855

[2]MLN/169/3. Milne actually joined *Crocodile* at Barbados.

[3]Sir David Milne to Minto, 11 April 1839; Minto to Sir David Milne, Private, 8 May 1839 (Scottish National Library Manuscripts collection, Acc. 7467, Box 1, no. i). Minto's reference to the promotion being one of his last acts as First Lord was owing to Lord Melbourne's resignation on 7 May following a near defeat over the state of Jamaica's government. The ensuing 'Bedchamber Crisis', however, brought the Whigs back to power for another two years, during which Minto remained at the Admiralty.

[4]6th rate, 28 guns, 500 tons, builder's measurement. Launched at Chatham, 28 October 1825; sold 22 November 1861.

[5]MLN/102/6: 12 March 1839. Milne's commission as Captain was backdated to 30 January 1839, the day on which Sir Charles Paget died.

[6]MLN/101/10: 16 April 1839.

Crocodile, a frigate of 28 guns, was a larger vessel than *Snake*, but Milne's duties in his new command were little different from those undertaken over the previous two years. These were recounted to David in a manner which conveyed the general monotony of life at sea [**71**]. There were, to be sure, occasional exciting episodes to interrupt the routine. On 13 April 1840 *Crocodile* stopped the Spanish-flagged schooner *Mercedita* north of the Cayman Islands and found on board no slaves but abundant evidence that they were the intended cargo [**74**]. Unlike Britain's anti-slavery treaty with Portugal, which limited prize seizures to vessels actually carrying a human cargo, that with Spain permitted ships like *Crocodile* to make prizes of those carrying the accoutrements of slave-trading. The following January, while shaping a course eastward from St Thomas, Milne sighted a suspicious vessel. She proved to be a Spanish-flagged schooner, *Secundo Rosario*, carrying 288 slaves [**96**], and for the fourth time a prize crew was detailed to sail the capture to Havana for adjudication by the Mixed Commission Court [**97**].

But Milne's chief occupation during his final two summers on the station was very different from anti-slavery patrol: protection of the Newfoundland (1840) and Gulf of St Lawrence (1841) fisheries.[1] This lucrative industry was of ongoing importance to Britain and Milne was neither the first nor the last officer to be charged with the job of upholding national economic interests. The factors that made these duties both so valuable and so onerous were tied to the fisheries' complex international legal status. Citizens or subjects of any nation could, of course, fish in international waters, but two countries – France and the United States – had special privileges granted by treaty. France, indeed, still ruled (and rules) St Pierre and Miquelon, two small islands barely ten miles from Newfoundland's south coast. The Treaty of Paris (1763) furthermore granted French fishermen extensive rights to pursue their vocation on the entire west coast of Newfoundland (which was widely termed 'the French coast' as a consequence) and on the north coast north of 50N latitude. By an 1818 treaty with the United States, that nation's mariners also had limited fishing privileges along the southern Labrador coast (today part of Quebec). The presence of foreign fishermen, in turn, led to widespread accusations of encroachment on British fishing grounds as well as equally common charges of smuggling. Enforcement of the treaty stipulations, to say nothing of preventing smuggling, was made all the more daunting due to the vast expanse of

[1]MLN/102/7: 'Sailing Orders for the Protection of the Newfoundland Fisheries', 25 May 1840, 23 pp.

coastline to be patrolled. Milne's job, therefore, called for both energy and discretion.

Milne's lengthy reports on the fisheries [**86**, **102**] deserve attention for numerous reasons, among them his diligence, powers of observation, and analytical skills. They also reveal the degree to which the scenes of his activity were still very much on the frontier. Both conclude with succinct summaries of the overall situation as he perceived it and recommendations for extending the rule of law. He was not hesitant to exceed the scope of his instructions, for instance complimenting both American and French industriousness, and urging that Admiralty navigational charts be made more widely obtainable so as to reduce the number of shipwrecks.

On 30 October 1840, Paget's successor, Sir Thomas Harvey,[1] placed Milne in temporary command of *Cleopatra*,[2] which, although carrying two fewer guns, was a much larger vessel than *Crocodile*.[3] Milne subsequently applied to Lord Minto for permanent appointment to *Cleopatra*, but the latter was unable to oblige, although he assured Milne that he held him in high regard [**94**]. Milne thus returned to *Crocodile* (17 February 1841), but Minto's compliment, and the Board's approbation for his conduct while engaged in fisheries protection, may have been remembered when the Whigs offered him a seat at the Admiralty in late 1847.

Upon submitting his report on the Gulf of St Lawrence fishery to Sir Charles Adam,[4] Milne was ordered to proceed without delay to Spithead, after almost four and a half years in American waters. *Crocodile* made a speedy passage across the Atlantic, sailing from Halifax on 23 October and reaching Spithead on 10 November. There Milne reported to the Port Admiral, Sir Edward Codrington, only to learn, to his frustration, that his ship was to be paid off at Plymouth. Before leaving Spithead he had time to write his brother [**105**], and while making the passage he penned a missive to his father [**106**].

On 17 November he informed Devonport Commander-in-Chief Sir Graham Moore[5] that the *Crocodile* would be ready to pay off on the

[1]Sir Thomas Harvey, C.B., K.C.B. (1775–1841). Entered, 1787; Lt, 1794; Cmdr, 1796; Capt., 1797; Rear-Adm., 1821; Vice-Adm., 1837.

[2]6th rate, 26 guns, 905 tons, builder's measurement. Launched, Pembroke, 28 April 1835; broken up, February 1862.

[3]MLN/101/15: 31 October 1840. In a letter to his brother of 31 December 1840, Milne alluded to his new command. See below [**93**].

[4]Sir Charles Adam, K.C.B. (1780–1853). Entered, *c*.1790; Lt, 1798; Cmdr, 1798; Capt., 1799; Rear-Adm., 1825; Vice-Adm., 1837; Adm., 1848; M.P. 1831–32, 1833–41; Lord of the Admiralty, 1834, 1835–41, 1846–47. Harvey died while Milne was protecting the fisheries in the Gulf of St Lawrence and Adam replaced him.

[5]Sir Graham Moore, K.C.B., G.C.B. (1764–1843). Entered, 1777; Lt, 1782; Cmdr, 1790; Capt., 1794; Rear-Adm., 1812; Vice-Adm., 1819; Adm., 1837.

25th. That day he also wrote his brother again, lamenting *Crocodile* 'looks sadly changed – her masts all down & guns dismantled' [**108**]. He admitted, too, that the life of a naval officer was 'a very solitary and queer sort . . . full of anxiety & annoyance from beginning to end', yet he was eager for further employment: 'if any active service is going I wish to see the Pendant going.'

On 1 December he again wrote his brother as 'a gentleman at large' [**109**]. *Crocodile* had been paid off, and Milne had travelled to London to wait on Sir George Cockburn, now First Naval Lord, and First Lord of the Admiralty Lord Haddington.[1] His object, as he put it, was 'to make my bow and ask for employment', but prospects were poor, given the glut of officers seeking active service, coupled with the lengthy commission that he had just completed. There was, however, one possible route to employment: persuading Sir David to apply for employment as Port Commander at either Portsmouth or Devonport. A subsequent letter to David [**110**] reiterated this theme.

The following documents provide an unusually detailed picture of the Royal Navy's tasks as a maritime police force during the *Pax Britannica*. In order to make that picture as complete and balanced as possible, several letters not mentioned in this introduction have been included so that the reader may understand and appreciate the administrative responsibilities and tasks facing a small ship's commanding officer during the waning days of sail.

[1]Thomas Hamilton, ninth Earl of Haddington (1780–1858). Commisioner of the Board of Control, 1809; Lord-Lieutenant of Ireland, 1834–35; First Lord of the Admiralty, 1841–46; Lord Privy Seal, 1846.

[**46**] *Milne to David Milne*

Colonnade Hotel, Charles St.
London, 21 December 1836

My dear David

Here I am at last after the perils of the sea & all the Saints in Holy Island.[1] On Saturday night we bumped[,] & that very hard & there we remained until Sunday at noon[.] Hard work it was. I landed at 2 A.M. on Sunday & wrote for assistance to Berwick[,] having to walk from the Coos [*sic*], the place where we struck[,] to the town & before day light I was on board again . . . The Bower anchor & chain was carried out, by aid of Holy Island Boats, & with their aid the ship was hove off with [the] top of [the] rudder, [and] most of the pipes which pass through the ship to boiler & engine broken off; a few holes in the bottom there must have been, as she leaked faster than the pumps could act, & therefore they were obliged to lay her on the beach at Holy Island, from whence I sent an Express to . . . Soho[.][2] I took a great deal of trouble about the business[,] as I was bound to do[,] & had the wind shifted it would have been all up with *London Merchants*.[3] I came up by [the] Mail, having stayed all night at Bedford, & arrived here this morning much fatigued & will go to bed early.

I saw Sir C. Adam. I am to have the *Snake*, a Brig of 400 tons, & my Commission will be ready possibly on Friday, when I will go down to join [her]. Lord Minto I have not seen[,] but will probably do so some day soon[.] I wrote to Sir G. Cockburn offering him the nomination of First Lieut: this afternoon. I have no news. Farewell my dear David & with kind love to Jean . . .

[**47**] *Milne to David Milne*

Sheerness
1 January 1837

My dear David

I write now after some delay; not from want of will have I delayed it so long, but from downright hard work, & not a moment to oneself. I received my commission [*sic*] last Monday and to my satisfaction once

[1]Lindisfarne. For information on this stranding, see *The Times* (London), 24 December 1836, p. 6.

[2]Grace Milne Home added a question mark after Soho, which may have been a reference to the Soho steam engineering works of Boulton and Watt.

[3]The name of the vessel on which Milne was sailing.

got the sheepskin they could not get it back, & once the Pendant hoisted,[1] they could not get it down! So after my Commission the next thing to do was hoist that said Pendant [onboard the brig], but the snow had blocked up the roads, & the wind had wrecked the Steamers[,] so I was fairly done, & heard only of a chance Steamer going down with anchor & cables to a convict ship here, so aboard I went & although I had to weather it out without a bed[,] yet my big coat answered all the purpose [*sic*], and I got here on Friday, shipped the Uniform & Cocked hat & sallied forth to the Admiral's – which done & having reported myself, I sallied forth to the Brig, & then hoisted the Pendant under the command of Admiral Fleeming.[2] A stiff chap he is.

I have done nothing more except house myself in lodgings and amuse myself with a budget [*sic*] of orders, circulars, instructions, appointments, and memoranda, as also sundry & various applications of all sorts & sizes – so I manage to pass the day, as none of my officers have yet made their appearance[.] Last post however carried to some of them a gentle hint to be here as soon as possible[.] The Marines come down from Chatham on Wednesday[.]

The Brig is large & roomy & I am much pleased with her. She is now coppered, but no masts nor ballast in. We will be at work on Thursday – first to get the snow off her Deck, which makes her look miserable, but she must sail, & sail she shall, for she is a beautiful model, & a regular clipper[.]

I have just received an order to convey a Mr Nichols out to join the *Belvidera* in the West Indies – a way of letting you know your destination. So much the better. I rather like the idea, – a fine extent of Coast including Canada & Mexico and all the Islands, lots of Slavers, if we can catch them & get £5 a head for them[.] Sir P. Halkett will give me the best station I dare say. I have just received your letter of the 27th[.] I had no idea of my name being so conspicuous[3] – & I regret it. Old Col: Wright sent me 2 papers & also Sir David – the Warder [*sic*] & a letter.

I have got fine sounding names for my Lieutenants – 1st Lieut: Horatio Jauncey,[4] 2nd Talavera Vernon Anson:[5] – Master is not yet

[1]Onboard HMS *Fisgard*, Flagship of Woolwich Dockyard's Commodore-Superintendent.

[2]Charles Elphinstone Fleeming (*c.*1773–1840). Entered, *c.*1785; Lt, 1793; Cmdr, 1794; Capt., 1794; Rear-Adm., 1813; Vice-Adm., 1821; Adm., 1837; M.P., 1802–12, 1832–34.

[3]This was perhaps in connection with the incident described in the previous letter.

[4]Horatio Jauncey (*c.*1804–65). Entered, 1816; Lt, 1830; Cmdr, 1843; Capt. (Ret.), 1860.

[5]Talavera Vernon Anson (1809–95). Entered, 1824; Lt, 1832; Cmdr, 1838; Capt., 1841; Rear-Adm. (Res.), 1861; Vice-Adm. (Res.), 1866; Adm. (Res.), 1872.

appointed;[1] Surgeon Dr [James] Bankier, Purser, Mr [George] Doubt, a regular old fellow & as deaf as a post, Ass[istan]t Surgeon, Mr [Joseph] Hobb, Mate, a Mr Godfrey Graham, cousin of Sir James Graham, Mid: Mr Collingwood – Grandson of Lord Collingwood, Volunteer – Mr Jones, son of Sir P. Jones & old Saltouns [*sic*] of Bermuda's Grandson. I have still a Mid: vacancy & 3 College gentry, but I will take Seamen instead of them if I can. They [naval college graduates] are useless for the first year[.]

This is a precious place! cold, bleak, raw, miserable & straggling, not a tree within 3 miles, but that matters not if there is plenty of wood & cordage!

I propose reporting the ship ready for sea Feb: 11th[.]

With love to Jean & Bairns & my congratulations & good wishes for all health & prosperity . . .

[**48**] *Milne to David Milne*

HMS *Snake*, Sheerness
c. 20 January 1837

My dear David

I now write you a few hurried lines which I have long intended to do, but delayed that you might receive some congratulations from your brother on the 22nd. Accept therefore my kindest wishes, & that you may long enjoy many happy returns of the day will ever be my ardent wish.

I have been too busy with many matters here to write you before, & now in the interval of the men's dinner I have taken up my pen. We are getting on slowly, but surely[,] doing nothing that can be or rather ought to be undone. Our masts are in & to day our anchors, our water tanks are also stowed & I hope they will be filled this evening. To morrow we will get our chain [?cables], but in our rigging we are behind for want of men – our men consisting of 4 [seamen] & 6 boys with 20 Marines and volunteers are scarce. The Surgeon joined yesterday – a nice sort of person[.] Sir P. Jones is also here with his son. I have demanded 4 months provisions, which will be here in a few days. Our time of sailing is quite uncertain though down for 5th Feb: & no doubt the Admiral will hurry us. Sir Robert Otway comes here to relieve Admiral Fleeming, but I have not heard when – probably soon. Sir C[harles] Paget goes to our station – West Indies – to relieve Sir P.

[1]Henry Mapleton (d. 1879) – Master, 1838; Staff Cmdr (Ret.), 1863 – was subsequently appointed.

Halkett, which I regret as I expected to have got good cruizing grounds from him, & I do not know Sir Charles.

I know not how all my scientific researches will come on, for at present I have so much to think about & am so engaged what with Admiral, Dockyard, Ordnance, Boats &c that I am almost bewildered & find no time for anything but my duty.

The weather is infamous[:] wet & raw, not to say cold. My cabin is nearly finished but not yet painted. I have made it as comfortable as I can, but I will likely want room for all my traps & I am in daily expectation of my things[.]

There are [an]other two ships fitting out here. One has gone from the yard basin to day & sails next week on trial[.] Col. Wright has sent me a paper with all the business at Glasgow.[1] Thank him from me[.] It is the only account I have seen. I am in hopes of seeing Sir David before I sail[.] I shall be in London in about 10 days time to get my stock [of personal provisions][.] I have a steward coming from Portsmouth[,] a Coxswain from the Flag Ship here & also a Fiddler, so we shall have music[,] having also a Fifer & Drummer.

I hope Jean is well & also the young ones[.] Give my love to her &c. . . .

[**49**] *Milne to David Milne*

HMS *Snake*, Sheerness
9 February 1837

My dear David

You will be expecting my departure from this, but it will not be yet for some time as I cannot get ready. I am now reported for the 25th, but I cannot get away so soon & it may probably be March 1st. All will depend on our getting men &[,] as we are 47 short of compliment [*sic*] we may be unable to complete. I have a Capt King going out – a passenger to join a ship in the West Indies, I will therefore most likely go direct there – to Jamaica. The Admiralty had ordered another, but he is now to go in the packet of which I am glad – two is one too many[.]

I have been in London for two days & met Hugh Ross[2] looking miserably ill – also Capt Beston[3] who has been laid up with Influ-

[1]Grace Milne Home added on page opposite: 'I think the business in Glasgow was a political demonstration, 3,000 people having invited Sir Robert Peel to a dinner in December 1836.'

[2]Possibly Hugh Ross (*né* Hugh Rose, 1767–1846) of Glastullich, Ross and Cromarty or his son Hugh Munro St Vincent Ross (1800–67) of Glastullich and Tarlogie, D.L., J.P.

[3]Perhaps A. Beeston of the Royal Marines, with whom Milne had served in *Conway*.

enza[.] The epidemic has been more severe than the Cholera, and in one month 98 died in Greenwich Hospital[.] None of our men have suffered to any extent[,] although several were laid up[.] My 2nd Lieut: is appointed to a larger ship & another in his room will join in a few days – a person of the name of Miller[1] & a very fine young man, only promoted last month. . . .

I must conclude with kind love &c. . . .

[50] *Milne to David Milne*

HMS *Snake*, Sheerness
1 March 1837

My dear David

Excuse a few hurried lines, but I am hard run[.] Our orders are down for sea & I go out of Harbour in the morning & sail on Saturday for Portsmouth[.]

I was in London for two days with Sir David[,] who is looking very well[,] & I came back last night in a hurry as both Admiralty & Admiral were in a slight ferment[.] I am going to the North American and West Indian Station. At both I will be employed in turn, but I believe I go to Barbadoes [*sic*] or Jamaica first[,] and then I suppose I will be employed after Slavers about the Islands, but not having my final orders I can in no way speak for certain. When do you come up[?] If you leave on Saturday first, you might see me at Portsmouth[,] as I may not leave that place before Wednesday[.] I may also be at Plymouth on my my [*sic*] way . . .

[51] *Milne to David Milne*

HMS *Snake*, Spithead
22 March 1837

My dear David

As I shall be some time absent from Scotland[,] I will thank you to act as my factor with regard to the small property in Peebleshire I bought from Mr Dearkes [*sic*] &c[.]

I can only say Good bye. God bless you & all belonging to you & may you, Jean & they enjoy every prosperity & happiness . . .

[1]Robert Boyle Miller (*c.*1809–73). Entered, 1821; Lt, 1837; Cmdr, 1854; Capt. (Ret.), 1866.

[52] *Milne to David Milne*

HMS *Snake*, Barbados
24 April 1837

My dear David

Here we are on our new Station[.] We arrived on Saturday last from Madeira which place we went to for the purpose of setting up our rigging. I sailed from Spithead as you know on the 22nd & that evening got clear of the land. So far lucky[,] as before 2 A.M. it came on to blow most violently from the S.E.[,] accompanied with thick snow & were I nearer the land I would have returned to St Helen's or gone to Portland[.] The wind shifting however allowed us to go down Channel with a fair wind, but it was so cold & so severe with the strong wind & snow that our men were unable to face it & were at times perfectly frozen. We soon however got into milder weather & arrived at Madeira in 12 days. We remained there for 36 hours & I had not time to go far into the country. It however is most beautiful; the whole scenery is wild and beautiful[;] vines are trained in every direction among the rocks, – Peaches were in full bloom & other varieties of fruits[,] presenting contrast to England quite wonderful & astonishing, whilst the sun's heat was perfectly overpowering[.] I went a few miles into the country before we sailed, & was surprised at the whole system of cultivation. The faces of the hills are exceedingly steep & are divided into narrow spaces by stone walls. Between these walls are the vines[,] trained on horizontal Bamboos[,] & beneath are various plants & grapes which come to maturity before the vine leaves are sufficiently grown to shade them. I had no time for geology. My hands are indeed well filled without any scientific pursuits[,] but still I endeavour to do some little business[.] The Bar & Symp,[1] Temperature of air & sea have been taken at 8 A.M. & at 8 P.M. every day. Bottles have been hove overboard nearly every third day[,] enclosing a note on His Majesty's Service with Lat: & Long: for determining the set of the Current – observations every evening of obtaining the Magnetic variation[,] and at Madeira for the dip[,] & I hope to be able to fight through many difficulties in following out my intentions. The ship pleases me in sailing[.] My crew are indifferent[;] the officers a [*sic*: &] mid[ship]men & I have been obliged to be severe on some of the Juniors [boys] to check their tricks at the beginning[.] The crew are a useless set of Portsmouth watermen[.] We do well however & from the Commodore

[1]Sympiesometer: a barometer which contains air or another gas above the liquid, rather than a vacuum.

or Senior Officer[1] here have received commendation, – that the *Snake* is better rigged, looks better than ever she did before & has come into Barbadoes in better style than any vessel they have ever seen arrive from England & the log shews only one punishment & that my cook for being insolent to [the] 1st Lieut – All this is satisfactory[,] though perhaps not so to Cookey! While I feel flattered by all this, still I labour under considerable annoyance & distress, as we have been unfortunate in losing a fine little boy. Poor thing, he fell from the Rigging – ship going 8½ miles an hour before the wind & he was drowned. I did all & everything, but alas to no purpose. He was I will say a favourite of my own, a recommendation of Admiral Fleeming's, & an active fine little fellow as ever was on board a ship & one who worked all our masts for rigging during our fitting out[.] The sensation to myself at the time was dreadful, but to myself it can be nothing in comparison to those of his friends. Poor thing! He is gone!

We are all well, but really annoyed with the changes of climate[.] The Ther: now in my cabin at 8 P.M. is 84° & [it is] sultry and close[.] Barbadoes is a nice place although barren in appearance, yet its climate is cooler than other islands[.] The hurricanes which are severe here in August have sadly devastated the place & few trees remain – But [*sic*] Cocoa nut & Banana trees – also the Tamarind still exist in some places & give a beautiful appearance to those few spots of interest. I start to night for Bermuda with despatches for Sir P. Halkett &[,] if he is not there[,] shall go on to Halifax[.] The Admiral was here in February about the Carthagena business[2] but that is now settled by their paying £1000 & apologizing to the Consul . . .

I will write as soon as conveyance offers[.] Though far separate[,] yet to you my dear David & yours[,] I am[,] I assure you[,] present & wishing all health[,] happiness & prosperity . . .

[1]John Leith (c. 1791–1854). Entered, 1803; Lt., 1809; Cmdr., 1815; Capt., 1825; Rear-Adm., 1854.

[2]Panamanian authorities had imprisoned the British Consul – a Mr. Russell – in mid-1836. When he learned of this action, Foreign Secretary Lord Palmerston dispatched a set of demands to the government of New Granada on 31 August (they were delivered 28 November). When New Granada failed to meet these demands, Commodore Peyton instituted a blockade of Cartagena. See *The Times* (London), 11 March 1837, p. 6; 22 April 1837, p. 6; 10 May 1837, p. 2; and 'Correspondence with the Government of New Granada, relative to the Imprisonment of Mr. Russell', *Parliamentary Papers*, 1837, vol. LIV, p. 573.

[**53**] *Declaration of Capture of* Arrogante, *Portuguese Slaving Brigantine*

HMS *Snake*, off the Southwest Coast of Cuba
23 November 1837

I[,] Alexr Milne[,] Commander of HBMS *Snake*[,] hereby declare that on the 23 day of Nov. 1837[,] being in about latde 21.27N and long 84.53W[,] I detained the vessel named the *Arrogante*[,] sailing under Portuguese colours[,] armed with one gun 12 pr[,] Commanded by Augusto Caesar de Medina[,] who declared her to be bound [from] Rio Gallinas[,] coast of Africa to Havana with a crew consisting of 35 men, 1 boy – supercargo, 7 Passengers . . . and having on board 406 slaves[,] said to have been taken on board at Rio Gallinas on the 12th day of October last[,] and are enumerated as follows viz.

Men 101
Women 57
Boys 144
Girls 104
40 to 50 being sickly

I do further declare that the said vessel appeared to be sea worthy and supplied with a sufficient quantity – stock of water and provisions for the support of the said Negroes and Crew on their destined voyage to Havana. I do further declare that by inspection I found the said vessel to be most complete in every way, being well found in rigging Sails &c, apparently a new vessel[,] and the slaves apparently healthy and well attended to . . . [1]

[**54**] *Declaration of Capture of* Matilda, *Spanish Slaving Schooner*

HMS *Snake*, off the Southeast Coast of Cuba
4 December 1837

I[,] Alexr Milne[,] Comdr of HMS *S*[*nake*,] hereby declare that on the 4th day of Decr 1837, being in or about the Latde – N Long 77.12W[,] I detained the vessel named the '*Matilda*'[,] sailing under Spanish colours, armed with 3 Guns[,] one 18 P. Long, & 6-P Carronades[,] commanded by Deiho Curnerno[,] but in charge of I. Sugadar, who

[1]See Milne's letter of 31 January 1838 to David Milne ([**57**] below), for a more candid assessment of conditions on board the slaver.

declared her to be bound from Ambris[1] to St. Jago de Cuba with a crew consisting of 37 men & boys – supercargo – Passengers . . . and having on board 259 slaves, said to have been taken on board at Ambris on the 15th day of October 1837 and are enumerated as follows, viz.

Men – 56 Boys – 93 Girls – 48
Women – 45 Children – 17

I do further declare that the said vessel appeared seaworthy and was supplied with a sufficient stock of water and provisions for the support of the said Negroes and crew on the destined voyage to St. Jago de Cuba. I do further declare that the said *Matilda* appeared a fine vessel and the slaves very healthy[,] but [I was] obliged to victual her for her voyage to Havanah. . . .

[PS:] I am inclined to consider the person representing himself as captain is not the person stated in the manifest.

[**55**] *Milne to Jauncey*

HMS *Snake*, off Cuba
[5 December 1837]

You are hereby required & directed to proceed on board the Slave Schooner *Matilde* [*sic*] and proceed with her & her cargo of Slaves to the Harbour of Havana[.] immediately on your arrival at that port[,] you will lodge in the Court [of] Mixed Commission the papers which I now forward to you[,] viz.

The Declaration of Capture
The Papers belonging to the Vessel
The Log Book and Track Chart

and [*sic*] you will be required to deliver a paper into Court signed by yourself and verified upon Oath[,] stating the changes which have taken place in the Vessel since the detention[.] I confide entirely upon your judgement for acting in a manner for the interest of the service upon which you are engaged[,] and am of opinion you should remain at Havana until you hear from me[,] unless you have any direct opportunity of returning to Jamaica[.]

The Crew named in the margin[2] have been sent on board and I trust you will use every precaution to assure the safety of the Vessel

[1]Ambriz, in northwestern Angola.
[2]Not copied to *Snake*'s letter book.

and guard against any attempt at mutiny among the Crew left on board . . .

[**56**] *Milne to Peyton*

HMS *Snake*, Port Royal, Jamaica
10 December 1837

. . . On the 23 Nov. [1837] at daylight we made Cape [San] Antonio[1] and at the sametime [*sic*] saw a strange sail to the SE which appeared suspicious[.] We cast off the *Fountain* [tank vessel, which was under tow] and made sail in chase[.] on observing her from the masthead[,] she was evidently using her sweeps[,] which confirmed our former opinion suspicions [*sic*], we accordingly continued in chase and rapidly clos[ed on] her with a fresh breeze in squalls from the NW[war]d. It however fell nearly calm about Noon and obliged us to have recourse to our sweeps[.]

The slaver now being within range[,] several shots were fired from the two long guns when she hoisted Portuguese colours and shortened sail. At 1:40 we took possession of the Portuguese Brigantine '*Arrogante*' [,] Augusto Caesar Medina Capn . . . [She] had cleared out from Cape de Verdes for Havanah, but was actually from the Rio Gallinas coast of Africa with a cargo of 406 slaves . . .
Number Shipped 473[2]
This is as near a statement of the slaves shipped on the 13th of October as I have been able to obtain[.] Having taken out 25 of the crew and all the Passengers[,] I placed Lt. Miller[,] the 2nd Lt.[,] in charge of the Prize and directed him to proceed with all dispatch to Port Royal[,] Jamaica. I then proceeded to Jagua[3][,] a H[arbou]r situated in the bight eastward of the Isle of Pines Cuba, where I landed the Prisoners and Passengers[,] communicating the circumstance by letter to the Gov[erno]r of the Fort. On the day following the Cap[tur]e of the *Arrogante* we boarded the Portuguese Sch[ooner] '*Maria Therese*' bound to Havanah from the Cape de Verdes. She had made the land near Cape Cruz[,] where she undoubtedly landed her slaves.

From the Port of Jagua [we] stood to the Southd and[,] having taken the *Fountain* in tow[,] made sail to the SEd[,] and on the 2nd Decr stood close in to the H[arbou]r of Falmouth[,] Island of Jamaica but finding on

[1]The westernmost tip of Cuba.
[2]*The Times* reported only 330 alive by the time the prize crew brought her into port, dysentery having broken out.
[3]Cienfuegos lies the head of Jagua harbour, and is the commonly used name today.

the following morning we had lost ground from a strong westerly current, stood towards the coast of Cuba[.] In so doing we fell in with our Prize[,] the '*Arrogante*'[,] and directed her to proceed to Montego Bay and land the slaves. The wind continued light and variable during the 3rd and on the 4th at 4 PM[,] a sail was reported on the Lar[board] Bow we considered suspicious[,] from her being a Two Topsail Schooner and having altered course to near the land. At dark (c.6:10) [we] cast off the *Fountain* and tacked in shore in chase[;] at 7:15 lost sight of the *Fountain* astern[.] At c.11 oclock lost sight of the chase[,] having been able to see him only with the night glass since we tacked[.] At c.1:40[,] however[,] we again discovered the chase from the maintop[,] close on the Lar. Bow. [We] bore up and made sail and[,] having got inshore of her[,] tacked. she [*sic*] did so likewise on observing us[.] At 3 oclock am came up on and hailed a Two Topsail Schooner which proved to be the '*Matilda*'[,] having on board 259 slaves (men – 56. Women – 45. Boys – 95. Girls – 48. Children – 17 = 259)[,] bound from the coast of Africa to St. Jago de Cuba[,] but [who] had overrun his port. By his manifest[,] his crew consisted of 37 men[,] only 27 however were on board, was armed with a long 18 Pr [and] 2–6 Pr carronades[.] Having sent Lt. Jauncey[,] the Senior Lt[,] and a prize crew on board and supplied her with water & flour, I directed that officer to proceed direct to Havanah and[,] having taken out 21 of her crew[,] proceeded working to the Eastward along the coast of Cuba to land the prisoners, which I did about 15 miles west of St. Jago de Cuba. The evening before doing so [we] chased another suspicious vessel (schooner)[.] She was a Portuguese schooner called the *Constitution* [bound] from St. Jago de Cuba to Havanah, and had landed her slaves. From information received from the prisoners we had on board[,] I was enabled to find out that a Brig with 600 slaves on board sailed two days before them for Cuba[,] also several schooners with Cargoes[,] and an American [vessel] was getting wood and water on board preparatory to taking on board slaves . . .

[57] *Milne to David Milne*

HMS *Snake*, off the South Coast of Cuba
31 January–17 February 1838

My dear David

Since my last letter to you we have had many adventures[.] You know of my visit to Santa Martha & Carthagena[1] & after that came my

[1]That letter is missing from the MLN/169/3 compilation.

visit to Sisal[,] which has proved a source of annoyance to me [by] not having found what I went to look for[1] & having [lost] all my anchors[.] Every body says they expected it for one going down in the Hurricane months. It was a hurricane[,] or the end of one[,] we experienced called the Cayman hurricane from the devastation made on those Islands[,] about 70 miles west of Jamaica, but we shared [*sic*: fared] better than our neighbours – The [*sic*] *Racer* was hove on her beam ends, her Tops [*sic*] were in the water[,] & luckily her Bowsprit went & then her masts. She had not sail set & top[2] Masts on deck[.] Her chain cable in the hold was thrown into the Purser's cabin[.]

This however happened the last week in September[,] & at the same time the *Comus* near Bermuda was nearly lost[.] Capt Bennett[3] of the *Bamboo* said – if *Snake* or any of Symonds Brigs had been there they would have foundered.

Whenever I cruise in the hurricane season[,] I shall always look out for a harbour[.] I understand Capt Hope[4] of the *Racer* says – The [*sic*] Barometer never fell & there was no warning given. I have found generally that the Barometer does give warning[,] except [if] the wind blows hard in the same direction as the Trade[:] E.N.E. Then it is hardly affected, nor is it so with a North wind as a S.W. one[.] The greatest fall last August was to 29.89[.] The mean fall for Barometer is about 30.5[.] The mean height at 8 A.M. has been about 30/266°[.] When down to 30.1[,] there will be a change[.] The diurnal variation from 8 A.M. to 4 P.M. is very perceptible & regular[.] When the weather begins to change, the Bar[ometer] does not rise after the fall at 4 P.M.[,] but continues to subside for a day or so before the change. This is the earliest warning[.]

The heat at sea is not great[,] averaging 76 to 79°. In Jamaica in the shade [it averages] 86° at Noon, & in Havanah 70 to 69 & even down to 56° [owing to] the cold wind coming from America[.] So much for Meteorology.

Many thanks for your book on navigation[.] It is very amusing & late observations there given are useful here as a companion. The only place I have not observed the Dip & Intensity was Havanah[.] They are so jealous, so watchful & so bigoted that I would not ask leave to observe at all from the Capt General[.]

[1]Grace Milne Home interjected '(Slavers)' but Milne was referring to a shoal on which HMS *Madagascar* had earlier grounded, that he had been sent to locate and survey.

[2]Somebody, perhaps Milne himself, wrote '(gallant)' after top.

[3]Thomas Bennett (1785–1870). Entered, 1797; Lt, 1803; Cmdr, 1814; Capt., 1828; Rear-Adm., 1855; Vice-Adm., 1862; Adm., 1865.

[4]Sir James Hope, C.B., K.C.B. (1808–81). Entered, 1820; Lt, 1827; Cmdr, 1830; Capt., 1838; Rear-Adm., 1857; Vice-Adm., 1864; Adm., 1870; Adm. of the Fleet, 1879.

Havanah is the most civilized place I have yet seen – A fine town & noble harbour, most strongly fortified & at present a healthy place – but in the summer not so. We have had a few cases of common fever since leaving it, & one death – a man who entered at Jamaica & who had been drinking hard there during Christmas & never complained here for a week after[,] till he was taken ill.

At Havanah I counted 10 Slavers all nearly ready for sea under Portuguese colours. We cannot touch them unless they have actually slaves on board[.] The Spaniards we can seize if they have a slave deck or Irons or Mess Tubs or large Water Casks[.] Consequently[,] they carry it on under the Flag which gives most protection[.] 40,000 Slaves are landed yearly in Cuba[,] which divided into 400 gives about 100 vessels engaged in the traffic[,] & the English vessels[,] which are seldom cruising[,] don't capture more than 800 per year. The risk of landing is therefore not great, particularly as you cannot touch them if within shot of the Batteries on shore.

The '*Mathilda*' [*sic*] has been condemned & all correct in papers &c[,] & I am now clear of her – not so the '*Arrogante*'. She has gone to Sierra Leone to be condemned[.] Her Capt & 30 of her crew have gone in her[.] Capt Fraser[1] took a Prize with 130 slaves & Brig[,] Portuguese[.] She would have gone to the same place if sea worthy but is condemned[.] The officers & men have gone over in *Arrogante*. I hope to get her (the *Arrogante*) back with the men & sell her here[,] if the Commission will allow her [*sic*]. She was in a most wretched state – I could not have believed it – with 406 slaves on board[,] 100 men in Irons. None but the children had been on deck since leaving the Coast[.] They were all actual skeletons with death in their countenances[.] When I went on board, I was shocked[.] Dead children lying about the deck – others just in the last stage, all calling for food & water & pointing to their mouths. The weather was cold & wet and [they had] not a stitch of clothes on & [it was] blowing hard[.] With all the assistance we could render & all the attention we could pay with an Asst Surgeon I sent on board of her, 74 died between the 23rd November & 2nd Dec. They had nothing but rice to eat & were in that state that they refused food. 17 had died in Irons one night, the vessel battened down from bad weather[.] Two of the slaves spoke English as they belonged to Sierra Leone[.] It was a most awful picture of slave dealing I ever beheld or ever wish to see[.]

The other vessels were all healthy & well fed on Beef & Farina[,] but[,] being short of the latter[,] I supplied them with flour. They had

[1]John Fraser (*c.*1793–1861). Entered, 1805; Lt, 1813; Cmdr, 1831; Capt., 1841. Fraser was then captain of the *Nimrod*.

puddings every day[,] much to their delight. They are all gone to Honduras – Some [*sic*] drafted into West India Regiments[.]

Your long letter about stowage & the plan is amusing – but I cannot venture to write about it – only I admit the principle of pitching & rolling can be shown by a model, but velocity is another point altogether, in which stability is involved, also the balance of the sails before & abaft the centre of rotation or flotation. However the *Snake* is a Flyer [*sic*] & of that there is no doubt! Last night[,] Feb: 4th[,] I chased a Brig called the *Esther* of Greenock[.] We were going 9.2 [knots] on a Bowline[,] with Topgallant sails set[,] & of course came up to her[,] much to her annoyance[.]

Sir David's brass swivel [gun] is a fine fellow for bringing vessels to. They [*sic*] heave a shot a long way & make plenty of noise[.] We had an exercising day for the great guns with shot a few days ago. Most beautiful firing at 800 yards[.] We knocked a small half hogshead to pieces & washed the face of another at 1000 yards.

Feb: 17th Jamaica
I arrived here yesterday from my cruises – unsuccessful. I found the *Madagascar* ready for sea, going to England, so I hasten to finish this.

Do not think[,] my dear David[,] that I forgot the 22nd January[.] Although I dined solitary & alone, yet my thoughts & my kind wishes of happiness & prosperity were directed towards you & yours[,] & may you long have to enjoy the return of the day & receive the congratulations of your brother. Kind love to Jean &c &c . . .

[**58**] *Milne to the Governor of Santa Marta, Colombia*

HMS *Snake*, Santa Marta, Colombia
7 March 1838

Sir

Having been informed that Four British Subjects are at present confined in the Prison of Santa Martha, I have to request you will be pleased to inform me, for what crime they have been incarcerated[,] and whether in violation of the laws of the Colombian Government . . .

[**59**] *Leith to Milne*

Port Royal, Jamaica
2 April 1838

An application having been made to the Commander in Chief by the Merchants of Kingston for a Man-of-War occasionally to visit St Jago de Cuba for the purpose of forwarding the mercantile interest [you are to proceed to that port] . . . While at St Jago de Cuba[,] you will wait upon the Governor, and enquire whether the man who attempted to assassinate one of the Crew of HM Sloop *Ringdove*[,] while on shore on duty[,] has been punished. should [*sic*] he not have been so[,] you will demand that he may be . . . A complaint having been made of the treatment of the Captain and Crew of the British Sloop '*Sarah Anne*', and also the detention of the Vessel at St Jago de Cuba, you will make strict enquiry into the circumstances, and[,] if necessary[,] have a correspondence direct with the Governor on the subject, using that discretion which the amicable relations of the respective countries require . . .

[**60**] *Milne to Leith*

HMS *Snake*, Port Royal, Jamaica
[*c.* 12] April 1838

Sir

In pursuance of your Instructions dated the 2nd day of April[,] I sailed from Port Royal on the morning of the 3rd in HM Sloop *Snake* under my command[,] with the mail for St. Jago de Cuba[,] and arrived at that Port on the afternoon of the 6th[.] on the following day I waited on the Governor[,] accompanied by Mr. Hardy[,] Her Majesty's Consul[,] and communicated with his Excellency in reference to the Criminal who attempted the assassination of the Seaman belonging to HMS *Ringdove*[.] His Excellency expressed himself personally willing to afford every assistance to obtain the punishment of the offender[,] but the case was judicially entirely out of his jurisdiction[,] being in that of the Captain of Marine[,] to whom I accordingly made application and received the following information[:] That the prosecution of the Criminal has been delayed for a considerable time in consequence of Captn Nixon[1] not having returned to confirm his former declaration[,] that on the receipt of Commodore Sir J Peytons dispatch it was supposed

[1]Horatio Stopford Nixon (*c.*1798–1838). Entered, *c.*1810; Lt, 1918; Cmdr, 1829. See also [**67**].

Captn N[ixon] would not return and the case had again been taken [i.e., resumed][,] The prosecution is no[w] closed and the Prisoner has to make his defence. the [*sic*] Captain of Marine stated there could be no doubt, but that the man would be punished[,] which by Spanish law is six years hard labour in chains.

The next subject to which I directed His Excellency's attention was the seizure and imprisonment of three British Subjects belonging to the Sloop '*Sarah Anne*' of Kingston[.] His Excellency stated that in so doing he had no alternative[;] that he is ordered by the Captain General of Cuba to confine all coloured people of every nation immediately on their arrival at St. Jago de Cuba[,] and keep them confined until the vessel is ready for Sea[, and] that his order has been equally enforced against Spanish, American and French Subjects in their respective vessels[.]

In reference to the Seizure and condemnation of the English Schooner '*Red Rose*'[,] I applied to the Captn of Marine, who stated that she had been found at anchor at Cumberland [*sic*] harbour by a Schooner of War[,] and had been detained upon two charges[:] 1st[,] For her being in a Port of Cuba not a Port of [?Refuge][,] 2nd[,] with having articles of commerce on board not specified in her papers[.] She was tried at St. Jago but[,] not wishing to act with severity[,] the papers were forwarded to Havana[,] which were immediately returned with a censure to the Court for not having condemned the vessel at once[.] I stated the circumstances of the vessel putting in, in distress from weather and want of ballast[,] but further information[,] the Captn of Marine stated[,] could be furnished only thro' the respective Cabinets[,] altho' the Spanish Admiral at Havana might give some information.

I sailed from St. Jago on the evening of the 9th Inst and have the Honour to inform you of my arrival at this Port.

[**61**] *Leith to Milne*

Port Royal, Jamaica
15 April 1838

You are hereby required & directed to put to Sea in HM Sloop under your command to-morrow morning to cruize for the protection of British Commerce, the suppression of Piracy, and of the traffic in Slaves, and you will return to this port by the end of May. [Milne was also instructed to touch at Annotto Bay], it being reported that there are some deserters there from the Squadron[.] [*Snake* was then to proceed via the Crooked Island Passage to Abaco] where it seems likely the

Slavers are at present steering for on their passage home. [Following that, Milne was to proceed to Nassau, communicate with the Governor there, and] while there I wish you to examine the Buoys that were sent up to be placed in the channel for Cochrane's Anchorage, if they have not been laid down, so as to be able to report to me on your return the condition in which you may find them. From there you will proceed according to your own judgment and the information you may receive, either to round Cape [San] Antonio and to cruize up the south side of Cuba[,] or by any other track by which you think the object of your cruize will be best effected.

[**62**] *Milne to David Milne*

HMS *Snake*, Jamaica
15 April 1838

My dear David

Here we are again[,] having arrived on Thursday last from St. Jago de Cuba[,] having left this on the 3rd for that place[,] and where we remained three days. I was sent there to demand punishment of the vagabond who stabbed *Ringdoves* Seaman[,] and I believe he will [be] sentenced to six years hard labour in chains, also to demand satisfaction for the Seizure of an English schooner for Smuggling and [to protest detaining] all coloured men belonging to ships who enter the port. but [*sic*] to these two questions I was informed that it must be settled between the respective Cabinets. So I came back and sail tomorrow on a month's cruise[,] to call during that period at Nassau[,] where Colonel Cockburn is Governor. I shall therefore proceed round the E. end of Cuba[,] thru the Crooked Island passage[,] and to Nassau[,] then going to Havanah and round the W end of Cuba & home[,] after which I proceed to Bermuda to clear out the brig, and[,] I suppose[,] return here, but all will depend on the Admiral or Senior Officer there. The Adml I believe proceeds to Quebec on account of the Canada business,[1] but I am attached to Jamaica division of the station with 9 or 10 others, therefore all letters must come directed here. Since I last wrote you I have been down at Santa Martha and Carthagena with the mails[,] remaining at each place the limited time of 72 hours, which[,] after the

[1]Almost certainly a reference to the Canadian rebellion of 1837. The rebels had support from across the border and during 1838 several small invasions were staged from the United States. These, along with a Canadian raid that burned the American vessel *Caroline* (29 December 1837), generated a severe crisis in Anglo-American relations.

preliminaries of calling on the Governor[,] Mails, & Freight[,] leaves little time for other avocations. In the way of Geology[,] indeed[,] I have done nothing, the climate is sadly against it. Soon after the sunrise the heat is insufferable and continues so until near sunset[,] and during that time walking is out of the question and[,] what is still more important[,] I find matters go much better on me when I am [a] little on shore . . . which is seldom the case. I paid a visit[,] however[,] to a Sugar Estate here sometime back[,] and was delighted with 36 hours vacation among the Blackeys[,] who appear very quiet[,] altho the planters are much afraid of the approaching August[,] when part are made free and a part remain slaves. The dread is from the latter, but I dont [*sic*] suppose there will be any dissatisfaction[.] the planters[,] however[,] wish the men of war to be in the different harbours at the time[,] to awe them a little[.] I sent home a week or two ago two boxes of Havanah [?Sweets], one for Lady Milne and the other for Jean[,] which I hope will arrive safe and not in a leaky state . . . I wish you to send a paper now and then[;] the Edin[burgh papers] are a great treat when at sea. I see the gardener at Inveresk keeps up the Register, and by it the Ther[mometer] has been as low as 5°. it [*sic*] must have been very severe [this winter], indeed the papers contain long accounts of Snow Storms & ice[,] a little of which would be agreeable here. the [*sic*] heat is now excessive[:] no sea breezes nor land winds[,] and heavy close atmosphere[.] if it lasts we will have sickness, but at present we are all well[,] indeed better than ever. no [*sic*] sick list to mention viz. 3 with accidents. I have an additional Lieut appointed in lieu of the one gone to the coast, but only during his absence. Where is Tommy Cochran[,][1] is he still in Asia[?] he is far better there than here[,] but I am now short of Mids, & certainly would rather be without than have a repetition of thick headed fellows I have had, who were a constant worry to me &[,] I suppose[,] me <u>to them</u>, for I never can help telling them what I <u>think</u>[,] sometimes not very palatable. Tom Hope[2] is out here in *Sappho* and is a fine strong fellow[,] looking very well when I last saw him[.] he is now out cruising off Cuba for 3 months, as also 3 of us <u>Symondites</u>. *Snake* however yields the palm to none either in look[s] or sailing[,] and such is the general opinion as well as <u>my own</u>. I hope to nab a slaver this cruise if I can[,] but Lord Brougham appears to have a poor

[1]Thomas Cochran (*c.*1821–89). Entered, 1833; Lt, 1844; Cmdr, 1851; Capt., 1857; Capt. (Ret.), 1874; Rear-Adm. (Ret.), 1875; Vice-Adm. (Ret.), 1879. Cochran was the son of Archibald Cochran of Ashkirk and brother of Euphemia Cochran and hence, Milne's first cousin and future brother-in-law.

[2]Thomas Hope (1810–67). Entered, 1825; Lt, 1832; Cmdr, 1841; Capt., 1852; Rear-Adm., 1867. Hope was First Lieutenant of HMS *Sappho*.

opinion of us[.][1] I only hope they wont [*sic*] do away with the prize money[.] It is a reasonable assistance for all our hard work, which is no sinecure; often I get no sleep, the officer of the watch constantly calling me, 'Another Sail in Sight.' then [*sic*] we chase and examine, no sooner done than after another, and so on. I tryed [*sic*] to gain information at St. Jago de Cuba, but I cannot confide in them. I saw the proprietor of the '*Matilda*.' He looked very black at me[.] each of the seamen belonging to that vessel had 580 dollars due to them[,] viz. 7 months wages at $40[,] and a dollar for each slave landed. Capt. [?Sharpe] is to be at Bermuda with troops for Canada from Gibraltar. I hope I may meet him. There is a talk [*sic*] here of a war with America[;][2] they are fitting out a number of vessels in a great hurry but cannot get men, one of [?their] men of war . . . was there lately and came here direct. by [*sic*] last packet I had no letters. disappointed! [*sic*] I will write Sir David from Nassau and must now conclude this scrawl. Kind love to Sir David and Lady Milne and Jean . . .

[**63**] *Milne to Leith*

HMS *Snake*, Port Royal, Jamaica
[June 1838]

Sir

In pursuance of your Instructions dated 15th day of April last, I put to Sea from Port Royal on the morning of the 16th of the same month, and proceeded off Anotta [*sic*] Bay; from thence reached over to the Island of Cuba and rounded the Eastern end of that Island; from thence passed thru the Crooked Island passage and made Abaco Lt. House on the evening of the 26th[,] off which position I remained cruising for several days[.] from there proceeded to Nassau where I arrived on the 3rd of May[.] in obedience to your orders to report on the Buoys intended to be laid in Cochrane's Anchorage, I beg to state that they are all in want of considerable repair viz. a general caulking, and the Hoops redrove [*sic*]. In some, several planks will require to be shifted, and if not put in repair, in a short time they will become entirely rotten. I put to sea from Nassau on the 7th May and cruised between Abaco

[1]Peter Henry Brougham, Lord Brougham and Vaux (1778–1868). Lord Chancellor, 1830–34. Brougham had recently advocated the abolition of 'head money' paid for each slave, arguing that it encouraged officers on anti-slavery patrol to wait until slavers had loaded their human cargo, thus contributing to the barbarity of the trade. See *Hansard's Parliamentary Debates*, 3rd ser., vol. 40, cols. 599–600.

[2]Over support in the United States for the Canadian rebels.

and the Great Isaac [Island,] from thence along the Western edge of the Bahama Bank and communicated with Havana on the 17th Inst[.] from thence [we] have worked up along the South Shore of Cuba without having seen any suspicious sail[.] We left at Nassau HMS *Sappho* and two Portuguese slave Brigs[,] one the prize to [*sic*] the *Sappho* with 575 slaves[,] the other to HMS *Pearl* with 475, all of which were landed at Nassau[.] . . .

[**64**] *Paget to Milne*

HMS *Cornwallis*, [Halifax]
29 August 1838

Dear Sir

I am much obliged to you for your letter giving me the details which it contains. As soon as you are ready for Sea you cannot[,] I believe[,] do better than return to the Jamaica Station[,] Where [*sic*] I hope you will Continue to Enjoy Health and meet with Success. I feel very thankful for the Satisfactory Report you have been so good as to make in regard to my Son[1] having passed a creditable Examination. He tells me that the *Snake* Sails very fast[,] and I hope your zeal may be rewarded by the Capture of some Slavers. I am told they have for some time past adopted a new course of proceeding, to avoid our Cruisers, keeping to the Southward of the Pedro Shoals[2] til they run down the Longitude of the Isle of Pines, when they strike over. You had better try this. At all events I wish you luck . . .

[**65**] *Milne to Wood*[3]

HMS *Snake*, Port Royal, Jamaica
16 September 1838

Sir

I beg to state to you for the information of My Lords of the Admiralty[,] that the Officers and Ships Company of HMS *Snake* under my

[1]Brownlow Henry Paget (1819–43). Entered, *c.*1831; Lt, 1838.

[2]South of Jamaica, 17N lat., 78W long.

[3]Sir Charles Wood, 1st Viscount Halifax (1800–1885). M.P., 1826–66; Joint Secretary to the Treasury, 1834–35; Admiralty Secretary, 1835–39; Chancellor of the Exchequer, 1846–52; President of the Board of Control (India), 1852–55; First Lord of the Admiralty, 1855–58; Secretary of State for India, 1859–66; Lord Privy Seal, 1870–74.

command have subscribed the sums named in the margin[1] to the monument to be erected in London to the late Lord Nelson[,] and I have to request their Lordships will permit me to charge the sums specified against the individuals on the Ships Books[,] and to remit to the Secretary for the Building [of the monument] a list of men subscribing[,] and to request that their Lordships will grant an order for the sums being paid on the receipt of the above list in London . . .

[**66**] *Douglas to Milne*

Port Royal, Jamaica
16 September 1838

You are hereby required and directed to complete the Water and Provisions of Her Majesty's Sloop under your command to three months, and[,] being in all respects ready to put to Sea on Tuesday morning . . . run down the South Side of the Pedro Shoals, and cruize between the West of them to Cape Cruz, Isle of Pines, Cape [San] Antonio, and the Colorades,[2] for the Protection of British Commerce [&] Suppression of Piracy and Slavery, or in such position or situations as from information or otherwise you may think fit for the Capture of Vessels engaged in the illegal traffic of Slave dealing[,] and you will call at Lucea Bay [Jamaica] on or about the 15th of October for any orders that there may be from me, or to send me any information that you may have obtained. Should there be no orders[,] you will complete your water and resume your cruize, returning on the 7th of December to this Port for further orders.

[**67**] *Milne to David Milne*

HMS *Snake,* Havana
November 1838

My dear David

I wrote you from Halifax[3] in July or August. Thence we went to Bermuda & since then have been cruizing about[,] save when we went into the harbour of Lucia [*sic*] Jamaica[,] where our letters were for-

[1]'Cmmd (&) Officers with Mastr, Surgeon & Purser 4 days [salary] each[;] Mates &c and Warrant Officers 2 days each[;] Seamen Boys and Marines 1 day each'.

[2]De los Colorados, off the west coast of Cuba, northeast of Cape San Antonio.

[3]Missing from MLN/169/3.

warded to us. I received one from Jean, by which I was glad to hear good accounts of No 10[.][1]

Our cruize has been a very stupid one, not having caught any slavers, only [having] seen one a long way off, which escaped from the fascination of the *Snake* by aid of a dark night, but we have still a month before we go home – i.e. to our head quarters Port Royal[.]

Cruizing is very pleasant in fine weather but we have had about a month's daily rain & since then constant gales from the Northward, & as we are blockading a Harbour near Havanah on a dead lee shore, it becomes somewhat tiresome[.]

The three harbours are Mariel, Cabanas & Bahia Honda, which I suppose to be the places where the slaves are landed[.] It is most difficult to say where it is best to search for them, & I could take any station I liked, & therefore chose this[.]

The villains are so cunning & so cautious that they are rather difficult to find, but more difficult to capture[.] I go into Havanah to morrow [*sic*] for 48 hours to procure water &c[,] & I intend proceeding direct[ly] around the West End of Cuba & thence beat off for Jamaica[,] where I am to be Dec: 7th[.] After that I do not know my destination, but I should like to [go to] St Jago de Cuba, Carthagena or St Martin [Santa Marta] & thus complete a survey of the latter place which I commenced when last down there[,] when our stay was limited to seventy hours, which did not give us much time for either surveying or geology.

I was never a great hand for solitary walking in search of Geological Phenomena[,] and I am not a bit altered[.] I have never been keen on any excursion more that three days together & that generally at Halifax for fishing, &[,] as to Geology, here you are roasted by 7 A.M. & would be burnt & dried up by 2 P.M.[,] & the only locality for observation is the Sea Beach, the whole of Cuba being an impracticable forest. Yesterday my sympiesometer was smashed[,] much to my mortification & from the neglect of my Servant[.] The ship took a heavy lurch & out came a drawer from the highest nest [*sic*] and smashed my companion[,] & very nearly made a vacancy for the Admiral in your humble servant. We are all well on board, though I lost a boy overboard a month back & another is just dying of consumption[.] *Sapphire* has had a severe touch of fever – upwards of 70 cases[.] Hope[2] I believe was laid up, but there was only one death[.] The slaves at Jamaica are in an unsettled state, and I think it very doubtful how matters will end. The slaves are now free & the proprietors hire them by the day[.] The price

[1]Grace Milne Home added '(York Place)'.
[2]Thomas Hope.

varies. The estates cannot afford more than about 12 to 15 pence. The Saints[1] advise them to hold out for ½ a dollar 2d/[,][2] & accordingly there is a great deal of bad blood between the planters & negroes not working more than 5 to 6 hours. They get up at 7 o'clock, work until 9, go to breakfast, return at 9:30 A.M. & at 12 they throw down their hoe[s] & say, [']there is 15 pence I work no more this day[',] & most probably will not work for 2 days to come. The Planters are in a complete hobble, as these gentry don't care about money. I dined with a gentleman at Lucea. His servant said to him to day [*sic*] he was engaged for the day & he intended going away, & that if any gentleman was coming, he must get some one else to attend, as he could not stay. Such is Jamaica[.]

I was at a very fine Estate belonging to Wallace of Kelly.[3] The carts on the farm had not been moved since the 1st August[,] & this was the 20th October, & I was informed that on many of the Estates the whole produce will not pay for the labour of the negroes[.] Some change must take place[.] I heard two stories at Lucea, first a certain rebellion[,] 2nd nothing but quietness, The [*sic*] former from the Coroner, the second from the Chief Magistrate, who gave us a grand Ball the evening before we left[.]

My two years of Commission are now nearly expired, but I have of course another 12 months certain[,] & probably 18 months more[.] I wish there was some society, some amusement when in harbour at Jamaica[.]

I have only been in one man's house. Never did I meet such uncivil people.

The only change in my monotonous life is being a member of the Royal Artillery Mess, which is always a change[,] & a very agreeable set of gentlemen they are[.]

I want to see the black President of Port au Prince & must endeavour to meet him[.] A ship goes there every three months to look about[.]

The French have a large Squadron here. They have nearly 1000 men laid up with Scurvy, which is unknown in our service. On board the *Snake* our men have about 10 days Salt provisions to 1 of fresh[,] & yet we are all quite well.

Saturday was my birthday & a precious day it was, a hurricane of wind & rain under close reefed top sails[,] & as miserable as possible from the ship kicking about most famously. The Saturday before was

[1]Black preachers.

[2]That is, a half-dollar plus tuppence.

[3]Robert Wallace (1773–1855). See *DNB*, vol. XX, pp. 561–2.

Jean's birthday and Jan 22nd is advancing[.] I wished her many happy returns and received the same from my dear David[.]

Nov: 17th

I sail to morrow for Jamaica[.] This place[1] has civilization & is a splendid town. Nixon of *Ringdove* has shot himself[.] Reasons are only known to himself [*sic*][.] His conduct would [not?] have come before a Court Martial, but he never could have got over the Stigma.[2] When we arrived here we heard of the death of Sir C Paget[,] also before him of Captain Polkinghorne[3] of the *Crocodile*.[4]

[**68**] *Milne to David Milne*

HMS *Snake*, Vera Cruz, Mexico
30 January 1839

My dear David

I have scarcely time to write even a few lines[,] as I have ample employment all hours of the day, but as it has set in for a gale of wind[,] I can take advantage of the blow[.] It is now sometime since I last wrote you[.] My last was in November from Havanah – from which place I went to Jamaica – cruizing on my way & looking for slavers – but my cruize proved a blank[.] Two days after reaching Jamaica[,] the Admiral[,] Sir C. Paget[,] arrived from Bermuda, but so ill that he could not leave his cot, having lost the use of his limbs[.] He remained there a few days & then a Squadron was selected from the ships arrived from England & part from the Squadron there[,] & placed under the com-

[1]No location specified.

[2]See ADM1/302, Paget to Admiralty, 20 November 1838. Paget reported that Nixon had shot 'himself through the head with a Pocket Pistol between the night of the 6th & morning of the 7th Ultimo in consequence of the charge preferred against him by Henry Avery[,] a Boy serving on board that Sloop [*Ringdove*] of his having attempted to commit breaches of the 29th Article of War on the person of the said Boy': Nixon left a note claiming that he was 'the victim of an infamous conspiracy' and Paget subsequently court-martialled Avery 'for falsely accusing the said late Commander . . . '.

[3]James Polkinghorne (Puckinghorn) (*c.*1788–1839). Entered, *c.*1800; Lt, 1808; Cmdr, 1814; Capt., 1828.

[4]David Syrett and R.L. DiNardo list 29 January 1839 for Paget's death and 9 January 1839 for Polkinghorne's (*The Commissioned Sea Officers of the Royal Navy 1660–1815* [Aldershot, Hants, 1994] pp. 343, 368). Either the report Milne received of both men's demises was erroneous or, more likely, Grace Milne Home mistakenly transcribed the last few lines of a later letter onto this one. Milne himself referred to Paget's illness in a letter of 30 January 1839 (see below [**68**]).

mand of the Commodore at Jamaica.[1] We sailed thence & arrived here Dec: 29th, The [*sic*] Squadron consisting of two 74 guns [*sic*] – one small frigate 28 guns, 2 corvettes & 3 brigs[,] & we met here two more frigates & 2 more corvettes, which made our force greatly superior to the French[.][2] The two 74 guns have however proceeded to Havanah, as it looked rather too much like a compulsory mission than a mediation on our part, but John Bull is as usual always too late, for the Castle had been taken exactly one month before our arrival[.] This will[,] I suppose[,] make [i.e., generate] some outcry among the Mercantile Body in England[.] The French are still here, wishing to treat with the Mexicans, but I rather suspect the Mexicans will have nothing to say to them, or enter into any treaty whatever, but[,] having declared war against France[,] will issue letters of Marque to destroy her trade[.] This will annoy the French dreadfully. The Mexicans are so inveterate against them, that they have turned them all out of the country, & they flock down here by [the] hundreds. The famous fort of St. Juan de Ulloa was bombarded by the French Squadron – but it was not fit to stand any action. The guns run on rotten carriages & they have scarcely any powder to defend it[.] The guns themselves are not numerous[,] but they are of the most beautiful work & were cast about the year 1550 & are of brass[.] I have been occupied for the last fortnight in wrecking[.] I have however saved a fine Spanish Barque from destruction & also all of her cargo[.] She was on shore for three days before we could get her off[,] & now I am busy heaving her down to the *Snake*[,] which is a business of great responsibility & risk, more particularly when I find both her masts are rotten[.] I have hove her down three times on one side.

We have an American Corvette & two French Men of War here[,] with whom we amalgamate & dine with each other by rotation[,] which makes it very pleasant[,] as we seldom meet except on an occasion like this[.] But our mediation between Mexicans & French is not likely to prove successful[.] I wish to be away as soon as possible[,] as the Slavers now have it all their own way – no one looking out for them. The *Wanderer* captured a fine Brig with 200 slaves[:] 500 had died on the passage[.]

The Yellow Fever has been very bad in Jamaica – many have died & the Admiral was given over, but has rallied. I have invalided several

[1]On the reverse Milne added the lines quoted in the introduction regarding the circumstances of his promotion to post rank.

[2]The British squadron was dispatched to Vera Cruz in an attempt to mediate the dispute between France and Mexico. On the French attack, see *The Times* (London), 10 January 1839, p. 6; 18 January 1839, p. 4.

men from severe rheumatism, which I scarcely believe they will recover from[.]

I wanted to have gone into the country to have seen something of it, but I cannot get leave at present, & if the Interior is not better than the Coast[,] I have little to lose, as Sandy hills are the only visible object[s] with a few stunted trees & shrubs.

Our only anchorage is under the reefs of Sacrificios consisting of Coral[.] These [*sic*] are our only protection against the heavy set [*sic*: 'swell'] which sets in from the Northward with a most strong Lee current. I am afraid the last gale has made some poor fellows go to pieces, as we have picked up sundry pieces of wreck [*sic*] & several bodies on the shore[.]

Many happy returns of the New Year & also of the 22nd which I did not forget. What an old chap you are getting. Give my kind love to Jean & her flock . . .

[**69**] *Milne to Douglas*

HMS *Snake*, Port Royal, Jamaica
2 April 1839

Sir

In remitting to you the Warrants and Abstract of Punishments on board of the Sloop '*Snake*' under my command for the Quarter just ending[,] I feel called upon[,] on account of the number of punishments[,] to lay before you the cause of such apparent severity. From the Ships Company of HMS under my command[,] as also those of others then laying at Vera Cruz [men are] employed in rendering assistance to vessels in distress; it was observed that drunkenness to a very serious extent became general among the men employed on this service[,] so much so as to call upon me to take strong measures for suppressing so great an evil. This was done by placing sentinels at the different Hatchways. These very sentinels[,] I regret to say[,] were the first to forsake their stations and permit depredations on the cargo and to join in the scene of drunkenness. As I was eye witness to these excesses[,] so infamous in themselves and so subversive of order[,] that [*sic*] I would consider I would neglect my duty if an example were not made to check this conduct[.] I trust this explanation will be sufficient to satisfy you that I have not acted harshly[,] but solely called upon to do so through sheer and absolute necessity . . .

[70] *Adam to Milne*

Admiralty, London
13 August 1839

My dear Sir

. . . It was the source of much satisfaction to me to find that Commodore Douglas from his high opinion of your merit as an officer had put you in a position to be promoted[.]

[71] *Milne to David Milne*

HMS *Crocodile*, Antigua, Barbados, and Jamaica
6–12 November 1839

My dear David

I must make this a joint letter [to both David and Jean Milne Home] as I am so long in debt & I think it will be best to pay you both off at once[.] The Last received from you was dated July 12th 1838[.] Your letter was in the box which you were so kind as [to] send me[,] & which I heard of when I was last at Jamaica &[,] having been forwarded to Halifax[,] I received it there & had it immediately opened to relieve the inmates from their confinement!

The coffee pot appeared first in good condition – then came out Her Majesty[,] also in good case [*sic*] & now incased [*sic*] in a frame & staring me in the face.[1] . . . So much for the box & many thanks for my friends' recollections[.]

Here I am on the incessant swing, winging my way from one clime to another[.] We cruized from Halifax to Newfoundland[,] thence to Barbadoes[.] I called at Antigua & then went to Barbadoes[,] arrived there the 23rd Oct: & there I caught the fever, was cautious & got the Doctors in time[.] A few hours makes all the difference in this climate[.] They bled me & what [not] with Calomel &c[.] I am now well, but had a sharp attack. They talked of blisters, I did not. I have therefore saved that part of the play for another time, but I expect to have no more; once in one station is quite enough, & this ship as yet is exceedingly healthy[.] The *Satellite* however has lost several men – a Lieut: and a Mid: & the only officers doing duty were the Capt[,] Purser & Surgeon.

Sunday was Nov: 3rd. I did not forget to wish Jean's health in a glass of toast & water [*sic*] – very poor stuff – but the birthdays are

[1]Grace Milne Home added: '(Then comes an enumeration of various eatables enclosed)'.

now becoming so numerous, that I find no small difficulty in keeping count.

Nov: 11th Jamaica

I anchored here last evening from Barbadoes & now prepare this for the packet[.] I am quite well, but the weather here is very unfavorable – not to me, but I mean in general – sickness prevails[.] I visited the Hospital & spoke to 24 cases of Yellow Fever &[,] as there are no other ships in harbour, it is a daily duty, and I think a very proper one[.] Some Captains dislike the idea & more so the duty[.] If a duty, it should be properly done, as it gives confidence to the men, & shews a proper attention to their misfortunes.

There is no news here[.] The Governor Sir T. Metcalfe[1] has arrived[.] He gives a Ball on the 21st[,] but as he does not offer either a conveyance or a bed[,] I do not intend [on] going unless he does so[.]

I have been landing my magnetic needle at a Storehouse in the Dockyard – the one that used to be in my room at Milne Graden [–] for the diurnal variation & aurora, &[,] as I may be here for a fortnight[,] I hope to get a series of observations which I have been unable to do before, but it is tedious doing anything in a climate like this. The Ther: in my cabin now is at 87° & not a breath of air, & observing in the sun is to roast oneself entirely.

I have some intention of paying a visit to the Mountains & see them ere I return home, as I have never been 20 miles, nay, not 5½ into the interior, and only once at Spanish Town[,] the seat of Government, & only 3 or 4 times at Kingston[,] which is the Seaport town, about 4 miles from this[,] higher up the harbour[.]

I don't know a person on the Island & therefore have paid no visits[.] My stay in the West Indies will probably be till March or April &[,] as I go to Newfoundland for certain next summer[,] I do not suppose I will again visit this region of heat & fever . . .

[**72**] *Milne to Douglas*

HMS *Crocodile*, Jamaica
27 December 1839

Sir,

In Pursuance of your Instructions of the 28th November 1839[,] I proceeded to sea from Port Royal in HM Ship under my command for

[1]Charles Theophilus, Baron Metcalfe (1785–1846); Governor of Jamaica 1839–42.

St. Jago de Cuba on the morning of the 30th[,] but owing to light W[esterl]y winds and calms[,] did not arrive at that Port until late in the evening of Saturday the 7th Decr 1839[.] on the following Monday I waited on His Excellency the Governor in company with Mr. Wright[,] HM Pro Consul at that Port[,] for the purpose of communicating with him on the subject contained in your Instructions relative to the four boys kidnapped from Jamaica and sold at St. Jago de Cuba. I have to acquaint you[,] relative to this transaction[,] that 3 of the boys have already been recovered and were sent to Jamaica in June last by HM Pro Consul[,] one of them stating to him at the time that his name was Wellington[,] and a receipt granted to the Authorities of the Province. On the boys being examined at Jamaica[,] this statement did not prove to be true. The boy Wellington therefore remains undiscovered[,] nor can any trace be found where he is. The Person[,] Garcis[,] it is said a Frenchman by birth[,] who purchased the boys had been Arrested and Prosecuted[,] but has since escaped from Prison. His Brother in Law[,] a baker in whose yard the Boys were detained[,] was also examined [but] he has also fled from St. Jago[,] and the Government Authorities have been unable to trace them or obtain any further information relative to this transaction. It is presumed that on examination of the boys already sent to Jamaica[,] with whom the boy Wellington was associated[,] some information may be obtained relative to Wellington's present residence[;] whether he was sent to any other part of the Island, sold or died; and should any clue be obtained from such examination[,] His Excellency the Governor has expressed his determination to cooperate in any way possible with HM Pro Consul[,] who has devoted great attention to this transaction in the recovery of the individuals and Punishment of the offenders.

Government Prosecutions and Investigations[,] copies of which will[,] I believe[,] be sent to Jamaica[,] have been carried on against the Individuals mentioned for some years (1835) up to this Present Month[,] to endeavour to trace those who have been associated in the guilty transaction[.] Garcis having escaped from Prison[,] the Gaoler has been substituted for him[,] and has been in prison for some months. I also brought before His Excellency's notice the case of the Boy sold at [?Jucaro] [,][1] a Port 20 Leagues East of Trinidad[,] but that place not being in the Province under His Excellency's command nor in the jurisdiction of the Pro Consul[,] the subject could not be taken up[.] HM Consul at Havanah has been made acquainted with the transaction

[1]Jucaro is about 60 nautical miles east of Trinidad, and thus corresponds to the location. *Crocodile*'s letter book appears to read 'Elio'.

and[,] I believe[,] has already taken measures on the subject. As no further steps could be taken[,] nor information procured until the examination of the boys at Jamaica was remitted to St. Jago[,] I did not consider it would be of any benefit my returning to that Port as directed by your Instructions[.] I therefore proceeded to sea on the 11th Decr 1839 for Port au Prince[,] St Domingo[,] where I arrived on the 16th and delivered your despatch to Captain Courtenay[,][1] H Majestys Charge de Affaires. It was my intention to have left that Port on the 20th[,] agreeably to your Instructions[,] had not Captain Courtenay requested me to remain a few days[,] as he considered HM Ship remaining there was of importance at the present time. I have therefore to state that I left that Port on the 22nd[,] passed a French Man of War of 20 guns off Cape Dama Marie[,] apparently bound to Port au Prince[,] at which place the French Admiral is daily expected[,] and [I] have to acquaint you with my arrival this day . . .

[**73**] *Thomas Harvey to Milne*

Port Royal
15 February 1840

. . . you are hereby required and directed to complete the Provisions of Her Majesty's Ship under your Command to three months and[,] having done so[,] and being in all respects ready to put to sea . . . to cruize around Cuba either to the Northward or the Southward[,] as you may deem best from any intelligence you may receive, for the protection of British Interests and the suppression of the Slave Trade until the 20th of April[,] when you are to return to Port Royal for further orders . . .

[**74**] *Declaration of Capture of* Mercedita, *Spanish Slaving Schooner*

HMS *Crocodile,* off the Cayman Islands
13 April 1840

I[,] Alexr Milne[,] Captain of Her Britannic Majestys Ship '*Crocodile*' hereby certify that on this 13th day of April 1840, being in or about Lat 19.30[N] and Longitude 81.41[W,] I detained the Schr *Mercedita*[,] sailing under Spanish colours[,] armed with one gun ——

[1]George William Conway Courtenay (1795–1863). Entered, 1805; Lt, 1813; Cmdr, 1823; Capt., 1828; Rear-Adm., 1854. Courtenay was British Consul-General to Haiti 1832–42.

pounder[,] commanded by Matia de Lulueta[,] who declared her to be bound from Trinidad de Cuba to Caho Lopes con escalain [*sic*] Rio Gabon[,] with a crew consisting of fifteen men and one passenger and having on board no slaves but detained for trial before the Mixed Commission Court at Havana for having certain Articles on board contrary to the Tenth Article of the Treaty existing between Great Britain and Spain[,] namely under the fifth section of the said Article for having open gratings for the Hatchways[,] instead of being close as usual in Merchant Vessels.

Under the sixth section of the above Article for having an extraordinary number of Water Casks (although some shook[1]) in her hold and not specified in the certificate of her cargo.

Under the eighth section of the above Article for having a boiler of unusual dimensions stowed in the Hold (independent of the one on deck) also not specified in the certificate of her cargo. as [*sic*] the above Articles appear to me to be in violation of the Treaty existing between Great Britain and Spain . . . I have therefore sent her in charge of Lieutenant Thos C Woodman[,][2] Third Lieutenant of Her Majestys Ship '*Crocodile*' under my command[,] who will lay before the Mixed Commission Court the requisite Documents. I do further declare that the said schooner appeared to be seaworthy and was supplied with a sufficient quantity of Water and Provisions for the support of her crew for her voyage.

[**75**] *Milne to Woodman*

HMS *Crocodile*, at sea
13 April 1840

You are hereby required and directed to repair on board the Spanish Schooner *Mercedita*[,] detained by me this day in contravention of the 10th Article of the Treaty existing between Great Britain and Spain[.] you will take with you the officers and men named on the other side[3] and proceed with all possible expedition to the Havana[,] where you will lay before the Court of Mixed Commission, the enclosed documents and proceed in the condemnation of the said Vessel[.] you will[,] on being superseded for the Vessel by the authority of the Mixed

[1]'A set of staves and headings sufficient for one hogshead, barrel, cask, or the like, prepared for use and bound up compactly for convenience of transport' (*Oxford Universal Dictionary*, 1955 edn, p. 1877).

[2]Thomas Copeland Woodman (*c.*1821–49). Entered, 1833; Lt, 1839.

[3]A mate, quartermaster, six sailors and four marines were detailed as prize crew.

Commission Court[,] repair on board HM Ship '*Romney*' where you will remain with the crew until my Arrival[.] you are to be careful to keep your men armed[,] to avoid sending too many men aloft at one time[,] and be prepared to avoid surprise. I expect from you a zealous performance of this duty intrusted to your charge.

[**76**] *Milne to Douglas*

HMS *Crocodile*, Port Royal, Jamaica
22 April 1840

Sir,

I beg to acquaint you that[,] in pursuance of Instructions from Vice Admiral Sir Thos Harvey K.C.B. Commander in Chief[,] I put to sea from Port Royal in Her Majesty's Ship '*Crocodile*' under my command on the 17th day of February last, for the purpose of cruising on the coast of Cuba, to protect British Interest and suppression of slave dealing. I continued to cruise from the above date until the 12 March in the vicinity of Trinidad, St. Jago de Cuba, and Cumberland Harbour, both of which latter ports I put into for information; from there I stood to the Westward off the Isle of Pines[,] round Cape Antonio, and was off Havana on the 21st in company with Her Majesty's Ships '*Cleopatra*', '*Satellite*', and '*Racer*'. from [*sic*] there I proceeded off the Cay Sal Bank,[1] and Anchored at the Island of Cal Sal[,] where a settlement had been found but no inhabitants; in pursuance of [standing] Instructions on the station[,] the Houses were destroyed. on [*sic*] the morning of the 25th March we parted our chain cable when getting under weigh from the above Anchorage[,] in consequence of a heavy swell setting in; proceeded to sea during the succeeding gale from the SW and returned on the 28th[,] picked up our anchor, and proceeded to Havana where I arrived on the following day (29)th [*sic*][.] Having completed water, I again put to sea on the 2nd Instant leaving in Harbour Her Majesty's Ships '*Cleopatra*' and '*Romney*'. Her Majesty's Brig '*Pilot*' proceeded on the same day to Galveston . . .

[1]Between Cuba and Florida in the Florida Strait, approximately 24N lat., 80W long.

[77] *Milne to Douglas*

HMS *Crocodile*, Havana
7 May 1840

Sir,

I beg to acquaint you that, in pursuance of your Instructions of the 25th April last[,] I immediately on my Arrival [*sic*] at this port made myself acquainted from . . . HM Consul with the application he had made to the Spanish Government relative to HM Ship *Rover*'s boat having been fired upon near the Isle of Pines. I found the Spanish Government[,] in their various communications which had taken place [*sic*][,] had evinced an anxious desire to forward the enquiry, and[,] as the matter is at present undergoing judicial investigation under the orders of the Captain General; and there appears no delay or wish to evade enquiry on the subject, I did not consider any application on my part could be of any use in forwarding your views of the subject, and therefore made Application to the Spanish Government[,] but left the matter entirely in the hands of Her Majesty's Consul . . .

[78] *Milne to Thomas Harvey*

HMS *Crocodile*, Bermuda
23 May 1840

Sir,

I have the honour to inform you that on the passage from Havana to Jamaica . . . when off the North side of the Grand Cayman on the 13th April, I fell in with a suspicious Sch[oone]r running to the West[war]d[.] having alt[ere]d course for the purpose of closing with the stranger[,] it was observed he made all sail to avoid our closing, upon which I made sail in chase to the Westward and[,] after a Run of 38 miles succeeded[,] by firing from the long gun[,] in bringing to a Schooner under Spanish colours called the '*Mercedita*'[,] three days out from Trinidad de Cuba[,] bound to Cape Lopez Rio Gabon Coast of Africa[.] there being no slaves on board[,] I directed the hold to be opened and found 1st[,] Boilers of an unusual size in which were stowed biscuit. 2nd[,] Leagers[1] of large size[,] some shook and marked[,] ready for being put up; neither had she close hatches fitted to her Hatchways[,] and[,] as these several articles were in violation of the 10th Article of the existing Treaty between Great

[1]Water casks.

Britain and Spain for the suppression of the Slave Trade, determined me [*sic*] to send her in for trial before the Mixed Court of Commission at Havana. she [*sic*] was accordingly placed in the charge of a Prize Crew under command of Lt Woodman[,] to whom I delivered the necessary papers required by the Act of Parliament and[,] on his Arrival at Havana[,] he produced them before the Court; the trial was immediately commenced, and the vessel condemned as a legal Prize to the ship under my command. I have received the necessary Receipts for her, from the Mixed Court of Commission, a survey of the stores, as [*sic*: 'and'] also an inventory of Cargo[,] consisting of the Articles herewith specified[,] was delivered with the vessel and I intend by HMS '*Pluto*' to transmit to Messrs Halford and Co. Navy Agents[,] the Copy of these papers and the necessary documents to claim Prize Money.

[Cargo]

68 Kegs fine powder 3 not quite full
1 keg of filled Cart[rid]ges
4 Cases of Musquets [*sic*] each containing 20 and Bayonets and 12 loose in the Cabin
10 Pipes of Aqua vitae one of which leaks a good deal
11 Half Pipes of Aqua vitae
55 Barrels of Do
1 Half Pipe of Wine
30 Square Packages of Tobacco
9 Casks of Salt Meat
6 " " Biscuit
1 " " Vinegar
7 " " Manioc[1]
1 " " Sugar

60 Pair slave irons
3 Compasses
1 Box Coloured Beads
1 case of Medicine
1 Box of Vermicelli
1 Bag Coffee
1 Copper
2 Boilers
2 Hides
10 Leagers shook
100 Hoops for Do Iron
4 Boxes of Handb[ill]s Coloured
1½ Cask of Rice
8 Boxes Salt Herrings
16 Tin Dishes for [?Crew]
1 Large Copper Pump
1 Tin Pump
2 Flags
1½ Coil New Rope

2 Hand leads
2 Bags of Beans
1 Boat
7 Beams
20 Broad Plank
27 Round Shot
10 Grape and bags of musquet balls and about 3 or 4 cords of Fire Wood

[1]Cassava.

1½ Kitts[1] of
Stock Fish
16 Jars of Oil
1 Bag of Salt

[**79**] *Milne to Prescott*[2]

HMS *Crocodile*, St. Johns, Newfoundland
7 June 1840

Sir,

I have the honour to acquaint you that I have received Instructions from Vice Admiral Sir Thos Harvey[,] Commander in Chief on the N American and West India Stations [*sic*][,] to proceed to Newfoundland in HM Ship under my command, for the protection of the Fisheries, around its Coasts, and also the Coast of Labrador. 'By the tenor of the said Instructions', I am directed to make application to your Excellency relative to the payment[,] by the colony[,] of the Expenses [*sic*] for the lodging of the Boats Crews, which I may find it necessary to leave on various parts of the Coast, for the protection of the Fisheries, during the fishing season, and also to intimate to your Excellency how much preferable the Commander in Chief considers it would be, if the Crew [*sic*] required to remain at fixed Stations as Armed Boat Crews, to prevent infringement of French Fishing Vessels, were wholly hired and appointed by the Island Government, leaving HM Ships with the entire complements to render their full and efficient countenance and cooperation towards the future effectual security of the Coasts in question from exterior molestation and interference of any kind. I am further directed to act throughout my continuance on this service, as far as may be possible[,] in entire and perfect concert and cooperation with your Excellency, as Governor of Newfoundland[,] not only as relative to the fishings [*sic*], but to any other matters which your Excellency may bring before me on the spot, for the security and advancement of the Interests of the Colony and its fisheries. I have therefore to acquaint your Excellency that I shall be glad to receive any suggestions which you may consider necessary for aiding in the protection of the respective fisheries, or on

[1]A wooden or straw container or basket.

[2]Sir Henry Prescott, C.B., K.C.B., G.C.B. (1783–1874). Entered, 1796; Lt, 1802; Cmdr, 1808; Capt., 1810; Rear-Adm., 1847; Vice-Adm., 1854; Adm., 1860; Naval Lord of the Admiralty, 1847. Prescott was governor of Newfoundland from 1834 to 1841.

any other matter in which I can be of service to the interests and welfare of the Colony of Newfoundland.

[**80**] *Prescott to Milne*

St. Johns, Newfoundland
10 June 1840

Sir,

I have the honour to acknowledge the receipt of your letter of the 7th Inst. as also to thank you for submitting to my perusal the orders under which you are at present acting, and for the expression of your desire to pursue the objects thereof as much possible in accordance with my wishes.

I shall, in the first place, be prepared to defray the expenses of the Lodgings of such Boats' Crews as you may find it necessary to leave on the coast for the protection of the fisheries during the Fishing season.

As only one Ship of War is employed on our shores[,] I think that no improvement can be made upon the first Six Paragraphs of your instructions.[1] It will certainly be desirable that I should communicate with you on your return from the Southward and Westward, either by boat from the offing, or by your coming into the Port with your Ship, as you may think best.

Supposing no particular matter to have occurred, I should then recommend you fulfilling the Services prescribed in the 7th Paragraph,[2] but unless some unforeseen necessity should arise for your immediate return here from Cape St. John[,] I would recommend your proceeding thence to that part of the Labrador which is within the limits of this Government, that is to say, from Blanc Sablon[,] in about 57 W. Long. Northward[,] at least as far as Sandwich Bay[,] and further if you find that our Settlements are still more extended, as the whole coast to the entrance of Hudson's Straits is included in my Commission.

You will observe that the part of Labrador named in the 11th Paragraph of your orders[3] forms no portion of the abovenamed limits[,] and that while stationed there you cannot be considered as protecting the Newfoundland fisheries.

As respects that branch of the service[,] it would probably be desirable to commence with Sandwich Bay and[,] having proceeded thence

[1]Those relating to fisheries protection on Newfoundland's south coast.

[2]Surveying the coast north of Cape St John.

[3]The north shore of the Gulf of St Lawrence west of Blanc Sablon, which is part of Quebec.

Northward as far as may be found needful, to return alongshore . . . passing thro' the Straits of Belleisle to visit that remaining portion of Labrador belonging to this Government, the other portion mentioned by the Commander in Chief – What is termed the 'French Shore' in Newfoundland – and then[,] again shewing yourself at St. Pierre's and the adjacent coast[,] to proceed leisurely back to St. Johns . . .

[**81**] *Milne to the Governor of St Pierre's and Miquelon*

HMS *Crocodile*, St. Pierre
20 June 1840

Sir,

I have the honour to acquaint your Excellency that I have received Instructions from Vice Admiral Sir Thos Harvey[,] Commander in Chief on the N American and West India Stations [*sic*], to protect the British Fisheries of Newfoundland from all infringement on the part of Foreign Vessels [and] of the limits prescribed to such vessels for their fisheries on the above Coast, by the existing Treaties with Great Britain.

I have therefore to express my hope, that your Excellency will be pleased to issue such notices, and directions, to the French Fishermen of St. Pierres, on their coming to that Island, as will prevent my being compelled[,] whilst in the execution of this service, to any severe measure towards them, in consequence of their attempting to renew the infringements complained of in former years, relative to their taking Bait or Fish on the southern Coasts of Newfoundland, in parts whereby the existing Treaties they are prohibited from approaching.

[**82**] *Milne to the Officers of HMS* Crocodile

[HMS *Crocodile*
July 1840]

The officers sent on detached service, are [?amicably] to obtain Answers to the adjoining Queries, from the principal inhabitants of the Settlements[,] or other person competent to give it; the name of the informant and principal family to be noted. The Bishop of Newfoundland wishes Answers to his Queries[,] which the officer will also fill up.[1]

[1]See the following document, [**83**].

1st Name of the Settlement ______
2nd Number of Inhabitants Male and Female ______
3rd Whether there is any resident Magistrate ______
4th Whether the Settlement is increasing, or decreasing ______
5th Whether any Vessels belong to the Settlement, and how employed ______
6th What fisheries are in the Vicinity ______
Cod, Salmon or others ______
7th Whether the fisheries are on the increase, or decrease, within the last three years ______
8th By whom are the Salmon fisheries owned, and are any of them fished by French fishermen ______
9th Do the French encroach on the Fisheries, or on the Coast for taking Bait ______
10th At what places, and at what period of the year ______
11th Do the French, or Americans, carry on a Barter Trade on the Coast, in this Vicinity ______
[12th] What are the adjoining Settlements ______
[13th] What Number of Inhabitants do they contain ______

[**83**] *Bishop Spencer*[1] *to the Officers of HMS* Crocodile

[St Johns, Newfoundland
July 1840]

In any Settlements where a congregation of two hundred persons or more belonging to the Church can be regularly assembled and where the residents are prepared to provide residence together with a salary of £30 or 20*l*. towards the maintenance of a Clergyman, The [*sic*] Bishop will appoint a Missionary with a stipend of £150 or £200 per Annum from the Society for the propagation of the Gospel in Foreign parts.

1st How many Protestants belonging to the Church of England, or willing to attend divine Service in the Church[,] within the Settlement ______
2nd Is there any Church or building appropriated to divine worship within the Settlement, if not[,] to what extent would the people contribute to the erection of a Church ______
3rd If there is a Church already built in the Settlement, is it in good repair [and] has it been consecrated ______

[1]Aubrey George Spencer (1795–1872), first bishop of Newfoundland.

4th Is the Settlement periodically visited by any Clergyman of the Church of England, and if so how frequently ______

5th In the absence of a Clergyman[,] is divine Service performed on Sunday, and [if so] by whom ______

6th Are the people willing to contribute towards the maintenance of a Clergyman, and to provide him with a Residence ______

7th What number of Schools [are there] in connection with the established Church? The number of pupils, and the funds by which they are maintained. ______

[84] *The Captains of the French Brigs* Binicos, Sometre, Alcide, *and* Frainida *to Milne*

Pacquet Harbour, Newfoundland
30 July 1840

Sir,

Yesterday, at the moment of your entrance into this harbour, we were in a hurry to hoist the French flag at the establishments which we have a right to occupy in the business of the fishery. It was with the greatest astonishment that we received immediately the orders on your part to strike the colours of our nations. That we have the right, or that we have it not, is not for us to decide.

We hoisted our flag for the purpose of saluting that of a friendly nation; had we not done so, we should have thought that we had essentially failed. In giving us to understand that the Island of Newfoundland, not being French property, we are desired to hoist our flag on board of our vessels; but our vessels are in different parts, very far removed from the residences; we must therefore not answer the salute of any vessel whatsoever during our stay on the coast, and conceal, if we may so express it, the French flag. If the Island does not belong, as we fully believe, we are even certain that the habitations which we occupy are French occupancies, during the season of the fishery, and that no person has the right during that time, to hinder us from exhibiting the French flag on them.

To the moment that you shall receive our letter we have, then, decided to hoist our Flag, and we shall not strike it, but on a new order on your part.

It is with pain, Monsieur le Commandant, that we see ourselves compelled to give you this trouble; but we should fear that we had failed in national honour, if we made not every effort in support of the colours that 1830 restored to us, and of which every Frenchman is proud.

We have the honour to salute you, Mon. le Commandant, with consideration.

[85] *Milne to the Captains of the French Brigs* Binicos, Sometre, Alcide, *and* Frainida

HMS *Crocodile*, Pacquet Harbour, Newfoundland
30 July, 1840

Gentlemen

I have to acknowledge the receipt of your letter of this morning's date[,] complaining and also protesting against my order of last evening 'That the French National Colours which are hoisted on the Establishments on Shore should be removed' (at the same time acquainting you that you had the opportunity of displaying your National colours on board your respective vessels now at anchor in this Port) not one of which have hoisted their national colours since my arrival[,] and therefore I can only suppose that they are French.

I regret that there should have been any misunderstanding on the subject; no disrespect being intended to the National Flag of France[,] but I cannot permit it, or any other Foreign National Flag whatever, to be hoisted on the shores of Newfoundland a colony of Great Britain . . .

[86] *Milne Report on the Newfoundland Fisheries*[1]

HMS *Crocodile*
7 June–13 August 1840

The first communication with the shore after leaving the H[arbou]r of St Johns on the 16th June was on the South Coast at Cape Lance[2] near Cape St Mary's. The place of landing was at a small bay called Little Pine; here I found Mr Littler, and his family occupying a pasture [*sic*] farm. There are no fishing establishments at this bay from its exposed situation; the nearest is Branch[,] about eight miles to the NE of Cape Lance. The Bay of Little Pine is yearly frequented by Caplin towards the end of June; and resorted to by our fishermen for the purpose of procuring them for Bait. In answer to my enquiries[,] I was informed that French Vessels never visit this part of the Coast; nor had he ever heard of their encroachments in the neighbourhood.

[1]The copy of this report submitted to Sir Thomas Harvey can be found in ADM1/5495.

[2]Point Lance.

When visiting different parts of the South Coast[,] I have been informed that the fishing for Cod in the vicinity of Cape St Mary's was considered very good; the fish being abundant, and of a larger size than those caught further to the West. Individuals belonging to Fortune, Lamelin and other establishments who can afford to purchase, or build Schooners from 20 to 30 Tons[,] send them to Cape St Mary's to fish and return with their cargoes to cure them.

20th June At St Pierre's. I arrived on the 20th June and found the outer roads, and likewise the inner Harbour[,] filled with French Vessels, there could not have been less than 80 or 90[,] averaging from 120 to 300 Tons[.] They were chiefly Brigs[,] lately arrived from the Banks with their cargoes[,] which they were then discharging and making preparation for again departing for the banks for the fishings of July, August, and September[.] many[,] if not all[,] were delayed in harbour in consequence of the want of Bait (Caplin)[,] the supply afforded by the Bays of St Pierres and Miquelon having been nearly exhausted[,] and inadequate to the great demand which the number of French Vessels (this year amounting to about three hundred) require; in former years when this scarcity of Bait occurred[,] it was common for the French Vessels to proceed to the Bays on our coast and there haul for Caplin, in violation of the limits, as defined by Treaty. This practice they have almost entirely given up, in consequence of the risk of capture, and the fear of punishment, and also from their being now enabled to procure a sufficient supply of the required Bait[,] brought over from Fortune, Grand Bank, and other settlements on our coast by our Fishermen. The small schooners belonging to the above ports and those belonging to other settlements supply the great demand which the French require. the [*sic*] Trade is conducted in an illegal manner.
1st[:] By the registered Vessels not having a Custom House clearance[,] in Violation of the Act 3rd and 4th William 4th Cap 59.
2nd[:] by boats not registered[,] who have therefore no right under the same act to carry on a Foreign Trade.

At St Pierre's on the 22nd June 5 Schooners left that port[,] all of whom I detained and they all admitted their having brought Caplin over[,] but pleaded ignorance of its being illegal. I however released them[,] warning them of the illegal trade they were carrying on; the punishment to which they are liable [&] the determination to seize all vessels which I should in future find under similar circumstances[.] since that time I have been informed that 20 Schooners went to St Pierre's loaded with Caplin about the beginning of July[,] and that this

trade is daily carried on to a great extent. It is obvious the British Trade in fish must suffer by permitting this Traffic to Continue[,]
1st[:] By the quantity of Fish which the French Vessels are enabled to take from the great supply of Caplin they can procure so easily, by which means they now supply Foreign Markets to a greater extent than formerly. The success with which they prosecute their fishing, is entirely owing to this supply of Bait[,] therefore giving encouragement to an increase of their fishing Vessels[,] which is actually the Case.
2nd[:] The boats being employed taking Caplin for the supply of the French Bankers[,] they do not prosecute the Cod fishing as formerly[;] the quantity of fish actually taken by British fishermen will consequently be on the decline[,] and therefore our Foreign exports.
3rd[:] The consequence of a trade in Caplin to St Pierre's has been the means of increasing a Smuggling Trade along the Coast[,] for in return for the supply of Caplin[,] the fishermen are paid with money which is laid out in St Pierre's for Tea, Brandy and other prohibited Articles[,] which are brought over and smuggled into the various Settlements along the Coast[,] paying no duty, by which means the Revenue is defrauded[,] the British Merchant is not employed for those necessaries of life, and perhaps is not even paid for any advances of necessaries, which he may have given for the previous winter.

<u>23rd June 1840</u> <u>Little St Lawrence</u>
The settlement at this port is extremely limited[,] consisting of only one permanent resident[,] Mr Thorne and his family[,] who conduct a fishing establishment[.] there are several others on a limited scale by persons who come there for the season, disposing of their fish to Mr Thorne. The principal settlement is at Great St Lawrence[,] about two miles to the Westward[.] the number of inhabitants averages at present about two hundred[,] including children[,] and is slowly on the increase. There are about sixty small fishing boats employed on [*sic*] this settlement in the Cod fisheries[,] the produce being disposed of either to Mr Thorne at Little St Lawrence or at the establishment of a Jersey House at Great Laun. The Inhabitants complain of the fishermen at Fortune Bay coming to the Harbours of the St Lawrences with large Sch[oone]rs (which they cannot afford to procure for themselves)[,] each having 2 or 3 punts with them for the purpose of the inshore fishing, while the schooners are employed in the offing, by which means the fish are prevented from coming in shore[,] or are driven off the Coast before they in their small boats are able to catch them[,] and when the fish are scarce, or will not bite, these Fortune Bay fishermen haul Caplin on their shores and Bays[,] with which they load their schooners and

proceed to St Pierre's[,] dispose of their cargo, and again return to prosecute the Fishery at a more favourable period. The Inhabitants alledge [*sic*] that in consequence of the Fortune Bay people coming to the St Lawrences[,] their fishing is on the decline. at [*sic*] Little St Lawrence Salmon are taken in nets laid out from the rocks and moored with an anchor in which the fish mesh themselves[,] a common manner of fishing all along the coast. In answer to enquiries relative to encroachments by the French[,] I obtained information that the French now and then do encroach for a day or so for the purpose of taking Caplin early in the season[,] but they do not fish in the neighbourhood for Cod.

<u>25th June 1840</u> <u>Great Laun</u> [Lawn]
is [*sic*] situated about 11 miles to the Westward of the St Lawrences[.] it is a settlement consisting of about 120 to 150 Inhabitants[,] all employed in the Cod fisheries. The settlement is slowly on the increase[.] this[,] I believe[,] is owing to settlers coming from Fortune and Grand Bank[,] where the harbours are not so good nor the fisheries so productive. At this port the principal permanent resident is a Mr Connor[,] carrying on an establishment for Cod and Salmon. The house of Nicholle and Co. of Jersey have also a fishing establishment at this port under the charge of Mr Cloke. There are a number of small sch[oone]rs belonging to the Inhabitants[,] which proceed to the Laun Islands (about 7 to 9 miles distant) to fish[,] whilst the small punts are similarly engaged at the entrance of the H[arbou]r. The fisheries are on the increase within the last three years. as [*sic*] many fish have been taken this season (ending June) as during the whole of last year[.] the Caplin had set in early and abundant. The Salmon fishing is carried on by Bar Nets across the entrance of two small rivers[,] but this year a sch[ooner]r from St Johns is prosecuting this fishing with great success, having brought several large nets which are laid straight out from the points in the H[arbou]r with Anchors[,] in which the fish mesh themselves as they run along shore[,] and the number daily taken is from 20 to 40, which are salted for exportation. This fishing has entirely destroyed the fishing at the entrance of the rivers fished by Mr Connor. relative [*sic*] to encroachments by the French[,] the following replies were received in answer to queries on the subject[.] That the French occasionally encroached for Caplin and Cod[,] two Sch[oone]rs having been hauling for the former in Little Laun Bay early in June[,] and that they sometimes fished for the latter off the Laun Islands in the same month. I may here remark that the above observations relative to the French were only elicited by questioning Individuals[:] no com-

plaint was ever made of such or [of] any encroachments, and I am inclined to think that there is rather a dread of giving information, or an understanding between the residents themselves and the French; as it was hinted to me by a person not connected with the locality, that to give information of the French encroachment was to risk one's life. I have since heard that Mr Connor has a niece married to a French fisherman, and another resident[,] about eighty years old and blind, has also a daughter married to a French man engaged in fishing; that those individuals fish off the Laun Islands; come into Laun, clean their fish, and then carry them to St Pierre's. Mr Connor has several French people engaged in his service for curing fish; it was also mentioned that sometimes 12 to 20 French Vessels will be fishing off Laun[,] and yet no complaint of encroachment was [*sic*] ever made. I may also here state that the period of the year when the French encroachments are more generally felt is early in June[,] when the Caplin first strike upon the Coast. if [*sic*] the Bays are then hauled for them, before spawning[,] they are very likely to leave the Bay entirely. All the inhabitants are Catholics except about 14 to 20.

<u>6th July 1840</u> <u>Lamelin</u> [Lamaline]

There are two settlements at the Lamelin Islands close together and therefore may be considered as one. The number of Inhabitants[,] including children[,] is about 400 and is on the increase by settlers from Fortune Bay: about 70 fishing boats are owned by the inhabitants[,] entirely engaged in the Cod fishing. Their fishing ground extends from P[oin]t May to Lamelin and from thence to the Laun Islands, but their largest Sch[oone]rs proceed to Cape St Mary's, returning to Lamelin to cure their fish. The fishings [*sic*] of this year have been very productive[,] as on other parts of the coast, and as an instance of the quantity of fish[,] I may mention that at one haul of a Cod seine 140 quintals of Cod were taken at this place. As Lamelin is the nearest settlement to St Pierre's and the coast from it to Pt May is only 10 miles distant from that Island, it is natural that this part of the coast should be more subject to encroachment by the French fishermen than any other. Mr Pitman[,] and [*sic*] old fisherman and the principal resident[,] stated that the encroachments are not so numerous as formerly in consequence of Caplin being carried to St Pierre [*sic*] in sufficient quantities for the French Bankers: that they did encroach for Bait at times between Pt May and Lamelin[,] and also to fish for Cod off Pt May: that the coast being so very close to the Island, the French Sch[oone]rs run over from St Pierre's early in the morning, and are back again with their boat[s] full of fish in five to six hours. this [*sic*] speedy dispatch of business renders it difficult to detect them, and more especially as the English and French boats are similarly rigged, there being no feature to distinguish them from each other. No ship could attempt to chase a Sch[oone]r or fishing boat near the line of limit, from the danger of the Navigation caused by the Lamelin ledges running off the coast for several miles: the constant fogs in which this part of the coast is so suddenly enveloped; and the strength and uncertainty of the currents; from the great number of boats in sight at one time whose nationality you cannot know without boarding; the excuses offered of beating up for St Pierres, and not finding them in the act of fishing renders it a difficult matter to detain them legally. It may be asked why the French boats encroach on our shores at all, when the fishing off St Pierres and Miquelon are [*sic*] so productive, and as close to the doors of their own curing houses. The answer given is that the fish are better, it may be so, but from my own observations, I could observe no difference, or otherwise, nor did I observe[,] in passing thro the channel to Fortune, any boats fishing near Pt May, but vast numbers off the H[arbou]r of St Pierre and [off] Miquelon. I am therefore of opinion that the encroachments are chiefly to obtain an early or also a continued supply of Bait, and that it is when first the Caplin set in on the Coast that protection is chiefly required[:] from the end of May to the end of June, by that means to prevent the Caplin being driven from the bays they resort to for the purpose of spawning[,] and I have been told that after the first fortnight when the Caplin have set in[,] all the hauling of the French would do little harm. To leave an officer and boats crew at Lamelin I did not consider would have been of any material benefit at this late season of the year[,] but should any ship visit the Coast in May[,] I would recommend a fishing Sch[oone]r to be hired[,] of sufficient size to keep the sea in case of bad weather, to render sufficient comfort for the crew; as it may most likely happen that[,] instead of being able to return to their H[ea]d Q[uarte]rs at Lamelin[,] they may be absent for days either to the East or West according to the gales[,] and an open boat would be unsafe and unfit for such a purpose[,] and to render efficient service for the protection of the Coast and safety of the Vessel[,] a pilot would be required[,] acquainted with the various localities where encroachments are made, [&] where security may speedily be obtained on the sudden setting in of the fogs, or bad weather. Her cruising ground would extend from Fortune to Pt May and from thence to Little St Lawrence[,] in all which extent of Coast consisting of 45 miles [*sic*] there are bays in which Caplin resort[,] and if any Vessel differing from those on the coast were employed in this service[,] be assured it would be readily distinguished by the French men and while absent on her avocations at Fortune, Caplin would be hauled by them at Lamelin. But what do the Lamelin people themselves say on the subject.[?]

'We are in great want of some person having the authority of a magistrate[,] not only to settle disputes among ourselves, but having authority to remove the French from our fishing grounds[.] when we go to them and tell them you must leave this, you are on our grounds, they reply ["]who are you, you may be Americans and therefore we have as much right to fish here as yourselves. produce [*sic*] your authority and we will leave.["] It is this authority we want, we will man our boats for the purpose[,] only let us have an authorized person.'

At this place all the Inhabitants are Protestants; they are very anxious to obtain a Clergyman[,] provided he will undertake to instruct a school, but if not, they would prefer a School Master for their children[,] who would also read prayers on Sundays. their [*sic*] wishes are certainly worthy of consideration[,] as I found at Great Laun and St Lawrence Roman Catholic Schools established; and the visitations of the Roman Catholic Clergy frequent[,] and many of the Protestant Inhabitants along the Coast have become Catholics owing entirely to the want of Protestant Clergymen.

<u>7th July 1840</u> <u>Grand Bank</u>

The number of Inhabitants at Grand Bank are about 300 and rather on the increase. There are 4 registered sch[oone]rs belonging to the Port[,] and also a number of [the] smaller class occupied in the fishings[,] not in Fortune Bay on account of the scarcity of fish[,] but [they] proceed to Pt May[,] off Laun and the St Lawrences. The registered vessels are engaged in the Coasting trade[,] collecting fish or carrying it to H[arbou]r Briton[1] or St Johns. The fishings have not improved for the last three years, I should presume this to be the case from their boats being more engaged in the Caplin Trade to St Pierres than the fishings, and I observed very little fish drying at the establishments; there are Salmon fishings at this small port, as at others where a small rivulet communicates with the sea; and the same means adopted for taking them as at other places. Mr Evans[,] the Magistrate[,] mentioned that the French had made occasional encroachments about Point May for the purpose of obtaining Bait[,] but did not trouble them much. I communicated with him on the trade carried on between Grand Bank and adjoining settlements with the French Island of St Pierres – alluding to the non

[1]Harbour Breton, across Fortune Bay.

clearance of the Vessels, he then mentioned the impossibility of doing so with a cargo such as Caplin, when the nearest custom house was at H[arbou]r Briton, or Burin, distant 23 and 40 miles, and as the Caplin would be unserviceable in 24 to 48 hours, their attempting to proceed to the above places to clear would render them useless and the Trade impossible.

I have formerly alluded to the difficulty of distinguishing between the English and French Schooners[,] and would remark that none of the vessels or boats belonging to any of the Ports along the coast have their names or Ports they belong to painted on their sterns[,] which Custom House regulation ought to be inforced [*sic*], as it would most materially assist in distinguishing French Vessels, and those engaged in illegal trade. The settlements to the NE of Grand Bank are Little Barrasway[1] and Grand Beach[,] containing together about 60 to 70 souls.

<u>8th July 1840</u> <u>Fortune</u>

A settlement consisting of 240 persons: it remains nearly in the same state as to number[,] neither increasing or decreasing. there [*sic*] are about 25 Vessels employed in the fishing and under the same circumstances as at Grand Bank. The fish[,] as at Grand Bank[,] are disposed of principally at Harbour Briton. No complaints of encroachment by the French were made: it was however stated in answer to queries on the subject that they sometimes encroached during the fishing season at Pt May and Cape Cruz[,][2] opposite to St Pierres.

<u>11 July 1840</u> <u>From Connoire Bay</u>

When the ship anchored[,] a boat was dispatched to the Burgeo Islands: from the report given by Lieutenant Woodman[,] it appears that there are two settlements called Upper and Lower Burgeo, distant from each other about three miles[,] the combined numbers of Inhabitants being about 650. The settlement[,] by the statement of Mr Cox[,] the principal resident[,] is increasing from settlers coming from Fortune Bay, the fisheries of this place being more productive. There are about 10 registered Vessels belonging to the settlement prosecuting a coasting trade, and carrying fish to Markets[,] and the small schooners are engaged in the fishing [*sic*] among the Islands. The Cod fishing has been very successful, having already averaged 100 quintals per man[,] and has increased during the last three years. There are also Salmon fisheries in

[1]This reference is unclear. Milne subsequently refers to another Little Barrasway [*sic*], west of Connoire Bay. There is also a Barasway Bay, *east* of Connoire Bay. No settlement named Little Barasway survives today on the Burin Peninsula.

[2]Cape Crewe.

the vicinity[,] fished by the inhabitants and also by the Indians[,] there being a settlement of about 100 of them a few miles to the West at Little Barrasway[,][1] who trade with the inhabitants of the Coast and Burgeo Islands[,] exchanging Salmon, Geese, and Furs for Clothing, Spirits, and [?Porridge]; Herrings are also abundant[,] more so than has been known for many years past, and [they] arrived earlier on the Coast. they [*sic*] are used for Bait, the Caplin having gone into deep water. At both Upper and Lower Burgeo's [*sic*] the inhabitants expressed the great want of a Magistrate in so extensive a settlement[,] not only to administer justice among themselves[,] but for the purpose of preventing the extensive encroachments of the French which commence at the fall of the year in the various harbours from that of Jersey to White Bear Bay. In all the intervening Ports they are throughout the whole winter engaged in cutting and carrying away great quantities of timber of the largest size[,] and do great damage to the young trees. That during all April [*sic*] and the beginning of May they encroach at the Barrasways[,] to the West of the Burgeo Islands[,] and yearly continue as formerly to dig shell fish for Bait and this year[,] in consequence of the continued encroachments[,] the shell fish have almost entirely disappeared[,] scarcely any having been procured by the inhabitants; about 50 French Sch[oone]rs had been digging Bait at the Barrasways this Spring. They do not encroach for the purpose of Cod fishing[,] being too far from St Pierres. The Inhabitants at these Islands are all Protestants[,] and are most anxious to obtain a School Master for their Children and a person who[,] at the same time[,] would read prayers on Sundays. The wishes of so large a community settled in the locality certainly deserve attention.

Not considering it requisite that I should proceed further to the West at this advanced season of the year[,] I left Connoire Bay on the 15th of July and shaped a course to the Eastward and[,] on passing the Islands of Miquelon and Langley[,][2] a boat belonging to an English Merchant Brig came off from the latter[,] acquainting me that their Vessel[,] the '*Roden*' of Sunderland[,] had been wrecked on Langley Point on the night of the 1st of July in thick W[eathe]r[, the] crew saved, and part of the materials[,] and requesting that information might be forwarded to England by the first opportunity. On the 17th we passed Cape St Mary's and Cape Freels[3] off which numerous small schooners were engaged in

[1]Barasway.

[2]The island of Little Miquelon was frequently called Langley Island.

[3]Confusingly, Newfoundland has two Cape Freels, one on the point of land between St Mary's and Trepassey Bays on the southeastern coast, the other on the northeast coast between Bonavista Bay and Hamilton Sound. Milne was referring to the former.

fishing: they belong to Fortune Bay and other parts of the South Coast[,] and also to the Settlements on the Eastern Coast, South of St Johns. The fishermen stated that no French Vessels were engaged [in] fishing at the above place[,] nor did they ever encroach on that part of the Coast. The same evening we rounded Cape Race and on the following day[,] the 18th July[,] Anchored [*sic*] in St Johns. Having acquainted his Excellency the Governor with my proceedings on the South Coast and remitted to him a copy of this report, I again put to sea on the 24th July[,] to proceed in execution of the 6th Section of your Instructions[,] namely to visit the Coast in the vicinity of Cape St Johns and afterwards to proceed to Labrador and visit the Northern part of that Coast[,] as requested by His Excellency the Governor of Newfoundland in his letter to me of the 10th June. On the 29th communicated with Nippers H[arbou]r[,] which is situated towards the entrance of Green Bay and about 20 miles to the SW of Cape St Johns.

<u>29 July 1840</u> <u>Nippers Harbour</u>
is [*sic*] a small settlement[,] but the only one of any consequence near the limit defined by Treaty to the Southward of which the French Vessels are not permitted to prosecute the Fishery: it contains about 130 to 140 Inhabitants who resort there during the summer season for the Cod fishing and in the spring for seals[,] but during the winter months either proceed to St Johns or Ports they belong to, or retire into the woods in the various Bays which abound in the neighbourhood[,] where they seek shelter from the inclemency of the weather. The Cod fishing on this part of the Coast this year has not been so productive as usual. Caplin also have been exceedingly scarce; Salmon are taken at Nippers H[arbou]r and the Bays adjacent in the same manner as already mentioned on the South Coast. It was stated that the French sometimes fished round the South side of the Cape[,] but they never disturbed the Inhabitants in the least. I should presume from what evidence was collected that when NW winds prevail[,] the French fishermen from the H[arbou]r of La Scie[,] being unable to remain on the W[es]t side of the Cape[,] proceed round to the smooth water under the lee and there fish, and also in Shoe Bay[,][1] but there is no continued encroachments [*sic*]. From Nippers H[arbou]r we bore up for Cape St Johns[,] passing several Bays and Inlets, none of which afforded Anchorage or security for large Vessels[,] and are only resorted to by Fishing Sch[oone]rs which come there for the season from Conception Bay, Fogo & Toulinquit[2] and other parts of Newfoundland.

[1]Shoe Cove.
[2]Toulinquet Island, south of Cape St John.

Round Cape St Johns and hauling up for Pacquet H[arbou]r[,] we passed the harbour of La Scie[,] 5 miles from the above Cape[,] and the first harbour on what is currently called the French Shore. in [*sic*] it we observed 10 or 12 Vessels principally Brigs[,] presumed to be all French[.] on the same evening we anchored at Pacquet Harbour.

29th July 1840

At this port I found five French Vessels at Anch[o]r and there were four French Establishments on shore[,] on each of which was flying The [*sic*] French National Flag. Conceiving it [to be] illegal that[,] on the shores of a Colony of Great Britain[,] any Foreign national Flag whatever should be hoisted, and following the same line of conduct as my late predecessor in this Ship[,] I sent on shore Lieutt Woodman to inform the head people of the Establishments that their Ensigns must be removed and[,] if hoisted at all, it must be on board their respective Vessels now in Port: the Flags were accordingly immediately removed, but the following morning a letter was presented to me[,] signed by the Captains of the respective French Vessels in Port, complaining and protesting against the order I had considered it my duty to issue on the previous evening; and their unanimous determination to rehoist their Ensigns and not haul them down unless ordered by me. This decision on their part they accordingly complied with the moment the letter was delivered on board. I considered it therefore my duty to inforce [*sic*] the order of the previous evening: and they were hauled down on my again sending Lt Woodman on shore. But to prevent all disputes that might hereafter occur, and to show no insult was intended to the French Flag, I answered their letter which had been addressed to me, copies of which are attached hereto for your information. I have at the same time to acquaint you that during my stay in the above Port, not one of the French Vessels ever hoisted their Colours.

The French resort to this Coast in Spring[,] bringing with them in their Vessels (which are chiefly Brigs of 100 to 200 Tons) a cargo of salt for curing their fish, as also their implements of fishing. Having moored their Vessels in security, they commence the repair of their salting houses, drying stages, and likewise the Huts for the abode of the Crew, the former are covered with canvas. The Ships Bell is landed, and shipped in its former cranks near the Superintendants [*sic*] house. the [*sic*] large boats which were hauled up in places of security at the close of the last year['s] fishing, are launched, repaired, and fitted. In all their arrangements and mode of prosecuting the fishing[,] there was displayed system and neatness, which we observed no where [*sic*] else:

each vessel has from 6 to 10 of these boats, according to the number of her crew, they are of large dimensions, being about 25 to 30 feet long with great beam and all rigged alike with two lug sails: their crew consists of two men and a Boy, they start early in the morning to their fishing grounds[,] which are generally at the entrance of the harbour, and continue to prosecute their avocations with Hooks and Line until they procure a cargo, when they return to their Establishments[.] the crew are then relieved and the fresh hands immediately commence throwing the fish into the salting house, where the process of splitting, cleaning, boning, and salting is prosecuted with amazing quickness. the [*sic*] fish are not laid out to dry until about three weeks before their departure for France, so certain are they that[,] on this N[orther]n Coast[,] no fogs[,] which are so prevalent, and so dense on the South Shore of the Island, will continue [i.e., intervene] to interrupt the principal process of the fishery. The West Shore[,] which is also called the French Shore from their right of fishing extending along the whole of that Coast[,] is not liable to fog nearly so much as the SE and S[,] where they are not only exceedingly dense, but may continue for weeks together with scarcely a day's clear weather. It is on this account that the French Fishing Ground is considered so much more valuable than the English. There was a peculiarity noticed in the French boats at Pacquet H[arbou]r which I have never observed elsewhere[,] namely both oars being pulled on the larboard side[,] and no oar at all on the starboard[,] but the third person used a oar fitted into a Crutch placed broad on the Starb[oar]d Q[uarte]r with which he pulls the stern around against the power of the two larboard oars, and thus steers her course.

Besides the hook and line[,] large Cod seines are also used[,] with which they take immense quantities of Cod. There is only one English resident at Pacquet[,] who sells his fish to the French and[,] during the winter[,] takes charge of their abandoned Establishments until their return in spring. Having completed the water of the Ship under my command[,] I again put to sea on the afternoon of the 1st August and proceeded direct to the coast of Labrador[.] on the 4th August[,] communicated with the fishermen engaged in fishing off the Black Islands in Lat 54. They were part of the crews of 23 Vessels then at Anchor in Grady's Harbour at the Black Islands: they were principally from Conception Bay and the Island of Fogo[,] Newfoundland, Nova Scotia, and several American[s] from the State of Maine were at the same Anchorage[,] also engaged in fishing on the same ground with the Inhabitants of Newfoundland and Labrador[,] as granted to them by Treaty. From information which was afterward obtained at Dumplin Island, and Round

Island near Sandwich Bay[,] and at Indian Island[,] further to the South[war]d, The [*sic*] number of American Sch[oone]rs resorting to this part of the Coast this year is upwards of 100, many of them having been previously fishing in the vicinity of Red Bay, Lance Loup,[1] and other Ports on the South Coast of Labrador, and had [*sic*] come to the North on account of the scarcity of fish on that part of the Coast[.] here also they had been unsuccessful; indeed on the whole Coast of Labrador the Cod fishing this year has been as yet very unprofitable and the Caplin[,] whose yearly strike is looked forward to with so much importance [*sic*][,] have only been three or four days on the Coast. Herrings had set in for a few days[,] but again left the shore. The fishermen are in consequence deprived of their principal bait, and were instead making use of Lance and species of small smelt about three inches long. The fishermen were[,] however[,] still in expectation that the Autumn fishing might prove productive[,] and many of the Schooners had consequently gone further North towards Cape Harrison[,] Lat[itude] 55[,] to try their success [*sic*] and would again return in Sept[embe]r to the Black Islands and vicinity.

6th August Dumplin Island[2] was the northmost settlement at which I communicated[.] it is at the entrance of Sandwich Bay[,] and situated between Huntingdon and Henrietta Islands[.] on this latter Island there were formerly many summer settlers and numerous stages[,] v[iz] – for prosecuting the Cod fishery. These have been entirely abandoned and the only Establishment remaining is the one on Dumplin Island[,] belonging to Messrs Hunt[.] their principal and almost only fishery is Salmon[,] taken in the Eagle and other rivers which are 20 miles from the establishment[; they are] packed in tin cases, sent down to Dumplin Island[,] and from thence shipped for England direct. The people who fish the rivers, cure and pack the fish in Tin cases are b[r]ought out from England in the spring and again return when the Salmon season is over, which is the beginning or end of August. There are a few Indians in the vicinity who have come from the Moravian Settlements[3] to the North[war]d[.] they assist in the fisheries during summer[,] are engaged in procuring furs during the Autumn and winter[,] and in the spring [are] employed in the seal fishery, and all in the service of the establishment of the Messrs Hunt. Between the Black Islands and Huntingdon Island at Sandwich Bay; there is also an Establishment on

[1]L'Ance-â-Loup.

[2]Dumpling Harbour is at 53:51N lat., 56:59W long.

[3]Moravian missionaries had established a number of settlements along the Labrador coast during the late eighteenth and early nineteenth centuries.

Round Island for the Cod fishery[.] it belongs to Mr Wills[,] a resident in England, and under the superintendence of a Mr Goodridge.

12th August 1840. At Indian Island
further [*sic*] to the Southd there are also one or two Establishments[,] entirely for the Cod fishery; the principal belonging to Mr Warren[,] also resident in England; superintended by his son who resides there in summer: it is connected with St Johns Newfoundland[,] from which place the people come every year in spring; and return in Sept[embe]r or October. Between the above ports and Belle Isle there are numerous Harbours and Bays, resorted to by Sch[oone]rs from Newfoundland[,] Nova Scotia, and America. having [*sic*] securely moored their Vessels, they hoist out their boats, each Vessel having 3 or 4, and commence fishing: the Americans salting their fish in Bulk; whilst the Newfoundland people carry them to some harbour on the Coast on the shore of which they have stages for drying their cargoes. Should the fish prove abundant[,] they remain there until they have completed their cargo, but if scarce[,] they immediately proceed to sea, and grope their way to some other harbour, where the fish are more abundant. It is surprising how they manage to find their way among the numerous Islands, and dangers which fringe this barren coast and that[,] during the dense fogs in which it is sometimes engulfed[,] they are not more often wrecked, especially when they have neither chart, Quadrant, or Book of directions to guide them on their way. I am not aware that there is any settlement properly so called on this part of Labrador. The word I conceive to mean a number of houses with inhabitants permanently residing in one locality, but there are I believe numerous establishments, the same at Dumplin, Round, Black and Indian Islands along the coast from Belleisle [*sic*] Northward, these establishments consisting of one principal house. It is in general a store for the sale of the various necessaries of life and implements of fishing &c[,] and for the purpose of purchasing fish, from any casual fisherman who come there. The superintendants [*sic*] of these establishments generally come to their houses every spring, bringing with them a number of fishermen, to prosecute the fishing[,] all of whom reside in temporary huts during the season, and when it is concluded[,] return to England, St Johns, or their native place until the season commences in the following spring, The [*sic*] houses being left in charge of some trustworthy person of the establishment who continues [*sic*] to hold communication with a few Indians and some people who remain to procure seals during winter and spring. There is a circumstance which has come to my knowledge connected with the Island of Belleisle[,] which I consider my duty to

lay before you. It appears from information obtained on the Coast, that the fishings on the shores of this island are exceedingly productive[,] and are resorted to every year by our fishermen, as also Americans[,] to pursue their lawful occupation. Of late years they have been entirely prevented from going near the island by the interference of the French, who will not permit any of our fishermen to fish there, and that consequently they have been obliged to give up a fishing ground which to they was not only convenient from its locality, but also productive. The Question is whether Belleisle Island belongs to Newfoundland, and therefore to the French shore[,] where they have the right of fishing; or whether it is an Island of the Labrador Coast[,] to which it is more nearly situated than Newfoundland. If it belongs to Labrador, the French have no right there whatever[,] and even if it belongs to Newfoundland[,] the right of the English to fish comes under the 9th Section of your Instructions.

Having laid before you the foregoing statement relative to the fisheries on the South Coast of Newfoundland and Eastern part of Labrador, so far as information could be obtained at the ports visited by HM Ship under my command, and having received your Instruction per HM Sloop '*Snake*'[,] when at Indian Island[,] to proceed immediately to Quebec, It [*sic*] will be out of my power to afford you any information relative to the West shore of Newfoundland, or South Coast of Labrador, neither of which have been visited. But before bringing this statement to a close[,] I consider it my duty to lay explicitly before you what I[,] in my opinion[,] consider is principally required from HM Ships in the protection to be afforded to the British Interests [*sic*] on that Coast called the Newfoundland fisheries.

The first point of consideration is the period of the year a Vessel of War is required for the above purpose.

I should most decidedly say that any Vessel intended for the protection of the above Coast should be at the Burgeo Islands about the middle of April, for it is at that period of the year[,] at those Islands and the Barrasways in the Vicinity (Harbours that are dry at low water)[,] the first encroachments are made by the French for the purpose of digging Bait, to the prejudice of our settlers and fishermen.

By the 2nd Section of your Instructions[,] I am directed to proceed to the Burgeo Islands, and there make inquiry relative to the encroachments complained of in 'An address (of which you were pleased to lend for my information and guidance) from the House of Assembly [*sic*] of Newfoundland to His Excellency Captn Prescott[,] Governor of that

Colony.' I have to acquaint you that[,] from the statements of the residents of the Burgeo Islands[,] these encroachments, [*sic*] continue to be repeated without intermission year after year, during the months of April and May. The next part of the Coast which will require the attention of HM Ships will be the vicinity of Fortune Bay, Grand Bank, Lamelin, Laun, [the] St Lawrences and the bays of Placentia and St Mary's. This must be divided into two divisions. In the 1st, Fortune Bay, Grand Bank, Lamelin, and the St Lawrences[,] because they are close to the French Islands of St Pierres and Miquelon[,] and the duty required is to prevent the French from sweeping our bays of the Caplin, which set in on the Coast in early June, to prevent the French from fishing on our shores for Cod, and to check the illicit traffic carried on by our fishermen with St Pierres. Lamelin would become the head quarters [*sic*]. To perform this service[,] the ship herself could not be employed[,] as the Navigation of the Coast from numerous shoals, and the prevalence of fogs, would render it unsafe for her to remain at sea, and there is no anchorage nearer than Great Laun[,] 12 miles distant. The duty could be better performed by vessels hired for the purpose, capable of affording accommodation for the officer and men, and fit to keep the sea in case of bad weather, when unable to attain a secure Anchorage. Whilst the small vessels [are] engaged for the season in protecting this part of the Coast: the Ship might visit the 2nd division of this shore, namely Placentia and St Mary's Bay[,] via St Johns and the East Coast of Newfoundland, [&] to visit Cape St John. here [*sic*] of late years, there have been no complaints of encroachments beyond the defined limits[,] but the presence of a Man of War in the vicinity would be of service, if only to show the French her [*sic*] watchfulness over the British Interests. The remaining and most extensive part of the Coast is the Labrador. I have been informed by proprietors of Vessels engaged in the Cod fishery, that numerous French Vessels from Newfoundland constantly fish in the Bays of that Coast, about Bras d'Or [*sic*] Harbour[1] and Lance Loup &c[,] to the annoyance, and in many cases prevention of our fishermen from pursuing their avocations. This has been stated to me by more than one person[:] indeed almost all those who frequent this part of the Coast have given the same statement[,] and that these encroachments are during the end of April, May and June, and I see no reason to doubt their information. Looking therefore at this vast line of Coast extending from the River of St John, to Belleisle[,] and from thence Northward[,] in the whole range of which

[1]Perhaps a reference to Brador Bay, just across the border from Labrador in extreme southeastern Quebec.

are innumerable Bays and Harbours yearly frequented by swarms of American Schooners who come there for the Fishery and[,] whenever opportunity offer[s,] encroach on our shores, I consider that the superintendence of one Man of War alone would not be more than sufficient [*sic*] to prevent the encroachments of the French and check the lawless conduct of the Americans on that shore alone.[1]

Continuation of the Report on the Newfoundland Fisheries[2]

As only one vessel is employed on the Newfoundland fisheries[,] it must be obvious on consideration that so vast a range of coast as there is included within its limits[,] extending around the Island of Newfoundland along the South shore of Labrador from 64.4 West Long to the Straits of Belleisle, and from thence indefinitely to the North[war]d[,] cannot possibly be efficiently controlled[,] or even visited by HM Ship employed on that service, not even if a portion of her officers and crew are left on those parts of the Newfoundland Coast (viz. Burgeo and Lamelin Islands), for the purpose of manning boats to assist in her assigned duties. During this year I did not consider it requisite to comply with this part of your Instructions, on account of the late period of the year I arrived on the Coast, yet I cannot refrain from mentioning the distressing situation in which the Captain of HM Ship may be placed at being deprived of the efficient services of so many of his officers and crew[,] sent from the Ship for so long a period. I trust any allusion which I have here made may not be considered by you as an attempt on my part to throw difficulties or objections in the way of any service on which you may be pleased to order HM Ships[,] but that you will solely attribute it to an anxious wish on my part to point out the situation in which HM Ships may be placed[,] not only on an almost unknown and a dangerous shore[,] but when in company with Men of War[,] fully manned[,] belonging to France, and the United States,

[1]There follows a section of the Report which has been crossed out, to which has been appended the words 'within the above limits,' inserted between lines, but with no indication whether it was intended to be inserted in the last line of the report or the first line of the crossed-out section. The crossed-out section, parts of which are essentially duplicated in the following paragraphs, reads: 'Indeed[,] the Ship employed on the South Coast[,] instead of proceeding from St Johns Harbour to Cape St Johns on the East Coast[,] would be employed with more advantage to the British Interests [*sic*] if she were to return to Lamelin (where she has hired vessels for that season) [and] from thence proceed direct to Mingan [on the Quebec coast, in 64W Latitude][,] along the Labrador shore to Belleisle[,] and then visit Cape St John if considered necessary[,] or instead pass down the West shore of Newfoundland again to revisit the South shore, pick up her Boat crew left at Lamelin[,] and proceed to St Johns before returning to Halifax at the conclusion of the fishing season . . . Continued.'

[2]Seven blank pages lie between the end of this sentence and the report's continuation.

employed on the same coast; and similar service[,] and therefore the propriety of urging upon the Colonial Government of their either employing small Vessels for that purpose, or having local authorities, at those places, where the principal encroachments are made and complained of.

Your Instructions[,] by which I have been guided[,] directs [*sic*] my attention to the protection of the British Interests [*sic*] [in] general and especially the Fishing Grounds on our shore from all interference by Foreign Vessels[.] you have also directed my attention[,] in the 22nd Article of the above Instructions[,] to the prevention of all illicit trade, I am therefore called upon to allude especially to the Trade now regularly but illegally carried on with our shore and the Island of St Pierre. This trade in Caplin and Contraband Articles, as already pointed out in the former part of this Report[,] is[,] I understand[,] on the increase[,] and unless the Home or Colonial Government take some means to punish those engaged in it, or adopt expedient means to stop it, and protect its own Coast[,] it will continue, and I consider it quite a vain attempt for the Captain of HM Ship employed on the fisheries even to check, much less to suppress[,] this contraband trade. He may [only] afford assistance to whatever system the respective governments may adopt for the protection of the Coast as his short sojourn in the vicinity, and his duties requiring his presence [*sic*] at other stations[,] can only render his interference a matter of secondary importance. I have also been made acquainted that smuggling to a very considerable extent is carried on along the South Shore of the Labrador (which has not been visited by HM Ship under my command) by American Vessels resorting to that Coast for the Fishery. This illegal trade consists of provisions brought from the United States in greater quantity than sufficient [i.e., necessary] for their own consumption during the season, and therewith secretly carrying on an illicit Trade in every Port and River on the above shore. Nor do I see any means by which so extensive an evil to the interests of the British Merchant, and to the colony[,] can be possibly suppressed[,] unless by the interference of the Home Government. It may be required that some reason should be assigned for the want of accurate detail and the meagre information conveyed relative to the Fisheries on the shores of which I have been employed. It must however be remarked that no accurate information can be obtained or any estimate formed of the present state of the Fisheries[,] until after the termination of the fishing season, when the returns from the respective Custom Houses and Establishments are made up. Where I have stated the increase or decrease of fishing or settlements, it has been derived from the principal residents of the Place visited, given by them as matter of opinion founded on their own local knowledge[,] and without any reference to official documents.

In respect to the South Shore[,] where the encroachments of the French are generally made[,] I was unable to derive better information. There was invariably an unwillingness on the part of Individuals, to give any information whatever (except at Lamelin and Burgeo Islands) or to admit that the French ever encroached, even denying the fact, when I afterwards found that the French Vessels were in the habit[,] not only of fishing off those very harbours; but resorting to them for the purpose of curing their fish, before returning to St Pierres. The concealment on the part of the Inhabitants has certainly confirmed an opinion. I then found that an intercourse exists between them for their mutual benefit, and that individuals are deterred from giving information for fear of the resentment of those who carry on a contraband trade.[1]

[**87**] *Milne to Prescott*

HMS *Crocodile*, St. Johns, Newfoundland
6 October 1840

Sir,

I beg herewith to forward[,] for Your Excellency's information[,] a Copy of the Statement relative to the Fisheries on the NE Shore of Newfoundland and East Shore of Labrador as forwarded to Vice Admiral Sir Thos Harvey[,] KCB[,] Commander in Chief &c. I regret the limited time which I was employed on the Coast prevented me from obtaining more general and useful information, and that the exigencies of the service required HM Ship under my command being ordered to Quebec from Indian Harbour[,] by which the Southern Shore of Labrador and also the Western Coast of Newfoundland has [*sic*] not been visited. I have more especially to draw your attention to the circumstances detailed in the case of Pacquet Harbour[,] relative to the French National Flag[,] and I trust the line of Conduct I pursued at a Port under your Excellency's Government will meet with your approval[,] and that some definite Instructions will in future be given from H Majestys Government relative to the common custom of the French Ensigns being displayed on the shores of the Colony. I am directed by the

[1]Milne's report was subsequently cited in another Report, this by the Committee on the Deep Sea Fisheries of Nova Scotia to the Newfoundland legislature. The whole of his Report was printed as an appendix, and the Committee's Report made specific reference to his recommendations.

Commander in Chief to apply to Your Excellency to defray the expenses of Lodging, Fuel and Boats for the protection of the Fisheries in the ensuing year[,] as these boats must be hired at Burgeo or Lamelin previous to the Captain of the ship employed on that service communicating with Your Excellency at St Johns.

[**88**] *Prescott to Milne*

St. Johns, Newfoundland
9 October 1840

Sir,

I have the honour to acknowledge the receipt of your letter of the 7th Inst[,] inclosing [*sic*] for my information [a] Copy of your Report to Sir Thomas Harvey respecting your Proceedings on the Northern Shores of Newfoundland and on the Coast of Labrador[.]

For this Report[,] as well as for that previously supplied upon the state of the Fisheries and other Circumstances on the Southwestern portion of the Island[,] I beg you to receive my best thanks.

Your suggestions are extremely valuable[,] and shall be made known to the Legislature when next in Session[,] with a view to the correction of evils in that Locality.

I shall be prepared to defray such expenses as may be incurred for Lodging and Fuel for Boats Crews employed in the protection of the Fisheries in the Neighbourhood of St. Pierre's and for the prevention of Smuggling – as also the hire of such Shore Boats as it may be absolutely necessary to engage for these important Objects.

Your temperate notice of what I believe to be an irregular proceeding on the part of French Subjects in Pacquet Harbour shall be brought without delay under the notice of Her Majesty's Principal Secretary of State for the Colonies[,] as well as your Observations respecting Belleisle.

[**89**] *Milne to Thomas Harvey*

HMS *Crocodile*, Bermuda
19 October 1840

Sir,

I have the honour to forward herewith the Report on the fisheries of Newfoundland, having added some observations relative thereto, since it was delivered to you at Quebec. I have more especially to direct your attention to the circumstances which occurred connected with the French Flag at Pacquet H[arbou]r and trust my conduct on that occasion has met with your approval.

[**90**] *Thomas Harvey to Milne*

HMS *Winchester*, Bermuda
6 November 1840

Sir,

I have to acknowledge the receipt of your Letter of the 19th Ultimo[,] enclosing Copies of Correspondence with His Excellency Captain Prescott Governor of Newfoundland, also enclosing to me a Copy of your proceedings while protecting the Fisheries around Newfoundland and I have to acquaint you in reply that I fully approve of the whole of your proceedings detailed therein.

[**91**] *Milne to Axholm, Governor, Danish Virgin Islands*

HMS *Cleopatra*, St, Thomas, Virgin Islands
27 December 1840

Sir

I have the honour to acquaint Your Excellency that[,] acting under the Instructions of the Senior Naval Officer of Her Britannic Majesty's Squadron at the Island of Barbadoes, I have been directed to proceed to this Island for the purpose of communicating to Your Excellency certain circumstances connected with the Danish Men of War cruising in the vicinity of the British Virgin Islands[,] which has called forth the attention of the Inhabitants and representations from the Government. It has been observed by the Inhabitants of these British Islands that[,] of late[,] the Danish Vessels of War have cruised cruised [*sic*] along the Coasts of the British Colonies much more frequently[,] and have approached nearer to these shores than had hitherto been their practice[;] that they have anchored close under the Kays [*sic*] and out[er] islands[,] and that their Armed Boats have been seen running close along the shores and even lying within the surf at night.

These proceedings are not of a nature which[,] under ordinary circumstances[,] would have attracted any uncommon degree of attention, from the Vessels of War belonging to a nation in amity with Great Britain[,] and even were this not the case[,] the two Governments are in such close vicinage [*sic*] as to render it almost impossible for the ships of the one to cruise on their own Coasts without approaching those of the other. but [*sic*] while I admit these facts to Your Excellency, I must observe that such a construction can hardly be applied to Armed Boats. that [*sic*] so long as the British Government has no grounds of entertaining any ulterior suspicion of the movements of the Danish Men of War on the Coasts, no question was raised[,] no suspicion was entertained, but Your Excellency must be fully aware such grounds have unfortunately been established by certain proceedings of an aggravated nature which took place at Thatch Island [*sic*], one of the British Virgin Islands[,] on the 4th of August last.[1] I do not bring this act of aggression before Your Excellency's notice further than to adduce it as the occasion which has involved[,] as natural consequence, the jealousy with which the Government of these British Islands has since received the species of surveillance lately observed by the Danish Vessels of War and their Armed Boats on the Shores of their Islands. In laying this subject before Your Excellency's notice, I feel confident it will meet with immediate attention and that Your Excellency will adopt such measure [*sic*] as will prevent a recurrence of similar complaint from the Governor of the British Virgin Islands[,] and [which] will be the cause of allaying any jealous feeling which might arise to disturb the amity which prevails between the Inhabitants of the respective Islands of both Nations.

[**92**] *Barrow to Thomas Harvey*

Admiralty, London
29 December 1840

Sir,

Having laid before my Lords Commissioners of the Admiralty your letter of the 5th of last month, No. 221, with the report from Captain Milne of the *Cleopatra* upon the subject of the Newfoundland Fisheries therein referred to; I am commanded to signify to you their Lordships direction to convey to Captain Milne their approval of the intelligence and activity shewn by him in the report of his proceedings, and in the execution of his instructions.

[1]No information appears to have survived in the Admiralty's records relative to this incident.

[**93**] *Milne to David Milne*

HMS *Cleopatra*, off the northeast end of Puerto Rico
31 December 1840

My dear David

Before this year closes its last evening &[,] after the labours of the day, I sit down in my solitary cabin to convey my Brother the best wishes of the season & that you may long live in happiness & prosperity to enjoy those that are to follow, & in wishing you all the happiness that this life can bestow, be good enough not to assume it is entirely to yourself, but I freely extend it to your better Half [*sic*] & family. I wish indeed I could once more enjoy the happiness of a family circle towards the close of each year[,] as formerly. This is now the fourth [year] of my absence[,] & when we shall again meet, no one can say. My first ship some months ago has arrived in England, my second will probably follow in a few months, but when the *Cleopatra* will turn her head toward England is uncertain. 15 months must certainly elapse and probably 2 years[.] If I am confirmed in the command of the ship[,] that time must elapse before I once more behold the North, unless sickness should bring me away to a more bracing climate. I however stand well & manage to retain my health when many are obliged to seek refuge in England[.] One of my Lieutenants goes home in this packet from their [*sic*] debility. Here I am among strangers, no friends, no one to associate with[.] Such is discipline, both for officers & men[,] but I really think as much for the Captain[.]

You may have heard I have exchanged a 500 ton ship for one of 960 & 205 men, increasing the vexation & annoyances of command, especially when all have been permitted to do exactly as suited them best. Unfortunately for them, my ideas are very different & severe examples have become requisite, & at last matters are assuming a different aspect, but still it won't do yet. My first Lieut[,] Mr Fordyce[1][,] is an Aberdeen man, & wrote a book on Naval routine, but theory & practice are often at variance[.] He is[,] however[,] a nice quiet gentlemany man & a great comfort to me because[,] to a certain extent[,] I can associate with him & generally introduce him wherever I go.

I took command of this ship in Bermuda Nov: 1[.] I was in bed for 4 or 5 days with a most severe attack of Lumbago, having been half killed with the kindness of the Bermudians[.] From Bermuda I came to Barbadoes to be under the command of Capt Leith[,] & from thence

[1]Alexander Dingwall Fordyce (1800–1869). Entered, 1813; Lt., 1826; Cmdr., 1841; Capt. (Ret.), 1857.

went to Antigua to refit the ship – returned to Barbadoes Nov: 16th, & thence sailed for the Danish Island of St Thomas, where I remained for 3 days, & a nice set of people the Danes are & the Governor very attentive[.] I believe he is going to give us a ball on our return there about the 19th[,] & he dines on board here to the best turn out I can give him.

The *Ringdove* – Capt Stewart[1] – was with me at St Thomas's [*sic*]. I hailed one of our Steamers this morning[,] who told me *Ringdove* took a Slaver last night with 250 slaves & she is now at anchor at Santa Cruz. What luck! I am now on the look out for slavers[,] alias £[,] which would prove very acceptable in these hard times, especially as the [new] Commission has not increased our pay[.] I hope to be enabled to make arrangements to get to the North during the ensuing summer, which is a very great treat, not only for the comfort of a good cold day, & amusement, but to avoid the hot rainy weather of the West Indies & its attendant Yellow Fever, by no means an agreeable companion on shore, and still less so on board[.]

I am glad we are all healthy & the Squadron also[,] although at times there are detached [*sic*: 'isolated'] cases. I wish you would send me out Sabine's last work on magnetism[.][2] I believe there is something quite new in it – relating to the construction of Magnetic Needles for the determination of the Dip[.] My long absence and want of seeing the periodicals connected with different Societies has kept me at a standstill. I waste away however [*sic*: 'therefore'] in a professional way, but the duties of the ship occupy me daily & by being always on the 'Qui vive' I keep matters square. A Captain always on those [i.e., one too occupied with studying] can never have his ship in proper order.

I must now say farewell – as we see the packet running down to us. It is near the dawn of Jan: 2nd. Many happy returns of the New Year & of the 22nd & with love &c. . . .

[P.S.:] I hope young David is now in perfect health[.]

[1]Keith Stewart, C.B. (1814–79). Entered, 1827; Lt, 1833; Cmdr, 1838; Capt., 1842; Rear-Adm. (Res.), 1862; Vice-Adm. (Res.), 1867; Adm. (Ret.), 1875. Stewart's relatively rapid rise through the ranks may have owed something to his being Sir James Graham's cousin. See below, Graham to Milne, 19 March 1859, [**654**].

[2]This probably refers to Edward Sabine's *Report on the Variations of the Magnetic Intensity observed at different points of the Earth's Surface* (London, 1838).

[**94**] *Minto to Milne*

Admiralty, London, Private
3 January 1841

Sir

I very much regret that my arrangements did not admit of my attending to your wish for an appointment to *Cleopatra*. I beg you[,] however[,] to be assured that I shall at all times be most glad to mark my sense of your merit.

[**95**] *Milne to Axholm*

HMS *Cleopatra*, St. Thomas, Virgin Islands
26 January 1841

Sir,

I have the honour to thank Your Excellency for your kindness in procuring for me Translations of the Declaration forwarded from the Captains in command of the Danish Vessels of War on this Station[,] relative to their cruising in the vicinity of the British Virgin Islands.

These Officers appear to insinuate that the Government of these Islands is finding cause of complaint at their casually Anchoring [*sic*] under their Cays and in their Harbours. I therefore feel called upon to state to Your Excellency that the Government has no such view, that they have and always will continue to afford any assistance, and show attention to Men of War of the Danish and other Nations that may arrive within their Ports; or at their Islands; nor could it be possible that any complaint or remark would be made relative to Men of War Anchoring either under their Cays or in their Harbours or encroaching on the Shores when their Men of War are casually passing.

But it is the Surveillance of cruising Men of War[,] permanently stationed in their vicinity[,] and continually employed on their coasts[,] that has called forth the Statements which I have brought before Your Excellency's notice, at the Instigation of the Governor of the British Virgin Islands and the Officer in Command of Her Britannic Majesty's Naval forces.

I have therefore considered it my duty to lay this Statement before Your Excellency[,] that the Governor General may be aware that there is no wish on the Part of the British Government to look for cause of Complaint.

[96] *Declaration of Capture of* Secundo Rosario, *Spanish Slaving Schooner*

HMS *Cleopatra*, East of the Virgin Islands
[27 January 1841]

I[,] Alexander Milne Esquire[,] Captain of Her Britannic Majesty's Ship *Cleopatra*[,] hereby declare; that on the 27th day of January 1841; being in or about Latitude 18.5.N. Longitude 64.40.W.[,] I detained the Schooner named the *Segundo* [*sic*] *Rosario*[,] Sailing under Spanish Colours, armed with No Guns ____ Pounders; Commanded by Captain Francisco Perrano[,] who declared her to be bound from the Rio Pongos to Porto [*sic*] Rico with a Crew consisting of 17 Men 4 Boys ____ [no] Supercargo; 7 Passengers . . . and having on board 288 Slaves; said to have been taken on board at Rio Pongos on the 3rd day of January 1841, and are enumerated as follows viz.

	Healthy	Sickly
Men	166	4
Women	60	None
Boys	47	None
Girls	15	None

I do further declare that the said Schooner appeared Sea worthy [*sic*][,] and was supplied with a sufficient stock of water and Provisions for the support of said Negroes and Crew for their destined voyage to Porto Rico. I do further declare that I have supplied the said Schooner with Two Casks of Peas, Two Casks of Flour[,] and Five Casks of Water for the use of the Slaves in case their Provisions should run short on their voyage to Havana . . .

[97] *Milne to Gordon*[1]

HMS *Cleopatra*, off the Virgin Islands
28 January 1841

You are hereby required and directed to proceed on board the Slave Schooner *Segundo* [*sic*] *Rosario*[,] and proceed with her and her cargo of Slaves to the Harbour of Havana[.] immediately upon your Arrival [*sic*] at that port[,] you will lodge in the Court [of] Mixed Commission the papers which I now forward to you[:]

[1]Alexander Crombie Gordon, Mate of *Cleopatra*.

No. 1. Custom House Paper or List of Cargo
" 2. Passport of Navigation No. 441
" 3. Half a register Havana March 27 1840
" 4. Official papers relative to the Spanish Merchant Vessel with Port Regulations
" 5. List of Crew of Schooner *Segundo* [*sic*] *Rosario*
" 6. Certificate of a Black Man
" 7. Various letters
" 8. Log Book

and you will be required to deliver a paper into Court[,] signed by yourself and verified upon Oath[,] stating the changes which have taken place in the vessel and cargo since her detention[.] you will also be required to make a strict Survey of all her Stores in proper form[,] and deliver it with the other documents to the Mixed Commission. on [*sic*] your been [*sic*] superseded from this vessel by Authority of the Mixed Commission Court[,] repair on board H.M. Ship '*Romney*'[,] where you will remain with the crew until you have an opportunity of returning in a Man of War to Jamaica.

The crew named in the Margin[1] have been sent onboard and I trust you will use every precaution to ensure the Safety of the Vessel and guard against any attempt at Mutiny among the crew left on board.

[**98**] *Milne to Leith*

HMS *Cleopatra*, Barbados
5 February 1841

Sir

I have the honour to inform you that in furtherance of your orders of the 18th December last[,] I put to sea from Barbadoes in H.M. Ship under my command on the 19th of the same month and proceeded off Fort Royal[,] Martinique[,] from thence off Guadeloupe[,] off St. Eustatius & St. Bartholomew[.] observing no suspicious vessels at Anchor off the latter Island[,] I proceeded to Tortola where I Anchored on the 23rd of December and communicated with the President of that Island[,] as directed by your Instructions. From Tortola I proceeded on the 26th to the Island of St Thomas[,] where I arrived the same afternoon and communicated with His Excellency Colonel Axholm[,] the Governor.

On the 29th I proceeded to sea and cruised off the NE side of Porto [*sic*] Rico until the 3rd of Jany 1841[,] when I put into St Juan's [*sic*] to

[1]Not copied to *Crocodile*'s letter book.

complete water[,] and again sailed on the 6th. Worked to Windward, and afterwards bore up round the east side of Porto Rico for the South Coast[,] where I continued cruising off Ponce & Salinas until the 16th and then beat up for St Thomas, where I Anchored on the 18th.

I then received from His Excellency the Governor the papers now enclosed, which had been forwarded from His Excellency the Governor General of the Danish West India Islands at Santa Cruz, but did not procure the Translations until the 25th, when I put to sea on the 27th and the same evening captured[,] between Norman Island and Santa Cruz[,] the Spanish Schooner '*Secundo Rosario*' with 288 Slaves from 'Rio Pongo'[,] West Coast of Africa, bound to Porto [*sic*] Rico . . .

[**99**] *Milne to John Harvey*[1]

HMS *Crocodile*, Halifax, Nova Scotia
5 April 1841

Sir,

I have the honour to acquaint you with the arrival of HM Ship under my Command on the North American division of the West India Station [*sic*][,] having been dispatched from Jamaica on the 10th Inst by Vice Admiral Sir Thos Harvey[,] to proceed to Halifax and from thence to the Gulf of St. Lawrence for the protection of the Fisheries.

It is my intention to proceed to Prince Edwards Island in about ten days[,] where I shall be glad to receive any communication from you relative to the Fisheries on the shores of New Brunswick in the Gulf; or to afford any assistance on that Coast which you may consider requisite.

[**100**] *Milne to FitzRoy*[2]

HMS *Crocodile*, Charlotte Town, Prince Edward Island
28 April 1841

Sir,

I have the honour to inform your Excellency that HM Ship under my command has been dispatched to this Station by Vice Admiral Sir Thomas Harvey[,] K.C.B.[,] the Commander in Chief[,] for the purpose

[1]Major General Sir John Harvey, Governor of New Brunswick and C-in-C of Her Majesty's Forces.

[2]Sir Charles Augustus FitzRoy, K.C.B. (1796–1858). FitzRoy was Lt Governor of Prince Edward Island 1837–41.

of affording protection to the British Fisheries in the Gulf of St. Lawrence during the ensuing season.

As the shores of Prince Edwards and [the] Magdalen Islands under your Excellency's Government are yearly resorted to by American fishermen for the purpose of carrying on the fishery[,] I shall be glad to receive any information relative to the encroachments by them on the shores of the Province under your Excellency's Government, or such other information which your Excellency may possess, which may enable me the more effectually to protect British subjects from foreign interference in violation of the existing Treaties.

[**101**] *Milne to FitzRoy*

HMS *Crocodile*, Charlotte Town, Prince Edward Island
20 July 1841

Sir,

In compliance with Your Excellency's request[,] I beg herewith to forward my opinion respecting the Harbour Light at Charlotte Town.

The term 'Harbour Light'[,] as mentioned in the Act of the Assembly[,] clearly defines a Light House to point out 'the entrance of a Harbour' and if the literal meaning be taken as applicable to the Harbour of Charlotte Town, there can be only one situation where the Light House can be erected, viz. on the 'Black House Point.' But having understood that the House of Assembly proposed that the Light House should be on Governor's Island, I presume its position is intended for any part of the Bay where it can be of the utmost service to vessels trading to & from the Harbour of Charlotte Town. Under this supposition[,] I am decidedly of opinion that if the Light House should be erected on Point Prim it would be of more general use to navigation and to the trade of the Port of Charlotte Town & Hillsborough Bay than if placed either on the Black House or Governor's Island.

In this position it will be an excellent guide to all vessels approaching Hillsborough Bay from the Westward and Eastward[,] and will be a leading mark to clear the Rifleman Shoals. By it Point Prim itself will always be clearly defined[,] and the shoal which extends from that point will be safely rounded in the darkest night. The light so placed[,] combined with the use of the Lead [*sic*][,] will be of equal service in guiding vessels clear of the shoals which extend from the Island of St Peters[,] and likewise Governors Island[,] as if the Light House was on the Black House Point. By its position on Point Prim you can make certain of seeing and approaching the Light House before you approach any of the dangers which extend between Point Prim and the Harbour of Charlotte Town & [it] will not only serve as a Light House for that Harbour[,] but will be of general utility to all parts of Hillsborough Bay and the adjacent coast[,] and will likewise enable vessels to take up a secure Anchorage under Point Prim in case of bad weather, Whereas [*sic*] if no light was on that low and ill defined point[,] I am of opinion no person would venture to round it in a dark night[,] & if vessels would not round it during the night the Light on Black House Point would be of no use except to those vessels who have [*sic*] rounded Point Prim before dark[.]

If the Light House was erected on Governor's Island[,] it must be obvious its sphere of utility would not be as extensive as if placed on Point Prim[.]

[**102**] *Milne Report on Protection of the Gulf of St. Lawrence Fisheries*

HMS *Crocodile*, Halifax, Nova Scotia
2 October 1841

Sir,

I have the honour to acquaint you that HMS *Crocodile* under my command sailed from Halifax on the 19th April last for the Gulf of St Lawrence under Instructions from the late Vice Admiral Sir Thos. Harvey K.C.B.[,] Commander in Chief [,] 'To afford protection to the Fisheries and Trade of HM Subjects within the said Gulf Westward of 60. West Longitude' [.]

HM ship arrived in the Gulf of St Lawrence on the 20th but it was found to be impracticable to expect a passage thro[,] in consequence of St Georges Bay being blocked up with the winters Ice[.] I was therefore compelled to put back and anchor in Sea Coal Harbour[,][1] Inhabitants Bay[,] where I remained until the 23rd. I then proceeded as far as Pictou Roads[,] the field Ice of St. Georges Bay having receded to the North[war]d and left a passage about 3 miles wide between it and the shore of Nova Scotia. From Pictou I proceeded to Charlotte Town[,] Prince Edward Island[,] where I arrived on the 27 April and[,] having landed in the Commissariat Stores the Surplus provisions embarked at Halifax for the use of HM Ship until October[,] put to sea on the 7th May to visit those parts of the coast where I conceived I could be of most service in fulfilling the object and tenor of the orders under which I was acting.

[1]Sea Coal Cove, 45:34N lat., 61:17W long.

Before however proceeding to mention the places visited and the information obtained relative to the fisheries[,] I will have the shores comprehended within the Gulf of St Lawrence and state what Fish are taken on those Shores which are [a] source of Trade to Her Majesty's Subjects.

The late Commander in Chiefs Instructions direct[ed] me to proceed to the Gulf of St Lawrence to the Westward of 60 West Longitude. On referring to the accompanying chart[1] containing the Track of HM Ship whilst employed in the Gulf, it will be observed that the West shore of the Island of Cape Pictou[,] the North shore of Nova Scotia & New Brunswick[,] extending from the Gulf of Canso to the Island of Miscou, & the North shore of the Bay of Chaleur to the entrance of the River St Lawrence[,] on from thence along the Labrador shore under the Government of Canada to the limit of 60 West[,] are comprehended within the limits of the Gulf of St Lawrence, together with the Islands of Prince Edward, Anticosti and the Magdalens.

Along this range of coast, the British fishing is prosecuted, and [the] Foreign nations of America & France have certain fishing privileges granted to them by Treaty. The Treaty with America was signed in 1818[,] of which the following is an extract[:]

'It is agreed between the High Contracting Parties that the Inhabitants of the United States shall have for ever[,] in common with the Subjects of His Britannic Majesty[,] the Liberty to take fish of every kind on that part of the Southern coast of Newfoundland which extends from Cape Ray to the Rameau [*sic*: Ramea] Islands, on the Western and Northern coast of Newf[oundlan]d from the said Cape Ray to the Quirpon Islands, on the shore of the Magdalen Islands[,] and also on the Coasts, Bays Harbours and Creeks from Mount Joli [*sic*] on the Southern coast of Labrador to and thro the Straights [*sic*] of Belleisle[,] and thence northerly indefinitely along the Coast without prejudice[,] however[,] to any of the Exclusive rights of the Hudsons Bay Company: and that the American fishermen shall also have the Liberty for ever to dry and cure fish in any unsettled Bays, Harbours & Creeks of the Southern part of Newfoundland here above described[,] and of the Coast of Labrador, but so soon as the same or any portion thereof shall be settled[,] it shall not be lawfull [*sic*] for the said fishermen to dry or cure fish at such portion so settled without previous agreement for such purpose with the Inhabitants[,] proprietors or possessors of the ground, and the United States hereby renounce for ever any Liberty heretofore enjoyed or claimed by the Inhabitants thereof to take[,] dry or cure fish

[1]Not included with this copy of the report.

on or within three marine miles of any of the Coasts[,] Bays, Creeks or Harbours of His B. Majesty's dominions in America not included within the above mentioned limits, provided[,] however[,] that the American fishermen shall be permitted to enter such Bays or Harbours for the purpose of shelter or repairing damage therein, of purchasing wood[,] of obtaining water & for no other purpose whatever: But [*sic*] they shall be under such restrictions as may be necessary to prevent their taking[,] drying or curing fish therein[,] or in any other manner whatever abusing the privileges hereby reserved to them[.]'

From the above Extract of the Treaty with America[,] it is clearly defined that the Americans cannot approach any part of the Shore of the Gulf of St Lawrence to prosecute a fishery [*sic*] the distance of three marine miles, save & except on the Shores of the Magdalen Islands and on the Shore of Labrador East of Mount Joli.

French Vessels had formerly the privilege of fishing in the Gulf of St Lawrence[,] but in the year 1763 a Treaty was signed at Paris[,] by the V Article of which the limits were clearly defined beyond which French Vessels could not pass. The following is the V Article.

'And His Britannic Majesty consents to leave to the Subjects of the Most Christian King the Liberty of fishing on [*sic*] the Gulf of St Lawrence on condition that the Subjects of France do not exercise the said fishery but at the distance of three leagues from all the Coasts belonging to Great Britain[,] as well those of the Continent as those of the Islands situated in the Gulf of St Lawrence.'

This Treaty has been confirmed by all subsequent Treaties, and clearly points out the boundary of the fishing grounds. These two nations are the only ones permitted to fish on the Coasts of America[,] & I shall hereafter mention any instances of encroachment which may have occurred[,] and what complaints were made against infringement of the above Treaties by the Inhabitants on the Coasts.

The Fish taken in the Gulf of St Lawrence which are source of trade [*sic*] to H.M. Subjects may be classed under the following.

Herring. This fish is[,] I believe[,] somewhat smaller than those taken on the Coasts of the British Islands[.] They are the first to run on the Shores of the Gulf[,] about the 15th May[,] and generally remain in the Bays & vicinity of sandy beaches until the beginning of June[,] when they leave the Coasts for deeper water[.] They are taken in large quantities with Seines & hanging nets and are cured for exportation and likewise used and considered to be the best bait for Cod. These fish again return to the shores in the middle of July or beginning of August[;] they are then called the Summer Herring [and] are in much better condition than the spring[.] after running on the coast about a fortnight[,] they again return to the deep water and at some places return a third time to the shore[,] when they are called the Fall Herring. Their periodical visitations to the Bays is [*sic*] presumed to be in pursuit of food[,] which is a species of very small shrimp called the 'Herring bait.'

Cod. This fish[,] the most abundant of any on the Coasts of the Gulf and the great source of the fishery and trade[,] generally strike upon the Coasts towards the third week in May and remain until October and November[.] It is supposed they come upon the Banks and in shore [*sic*] in pursuit of food and that they follow the schools of Caplin and Herring from the deep water towards the Bays and entrance[s] of Rivers where the former fish resort annually to spawn. When these fish and the Herring forsake the shores and return into deep water, it is found that the Cod likewise return to deep water and the Outer Banks &c. When such is the case[,] the fishing boats have to proceed further from the shore to pursue their occupation than during the early part of the season. In all parts of the Gulf of St Lawrence[,] Bay of Fundy, Banks of Nova Scotia and around Newfoundland do these fish abound[,] not only on the shores but likewise in the open sea & in all parts where there is less than 100 faths water they can be taken with Hook & Line. Their vast numbers is [*sic*] beyond all conception[,] and what points this out is the manner in which these fish are taken on the Coast of Newfoundland. When Bait cannot be procured, they are then jiggered, two Hooks are secured back to back and run over with lead to sink them. With this simple apparatus are fish taken in large quantities on the Coasts[,] & Schooners of 20 Tons may constantly been seen drifting along the Newfoundland shore in 20 to 30 fathoms water, completing their cargoes.

Salmon. This fish is common to all the Rivers of North America and has this season run more abundant [*sic*] than for the last 10 years. They enter and ascend the rivers soon after the breaking up of the Ice[,] and continue to do so until the middle of August[,] by which time the fishery is over[.]
The fish are apparently of a coarser species than those frequenting the Rivers of the British Islands[,] and in taste decidedly not so highly flavoured[.] They are taken in fixed nets in most of the Rivers and along the Shores of the Harbours and are salted in tierces[1] containing each from 40 to 45 Salmon. They are exported for the American and West India Markets.

[1]A cask of 42 gallons' capacity.

Sea Trout abound in all the Rivers on the American Coasts, and are generally to be found in larger schools where the Salt & Fresh water meet[,] or off the Sandy Beaches at the River mouths, in June & July. In August they ascend the Rivers and are then found above the Rapids or in the lakes. They are taken in large numbers with the Artificial Fly, but never taken or cured by the Inhabitants[,] either for home consumption or exportation[.]

Caplin. This is a small fish about 4 to 5 inches in length and ¾ of an inch deep [*sic*] and having the silvery character and appearance peculiar to the smelt. It arrives on the coast soon after the Herring[,] in or about the middle or third week in May[,] and remains in large shoals along the sandy beaches and near the Entrance [*sic*] of Rivers until the 2nd or 3rd week in June. They appear to visit the above localities for the purpose of spawning and then return into deep water[,] never again appearing until the following spring. They are taken in large quantities for Bait[,] but are not an Article of General Commerce except by the fishermen of Newfoundland[,] who sell large quantities to the French at St Pierre[.] besides the Caplin there is also a smaller fish called

Lance, also used as bait when Caplin & Herring cannot be procured. They derive their name most probably from their peculiar form[,] being about 3 inches in length and the size in [*sic*] bulk of a large quill. They have also the silvery appearance of the smelt[,] and are taken near the Entrance [*sic*] of the Rivers, about the time that the Caplin leave the Coast. It is supposed that they do not migrate the same as that fish, but remain nearly in the same locality, during winter and bad weather <u>burrowing</u> in the sand & mud[,] their tails alone being visible. I rather doubted this circumstance until I observed the Crews at Mingan digging them out of the Sand on the beach, above the <u>reach of the water</u> on an Ebb Tide[.]

Mackerel. This fish frequents the shores of the Gulf in August and September[.] they are chiefly found in large shoals on the North Shore of Prince Edwards Island, [the] West Shore of Cape Breton[,] and also around the Magdalen Islands[.] They are eagerly sought after by the Americans, who take them in large quantities, their value in the United States being more than double that of the Herring[.]

Whale. Whales are taken in different parts of the Gulf[,] but chiefly on the shore of Labrador near the Straight [*sic*] of Belleisle and vicinity of Gaspe[,] at which place there are several small schooners employed in their pursuit. The species taken are small[,] called the ‘hump backed whale'[,] yielding about 20 to 30 Barrells [*sic*] of oil[,] each barrell containing 18 to 20 Gallons. The chief time for taking them is during the Herring Season[,] as they live on and follow the 'Herring Bait.' The fishery this year has been successfull [*sic*].

Besides the fish now mentioned, Haddock[,] Halibut and Rock Cod are taken[,] but only casually[,] except the Haddock[,] which is now become numerous in the in shore fisheries[,] for instance in Gaspe Bay. they [*sic*] are salted and cured in the same manner as the Cod.

Having already mentioned that I put to sea on the 7 May[,] I communicated the same evening with Pictou[,] sailed on the following morning for the Eastward[,] and beat up between the Islands of Prince Edward and Cape Breton[,] and from thence proceeded to the Magdalen Islands[,] where we anchored in Pleasant Bay on the evening of the 10th.

The Magdalens are a chain of Rocky Islands[,] evidently of volcanic origin[,] connected together by low sandy beaches[,] most probably deriving their origins from the wash of the sea and accumulated to their present height by the agency of the wind and binding influence of vegetation. They extend in a NW direction for about 35 miles. The principal settlements are on Entry[,] Amherst, Grindstone & Allwright[1] Islands on the SE extreme of the range. Their population is said to consist of 300 families[,] all of Canadian French extraction and only speaking the French Language[,] deriving a scanty subsistence from employment in the fisheries. Entry Island is the only one on which Agricultural [*sic*] pursuits are the chief occupation. I believe all these Islands are private property and now belong to the Heirs of the late Sir [?Jeane] Coffin. They are under the Government of Canada[,] but measures have been taken to have them transferred to the Government of Prince Edward's Island.

In Amherst Island Harbour several American Schooners were at Anchor[,] in all about 21. They had recently arrived from various ports in the state of Maine[,] and annually resort here at this season for the spring Herring fishery[,] which had already commenced[,] and most of the vessels were loaded. The Herring taken at these Islands are not considered by the Inhabitants as Marketable fish[,] and are consequently cured in small quantities for their own use[,] the neighbouring colonial markets[,] and for the purpose of Bait for Cod. For this reason[,] the Schooners belonging to these Islands proceed to St Georges Bay on the West Shore of Newfoundland for the Herring fishery[,] where they are of a much finer quality and likewise very abundant. St

[1]Alright.

Georges Bay is situated on that part of Newfoundland commonly called the French Shore, where it is said the French claim an exclusive right of fishery and prevent our fishermen from taking fish. Such has appeared in a publication a few years ago, but one of the Magdalen Island Merchants informed me that he was at St Georges Bay that spring whilst a French corvette was there but [*sic*: and] they never prevent the English from fishing there[,] altho they do the Americans.

At this date[,] May 11th[,] no Cod fishing had commenced at the Magdalen Islands[,] but the fish were looked for in about 10 days.

Having been directed by the Second Article of my Instructions to proceed to Gaspe Bay as soon as circumstances would admit after my arrival in the Gulf[,] and 'there make inquiry relative to complaints of encroachment by American vessels' contained in a letter from the Sub Collector of HM Custom at that Port[,] which the late Commander in Chief forwarded for my guidance[,] I beg to acquaint you that on the 13 May I anchored off Douglas Town[.] The same evening the Ice broke up on the Bar of Gaspe Harbour[,] enabling HM Ship to anchor in that Harbour on the following day[.] It is situated at the head of Gaspe Bay[,] an inlet of the sea 14 miles deep and about 4 broad[,] & is one of the most secure and extensive harbours I have seen anywhere on the coast of America[,] sufficiently capacious to contain a numerous Fleet in perfect security[,] & extending from this Harbour is an inner Basin with 7 to 8 fathoms water.

There are several Settlements on the Shore of Gaspe Bay which will be mentioned hereafter as connected with the fishery. At none of them were any Boats launched nor any preparation commenced for the fishery[.] Even in Gaspe Basin the Schooner's [*sic*] retained their winter moorings and [were] still frozen in with the last remains of the winters Ice[.] we were much too early in our visitation to this part of the Coast & could be of no service except to show the Anxiety [*sic*] on the part of the Commander in Chief to afford early protection to the fisheries in the Gulf[.] Having completed water[,] I put to sea on the 20th May and proceeded to the North Cape of Prince E. Island[,] from thence along the South Shore thro Northumberland Straits and Anchored [*sic*] at Charlotte Town on the 23rd without having seen any vessel whatever engaged in the fishery.

On the 7 June I again put to sea from Charlotte Town[,] run [*sic*] down the Coast as far [as] the Entrance of the Gulf [*sic*] of Canso[,] looked into Port Hood without seeing any fishing vessels[,] and from thence run [*sic*] over to the East Point of Prince Edwards Island and along to [*sic*: the] North Shore[.] Off this coast we first saw American fishing Schooners employed in the fishery[.] Several were at Anchor from 4 to 6 miles from the Shore and consequently from 1 to 3 miles outside the defined limits. The one boarded had lately arrived from the States [&] was salting the fish in bulk[.] The Bait used by them was salted clams. Each vessel brings from 30 to 40 Barreles [*sic*] with them[.]

(In my report of last year on the fisheries of Newf[oundlan]d[,] I allude to encroachments by the French from St Pierre & Miquelon for the purpose of procuring clams at the Burgeo Islands to the prejudice of our own settlers.)

Few vessels were however seen on the Northern Shore of P. Edwards Island[,] which was sufficient evidence that even at this date[,] 8th June[,] the fishery had scarcely commenced. From Cape North I stood over towards the New Brunswick Shore[,] made the Island of Shipegan[,][1] and on the following morning[,] 9th June[,] anchored off Miscou Island[,] the SE extreme of the Bay of Chaleur.

At this Island are several Establishments for conducting a fishery[.] The Population amounts to about 100 summer residents[,] who resort here early in spring from the upper parts of the Bay. The fishery had commenced, Herrings having set in abundantly about the 15th May[,] Caplin soon after[,] and Cod had recently come upon the coast. Every description of fish were abundant and gave indication of a successful season.

It was stated by the residents 'That the fishery had been much better for the last three years[,] in consequence[,] it was alleged[,] of few Americans having been on the Coast and no Encroachments having taken place during that period'[.]

Such was the satisfactory information obtained at the Island of Miscou[.]

From Miscou Island I proceeded along the North East Shore towards Percie[,][2] at which place I Anchored [*sic*] the same evening I had anchored at Miscou. Percie is a beautifull [*sic*] settlement on the Main Shore[,] opposite to the Island of Bonaventure[.] More neatness and cleanliness was employed at the Establishments at this place than at any place I had yet seen in the provinces of North America[.] The Settlement contains about 400 Inhabitants[,] and is by the statement of the residents on the increase[.] about 150 Boats are employed in the fishery[,] which is close to the beach[.]

The quantity of fish taken yearly remains nearly in the same state[,] without any sensible decrease or increase for the last 4 years. From

[1]Shippegan.
[2]Percé.

inquiry I am able to state that no Encroachment took place by American or any other vessels on the Coast last year[,] nor have the residents any complaints to make against the Americans[.] They were[,] however[,] in the habit some years ago of frequently coming within the limit[.] The Establishment at this place belongs to Messrs Robins & Co of Jersey[.] They appear to hold Establishments at almost every place visited by HM Ship.

St Peters[1] was the next settlement visited[.] it is situated on the extreme SE point of Gaspe Bay[,] [&] contains a permanent population of about 80 people[,] but during summer nearly 200 fishermen come there from various parts of the Country to assist in the Cod fishery[,] the only species of fish taken at this place. The fishery had commenced but as yet the fish were scarce and[,] from the statement of the residents[,] it appears that of late years the quantity of the fish taken was on the decrease[.]

'No Americans they said had visited this place or neighbourhood for two or three years.' Nor can we assign any reason for the decrease of the fishery[,] unless it is owing to the great quantity of fish taken of the Outer banks by the Americans. At this place I learned of an English Barque being on shore on the South side of Gaspe Bay[.][2] I therefore proceeded to her assistance and Anchored [*sic*] off the '*Belvedere*' of Newcastle[, she] having run on shore during the night[,] steering NW . . . to the Northd of Cape Rozier[3] & steering up the Estuary of the St Lawrence[.]

A party of Hands was sent on board & H.M.S Stream anchor and cable laid out[,] and part of her cargo discharged[.] On the following morning she was hove off[,] the tide having risen a foot to fifteen inches higher than the previous evening. The Master was part owner[,] but showed little symptoms [*sic*] of obligation for the trouble we had taken.

On the North Shore of Gaspe Bay is the thriving settlement of Grande Greve[,][4] containing about 230 permanent Inhabitants[,] and in the fishing season upwards to 200 fishermen resort there. The chief fishery is for Cod[,] to prosecute which upwards of 100 boats are employed[,] and likewise several small coasting schooners. It is said that the fishery at this place has likewise decreased and the same reason is assigned for it as at St Peters.

[1]Pointe-St-Pierre.

[2]Milne meant Gaspé Passage rather than Gaspé Bay, as the location he subsequently described is outside the bay itself, to the northeast.

[3]Cap-des-Rosiers.

[4]Grande Grève. Again, Milne must have meant Gaspé Peninsula rather than Gaspé Bay; Grande Grève is outside the bay.

Gaspe. we [*sic*] again anchored in this Harbour on second visitation on the 11th June[,] when I communicated with Mr McConell[,] the Sub Collector of HM Customs[,] and from him received the following statement. 'The County of Gaspe contains in all about 4000 Inhabitants[,] the most populous [areas] being the vicinity of the sea coasts[.] about 12 square rigged vessels and 950 Boats are owned in the County[,] and all are employed in the fishery[,] which commences early in June and continues until November. The Cod fishery has decreased in quantity for sometime [*sic*] and it is alleged that it is in consequence of the mode of fishing adopted by the Americans'[.]

'No Americans have encroached here since men of war have been in the habit of visiting Gaspe Bay.'

Herrings were formerly taken here in considerable quantities[,] but within the last 10 years that fishery has entirely failed[.] They are now only taken in sufficient quantities for bait. Salmon are taken here in great numbers in hanging nets moored from the various points in the Harbour[.] this fishery is only carried on by the Inhabitants off the Shore of their own farms. At this period they are more abundant than has been known for many years. They are salted and sold to the merchants in payment for goods received during the previous winter[,] For [*sic*] I believe it a very common circumstance that all the Fishermen[,] Farmers[.] &c are always in debt for supplies granted in advance. The Merchants of Jersey are the chief owners of the Establishments in the Bay of Gaspe. Their Fish[,] towards the close of the season[,] is shipped direct to foreign markets[,] principally Brazil.

On the 17th June I proceeded to sea from Gaspe Bay and stood over towards the shores of Anticosti[,] worked up along its coast[,] and from the western extreme stood over towards the River St John[,][1] and from thence to Mingan[,] where I anchored on the 19th without having seen any vessel whatever resembling a fishing schooner.

Mingan is situated on the coast of the Labrador[2] in 64 West Longitude[.] [It] is an Establt of the Hudson Bay Company. Their Charter was granted to them by Parliament in the year 1669[,] and limited their trade and commerce to the shores which lie within the entrance of Hudsons Straits. I was therefore at a loss to know on what grounds they held an Establishment in this locality. From Information subsequently obtained[,] it appears that the Co. rent the Seignory of Mingan from the Canadian proprietors at a lease of 21 years and an [*sic*] yearly rent[,] it is said[,] of £500[.] This Seignory extends from near

[1]Rivière St Jean.

[2]Now Quebec.

the River Moisie[1] to a few miles Eastward of the Musquaro River[,][2] running parallel with the shore and at a distance from it of three leagues. The chief object of the Establis[hmen]t is to promote a fur trade with the Indians[,] who receive their supplies entirely from the Head [*sic*] port at Mingan and out port at Musquaro. These Indians arrive at the port from the interior early in June[,] some coming even from as far as the G[rea]t Bay of Esquimaux. They bring with them the furs which they have taken during the winter[,] which consist of Black, Silver, & Red Fox, Wolverine, Beaver, Martin [*sic*: 'Marten'], Muskrat, Deer Skins and Eider down[.] These are taken by the superintendant at a certain valuation, receiving in lieu cloth, powder, shot sugar &c. At this present time 20 families have arrived[,] where they remain about 10 to 14 days. [They are] entirely devoted to the observance of their religious rites under the supervision of a Catholic Priest from Quebec[,] who yearly visits the Port for the purpose and receives a salary from the Company.

All the Indians of the Seignory have taken the temperance pledge and requested the Superint[en]d[ent] to send all the spirits away from the Ports. This is certainly disinterested on their part[,] as it was always given to them Gratis by the Company. During the months of June & July they migrate with their families to the numerous Islands along the Coast for the purpose of shooting Seals[,] Ducks &c. The former they convert into oil & sell to the Company on their return to the Port in Aug[us]t[,] when they receive their winters stores and take their departure for the interior[,] where they wander from place to place during the long and dreary Canadian winter in pursuit of Furs[,] and never remain beyond two or three days in one locality. The only fishing carried on here is for Salmon in the River Mingan by [the] H. B. Co. They have people also employed in a similar manner in all the rivers of the Seignory. Altho no fishery except Salmon is prosecuted[,] I believe fish of other descriptions may be taken[,] as there are excellent cod Banks off the River St John & I should suppose Herring might be taken in the proper season.

From Mingan I proceeded to the Eastward along the Labrador Shore and among the extensive chain of the Mingan Islands, Anchoring [*sic*] at Esquimaux and also at Charles Island and proceeding from there to the Small [*sic*] Harbour of Natashquan. At this H[arbou]r we found at Anchor [*sic*] two small schooners belonging to the Magdalen Islands employed in Cod fishing & salting their fish in Bulk. From the Fisher-

[1]Some 75 miles west of Mingan.
[2]Some 125 miles east of Mingan.

men employed in the Natashquan river I was informed that no American vessels had been seen on the coast this season[,] but it was customary for them to visit this shore in spring and to use the Harbour of Natashquan. I have no doubt the visits of HM Ships to this place has deterred them from revisiting it. Mount Joli[,] the position on the coast which defines the limits where the Americans have the privilege of landing to cure their fish[,] is close to Natashquan River. From Natashquan H[arbou]r I proceeded to Kegaska Bay and anchored there on the 30 June[.] it is a small port[,] 18 miles to the Eastward of Mount Joli. No vessels were seen at this port nor any on the coast.

The range of coast from Mingan to Kegaska is a wild sterile country composed of rocks of the primitive formation[,] in parts thickly covered by dwarf trees of the spruce species[,] almost impenetrable[,] and infested with myriads of Mosquitos [?locust] & sand flies. No vestige of a Habitation [*sic*] exists along all this shore . . . except one or two Log Hut [*sic*] erected at the Entrance of the Rivers to afford shelter to a few fishermen belonging to the H. B. Company during the the [*sic*] Salmon Season in June and July.[1]

Having completed water at Kegaska[,] I put to sea on the 3 July for the Magdalen Islands[,] where I arrived on the 5th and anchored off their NW extreme, from thence proceeded to Pleasant Bay on the following morning[,] where I communicated with the shore &[,] finding the fishing proceeding without molestation or encroachment[,] & that the services of HM Ship were not required[,] proceeded in Co. with HM Sloop *Ringdove* to Charlotte Town for any orders which might be forwarded for H.M.S. consequent upon the melancholy death of Sir T. Harvey[,] the Commander in Chief.

H.M.S. *Ringdove* having arrived in the Gulf early in June[,] had proceeded during the *Crocodiles* absence at Labrador, along the North Shore of P. E. Island[,] visited the Coast about Miramichi[,] the Island

[1]Milne then added a note on navigation which he subsequently crossed out. The text of this section reads: 'This coast has always be[en] viewed as one of great danger to navigation. That[,] however[,] has now been dispelled owing to the publication at the Hydrogh [Hydrographic] Office of the late Surveys of Captain Bayfield. by [*sic*] their existence we were enabled with great facility to navigate among the Islands & Enter the Harbours[.] The great extent of the Coast which has been surveyed and its peculiarly rugged form[,] caused by the numerous Islands and shoals with which it is fraught[,] must have rendered it a task of more than ordinary difficulty, but in every locality I have visited on the Coast and among the Islands[,] every small rock and feature of the Coast [has been] most accurately laid down[,] & I feel confident the Survey of the Gulf of St Lawrence[,] when completed[,] will prove one of the most usefull [*sic*] and at the sametime [*sic*] beautiful records of Nautical Surveying in the Hydrographical Office.' Reference to Bayfield's achievement is made at the end of the Report, and some of the language of the above passage is repeated there.

of Miscou, Paspébiac in the Bay of Chaleur, Percé, St. Peters[, and] from thence returned along the shore of P. E. Island to the Magdalens without having observed or heard of any encroachments by American or other vessels.

Having arrived at Charlotte Town on the 10th July[,] and finding no further Instructions[,] I again put to sea on the 15 (July) and proceeded in Co with HMS *Ringdove* to the Eastward. I then visited the vicinity of the West Shore of Cape Breton[,] looking into Port Hood[;] from from [*sic*] thence worked up alongshore [*sic*] to [Sea] Wolf Island[,][1] where I communicated with two Schooners at Anchor [*sic*] and likewise with the Shore. From them I hear that no Americans had been upon the Coast[,] but that they came there in August & September for Mackerel. They mentioned they had no cause of complaint against them, & one Schooner belonging to Arichat said, 'I have only seen two American vessels this season and we have more cause of complaint against the Nova Scotia Schooners & fishermen from the Westward than the Americans.'

From [Sea] Wolf Island I went to Chetican[,][2] a small harbour on the West Shore of Cape Breton [and] from the residents was made acquainted 'that there are about 150 families in the neighbourhood[;] that 10 or 12 Schooners and a few small boats are owned by them[,] all of them engaged in fishing for Cod[,] Herring[,] and Mackerel[.] The fishing as yet has been indifferent and we have no complaints to make against the Americans; but a great number of them come on this coast to fish for Mackerel in August' & it was added 'The Americans sometimes fish here with permission from the Inhabitants.'

On the 22 July I anchored in Pictou Roads &[,] having communicated with the Shore[,] proceeded in Company with HMS *Ringdove* to Charlotte Town[,] where we arrived on the 23rd.

Having found the Foremast of HM Ship badly sprung & being under the necessity of being taken out, It [*sic*] was landed and repaired on shore and on the 6th August again restepped.[3] The same afternoon Instructions were received from Commodore Douglas[,] Commander in Chief, directing me to proceed without a moments delay to Halifax. I sailed on the following day and arrived at Halifax on the 11th. The services of HM Ship not being further required at that port[,] I was directed by the C in Chief to resume the duties in the Gulf of St Lawrence. [I] Sailed from Halifax on the 19th and arrived at Charlotte

[1]Sea Wolf, or Seal Island, as most maps call it, is just south of Margaree.

[2]Chéticamp.

[3]It was damaged 'between Hounds and Head,' that is, between the staples used to bind the standing rigging to the mast and the mast head.

Town on the 24th. from [*sic*] thence I put to sea on the 28th and arrived at the Magdalen Islands on the 30th. The Settlements at Amherst and [?L'Etang-du-Nord] on Grindstone Island were visited[.] at the former Harbour were about 15 vessels[,] principally Schooners from Quebec[,] taking on board salted fish from the correspondents of the Merchants houses at that place. From the Magistrate I was informed that about 50 or 60 American Vessels had been there during the season, That [*sic*] everything was going on well and quietly. The fishing had been very productive[:] too much so say the Merchants 'as it will cause the prices to depreciate' and 'the markets in consequence of a decreasing demand will be overstocked'; The 7th Article of my Instructions alludes to the Americans drying and securing [*sic*] their fish on the Magdalens, Which [*sic*] is not authorized by Treaty &c &c. I made inquiry relative to this subject to find that a few American vessels fishing in the neighbourhood of the Islands are in the practice of landing their fish. That they are dried and cured by the Inhabitants for them[,] and they [the Inhabitants] received in payment for their trouble 8 to 10 p[er] c[en]t of the cured fish. It would be impossible for the crews of these A[merican] vessels to land and cure their own fish[,] as they would then lose all their time for catching them unless they brought people from the States with them; In [*sic*] Grindstone and Amherst Har[bour]s were several small French [*sic*] Schooners belonging to St Pierre and Miquelon[.] having landed myself at the latter Harbour, I endeavoured to obtain every information relative to their visits to these Islands[,] where they have no right [to be.] From the Sub Collector of the Customs I was informed that they come there for the purpose of procuring bait and take that opportunity of [*sic*] smuggling, one vessel a short time since having landed 6 Casks of Brandy[,] and that they always fish off the Northern Range of the Magdalen Islands. I therefore took the opportunity of Explaining [*sic*] to the Crew of the *Madelaine* of Miquelon that they had no right to fish where they had been[,] and towed his [*sic*] vessel out of the Harbour[,] and placed the accompanying notice on his fishing license [']This vessel was found at Anchor at the Magdalen Islands and had been fishing within the British limits. I have refrained from sending her before a Court for Condemnation[,] feeling convinced the Governor of St Pierre will punish the Master & Crew to deter others from Encroaching with[in] the limits[.]

Signed A Milne Captain[']

No complaints were made against [them] by the Inhabitants [of the Magdalens,] altho by one person it was stated that they did at times commit wanton mischief on shore by setting fire to the woods, stealing oil, staving boats, and other such misdemeanors, all of which I verily believe[,] having heard of similar outrages last year on the Shores of Labrador. I recommended in all such cases to obtain the name of the vessel to which such people belonged[,] and make complaint of the facts [to] the Magistrate[,] whose duty it should be to represent it to the Governor of the Colony to which the Islands are attached, to the Captain of HMS visiting the Port[,] or [the] Collector of Customs, that steps might be taken against the Individuals.

To whatever government these Islands are ultimately transferred, I am fully of opinion circuit courts should be formed and some law and order established, for at present there appears to be very little of either[,] and the Sub Collector of HM Customs[,] being there 'solo'[,] is afraid or unwilling to act[,] & being likewise the Magistrate[,] is probably very much in the same position[.] From the Magdalen Islands I returned to the N Shore of P. E. Island[,] making the land at Cape Tryon[,] from thence run [*sic*] along the shore to the Westward[.] Several American Vessels were passed 20 miles from the land. They were all looking for Schools of Mackerel[,] but appeared unsuccessfull [*sic*] from their constantly shifting their births [*sic*] from place to place. Two Schooners were observed going into Richmond Bay[,][1] and about 7 to 9 miles directly up it we observed 19 sail of American Schooners. They were all evidently busy fishing for Mackerel[,] but being Sunset we could not have reached them before dark. From the North End of P.E. Island we stood over towards the New B[runswic]k Shore[,] made Shipegan [*sic*][,] off which some Boats from that Island were fishing. It was my intention to have visited Miscou, but in consequence of a dense fog setting in[,] apparently with bad weather[,] was unable to do so[,] but proceeded [instead] to Gaspe Bay[,] Anchoring [*sic*] off Douglas Town on the 2nd September.

Douglas Town is a Settlement on the South Shore of the Bay of Gaspe[.] I have not mentioned it before[,] in consequence of not having called there in the previous visits of HM Ship to the Bay; it is situated at the Entrance of the River St John[,] contains a population [of] between 50 and 60 families and[,] besides the fishery, which is carried on extensively, by each family for themselves, possesses a considerable extent of cultivated land.

This was the third visitation of HM Ship to this [Bay] and from the Sub Collector of H.M. Customs [I] received the satisfactory intelligence that no case of Encroach[men]t had taken place this season, nor had the fisheries been molested in the slightest manner. The Fishing throughout the survey under his charge had been most unprecedentedly

[1]The original name of Malpeque Bay.

successfull [*sic*], much beyond the average of the last several Years. Similar Statements were also made by other individuals, who likewise mentioned that only two American Vessels had been in the Bay for Wood & Water during the Season[.]

On the 4 Sep[tembe]r I sailed from Gaspe Bay, stood over towards the S.W. Shore of Anticosti[,] along that shore to the Westward[,] and from the N.W. Extreme of the Island stood over towards the Entrance of the River St John[,][1] and from thence proceeded to Mingan Harbour[,] where I anchored on the 6th.

I was told by the resident of the Hudsons Bay Co that since our previous visit to this place in June, Several [*sic*] American Schooners had visited the Harbour for the purpose of obtaining Bait and likewise Wood and Water[.] These vessels had been fishing off the Entrance of the River St John[,] but had left the Coast some weeks [earlier.] Nothing was doing at Mingan[.] The Salmon fishery was over and the Indians[,] having returned from their summers cruise among the Islands in pursuit of seals &c[,] had proceeded into the interior. The Salmon fishery on the coast had been successfull [*sic*] altho some of the Rivers which had formerly been the most valuable had this year almost entirely failed, a circumstance which likewise occurs in the Rivers of the British Islands.

From Mingan I proceeded to Kegaska and from thence to Cuacuacho[2] Bay in 60½ West Longitude[.] The only persons we saw in this range of Coast were a few fishermen returning to their Homes at the River St Augustine on the Labrador after their summer fishing for Salmon in Coacuacho [*sic*] River. from [*sic*] them I was told that no American or other Vessels ever came to that part of the Coast to fish. That there we[re] no fish to be caught[,] or only in small quantities[,] 40 or 50 pr day[.] That it was not worth their trouble. That there were Herring & Mackerel on the Coast but few in quantity[.] That they kept in too deep water to be taken in nets, and that on this coast they would not take the bait.

At this point is the boundary of the Gulf of St Lawrence fishery, and from this I proceeded direct to the coast of Bryon Island[3] and then run [*sic*] along the West Shore of the Magdalens, under which Islands were several American Schooners at Anchor and wherein [*sic*] 18 off Bryon Island[,] fishing for Mackerel[.] From the Magdalen Islands I stood over to the North Cape of Cape Breton[,] run [*sic*] down its Western

[1]On the Quebec shore.
[2]Coacoachou.
[3]Brion.

Shore within three miles of the Coast without seeing any Foreign Vessels[,] and from thence stood over to Pictou[,] where I anchored on the 20th Sept. Having completed water at that port[,] I proceeded from there to Charlotte Town to Embark old guns belonging to the Fort[,] as directed by Instruction from the Commander in Chief.

Having brought to a close the foregoing statements relative to the places & coast visited by HM Ship in the Gulf of St Lawrence, I will now[,] in furtherance of the 11th Article of my Instructions[,] allude to the State of the various Fisheries &c[.]

The British Fisheries may be classed under two heads. 1st[:] The In Shore fishery[,] which is carried on by small boats with two men close to the shore & to the fishing Establishments[,] at which the fish are landed several times during the day. This fishery is carried on chiefly on the coast of the Bay of Chaleur at Miscou, Paspébiac[,] from thence along the coast to Percie, St Peters & [the] Bay of Gaspé, the Magdalen Islands & Chetican [*sic*] & Port Hood on the West Shore of Cape Breton. At these Establishments are Storehouses belonging to Merchants in England[,] Nova Scotia, New Brunswick & Canada, who supply the Inhabitants with Clothing[,] Provisions, linen &c during the winter months and[,] in the Ensuing [*sic*] summer[,] receive from these people their fish at a certain fixed price in payment. The outer or Bank [fishery] is prosecuted in small schooners either belonging to the above Establishments, or the various ports of Nova Scotia[,] New Brunswick or Cape Breton, and generally proceed to a distance to fish[,] as at the Magdalen Islands &c[,] even at the Labrador. It is customary for their fish to be cleaned and salted on board, & they only return to their Homes, when their cargo is complete. I have found it impossible to form any estimate of the number of people employed in the British Fisheries, in consequence of the manner in which the Coast is populated in every small creek which affords shelter to a Boat[,] and in consequence of the manner in which the fishermen move about from place to place in search of more productive fishing grounds, nor can I form any estimate of the quantity of fish taken. To do so is impossible[,] nor can such a return be obtain[ed] until the final close of the fishing season and then only thro the returns of the respective Custom Houses and Fishery Establishments.

It is[,] however[,] satisfactory for me to state that throughout the Coast the fishing has been most productive and beyond the average of the last few years.

P. E. Island may be said to have no fisheries[,] altho situated in that part of the Gulf the most favourable for their prosecution[,] and possessed of harbours of great security[,] Easy [*sic*] access[,] and so close to the most approved fishing grounds that it would be supposed on its shores large fishing Establishments would be found. Such however is not the case; There [*sic*] is no regularly Established fishery[,] In so [far as] I can hear, and moreover the Import of fish exceeds the Export. To what cause can this be assigned[?] I believe the State of the Island with regard to population, that the few settlers find more inducement to pursue the pursuits of Agriculture [*sic*] than those of the fishery[,] and whenever an attempt has been made to Establish one, The [*sic*] people employed have invariably retaken themselves to the cultivation of the soil. nor do I think any fishery will be established until the profit derived from it exceeds what they can procure by Agriculture. It must, however[,] be stated that throughout most parts of the Shores of the Gulf of St Lawrence[,] the pursuits of Agriculture are somewhat continued [i.e., simultaneously pursued] by the resident farmers whose lands are chiefly cultivated on the Sea Shore. These people build their own Boats. They set their nets for Herring[,] Mackerel and Salmon[,] and when when [*sic*] the period of the year will admit of them leaving their fields and crops[,] will be engaged in Cod fishing[.] their take is however limited, and chiefly for their own consumption and winter Store, but [they] most probably dispose of their Herring[,] Mackerel & Salmon [*sic*]. This system of fishing is perfectly independent & on quite a different footing from the regular Establishments.

The Trade of the Gulf of St Lawrence[,] besides the fishery[,] is principally in timber Exported in vast quantities from the St Lawrence, Bay of Chaleur, Miramichi, the various small ports of the North Shore of Nova Scotia[,] & likewise from P. E. Island[,] to the Ports of Great Britain. The trade of Pictou is likewise extensive by American [*sic*] vessels who resort there for coal. Quantities [of coal] are likewise shipped for the Nova Scotia Markets.

I have endeavoured by repeated inquiry to obtain the best information relative to the number of American Vessels frequenting the Gulf of St Lawrence to prosecute the fishery. By some people['s estimates] it has been upward from 2 to 3 & 400 sail[,] and by others the number has been extended even up to 500. I am however of opinion that between 3 & 400 is nearly the Amount. The opinion is however very prevalent that of late Years the Number of American Schooners have [*sic*] very much decreased. They receive from the United States Government one bounty, and that bounty is on the fishing license[,] which license prevents them from carrying on any trade whatever for four months. The bounty is 4 dollars for each ton of the vessels burden.

It is early in May that these vessels first arrive in the Gulf[,] resorting to the Magdalen Islands[,] which may be considered their head quarters. here [*sic*] they await the setting in of the Herring and[,] with their own Seines[,] which they lend to the Inhabitants[,] haul for those fish on the shores[,] with which they soon complete a cargo salted in bulk and then proceed with all expedition on their return to their own Ports[,] that they may again revisit the Gulf in sufficient time for the 'Cod fishery'[.] it is only these early spring vessels that ever make a second voyage during the fishing season. In June and July the more numerous part of these vessels arrive in the Gulf to fish for Cod[.] they generally bring with them Salted Clams & Herrings for bait and take up there stations on the various banks surrounding our shore. They may be seen at Anchor [*sic*] in fleets Extending [*sic*] along the N. Shore of P. E. Island[,] on the Orphan and Bradelle Banks (both favourite places with them) around the Magdalen Islands, Seldom [*sic*] on the W. Shore of Cape Breton[,] and should the fish prove scarce on any one locality[,] will move about from place to place & will even proceed along the Labrador Shore thro the Straights [*sic*] of Belle Isle [*sic*] as far as 55 North Latitude. By the month of August these vessels have probably completed their Cargoe's [*sic*] when they return homeward, but at this time another squadron have arrived for the purpose of obtaining Mackerel[,] which with them is a valuable fish, and in their manner of taking them a peculiar mode is adopted which has called forth observation from the Inhabitants of our shores. The Schooners engaged in this fishery have each a Bill made with spike nails for the purpose of grinding up salted or other fish in very small pieces. when [*sic*] in this state it is placed in troughs fitted to the vessels side & the vessel[,] it is said[,] 'proceeds within the limits in search of the Mackerel School[']. When they find it[,] this bait is thrown overboard and the vessels head put towards the Sea[,] and by means of the bait the Mackerel follow the Vessel beyond the limits[,] where they are quickly taken in large quantities with jiggs [*sic*] & bait hooks, The [*sic*] milled bait from the vessel keeping the mackerel close to the surface of the water[.] in this manner are the Cargoes of the A[merican] vessels completed[,] but it is obvious that whilst individuals are benefitted by so easy and expeditious a method of obtaining a cargo[,] much damage is done to the fishery in consequence of the Mackerel Schools bein[g] broken on their way to our shore[,] by which our inshore fishermen are partly deprived of this profitable fishery[,] and the fish which are wounded and die from the mode adopted in taking them will ultimately cause a falling off of the fish themselves.

Whether such is the case or not[,] I am not adequate to form an opinion[,] but those whose knowledge of the subject entitles them to form one[,] state the above to [be] the facts.

Much has been said and written on the Encroachment of American vessels on our Shores[,] and I have heard observations made of these continued transgressions of the defined limits[.] Insofar as my own observations go[,] I shall allude to the transgressions which I have observed and the Answers I have received from the residents at the fishing Establishments I have visited to the Question [']Do the Americans or French Encroach on the Fisheries either for fishing or obtaining Bait?[']

In my various cruises round the shores of the Gulf I have seen numbers of American Vessels pursuing their lawfull [*sic*] avocations. I have run down the above shores in thick weather[,] but in no instance have I witnessed a decided violation of the Treaty. I do not mean by this that it should be inferred that no Encroachment has taken place, because I think it not unlikely that slight transgression may have occurred, but the outcry against American vessels is caused more by individuals than general acts of Encroachment[.] observations have likewise been made relative to the American Schooners frequenting our Harbours[.] by some of our Inhabitants it has been looked upon as illegal[,] they being ignorant of the Treaty which admits of all our Harbours being open to them under certain restrictions; for the purpose of obtaining shelter, and likewise wood & water. It is said that under this plea they constantly enter our ports for the purpose of illicit trade[.] I am unable to form any opinion or to say whether such is the case or not[,] nor am I aware whether any restriction or authority is [*sic*] imposed on these vessels when they enter our ports. Such should certainly be the case, which of course rests with the respective Colonial Governments and the officers of HM Customs and[,] should HM Ship be in any Port to which American Vessels resort[,] as at Richmond Bay, P.E. Island[,] her authority might in such a case be rendered available[,] but I conceive her duties are chiefly to exercise[,] by her presence on the coast[,] a moral influence over American & other vessels in the Gulf to maintain [i.e., uphold] their respective Treaties[,] & it cannot be expected that HMS should enter the various ports on the shores of the Gulf to watch illicit trade, at all times difficult to detect but especially with regard to American Vessels[,] as it is only when taken in the actual fact [i.e., act] of Smuggling that the Custom House will take cognizance of it[,] or that condemnation will follow. But independent of not having observed any decided violation of the Treaty, The [*sic*] residents at the Establishments have in every instance borne testimony to 'no Encroachment having taken place' & 'having no complaint against American Vessels.' Another source of general outcry against American Vessels is the manner in which they fish. This alludes to the manner in which they take

Mackerel[,] and to their heaving overboard the Gurry or offal of the fish they take on the fishing Banks, by which[,] it is said[,] the fish (Cod)[,] finding food on those Banks[,] do not approach the shore in pursuit of food[,] and that the offal is deleterious to the fish. The Treaty certainly does not define the mode in which the fish are to be taken nor whether the offal is to be landed or not, nor are any Colonial acts relative thereto, and as the English[,] French & American Fishermen all pursue the same system when it suits their convenience[,] and even at the fishing Establishments on shore the Gurry falls from the stages erected on the beach[,] to be washed into the sea by the reflux of the tide[,] I see little little [*sic*] reason for one party to complain more than another, but am somewhat inclined to view the complaints against A[merican] Vessels in light of a jealous feeling towards them engendered in our Inhabitants by being envious of the zealous perseverance in pursuit of their fishing[,] which is highly commendable[,] and if some of their active spirit of Enterprise [*sic*] was instituted into the habits of our own fishermen[,] it would add much to their individual benefit & prosperity.

Amongst a large number of vessels congregated in one place as those of the United States are in the Gulf of St L[awrence,] some misconduct is likely to occur among them[,] & I am inclined to entertain the opinion that wanton mischief may sometimes be committed[;] that we know such to be the case even in Communities whose law is Established and Enforced [*sic*], and therefore where there are neither the one or the other[,] it is more than likely some evil minded people will break out [*sic*][,] but in all such cases where I have heard of it & have [?examined] the parties[,] no satisfactory answers could be obtained[,] & no remedy will or can be adumbrated until the settlements become more numerous so as to attract the attention of Government[,] & law & order firmly Established.

The only place where the French fish in the Gulf is at the Magdalen Islands, where in August they resort from St. Pierre's. They at this time enter the harbours of the Magdalen Islands in order to obtain bait & there smuggle Brandy & Tea. This was told me by the Magistrate & Sub Collector of HM Customs, who appeared to view it as a regular established yearly trade. I could not help asking him if he was the Collector & [if so] why he permitted them to enter the ports, to which he said, they would heave him overboard if he interfered. So much to [*sic*: 'for'] the Law of the Magdalen Islands.

The Light Houses in the Gulf of St. Lawrence are the following.

On the Island of St. Pauls[,] to the Northd of the Island of Cape Breton, but not seen by HMS *Crocodile*.

A Revolving Light on the point of Anticosti. This Light House was twice seen, it is [a] clear well defined light[,] and observed at a distance of 15 to 20 Miles. The Light House[,] from its Whitish colour[,] is an Excellent Land Mark by day. Another Light H[ouse] has been constructed on the East point of the Island, but has never been lighted in consequence of want of funds. This is somewhat surprising[,] considering the immense trade of the St. Lawrence and the very dangerous navigation of this part of the Gulf in Spring and Autumn.

Pictou Harbour Light was the only other light we observed. it [*sic*] is a small light of quite sufficient power for the purpose intended, viz. guiding vessels into the Roads and likewise [the] Harbour of Pictou. Funds have been voted by the House of Assembly of P. E. Island for the Erection of a Light House for the Harbour of Charlotte Town. Some difficulty will however occur, as the funds voted are certainly not adequate to the purpose[,] & there exists some difference of opinion relative to its intended position. I recommended Point Prim[,] at the Entrance [*sic*] of Hillsborough Bay; should it be erected in that position – It [*sic*] would be a light not only for the Harbour but likewise for the adjoining coast.

The navigation of the Gulf of St Lawrence has been rendered much more certain than formerly[,] in consequence of the publication of the Surveys of Captain Bayfield by the Hydrographical Office[.]

The Magdalen Islands[,] with the various shoals which are in their vicinity[,] are now accurately laid down, The [*sic*] St Lawrence has been completed[,] and likewise its Southern Shore extending to the Bay of Chaleur. The [*sic*] dangerous coast of the Labrador[,] formerly almost unknown and looked upon with dread[,] is now rendered easy of access[,] and by the assistance of the new charts we were enabled with perfect confidence to navigate among the numerous Islands and reefs which fringe this coast[,] and to enter its Harbours with safety. One oversight was alone detected[,] viz. a shoal not laid down in Cuacoacho [*sic*: Coacoachou] Bay. In all other localities every feature of the coast appeared most accurately defined, a task of no ordinary difficulty from the very peculiar character of the coast[,] being entirely bounded by a continuous rim of numerous Island[s][,] Rock[s] & reefs extending sometimes to nearly three miles from the shore[,] & I feel confident; when the shores of Nova Scotia & Prince E. Island are completed[,] the Survey of the Gulf of St Lawrence will prove to be one of the most usefull [*sic*] and beautifull [*sic*] records of Nautical Surveying in the Hydrographical Office[.]

But It [*sic*] is much to be regretted that the usefull [*sic*] labours of our Nautical Surveyors are not more generally known[,] and the Admiralty Charts more generally diffused among the Mercantile Marine of the country. I should presume the sale is limited on account of only one Agent in London being appointed, but am of opinion[,] if branch agents were nominated at our principal sea Ports & Colonies[,] these most usefull [*sic*] and valuable Charts would be in more circulation [*sic*] than they are at present. Their Existence is not know[n] but to a few, and these are the officers of HM Ships – and when I had shown them to the fishermen on the shore of the Gulf[,] they have been most anxious to obtain them[,] especially the Labrador Shore. This diffusion among our Mercantile Marine might lessen the numerous shipwrecks which yearly happen, but a more certain means of reducing the sad catalogue of these shipwrecks would be [the] placing of more eligible people in Command of Ships. This summer I have observed 4 vessels on shore – viz. 2 on the Magdalen Islands, one on P. E. Island [&] one in Gaspe Bay, and have heard of several others on the Island of Anticosti, where many lives were lost.

Having in the foregoing report detailed my proceedings in the Gulf of St Lawrence since April last, and complied in so far as I felt capable of doing with the tenor of the Instructions under which I was acting, It [*sic*] only remains for me to acquaint you that I sailed from P. E. Island on the 28th Inst and have the honour to inform you with [*sic*] my Arrival [*sic*] at Halifax.

[**103**] *Adam to Milne*

HMS *Winchester*, Halifax, Nova Scotia
22 October 1841

Sir

I have to acknowledge the receipt of your letter of the 2nd Instant with its annexed report of the state of the Fisheries &c in the Gulf of St. Lawrence, and of your proceedings during the period of Her Majestys Ship *Crocodile* being employed in that quarter; I have much satisfaction in acquainting you, that I highly approve of your proceedings, and that I have transmitted your very able report for the information of my Lords Commissioners of the Admiralty.

[**104**] *Adam to Milne*

HMS *Winchester*, Halifax, Nova Scotia
22 October 1841

You are hereby required and directed to put to Sea in Her Majesty's Ship *Crocodile* and proceed without loss of time to Spithead, reporting your arrival for the information of the Lords Commissioners of the Admiralty.

[**105**] *Milne to David Milne*

HMS *Crocodile*, Spithead
14 November 1841

My dear David

We sailed from Halifax on the 23rd[1] & have had a fair passage across the Atlantic. We are now about to sail for Plymouth[,] where the ship is to be paid off[.] I had rather it had been at this place, but must make the best of it[.] My further movements are of course uncertain & will entirely depend on the period when the *Crocodile*'s Pendant is hauled down[,] which will be a week after our arrival in Plymouth Harbour. Everything is so much changed since I left England, that I find myself a perfect stranger. I shall go to London & thence come north[,] but by which route I know not – but I think I will keep to the land journey[.]

Write me a line as soon as you can[.]

[**106**] *Milne to Sir David Milne*

HMS *Crocodile*, off Start Point
15 November 1841

My dear Father,

We are now close to the End of our final destination[,] and I hope this afternoon we may be enabled to reach the [Plymouth] Sound[;] if not I think I may make certain of being there tomorrow morning[,] and I trust in Harbour on the following day. We left Spithead yesterday afternoon about 4 oclock. It blew so heavy between that hour and one oclock that I would not venture to Sea[.] towards the latter hour it

[1]Grace Milne Home added: '(Oct: I suppose)'.

moderated and we made a start thru St. Helens, stood down Channel on a wind under treble reefed Topsails & reefed Courses on the Starb Tack[.] before morning the wind fell almost to a calm and then sprang up[,] blowing fresh from SW, with snow and sleet. We found it very cold and disagreeable[,] and are all anxious to reach our journeys end. I am all ready in the way of ships books & to be paid off[,] and I think 6 or 7 days from the time of our going into Harbour will see the Pendant hauled down[.] I will then start the same evening for London, probably by way of Exeter or Southhampton[,] as I dont [*sic*] want to be staying either at Capt. Revans's or any other friends. He wants me to pay him a visit[,] but I have done all I can to avoid going there[,] not wishing to be detained. I have a letter from Sir. C. Adam to Sir George Cockburn[,] but have not forwarded it as it appears a letter of introduction. G. Seymour[,][1] who is my first Lt[,] had a letter from his father yesterday morning in which he says 'The promotion is at present very doubtfull,' but I suppose the Queen herself will be anxious for one. In the Navy the promotion during the last few years in the junior branches has been rather extensive[,] caused by the proceedings at Acre and in China, but there have been few Captains promoted to Flags. Sir Graham Moore is the Admiral at Portsmouth. I think I have often heard you mention his name as an old cruising friend when in Command [*sic*] of Frigates[,] and I once called at his house when staying at Cobham with Sir Thomas Thompson. I am sure Portsmouth Dock Yd is active at the present time in consequence of the number of vessels fitting out[.] Lord John Hay[2] has a most splendid frigate[:] The *Warspite*[,] 74 cut down[.] all his [ships] boats are now building on models of his own[,] taken from Spanish launches[.] They appear fine Boats[,] very roomy and it is said quite remarkably [?mill.][3] The most curious thing I have yet seen is the process of coppering by Galvasion [*sic*]. The Experiment [is] about to be tried on the *Warspites* Launch by a Chemist at Portsmouth[.] The boat is floated in a solution of Sulpte [sulphate] of Copper and [a wire from] the negative pole of a Galvain [*sic*] battery is put [i.e., wrapped] round the Boat and touches the solution in which she floats[.] The other wire is put direct into the solution, and the copper of the solution in which the boat floats goes to the negative wire on the vessel and

[1]George Henry Seymour (1818–69). Entered, 1831; Lt, 1838; Cmdr, 1842; Capt., 1844; Rear-Adm., 1863; Vice-Adm., 1869; M.P., 1865–69; Naval Lord of the Admiralty, 1866–68. Seymour was the son of then-Captain George Francis Seymour.

[2]Lord John Hay, C.B. (1793–1851). Entered, 1804; Lt, 1812; Cmdr, 1814; Capt., 1818; Rear-Adm., 1851; M.P., 1826–30, 1847–50; Naval Lord of the Admiralty, 1847–50.

[3]This passage is obscure. Perhaps Milne meant manoeuvrable, one meaning of 'mill' being quickness in turning.

coppers her; in 60 hours the copper is on as thick as is requisite. I saw several small models undergoing the process.

Sir W. Symonds[,][1] I understand[,] has made some changes in his vessels by given them <u>ten</u> feet greater length upon the same beam[.] This is what they require so to be a little fuller under the water line. I hear he is very crusty with anyone who gives an opinion about his ships. he [*sic*] may do himself harm by it[,] as his Squadron are not so popular as they were. I should not be surprised to see an inquiry about them by the appoint<u>t</u>. of a Committee.

Nov 16. Plymouth
I anchored this morning at 4 oclock and now[,] with this P.S.[, am] in [the] Admiral's Office. I am coming into Harbour this afternoon or as soon as a Steamer arrives to tow us[,] as it is calm. Sir G. Moore I have not yet seen, but [I] must conclude this to be in time for [the] Boat[.] With kind love to lady Milne . . .

[**107**] *Milne to Moore*

HMS *Crocodile*, Hamoaze
17 November 1841

Sir,

I beg to acquaint you that HM Ship under My Command will be ready for paying off on Thursday next the 25th Instant.

[**108**] *Milne to David Milne*

HMS *Crocodile*, Plymouth
17 November 1841

My dear David

The *Crocodile* will be paid off on the 25th[.] She looks sadly changed – her masts all down & guns dismantled. When my next appointment will take place I know not, but if any active service is going I wish to see the Pendant flying[.] It is however a very solitary & queer sort of life, full of anxiety & annoyance from beginning to end – and all the precautions in the world won't check the inclination Jack has for his Grog, & then follows all sorts of punishments – by no means a pleasant duty.

[1]Sir William Symonds, Kt., C.B. (1782–1856). Entered, 1794; Lt, 1801; Cmdr, 1825; Capt., 1827; Rear-Adm. (Ret.), 1854. As Surveyor of the Navy (1832–47), Symonds was responsible for several controversial innovations in warship design.

So many changes have taken place since I left England, I scarce know what to ask, or what to say. It appears to me like a dream! Even the penny postage appears so odd.[1]

I hope to be in London on the 28th: Please write me a few lines what is going on, & with kindest love &c . . .

[**109**] *Milne to David Milne*

United Service Club, London
1 December 1841

My dear David

I am in debt to you several letters[,] but I have been so busy, I have scarce time to write[.] I came to town on Friday last, having got clear of the *Crocodile* & I am now a gentleman at large. I have seen Sir George Cockburn, who has been very flattering in his reception[.] I have not yet seen Lord Haddington, but will do so[,] if possible[,] to morrow [*sic*], but I have little to say, only to make my bow and ask for employment, which I cannot expect at present[.] I have been writing to Sir David to apply for the Portsmouth or Plymouth Command[,] & to do so as soon as possible[.] But he does not appear inclined, which I regret exceedingly, as it would not only give him occupation, but likewise give me employment, so I have just written to ask him to come to London[,] which I hope he will do, and see Lord Haddington himself[.] There is nothing to be got without asking, & now is the time[.] I cannot expect anything by myself after having been so much employed . . .

[**110**] *Milne to David Milne*

United Service Club, London
6 December 1841

My dear David

. . . My movements are at present uncertain[.] I wish much Sir David would apply for employment, but he hesitates & wishes to have communication with the Cockburns before doing so. But all of this is to no purpose, so I have written to him to day to say 'Write direct to the first [*sic*] Lord at once'[.] My movements will consequently be guided by his, but I cannot leave this for a week[.] Give my kindest love to Jean & Maggie . . .

[1]Penny postage had been introduced in 1840.

PART III

FLAG CAPTAIN, 1841–47

Milne's entreaties to his father, as related in the previous section [**109**, **110**] bore fruit. With the Tories back in office, and Sir David Milne's friend Sir George Cockburn now First Naval Lord, the former's request for a Port Admiral's command received prompt and favourable attention. On 23 April 1842 Admiralty Secretary John Barrow informed Sir David Milne that 'Captain Alexander Milne has been appointed to H.M.S. *Caledonia* at Devonport, when recommissioned' [**113**]. Such behaviour would today be termed out-and-out nepotism, and so it was increasingly called (and denounced) by contemporary critics. One must not, however, lose sight of two circumstances connected with Milne's appointment. First, in the absence of a formal review process to ascertain officers' qualifications for active service, a patronage-based system of preferment was the obvious alternative. As an ancillary to this situation, it is further worth noting that at least part of both Sir David's and Alexander's standings with the Tory Board, in particular Cockburn, was owing to their professional attainments; it is indeed doubtful that Cockburn would have been as close to the elder Milne personally had the latter not distinguished himself in the French Wars. Moreover, it must be borne in mind that once at the Admiralty himself, Milne devoted much time and energy to reforming both the system of officer training and education, and the methods of testing junior officers' professional competence.[1] Although a beneficiary of the 'old' system, Milne was by no means eager to perpetuate it.

That said, his experience as Flag Captain for first his father (1842–45), then, in succession, Sir Charles Ogle (1846–47) and Sir Charles Napier (1847) was a notable departure from previous commissions. The last time Milne had served in a flagship was as a midshipman in HMS *Ganges*, 15 years prior to joining *Caledonia*. Since that date, the largest vessel in which he served was *Cleopatra*, a 26-gun frigate of less than 1,000 tons. *Caledonia* was a 120-gun three-decker of 2,616 tons. At the time he captained her she was, as he proudly wrote to his brother David, the second largest ship in the Royal Navy [**127**].

[1]See below, [**224–7**, **596**, **610**, **613**, **617**, **659–60**].

Of equal contrast, *Caledonia* was a Port Admiral's Flagship, rather than a private vessel in commission at sea. Aside from the lengthy interval *Snake* tarried at Sheerness while filling out her crew, she never spent more than three weeks at one place while under Milne's command. His experience in *Crocodile* was similar; the longest stretch she spent in port during Milne's tenure as Captain amounted to about four weeks. By way of comparison, from April 1842 until August 1843, when she was ordered to sea to cruise in an *ad hoc* Channel Squadron under the command of Admiral Sir Charles Rowley, Commander-in-Chief at Portsmouth, *Caledonia* never left Plymouth Sound.

The difference carried over to Milne's duties as well; *Caledonia*'s chief function was as a Receiving Ship. To be sure, the continuous service system that made such vessels essential as floating barracks for temporarily unassigned or newly-recruited enlisted personnel in all major naval ports was still years in the future.[1] Nevertheless, there was still a pressing need for a vessel to provide short-term accommodations for midshipmen, boys (apprentice seamen), and warrant officers whose vessels had been paid off. These men, unlike both ordinary and able seamen on the one hand, and commissioned officers on the other, served continuously, and thus had to be maintained in the interval between one ship's decommissioning and assignment to another in the process of commissioning.[2]

As a consequence, most of the material found in *Caledonia*'s private letter book is routine and fairly trivial. Unlike *Snake*'s and *Crocodile*'s corresponding volumes, it relates predominantly to personnel matters: 'the boy named in the margin is hereby discharged to HMS *Albion*', and the like. Milne himself wrote his brother David not long after hoisting his flag 'there is nothing going on save the routine of Harbour duty' [**116**]. The bulk of these letters have been omitted from this collection for the sake of readability (to say nothing of interest). One significant duty entrusted to Milne as Captain of a Port Admiral's Flagship was that of conducting experiments on items forwarded by the Admiralty for testing. In the course of his commission, therefore, Milne reported his findings on a variety of items ranging from a novel compass, to cocoa, to hammocks and washing powder [**129**, **140**, **141**, **144**, **145**, **147**].

The mundane routine of harbour service, however, was interrupted frequently from mid-1843 onward. On 17 August of that year *Caledo-*

[1]Continuous service was introduced generally in 1853, following the recommendations of a Committee on Manning. See R. Taylor, 'Manning the Royal Navy: The Reform of the Recruiting System, 1852–1862', *Mariner's Mirror*, 44 (1958), pp. 306–8. Milne was instrumental in having the Committee appointed (see below, [**238**, **240**]).

[2]Marines, who also served continuously, had barracks ashore.

nia was ordered from Hamoaze to the Sound to prepare to put to sea.[1] The reason for this late summer cruise was ceremonial rather than warlike. Secret instructions directed Milne to escort Queen Victoria from Plymouth to the French coast, and from thence to Brighton.[2] Following this service as royal escort, *Caledonia* was dispatched to the Irish coast, a voyage Milne described in a lengthy letter to his sister-in-law [**124**], but soon returned to Plymouth, only to be again ordered to Cork on 13 November.[3] Daniel O'Connell's campaign for repeal of the 1801 Act of Union was then at its height and, as Milne put it to his brother, the ship was present in the event that the situation in Ireland got out of hand [**127**, **128**]. Milne and his command were to remain at Cork until 29 January 1844.[4]

On 2 July 1844, the Admiralty ordered *Caledonia* to proceed 'with all convenient expedition' to Tangier in the Straits of Gibraltar. Milne expressed his own surprise at these orders in a letter to David [**130**], but France had sent a powerful squadron under the Prince de Joinville[5] to Morocco owing to a crisis in the relations of those two countries[,] and the Royal Navy's Mediterranean Squadron was being hurriedly strengthened to maintain its deterrence value and to uphold British commercial interests.[6]

Caledonia's sojourn in the Mediterranean was both brief and uneventful. Milne lamented to his brother on 27 July that he would not 'be there to see the fun' if the French bombarded Tangiers (which they did), having been detailed to remain at Gibraltar [**132**]. Worse still, if that were possible, the same day that the assault took place Sir Edward Owen ordered *Caledonia* to proceed to Lisbon to carry dispatches to the British Ambassador to Portugal, and to remain there pending further instructions from the Admiralty.[7] Milne and his crew remained idle at Lisbon until 2 October.

[1]MLN/102/8: Sir David Milne to Milne, 17 August 1843.

[2]MLN/102/8: Rowley to Milne (Secret), 1 September 1843. The Queen and Prince Albert departed from Southampton aboard the Royal Yacht on 29 August 1843, cruised down the Channel to Devonport on 31 August, where they were saluted by the ships in Plymouth Sound, *Caledonia* among them, and toured the dockyard in the company of Lord Haddington, Sir George Francis Seymour, Lord Aberdeen, and Sir David Milne, among others. The royal couple then cruised back up the Channel before departing for France on 4 September, from whence they returned on the 7th.

[3]MLN/102/8: Admiralty to Milne, 13 November 1843.

[4]MLN/102/8: Admiralty to Milne, 29 January 1844.

[5]François-Ferdinand-Philippe D'Orleans, Prince de Joinville (1818–1900). Entered, 1833; Lieutenant de Frègate, 1835; Lieutenant de Vaisseau, 1836; Captain de Corvette, 1838; Captain de Vaisseau, 1839; Contre-Amiral, 1843; Vice-Amiral, 1844.

[6]MLN/102/8: Admiralty to Milne, 16, 22 July 1844.

[7]MLN/102/8: Owen to Milne, 6 August 1844.

On 13 October 1844, following *Caledonia*'s return to Plymouth, Rear-Admiral William Bowles wrote to Milne to acquaint him with plans for Bowles to hoist his flag in the ship and proceed to sea for a short trial cruise to test the sailing qualities of HMS *Albion* and *Queen*, two of Surveyor of the Navy Sir William Symonds' controversial designs [**137**].[1] Milne himself was not enthusiastic about this task, but vented his displeasure only to his brother [**138**].

The following January Milne requested and was granted leave for a visit to Scotland, the purpose of which is unknown. By the time he returned to Plymouth, *Caledonia* was nearing the end of her three-year commission, and most of his correspondence during March and April 1845 related to her decommissioning. *Caledonia* was duly paid off on 28 April 1845 and the Milnes set out first for London and ultimately Milne Graden. Sir David, however, never reached his home. The old sailor was ill, and Alexander's alarm at his state surfaced in a letter to his brother written from London on 2 May [**151**]. The family had booked passage to Granton, on Edinburgh's waterfront, but Sir David died on board the steamer *Clarence* on 5 May, before reaching Scotland. He was buried in the Inveresk Kirkyard, where his memorial reads:

> In memory of Admiral Sir David Milne, GCB &c. For 60 years he served his country in the Royal Navy; his gallant deeds are recorded in her annals. In all the relations of private life he was upright, exemplary, and esteemed . . . [2]

Milne inherited his father's estate at Inveresk, which remained his seat for the rest of his life (he shared it with his stepmother until her death). It was while he was there, in early September 1846, that Admiral Sir Charles Ogle, Commander-in-Chief at Portsmouth wrote, inviting Milne to be his Flag Captain, owing partly to his high service reputation and partly to Ogle's esteem for Sir David [**152**]. Milne was in Portsmouth by 17 September, but some delay ensued before he could actually take up his new duties [**156**]. No sooner had he done so, than orders arrived from the Admiralty to prepare immediately for sea. Milne accordingly reported his command ready the following day. In a mis-

[1]On the Experimental Squadron's cruise, see *The Times* (London), 4 December 1844, p. 5, and 'Copies of the Several Reports from Rear-Admiral Bowles, C.B., Commander Corry, and Captain Thompson, R.N., of the Sailing and other Qualities, as exhibited during the late Trial Cruises of Her Majesty's Ships "*Queen*," "*Caledonia*," "*St. Vincent*," "*Camperdown*," "*Albion*," "*Espiègle*," "*Daring*," "*Flying Fish*," "*Mutine*," "*Waterwitch*," "*Pantaloon*," "*Osprey*," and "*Cruizer*;" with the Names of the several Constructors of the same', *Parliamentary Papers*, 1845, vol. XXX, pp. 133–87.

[2]'Royal Navy Veterans Memorials', http://redcoat.future.easyspace.com/navyz1.htm

sive to his brother he guessed that Lisbon was *St Vincent*'s intended destination, but added that he doubted orders to proceed to sea would be immediately forthcoming [**157**]. He was right on both counts.

St Vincent remained at Portsmouth through the rest of 1846, Milne staying with his ship through the Christmas holidays, carrying out the same sorts of routine tasks that he had while at Devonport. As he complained to David in late January, 'it is hard work all day, & I may say every day in prospect . . . ' [**161**]. Two months later he speculated that *St Vincent* might be sent to Lisbon during the summer on account of chronic political instability in Portugal, but his principal concern was the distress in Ireland [**165**].

Only in mid-May did he learn that his suppositions were right; *St Vincent* was to be sent to the Tagus [**166**]. This confirmation, however, was accompanied by the unexpected news that Ogle was to be superseded by Rear-Admiral Sir Charles Napier. Napier had a reputation both as a bold and enterprising officer ashore and afloat – he had achieved great renown in the 1840 campaign against Mehemet Ali's forces on the Syrian coast[1] – and as a contentious, not to say quarrelsome, individual. As M.P. for Marylebone during the early 1840s he had been a tireless and often extravagant critic of virtually all aspects of British naval administration, and Milne flatly informed his brother on learning of Napier's appointment, 'I am horrified at the <u>man</u>', although he characteristically added that he had to 'make the best of it'.

Napier hoisted his flag in *St Vincent* on 17 May [**168**], but she did not sail for Portugal until August. In the interval, Milne carried on with the familiar duties as Captain of a Harbour Service ship. Even after arriving at Lisbon, *St Vincent* seems to have maintained the ordinary routine as if she had still been at Portsmouth; almost all of Milne's correspondence relates to personnel matters of the sort which consumed much of his time while in *Caledonia*.[2]

It is plain, however, that he also gave much attention to the more warlike aspects of command – gun drill and sailing exercises. Moreover, it is equally clear that, regardless of his trepidation, Milne and Napier got along very well, and that the latter was much impressed with the smartness of *St Vincent*'s crew. Indeed, when Milne was super-

[1]See *DNB*, vol. 14, pp. 41–3; Clowes, *The Royal Navy*, vol. 6, pp. 308–23; Priscilla Napier, *Black Charlie: A Life of Admiral Sir Charles Napier, 1787–1860* (Wilby, Norwich, 1995), pp. 85–107.

[2]Most of the routine correspondence relative to Milne's command of *St Vincent* has not been included in this volume. That relating to his service under Napier is contained in the Napier Papers, BL Add Mss 40042, fols. 139, 150, 278, 302, 307, 313, 323, 381, 404, 440, 447.

seded in command and reassigned to HMS *Victory* in December 1847 (Ogle's flag as Commander-in-Chief at Portsmouth having been lowered in September), Napier penned an exceptionally complimentary letter [**172**], and simultaneously wrote to Lord Auckland, urging him to bestow a knighthood on Milne, adding 'it would gratify him'.[1]

Milne had noted to his brother, when offered command of *St Vincent*, that it was unusual for an officer to serve as Flag Captain at both Plymouth and Portsmouth [**154**]. The tasks associated with those important commands gave Milne an unusual amount of administrative experience for a relatively junior Captain. This experience, coupled with Napier's praise, ensured that Milne was immediately employed upon his return to England, rather than enduring another stretch on half-pay. His new employment, however, would be in marked contrast to seagoing or even harbour service, for on 14 December he reached Portsmouth to be greeted with Lord Auckland's[2] invitation to join the Board of Admiralty as Junior Naval Lord. He would remain at Whitehall for the next eleven and a half years.

[1]Add Mss 40040, fol. 40, Napier to Auckland, 9 December 1847.

[2]George Eden, Earl of Aukland, G.C.B. (1784–1849). Pres. of Board of Trade, 1830–34, 1835; First Lord of the Admiralty, 1834, 1835, 1846–49; Gov-General of India, 1835–41.

[**111**] *Gage*[1] *to Milne*

Admiralty
20 March [1842]

My dear Captain Milne

On Saturday evening Sir George Cockburn told me, that by his recommendation, Sir David had been kind enough to accept the services of my Cousin Mr Kemble[2] [*sic*] as his flag Lieut. Having no claim to such a mark of his regard, I cannot receive it without offering him my very grateful thanks, which I beg you will have the goodness to convey, as I think he will be best pleased not to receive a letter from me on this occasion. I trust he is gaining strength & that this fine weather will set him up.

Mr. Kemble will leave Portsmouth immediately & his commission goes to Devonport this evening. Any little kindness you may have it in your power to show Lieut Kemble I shall feel much obliged to you for[.]

[**112**] *Barrow*[3] *to Sir David Milne*

Admiralty
21 April 1842

Sir

I am commanded by my Lords Commissioners of the Admiralty to acquaint you that they have been pleased to sign a Commission appointing you Commander in Chief of the Plymouth Station, and that your Commission is with the Chief Clerk of this office.

[1]Sir William Hall Gage, Kt., K.C.B., G.C.H., G.C.B. (1777–1864). Entered, 1789, Lt, 1796; Cmdr, 1797; Capt., 1797; Rear-Adm., 1821; Vice-Adm., 1837; Adm., 1846; Adm. of the Fleet, 1862; Naval Lord of the Admiralty, 1841–46.

[2]Frederick Kemble (1815–88). Entered, 1829; Lt, 1841; Cmdr, 1845; Capt. (Ret.), 1864. Kemble was appointed Flag-Lt to Sir David Milne in HMS *Caledonia* on 20 March 1843. He received his promotion to Commander on 29 April 1845 as a consequence of Sir David's hauling down his flag.

[3]Sir John Barrow (1764–1848); Admiralty Permanent Secretary 1804–06, 1807–45.

[**113**] *Barrow to Sir David Milne*

Admiralty
23 April 1842

Sir

In reply to your Letter of the 22nd Instant, I am commanded by my Lords Commissioners of the Admiralty to acquaint you that Captain Alexander Milne has been appointed to H.M.S. *Caledonia* at Devonport, when recommissioned.

[**114**] *Milne to Barrow*

HMS *Caledonia*, Hamoaze
27 April 1842

Sir

I have the honour to acquaint for the information of the Lords Commissioners of the Admiralty that I have this day assumed the command of Her Majestys Ship *Caledonia* at Devonport[.]

[**115**] *Milne to David Milne*

HMS *Caledonia*, Devonport
7 May 1842

My dear David

Many thanks for your letter, which to my surprise I received yesterday. I had no idea you were coming up, but most delighted we shall see you here next week[.] Sir David is remarkably well, & gets on famously with the duties, although still a stranger to the many changes which have taken place in the navy. Lady Milne & the party arrived here last night, tired with their journey, but all quite well.

[**116**] *Milne to David Milne*

[HMS *Caledonia*, Devonport]
10 June 1842

There is nothing going on save the routine of Harbour duty – all matters on board *Caledonia* going on fair & square & I hope they will continue so[.] Sir David is very well, but complains of the Office hours confining him to the house during the greater part of the day[.] He goes out in the Tender about 2 o'clock & returns about 5.

I find plenty to do in many ways, in fact can scarcely get time to look round me, from various small matters in the Ship[,] Office & house, but must plod on the best way I can[.] I must own I find it different from my last seagoing ship & wish much I was again on the Coast of Newfoundland[.]

[**117**] *Milne to Sir David Milne*

HMS *Caledonia*, Hamoaze, Plymouth
21 June 1842

Sir

Having found that no Sick Bay Mess has ever been established on board this ship for the benefit of the Men on the Sick List, who are not considered Hospital Cases[,] and especially for the comfort and use of the many supernumeraries who are sent to this ship from the various outports on the coast[,] whose destitute condition & poverty prevent them from obtaining those comforts whilst on the Sick List, which would conduce to their more speedy and certain recovery, and which a Sick Bay Mess should supply, I have to request you will be pleased to move my L[ords] C[ommissioners of the] A[dmiralty] to grant such a sum of money as they may see proper to enable a Sick Mess to be established on board, which I feel confident will prove of much benefit to the Service . . . I beg to acquaint you almost 3600 persons have been Victualled during the last year.

[**118**] *Milne to David Milne*

HMS *Caledonia*, Plymouth
1–9 July 1842

When do you again pay a visit here[?] We want some Scotch friends to change the tune[.] Sir David has been very low of late, & complaining most terribly about his eyes, but under the Doctor's prescriptions they have decidedly improved[.] He feared he was losing the sight of the right one[.] Lady Milne has been seriously ill – but is some what better[.]

July 9th:
We have beastly rainy weather & luckily the *Sylph*[1] is in the hands of the Dockyard, having a requisite change made in the cabins & a Ladies cabin in addition [*sic*] . . .

[119] *Milne to Sir David Milne*

HMS *Caledonia*, Devonport
27 July 1842

Sir,

I beg herewith to enclose a letter I have this day received from Mr Raimbach[2] Naval Instructor of HMS *Wellesley*[,] requesting to be appointed to HMS *Caledonia*.

I have to request you will be pleased to move my Lords Commissioners of the Admiralty to grant his request[,] as the services of a Naval Instructor are much wanted on board for the Instruction of the Youngsters.

[120] *Milne to David Milne*

HMS *Caledonia*, Devonport
14 November 1842

My dear David

Many thanks for your kind letter & remembrance of Nov: 10th[.] It is the first birthday which I have passed in the family for six years[,] & I would have been sincerely glad if you, Jean & your little ones had been here or if we had all been in the North[.] I have not written to you for a long time, perhaps scarcely to be avoided[,] & yet a most un-natural proceeding my doing so[.] We are all well here just now & Sir David better & calmer than I have seen him since our arrival here. He has had a very severe illness & looked dreadfully ill & much reduced, but he has become much better during the last fortnight.

There is nothing going on in the Navy way[.] *Caledonia* is now to have 620 men but we are 160 short of complement[,] but we pick up men easily[,] & as far as the ship goes, we go on smoothly enough. I am organizing a band for the amusement of all, but I have only got six at present[.]

[1]Tender to the Devonport flagship.
[2]Michael T.S. Raimbach, M.A. (d. 1887); Naval Instructor, 1837.

I have been writing for the last 5 hours & I am quite tired out[.]

Please thank Jean for the beautiful slippers[.] They are much too handsome to wear but I will keep them in recollection of her remembrance of the 10th[.] Give my kind love &c. . . .

[**121**] *Hamilton*[1] *to Milne*

Admiralty
12 January 1843

Dear Milne,

Lord Haddington has promoted Lieut. Thurtell[2] to the rank of Commander.

Let me have a line from you to say if you still want Lt. Jauncey[3] to be appointed to the *Caledonia*.

[**122**] *Gage to Milne*

Admiralty
16 January 1843

My dear Sir

Lieut Jauncey shall be appointed as you wish[,] altho' it does interfere with my arrangements; the Gunnery Officer I had destined for the first vacancy in *Caledonia* was a Lieut. perfectly unknown to me[,] excepting by high testimonials and the misfortune of having lost a leg in China[.] however[,] he shall have the next vacancy[,] and I bespeak your kind disposition towards him provided he proves deserving. . . .

[1]William Alexander Baillie Hamilton, (1803–81). Entered, 1816; Lt, 1823; Cmdr, 1826; Capt., 1828; Rear-Adm., 1855; Vice-Adm. (Res.), 1862; Adm. (Res.), 1865. Hamilton was Private Secretary to Lord Haddington, First Lord of the Admiralty, 1841–45 (the two were second cousins), and subsequently served as Admiralty Permanent Secretary, 1845–55.

[2]Charles Thurtell (1796–1856). Entered, 1807; Lt, 1821; Cmdr, 1843. Thurtell was appointed *Caledonia*'s First Lieutenant on 26 September 1842, and promoted to Commander the following 12 January.

[3]Horatio Jauncey, who had been Milne's First Lieutenant in HMS *Snake*, 1836–39. Milne did request Jauncey's appointment to *Caledonia*, as the following letter [**122**] suggests. He was appointed Senior Lieutenant on 17 January 1843, and promoted to Commander on 25 September in honour of the Queen's visit to *Caledonia*. Cmdr William Hood was promoted to Captain the same day. For Milne's impression of the Queen, see below [**124**].

[**123**] *Milne to David Milne*

Admiralty House, Devonport
22 January 1843

My dear David

I cannot allow this day to pass over without writing you a few lines of congratulation on the return of the 22nd Jan[,] & to wish you[,] with every affecte & brotherly regard[,] many happy returns of the day[,] & that you & yours may long prosper in the land & have every blessing & happiness in your family circle[.] I should have written some days ago, but from constant occupation I missed the post[.] Most gladly would I go down for a short leave, but there is no one to undertake the duties in this house[.] I am now doing [the] Flag Lieut's duty as well as my own & have plenty of occupation[.] There are now 714 living souls on the Ship's Books & 60 more are coming to morrow from the *Cambridge*[.]

Sir David has been very well of late, better than I have seen him for the last twelvemonth & much more mild . . .

I look forward to our having a cruize in summer[.] Perhaps we may attend the Queen if she goes to Ireland[.]

We have been a good deal out of late – Dinners[,] Balls &c[,] & once a week always a dinner here of 18 to 20 people, besides now & then a smaller party by chance when any one arrives as a stranger in the place[.]

Never were matters so dull in the Navy way, nothing going on except the daily routine of post duties – not very interesting or entertaining – yet enough to give employment[,] and I do not complain at the quarterly bill coming in regularly, even minus the Income Tax[.]

I will now conclude with kind love &c. . . .

[**124**] *Milne to Jean Milne*

HMS *Caledonia*, Cove of Cork
23 September 1843

My dear Jean

Many thanks for all your congratulations on my being in command of so splendid a ship. I can scarcely credit it myself[,]f & sometime look upon it as a dream, but it is reality & now I am quite at home, although the first night we were on the wide ocean, I must acknowledge I was somewhat anxious[, it] being the first time I ever was at sea in so large a ship. What a responsible command, upwards of 800 men on the

Books, but only 777 on board[,] and what professional knowledge & attention it requires, and I have no assistance, the Commander not having been at sea since 1819 or 20[1] – but I feel great confidence in myself &[,] as yet[,] all has gone on well, our evolutions in line of Battle & our exercising at sails & guns everything that could be desired, but with all this there are drawbacks which are sources of annoyance[.] We have lost a boy having fallen overboard, he was drowned[,] and a man fell from aloft & was so much injured, that there was no hope of him[.] He died 12 hours afterward & was buried this morning[.] Poor fellow, it was a sad thing to see. He fell close to me and never spoke afterwards[.]

We remain here till Wednesday next when we proceed to sea – our destination unknown, but most probably to cruize for 2 or 3 weeks before returning to Plymouth[.] I like the fun very much & so says Sir Charles Rowley, but all the married men & others are anxious to get back. Sir Charles is an exceedingly pleasant man & a good officer & keeps moving[.] He commences making signals at 5 A.M. & goes on until dark[.] His last telegraph yesterday morning is rather amusing & gives us some occupation. 'Make a return of the age, weight, & height of your respective ships companies, particularizing seamen, marines & boys[,] & stating the average of each class'. So that we have every man to weigh & measure [*sic*]. This will probably take us 2 days at least[.] He of course has his object, but I think there is not a little humbug in it.

I have just returned from the shore having been walking about with Sir William Dickson[2] & Capt Brace[.][3] This is a beautiful place, but a dirty one in the town & swarming with beggars, but the Government Establishments are on a grand scale[.]

You asked about the Queen and Sir David[.] Her manner to him was quite beautiful[.] She went up to him on the Quarter Deck & with a loud voice said 'You have a fine ship here Sir David'. Her reception on the Quarter Deck of the *Caledonia* was most imposing. It was really what I could not have supposed[,] & she appeared to enjoy it. She came round to me twice & spoke about different things saying 'I understand Lady Milne and some ladies from the Admiralty House are here, go & tell Sir David he must present them'. I was quite charmed with her &

[1]William John Thompson Hood (1794–1857). Entered, 1805; Lt, 1815; Cmdr, 1828; Capt., 1843. Hood had actually served at sea most recently in 1829, although in a coast blockade ship.

[2]Sir William Dickson, Bt. (1798–1868). Entered, 1814; Lt, 1822; Cmdr, 1829; Capt., 1837; Rear-Adm. (Ret.), 1857; Vice-Adm. (Ret.), 1864.

[3]Francis Brace (*c*.1793–1850). Entered, 1805; Lt, 1813; Cmdr, 1818; Capt., 1827. Brace was Sir Edward Brace's nephew, and thus probably known to Milne.

also [by her behaviour] at the Downs,[1] Her [*sic*] passing all the ships there & our cheering her as she passed, with the guard officers on deck, yards manned, & the Band playing 'God Save the Queen'. She passed almost touching the old *Caledonia*, & bowed most condescendingly several times to your humble servant. She was leaning on Prince Albert's arm, & altogether it was a most delightful sight.

I will now say Good night – I am going to dine with Admiral Bowles – With kind love &c. . . .

[125] *Sir David Milne to Milne*

HMS *Albion*, Hamoaze
16 November 1843

The Lords Commissioners of the Admiralty have signified to me their approval of the alacrity with which the *Caledonia* was got ready for sea.

[126] *Milne to Bowles*

HMS *Caledonia*, Cove of Cork
17 November 1843

Sir,

In pursuance of orders from Adml Sir Dd Milne G.C.B.[,] Comr in Chief at Devonport[,] I put to sea in HMS *Caledonia* on the 13th Nov at 1:30 P.M. & made the best of my passage to this anchorage[,] where I have the Honour [*sic*] of reporting my arrival to you this day.

[127] *Milne to David Milne*

HMS *Caledonia*, Cove of Cork
18 November 1843

My dear David

Here we are back again in Paddy's land & for what purpose I really have not found out, but I suppose to overcome the Repeal[er]s here[,][2]

[1]When *Caledonia* had been part of the Squadron escorting the Queen across the Channel.

[2]Irish politician Daniel O'Connell was in the midst of a massive public campaign to repeal the 1801 Act of Union between Ireland and Great Britain which had eliminated the Irish Parliament.

& I presume we shall be here several weeks[,] & if Dan [O'Connell] is not obedient & quiet it may be for months[.] We shall lie within 300 yards from [*sic*] the shore, between the Dockyard & Main Island. We have not yet reached our final anchorage & are anxiously looking for a steamer to take us in tow – the channel is so narrow & curved, we cannot get through without a fair wind – or a steamer. We shall land one ship's company for daily exercise & get them well drilled for Dan's repealers[.] We have 950 men on board including Marines[.]

This is a large and responsible command[,] & I suppose I am the youngest Captain that ever had so fine a command – *Caledonia* being the 2nd largest ship in the British Navy[.] I wish you could take a run over here for a few days, it would do you a great deal of good[.]

The country in this neighbourhood appears quiet, but fires were burning on most of the hills two days ago[,] & from what Admiral Bowles said to me yesterday, I suspect there is a good deal of alarm among the heads of departments[.] I trust matters may remain quiet, if not what a sad loss of life must take place[,] & what an awful duty we shall have to perform, but it must be done, & the sooner the better if it is to be[.]

Sir David was very well when I left last week, but he is very deaf & worries himself about trifles.

[**128**] *Milne to David Milne*

HMS *Caledonia*, Cove of Cork
17 December 1843

I am here as I am named Flag Captain to Rear Admiral Bowles, a worthy[,] good man as ever lived [*sic*] & we get along famously together[.] Indeed I never quarreled with a Senior or Junior officer in my life & I don't see any reason to do so now[.] The ship is as she ought to be & everything goes well[,] considering the medley we have on board[.] How long we shall remain here I do not know, but I don't think the Admiralty will let this ship leave Ireland until after the trial of Dan 'the first'.[1] We keep a good look out in case of any outbreak, but all is perfectly quiet, & the Cove people are reaping a harvest from this ship alone. Admiral Bowles brought a party on board the ship on Tuesday[:]

[1]O'Connell was arrested 14 October 1843 and charged with sedition and with trying to subvert the loyalty of British Army units in Ireland. He was convicted in February 1844, fined, and sentenced to a year in prison. The verdict was overturned by the Law Lords on September 1844.

Lady Shannon,[1] Lord & Lady Ormond[2] [*sic*] & several others. They went all round, even into the holds, &[,] when at lunch[,] some expressed a wish to see the guns exercised, so we beat to quarters & in 5 minutes the ship was reported cleared for action, so down we all went to the Lower deck, & much to the amazement of the party, the exercise of the guns, cutlasses [&] Firemen was gone through, & they went away highly delighted after having been on board 2½ hours[.]

The ship is a great sight among the Paddys & on one day we had upwards of 1000 people on board[.] But this cold weather[,] I am glad to say[,] keeps them away & I have found out another mode of keeping them out, which is, sending the Band on shore twice a week to play for two hours in the afternoon, & this brings all the families for miles round[.] I believe it is more for the pleasure of hearing the band, than seeing the ship, that they come . . .

What with Ship's duty – official correspondence &c[–] I have not a spare moment to myself[,] & have never been away 30 hours since the flag was hoisted in April 1842, but I am determined to take a few weeks leave when I get back to Devonport.

Give my kind love to Jean & all the family circle[.] I wish I was one of the party . . .

[**129**] *Milne to Sir David Milne*

HMS *Caledonia*, Plymouth Sound, Plymouth
29 May 1844

Sir,

In pursuance of your order of the 13th April[,] directing me to report on a Steering Compass Card ordered to be fitted to this ship by the Lords Commissioners of the Admiralty on a plan proposed by Mr Walker[,] the Harbour Master at this Port[,] for trial against the ordinary Compass[,] I have to acquaint you that I have put the same to repeated trial in a Boat against one of the ordinary Compasses supplied by the Dock Yard and I have found it[,] when used as directed by Mr Walker[,] viz. by Clamping or fixing the Brass Cone which works on the needle in the Compass Bowl[,] and by Clamping the gimble which prevents its pitching motion[,] that it is much more steady & more serviceable than the ordinary Card now in use[,] which

[1]Emily Henrietta, wife of Richard Boyle, fourth Earl of Shannon (1809–68).

[2]John Butler, second Marquis of Ormonde, K.P. (1808–54) and his wife, Frances Jane.

are [*sic*] in constant motion from the jerk which is given the Boat by the sea.

I have not observed any Superiority in its action over the Compasses now being furnished by the Dock Yard when the Boat has been under sail[,] except what may be attributed to a better description of workmanship & superiority in the strength of the Magnetic Power given the Needle[.] But before giving any decided opinion on its merits[,] I consider it ought to have further trials of its action watched in every variety, and at sea[,] which I have had no opportunity of doing.

[**130**] *Milne to David Milne*

HMS *Caledonia*, Plymouth Sound
4 July 1844

My dear David

You will be surprised to hear that I sail to morrow morning for Tangiers & will be attached for the present to Sir Ed: Owen in the Mediterranean[.] This is something novel & most unsuspected. The orders came yesterday[.] The cause of this movement is the French Squadron under the command of the Prince de Joinville having been sent to the above part of the coast,[1] but what will be my future movements will depend on the Senior Officer I may meet there, & if there should be no ships there, I have sealed orders to open for my guidance[.]

I am surprised at the Admiralty having allowed me to retain command of this ship, & it is something very much out of the common – so young an officer as myself being in command of so large a ship on a Foreign Station[,] & in contact with the French Fleet. However[,] I must do my best[.] We have a complement made up of 915 men by drafts from the Guard Ships & Marine Barracks[.] This cruize will be a delightful one[.]

I should have written to you long ago in answer to your last letter, but I have been very far from well & unable to write with spirit of inclination[,] & have been a complete fixture[,] without any satisfaction to myself [*sic*].

Sir David has been very well of late, better than I have seen him for a long time & has been much engaged in entertaining Royalty[.] The King of Saxony was here on Tuesday[.] He went with Sir David to the Dock-

[1]Joinville's Squadron was sent to the Moroccan coast in support of French land operations in retaliation for Moroccan raids along the Algerian frontier.

yard – came to the Admiralty House for lunch – thence went to the Breakwater[,] & all over the *Caledonia*[.] He is a very pleasant agreeable man. He was not received as Royalty but as Count Hockenstein[.] I was too busy preparing for sea to have much to say to him[.]

July 5th 5 A.M.

I am up early to prepare for our departure[.] The wind is North & the day is fine[,] so we shall get away with favourable weather[.] I am going ashore to breakfast & shall sail before noon[.] Write to me to Gibraltar[,] care of Sir John Sinclair[.][1] I lament much I have been unable to get north to see you all, but ever since April 11th the orders have been, to keep the *Caledonia* in readiness for sea[.]

I must now conclude with kind love to yourself[,] Jean & your children & with every good wish for prosperity & happiness . . .

[**131**] *Sir David Milne to Milne*

HMS *Sylph*, Hamoaze
6 July 1844

Sir,

The Lords Commissioners of the Admiralty have expressed to me their approbation at the expedition with which their Lordships orders with respect to the *Caledonia* were carried into execution.[2]

[**132**] *Milne to David Milne*

HMS *Caledonia*, Gibraltar
27 July–10 August 1844

My dear David

Here we are fixed for the present[.] The Admiral[,] Sir E. Owen[,] is here – the *Albion* & *Warspite* have gone to Tangier[,] where the Prince de Joinville smuggled off the French Consul General, but the Moors wont [*sic*] give up the Vice Consul. The Prince has threatened to bombard the town – gave 3 days respite[,] which is now extended to 8, & then he says he will burn & destroy. The Ships of our Flag have gone to protect British property, & our Consul has embarked[.] He will take

[1]Sir John Gordon Sinclair, Bt. (1790–1863). Entered, 1799; Lt, 1809; Cmdr, 1812; Capt., 1814; Rear-Adm., 1849; Vice-Adm., 1856; Adm., 1861.

[2]*Caledonia* reported ready for sea within 24 hours of receiving the Admiralty's orders.

nothing but a decided neutral part & therefore the Moors will get a jolly good threshing [*sic*]. I am only sorry I won't be there to see the fun[.]

Our destination is not known[,] but we are under immediate orders for a start at a moments notice – our guns all loaded, but not shotted, so we are prepared if His Royal Highness Prince de Joinville should mistake us for the Hill of Tangier, for as Capt Lockyer[1] says[,] to see the *Caledonia* under weigh it might be supposed to be the Rock of Gibraltar!

August 10th 1844

As to matters here, we might have been as well in England, & the Governor here has been most completely humbugged[.]

Your would [*sic*] see in Parliament,[2] he had gone over to the Morocco Coast of his own accord, for which he got a severe rap from Lord Stanley,[3] but he is a queer chap – interfering with everything and everybody. On Tuesday last he received his dispatches[,] which induced him to despatch a Courier to Madrid, that all the affairs between France and Morocco were settled & peace was certain – and at that very moment the Prince de Joinville was battering down Tangier[.]

It is only 33 miles from this and we heard the guns[,] and the Bombardment was seen from the top of the Rock, so the next morning the Governor had to despatch a Courier again to Madrid with the accounts of War, War, War!

The state of affairs now is worse than ever. The Emperor of Morocco wont [*sic*] have anything to do with the French, he won't treat[,] & accordingly Mareschal Bugeaud[4] sent instructions for the Prince to act. He lost no time about it, & next morning [6 August] at daylight he was towed in by his steamers there[:] 3 ships of the line, 1 Frigate 2 Brigs & several [smaller vessels.]

They commenced firing at 8:30 A.M. & left off at 2 P.M. The Moorish Forts are a good deal hurt, but not so much as they ought to have been. The Moors only acknowledge to [*sic*] 4 killed & 30 wounded & the French 12 killed & 20 wounded[.]

The French Squadron have sailed from Tangier & have gone[,] it is reported[,] to Cadiz, but I suspect they are going to attack Mogador &

[1]Nicholas Lockyer (1782–1847). Entered, 1790; Lt, 1803; Cmdr, 1806; Capt., 1815. *Albion*'s Captain.

[2]Milne was mistaken; no mention of the incident was made in Parliament.

[3]Colonial Secretary Edward Stanley, styled Lord Stanley, later the fourteenth Earl of Derby.

[4]Thomas-Robert Bugeaud, Marquis de la Piconnerie, Duc d'Isly (1784–1849); Commander of French military forces which had defeated the Moroccans at Isly on 14 July.

every town on the Coast, but they will not land, only destroy the Fortifications[.]

We remain perfectly neutral. I have been under orders for several days to proceed to Lisbon & there wait for instructions from the Admiralty, but a strong West wind has prevented us moving. I hope to get away to morrow evening[.] I am pretty well tired of Sir E. Owen[,] although he is a most excellent officer[.] He is famed for his correspondence & his orders would fill a good sized volume! All officers have to leave the shore by 8 P.M. during West winds & 9 during East, which bars all dining on shore[.] I have been obliged to decline all invitations – even the Governor's.

You ask me about Capt Warner's [*sic*] invention.[1] I can only judge from what I see in the papers[,] & there is certainly a most formidable power at his command, but by what means it is applied none can tell. I don't think it is a Torpedo. It may be something fired from a Musket which[,] on reaching the water [is] exploded by chemical agency. No doubt [the] Government will now take the subject up. I am sorry to see so dreadful a power coming into use[.] Our shells are bad enough[,] which we fire from our long 68 pounders [*sic*][.]

We are all well on board & the ship in capital working order for anything, but we have no chance of a brush at present, but no saying what a few months may bring forth for as Prince de Joinville said to Capt Wallis[2] [']If we go to war with Morocco there is no saying where it may end![']

Since writing this the Gibraltar Mail Steamer has arrived, by which I have a letter from Lady Milne, in which she mentions Sir David had been complaining – but I don't think it is anything material[.]

With kind love &c &c. . . .

[1]Samuel Alfred Warner (d. 1853). Warner claimed to have invented two secret weapons, one called an 'invisible shell' and the other the 'six mile range' or, more simply, the 'long range'. John Knox Laughton states in his *DNB* entry on Warner, that both, according to the inventor, were 'capable of producing the immediate and utter destruction of any enemy's ships or forts' (*DNB*, vol. XX, p. 859). Warner never revealed the secret of either device but spent years arguing for their adoption. A sample of his correspondence can be found in *The Times* around the period that Milne mentioned his name; see 10 August 1844, p. 6 and 29 August 1844, p. 6. *The Times* also reprinted an article from the *Polytechnic Magazine* (17 October 1844), which speculated that the 'invisible shell' might contain fulminate of mercury. Warner's claims and ceaseless publicity generated a number of Parliamentary enquiries. See *Parliamentary Papers*, 1844, vol. XXXIII, p. 419; 1846, vol. XXVI, p. 499; and 1847, vol. XXXVI, p. 473.

[2]Provo William Parry Wallis, K.C.B., G.C.B. (1791–1892). Entered, 1795, Lt, 1808; Cmdr, 1813; Capt., 1819; Rear-Adm., 1851; Vice-Adm., 1857; Adm., 1863; Adm. of the Fleet, 1875.

[**133**] *Milne to Lord Howard de Walden*[1]

HMS *Caledonia*, Lisbon
21 August 1844

My Lord

I have the honour to inform you that[,] in pursuance of Instructions from Vice Adml Sir Ed. Owen[,] G.C.H. G.C.B.[,] Commr in Chief in the Mediterranean[,] I have proceeded with HMS *Caledonia* under my command to this port from Gibraltar[,] from which place I sailed on the 12th inst[,] and am directed by my Instructions to acquaint your Lordship with my arrival[,] and to fulfill your wishes for the Service of Her Majesty as I can do so.

[**134**] *Milne to David Milne*

HMS *Caledonia*, Lisbon
3 September 1844

My dear David

Here we are uncertain of our movements & future proceedings, but the Packet from England is now entering the river & I expect a letter of instructions from the Admiralty. My own impression is that we shall remain here to watch passing events. The French Squadron has been reinforced with another 74 & a Frigate, but what they are going to do I do not know. The Prince was going to Cadiz yesterday with his Flag on a Steamer[,] but I believe he sails to day for Mogador, though report says the French Squadron are all expected at Cadiz[.] They lost one of their newest and finest Steamers on the Coast of Morocco – she went on shore in a fog & the Moors came down with Musketry – fired upon them & killed several men[.] The Prince came to the spot afterwards & burnt the vessel[.]

The Mail from England has just arrived & I am to remain here for the present. I have some official letters to write & not much time, as a party are coming to see the ship, consisting of The [*sic*] Duke Villa Real, Duchess of Forrea [*sic*] and Puhnella [*sic*] &c – so I must conclude with kind love to Jean &c. . . .

[1]Charles Augustus Ellis, sixth Baron Howard de Walden and second Baron Seaford, G.C.B., K.T.S. (1799–1868). British representative at Lisbon 1833–46.

[**135**] *Milne to Herbert*

HMS *Caledonia*, Lisbon
1 October 1844

Sir,

I have the honour to acknowledge the receipt of Sir John Barrows letter of the 24 Sept '/44[,] directing me to proceed on the receipt thereof with HMS *Caledonia* to Plymo [*sic*] Sound[,] and there wait for further orders. I have to inform you that I will put to sea in execution of their Lordships Instructions tomorrow afternoon at 1 oclock[.]

[**136**] *Milne to Sir David Milne*

HMS *Caledonia*, Plymouth Sound
12 October 1844

Sir,

I have the honour to acquaint you that[,] in pursuance of the enclosed Instructions of the 26 Sept last[,] received from Sir John Barrow on the 30th Sept[,] I put to sea from the Tagus in HMS *Caledonia* on the afternoon of the 2d inst[,] and have to acquaint [you] with my arrival at this Port. . . .

[**137**] *Bowles to Milne*

London
13 October 1844

Dear Captain Milne

I do not know whether[,] amidst all the bustle of tomorrow [*sic*][,] Sir G. Cockburn will have time to mention to you the probability of your having my flag again hoisted on board the *Caledonia*, but[,] it being very desirable to ascertain without further delay the qualities of the *Queen* and *Albion*[,] I have offered my services to my colleagues for this purpose, and have very naturally selected you for my Captain, which I hope you will not dislike.

As far as I can conjecture[,] the whole business ought to be over in a month, if we are at all fortunate as to weather, and as winter is approaching, and the days shortening fast, the sooner we are off the better.

The ships ought to go to sea in their best sailing trim, and on no account to be overloaded with provisions or water. Three months [stores] at this time of year I should consider sufficient.

With respect to myself[,] I should ask you to lay [on] a sufficient stock of everything, wine included, for our cruise – as we shall not have much else to amuse ourselves with in the Bay of Biscay[,] we must take care to have good breakfasts and dinners.

I shall bring one servant, and nothing more except what you may wish. I know nobody now at Portsmouth, so that I leave the selection of tradesmen entirely with you, if you will be kind enough to undertake the office of caterer, and I will pay everything when I come down . . .

Perhaps you will come to town for a few hours, in which case we may talk anything over which I have left unsaid. You will soon find out when the *Queen* and *St. Vincent* can be ready . . .

Lord Haddington must give his consent to this plan before we actually begin operations[.]

[**138**] *Milne to David Milne*

HMS *Caledonia*, Spithead
13 October 1844

My dear David

I hasten to send you these few lines to mention my arrival here, having sailed from Lisbon on the 2nd & anchored in Plymouth Sound on Friday night[.] This was unexpected[,] I suspect[,] at the Admiralty House, as at day light up went the signal to proceed directly to Spithead, so I got under weigh immediately & arrived here at 9 A.M.[,] after a most stormy disagreeable night. I did not land at Plymouth[,] being only there [*sic*] 6 hours during the night[,] but I had a line from Sir David just as we were going out.

I understand the Queen comes here to morrow to see Louis Philippe away & then she goes to the Isle of Wight[.] I hear we are to cruize in the Channel – perhaps only for two weeks with the *Queen* & *St Vincent*[.] I must say I wish it was over & the ship moored in her own harbour[.] We are all getting tired of being on the move continually, especially as we have been in a constant gale with rain, ever since we were off Cape Finisterre on the 6th[.]

I hope you are all well[,] & that you will drop me a line soon, as I am anxious to hear of you all. I am tired, tired, tired & am now writing this at the George Inn, having just come on shore & I dine with Sir Charles Rowley, where I am to receive orders about our duties to morrow[.]

I have neither wax nor envelopes & can't get anyone to answer the bell[.] Farewell just now & with kind love to all. . . . [1]

[**139**] *Milne to Rowley*

HMS *Caledonia*, Spithead
14 October 1844

Sir,

I have the honour to acquaint you that[,] in pursuance of a Signal made by the Comr in Chief at Devonport[,] 'ordering me to proceed immediately to Spithead'[,] I weighed from that Port immediately after the Signal and proceeded with HM Ship *Caledonia* under my command to Spithead[,] & I have the honour to report my arrival this day.

I beg further to acquaint you that I sailed from Lisbon on the 2d inst and arrived in the Sound at 12 o'clock on Friday night.

[**140**] *Milne to Meek*[2]

HMS *Caledonia*, Plymouth Sound
28 November 1844

Sir,

A supply of Chocolate manufactured by a different process from that heretofore adopted having been sent to this ship from the Royal William Victualling Yard at this Port, and the said chocolate having been issued to the Ships Company at various periods from May until Nov. 1844 –

I have to report that it has been most highly approved of, it is considered much superior in Quality and flavor [*sic*] to that formerly supplied, and it has kept perfectly good for the 6 months it has been in this ship[,] whilst employed at Gibraltar[,] Lisbon &c.

[1]Here Grace Milne Home wrote:
(I find no letter after this about the cruize or return to Plymouth – but in January 1845 there was leave obtained to go to Scotland for about a month – & there are letters from Berwickshire written to 10 York Place Edinburgh – where the writer of these letters proceeded before returning to Plymouth. In April 1845 Sir David was very poorly & there are letters about his health, but the Doctors said no vital organ was affected, that it was a case of indigestion[,] & Dr Nelson said on April 6th that 'there were no bad symptoms at all & not to be alarmed['] and Sir George Magratt concurred.

Sir David was[,] however[,] much reduced by his illness[,] though he recovered so far as to be able to leave Plymouth, at the close of his command [at] the end of April 1845 . . .

[2]Sir James Meek, Kt. (1778–1856). Comptroller of Victualling, 1830–51.

[**141**] *Milne to Admiralty Secretary*

HMS *Caledonia*, Devonport
21 December 1844

Sir,

With reference to your letter of the 7th inst[,] directing me to make a further Report for the information of the Lords Commissioners of the Admiralty on the remaining Cotton Hammock Cloths sent home from N America and fitted to this ship in Dec '/42 – I have the honour to acquaint you that these Cotton Hammock Cloths which were continued on further Trial when those made of Flax Canvas were condemned in Oct '/43[,] were found unserviceable and Condemned at this Dock Yard in Feb. 1844[,] in consequence of their being much worn and defective from want of a renewal of Tolmans Composition to repaint them – none having been supplied for that purpose[,] but I am of opinion that[,] altho the Cloths were exceedingly soft and pliable, they admitted the Damp thro' them with more facility than those supplied from HM Dock Yards, and when any strain came on the Cloths by their being drawn tightly over the Hammocks[,] the composition cracked and admitted the Wet.

[**142**] *Milne to Briggs*[1]

HMS *Caledonia*, Devonport
23 December 1844

Sir,

I have the honour to enclose a letter from Mr. [James Hope] Burgess, Paymr & Purser of this ship[,] also the Lisbon Vouchers for Purchase made between 1 Sept and 1 Oct last[,] and also those for the Payment of Savings ending 30 Sept'/44[,] transmitted to me in your letter of Oct. 22d[, but] only received a few days ago, and in reply,

I have the honour to refer you to Mr. Burgess['s] communication on the Subject[,] and I have to acquaint you that the reason of [*sic*] the Vouchers being made out in the old Form was in consequence of the ship having sailed from England before the [new] forms were received at the Out Ports.

I have directed Mr. Burgess to forward a List of Casual payments of the Ships Co. and Boys – which is now enclosed[,] and at the same time

[1]Sir John Thomas Briggs, Kt. (1781–1865). Accountant-General of the Navy, 1832–54.

I cannot help expressing my regret at the inefficient and careless manner in which the Paymaster & Purser's Duties are conducted onboard this ship[.]

[**143**] *Bowles to Milne*

Admiralty
29 December 1844

Dear Captain Milne

Between ourselves I entirely agree with all you say about the Brigs trial[1] with which I had nothing to do; and you will be glad to hear that three of the fastest are to have another trial, the result of which I shall look forward to with much curiosity and interest. If I can have my way[,] you will command the squadron, but as this is not always the case, I only mention it confidentially as a possible occurrence.

Poor Lockyer will[,] I am afraid[,] be extremely annoyed at this sudden reduction of complement, of which I knew nothing until yesterday evening after all was settled, and I shall be much obliged to you to tell him this, as I should be very sorry he should imagine I have had anything to do with an arrangement I think very objectionable.

We have such fogs here that it is hardly possible to see[,] even at noonday[,] and the Easterly wind seems interminable.

[**144**] *Milne to Sir David Milne*

HMS *Caledonia*, Devonport
31 December 1844

Sir,

I have the honour to submit the following Report on Mr Walkers Compasses[,] sent for Trial onboard this ship against the Common Compasses supplied from HM Dock Yards, The [*sic*] Principal [*sic*] of Mr Walkers Compass being a double suspension – Viz. a Cone moving on the Point or Needle [*sic*] in the Compass Bowl[,] & and on the Cone there is fixed a Point or Needle on which the Compass Card moves.

[1]For Reports on the Brigs trials, see 'Copies of the Several Reports from Rear-Adm. Bowles, C.B., Commander Corry, and Captain Thompson, R.N., of the Sailing and other Qualities, as exhibited during the late Trial Cruises of Her Majesty's Ships . . . ', *Parliamentary Papers*, 1845, vol. XXX, pp. 156–9, 185.

These Compasses have been in constant use during the period this ship has been at sea during the last six months, and it has been found that[:]

In Moderate Breezes and fine Weather with the sea moderately smooth and this ship not having much motion –

Mr Walkers Compass was found superior to the Dock Yard Compass[,] being steadier & more free in its action[,] and attaining its true direction with more rapidity and precision[.]

In Rough Weather and the Ship having a Rolling Motion[:]

Under these circumstances Mr Walkers Compass did not prove so serviceable as that furnished by the Dock Yard, in consequence of the Rolling Motion of the Card, which Vibrated upwards of a Point and a Half on each side of the Lubbers mark on the Compass Bowl, Whereas [*sic*] the Ships Compass did not vibrate Half that Quantity[,] and when the moveable Cone of Mr Walkers Compass was Clamped as directed[,] the Compass was quite unserviceable.

When used in a boat Pulling & under Sail[,] Mr Walkers Compass [was] decidedly superior and much more serviceable than the Dock Yard Compass.

Under Sail, [it was] not superior to the Dock Yard Compass except what may be attributed to better description of Material & Workmanship.

When the Ships Company was exercised at General Quarters firing Blank Cartridges from all the Guns –

It was found that Mr Walkers Compass was steady and serviceable until the Quarter Deck Guns were fired, when it began to vibrate thro' a large arc – but the Ships Compass was quite unserviceable when the Main Deck Guns were fired – The [*sic*] Card making rapid Revolutions[.]

I am of opinion that if the Compasses supplied from HM Dock Yards were manufactured with the same care and attention as Mr Walkers[,] and made of equally <u>good</u> material, they would prove of the best description for H.M. Service[,] except in pulling in a Boat[,] when Mr. Walkers was found [*sic*] to be decidedly superior.

[**145**] *Milne to Sir David Milne*

HMS *Caledonia*, Devonport
5 January 1845

Sir,

I have the honour to acquaint you that[,] in pursuance of the accompanying letter from Rr. Adml. Sir Saml. Pym[,][1] requesting my opinion as to whether the Dresden Blue Dinner Service is preferred to the White Opal Service supplied by HM Dock Yard[,]

I have to acquaint you that I have examined the above[,] and would decidedly recommend the Blue Service, and I take this opportunity of stating that the White Service now furnished from this Dock Yard is of a very inferior Quality, easily broken[,] and also Cracks when heated.

[**146**] *Bowles to Milne*

Admiralty
9 January 1845

I have been watching all day for Captain Hamilton in hopes of finding out from him what has been finally decided about the brigs, and perhaps I may still see him before I close this letter, but if your business in Scotland is urgent and cannot be delayed[,] I fear there is nothing more to be done. The notion here was to give you the *Locust* for the cruize. It seems as if the *Daring* would not be ready for some time.

I do not know for what service the *Amazon* is intended – I dare say everybody else does.

Pray let me know the amount of my debt to you before you go, and I will then pay your banker or agent here . . .

Captain Hamilton will write himself if he [has] anything further to add.

[1]Sir Samuel Pym, C.B., K.C.B. (1778–1855). Entered, 1788; Lt, 1795; Cmdr, 1801; Capt., 1802; Rear-Adm., 1837; Vice-Adm., 1847. Pym was Adm.-Superintendent at Devonport Dockyard 1841–46.

[**147**] *Milne to Sir David Milne*

HMS *Caledonia*, Devonport
8 April 1845

Sir,

With reference to your Memo of the 8th March desiring that[,] in pursuance of orders from the L[ords] C[ommissioners] [of the] A[dmiralty,] that a limited Trial should be made onboard this ship for the period of one month[,] on a Method for Washing Linen in Salt Water proposed by Mr. Caldecott of Bath, I have to acquaint you that three Messes were selected for the purpose of carrying out the above Trial, and[,] as directed in your Memo of the above date – 'one Pound of Crystallized Soda was dissolved in a Gallon of Pure Salt Water, Cold, and the Linen intended to the Washed well rubbed with Yellow Soap previous to immersion'[.]

It has been found that the Soap does not mix with the Liquid[,] and the Clothes are not properly Washed, also those of a White or Light Color [*sic*] are turned Yellow[,] whilst those of a Blue Color [*sic*] partially bleached. I have interrogated the men upon the advantages which this process may possess[,] but they all state that they would prefer washing their Clothes in Salt Water with the Common Ships Soap, to the mixture now on Trial[,] which I do not consider is fit to wash their Clothes in. it [*sic*] is[,] moreover[,] so astringent that when men with thin skins immerse their Hands in it the skin is taken off, and one man's arms were bleeding from mere[ly] Washing his Clothes in it. under [*sic*] these circumstances I do not consider any advantage would be gained by its adoption.

[**148**] *Gage to Milne*

Admiralty
10 April 1845

My dear Sir

I was very glad to learn by a note from Sir David to Sir Geo Cockburn he was so well again, & I trust he may enjoy himself many years[.]

I can now tell you privately, that the *Caledonia* will be paid off[,] all Ratings[,] and will take the place of the *San Josef* [as Guardship of the Ordinary]. I should wish to remove the second Master or Mr Underwood[1]

[1]James Underwood, *Caledonia*'s Master.

immediately to the *Queen*, which ever you liked [*sic*][,] until the *Caledonia* is put out of commission as she [*Queen*] is to be the Flag Ship at Devonport. Mr Underwood will be allowed to complete his 3 years but the same indulgence cannot be extended to Mr Burgess. you [*sic*] have contrived to keep him straight, but the gentlemen of Somerset House complain so much that[,] as he has but little time to serve, it will not be worth while for him to open new Books.

Sir B. Walker has been put into the *Queen* at the express desire of the Surveyor[,] who has had his own way completely. he [*sic*] thinks Sir B. Walker will make her superior to all others, but I should think he depends somewhat upon the alterations[,] such as adding filling pieces to the bows[,] giving the ship more gripe [*sic*], adding to the size of the rudder[,] and many internal alterations, to improve her sailing qualities, as much as to a new Captain. before [*sic*] the ship went to sea last autumn[,] Sir W Symonds considered the *Queen* perfect[.]

If any of your men should wish to volunteer for the *Queen*[,] they should be sent round to her[,] I mean when you are paid off.

Will you have the goodness to tell me which of the two[,] viz. Mr Underwood or the 2nd Master[,] you can spare. I conclude the latter . . . but so soon as both can be allowed to leave the ship the sooner the *Queen* will be fitted. I hope you [will] be able to give good certificates to the Master 2nd Do & Masters Assistants, and also to the Warrant Officers. I know you will deal fairly by all, but remember the Service has also its <u>claim</u>.

[**149**] *Bowles to Milne*

Admiralty
17 April 1845

Dear Captain Milne

I am curious to hear how the reduced complement is answering in the *Albion* and *Superb*, and what sort of men your Devonport ships are getting. It is[,] I believe[,] arranged that the *Queen* is to be the future Flag ship there after her trial is over[,] and by this means I should hope she will get volunteers from the *Caledonia* when you pay off. She is to be commanded by Sir B. Walker[,] who will afterwards be appointed to some other command.

I hope Sir David is better, and that we may have the pleasure of seeing you all here on your way to Scotland.

[**150**] *Gage to Milne*

Admiralty
21 April 1845

My dear Sir

I am exceedingly obliged for your letters[.] I have written to Sir B. Walker respecting the men likely to volunteer from the *Caledonia* to *Queen*, if there should be vacancies for P[etty] Officers. Mr Underwood has been appointed[,] as the ship is getting in a forward state[,] and also Mr [William B.] Edwards[,] the [*Caledonia*'s] second Master[,] as you can spare him. I will arrange tomorrow with reference to the tenders[,] and let you know what is to be done with the gentlemen who command them[,] and also their crews.

I hope the weather may be fair & warm when Sir David returns to Scotland. he [*sic*] has been so long in the south he may feel a difference.

I beg he will accept my thanks for his exceeding kind attention to my relation[,][1] who has duly recorded it to me, & I must extend the same to you. I only hope he has done his duty[,] such as it was[,] to the Admirals satisfaction.

[**151**] *Milne to David Milne*

United Service Club
2 May 1845

My dear David

I do not know when Sir David last wrote – but I write a hurried line to say we leave this for Granton to morrow evening by the *Clarence*[.] Sir David, Lady Milne & the Cochrans[2] left Devonport on Tuesday last & I came away the following morning – met them at Exeter & came on here[.] Sir David[,] ever since his late illness[,] has never been well[.] He has never regained his strength & I am sorry to say is in a very debilitated state. He is very low & desponding & even alludes to his never reaching home. I am very much concerned about him & indeed far from satisfied about his state[.] He is unable to move or walk & it is with difficulty he can get upstairs to his bed. His breathing is oppressed

[1]Frederick Kemble. See above, [**111**].

[2]Almost certainly the family of Alexander Cochran of Ashkirk (1814–1903). Alexander's mother, Margaret Purves Cochran, was sister to Sir David Milne's first wife, and his sister Euphemia would subsequently marry Alexander Milne.

& he is altogether quite in an exhausted state[,] with no appetite[.] However we must endeavour to get him home[.] We are all staying at Stevens Hotel[,] Bond St[.] The Cochrans come down with us. I must now conclude with kind love . . . [1]

[**152**] *Ogle to Milne*

Admiralty House, Portsmouth
2 September 1846

My dear Sir

Sir Thomas Borchier[,][2] my [Flag] Captain is to be appointed the Superintendent of Chatham Yard. I am therefore induced from the high Character you bear in the Service, and from bringing to my [?recollection] the gallant Services I saw your Father perform when I was a very young Lieutenant in the West Indies[,] to ask you to allow me to apply to the Admiralty for you to be appointed my Flag Captain on board the *St Vincent* when she arrives at Spithead from the Cruise.

[**153**] *Milne to David Milne*

Inveresk, Musselburgh
5 September 1846

My dear David

I have been so unwell for some days past, that I have been confined to bed since Wednesday, & have only got up this morning – sooner than I should have done[,] but I have much to do before my departure for Portsmouth to assume the command of the *St Vincent* as Flag Captain to Sir Charles Ogle[,] from whom I received a letter this morning[,] offering me in very handsome terms the appointment, not only on account of my own name, but in recollection of Sir David's gallant & distinguished services in the West Indies. It is a most flattering letter & of course I cannot doubt for one moment the course I am to pursue – i.e. to accept this afternoon[.] I am very weak & hardly able to write[,] therefore you must excuse this short note.

[1]Grace Milne Home inserted: '(Sir David died on board the Steamer *Clarence* early on May 5th: 1845 before reaching Granton) G.M.H.'

[2]Sir Thomas Bourchier, C.B., K.C.B. (1791–1849). Entered, 1800; Lt, 1808; Cmdr, 1822; Capt., 1827.

[**154**] *Milne to David Milne*

George Hotel, Portsmouth
17 September 1846

My dear David

Thanks for your letter from Inverness & for your most kind and affecte congratulations on my appointment[.] It is of course a most pleasing & complimentary one to myself, who only saw Sir C. Ogle twice in my life[.] It is a curious circumstance & an unexpected one, that I should be Flag Capt: at the two principal ports in England[,] & I feel pleasure in telling you, that Sir C. Ogle told me yesterday, that Lord Auckland congratulated him on having obtained me as Flag Capt:[.]

I am so tired to night [*sic*] I cannot enter into a history of my proceedings here[.] At the request of Sir C. Ogle[,] I have been shewing the Lions [*sic*] from 10 till 4 o'clock to your friends of the British Association[.][1] Sir Charles is most sadly annoyed with the President[,] Sir Roderick Murchison[.][2] Sir Charles had invited him & a few of his intimate friends, leading men of the Society[,] to come down to luncheon with him, & he asked me to be civil to them, expecting from 20 to 30 people[,] & a most splendid dejeuné was laid out in the Admiralty House[.] Sir R. Murchison brought about 90! I requested him to separate his friends to the amount of 25[,] as that was the number for which the Admiral had prepared. He said, [']you know very well luncheon for 25 is quite enough for more than double that number[']! I did not venture to tell the Admiral this, for he is furious enough already at having been imposed on[.]

I arrived here in Monday & dined with Sir Charles on Tuesday[.] I had a long talk with him yesterday on the subject of my duties, the discipline of the *St Vincent's* youngsters, officers &c[,] & our views appeared entirely to agree[.] He is terribly afraid of rows in the ship & too much severity. I told him there was not the least occasion for severity[,] but of course officers & all must do their duty[,] & I was quite sure I would give him satisfaction on that point[.] To morrow I dine with Sir Charles to meet Lord & Lady Colville[.][3] I have been placed at the foot of his table from the first day I arrived[.]

[1]The British Association for the Advancement of Science, founded in 1831.

[2]Sir Roderick Impey Murchison (1792–1871). Murchison was a prominent geologist, and at that time President of the Geographical Society as well as the British Association.

[3]John, Lord Colville (1768–1849). Entered, 1775; Lt, 1793; Cmdr, 1795; Capt., 1796; Rear-Adm., 1819; Vice-Adm., 1830; Adm., 1841. Colville was one of Scotland's elected representative peers in the House of Lords.

I am looking out for lodgings near the Dockyard, as[,] though Sir Charles[,] besides a general invitation to breakfast & dine every day[,] offered me a bedroom in his house, that would not answer[.]

Good bye just now & with love to Jean & all the young people. . . .

[155] *Milne to David Milne*

United Service Club, London
22 September 1846

My dear David

I came to town yesterday as I could do no good at Portsmouth[,] & I now wait here for the arrival of the *St Vincent* from Cadiz[.] I have been down to the Admiralty & seen all of the board in town, namely, Admiral Dundas,[1] Lord J. Hay,[2] & Capt B. Hamilton[.] There is nothing going on here, but matters do not appear satisfactory in Ireland. A company of Artillery & Engineers were sent there last night by express from Woolwich[.]

All this row that was made in the papers about punishment has been spreading to all departments of the service &[,] I presume[,] ere long our hands will be entirely tied up.[3] We are to rule & guide our Ship's Companies by civil words & conciliatory speeches; What [*sic*] will be the end of it I know not, but if ever the power is taken from us, the discipline of the Service is gone, & then Goodbye [*sic*] to the navy. I hear it is fast coming to this, but as yet, I am not in [on] the secret.

I wish I could be with you on the 25th: but there is no help for it. I think it is best to be on the spot – ready for Sir C. Ogle when he wants me[.] I know I shall have a more anxious time of it after the arrival of the Ship[.] There is much to do, & much to look after in a big ship & to control such a mixture of people – officers & all – they will come into harbour all anxious for the shore[,] &[,] as matters have not gone very smooth on board, they will break out again under a new Captain[.]

[1]James Whitley Deans Dundas (*né* James Deans), C.B., G.C.B. (1785–1862). Entered, 1799; Lt, 1805; Cmdr, 1806; Capt., 1807; Rear-Adm., 1841; Vice-Adm., 1852; Adm., 1857; M.P., 1832, 1836–38; 1841–52; Naval Lord of the Admiralty, 1841, 1846–47; First Naval Lord, 1847–52.

[2]Lord John Hay, C.B. (1793–1851). Entered, 1804; Lt, 1812; Cmdr, 1814; Capt., 1818; Rear-Adm., 1851; M.P., 1826–30, 1847–50; Lord of the Admiralty, 1847–50.

[3]The subject of corporal punishment in the services was much in the public eye during August 1846; see leading articles in *The Times* (London) on Lord John Russell's motion to abolish flogging: 3 August 1846, p. 4, 4 August 1846, p. 4, and 8 August 1846, p. 5.

I hope Jean continues well & that you are all together at Milne Graden[.] I wish I was one of the party, it is somewhat different to me here, where our poor Father used to be with me, & we were always together – & now I look round & see no relative, although some casual friends[.] I will even feel it worse [*sic*] at Portsmouth[,] when I compare it with Plymouth[.] It is[,] however[,] as well to dismiss these reflections[,] yet they have their advantages[.]

With love & my sincere wishes for prosperity, health & happiness to you & yours . . .

[**156**] *Milne to David Milne*

Portsmouth
14 October 1846

My dear David

Here I am still on shore[,] not having been able as yet to join the *St Vincent*[,] although the ship is in the harbour[.] She still bears the broad Pendant of Sir Francis Collier,[1] though it is usual on the arrival of a Flag Officer that he should strike his flag at sunset, & an order is always sent from the Admiralty for that purpose – but no order has come down[.]

I suspect there is a difference of opinion at the Board, & they do not know what to do with Sir F. Collier, who was taken away from his own command in Woolwich Dockyard to go out with the Squadron[.] Houston Stewart[2] is now there[,] & as Sir F. Collier will be made an Admiral on the 9th Nov:[,] they don't want to turn out Houston Stewart[,] & yet they do not know what to do with Sir F. C.[,] for he naturally says 'you can't put me on half pay. You took me away from my own station for your own purposes & therefore you must let me go back to it'. Sir Charles Ogle is not at all well pleased about it[,] & I think[,] as I told him an hour ago, that he ought to represent it to the Admiralty & say his Flagship is now in harbour & ought to bear his Flag[.]

Sir Charles is a very pleasant agreeable person, very active both in mind & body, & is exceedingly strict in all matters relating to the service[.] He consults me in all concerns about the Squadron[.] I am in very comfortable lodgings next door to where you & I lived formerly

[1]Sir Francis Augustus Collier, Kt., C.B., K.C.H. (*c*.1783–1849). Entered, 1794; Lt, 1803; Cmdr, 1805; Capt., 1808; Rear-Adm., 1846.

[2]Sir Houston Stewart, C.B., G.C.B. (1791–1875). Entered, 1805; Lt, 1811; Cmdr, 1814; Capt., 1817; Rear-Adm., 1851; Vice-Adm., 1857; Adm., 1862; Adm. of the Fleet, 1872; Naval Lord of the Admiralty, 1850–52.

when Sir David commanded the *Bulwark* & *Venerable*[.] Perhaps you may remember the names of the people – Hill & Perkins.

My love to Jean &c. . . .

[157] *Milne to David Milne*

HMS *St. Vincent*, Portsmouth
19 October 1846

My dear David

I have delayed writing for the last two days till I got more settled down in my new ship, but I am now in such a fuss[,] & such a vortex of business[,] that I do not know which way to turn[,] or even get time to write you. An order came down to day for the *St Vincent* to refit & prepare for sea with all possible despatch, & I have taken the last part of the order as my guidance & reported 'Ready to go out of harbour on Wednesday morning at 10 o'clock' &[,] had I received the order at 10 this morning[,] *St Vincent* would have been at Spithead to morrow[.] As it is, there are precious long & not very pleasant faces, but it is no use, I always laugh at them. The Admiral is very much pleased at the way I have taken all this[,] & at my having reported the ship so soon ready. If we go to sea, which I very much doubt[,] Lisbon will I believe be our destination, where there is a revolutionary row.[1] *Cyclops* & *Scourge* Steamers are ordered for immediate service.

[158] *Milne to David Milne*

HMS *St. Vincent*, Portsmouth
28 December 1846

My dear David

Thanks for your letter & the almanack[,] which I found a very useful one last year[.] I wish I could have got down to Inveresk[,] but it was not possible[.] In fact[,] I think it my duty never to leave Sir C. Ogle. He has[,] in a very complimentary manner[,] placed me here & it is my duty to do my duty to him[,] & that I will do[,] however much I must sacrifice my own private feelings for[.] I can assure you I find it often

[1]Revolution erupted in Portugal in October 1846. See *The Times* (London), 20 October 1846, p. 4; 30 October 1846, p. 5; 2 November 1846, pp. 4–5; 9 November 1846, p. 4; 16 November 1846, p. 3; 18 November 1846, p. 5; 27 November 1846, p. 5; 8 December 1846, p. 5. The last of these accounts reports 'total defeat of the insurgents', suggesting why *St Vincent*'s presence at Lisbon was not deemed immediately requisite.

very up hill [*sic*] work & I fight against it. There is one great satisfaction, that with Sir C. Ogle & Admiral Parker[1] I am on the best of terms[,] & nothing could go on better than the duty of the Port[,] & in being here I am in the highest station possible[.]

I hear a meeting is to be held at Musselborough for a subscription for the relief of destitution in the Highlands.[2] If you don't dislike it[,] & it is not inconvenient[,] would you attend it for me & give my support to it by any subscription you may think proper, either 5, 10, or 15 pounds. There will be a dreadful scene of suffering this winter, it is[,] I think[,] terrible to contemplate[.] The Government Mills here & at Plymouth are never stopped day or night, but are constantly grinding & quantities are shipped from here[.] I am just going to order a large working party from the *St Vincent* to fill the *Rhadamanthus* at Daylight – Love to all & many happy returns of the season &c &c. . . .

[**159**] *Milne to David Milne*

HMS *St. Vincent*, Portsmouth
31 December 1846

My dear David

This is the last epistle I can write this year – which will end forever in a very few hours. Time is going forward upon us all, which must make us all reflect on the past & on the future[,] &[,] I trust[,] with benefit to ourselves.

I cannot but feel regret that I am absent from all those who are now the only ties which I can have[,] & who are all met under one roof at Inveresk, but in that absence I am following out the profession in which I have embarked . . . which does not recognize the absence of those who carry on its duties[.]

I must say I have passed a most heavy Christmas time, having much to worry [about] & little to add pleasure to the daily toil of business. However in all cases, no matter what, it is right to make the best of everything. I send you a small & trifling token – an almanack & Jean a small present – I hope none the worse of its small intrinsic value[,] but I send it to remind her of 1847.

[1]Sir William Parker, Bt., C.B., K.C.B., G.C.B. (1781–1866). Entered, 1793; Lt, 1799; Cmdr, 1799; Capt., 1801; Rear-Adm., 1830; Vice-Adm., 1841; Adm., 1851; Adm. of the Fleet, 1863; Naval Lord of the Admiralty, 1834–35, 1835–41; First Naval Lord, 1846.

[2]Like Ireland, the Scots Highlands were suffering the consequences of crop failure and widespread famine in the late 1840s. See *The Times* (London), 6 October 1846, p. 5; 7 October 1846, p. 4; 25 November 1846, p. 2; 9 December 1846, p. 2, and John Prebble, *The Highland Clearances* (London, 1969), pp. 171–87.

Goodbye my dear David & with my sincere wish for many, very many[,] happy returns of the New Year to you & yours[.]

[**160**] *Auckland to Milne*

Admiralty
3 January 1847

Sir

In a conversation I had with you some time ago, we came to the understanding that you should gradually lower the number of men employed on board the *St Vincent* and substitute boys, of such an age as might fit them for a seaman's education, in the proportion of three boys for two men. I believe that no formal orders have been issued to you, to the above effect, and I would see my way more clearly, than I do at present, to the details of the system which I wish to see established before I would direct the issue of such orders, but I trust that you are acting upon the suggestions which I made to you, and I shall be glad to hear from you whenever you may be able to report progress – and particularly I would have you lay down such general principles as have occurred to you to be fitting, so that in establishing similar Naval schools, on board of other ships, there may be some uniformity of proceeding. 1st[,] as to the age of the boys, I think that they should not, on entry be less than fourteen, or more than sixteen years of age – and 2nd[,] that it would be well if their term of engagement were for seven years. This term would be sufficient to allow them from one to two years of instruction and from five to six years of actual service, and they would not upon their return from their first voyage, be thrown on the world or enticed to leave the Navy – 3rd[,] you will have to consider the number of boys whom you could admit on board the Guard ship without an increase of expense and without materially impairing her efficiency[,] and I apprehend that the system will work much more easily after it has been some time in force, than it will in the beginning. I believe that on board the *St Vincent* your complement has been 620 men and 60 boys, and you would in the beginning be weak if you had only 570 men and 135 boys uninstructed and under the age of 16 – but if your men should be only gradually reduced, and boys but gradually admitted[,] you will always have a large portion of the latter well instructed and growing into manhood and your strength will not be impaired – 4th[,] I think that the term of instruction should be from eighteen months to two years, and I should hope that you might in every month draft off to the sea-going ships six or eight boys capable of ratings as 1st Class Boys.

These frequent drafts upon your crew may be regarded by you as taking from the efficiency of your ship, but you must consider yourself as working not for one ship alone, but for the Navy generally, and[,] as the *St Vincent* is likely to be much in port, she may well be used for the foundation of a beneficial system, under your direction – 5th[,] I would have established a good and well defined system of instruction. There must, of course, in the first instance be care of morals and religion and order and cleanliness, and there must be enough and not too much of reading and writing & arithmetic, and instruction in the principles and rudiments of navigation and gunnery[,] and in the use of arms, and practice in all the duties which regard the ship and boats, and the boys should be all taught to swim, and I would give them some practice in fishing as well as in sailing and rowing and they might also have some knowledge of the engine room of our Steamers – 6th[,] the system of discipline with boys need never be severe and there may be promise of rewards. The best boys may work to good early ratings, or to being sent as gunnery boys to the *Excellent*, or to apprenticeships to engineers, armourers or [?New] Naval Artificers. I would have the boys leave their school-ship for sea at the age of 17 or 18, and I should like that they might then be qualified to be rated as 1st Class Boys, and in two years afterwards as Ordinary Seamen. They should be intitled [*sic*] to be so, even though there may not be a vacancy for them, if they should exhibit merit and good qualifications.

It might perhaps seem best that separate ships be appropriated exclusively to schools, but the establishment of such ships would be more expensive[,] and it may be well that the experiment be tried in the first instance, by us, and I shall be much gratified if[,] under your good care[,] the *St Vincent* should become one of our model schools for the example of others. It is the more essential that we should have a good model school, as I understand it is to be in contemplation that the guardians of some of the Poor House Unions, situated near to the sea ports, should establish floating schools for the instruction of boys for the Naval and Merchants' [*sic*] service[,] and we may find these schools and our own mutually subservient to the uses of each other.

I think it essential on board our ships that the boys' messes should be in classes, of from 16 to 20, under a petty officer, separate, and under a separate purser's account, from the messes of the men – and, above all things there should be an absolute prohibition against the serving out of spirits to the boys, and the value of the spirits in money should be added to their pay – I will beg you to consult Sir Chas Ogle upon all these points, and to favour me with your opinion upon them and[,] as soon as I receive your answer[,] I will frame official instructions.

[**161**] *Milne to David Milne*

HMS *St. Vincent*, Portsmouth
20 January 1847

My dear David

I write to offer you my most sincere congratulations & many happy returns of the 22nd[.] I wish I could have been in York Place & joined your party on the 22nd[.] It would be a great pleasure & satisfaction to me, as I have no tie here, nor any friendly association[.] It is hard work all day, & I may say every day in prospect, & the last affairs here in way of Courts Martial have not been agreeable. We dismissed a Lieut: yesterday for drunkenness; & the loss of the new Steamer *Sphinx* commanded by my friend Cragg[1] has cast a gloom over us all.[2] She is on shore at the back of the Isle of Wight under a perpendicular cliff[,] & yesterday the sea was breaking over her & there is little or no hope of saving her[.] The *Scourge* lost a man drowned there on Monday & two other gigs are amissing [*sic*][,] and I am afraid all are drowned[.] Cragg will of course be tried by Court Martial and Capt Onslow[3] of the *Daphne* writes me he believes he & his Master will also be tried for getting on shore at the back of the Isle of Wight when coming here from South America.

I have been very unwell with cold & influenza . . .

[1]John Bettinson Cragg (*c*.1797–1878). Entered, 1809; Lt, 1828; Cmdr, 1842; Capt. (Res.), 1856; Rear-Adm. (Ret.), 1875. Cragg served on the North America and West Indies Station during the late 1830s.

[2]HMS *Sphynx* ran aground on 16 January 1847; see *The Times* (London), 19 January 1847, p. 5. Milne was a member of the subsequent Court Martial, which found Cragg and Sailing Master Joseph Wallis guilty of negligence in failing to take soundings. Cragg was dismissed from command of *Sphynx* and his name placed at the bottom of the Commanders' List. Wallis was reduced from Master to Second Master and made ineligible for promotion for a year. See *The Times* (London), 15 February 1847, pp. 5–6.

[3]John James Onslow (*c*.1798–1856). Entered, 1810; Lt, 1816; Cmdr, 1822; Capt., 1834.

[**162**] *Ellenborough*[1] *to Milne*

Francis Hotel, Upper Belgrave Street, London
2 February 1847

My dear Sir

I rejoice that Arthur Villiers[2] is to be[,] in the first instance[,] under your care on board the *St. Vincent.*

Mr Law[3] tells me you think £50 a year a proper Allowance. I have instructed my bankers[,] Messrs Hoare of Fleet St.[,] to honour the Boy's drafts[,] upon one countersigned by you, but to save trouble in the first instance I take the liberty of enclosing £15 on account of his Allowance.

It is probable[,] as I heard from Lord J. Hay[,] that he will soon [be] sent out to join the *Thetis* or some other Ship on a Foreign Station.

[**163**] *Milne to David Milne*

HMS *St. Vincent*, Portsmouth
5 February 1847

My dear David

. . . I will be at the first levée with the Admiral[.] We are all busy here with meal for Scotland & Ireland. The *Porcupine* was coaled and loaded yesterday & started off for Oban[.][4]

[1]Edward Law, second Baron and first Earl Ellenborough (1790–1871). Lord Privy Seal, 1828–29; President of the Board of Control, 1828–30, 1834–35, 1858; Junior Lord of the Treasury, 1834; Governor-General of India, 1841–44; First Lord of the Admiralty, 1846.

[2]Arthur Julian Villiers (*c.*1835–79). Entered, 1847; Lt, 1855, Lt (Ret.), 1871. Villiers subsequently commanded the gunboat *Snapper* at the bombardment of Sweaborg in 1855 and the *Starling* in the Second Opium War. He was removed from Acting Command of HMS *Hardy* and sent to England on account of *delirium tremens* in February 1863 and refused further employment in December 1867.

[3]Ellenborough's brother and private secretary.

[4]Oban, in Argyllshire, on the west coast of Scotland. *Porcupine* was presumably carrying food to alleviate distress in the Highlands, as mentioned in [**158**].

[**164**] *Milne to David Milne*

HMS *St. Vincent*, Portsmouth
8 March 1847

There is not much novelty here, but a great deal of hard work & disagreeable work[,] for I am much worried with the Ship's Co[.] I am in hopes[,] however[,] I have got quit of some of the bad ones, having again been obliged to punish a man & discharge him with disgrace, for theft & continued bad conduct[.] I have been pretty sharp with them[,] & yesterday I wrote for a Court Martial on a man for desertion[,] having found him in the forepeak of a Schooner about to sail for Ireland. All these matters keep one in constant excitement of a very disagreeable kind, but I now hope I have broken the system & things will go better[.]

We are all in a Hulk, where we will be for 6 weeks . . . in which period we will be refitting the *St Vincent* & getting her ready for sea.

[**165**] *Milne to David Milne*

HMS *St. Vincent*, Portsmouth
30 March 1847

As to our summer movements in *St Vincent*[,] I should not be at all surprised if we were sent to the Tagus, as no doubt some ship will have to be sent there, even if the political warfare is settled[.] I see they have been seizing British vessels. they [*sic*] had better leave that alone or they will burn their fingers[.]

I am sorry to see your account of scarcity of provisions & fodder for cattle. It is a very serious business in Ireland[.] Several large steamers are embarking large quantities of seed for Ireland[.]

The levée will probably be about the 10th April, but whenever it is I will go up to town to meet you[,] & hope you will run down here for a few days &c &c . . .

[**166**] *Milne to David Milne*

HMS *St. Vincent,* Portsmouth
13 May 1847

My dear David

Thanks for your letter. The day after you left I had a letter from Sir Charles Napier saying he was going to hoist his Flag in the *St Vincent*[,] to proceed to Lisbon & to command the Squadron. It was a secret letter, & now it is all out through Mrs Warren[,][1] who had a letter from a Lord of the Admiralty[.] I am horrified at the man, but must make the best of it[.] I suppose the orders will be down to morrow, & that we will sail as soon as possible . . .

I had a party on board when the *Queen* came into Harbour[.] The Admiral came on board, & it went off well.

[**167**] *Milne to David Milne*

HMS *St. Vincent*, Portsmouth
16 May 1847

My dear David

We have been in a precious mess to day in going out of harbour[.] The Hawser [*sic*] attached to the Steamer carried away just before we came to the narrows[.] We made sail on the ship, but the wind headed [*sic*] & we had to anchor in the entrance of the harbour, & nearly popped our Jib boom into the Quebec Hotel! We were in a very precarious position[,] & luckily got her stern hove over on the opposite side of the harbour & returned to our moorings. If the tide had left us, we should have fallen over. The Master Attendant was in charge[,] not me, also a pilot on board & leads in the chains. We will go out to morrow if moderate, & sail for Lisbon about to morrow week.

I hope to be home again in the summer, as the Flag is to be here for a temporary service only.[2]

[**168**] *Milne to David Milne*

HMS *St. Vincent*, Spithead
16 May 1847

My dear David

What with the *St Vincent*, Sir C. Napier & Sir C. Ogle[,] I have really had no time to look about me or answer letters. Sir Charles Napier hoists his flag in the morning & I then become his flag Capt:, which I did not bargain for, when I came here, & Sir Charles Ogle does not

[1]Milne may have been referring to Mary Laird Warren, wife of Vice-Adm. Frederick Warren (1775–1848), who resided at Cosham, near Portsmouth.

[2]Here Grace Milne Home added: '(I can find no letter after this explaining the delay of the expedition to Lisbon which it will be seen from [the] following letter did not take place till August.)'.

much like it. However the service must be carried on[.] The Commander[1] is as downcast as ever & is talking about trying to resign, but it won't do. I am afraid he & Napier will fall out & then a fine row will take place[.] I am quite done up, having been hard at work since 6 A.M. getting in powder – 30 tons, lower deck guns, provisions for 5 months – Love to all &c . . .

[**169**] *Milne to David Milne*

HMS *St. Vincent*, Portsmouth
22 May 1847

Here we are still & no orders to move! If we remain till to morrow I will[,] if possible[,] go to London to see Lady Milne[,] but it will all depend on our orders[.] As for Sir C. Napier[,] whose flag is flying in the *St Vincent*, I do not know where he is or anything about him!

[**170**] *Milne to Hamilton*

HMS *St. Vincent*, Spithead
26 July 1847

Sir

I consider it my duty it bring under your notice for the information of the Lords Commissioners of the Admiralty[,] the very great expense of the Government Articles of Furniture which are supplied on demand from the Dockyard to the Officers of Her Majesty's Fleet.

I believe it to have been the intention of their Lordships[,] in the establishment of Government Articles[,] to enable officers of limited Income to obtain their outfit at a moderate expense[,] and without their being obliged to make a considerable outlay of Money on their commissioning a ship. But it appears to me that their Lordships Intentions[,] which would prove so highly advantageous to the Service[,] are likely to be frustrated by the very heavy charges which are made to [the] Government for the respective articles of crockery and Glass[,] which articles can be supplied by any manufacturer at nearly 30 pr ct less cost. To prove this assertion[,] I beg to annex lists of the Government prices, and also what the same articles cost from private dealers. . . . [2]

[1]Graham Ogle (1814–1871). Entered, 1827, Lt, 1838; Cmdr, 1846; Capt., 1856; Capt. (Ret.), 1866. Ogle was Sir Charles Ogle's nephew.

[2]The price of the articles from private dealers totalled £29.14.6, those supplied by the dockyard, £38.11.2.

[**171**] *Milne to David Milne*

HMS *St. Vincent*, Lisbon
28 August 1847

My dear David

We are here with a very large Squadron – the number you will see by the paper – certainly the most formidable I have ever seen together, & if any row should take place, depend upon it we shall be in the middle of it[.]

We arrived here this day week, & I think it not unlikely we may go to sea for a cruize about the 6th September, but we cannot long be absent, as the affairs of the country are in a very unsettled state &[,] if you may credit the rumours on shore, it is not at all improbable that another revolution may take place in October[.] It is not for want of the will, but for want of the cash. The country is ruined by a set of vagabonds, who get into the Ministry for no other plea [*sic*] than plunder, & a new Ministry has been formed since our arrival[,] with £480 in the Treasury to pay the expenses of Government. They will be all out again in a month, & then for a flare up! Sir Charles Napier is a leading man here, viz. – a Count Cape St Vincent & in high favour with the Queen[,] for she owes her throne to him[,] & all parties respect him. He has great influence[,] & I suspect he will take a leading part in all the present proceedings[.] We have all the Great Guns of Portugal on board, & fired more salutes than ever I saw before, on one day 108 guns[,] & as many the day previous[.]

I hope you will write direct to Lisbon via Southampton[.] The mails arrive & leave this every ten days[.]

Can I bring or send you anything from this[?] My love to Jean & all the children. I wrote to Jean for her birthday – & with kind regards to all at Paxton . . .

[**172**] *Napier to Milne*

HMS *St. Vincent*, Lisbon
8 December 1847

Sir

I cannot allow you to quit the *St. Vincent* without conveying to you my sense of the very excellent state of discipline of that Ship. Her Gun Exercise is equal to any I have seen – and in the Small-arms exercise the men are nearly perfect.

I beg, before you give up the command of the Ship, to offer you my sincere thanks for the great zeal you have displayed at all times since my Flag has been on board the *St Vincent*, and that you will convey to the Officers and Ship's Company my satisfaction at the state in which I found the Ship on my inspecting her yesterday.

PART IV

THE ADMIRALTY, 1847–53

In response to Sir Charles Napier's urging that Milne be awarded a knighthood, First Lord of the Admiralty Lord Auckland replied: 'You will have long since heard that much better has been done for Captain Milne, than given him a knighthood which is a foolish reward in any case, and not granted now for Naval Service. I think that he will make a good working Lord of the Admiralty and the selection of a young officer entirely on account of his professional qualities cannot be otherwise than creditable to the Government.'[1] By this point Milne's political neutrality must have been well established; his first Flag Captaincy had been a gift from Lord Haddington's Tory Board, but notoriously difficult-to-please Napier was a Liberal, and he too had been impressed by Milne's professionalism and abilities.[2] Still, the latter could not be unaware of the political dimension of naval administration in an era in which patronage was as yet routinely deployed in appointments and was anxious to avoid getting caught up in intrigues. Indeed, Milne, Auckland, and Prime Minister Lord John Russell agreed that he was to be spared any business related to politics or patronage: he 'was asked . . . to entirely devote' his 'whole time to Service details'.[3]

This insistence notwithstanding, it is doubtful that either Milne or Auckland foresaw that the former's tenure at Whitehall would last until June 1859, through five successive Governments, and that he would serve six different First Lords. Auckland brought Milne to the Admiralty, but when the First Lord died in late 1849 he was retained by Auckland's successor Sir Francis Baring.[4] More surprisingly, when Russell's Whig Ministry fell in February 1852, new Prime Minister

[1]Add Mss 40040, fol. 42: Auckland to Napier, 16 December 1847.

[2]Napier's self-description as an M.P. was 'Liberal'. Sir Charles Ogle, on the other hand, had been appointed Port Admiral at Portsmouth by Haddington's Board in 1845.

[3]MLN/145/5: 'Measures brought forward by Captain Milne when a Member of the Board of Admiralty, from December 1847', nd.

[4]Sir Francis Thornhill Baring, first Earl Northbrook (1796–1866). Junior Lord of the Treasury, 1830–34; Joint Secretary to the Treasury, 1834; Chancellor of the Exchequer, 1839–41; First Lord of the Admiralty, 1849–52.

Lord Derby and new First Lord the Duke of Northumberland[1] extended Milne an invitation to join the latter's administration. Milne was the only member of the previous Board to be retained and, as can be seen, played a vital role in sustaining Whig initiatives, especially regarding manning the fleet [**237**, **238**]

Milne was not the sole member of Northumberland's Board to be asked to join the subsequent adminstration of Sir James Graham;[2] Senior Naval Lord Hyde Parker[3] was also kept on, but the latter was elderly and in failing health, dying in June 1854, and again Milne seems to have furnished a crucial element of administrative continuity with regard to dockyard appointments and advancement [**255**]. When Graham left office in February 1855, his successor, Sir Charles Wood, elected to keep Milne and Captain Peter Richards[4] in their posts as junior Naval Lords. Sir John Pakington retained the former alone when he took up the First Lordship in March 1858. Only when the Tories fell from power in June 1859 did Milne finally leave office.

In theory, Milne's duties on the Board were narrowly defined. In 1832 Graham had, during his first stint as First Lord, carried out an extensive reorganisation of naval administration, abolishing the Navy and Victualling Boards, and creating in their place five permanent officers – the Surveyor of the Navy, Accountant-General, Storekeeper-General, Medical Director-General, and Comptroller of Victualling – to carry out the functions previously overseen by the two eliminated Boards. Four of these officers and their departments, in turn, were typically supervised by one of the Naval Lords (the remaining officer being under the charge of the Civil Lord). Milne's bailiwick was the Victualling Department, which also encompassed, thanks to the vagaries of Admiralty administrative development, the Transport Department, which was charged with conveying Troops and Stores overseas. This latter responsibility became Milne's chief concern during the Crimean War; prior to 1854 it was a fairly insignificant burden.

From the beginning, however, Milne's duties ranged well beyond supervising the Victualling Department. As Auckland intimated to

[1]Algernon Percy, fourth Duke of Northumberland (1792–1865). Entered, 1805; Lt, 1811; Cmdr, 1814; Capt., 1815; Rear-Adm., 1850; Vice-Adm. (Ret.), 1857; Adm. (Ret.) 1859; First Lord of the Admiralty, March–December 1852.

[2]Sir James Robert George Graham, Bt. (1792–1861). First Lord of the Admiralty, 1830–34, 1853–55; Secretary of State for Home Affairs, 1841–46.

[3]Sir Hyde Parker, C.B. (*c*.1784–1854). Entered, 1796; Lt, 1804; Cmdr, 1806; Capt., 1807; Rear-Adm., 1841; Vice-Adm., 1852; First Naval Lord, 1852–54.

[4]Sir Peter Richards, C.B., K.C.B. (*c*.1786–1869). Entered, *c*.1798; Lt, 1807; Cmdr, 1816; Capt., 1828; Rear-Adm., 1855; Vice-Adm. (Ret.), 1862; Adm. (Ret.), 1865; Naval Lord of the Admiralty, 1854–57.

Napier, Milne was to be a 'working Lord of the Admiralty'. He was consequently involved not only with the conveyance of Stores (which formed part of his brief), but also with the Admiralty's system of awarding contracts for their supply (which did not) [**176–7**, **202–4**].

Moreover, it is plain from the surviving record in both Milne's papers and the Admiralty Secretariat files that by early 1848 he was functioning as a one-man, ad hoc naval staff to the Board. In February of that year he was charged by Auckland[1] to draft a new scheme for manning the Ordinary Establishments (the personnel required to maintain the Ships in Ordinary) and harbour service vessels – port flagships such as *Caledonia* when he commanded her – in order to minimise the number of men assigned to the duties of the Ordinary and maximise the number available for immediate seagoing service in the event of an emergency armament [**179**].[2] Of perhaps even greater importance to national security, Milne was also asked to draw up regulations for a Steam Reserve. Those who decry the Admiralty's alleged conservatism and the officer corps's hostility to steam would do well to read the preface to Milne's proposals on the subject [**180**] and consider the attention he gave to working out the details of preparation and cost [**181–2**] in order to ensure that a substantial, well-maintained force of war steamers would be ready on the shortest possible notice.

Milne later claimed that 'the first measure I was asked to deal with was "What was to be done with the Vote of Parliament of £30,000 a-year, given for the benefit of the Petty Officers and Seamen of the Fleet?" I then submitted three plans, but strongly urged the introduction of the Good Conduct Badges and Pay. This was adopted, and I drew up the whole of the regulations.'[3] Actually, his work on the Ordinary Establishments and Steam Reserve predated that on the Good Conduct Warrant, and Milne was mistaken as to the impetus for implementing the latter: fellow Naval Lord Maurice Berkeley[4] urged the system[,]

[1]ADM1/5590: 'Papers Relative to the New Establishment of the Ordinary & Steam Reserve', 1 February 1848.

[2]Following an increased vote for Seamen and Marines in late 1852, Milne was assigned to revise the system he had devised in 1848. See [**250**].

[3]MLN/145/5: 'Measures brought forward by Captain Milne when a Member of the Board of Admiralty, from December 1847', nd.

[4]Maurice Frederick Fitzhardinge Berkeley, first Lord Fitzhardinge, C.B., K.C.B., G.C.B. (1788–1867). Entered, 1802; Lt, 1808; Cmdr, 1810; Capt., 1814; Rear-Adm., 1849; Vice-Adm., 1856; Adm., 1862; Naval Lord of the Admiralty, 1838–39, 1846–52, 1852–54; First Naval Lord, 1854–57. Berkeley was also deeply involved in efforts to put manning on a sounder footing and is credited by R. Taylor as being the chief impetus for the establishment of the continuous service system. See Taylor, 'Manning the Royal Navy: The Reform of the Recruiting System, 1852–1862', *Mariner's Mirror*, 44 (1958), pp. 302–13 and 45 (1959), pp. 46–58. The role played by Milne during the Duke of

whereas Milne initially dismissed it as impracticable. That said, he was right on the other particulars. He submitted the first memorandum on the subject [**184**], drafted a detailed set of possible uses for the money that Parliament had granted [**185**], and when Berkeley expressed his preference for a scheme not favoured by Milne [**186**], submitted a new memorandum [**188**], taking into account the views of the rest of the Board [**187**]. Moreover, it was Milne who worked out the probable cost of the innovation and who had charge of drafting the Circular announcing its institution [**193**].[1] At virtually the same time he was also charged with drafting regulations for entry of Seaman Riggers, a dockyard force intended to supplement seagoing personnel in the event of a crisis [**189–90**].

The two tasks that Milne undertook in early 1848 serve to illuminate the principal quandaries besetting naval administrators during the 1840s and 1850s. Numerous minor problems confronted Milne and the rest of the Board, as is evident from the following pages. Two, however, were of overriding importance. These related first to the material transformation of the fleet, and second to the necessity of fashioning a new system of recruiting, retaining, and advancing enlisted personnel; in short, transforming naval service into a viable (if not hugely popular) career option, not only for commissioned and warrant officers, but for enlisted men too.

The first of these topics – the fleet's technological transformation – was only intermittently within Milne's brief prior to the Russian War, although several of those exceptions are of immense significance for understanding the Admiralty's response to *matériel* innovation. In 1849 he composed, in conjunction with a general ship inspection form [**205**], a list of queries pertaining solely to steam vessels [**206**]. In September and October 1851 he generated a series of memoranda urging that junior officers be instructed in the fundamentals of steam engineering [**224–5**, **227**]. He further recommended that they face mandatory examinations on the subject; his colleagues on the Board objected to that policy [**226**].[2]

Northumberland's First Lordship in keeping the manning question before the Board (Berkeley being out of office) suggests that Taylor's assessment might be amended. See below, [**238**, **240–42**, **256–7**].

[1]Milne also vetted the proposal to Charles Napier. See Milne to Napier, 16 January 1848, [**177**].

[2]In October 1851 Milne also composed a memorandum advocating the development of a coherent and *manageable* set of steam evolutions. This paper appears in John Hattendorf et al. (eds.), *British Naval Documents 1204–1960* (Navy Records Society, 1993), document 370, pp. 629–30. As did many of his brethren, Milne grasped the fact that steam had transformed the tactical realm at sea to one potentially resembling the sophisticated manoeuvres of horse artillery. Unlike most who set pen to the subject, he also understood that such sophistication ran the risk of unprecedented confusion.

Equally important, not only Milne but also the remainder of the Board appreciated that steam had wholly transformed the logistical basis of British naval strategy. In the sailing era that strategy – combining blockade, convoy, and peripheral operations – had been carried out by vessels whose operational endurance was typically limited by victualling requirements and whose geographic reach was defined by the 'five fathom line' on an enemy coast, as the old adage had it. To be sure, maintaining large blockading squadrons mandated well-developed and relatively close support bases; the achievements of Cornwallis and his contemporaries could not have been achieved without the maintenance and supply infrastructure at the Nore, Portsmouth, Plymouth, Minorca, and Leghorn.

Even so, the logistical demands of a sailing fleet paled in comparison to those of its steam successor. Furnishing coal to ships engaged in blockade or offensive operations against enemy ports – the envisioned enemies were France and Russia – required the creation of a new logistical arrangement at each of the home ports. Characteristically, Milne was delegated to study the problem and recommend steps to ensure that wartime operations in the Channel and North Sea would not be hampered for want of coal. The report he produced in November 1851 [**228**] is a testament to his thoroughness and practicality. As Third Naval Lord Captain Houston Stewart minuted, 'Capt. Milne has evidently devoted so much attention to the subject that I think it may safely be left very much in his hands . . . '[1]

Moreover, by the late 1840s the application of steam to line-of-battle ships had raised questions about blockade's utility. More than one alarmist publicly decried Britain's defencelessness against a French steam invasion fleet and no less a figure than Lord Palmerston proclaimed that steam had 'bridged the Channel'. If this were so, then the foundation of all British naval strategy, not to mention national security policy, was no longer secure: command of the sea appeared to be at stake if an ancillary or alternative were not found.

Conventional wisdom suggests that British defence planners responded to this conundrum by abandoning a forward, 'blue water' strategy in favour of a defensive *mentalité*, the so-called 'brick and mortar school', which centred on building elaborate (and expensive) land fortifications around the country's chief naval arsenals.[2] Those who entertain this view

[1]ADM7/617, Cases; Extract from Case 136, Coaling Steamers, Stewart minute.

[2]See, for instance, Arthur Marder, *The Anatomy of British Sea Power: A History of British Naval Policy in the Pre-Dreadnought Era, 1880–1905* (Hamden, CT, 1940 and subsequent edns) and Michael Partridge, *Military Planning for the Defence of the United Kingdom, 1815–1870* (New York, 1989).

would be well advised to consult Milne's draft memorandum 'Naval Measures to be taken in Case of War' [**217**], probably composed around 1850–51, perhaps in response to Napoleon III's 1851 coup. Milne pointed to the strategy of coastal assault which was being adopted by the Admiralty as a complement to the traditional blockade.[1] And for those who, influenced by the scurrilous and inaccurate recollections of John Henry Briggs,[2] doubt the Admiralty's receptivity to steam, Milne's forthright statement 'Ships of the Line are useless for <u>checking</u> the rapid movements of a Steam Squadron . . . <u>Steam</u> power alone can be of service under such circumstances' should serve as a healthy corrective.

Whatever he was Milne was no radical; he was instead a capable and thoughtful officer who saw in steam immense offensive potential, substantial defensive threats, and serious logistical hurdles. For him, and others of like mind (in fact, most of the Navy's administrators), the first had to be realized, the second countered, and the last surmounted. Milne and the rest of the Admiralty in the late 1840s and 1850s were committed to achieving all three. That it took several decades to do so should be seen as a consequence of the limitations of steam technology until the late 1880s, rather than as the result of hidebound traditionalism.

When it came to utilising labour (and cost) saving technological, or, for that matter organisational, accounting, or other innovations in the dockyards, however, Milne was a thoroughgoing moderniser. In late 1848 Auckland appointed him to a Committee charged with Dockyards revision and reform, suggesting again the wide-ranging scope of Milne's tasks at the Admiralty.[3] Many of the Committee's recommendations were carried out, but one – establishing Board oversight of mechanical improvements – had been overlooked owing to personnel changes at Whitehall and Somerset House. Milne did not allow the subject to be

[1]For further discussion of this subject, see Andrew Lambert, 'The Shield of Empire', in J.R. Hill (ed.), *The Oxford Illustrated History of the Royal Navy* (London, 1995), pp. 161–97; John Beeler, 'Steam, Strategy, and Schurman: Imperial Defence in the Post-Crimean Era, 1856–1905', in Greg Kennedy and Keith Neilson (eds), *Far-Flung Lines: Essays on Imperial Defence in Honour of Donald MacKenzie Schurman* (London, 1997), pp. 27–30; *idem*, *Birth of the Battleship: British Capital Ship Design, 1870–1881* (London, 2001), pp. 89–91.

[2]*Naval Administrations 1827–1892: The Experience of Sixty-Five Years* (London, 1897).

[3]See ADM1/5591: Admiralty Committee on Revision of Dockyards, Report (Confidential), 14 December 1848, 49 fols. The members of the Committee were civil servant and future Accountant-General of the Navy, Richard Madox Bromley, Surveyor of the Navy Baldwin Walker, Parliamentary Secretary Henry G. Ward, and Milne. See also MLN/155/2: Printed copy of General Board Order and Minutes, 25 January 1849, relating to the revision of HM Dockyards. Milne annotated on cover 'Member of a Committee who for six weeks went round all the Dock Yards & made Enquiry into the working of these establishments; this set of orders & minutes is the outcome'.

forgotten. When the Duke of Northumberland came to office Milne wrote him, bluntly condemning the lack of innovation in the Dockyards [**249**]. Northumberland did not remain in office long enough to act on this proposal, but his successor, Graham, issued a minute [**258**] shortly after his accession which suggests that Milne had raised the subject with him too. Milne subsequently conducted a survey of Devonport Dockyard [**261**], which may have been the consequence of Graham's suggestion. Additionally, he brought before Graham's Board a lengthy series of recommendations [**263**] designed to enhance dockyard efficiency, most of which were adopted.

At about the same time he was first engaged in reporting on dockyard revisions (1849), Milne also turned his attention to ensuring greater oversight and better maintenance of the fleet in commission, as regards both *matériel* and personnel. The result was a pair of Ship Inspection Sheets [**205–6**]. These are so comprehensive – the general inspection sheet contains more than one hundred questions and instructions – that they deserve thorough scrutiny, but it is worth noting that they, especially those relative to steam and steam engines, are another manifestation of Milne's receptivity to technological change. They are also a testament to his desire to regularise the conditions of service, not only through maintaining the material infrastructure, but also personnel. The general inspection sheet, indeed, links together those two overarching problems confronting the Admiralty: technological transformation and the establishment of a modern system of enlisted service. Milne repeatedly stated that one of the chief obstacles to attracting the type of men that the Navy wanted and needed was the capriciousness of shipboard discipline, and the inspection sheet was designed to reveal such. He was equally solicitous that shore leave be regularly granted, that the men's pay and grog money be scrupulously accounted for, and about myriad other details related to the seamen's welfare. Four years later he returned to the subject of shipboard discipline, drafting an Admiralty Circular on Minor Punishments [**264**]. Not trusting entirely to individual officers' moderation, the Circular set clear limits on both the type of punishments permitted and their duration or extent.

Regularising discipline, however, was only one aspect of overhauling the conditions of service. During the late 1840s the Whig Boards on which Milne served began to wrestle with the task of devising a new system of manning the fleet. Instituting Good Conduct Pay was one manifestation of this effort. The whole question of enlistment, however, was of perplexing complexity, and when the Whigs left office in February 1852 the Navy still relied largely on the traditional system of recruitment by individual ships' captains for the duration of a vessel's commission. Milne was not the only Board member to be concerned over this issue, but he alone was kept on by the Tories, and thus played a vital role in ensuring administrative continuity. It was he who urged on Northumberland the appointment of a committee to consider manning the fleet in the summer of 1852 [**238**], and it was he who, aided by Northumberland's willingness to follow his advice [**241**], drafted the committee's instructions [**242**]. The 1852 Manning Committee's report is generally regarded as the first step toward the implementation of a modern continuous service system.[1]

Milne's activities in improving service conditions ranged well beyond those thus far described. He composed a lengthy minute [**208**] on Naval Lord Rear-Admiral James W. D. Dundas's 1849 proposal to reduce sailors' grog ration [**207**]. Although the condition of the executive branches was less frequently under Milne's purview, one notable exception concerned the state of the Officer Lists. Thanks to a vast surplus of officers, coupled with the absence of a mandatory retirement system, the lists remained clogged for decades after the end of the French Wars.[2] Of equal, if not greater concern than the expense of maintaining such a large officer corps, was the problem of glacially slow promotion, especially from Captain upward, where all advancement took place under strict rules of seniority and similarly strict regulations as to the maximum numbers permitted in each rank. By the late 1840s the problem was so acute that there was a shortage of qualified, active, and healthy Flag Officers for the Navy's top commands. Accordingly, Baring's Board turned its attention to the subject in 1850. Rear-Admiral Dundas produced a memorandum embodying his own views on the subject [**218**]. This was printed along with two earlier memoranda by Rear-Admiral William Bowles, who had wrestled with the problem while a member of Lords Haddington's and Ellenborough's Boards [**219–20**]. Bowles himself remained concerned about the topic even after his departure from office and wrote direct to Milne about it in November 1850 [**221**]. Milne himself then addressed the question with characteristic thoroughness in a lengthy memorandum [**222**], which contrasted Dundas's proposals with those introduced in a House of Commons Bill, and Baring's views, before putting for-

[1]See Taylor, 'Manning the Navy, pt. 1, pp. 307–09. See also 'Report on Manning the Navy by a Committee of Naval Officers, correspondence and Order in Council relating thereto,' *Parliamentary Papers*, 1852–53, LX, p. 9. Milne's gloss on the report, the accompanying Sea Militia Bill, and the probable cost of implementing the committee's recommendations can be found in [**256–7**].

[2]On this subject, see John Beeler, '"Fit for Service Abroad": Promotion, Retirement, and Royal Navy Officers, 1830–1890', *Mariner's Mirror*, 81 (1995), pp. 300–312.

ward his own recommendations. The meticulousness with which he calculated, among other things, the probable number of deaths among Flag Officers during the 1850s suggests more than passing familiarity with actuarial tables.

There were, in addition, other subjects on which he composed minutes or memoranda while at the Admiralty. Indeed, he seems frequently to have brought subjects to the Board's attention on his own volition, for instance urging the establishment of an Admiralty Library[1] in 1851 [**223**] and composing a minute on an 1852 Committee Report on the practicality of arming merchant steamers in wartime [**251**]. Curiously, too, he was assigned to draft two sets of orders for expeditions searching for Sir John Franklin and his men [**259**, **260**] in April 1853 and[,] in December of that year, when any hope of finding Franklin alive had faded, he submitted a minute questioning whether the vanished officers' names should be removed from the Navy List [**268**].

Another notable aspect of Milne's Admiralty service is suggested by his keeping the manning question before the Board's attention following a change in government. In this instance he functioned as what we would today call the Admiralty's 'institutional memory'. It was by no means a lone occurrence. In March 1852, soon after Northumberland took office, Milne drafted a list of Admiralty priorities [**237**] which summarised the previous Board's concerns. That same month he composed a memorandum detailing what had been contemplated with regard to the search for Franklin [**236**]. More prosaically, he furnished the Tory Board with two memoranda instructing them as to the purpose and protocol of Dockyard Visitations [**244–5**]. And when Graham took office Milne sent him a lengthy confidential minute on Entry and Promotion of men in the Dockyards, a minute informed not only by the Whigs' attempt to introduce merit promotion in the late 1840s, but also by the Tories' manipulation of entry and promotion for political purposes during Derby's short 1852 ministry [**255**].

[1]Those who have utilised the outstanding Admiralty Library collection (now part of the Ministry of Defence Library) should appreciate Milne's hand in bringing it into existence.

[173] *Milne to Napier*

London
16 December 1847

My dear Sir

The arrival of the Mail at Lisbon will[,] I think[,] cause you and the Squadron as much a surprise from the news it conveys, as I was on my arrival at Portsmouth on the afternoon of the 14th, When [*sic*] I heard I had not only been named for the Admiralty[,] but Her Majesty's sanction had been obtained[,] and that the further arrangements only required my consent. To this, of course, so highly flattering and honourable to myself, I could not say 'nay' and[,] for the purpose of seeing Lord Auckland[,] came to town early yesterday morning when the matter was finally arranged and the Patent ordered to be made . . . with all possible haste. I am so much surprised and astonished at this matter[,] which has come upon me so unlooked for[,] that I do not know from what source it can have originated or to whom I owe so deep a tribute of gratitude for having brought forward my name. To you[,] I am aware[,] I owe much and perhaps this extraordinary mark of the Admiraltys approbation may have in some measure originated with you. If so[,] pray accept my warmest acknowledgements[,] for I shall indeed ever feel grateful for the very handsome and flattering manner with which you have always treated me, since I had the proud position of serving under your Flag. I can assure you[,] your approval of my conduct[,] so publicly expressed before I gave up the Command of the *St. Vincent*[,] affected me most deeply[,] and my feelings were much gratified to think that[,] in the discharge of my duty[,] I had given you satisfaction, ever the most pleasing reflection which an officer can have when he serves under a superior.

I enter upon my new station with hesitation and[,] I may say[,] pain[.] it is so entirely different from my former life that I feel an inward foreboding of the future[,] but I enter with full determination to do my duty and use [*sic*] my utmost exertions to give satisfaction. I trust it may be so. Lord Auckland received me in the most cordial and kind manner and he assured me my name had been unanimously elected [*sic*][,] and independent of all political feeling.

The *Montrose* brought me home in quick style[.] we went 9 or 10 knots the whole way from Vigo and we were 73 hours from thence to the Needles[.] of news I can give you none, <u>at present</u>[,] as I dare say

Admiral Dundas[1] will drop you a line. Charles Eden[2] goes to the *Victory* in my place. I have made a terrible scrawl of this[,] but I am writing at my lodging in [*sic*] a December morning in England and in London[,] precious cold and disagreeable[,] and I am afraid my feelings have partaken of the same. Pray therefore excuse the hurried note[,] for I am off to Portsmouth immediately[.] be assured[,] however[,] that if I am incapable of expressing[,] I am capable of feeling the great kindness and attention which I have always received from you[,] and will ever look back with great pride [on the time] when I had the honour of serving as your Flag Captain [*sic*] . . .

[**174**] *Milne to Napier*

Admiralty
26 December 1847

My Dear Sir

I have at last commenced my duties here and feel most anxious[,] as you may well suppose[,] to carry them out with all diligence and zeal[,] but as yet matters appear so complicated in the details that I cannot see my way. Somerset House business is chiefly in my department[,] and the Store business and Transports the most requiring attention. I recollect what you said relative to 'Freight'[,] and will have a look into it if possible, but I hear these good people don't like their affairs to be looked into. The ship which brought the Provisions to Lisbon has a Charter party and could have been detained 40 days. He must have been a great rogue to have talked about demurrage after 12 days' detention. The *Terrible* is reported ready about the 1st[,] but I suspect she will be much longer before she is quite ready to rejoin your Flag; she had upwards of 2000 new Tubes in her Boilers. I am not aware of any news to give you but[,] as Lord Auckland has gone to drop you a line[,] you will hear all from Head Quarters. Mr Rogers[3] and Dickson[4] are promoted, also [the] Senior Lieutenant of *Caledonia*.[5]

[1]First Naval Lord James Whitley Deans Dundas.

[2]Charles Eden, C.B., K.C.B. (1808–78). Entered, *c*.1820; Lt, 1832; Cmdr, 1834; Capt. 1841; Rear-Adm., 1861; Vice-Adm., 1866; Adm. (Ret.), 1873; Naval Lord of the Admiralty, 1859–66.

[3]Henry Downing Rogers (*c*.1816–67). Entered, *c*.1828; Lt, 1837; Cmdr, 1847; Capt., 1854. Rogers was promoted to Commander on 23 December.

[4]John B. Dickson (1815–76). Entered *c*.1827; Lt, 1839; Cmdr, 1848; Capt., 1854; Rear-Adm., 1870; Rear-Adm. (Ret.) 1879. Dickson, *Caledonia*'s Commander, was promoted to that rank on 4 February.

[5]John Barnes (*c*.1790–1874). Entered, 1802; Lt, 1813, Cmdr, 1847; Capt. (Ret.), 1861. Barnes was promoted to Commander on 23 December.

Your Mail from Lisbon has not arrived and therefore you will not get answers by this Mail. With reference to the expenditure of Rope on the Plan you proposed[,] will you order a Survey to be held on the 31st December, and take on charge [*sic*] what remains to be expended according to your plan and[,] if you wish, an order will be sent out for the purpose[,] and likewise what rope you may wish on demand[.] I find no official notice has been taken of it here[.] Pray accept my best wishes . . . with many happy returns of the season . . .
The Board are or will be all out of Town this day[.]

[**175**] *Napier to Milne*

HMS *St. Vincent*, Lisbon
31 December 1847

My dear Milne

I congratulate you on your appointment to the Admiralty. I had nothing to do with it except having always had great pleasure in stating of you in my commendations as I thought you deserved[,] and I believe that you have seen enough of me to know that I never would praise an officer unless he deserved it. You must expect a great deal of heart burning amongst your seniors[,] but that cannot be helped. We have had a dull R's [*sic*] cruize with *Albion*[,] which has done us all good[,] but I wanted to have had her in a strong breeze with a sea; you will see my reports and also the private letters to Dundas and others. It is of no use repeating them here.

The *St. Vincent* is certainly very much improved in every respect and without a doubt the least rotten of the lot. She was caught in a heavy squall[,] Cdr Rushbrooke's[1] watch[,] and went over 20° – Courses and Top Gallant sails set. There is not one officer in the *St. Vincent* fit to take charge of a watch.

We broke our Hawsers in tow of *Dragon* and were obliged to make sail . . . and beat the ship beautifully, tacking 12 times, and then anchored after dark between *Canopus* and *Queen* and never moved[.] *Canopus* was as usual ½ a point out of her station. Biddlecomb[2] told me unless the ship was worked by the Commander or Captain he would not take her in . . . He is a valuable officer[,] much superior to Rogers[,] who is sulky[,] but I have not yet fallen foul of him.

[1]William Henry Rushbrooke (*c.*1815–83). Entered, 1829; Lt, 1841; Cmdr (Ret.), 1864. Rushbrooke was *St Vincent's* Acting Commander.

[2]Sir George Biddlecomb, Kt., C.B. (d. 1878). Master, 1835; Cmdr, 1860; Capt. (Ret.), 1867. *St Vincent's* Master.

I think in a little while we shall beat them all. I am also much pleased with Dacres[,][1] who is very zealous[,] and I think I have made a good choice. Be sure to send our stores[,] as we are getting short of Rope. *Queen*, tho' reported as the others were, with a twelvemonths stores in [*sic*], was reported by Bruce[2] to have sailed with 8 months. I do hope the Admiralty will give the Knight[3] a dressing [*sic*]. He deserves it. I am disgusted with his newspaper puffing and still more disgusted with Schomberg[4] [*sic*] puffing him in his speech.[5] I believe every officer and man in the ship were [*sic*] glad to get rid of him. Set the Admiralty right about the superiority of *Caledonia*[,] and now *Queen* has got rid of her harbour contrivances[,] which Bruce is very properly doing away [*sic*], she is not smarter than the others. *St. Vincent* will very soon beat them all. I hope the Admiralty will not promote that fool Ogle.[6] They had better keep his place open for Harper[7] and let him remain a Commander all his life. He has already got too much.

We have surveyed all our rope and begun on the 1st January [*sic*] the system I recommended and which Prescott[8] told me to carry out in *St. Vincent*.

I hope he has made a minute of it[,] otherwise it may cause a difficulty in passing Dacres accounts. I am quite sure it will cause more care and expense.

Dacres and Ozzard[9] desire to be remembered to you.

[1]Sidney Colpoys Dacres, C.B., K.C.B., G.C.B. (1806–84). Entered, 1817; Lt, 1827; Cmdr, 1834; Capt., 1840; Rear-Adm., 1858; Vice-Adm., 1865; Adm., 1870; Naval Lord of the Admiralty, 1866–68; First Naval Lord, 1868–72. Dacres replaced Milne as Napier's Flag Captain.

[2]Henry W. Bruce, K.C.B. (1792–1863). Entered, 1803; Lt, 1810; Cmdr, 1814; Capt., 1821; Rear-Adm., 1852; Vice-Adm., 1857; Adm., 1863.

[3]Napier was referring to Sir Henry John Leeke, Kt., K.H., K.C.B. (*c*.1791–1870). Entered, 1803; Lt, 1810; Cmdr, 1814; Capt., 1826; Rear-Adm., 1854; Vice-Adm., 1860; Adm., 1864. Leeke was *Queen*'s previous Captain, and had extolled her sailing qualities. See 'Copies of all Reports and other Information received from Vice-Admiral Sir William Parker and Rear-Admiral Sir Charles Napier, on the Sailing and other Qualities of Her Majesty's Ships "*Queen*" and "*Albion*"', *Parliamentary Papers*, 1847–48, vol. XLI, p. 308.

[4]Charles Frederick Schomberg (*c*.1817–74). Entered, 1829; Lt, 1838; Cmdr, 1844; Capt., 1851; Rear-Adm. (Ret.), 1867; Vice-Adm. (Ret.), 1873. Schomberg was Acting Second Captain to Sir Henry Leeke in *Queen*.

[5]*The Times* contains no reference to a speech by Schomberg.

[6]Graham Ogle.

[7]Napier probably meant George Harper (*c*.1816–50). Entered, *c*.1828; Lt, 1837; Cmdr, 1847.

[8]Sir Henry Prescott. Prescott, who was briefly (20 July–23 December 1847) on the Board of Admiralty, was the same individual whom Milne had encountered six years previously as Governor of Newfoundland.

[9]James W. Ozzard (1818–1902). Passed Clerk, 1838; Paymaster, 1845; Paymaster-in-Chief (Ret.), 1872; Napier's secretary on HMS *St Vincent*.

[**176**] *Napier to Milne*

HMS *St. Vincent*, Lisbon
9 January 1848

My dear Milne

You will have enough to do to dive into all the Somerset House business. I am quite aware there is jobbery there about the Contracts . . .

I hope you will send out our Stores[,] for we are beginning to get short and any merchant ship can bring them out without freighting a ship. I expect *Terrible* every day but I do not hear whether she is to remain here or not.

Schomberg has written out here to deny his speech[,] so I suppose Leeke concocted it himself.

I hope you will put all that to rights at the Admiralty and let them know when I mustered '*Queen*' I was obliged to order her to be drilled. No order has yet come out for the Inspecting Admiral to examine the Officers. I know I have the power to do it[,] but I am doing so much here that they are quite unaccustomed to that. the [*sic*] officers may think I am pushing them too hard and get disgusted. it [*sic*] is always better for the Admiralty to strengthen one's hands.

We are getting on very well and I think ere long this will be a most perfect Squadron. Rushbrooke nearly upset the old Ship the other day. she [*sic*] went over to 20°, under double-reefed Topsails, Courses and Topgallant Sails.

Rogers is made. I am glad of it, for he had some disagreeable qualities. I wish you would look out for a good first Lieutenant and one worthy of promotion. I have applied for Kinsman[1] and if they would remove Rushbrooke he would do; it is not right that a Flag Ship should not have one Lieutenant at least who is a Seaman. Rushbrooke is much disappointed[,] but I desired Dacres to tell him he was not fit for it. I have heard from Phelps'[2] Brother that his commission has not been sent out to him. I fear there is some jobbery in this. pray [*sic*] look to it. The Step of *Amphion*'s mast has given way. I am doctoring it. Let me hear from you and make my best regards to Lady Milne . . .

[1]Hugh Mallett Kinsman (*c*.1820–47). Entered, *c*.1832; Lt, 1841. Kinsman was First Lt in HMS *Avenger*, Dacres' ship prior to his appointment to *St Vincent*. He lost his life when *Avenger* sank on 20 December 1847.

[2]Henry Phelps (*c*.1820–1905). Entered, 1832; Lt, 1842; Cmdr, 1849; Capt., 1864; Capt. (Ret.), 1881. Phelps was Mate of HMS *Powerful*, Napier's ship at St Jean d'Acre in 1840, and had been appointed *St Vincent*'s Flag Lt on 2 June 1847.

[**177**] *Milne to Napier*

Admiralty, Private
16 January 1848

My dear Sir Charles

Many thanks for your letter[,] which I received late last evening[,] and I now write you a few hurried lines for this morning's Mail[,] which you will receive in a few days. I would have almost passed over in silence the late awful catastrophe which has caused so much sorrow and distress[,] but I must not let this leave me without offering my sincere condolences on the occasion; how little do we see before us and[,] when I last saw you[,] how little did we contemplate what has taken place.[1] It is an awful circumstance and has caused universal sorrow throughout this country[.] how little indeed do we know our own ways, and whether we go fast or slow. I am much afraid all hope of other survivors is now over[,] since the *Hecate* returned to Malta. I will[,] I can assure you[,] be very anxious to follow out your views with reference to freight. I have paid some attention to the subject and[,] as far as I can see[,] all is fair and correct for Stores &c, as in the case of the Transport to Lisbon; public advertizement is made and it is open to all parties to send in Tenders for the conveyance of so many Tons to the place required. These Tenders are opened in my presence and I accept the lowest tender, provided I consider the Ship fit for the purpose. The Admiralty have only to pay the sum per Ton to the place[,] and there is then an end of the transaction[,] and the Ship proceeds on her own business. 'The ship itself is not freighted[,] but only taken up to land so many Tons of Stores at such places as are required.' This is followed out for all Stores, Provisions &c[,] and many ships have been taken up within the last month to all parts of the world.

The Somerset House business is very heavy and responsible, more especially that part which relates to the enormous Contracts for Timber, and combinations exist to a great extent. Not a single tender was offered for English Oak on the 13th[,] because it is in the hands of one Man[,] who acts as an Agent to all the Timber dealers in England, and the question is how to upset this and get the Timber. it [*sic*] is a serious question[,] and the Board must settle what is to be done this week. The Stores for the Ships[,] according to Demand[,] were sent out in *Terrible*

[1]Milne was referring to the loss of HMS *Avenger*, which ran aground on 20 December 1847 on the Sorelli Rocks, southwest of Eoleba Island, while en route from Gibraltar to Malta. Only eight of 270 on board survived. Napier's stepson Charles Elers-Napier, *Avenger*'s Captain, was among those drowned.

and whenever you want anything I will take care they are sent out by the first opportunity. They must be kept in check[,] as in the Demands[,] for instance for Paint, Oil &c in comet [*sic*] was contemplated 25 Nov[embe]r and demands again [were made] in Dec[embe]r. I am very anxious to do what is right[,] and am determined to keep down the enormous increasing expense upon the Store Dept, from giving way to all sorts of people with patent inventions[,] who look upon the Govt as fair game. It is abominable to see the sums of money laid out in nonsense. Mr Porter[1] is in a devil of a way and has been at me[,] because I will not allow any more of his Anchors to be demanded at present. Rogers[2] was inclined to be abusive the other day because I would not give him an order to supply Deptford Yard[,] and it is extraordinary the round about way they get at information from the D[oc]k Yards and Ships abroad; they have correspondents in your Squadron, and I begin to find out who are the writers. I will look out for a 1st Lieut, and will take care no jobs are carried out with reference to the appointment. There is nothing doing here at present. it [*sic*] is an odd system, everyone works independently in his own dept and you know little what is going on. this [*sic*] is all wrong[,] but I suppose cannot be remedied. I mention all this privately by you [*sic*]. The plan of improved *Sidon*[3] has been sent out to you for your opinion. it [*sic*] will require you to consider it well. The great increase of beam and length appears to me unnecessary[,] and I am of opinion our Steamers are really becoming very unwieldy. in [*sic*] the event of their being attached to Fleets[,] I should say Vessels of 1000 Tons are in every respect sufficiently large[,] and to be considered heavy Gun Boats, at the same time fit for towing. those [*sic*] again for detached service should be about 300 Tons larger, and capable of transporting Troops. It is proposed to have a Steam reserve at each Port[,] & I have been drawing up an Establishment for the purpose[,] also regulating a new arrangement of the Ordinary and Reserve Ship[s] to be ready for sea, but the demur [*sic*] is it requires 360 more men in each Harbour. It must be obvious where you have so many valuable steamers in Ordinary, but ready for sea, you must have Officers and Men to take charge of them, but this has nearly stopped the business. whether [*sic*] it will grow [i.e., go forward] I do not know. I have proposed *Victory* as at present 172 men, Ordinary by itself and for no other purpose 450 men, Reserve Ship 120 [guns], with a complement of 400, *Blenheim* 190 men, to

[1]Patent holder and manufacturer of an anchor with the flukes mounted on a pivot – a 'tumbling fluke' anchor.

[2]Another anchor manufacturer.

[3]*Sidon* had been designed by Napier. See Lambert, *Battleships in Transition*, p. 20.

keep her clean and attached to her 6 other [*sic*] Steamers with 100 men in all. this [*sic*] includes Engineers and Stokers[.] Riggers in D[oc]k Yard subject to enter when wanted[:] 300 men. this is all private. this [*sic*] is the lowest possible limit[,] and yet the expense is complained of. as [*sic*] I told Lord A[uckland][,] to have such an Establishment, expense must be incurred, especially when we look at the cost of the Steamers and Machinery.

I have sent you a cask of Beer which I hope will reach you in safety . . .

[**178**] *Napier to Milne*

HMS *St. Vincent*, Lisbon
29 January 1848

My dear Milne

I thank you for your kind condolence. it [*sic*] is a melancholy subject and I shall say no more, except that we must bear up against it till time softens down our afflictions.

You will get the Contracts for Coal[,] Beef and Vegetables much cheaper than before. Why send out Bread here when we could at least save the Freight by getting it baked[?] would not wine also be cheaper than spirits?

Terrible brought us nothing but an Anchor for '*Canopus*'. so [*sic*] much for Laing's[1] [*sic*] fine Steamer. I have written to *Comet* to account for demanding Paint. I rather like each Lord working in his own Department, but when in doubt he can go before the Board.

I have got the plan for a new *Sidon* but I cannot Fathom it. it [*sic*] is not what I want. *Sidon* requires a little more stability and a little more room for a Frigate. one [*sic*] foot broader and 10 longer would I think do this. rising [*sic*] the floor a little, and a little more run would recompense [*sic*] the foot more beam in speed. I want no other change, at least I would not risk it. but [*sic*] this is an entire new plan, with a rising floor and only a 400 Horse [Power] Engine[.] now if this answers[,] she will be a much finer ship in all respects than *Sidon*, will carry more Coal by a great deal[,] and will be a wonderful ship[,] and I shall be delighted, but I feel quite certain she will not have the speed of '*Sidon*'. we [*sic*] are too fond of changes. we [*sic*] have a good vessel and I want that good vessel made better, but I do not think this will do it. Fincham[2] built *Odin* and *Sidon*. he [*sic*] has been told their faults and

[1]Oliver Lang, Master Shipwright at Woolwich Dockyard.
[2]John Fincham, Master Shipwright at Portsmouth Dockyard.

I think he can correct them, but I am sure this plan will not do it. they [*sic*] ought to know better than me, but I don't know how it has happened [*sic*]. they [*sic*] never succeed; if they cannot improve *Sidon* they had better let her alone[,] but both Henderson[1] and myself think she can be improved and we both agreed about the means of doing it. we [*sic*] may be wrong, and the Committee may be right, and I hope they are. I quite agree with you no Steamer unless a regular Frigate should be more than 1000 Tons and that even is too much.

I am sorry you are arranging the *Victory* as you are doing. it [*sic*] is neither so efficient or [*sic*] so economical as what might be[,] and what I mentioned to you. you [*sic*] say there is to be in *Victory* 172 men[,] and 450 to take care of the Ordinary[, &] a Reserve Ship with 400 men of 120 Guns. there [*sic*] is the Guard Ship system again. What I propose is this – take a 120 Gun Ship <u>efficient</u> for the Admiral, put into her the 450 men or more, to manage the Ordinary. Should you require an augmentation of the Channel Squadron (which I take for granted will be kept up)[,] I would order the Admiral and all of his officers and ordinary men to be turned over to another efficient 120 Gun Ship[,] and let him fit her out. a [*sic*] new Captain and officers should be appointed to the Ship he leaves, the Marines put on board[,] and the Boys[,] which you can always get, and the ship[,] being perfectly ready for sea and no work to do[,] the men would readily enter, and your Channel fleet would be reinforced by 3 sail of the line [*sic*] in no time.

Should you be in a great hurry[,] the 300 Riggers you mention would go from the Dock-Yard[,] and they should all be prime Seamen, with good Pay, which they ought to hold while embarked[,] and they should be considered the <u>Elite</u>.

Your system of *Blenheim* and Steamers attached to her is good, this plan will save you the *Victory* and her 172 men, and the Reserve Ship with the 400[,] who will be much better at sea increasing the crews of your Squadron of Evolutions [*sic*], and if half their Marines were on shore in peace and filled up with Sailors[,] on a sudden emergency you might turn one watch into another Ship, fill both up with Officers, Marines and Boys[,] and you would at once double your efficient force. The Marines put on shore would garrison the Sea-Port Towns and when they marched on board[,] the Militia should march in and take their place. turn [*sic*] this over in your mind and give me your opinion. I send you a couple of Biscuits . . .

[1]William Honyman Henderson, C.B., K.S.F. (*c*.1796–1855). Entered, 1808; Lt, 1820; Cmdr, 1835; Capt., 1838. Henderson was *Sidon*'s captain from August 1846 through March 1849 and had commanded several other steam vessels.

PS I am sorry to say we have got the Small Pox on board, and have between 30 and 40 men at the Hospital[,] and all the Fleet pretty nearly have the Influenza.
Many thanks for the Cask of Ale.

[**179**] *Milne Paper Relative to the New Establishment of the Ordinary & Steam Reserve*

Admiralty
1 February 1848[1]

Your Lordship having called upon me for an opinion with reference to the Harbour and Ordinary Establishment at the Home Ports, I beg to submit the following observations on the subject and would first draw your attention to the Flag Ships of the Comdrs in Chief[.] It has[,] I believe[,] been admitted that when these ships were considered as Effective Sea going ships, much inconvenience was Experienced [*sic*] by the removal of the respective Flag Captains[,] and the Harbour duties were transferred to the Flag Ships of the Ordinary to prevent a recurrence of this Evil[.] The Establishments of the Comdrs in Chief have been transferred to non Effective ships[,] viz. the *Victory* at Ports[mouth], the *Ocean* at Sheerness[,] and the *San Josef* at Devonport, and a Complement of 172 Men & Boys has been Established for Each as per the List in the Margin [not preserved], adequate in Every respect to carry on the Port duties[,] which consist in Embarking new raised men, Marines, Troops &s[,] Hospital Day Boats, rowing Guard, &c. I do not consider it advisable that the crews of these ships should ever be drafted to fill up the Compl[emen]ts of other ships, but that the men should be allowed to volunteer for ships fitting out after having been on the Flag Ships Books above 6 months, and it would be a great boon to allow men to enter for these Flag Ships who had been long on Foreign Stations & were anxious to have a run [*sic*] of the Shore for a few months.

These ships should likewise be the Education ships for the training of Boys for the Navy[,] and are admirably suited for the purpose.

Your Lordship having named the Establishment of a Reserved [i.e., ready-reserve] Ship of the Line at Ports[mou]th[,] the same as the *Caledonia* now is at Devonport, It [*sic*] becomes a matter of consideration what should be the Established Complement for Harbour Service[,]

[1]Two earlier drafts of this paper are found among Milne's own papers, and he revealed some of his thoughts to Napier in his letter of 16 January 1848, [**177**].

and at the sametime [*sic*] to keep the Ship so far advanced and prepared for Service[.]

The Ship should of course be Entirely [*sic*] rigged and her Guns on Board[,] so far as the Harbour will admit with reference to the draft of water. She should be ready to go out of Harbour at a few hours notice[,] and this should be always kept in view by the Comdg Officer[.] To keep a ship in this state of forwardness will require a considerable complement[,] especially if it is intended that she should go to Sea in the Summer months. I do not think that a smaller Compl[emen]t than 350 or 400 men can be named[,] and even then 450 men would be required to fill up her Compl[emen]t when ordered to sea[,] if it is to be a 1st Rate[,] and a difficulty may arise from whence this number of men is to be obtained without taking from the *Excellent*.

This Reserved Ship it is proposed should carry the Flag of the Adml Superintendent and be commanded by the Captain of the Ordinary during the period the Ship is in Harbour[,] but to have – a Commander app[oin]t[e]d to her for Service at Sea with —— Lieutenants, Master & 2 Medical Officers – 2 Sec Masters & 3 regular warrant officers[.]

Portsmouth[:]
The present Establishment at Portsmouth with reference to the Flag Ship and the Ordinary. It is proposed to alter this[,] from the inconvenience which has been found to exist when the duties of the Ordinary are combined with an Active Ship. [see the table opposite]

The *Victory* Establishment which should remain as at present

Officers	Petty Officers	Extra Petty Officers	A.B.&c.	1st Class Boys	2nd Class Boys	Marines	Idlers	Engineers	Stokers	Whole Complement
22	15	–	49	6	24	50	7	–	–	172[1]

The *Excellent* Establishment also to remain as at present[:]

Officers	Petty Officers	Extra Petty Officers	A.B.&c.	1st Class Boys	2nd Class Boys	Marines	Idlers	Engineers	Stokers	Whole Complement
81	10	–	370	109	34	61	27	–	–	692

The Ordinary Estab[lishmen]t within the *Blenheim*[,] which it is proposed to change[:]

Officers	Petty Officers	Extra Petty Officers	A.B.&c.	1st Class Boys	2nd Class Boys	Marines	Idlers	Engineers	Stokers	Whole Complement
24	19	30	451	–	108	41	11	–	–	684

Tenders *Fancy* & *Mercury*[,] The Royal Yacht & *Fairy*[,] not named or *Undine*[:][2]

Officers	Petty Officers	Extra Petty Officers	A.B.&c.	1st Class Boys	2nd Class Boys	Marines	Idlers	Engineers	Stokers	Whole Complement
2	2	–	19	–	–	–	–	–	–	23

[1]Milne's figures for the complement to be borne on both *Victory* and *San Josef* (see below) add up to 173 rather than 172.

[2]Milne was apparently in doubt as to the ship to be chosen to round out Portsmouth's complement of auxiliary vessels; in other words, either *Undine* or an as-yet unnamed ship would fill that slot.

Old Estab[lishmen]t[:]

Officers	Petty Officers	Extra Petty Officers	A.B.&c.	1st Class Boys	2nd Class Boys	Marines	Idlers	Engineers	Stokers	Whole Complement
129	46	30	889	115	166	152	45	–	–	1571[1]

New Arrangement. It is proposed that the *Victory* and *Excellent* should remain as above, But [*sic*] that the Ordinary and the Effective ship should be entirely independent of Each [*sic*] other. That an Ord[inar]y Ship for the Captain should be Estab[lishe]d[,] and that the number of men for the Ord[inar]y duties should be brought down to the lowest possible limit depending on the No of ships in Harbour[,] viz. about 60. [see first line of following table]

That men for the duties to be entered solely for the duty of the Ord[i]n[ar]y[,] and not to be removed to any other ship[,] and the men so entered ought to be steady elderly people who have pensions or long servitude[,] provided they are active and of good character[.] it will require the Captain to live on board & the ship to be moored in a Central position in the H[arbou]r Estab[lishmen]t.

The *Britannia* to be commissnd with a Captain, Comdr, 3 Lieuts &c[,] as per sheet[,] and to be considered a ship in all respects ready for sea. This will require sufficient crew to make a foundation for a Ships Co and will require – [second line]

The *Blenheim* to be Commissnd by a Comdr for the Superintendence of the Steam Reserve in the Harbour[,] and the Men required for them [*sic*] to be borne on the *Blenheims* Books. This Estab[lishmen]t must have such a number of men as will ensure due care of the valuable Engines &c. I cannot see that the *Blenheim* can do with less than – [third line]

And Each Steamer will require a number of Stokers &c[,] the accomp[an]y[in]g scale is for six – [fourth line]

New Establishment [fifth line]

Old Establishment [sixth line]

Difference [seventh line]

[1]Should be 1,572 owing to the miscalculation in the number of men and officers in *Victory*.

	Officers	Petty Officers	Extra Petty Officers	A.B. &c.	1st Class Boys	2nd Class Boys	Marines	Idlers	Engineers	Stokers	Whole Complement
Ordinary Ship	17	10	30	228	–	110	25	10	–	–	430
Britannia	25	34	–	227	15	20	70	9	–	–	400
Blenheim	11	10	–	26[1]	10	10	20	4	2	7	100[2]
6 Additional steamers	12	12	–	24	–	18	–	6	6	24	90[3]
New Establishment	158	93	30	943	140	216	226	63	8	31	1907[4]
Old Establishment	129	46	30	889	115	166	152	45	–	–	1571[5]
Difference	29	47	–	54	25	50	74	18	8	31	336[6]

[1]Milne originally put down ‘26’, but wrote in ‘50’ above it.

[2]Milne wrote ‘150’ in the margin beside ‘100’.

[3]Milne wrote ‘240’ in the margin beside ‘90’. 90 is also erroneous; he evidently failed to count either the 12 officers or 12 petty officers; the correct figure is 102.

[4]Milne’s sums for the New Establishment contain several minor errors; 1) the total figure of 1,907 is erroneous firstly because the number borne on *Victory* should be 173 rather than 172, and that on the six additional steamers 102 rather than 90. The total, therefore, is 1,897 if the number of A.B.s aboard *Blenheim* is figured at 26, or 1,921 if 50. 2) The number of officers in the New Establishment is 168 rather than 158; the number of Petty Officers 91 instead of 93; and the number of A.B.s is 924 if counting 26 on *Blenheim* and 948 if counting 50. By adding the correct sums along this line one arrives at the same figures as reached by adding the vertical column of the whole complement, i.e., either 1,897 or 1,921, depending how many A.B.s are credited to *Blenheim*.

[5]Should be 1,572.

[6]Owing to Milne’s miscalculations in the New Establishment, the difference in officers should be 39 rather than 29, that of petty officers 45 rather than 47, and that of A.B.s either 35 (assuming 26 aboard *Blenheim*) or 59 (assuming 50). The total difference, therefore, would be either 325 or 349, depending how many A.B.s were borne on *Blenheim*.

Note, I think the No. of men & Boys might be reduced in the Ord[inar]y Estab[lishmen]t[,] but it must depend on investigation on the spot.

Devonport[:]
The present Establishment at Devonport consists of the *San Josef* as the Flag Ship[,] with the *Caledonia* and the Ordinary Combined and the following is the present Establishment[,] which it is proposed to alter[,] in consequence of the great inconvenience of having an Efficient ship [?intermixed] with duties of the Ordinary[.]
<u>The San Josef</u> as Flag Ship to the Commander in Chief[,] the Estab[lishmen]t to remain as at present. – [first line of the following table]
<u>The Ordinary Establishment</u> with the '*Caledonia*' as an Effective Ship. – [second line]
<u>Tenders. Sylph & Netley</u>[.][third line]

	Officers	Petty Officers	Extra Petty Officers	A.B. &c.	1st Class Boys	2nd Class Boys	Marines	Idlers	Engineers	Stokers	Whole Complement
San Josef	22	15	–	49	6	24	50	7	–	–	172
Ordinary Establishment	24	19	30	471	–	108	41	11	–	–	704
Tenders *Sylph & Netley*	1	2	–	18	–	–	–	–	–	–	[21]
Old Establishment	47	36	30	538	6	132	91	18	–	–	876[1]

[1]Should be 898. Milne evidently failed to include the 21 officers and men aboard the tenders, and figured *San Josef* as carrying 172, rather than 173. 172 plus 704 equals 876, but if the figures along the bottom line are added up the figure is 898.

New Arrangement[:]

It is proposed that the *San Josef* should remain on the present Establishment, but that the Effective Ships should be entirely separated and independent of the Ordinary. That a ship should be Established for the Ordinary[,] and the Captain to live on board of her[,] and to be moored in a central position in the Harbour. [first line of following table]
That the Ships Co of this ship should be reduced to the lowest possible limit[,] and they should not be drafted into other ships, but retained entirely for the duties of the Ordinary ships. The Establishment to be [– second line]
The Caledonia to be kept ready for service as a reserve ship[,] and her Complt to be [– third line]
The Establishment for a Screw Ship of the Line under the Comd of a Commander[,] as at Portsmouth, and an establishment for a reserve of Steamers to be attached to this ships[,] Say for six vessels [– fourth and fifth lines]
New Estab[lishmen]t [– sixth line]
Old Estabt [– seventh line]
Difference [– eighth line]

	Officers	Petty Officers	Extra Petty Officers	A.B. &c.	1st Class Boys	2nd Class Boys	Marines	Idlers	Engineers	Stokers	Whole Complement
Ordinary Ship	1	2	–	18	–	–	–	–	–	–	[21]
Ordinary Establishment	17	10	30	228	–	110	25	10	–	–	430
Caledonia	25	34	–	227	15	20	70	9	–	–	400

Establishment For Screw Ship of the Line	11	10	–	26	10	10	20	4	2	7	100[1]
Six Additional Steamers	–	12	–	24	–	18	–	6	6	24	90
New Establishment	76	83	30	572	31	182	165	36	8	31	1192[2]
Old Establishment	47	36	30	538	6	132	91	18	–	–	876[3]
Difference	29	47	–	34	25	50	74	18	8	31	316

Note, I think the number of Men may be reduced in the Ordinary and also the number of Boys[,] but this subject would require investigation on the spot.

[1]Milne pencilled in 50 above this figure and calculated in the margin, also in pencil, as if 150 were the number.

[2]This figure, like that for Portsmouth, calculates the total on the basis of 172 men in *San Josef* and moreover omits the 21 men and officers in the Ordinary Ship. The correct figure is 1,214, as is seen by adding the numbers along the bottom line.

[3]Should be 898. The difference – 316 – is unchanged.

[**180**] *Milne Paper on Superintendence of the Portsmouth Steam Reserve*[1]

[Admiralty
1 February 1848]

Capt Austin[2] should be made acquainted that he is app[oin]t[e]d to the *Blenheim* for the purpose of superintending the reserve Steamers which will be attached to that ship at Portsmouth[.] at the sametime [*sic*][,] it is not their Lordships intention that he should be removed from the duties which he has heretofore performed Equipping &c in the trials of all new Steamers[,] and for the purpose of his carrying on these duties[,] a Comdr has been appointed to the *Blenheim*[,] to whom will be intrusted the general supervision of the Steam reserve under the orders of Cap Austin[,] whose absence will be required at Woolwich [*sic*].

Their Lordships views with reference to the Steam reserve are that six or more steamers are to be attached on [*sic*] the *Blenheim*[,] whose Ships Co of officers & men is to be so distributed as to take due care and charge of the said vessels, and Cap. A[ustin] is to apply to the Comdr in Chief for two warrant officers for each steamer[,] to be sent to the *Blenheim* for the care of those steamers which will be included in the 2d Class. Those of the 1st Class should have their regular warrant officers appointed.

Their Lordships consider that the *Blenheim* should be kept in every respect ready for service, Her [*sic*] running gear and sails fitted, Gun gear complete and water filled, Half [*sic*] her quantity of Coal on board[,] and in every respect prepared for being sent to sea at short notice, Having [*sic*] provisions on board for six weeks and kept up for that time.

The reserve steamers of the 1[st] Class to consist of 2 vessels[,] one as a Captain['s,] the other as a Comdrs[,] command. These two ships with their Estab[lishe]t[e]d warrant officers to be ready for sea, stores on board. Running rigging[,] after being rove [*sic*] and fitted[,] to be placed below, sails fitted & one sail on board [*sic*][,] gun gear fitted & complete[,] Boats on board and Half their stowage of Coal[,] but no Provisions. They are to be kept in a perfect state of efficiency.

2d Class. Six vessels to be kept in a forward state with their Running rigging all cut out[,] fitted[,] and deposited with all their fitted sails[,] in a Store at the Dock Yard[,] gun gear fitted[.] The Boats to be selected and

[1]This memorandum bears no date, but clearly accompanies the foregoing.

[2]Horatio Thomas Austin C.B., K.C.B. (*c*.1801–1865). Entered, 1813; Lt, 1822; Cmdr, 1831; Capt. 1838; Rear-Adm., 1857; Vice-Adm., 1864.

fitted[,] and then placed in readiness in the Boat House with the ships names [on them.] The Anchor[,] Cables, Shot[,] Guns & Carriages to be on board the ships[.] The [*sic*] Tanks to be stowed and filled if possible. The Lower Rigging to be over the Mast Heads[,] but the Topmast Rigging and fittings aloft to be put below[,] and also the Rigging of the Yards.
The Paddle Floats to be taken off and the Engines disconnected.
3. Class[.] To consist of those steamers in a less advanced state than the 2[d]. Class. These vessels should not be rigged[,] but their Lower & Topmast Rigging should be onboard or fitted in Store[,] and allotted as in the case of the advance[d] ships. Their sails likewise to be fitted and kept ready.
The Engines should be disconnected as much as possible[,] The [*sic*] Pistons & pumps drawn [?down][,] and The [*sic*] guns should[,] with their carriages[,] be fitted[,] but under cover at the D[ock]yard. The Tanks might[,] however[,] be on board[,] also the shot and Chain Cables & Anchors[,] with spare engine gear.
The duties connected with the steam reserve will require a daily inspection of the respective ships by the Captain or Comdr[,] accompanied by the Chief Engineer and the mate[,] as the Engines will require the especial care and attention of the officer in Charge[.] They are to be examined and a daily[1] report made of their state, in a printed form which will be supplied for the purpose from the Engine [*sic*] department[,] who should be called upon the [*sic*: 'to'] state what instructions are required for the guidance of the Estab[lishmen]t[.]
The Head Quarters of Cap Austin must be defined[:] whether he is to consider himself at Ports[mouth] for the *Blenheim*[,] or whether[,] as at present[,] for the duties connected with the fitting and general supervision of Steamers[.]
It also becomes requisite to define the Pay which he will receive[,] and under what rate the *Blenheim* is to be considered[,][2] bearing in mind that by whatever arrangement this may be fixed, the same will Extend [*sic*] to Devonport[,] & It [*sic*] must also be borne in mind that Cap Austin will be constantly moving from Ports[mouth] to the river[,] & it will require that some definite arrangement should be made as to provisions[,] and perhaps the best mode would be that he should be constantly checked on the Books with his servant[,] and allowed for this 1/6 per day[,] as at present[,] and also 1/6 for servant, and again[,] when

[1]Milne had not made up his mind on the frequency of inspection: 'weekly' is written in the margin.

[2]Milne added in the margin: 'Cap Austin at present is on the Pay of 3[d] Class or 4th Rate[,] £498.'

employed away from his ship[,] whether some allowance should be made for Lodging &c[,] and other incidental expenses (perhaps 15/– p day)[,] exclusive of traveling expenses.

[**181**] *Milne Estimate of the Personnel Costs Associated with the Steam Reserve at Portsmouth*

[Admiralty
1 February 1848]

Blenheim [personnel costs]	
Captain	£600
Comdr	300
2 Lieuts (2)	382.10
Master	212.18
Surgeon	255
P[aymaster/] Purser	91.5
Ass Surgeon	136.17
Second Master (2)	65.3
Clerk	56.5
Sup[ernumerary Do	56.5
Gunner	71.5
Bosun	71.5
Coxn	76
Ships Cook	34.11
8 P[etty] Officer	271.4
15 P[etty] Officer	439.10
1 P[etty] Officer	33.17
2 P[etty] Off.	58.12
1 P[urser's] St[ewar]d	26.14
30 Stokers	900
110 AB	2436.10
7 Stewards &c	155
9 B[oys] 1 C[lass]	83.14
12 B[oys] 2 C[lass]	99.12
Marines [no number given]	297.2

Expense of the *Blenheim* Estab[lishmen]t of 240 officers & man for one year[:]

Officers – Cap, Comdr, Lts	£1282.10
Master, Purser Surgeon	559.3
Ass. S[urgeon], 2d Master, Clerks, Warrant Off	598.7
Petty Officers	837.14

Stokers	900
AB	2436.10
Stewards, Boys	338.6
Marines	297.2
	£7249.12
Each Steamer	
2 Petty [Officers]	£60
4 AB	68.12
3 2nd [Class] Boys	25
	22.3[1]
1 Engineer	104
4 Stokers	120
Each Ship	£419.15

[**182**] *Milne Paper on Personnel Arrangements for the Steam Reserve at Sheerness*

[Admiralty
1 February 1848]

A Master of Steam Engines to be app[ointe]d [as an] add[itiona]l [Master] to the *Wellington*[,] for the supervision of the Steamers[,] ad[ditiona]l pay 3d rate.

Warrant officers to Each [*sic*] [ship] to be the permanent warrant officers of the respective ships[,] and to go to sea in them[,] and to be allowed Sea Time in those ready for Sea viz. Two [i.e., two are to be ready for sea][.]

Each vessel to have 3 Engineers[.]

Each vessel to have 4 Stokers – 3 AB – 3 Boys.

The duty of the Master will be to superintend the Steamers under the direction of the Superin[ten]d[en]t of the Dock Yard[,] from whom he will receive his orders[.] The Rigging [and] Sails of each ship are to be fitted entirely and[,] after being so fitted[,] the running Rigging to be remove[d] and put below. The Topmast Rigging also tallied [*sic*] up and put below. The Lower Yards got Fore & Aft[,] and in those ships which are in the second stage of reserve[,] to be unrigged[.]

The Tanks are to be stowed and filled[.]

The Men's gear entirely fitted and ready for service and put below.

The slides to be carefully d[r]ied after wet weather. The gun's [*sic*] moved on them & their position on the deck changed.[*sic*]

[1]It is not clear what this figure is for.

The sails to be aired occasionally.
The well to be kept dry and the ship aired with Stoves – care being taken to keep the ships in [a] clean dry state.
The Engines[,] when in order[,] to be coated with tallow. The Boilers to be dried out and on no account to be filled or any water put into them.
The Engines are to be moved by Tackles and the Steam not got up more than once a quarter[.]
The Funnel to be covered with a cover of painted canvas to prevent the wet coming down.
A daily inspection to take place[,] and the Engineers, Warrant Officers & Stokers, also Abs[,] are to go from ship to ship to afford any assistance which may be required.
The Boats & Carpenters Stores to be allotted to the respective ships and kept in a separate place in the Dock Yard[,] ready for issue . . .

[**183**] *Milne Memorandum on the Ordinary Establishment*

[Admiralty
1848]

The Ordinary Establishment at Portsmouth[,] as well as the other ports[,] requires the services of 3 men to each ship of three and two decks[,] and 1 man for the Frigates and smaller vessels[,] but taking into consideration the casualties by sickness &c[,] it may be assumed at 3 Seamen to each ship in Ordinary, to which must be added about 2 Boys for each ship, which will include the Boys required for the Ordinary depot ship and those of the Lieutenants of Divisions. There is also required a Boats Crew for the Commander and 4 Lieutenants.

The Duties of the Ordinary are arduous[,] and much attention is required to keep the Ships decks and holds constantly dried[,] particularly after and during wet weather. great [*sic*] attention is required to Stoves[,] and also to keeping the ship well aired by tricing up the Ports, Hoisting [*sic*] the windsails, spreading awnings &c. all [*sic*] these duties give ample occupation to the 3 Ship Keepers[,] who likewise keep watch at night and are moreover employed during the day or a portion of them [*sic*] in Scraping [*sic*] and cleaning ships after caulking.

The Captain superintends all the Ordinary arrangements[,] and has under him a Commander and Lieutenants[.] The Commander should reside in the Depot Ship, if the Captain should reside on board the reserve ship about to be brought forward, and the Depot ship should be at Moorings in the centre of the Ships in Ordinary[,] for the convenience of the Men crossing to the Depot ship to muster and also obtain provisions. The Lieutenants[,] or —— of them[,] reside in divisional ships[,] having each charge of so many ships.

The entry of men for this Establishment has of late years been a matter of difficulty[,] from their having been constantly drafted to fill up the Complements of the Guard Ships when sent to sea[,] and An Article [*sic*] in the Ordinary Instructions has also been a great cause of keeping men back[.] this Article . . . states that when men enter for the Ordinary[,] it must be under the condition that they are liable to be drafted into other ships when required.

I think the Ord[inar]y Establishment should be fixed at as low [a] rate as the Service will admit[,] with due consideration to the responsible duty which devolves in having the ships kept in such a state so as to prevent the Evils [*sic*] of decay[,] and that the men entered for this duty should not be drafted from, if [*sic*: 'since'] there being only sufficient men entered to do the duty[,] and if they were withdrawn[,] the duty would be neglected[,] but I would allow them always to volunteer for ships fitting out.

Besides the Seamen & Boys required for this Service[,] there are a number of Warrant Officers employed to take care of the ships and the following is the regulations –

Every Line of Battle Ship & 4[th] rate in good condition has a Carpenter attached and the 3 deckers [an]other two warrant officers[,] viz. a Gunner & Boatswn, all other 2 deckers and 4[th] rates [have] a Gunner or a Boatswn in addition to the Comdr. The Estab[lishmen]t of the Ordinary at Portsmouth will therefore be 1 Captain 1 Comdr —— Lieutenants[,] 1 Master[,] 1 Surgeon[,] 1 Asst Do, and[,] there being 58 Ships in Ordinary[,] it may be taken at 60.

	AB	Boys	Marines
60 Ships 3 men each	180		
" " 2 Boys "		120	
Boats Crews for the Comdr & Lieutenants	22		
Marines for the Ordy			44
	202	120	41

AB	202
Boys	120
Marines	41
	363
Officers	
Idlers	12

There are in the Ordinary at Portsmouth[:]

Gunners –	35
Boatswns –	59
Carpenters –	36 = 23 Emp[loye]d in Dyard

[**184**] *Milne Paper on Increase of Pay to Sailors of the Fleet*[1]

[Admiralty
February 1848]

With reference to the increase of Pay to the amount of £30,000 pr Annum[,] to be given to the Seamen of the Fleet with the object of inducing such seamen to enter more freely into the Service[,] and to look to it as a profession instead of the Merchant Navy, It [*sic*] must be borne in mind that this class of people[,] especially in early life[,] look to present pay and advantages more than to 'future pension'[,] and that the present rate of pay of the Merchant Seaman at £2.10 pr. Month[,] especially with vast improvement in their present allowance of provisions as established by the Merchant Seamens Act[,] is a greater inducement to them than the Navy Pay of £1.14 pr. month with the same provisions.[2]
It would therefore be advisable[,] if possible[,] to increase the pay of the A.B.s & to establish a new class of AB[,] to be called 1 Class Able Seaman[.] If[,] however[,] this be done and the pay of such a class be established at £2 pr. Month[,] the pay of the Petty Officers will likewise have to be increased. How far then will £30.000 pr A[nnum] carry out this object[?] there are 7,250 Petty Officers . . . and if their pay be increased £2 pr. Year[,] it would take £14,500, leaving only £15,500 for the new class of A.B.[,] whose pay[,] if increased from £1.14 to £2 pr month would be [increased by] £3.18 pr Annum, therefore £15.500 divided by £3.18[,] say £4[,] would give 3,875 1 Class A.B. for the Fleet[,] or around 16 men of the new Class in a Ship of the Line[.]

[1]Probably an early set of thoughts for the memo which follows in [**185**].
[2]Milne added in the margin:

Present Rates of Pay

1 C. Petty officer	£2.12 to £2.5
2 C "	£2.1 to £2.4
A.B.	£1.14– –
Ord[inar]y [Seaman]	£1.6
L[and]M[an]	£1.3
Boy 1[st] C[lass]	£0.14.3
2[nd] C[lass]	£0.12.9

This would never answer, as the number of 1 C[lass] A.B. should be more than double the No. of Petty Officers[.]
If the ABs of the Fleet were to have their pay increased by 6 shillings pr. Month[,] leaving the P[etty] O[fficers] their present pay[,] the sum of £30,000 would be quite inadequate to the object, see margin,[1] and therefore a general increase of pay is impossible with the sum to be granted. The Pay of the P[etty] Officers might be increased in such proportion as to allow the £30,000 to be expended by increasing their pay[,] and also a certain number of A.B.s[,] who should be called 1 C[lass] AB and be free from Corp[ora]l Punishment[,] wearing a Badge on their Arm. This alone[,] indep[en]d[en]t of increase of pay will[,] I feel assured[,] bring a number of Seamen into the Service. I therefore propose that the present pay of the 1[st] C[lass] P[etty] officer should be increased £1.5 pr Annum, 2[d] C[lass] P[etty] officer £1 pr Annum[,] and a 1[st] C[lass] AB [be] established[,] with pay of £1.16 pr month[,] to wear a Badge on the Arm and to be free from Corp[ora]l Punishment in the same manner as Petty Officers[,] the number of such 1[st] C[lass] AB[s] to be defined[,] & none to be rated unless thorough Seamen[,] capable of every essential duty.

I do not see how the general recommendation of the Committee can be further followed out[,] but I would allude to the late prize proclamation of 1846[,] where the scale of prize shares is not in conformity with the Admiralty Regulations as to the rank and precedence of Petty Officers.[2]

[**185**] *Milne Paper on Increase of Pay to the Sailors of the Fleet*[3]

Admiralty
21 February 1848

I have to submit the following observations with reference to the distribution of the £30,000 to be granted by Parliament for the encouragement of the Petty Officers & Seamen of the Fleet. There is much difficulty in coming to a decision on the subject, and I will therefore state the different views I have taken relative to the mode of distribution and the calculations I have made. The chief object to be attained is the encouragement of our Seamen to enter our service, or I should perhaps say to induce them to remain in it, instead of being led away by the Crimps at

[1]Milne calculated it would cost £38,668, there being around 9,667 A.B.s in the Fleet.
[2]In the margin Milne also worked out the pay increases for the various ranks.
[3]This version appears to have been debated by the entire Board.

the outports to enter into the American Navy[,] a system which is carried on to a considerable extent at Ports[mou]th where a person is employed for the purpose, and the number of Seamen wanted stuck upon a Post at the leading place on the Common Hard.

The different modes of distribution may be classified under the four following heads.

First – A general increase of pay to all the Petty Officers of the Fleet with the exception of the leading stokers[,] whose pay has lately been augmented.

Second – A partial or limited increase of pay to all the Petty Officers[,] and an increase of pay to the following[,] viz. Second Captains of the Forecastle and Top[,] Second Captains of the Afterg[uar]d[,] and Second Gunners Mates[,] also to the Coxswains of Cutters[,] who at present are only A.B.s[.]

Third – A progressive increase of pay to the petty officers & seamen of the Fleet[,] depending on an increased servitude and on a [*sic*] completion of a certain number of years time.

Fourth – No increase of pay to the Petty Officers, but a distribution of the sum voted to the men of good conduct[,] and on the principle of the good conduct warrant of the Army.

These are the four modes to which I will separately allude.

The First

There are by the Estimates about 6,800 Petty Officers in the Fleet, but it is perhaps advisable to err on the safe side and assume the number at 7,000. If we therefore devote the £30,000 to the increase of their pay it will stand thus[:]

7.000 men at an increase of £2 pr annum	£14,000 pr A
7.000 men at an increase of £3 pr. annum	£21,000 "
7.000 men at an increase of £4 pr. annum	£28,000 "[1]

The Second

A partial increase of pay may be given to the Petty officers[,] but I do not see any good reason to apply the whole £30,000 to that purpose[, for] it appears to me to be doing too much for one class without considering the others. I am strongly of opinion an increase of pay to the Second Captains of the Forecastle, Tops [*sic*] Afterguard & Gunners Mates[,] also to the Coxswains of Cutters[,] who are only ABs

[1]In the margin Milne added:
'7000 P.O. at 1d per day = £10,646
7000 P.O. at 2d per day = £21,292
Therefore under this mode of distribution[,] the pay of petty officers may be increased £4 pr ann = £28,000 . . . leaving a surplus of £2000.'

would be a most advisable and desirable measure[,] and would be considered a great boon to the men themselves[,] and place them in that position which they ought to be from the responsible duties they have to perform. The numbers will stand thus –

2 Second Captains of the Forecastle
2 Second Captains of the Foretop
2 Second Captains of the Main Top
2 Second Captains of the Mizzen Top
2 Second Captains of the Aftergd
2 Second Gunners Mates
<u>2</u> Coxswains of Cutters

14 Men, in all vessels ship rigged[,] 3 less in Brigs and those having only <u>one Cutter</u>, but assume 14 as the [rule]. Therefore[,] advance their pay 4s pr month[,] viz. from £1.14 to £1.18 and It [*sic*] will stand thus – 14 men at 4s pr month – £36.8 pr a[nnum,] and if the Ships in commission are as under[,] the amounts will be[:]

200 Ships at £36.8 pr a. –	£7,280
250 " " "	£9,100
300 " " "	£10,920

We therefore have an advance of £10,920 if 300 ships are in Commission[,] and by advancing the Petty Officers pay at the sametime [*sic*] £3 pr ann or 5s per month[,] it would amount to as pr First calculation
<u>£21,000</u>
£31,920

Being [*sic*] £1,920 above the Grant when 300 ships are in Commission, but I feel assured there will be quite sufficient funds for this purpose when we take into consideration that the greatest number of our ships in commission will not be allowed Second Captains of M[i]zz[e]n Top and only one Cox[wai]n of Cutter.

<u>The Third</u> – This mode involves a long series of calculations and even then the chief items are uncertain[,] as no fixed <u>data</u> can be obtained without reference to the Books at Somerset House, as the calculations are on the supposition of increase of pay by a progressive servitude of the seaman [*sic*]. Let the number of P[etty] Officers and men be assumed as pr [the] margin[1] and the grand total at 24,000, and that[,] after a servitude of 7 years[,] an increase of 1 penny pr day be granted to such seaman[,] provided he has not been absent from the Service 6 months at any one time or one year collectively[,] and further that[,] after a period of 14 years[,] service 2d pr. day shall be granted[,]

[1]'Petty Officers – 7000; AB 11,500; Ord[inar]y S[ea]men 5000 = 23,500.'

provided he has not be[en] out of the Service more than 9 months at any one time or 18 collectively[,] and that the Claimant has always maintained a good character in the Service[.] we [*sic*] may assume that[,] out of the 24,000[,] ¼ part have not 7 years servitude[,] that ¼ are above 7 years[,] and that ½ [are] above 14 years. The numbers will stand thus[:]

¼ under 7 years	6,000 men
¼ above 7 years	6,000 "
½ above 14 years	12,000 "

Under the first item[,] no add[itiona]l pay would be granted, but with reference to the others it would stand thus[:]

6,000 at 1d pr day	£9,125 pr A.
12,000 at 2d pr day	£36,500 pr. A
	£45,625

Being £15,625 above the Grant[.]

It is therefore obvious such an arrangement would not suit the Expense to which the Admiralty are limited[.] If[,] however[,] an increase of pay be granted after 12 years servitude at the rate of 1d pr day[and assuming the Number at ⅔ of our seamen as entitled to this advance[,] it would amount to £24,330 pr annum, but this will be almost a general increase of pay throughout the service.

The Fourth – The proposal in this fourth mode[,] for introducing the principle of the good conduct warrant as in the Army[,] would be highly advantageous to the men of good character[,] for in the present system of the service there is nothing to excite emulation or distinguish the seaman of exemplary character from those of indifferent character. To introduce this system into the Naval Service would in the first instance require a Good Conduct Book of the Seamen to be established in every ship[,] and likewise a classification of all crimes and punishments, and a series of instructions to be drawn up relative to the working of the whole system.

The view I take of the subject is to give every man who conducts himself well a good Conduct Badge[,] with 1d pr day add[itiona]l pay and[,] on being paid off[,] to receive a Certificate stating his being entitled to the privileges (viz. being free from corporal punishment)[,] so long as he was entitled by good conduct to wear the Badge, but after a great deal of consideration to the subject[,] I find it is so difficult to work out that I must abandon the idea at present[,] as it is not possible under some considerable time [*sic*] to draw out the regulations[.] In considering over the whole bearing of this subject [*sic*] and the fair distribution of the Grant for the benefit of the Service[,] I am inclined to give my decided opinion that what I have pointed out under the Second head will prove the most beneficial in every way[,] and will not only be highly useful but highly popular with both officers and men[.] The calculations will have to be modified to avoid the fractions of a penny[,] and this could at once be done if Lord Auckland and the Board should adopt these views[.][1]

Note[:] The Calculations are made at Somerset House on the principle of rejecting fractions of a penny & the calculations under the proposal recommended under the Second Head would be –

7000 P. Officers at 2d pr day	£21,292
2000 Seamen increased pay at an Advance of 2d pr day	£6,083
[Total]	£27,375

Being £2,625 under the Grant[.][2]
The number of person's [*sic*] now serving who would benefit by giving 2d pr day to 2d Cap[tains] of Tops, Forecastle, Afterguard, 2d G[unner's] Mates & Coxn of Cutters would by the present [number of] ships in Commission[,] be 1,968[.] I have taken it at 2000.
The 2d proposal[,] If [*sic*] adopted would stand thus[:]
An increase of 2d pr day to all the Petty officers of the Fleet with the exception of the stokers[,] whose pay has been lately augmented – and
An increase of pay of 2d pr day to the

2 Second Capt of the Forecastle
2 Second Capt of the Foretop
2 " " of the Main Top
2 " " of the Mizzen Top
2 " " of the Afterguard
2 Second Gunner's Mates
2 Coxswains of Cutters
14

The said men to wear a Badge on their Arms
1 Class Petty Officers to be increased 2d pr day[:]

Seaman Schoolmaster
Master at Arms
Sailmaker
Ropemaker
Caulker

[1]Milne added: 'I would give those men a Badge with the Single Crown[,] or some such mark[,] and free them from Corp[ora]l Punishment, but not call them 3d C. Petty officers.'

[2]He added next to this figure: 'This is the number of 2d Capt of Forecastle, Tops, Aftergd, &c'; these numbers are repeated in the subsequent calculations.

Blacksmith
Carp[enter's] Mate
Ships Corporal
Captain's Coxswain
Quarter Master
Gunners Mate
Boats[wains] mate
Coxn [of the] Launch
Captain [of the] Forecastle
" " Hold
" " Main Top
" " For Top
Capt Afterguard (from 2d Class)

Second C. Petty Officers to be increased 2d pr day[:]

Sailmakers Mate
Caulkers Mate
Armourer
Cooper
Yeoman of Signals
Coxn [of] Pinnace
Coxn [of] Barge
Cap [of] Mizzen Top
Cap [of Mizzen] Mast
Paymaster & P[urser's] Steward
Musician[s]

[**186**] *Berkeley Minute on Increase of Pay to Sailors*

[Admiralty
February 1848]

Having considered the method of reward established in the Army by the Good Service Warrant, I am inclined to establish in the Navy (assimilating the Principle as near as may be consistent with the different nature of Naval and Military Service) the same system of reward.

Adhering to Captain Milne's second proposition of increasing the Number of Petty Officers & First Ratings therein proposed[,] without an increase of Pay[,] substituting the good service warrant and its consequent increase of emolument with the distinguishing marks, in lieu of the increase of Permanent Pay [*sic*][.]

[**187**] *Board Minutes on Increase of Pay to the Sailors of the Fleet*

[Admiralty
February 1848]

[Lord Auckland:] I lean very much to the outline of the second plan of Capt Milne and am not able to give an opinion on it in detail. The subject should be brought before the Board for discussion.

[James Whitley Deans Dundas:] I quite approve of Capt Milne's 2d plan & Capt Berkeley's addition. The numbers of men had better be checked by Mr Briggs.[1]

[Maurice Frederick Fitzhardinge Berkeley:] I propose to adopt the second plan of Captain Milne with this one trifling alteration – to put the Captain of the Afterguard in the 1st Class Petty Officers rating.

[Capt Lord John Hay:] I have already given my opinion on this subject. I have no objections of Capt. Milne's second plan.

[**188**] *Milne Memorandum on Increase of Pay to the Sailors of the Fleet*

[Admiralty
February 1848]

In a former paper[,] some proposals were made for the distribution of the £30.000 to be granted for the benefit of the Seamen of the Fleet[,] and the idea of doing so in accordance with the principle of the 'Army Good Conduct Warrant' was stated but not followed out. On reconsideration of this subject[,] it is thought advisable to adopt this view and to modify the proposal for an increase of the New Ratings which were then considered advisable and [?requisite] and[,] with the residue of the Grant[,] to introduce into the Navy a 'Good Conduct Badge' and a small increase of pay in sea going ships to those men of exemplary conduct and character, who have now no encouragement or mark of distinction or merit to point them out from those of less deserving character.
It is proposed to adhere to the principle of the Army 'good conduct warrant' as near as the duties and details of the two services will

[1]Sir John Thomas Briggs, Accountant-General of the Navy.

admit[,] & it appears to me this can be done without at all interfering with the present Naval pensions or the principle on which they are granted; before the Good Conduct warrant was established in the Army there was a progressive increase of pay depending on the length of servitude of the Individual[.] this was altered to a fixed rate of pay and the increase then given was by the regulations to men of good conduct with servitude by

1d pr day after 5 years
2d pr day after 10 "
3 pr day after 15 "
4 pr day after 20 "
5 pr day after 25 " &c

but as our Seamen are now allowed to draw their pension after 21 years servitude[,] as well as their pay when serving[,] I see no necessity for carrying out the privileges of the Naval good conduct warrant beyond 3d pr day.

In the Army the Individual enjoying the privileges of the G Conduct pay has the rate of such pay added to his pension. In the Navy I do not see how this can be carried out[,] for want of funds[,] and I do not see that it would be required[,] because if a Seaman obtains the G C Badge & allowance it is more than probable he will become a Petty Officer and[,] of course[,] obtain a P.O. pension[,] The [*sic*] G. C. Warrant being only intended to apply to Able Seamen only[.]

In the Army there are about 100,000 men who are entitled to the privileges of the warrant[,] but out of this number there are only 19,196 who have the privileges[,] viz. about ⅕[,] and at an expense of £52,100 pr. A[.] In the Navy[,] with the present Establishment[,] there are only 20,000 men (AB & Ordy) who would be allowed the advantages, if it be admitted that one half obtained the Badge & allowance[,] and it is a very high estimate. The Sum of money required would be £28,890 pr Annum viz. say[:]

	4000 men at 1d	£6,083
	3000 " at 2d	£9,125
	3000 " at 3d	£13,687
[Total]	10,000	£28,895

That is assuming the proportional scale here given to be near the supposed number who would benefit by the warrant, but I consider the estimated numbers I have assumed [to be] very far above the actual number of men who would be granted the Badge and its privileges.

Besides the Good Conduct Badge[,] it appears to me requisite to alter a few of the ratings of the Petty Officers, whose position does not appear to me to have been properly considered[,] viz.

(1) The Captain of the Afterguard to be a First Class Petty Officer instead of Second Class. This will cost[,] on 200 ships[,] £1,022 pr Annum[.]
(2) A Chief Boats[wains] Mate is much required in all Ships of the Line. This will cost[,] on 26 ships[,] by an increase of 2d pr. Day[,] about £80 pr. Annum.
(3) The following new ratings of Second Class Petty Officers are required in Ships of the Line & 4th rates, viz.

1 Coxswain Barge cost	£118.12 pr A.
2 Second Captains of Forecastle –	£237.4
2 Second Cap. Main Top –	£237.4
2 Second Cap Fore Top –	£237.4
2 Second Cap Afterguard –	£237.4
2 Coxswain of Cutters –	£237.4
[Total]	£1186

being the above [*sic*: 'increased'] amount on 26 Ships[,] or on all the ratings[,] a yearly outlay of about £2,500[,] leaving therefore for the Good Conduct warrant about £27,500
To carry out the Good Conduct warrant, the following regulations will be estab[lishe]d[:]
(1) Any AB. who has served in the Royal Navy for a period of five year's [*sic*] with the ratings of Ordy and AB, and who shall have maintained a good character[,] shall be entitled[,] on the recommendation of the Captain[,] to the Good Conduct badge[,] viz. a St Georges Cross of Red Cloth to be worn on the left sleeve of his Jacket & to an allowance of 1d pr day in addition to his pay.
2d. Any AB who has served for a period of 10 years &c[,] shall be entitled to the Double Badge[,] viz. 2 Crosses, and 2d pr day in addition to his pay.
3d. After 15 years[,] to 3 Crosses and 3d p[er] day.
To obtain a record of those who may not be entitled to the privileges of this warrant, a correct return of all punishments is to be made in the Defaulters Book now ordered to be kept in all ships[.] A quarterly examination of this Book is to be made by the Captain[,] who is to take to his assistance [*sic*] the Comdr or Senior Lt or the Master[,] and to select those names who[,] by indiff[erent] conduct[,] may be considered unfit for the warrant[,] & these names are to be transferred to a separate List in each Defaulters Book.
When any person has obtained the Badge[,] he is to be free from Corp[ora]l Punishment[,] & it is not to be taken from him for any trivial offence[,] but only on such crimes being committed as would render him subject to Corp[ora]l Punishment, or from continued inattention or

neglect of duty[,] in which case the person may have the Badge removed on a Warrant of Removal being made out as in the case of Petty Officers[,][1] and If [*sic*] a Badge be removed for his [*sic*] conduct[,] it cannot be reconferred for a period of 12 months & then only by most exemplary conduct.

When a person is discharged from one ship to another with the Good C. Badge[,] the same is to be certified on the back of his certificate[,] as will [be] pointed out in the Appendix[.][2] The same is to be noted in Red Ink in the margin of the Muster & Description Book.

The same regulation applies to Seamen paid off[,] and they will receive the Badge & allowance on reentry by production of their Certificates, but will not be conferred where persons have lost their Certificates[.]

The Badge is to be granted after the first 18 months of the ship being in Commission[,] & those now on service are to correct this time from the 1 Nov 1847 if they were commissnd [*sic*] previous to that date[,] or if not commissnd before 1 April 1848[,] they are to reckon from the period of their being put in Commission.

Each ship to send a return home of the number of men who have the G[ood] C[onduct] B[adge] in the quarterly returns[,] and a separate List is also to be kept in each muster [book] with the Sums ag[ainst] their names.

No Seamen can be allowed the benefit of advance to the higher grades of the Badge unless they have worn the lower grade for a continued period of two years.[3]

[1]That is, to be reported in the Quarterly Report of Punishments.

[2]Not included here.

[3]There follows a single-page synopsis of the proposed changes. ADM1/5598 also contains two subsequent Board Minutes:

(**1**) [5 June 1848] 'The proposed scheme for the encouragement of the Petty Officers, and Able Seamen, of H.M.'s Fleet, by making certain additions to their Pay, & Pensions, after stated periods of service, upon the principle of the Good Conduct Warrant of the Army – with the Accountant General's Estimate of the Cost, amounting in all to £28,935. Approved, & Ordered, to be carried into affect on 1st Oct[obe]r next, if sanctioned by Parl[iamen]t when the Estimates are voted. H[enry] G W[ard]' [Parliamentary Secretary of the Admiralty].

(**2**) [30 June 1848] 'Read, & reconsidered, Captain Milne's Minute on increased Pay to Petty Officers, & Seamen with a view to adopting it to [encourage] the Entry of men from the Merchant Service. Proposed Additions approved & adopted. It is also Their L[ordshi]ps intention to make provisions, out of the £30,000 voted, for the application of the principle of the Good Service Warrant to the Royal Marines. HGW'

[**189**] *Milne Paper on Proposed Regulations for Entry of Seaman Riggers*

Admiralty
April 1848

The L[ords] C[ommissioners of the] A[dmiralty], having taken into their consideration a proposal for the extension of Extra Seamen-Riggers into HM Dock Yards for the purpose, and with the view, of forming a Reserve of Seamen at such Ports, have been pleased to issue the following regulations on the Subject[.]

1. The Seamen who enter as Seamen-Riggers must have served for a period of not less than six years in H.M. Service with the ratings of Ord[inar]y and AB; and must produce certificates of good conduct, and ability, from the Captain of the Ship in which they last served. They will be entered subject to the express condition of being called upon to serve in any of HM Ships, should any sudden emergency require their Services, but it is not intended that the Compl[emen]ts of HM Ships proceeding to Foreign Stations shall be filled up from such men, but only such ships as may be required to be suddenly manned & fitted for the Home Station[,] or to aid in the navigation of Ships from one port to another, or duties connected with the Home Ports, or to complete the Compl[emen]ts of the Exp[erimental] Squadron during a few months cruize.

2. For every 25 Seamen there shall be entered one Petty officer: – the pay of such P.O. to be 3/6 per day[.]

All ABs, who are willing to enter under such conditions, shall have the pay of 2/6 pr. day.

The Time of Servitude of such P[etty] Officers and Seamen shall be considered as Sea time, and be allowed to count for Pension[.]

3. all [*sic*] such Seamen Riggers shall be allowed to have the privilege of obtaining Slop Clothing from HM Stores, at the same price as now issued to the Seamen of the Fleet, on demands made out by the Master Att[endan]t, and app[rove]d by the Rear Adm[iral] Superinten]d[en]t of the Dock Yard, but not to a greater Sum than 20 shillings pr. month[,] the same to be deducted from their weekly wages.

4. That if absent from the Port to which they belong, their wives & families shall be allowed to draw weekly one half the pay due to the Seaman himself, provided such Seaman obtains a Certificate from the Com[man]d[in]g Officer of the Ship[,] which must be countersigned by the Master Att[en]d[an]t of the Dock Y[ar]d that such man is embarked on service[.]

5. That such Seamen Riggers are to be under the directions of the Master Attendant of the D[ock] Yard[,] and shall perform all such duties in the Yard as may be required.
6. That on going on board any of HM Ships on service[,] they are to be entered as 'Dock Yard Riggers on Special Service' and so long as they are so employed, they shall be granted the Established allowance of Provisions according to the Regulations of the Service in addition to their pay as Seamen Riggers, but this privilege is not to extend for a longer period than two months, when they will then be placed on the Ships Books according to their respective ratings and be paid accordingly.
7. The Period of Servitude as a Seaman Rigger shall not exceed 18 months at any one time, but if they have been at Sea during any time of such period, such sea time is to be granted over & above the 18 months.
8. That during the time of Servitude as Seamen Riggers[,] they may volunteer for any of H.M. Ships fitting out at any of HM Ports.
9. They are to have all the benefits of the Royal N[aval] Hospitals as the Seamen of the Fleet.[1]
10. In case of death by accident in the Execution [*sic*] of the public service, Their [*sic*] widows shall be noted for Entry [*sic*] as Nurses in the Hosp[ita]l Estab[lishmen]ts.
11. Their sons shall have the privilege of Entry [*sic*] as Boys in HM Service, provided they qualify by the regulations of the Service.
12. The Captains of H.M. Ships paying off to recommend men for entry.
13. Such men shall have the privilege [of entering] into the Ordinary[2] on vacancies occurring[.]
14. Should any Seaman Rigger refuse to proceed on board any of HM Ships when ordered to do so, he shall forfeit all claim to servitude & pension.[3]

[1]The following was written but scratched out in pencil: '& Pensions for Hurts and Wounds as in the case of HM Seamen afloat'[.]

[2]That is, joining the force that oversaw and maintained the ships in ordinary.

[3]Ward minuted on the cover: 'Mr. Purcell – these regulations are to go forward. They should be printed & Captn Milne will revise the Proofs[.] May 28[,] HGW'.

[**190**] *Milne Draft Certificate for Half Weekly Pay to Wife or Family*

Admiralty
April 1848

I hereby certify that
(Petty Officer or AB) is now serving on board HMS ______, that he belongs to ______ Dock Yard as an Extra Seaman Rigger[,] and he requests payment to be made to his (Wife Mother or Daughter) of the Sum of ______, being one half his weekly pay from the (Date)[.]
Signed (In charge of Dock Y[ard])
I hereby certify the above person ______ is embarked from the D[ock]yard & I see no objection to the above request (Master Att[en]d[an]t Dock Yard)[.]

[**191**] *Milne to Napier*

Admiralty
4 May 1848

My dear Sir Charles

I should have written to you long before this[,] but as I know you were in correspondence with Lord Auckland and Admiral Dundas[,] I could not be of any use in giving you any news from this relative to what was going on[,] but before I leave Town[,] which I do tomorrow for 10 days[,] I drop you a few lines before my departure to say that[,] as some alterations in the Signal Book will probably be taken into consideration by the Board, I would be very glad if you would submit your views on the subject. I am not aware who has taken charge of this subject here[,] nor does any one appear to know[,] but I intend on my return to look into the matter upon a correspondence which has come from Sir William Parker, recommending some alterations[,] but more especially additions to the present code[,] and I should be very glad to have the aid of your knowledge and experience on the subject. You wrote home from Lisbon about the Baulk[1] supplied to the ships in lieu of the Yard Arm pieces[,] & recommending one of larger size to those now in use[,] but I find it is scarcely possible to get them of the required size[;] it has been tried[,] but the Spars are not forthcoming and our Dock-Yards cannot supply them, and another difficulty is the great expense. In consequence of the business of the *Howe*'s towing

[1]A roughly cut beam of timber.

and the smallness of size of the present Establishment [*sic*] of Hawsers, I have had the Establishment entirely altered[,] which I hope will now meet the difficulty of Towing. The Establishment of *St Vincent* was 3 of 9 inch[es]. this [*sic*] has been altered by [*sic*] 2 of 9, one of 10[,] and an additional [one of] 12 supplied as towing Hawser, by which means the Hawsers may be used with the Stream Cable if requisite[,] or with each other. I have also had the men's shoes altered[,] which I hope will now be found more serviceable as I know frequent complaints were made about them. Those you wanted for *St Vincent* have been ordered[,] and I dare say are at Cork before this.

If I can be of any use in London or Edinburgh for the next ten days, I will be very glad to be of use [*sic*] . . .

[**192**] *Napier to Milne*

HMS *St. Vincent*, Cove of Cork
7 May 1848

My dear Milne

I am no great hand at Signals, but I find the present ones not very good, nor will Signals ever be good if they are concocted in an Office[.] if I had a blank Signal-Book[,] I should begin to put them down as I wanted them[,] and I should then bring all those together that bore on the same subject[,] so that there would be no hunting thru' the Book for them.

I send you my sheet for Evolutions[,] and you will see how few of them are in the Signal Book. As to Night Signals[,] there is none to wear in succession, what I mean is, the Headmost ship to wear and pass to leeward of the line, followed by the rest. Dixon[1] said it was a practice in the Channel fleet for the Headmost ship[,] after wearing[,] to pass under the Stern of the third ship, if they were to do that now they would make a mess of it. Every ship ought to be able to make a lower yard, but if you cannot get the span there is no help for it. a [*sic*] lower yard can always be made with spars, as we did the other day. I am glad you have improved the Towing Apparatus. it [*sic*] was much wanted.

I am glad you have improved the Shoes. it [*sic*] was wanted, and so are many other improvements, but you know the difficulty of getting

[1]Probably Manley Hall Dixon (1786–1864). Entered, 1794; Lt, 1802; Cmdr, 1809; Capt., 1811; Rear-Adm., 1847; Vice-Adm., 1855; Adm., 1860. Dixon was in command of *Caledonia*, 1845–47.

things done, which prevents people from recommending them. it [*sic*] is no easy matter to make six men agree. I wish we were at Spithead and I hope to see you when we come there. Best regards to Lady Milne . . .

[**193**] *Milne Draft Circular on Increased Pay to Petty Officers, and Introduction of the Good Conduct Badge*[1]

[Admiralty
June 1848]

Circular for Ratings &c[.]
The Lords Commissioners of the Admiralty having taken into consideration, [*sic*] suggestions which have been submitted to them for the benefit of the Petty Officers and Seamen of the Fleet, have been pleased to direct that the following alterations and additions to the Ratings and Pay shall take place form the 1st of October 1848.
In all Rates of H.M. Ships[:]
The Captain of the Afterguard is to be in future a First Class Petty Officer[,] with the pay of £2.5 pr. month.
In First, Second & Third Rates[:]
A New rating of Chief Boats[wains] Mate is to be established as a First Class Petty Officer, to be selected from the present number of Boats[wains] Mates allowed, but must have passed an examination for Boatswain. The Pay of this rating to be £2.9 pr month[.]
In First, Second & Third Rates[:]
The following new ratings of Second Class Petty Officers are to be allowed[,] with pay of £2.1 pr. month.

1 – Coxswain of the Barge
2 – Second Captains Forecastle
2 – Second Captains Main Top
2 – Second Captains Fore Top
2 – Second Captains Afterguard
2 – Coxswain of Cutters

In all Fourth Rates[:]
The following ratings are to be allowed[,] with Pay pr month as under

1 Coxswain Barge	£2.1
1 Coxswain Pinnace	£2.1
2 Coxswain of Cutters	£2.1

[1]This paper is undated; June 1848 has been chosen since it meshes with the minutes of 15 and 30 June on the subject.

Their Lordships have been further pleased to establish[,] for the benefit of the well conducted and meritorious Seamen of the Fleet, the following scale of 'Good Conduct Pay' with a Good Conduct Badge to be worn on the left sleeve of the Jacket or Frock[.]

First[:]

Any Seaman of the Fleet who has served for a period of Five years in the Royal Navy, with the Rating of Ord & A.B.[,] without being absent from the service for more than six months at any one time, and who has invariably conducted himself with sobriety and attention so as to merit a 'very good' character, shall be allowed to wear the First Good Conduct Badge.

The same privilege will extend to Seamen of the Merchant Service, who can produce five year's [*sic*] certificates of servitude (exclusive of apprenticeship time). [They] shall[,] after one years servitude in the Royal Navy with 'very good conduct'[,] be entitled to the same privilege[.][1]

Second[:]

Any Seaman of the Fleet who has served for a period of Ten years in the Royal Navy, (without being absent from it for a period of more than nine months at any one time, or two years collectively)[,] and who has maintained a very good character for the last 'two' years, shall be allowed two pence pr day in addition to his pay as AB[,] and shall wear the 2d Good Conduct Badge. The same privilege shall extend to Seamen of the Merchant Service, who can produce eight years certificates of servitude (exclusive of apprenticeship time) and certificates of two years very good conduct, subsequently served in the Royal Navy.

Third[:]

Any Seaman of the Fleet who has served fifteen years in the Royal Navy, (without being absent twelve months at anyone [*sic*] time or three years collectively), and who has maintained a very good character for the last two years, shall be allowed three pence pr. day in addition to his pay as AB.[,] and shall wear the 3d Class [*sic*] Good Conduct Badge.

The same privilege shall extend to Seamen of the Merchant Service who can produce 13 years certificates (exclusive of apprenticeship time)[,] with certificates of two years very good conduct during two year's [*sic*] subsequent service in the Royal Navy[.]

[1]Milne added in the margin: 'Those parts underlined appear to me doubtful[.] AM'

Fourth[:][1]
Any AB who has completed a period of Twenty one years servitude in the Royal Navy, and is entitled to a pension, shall be allowed one penny pr day in addition to such pension[,] provided he has worn the 3d Class Good Conduct badge for a period of one year or more, [&] provided it has not be[en] removed for any misconduct.[2]
Fifth[:]
No person can claim or be allowed to wear the 2d Badge until he has worn the First for a period of two years, nor the 3d Badge until they [*sic*] have worn the 2d for the same period.
Sixth[:]
Seamen who by continued good conduct have been awarded the 'Good Conduct Badge' shall[,] so long as they are entitled to wear the same, be free from the imposition of Corporal Punishment[,] except in cases of Mutiny[,] and the privileges of the Good Conduct pay and Badge shall not be taken away from such person [*sic*] unless by a warrant made out for the same, under the regulations as presently established for the disrating of Petty Officers, and to be reported in the periodical returns[,] and when by misconduct a person shall forfeit the Badge & Pay, it is not to be reconferred for a period of at least one year[,] and then only under circumstances of extreme [*sic*] good conduct.
Seventh[:]
When a Seaman is discharged from one ship to another or is paid off[,] the Captain of such ship is to certify on the man's parchment certificate in Red Ink the Class of Badge the Seaman is entitled to wear, or in case of not having sufficient servitude, he is to state his character, 'very good' being considered a claim to the Badge when sufficient time has been served according to the foregoing regulations. Annotation is likewise to be made on the margin of the Muster & Descript[io]n Book in Red Ink of the Class Badge the Seaman has been granted[,] with the date. All Seamen paid off with the Badge will be granted it on reentry on production of their Certificates[.]
The Weekly Accounts and Quarterly returns are to contain a notation in Red Ink of the number of men who have been granted the different Class Badges.[3]

[1]This clause was subsequently scratched out and next to it Milne wrote: 'This at the End'. See the following Board Minutes.

[2]Someone, perhaps Milne, although the script is unusually large for him, wrote in addition: 'Those persons who have worn the Good Conduct badge will be [that is, have it] considered in their claim for pension'.

[3]Milne added underneath this clause: 'When an AB is rated a Petty officer he loses the G[ood] C[onduct] B[adge] on his promotion'[.]

Eighth[:]
The 1st Good Conduct Badge is to be a plain St Georges Cross of crimson cloth as under[.][1]
The 2d to be a St Georges Cross of crimson cloth with [the] No II in the centre in gold numbers[.]
The 3d to be a St Georges Cross of crimson cloth with [the] No III in the centre in gold numbers[.]

[**194**] *Board Minutes on the Draft Circular on Increased Pay to Petty Officers, and Introduction of the Good Conduct Badge*

[Admiralty
June 1848]

[Lord Auckland:] I approve. We should have simultaneously an order for good conduct warrants to the Marines. The period at which this increase is to take place may be discussed at the first Board held at Somerset House.

[James Whitley Deans Dundas:] I think the draft of the Circular very good . . . [but] the 4th clause ought to be struck out. Pensions are awarded by Regulations & ought not to be tampered with.

[Maurice Frederick Fitzhardinge Berkeley:] I agree with Adml Dundas that the 4th clause should be struck out. The pension for good service should cover all. Mr Briggs should be consulted as to the time when the regulations may take affect [*sic*].

[Lord John Hay:] I agree with Adml Dundas[2]

[**195**] *Auckland Memorandum on Entry of Naval Cadets*

Admiralty
16 July 1848

I think that the Entry [*sic*] and career of Naval Cadets should be made the subject of a very particular consideration and revision. It is upon a good regulation of this branch of the Naval Establishment that the

[1]Milne also furnished a sketch of the proposed badge.
[2]The actual circular (Number 46, 16 January 1849) departs substantially from Milne's original draft, in terms of wording, but the premises behind it are unchanged.

efficiency of the Navy List in great measure depends, and the absence of such regulation has heretofore led to great embarrassment. In 1841 there were 539 mates upon the list[,] and men remained almost hopelessly for years in this rank before obtaining their promotion to that of Lieutenant. In 1842 and subsequent years promotions were largely made – from 1845 to this time the number of mates has been too small for the Service, and at present they are hardly sufficient to maintain the efficiency of the Lieutenants List. I would lay it down (subject however to frequent revision) that 80 mates in each year should be promoted to the rank of Lieutenant. That mates should ordinarily serve in that rank for at least two years[,] though some may[,] for exemplary conduct[,] be promoted sooner, and a Lieutenant receiving his promotion after only eight years of service might be expected to serve longer without looking for Commanders rank than he is at present, after six or eight years of service as mate. I further reckon that of first Entries[,] 2½ per cent may be expected annually to fall off[,] and that 100 young officers entering in each year would be reduced to 80 at the end of eight years service as Cadet & Midshipmen and Mate [*sic*]. This would allow of 100 entries in each year, and would give about 160 Mates, 352 midshipmen and 200 cadets, 712 in all. At present we have 51 mates and about 1000 Midshipmen and Cadets, and the present table of complements would require 1086 mates and Midshipmen and 286 Cadets. I should like these numbers to be revised by the members of the Board with regard to the number of promotions which may be required to maintain the Lieutenants List in efficiency[,] and with regard to the number of first Entries which may be allowed in each year. Between the 1st Jan 1840 and 1st Jan 1848 about 660 mates have been promoted, or upon an average [of] about 82 in each year, and this number does not seem to have been more than sufficient.

I further think that the career which Naval cadets are expected to run [*sic*], should be well considered and very carefully regulated. The age of entry should be defined, and no Cadet should be admitted at a more advanced age than 14. I have known entries of young men of nearly 17 years. I think[,] too[,] that there should be more strictness than seems to be enforced at present in the passing of Cadets to the rank of Midshipman[.] The qualification required should be sufficient and the examination strict, and the Cadet not passing should be rejected for three or six months. I think too that with the small number of Cadets &c proposed, every new entry should be to a Line of Battle Ship or other ship in which a Naval Instructor is entertained [*sic*], and where systematic instruction may be gained, and that subsequently the Midshipmen and Mates should be in great measure distributed amongst the smaller ships[,] where there is likely to be more of the practice of Navigation, and I would altogether discontinue the first entry of Cadets to Sloops & former [*sic*] vessels. Upon all this a question will arise upon the manner in which the service is to be performed which has been heretofore committed to Mates and Midshipmen, and I am clearly of opinion that less inconvenience will arise from a reduced number of these young officers than would be the result of the large & capacious entry of Cadets which has latterly taken place. Of the Mates, Midshipmen and Cadets now upon the List there are of the Year 1839 – 6. 1840 – 27. 1841 – 89. 1843 – 143. 1843 – 47. 1844 – 110. 1845 – 183. 1846 – 221. 1847 – 172 and 1848 – 39. 1037 in all. And it will require great care and very watchful proceedings to bring this part of the Naval Establishment to the Condition in which I should like to see it.

The Naval Estimates as at present taken, would admit of 509 Mates, 527 Mid[shipme]n, and 352 Naval Cadets, Costing [*sic*] about £55,000 annually. The [*sic*] reduced number which I would propose[,] would bring this charge down to little more than £30,000[,] and would give a sum of money by which a superior class of Petty Officer might be maintained[.] I would wish it to be considered whether a grade of this kind might not with advantage be created. It might be the ultimate object of rise [i.e., promotion] with the existing Petty Officers; it might be invested with higher authority than has hitherto been given to them[,] and might operate as a general means of encouragement. But the points which are first to be considered are 1st[:] The average period of service which are to be expected [*sic*] from Mates. I have suggested two years. 2nd[:] The number of promotions of mates, of from 20 to 22 or 23 years of age, which will be sufficient and not more than sufficient to keep the Lieutenants List in a state of efficiency. I have suggested 80. and [*sic*] 3ly[:] what shall be the number of Entries of Naval Cadets in each year[?] I have suggested 100. When these points are determined[,] other regulations may be framed as consequent upon them.

[**196**] *Milne Minute on Auckland's Memorandum on Entry of Naval Cadets*

[Admiralty
July 1848]

This paper of Lord Aucklands on the entry of Naval Cadets requires a good deal of consideration[,] as it is from their entry [that] all promotions flow thro the different grades to that of the Flag. His Lordship proposes to limit the entry to 100 pr. A[,] and by deducting the average casualties from death, and those leaving the service, there will probably remain at the end of six years, about 80 who will arrive at the rank of Mate, and in a further period of two years there will be about 157 of that rank on the list of the Navy. It is after two years servitude as Mate, that Lord A. proposes that they should be made Lieutenants, and about 80 in each year. Such being the case[,] it is easy to calculate how many officers of the rank of Cadet, Mid & Mate there will be available for the service of the Fleet. It will be as many as under[:]

Cadets.	196	in 2 years
Mid	348	in 6 years
Mates	157	in 8 years
Total	701	

That is[,] there will be 701 officers of those grades for disposal among the Ships in Commission, consisting[,] with reliefs[,] of about 220 ships. It must be at once obvious that so small a number of officers will be totally inadequate to the wants of the service, more especially if we contrast it with the present number required by the present Estab[lishmen]t[:]

	Cadets	Mates & Mid	Ships in Com	Cadets Required	Mates & Mid Required
1 Rates	6	22	14	224	756[1]
2 "	6	16	"		
3 "	5	16	"		
4 "	4	12	5	20	60
5 "	3	10	25	30	250
6	2	8	10	16	80
Sloops	2	4	45	90	180
[Total]			99	380	1326

I have here assumed a very low limit to form the above calculation[,] viz. 99 ships, and these 99 require[,] by the present Est[a]b[lishe]d regulations of Complement[,] 380 Cadets, and 1326 Mid & Mates. What is then to be done with the 701 officers of these grades to be distributed over our fleet, when we find it requires 1706 for 99 ships[?] Some ships will require to be without any, and our Line of Battle Ship[s] will have to be limited to about 1 Cadet, 2 Mid & 1 Mate. It is therefore perfectly obvious that such a limitation is in every respect

[1]This is the cumulative figure for all three rates combined.

inadequate for the duty, for a Ship of the Line at the lowest possible scale would require –

Middle Deck –	1 Mate
Main Deck	1 Do
Mates of Watches	6 Mates or Mid & 3 Cadets
Signals	3 Mates or Mid or [unfinished]
Boats Watering &s	2 Mates or Mid and 3 Cadets

19 in all[,] and so in proportion for other classes of ships, the present complement of a 1st rate being 28. If the service cannot afford to maintain a greater number of officers & bring them forward for the rank of Lieut, there is of course no help for it, but I do not myself see how the service is to be conducted; Lord Auckland has proposed a superior Class of Petty officers to fill up the place ('on duty') by the reduction in Mid[,] &c. I cannot see my way to this proposal. at [*sic*] present there is great difficulty in obtaining good steady est[ablishe]d warrant officers[,] more especially Carpenters[,] & every day this difficulty is getting worse[,] from having few good shipwrights in the service[,] the pay being so low in comparison with what can be obtained on shore, and the Widows pension having been taken away from the warrant officers. There is no inducement for them to obtain that rank, more especially since the Seamen can draw his pension when serving and the two combined are sometimes as much as the pay of the warrant officer.

I fully concur in Lord Aucklands view with reference to a limitation of age for Cadets. 14 is certainly a desirable age for entry[,] but I think it might be extended to 14½ and such a regulation should be adopted. . . .

The regulations relative to the periodical examinations require revision with reference to some points of when a Mid having served two year's [*sic*] & ought to be examined [*sic*]. he [*sic*] may be unable to do so[,] and there is no certificate required or any penalty if he does not[,] his time goes on and he passes at the end of six years[,] whether he has gone thro the examination or not.[1]

[1]The subsequent Board Minute (2 October 1848) fixed the number to enter every month at six. In MLN/145/5: 'Measures brought forward by Captain Milne when a Member of the Board of Admiralty, from December 1847,' nd., Milne stated that one of his accomplishments was having 'Proposed reduction of the entry of Naval Cadets to 100 in 1848, double that number having on one occasion been entered; this number subsequently reduced to 70; [and] a check put on the entry of Masters' Assistants and Assistant Clerks.' The papers reproduced here, however, suggest that the plan originated with Auckland.

[197] *Napier to Milne*

HMS *St. Vincent*, Cove of Cork
3 September 1848

My dear Milne

I send you a letter from Henderson with his warrant for Boatswain's and Carpenter's Stores, which I hope you will examine into[.] The *Sidon*[,] as you know[,] is not like other steamers and ought to be treated differently. There is some mistake in your Steam department. It appears *Sidon*'s Steam Chests were made both at Malta and at Portsmouth. when [*sic*] I urged them being sent out to her[,] it appears Parker[1] had written home to say he was making them at Malta.

All *Reynard*'s[2] Topmasts and Top Gall[an]t Masts are too small. She carried them away. I will examine her more particularly and report. You will see by my public letter that *Blenheim* does wonders[,] but I would advise you to halt about [*sic*] fitting any other until I and Chads[3] have had time to consider what changes are necessary.

We had three days and nights of weather not at all comfortable.

[198] *Milne to Napier*

Admiralty
6 September 1848

My dear Sir Charles

Thanks for your note and its Enclosures[,] which came in excellent time as I had the *Sidon*'s Establishment in hand with the Storekeeper General, in consequence of reports from Malta Dock Yard[,] and I will take due care to go into the whole matter in the course of a few days[,] and have the requisite Papers sent to Henderson and Malta Dock Yard.

We have been looking over your report. It is highly gratifying[,] and I feel assured it would be most satisfactory specially to report on the Screw vessels; I would also wish something official from you on the Wire Rigging[,] to enable us to come to an opinion with reference to *Arrogant*, *Ajax*, *Hogue* &c. It becomes a question whether its use should be continued . . .

[1]Adm. Sir William Parker, C-in-C of the Mediterranean Squadron 1845–52.

[2]Variously rendered *Renard* or *Reynard*.

[3]Henry Ducie Chads C.B., K.C.B., G.C.B. (1788–1868). Entered, 1800; Lt, 1806; Cmdr, 1813; Capt., 1825; Rear-Adm., 1854; Vice-Adm., 1858; Adm., 1863.

I hope to see you at Devonport about [the] 20th[.] we are to be at Portsmouth 14th[,] Sheerness tomorrow[, then] Chatham . . .

[**199**] *Napier to Milne*

HMS *St. Vincent*, Cove of Cork
9 September 1848

My dear Milne

. . . I have reported on the *Blenheim* and I hope it will not be put at the bottom of a chest as my Steam Table was, which is discouraging.

I am setting the *Reynard* to rights[,] and when she is ready and everything is in its place[,] I will inspect her more closely; she was hurried out too soon and [at] the first breeze away went her Fore Topmast and Main Top Gallant Mast. He[1] complains of the wire rigging stretching[,] but (entre nous)[,] I begin to find out he knows nothing about it. I do not believe he ever kept a Lieutenant's Watch more than a month or two, lots of zeal but no knowledge. It will take some time to decide about the wire rigging[.] Ramsay[2] has had some experience of it. You can trust to his reports. I certainly would not be in a hurry about fitting other Steam Ships with it, and when you do fit more Steam Ships[,] do get somebody who understands it. The Dock Yard know nothing about it [*sic*], and do pause before you build more *Reynards*. As far as Screwing [*sic*] goes she does well, but she is a shell and[,] I strongly suspect[,] when examined into, will show little or nothing[,] and she has been fitted in a Slop [*sic*] way in every respect as all vessels will be, when built by Edye[3] and fitted by Oliver Lang. He seems to have played her the same trick in masting as he did the *Sidon*. Those rival Gentlemen put the Country to great Expense and ought to be brought up with a round turn.

I am glad you are pleased with my report, but it is a pity that Ward[4] does not write me a public letter, for I am always in doubt whether I am doing right or wrong.

[1]Peter Cracroft (1816–65). Entered, 1830; Lt, 1841; Cmdr, 1846; Capt., 1854. Cracroft commanded *Reynard*, which, while still under his charge, was wrecked in Chinese waters on 31 May 1851.

[2]William Ramsay, C.B., K.C.B. (1796–1871). Entered, 1809; Lt, 1821; Cmdr, 1831; Capt., 1838; Rear-Adm., 1857; Vice-Adm., 1864. Ramsay was HMS *Terrible*'s captain.

[3]John Edye, Assistant Surveyor of the Navy.

[4]Sir Henry George Ward (d. 1860). Secretary to the Admiralty, 1846–49; Lord High Commissioner of the Ionian Islands, 1849–55; Governor-General of Ceylon, 1866–60; Governor of Madras, 1860.

[**200**] *Napier to Milne*

HMS *St. Vincent*, Cove of Cork
3 November 1848

My dear Milne

Dacres has shewed me your plan for ameliorating the conditions of the Petty Officers and Seamen; it does not go far enough to please me[,] but if you could get no more money you could do no more.

The Yeoman of Signals ought unquestionably to be a First Class Petty Officer. His situation is a most important one. I used to think it was quite right to reduce the Pay of a Flag Captain[,] but I have changed my mind; he has twice the work of any other Captain to do, if he does it, particularly with a squadron like mine, and the little time you were with me must satisfy you on that head. I suppose you know I sail on the 19th to resume my office of Dunce driving.

[**201**] *Milne to Napier*

HMS *Black Eagle*, Devonport
8 November 1848

My dear Sir Charles

Many thanks for your kind note[,] which I received two days ago[,] and I am glad you so far approve of the Good Conduct Warrant. It is a difficult and complicated subject[,] and one which requires very great caution and consideration[,] as its application to Seamen is so very different from the mode adopted in the Army[,] and our funds were and are limited. We are still going on with our Dock Yard Investigation[,][1] but leave this for Pembroke this afternoon and hope to reach London after visiting Liverpool and Manchester on Saturday week, by which I presume you will be starting for the groves of the orange and geraniums as Mr Cobden[2] considers them to be. Wishing you therefore a pleasant winter campaign in Dunce Driving . . .

[1]Milne was then part of a Dockyard Revision Committee.

[2]Radical M.P. Richard Cobden had recently denounced maintaining the Navy's overseas squadrons as a wasteful extravagance that allowed officers and men (as paraphrased by Henry Ward), 'an easy indolent existence, passed under groves of laurel and orange trees . . . '; see *Hansard's Parliamentary Debates*, 3rd ser., vol. 97, col. 787.

[202] *Napier to Milne*

HMS *St. Vincent*
18 November 1848

My dear Milne

Did it ever occur to you that when Stores &c are wanted in the Dock Yards[,] it would be as well to let the Superintendents advertize for Tenders and receive them at once[?] Slop Clothing[,] for instance[,] supplied would be much better attended to in the Yards than elsewhere [*sic*]. The Admiral could order them to be surveyed before they were received[,] and it would soon be seen which Dock Yard supplied the best; this would be a check on Jobbery and Roguery.

[203] *Milne to Napier*

Admiralty
19 November 1848

My dear Sir Charles

Thanks for your note and suggestions about the contracts for Clothing[,] and I will give it full consideration when we come to the revision of the Contract system; there is a good deal to be said on both sides of the question, more especially as the amount of Articles contracted for is very great[,] and we get the Articles from the manufacturer direct[,] whereas if we took the Contract at the Port, the Agents there would have to employ one of the great manufacturing Houses[,] and charge you the percentage. I have learned a few wrinkles on the cruise[,] such as boring out a rotten piece of wood in a log and setting in a false knot with rosin to resemble a real one[,] & also plugging up the rent ends of logs & sawing the end off 'fair & square'[,] to make it look like a solid piece[,] but no doubt in spite of all that may be put on paper in the way of stringent terms[,] the Contractor will find a way of humbugging us. No news. With best wishes for a pleasant cruise . . .

[**204**] *Milne to Napier*[1]

Deptford
30 November 1848

My dear Sir Charles

Thanks for your note[,] which I received this morning[,] and I am glad you have taken a walk thro 'Anchor Forest.' All yards are equally prolific in them and months ago (last February) I recommended that no more orders should be given, altho £30,000 was taken in the Estimates and[,] with the above[,] £122,000 for Chain Cables. I recommended a reduction of £30,000. This should have been done the year before, for we had more Anchors than can ever be used. As to the Rogers & Porters[,] it annoys me whenever I go into a Dock Yard to see so much money thrown away. I am in those Gentlemens Bad Books[,] as you will often see by the Papers, because I will not allow any Anchors to be ordered. In all our Stores much is required to be done[,] and I hope by degrees to be enabled to check the waste of Public Money. Recollect not to speak of these matters before Dundas[2] of *Powerful*[,] who is brother to [the] Storekeeper General[,] and who feels[,] I think[,] very sore at my interference and checking the unnecessary outlay of public money. Our Timber wants looking into[,] and it requires some one person to follow up a system of enquiry and endeavour to place matters on a more regular and economical footing. I find it difficult to do myself[,] and even what I have to do in the Storekeeper Gen[era]l, Victualling[,] Medical and other departments is not done satisfactorily to myself. It is too vast a field for one person, unless they are exclusively engaged on that duty which I am now, but I will do my best and I feel confident I will be able to reform in somethings. I will drop you a line now and then to let you know what is going on . . .

We finish here [Deptford] on Saturday[,] if possible which will close our Dock Yard labours just now. I am glad to hear Dacres is much better.

[1]It is noted in the margin that this letter was written in response to a letter Napier sent but did not have copied to his letterbook. Nor is it preserved among Milne's papers.

[2]Richard Saunders Dundas.

[**205**] *Milne Draft Inspection Sheet for H.M. Ships*[1]

[Admiralty
January 1849]

Inspection Sheet of HMS ________
Confidential Report and Inspection Sheet of HMS ________
Date ________
Date of last Inspection, and by whom? ________
Name of Captain or Commander, with date of his Appointment
Have you any complaint to make against any of the Officers of the Ship?
Have the Articles of War, and all Admiralty Circulars and General Memorandums [*sic*] been read publicly to the Ship's Company?
Have the Officers paid attention to the Admiralty Regulations and Instructions on all points connected with the Public Service?
Has Divine Service been regularly performed?
Have the regulations with regard to smoking been attended to?
Whether there is a Book of written orders for the Ship?
Whether the orders for the night are left verbally or in writing?
Defaulter's Book to be produced and thoroughly examined relative to punishments?
To furnish a List of all descriptions of Secondary Punishments?
Have Secondary Punishments of all descriptions, adopted and inflicted in the ship, been recorded in the Defaulter's Book?
By whom have these punishments been awarded?
Has the Captain delegated his authority to any Officer as to Secondary Punishments, or does he allow any Officer to award Secondary or Minor punishments without his authority?
If so, have these Secondary Punishments been inserted in the Defaulter's Book?
To furnish a List of all disratings of Petty Officers, and to what ratings, with the reasons for such disratings?

[1]MLN/145/4 contains four copies of the main inspection sheet, plus two ancillary ones relative to steamships (one of which is a handwritten draft of [**206**]). Three of the four of the former are identical, the fourth appears to be a working draft. One of the three identical sheets is reproduced here. Milne wrote in pencil on one of the printed inspection sheets (that copied here): 'This inspection sheet [was] drawn up and introduced in the Service by me'. On another copy he noted 'This was drawn up by me with the view of Establishing a proper Inspection Sheet for the Service. A Milne'. Beneath this notation he later added '1848–49' but no precise date is to be found on any of the copies; 3 January 1849, however, is clearly written on the subsequent inspection sheet for steam vessels, and it appears likely that the two were composed about the same time. Milne put an 'x' beside those clauses marked with an asterisk.

To furnish a List since last inspection of all Corporal Punishments and confinement in Gaol or Cells, with time of confinement and for what offences?
Desertions, to furnish a list of all deserters, with servitude of each person in the Navy with former character, as per Certificate?
Supposed reason on enquiry for such desertions?
Marines [deserted], from what Division?
Punishment Book, whether it is inspected by the Captain, or Officer in command?
Whether the Senior Marine Officer is permitted to punish the Marines by Secondary Punishment, independent of the Captain of the Ship?
If so, whether all and every such punishment is inserted in the Defaulter's Book?
What power of punishment is granted by the Captain of the ship to the Senior Marine Officer?
Leave, whether regularly given to the Ship's Company when in Harbour, and at what Ports, also when last leave was granted, and for what time?
Reasons why leave is not given?
Short allowance money, when it is usually paid to the men, periodically, or at what time?
When men are discharged from the Ship Books [*sic*] or the Supernumerary List, either to the shore or another ship, what means are taken to pay him his savings for provisions or for grog which might have been stopped?
Monthly money, when is this paid, monthly or quarterly, or depending on a ship's being in Harbour?
Has the monthly money been stopped as a Punishment?
Officers, have they kept their regular watches according to the regulations of the service, viz: in 3 watches?
Have they kept their Logs, &c. according to Admiralty Regulations?
Have they regularly submitted their day's work, and has the Admiralty Circular order ________ been enforced and attended to by them?
If not, from what cause has that order been disobeyed?
Have the Officers messes been conducted in an economical manner and commensurate with those Officers who can least afford it?
What is the amount of mess money paid each month, also if there is a subscription for a wine fund, and to what amount?
Are all out-standing claims against the respective messes liquidated?
Has card playing been allowed in the mess, if so, under what regulations, and has any acts [*sic*] of gambling or playing for high stakes been permitted?

Have the junior Officers been in regular attendance with the Naval Instructor?
Naval Instructor to be called in and questioned on the subject, and their [i.e., the junior Officers] Logs and Books to be examined.
Has a monthly examination day for the purpose of testing the improvement of the Cadets and Midshipmen been adopted?*
Also in knotting, splicing &c., heaving the lead, exercise in reefing and furling on mizen [*sic*] topsail yard and general duties in seamanship and rigging?
In Steam Vessels, have they been placed under the Engineer for instruction in the theory and working of the engine?*
What person takes charge of their money affairs, and by whom are their expenses checked?
The Log Books and Watch Bills of the Officers to be examined.
The Ship's Logs to be produced and examined, and to see whether all entries relative to discharges and receipt of men have been inserted, also the opening of provisions, &c.
Whether there is any complaint against the provisions and whether any condemnations?
To examine Muster, Slop and other Books[.]
Whether they are complete and are kept in a clean state, and do credit to the Clerk of the Ship?
Have they been regularly transmitted when due, and at what period of the Quarter, &c.?
Also with regard to Pursers Accounts, &c.
Whether Officers and Men are checked when on leave or absent[,] in accordance with the Instructions?
Whether they are regularly examined after each muster, the entries and discharges compared and signed by the Captain in the Muster Table?*
Whether Slop Clothing is always issued in a public manner, and whether the Officers of Divisions attend with their men?
Whether any men have been allowed to run into debt, by taking up a larger amount of Clothing than his [*sic*] pay would admit?
Whether the men are furnished with check notes of the charges against them on the Books, to enable them to rectify any apparent error before the Books are finally closed and transmitted, and if so, how often?*
When the boys are checked for their grog money, who takes charge of the savings, and how is it laid out, and what check is there on its appropriation?*
Is the Master at Arms allowed to sell articles of Clothing or Knives &c. to the Ship's Company, or advance money to them?

What duties does the Seaman Schoolmaster perform, and how many persons has he under his instruction, and at what hours?
Muster Ship's Company divisions to see if they are clean, also the Ship, and that the holds &c. are properly ventilated, and that the Officers are in proper uniform.
Muster the Ship's Company, by open List.
The Ships [*sic*] Company should be informed if they have any cause of complaint to come forward and make the same known whilst the Admiral or Inspecting Officer is on board.
As the men pass[,] to call their ratings, and ask whether the P[etty] O[fficers] actually perform the duties of their respective ratings.*
If any disrating from Petty Officer to Ordinary Seaman is noted in the Books, it is to be noticed, and explanation asked, being irregular, although common.
Ordinary [seamen], whether too long kept in these ratings or too soon advanced, whether they are mustered and examined once a quarter or oftener, to see whether they are fit for A.B. ratings?
Boys 1st Class[:]
Are any employed as Servants?
Are they regularly exercised aloft, at the lead &c., and do they take their regular turn at the wheel, if not, the reasons?
Are they all stationed in the Tops and Boats?
Boys 2nd Class[:]
How are they employed?
Do they regularly attend for exercise aloft, also at great gun, cutlass and musket exercise[?]
Do they attend the Seaman Schoolmaster[?]
In what manner has the Sick Pay Fund been laid out, and has there been any saving to the Government, if so state the amount[?]*
Has the Surgeon laid out the Fund in such a manner as to afford those comforts to the patients for which [*sic*] the fund was established[?]
Have the Warrant Officers been attentive to their duty, and are they persons in all respects fit for their situations?
Have their respective Expense Books been kept up, and by whom are they examined and submitted to you for inspection and approval?
Has any irregular expenditure of Stores taken place[,] contrary to the Regulations of the Service?
To inspect the Rigging, &c., and enquire, whether according to the Establishment, or if any change, from what cause a deviation has been allowed.
What Articles of Experiment are on board, and have they regularly been reported upon to the Admiralty?

Have you, or any of the Officers, any recommendation to submit with reference to the Ship, Armament, &c., which might be considered to render her more efficient[?]
To Beat to Quarters, and Flag Lieutenant to note time taken to clear the quarters, and the time each deck was reported, and also the general time when clear.
To Inspect the Decks, to see that all Spare Gear is at the Guns, and every thing in proper order.
Man one side[.]
Call duties and numbers[.]
Exercise[.]
Extreme training[.]
Transport Guns one Port forward[.]
Exercise[.]
Transport to proper ports[.]
Man both sides[.]
Exercise[.]
Select Officers to Exercise Guns[.]
Dismounting Guns, whether proper fittings [*sic*][.]
Quick firing with wads from Magazine, instead of Powder[,] Wad and Shot, to be placed in the Gun, continue 5 or 6 rounds. Mark time, draw the Guns.
Firemen, Divisions, Boarders, Rigging men, [&] Small Armed [*sic*] Men to be exercised by their Divisional Officers.
Whether the arrangements for extinguishing fires are judicious?
Have the Boys and those stationed at the Magazine passages been exercised at the Magazine exercise, independent of the general exercise[?]
Man the Boats, fire [the boats' guns] or not as convenient.
Whether the Arms are kept at or near the Guns, with proper fittings &c.
Secure Guns &c.
General observations on the state of discipline and preparation for battle.
Armament H.M.S ________

	No.	Prs.	Weight	Length	Rounds of shot on Deck for each gun
Gun Deck					
Middle Deck					
Main Deck					
Quarter Deck					
Poop					
Forecastle					
Total					

Boats ______

Ship's Complement[:]

	Establishment	Complement	Borne	Short	Remarks
Officers					
Subordinate do.					
1st Class P. Officers					
2nd Class do.					
A.B.					
Ordinary					
1st Class Boys					
2nd Class Boys					
Marines					

[**206**] *Milne Draft Inspection Sheet for Steam Vessels*

Admiralty
3 January 1849

Yard ______
18 ____
Form to be filled up on the completion of each Steam vessel for service, whether first fitted, repaired, or newly equipped, by the Engineer Department at the Port where the Works have been performed; the particulars, as to the Dimensions, &c., of the respective parts, to be ascertained by accurate Measurement.
(To be forwarded direct to the Comptroller of Steam machinery.)
Her Majesty's Steam [Ship, Sloop, etc.] ________
Draught of Water when Launched, or before receiving the Machinery
Forward
Aft
Ditto with Engines, Boilers, Masts, and Rigging
Forward
Aft
Ditto Load complete, with Stores for Sea
Forward
Aft
Engines, Manufacturer
" When new?
" If old, from what Vessel?
" Date of last thorough repair at a Factory
" Description, (whether direct, beam, oscillating, vertical, Horizontal [*sic*], &c.)

" Number of Cylinders
" Diameter of Cylinder
" Length of Stroke
Kind of Piston
Weight of Engines
" Boilers
" Water in ditto
" Paddle Wheels, or
" Screw Propeller
" Spare Gear
Total weight with all fittings
Number of Revolutions per minute
When tried light – Draft of Water
Fore ____ No.
Aft ____ No.
When tried deep – Draft of Water
Fore ____ No.
Aft ____ No.
Mean Pressure on the Piston by Indicator
When tried light ____ lbs.
When tried deep ____ lbs.
Boilers
Description of Boilers
Iron or Copper
By whom made
When new
Date of last thorough Repair, and where performed
Number of separate Parts
Height of top or Boiler above or below Load Water Line
Tubes, Number (Total)
" Length
" Diameter
" Thickness
" Whether with Ferrules or not
Tube plates, Thickness
" Distance between Tubes
" Iron or Brass
Number of Furnaces
Length of ditto
Breadth of Ditto [*sic*]
Pressure on Safety Valve
Number of Stoke Holes

Means of Ventilation
Number of Funnels
Diameter of ditto
Length of ditto
If made to strike, in what manner
Number of Masts
Position of Main Mast with relation to Funnels
Cubic Contents of Boxes
Quantity of Coals that can be stowed in Boxes, and of what Description
Ditto that can be stowed in other Parts
Cubic Contents of ditto
What number of Pipes are fitted in Boxes to ascertain the Temperature
Paddle Wheels
Description of Paddle Wheels
Diameter of the inner edge of outer Rim
How much Reefed [*sic*]
Total number of Paddles in each Wheel
Number of Paddles on the Arm
Breadth of each
Dip or Immersion of Paddle[1]
When tried light
ft. ____ in. ____
When tried deep
ft. ____ in. ____
Description of Disconnecting Apparatus
" " Brakes, or holding do.
Extreme breath over Paddle Boxes at the Spring Beams
Whether fitted with Paddle Box Boats?
Screw Propeller
Description of Screw Propeller
Diameter of do.
Length, (on the line of Keel)
Pitch
Multiple
Means for Disconnecting the Propeller
" for Hoisting do.
Description of Distilling Apparatus
" of turning round the Engines when cold
" of any other contrivances under trial

[1]Milne added in the margin: 'The immersion of the Paddles is to be ascertained by careful measurement, at the same time, of *both Paddle Wheels in Smooth Water*'.

What is the rate of Speed, both when at light Draught [*sic*] and when Deep, ascertained by measured distance, and where tried?[1]
When tried Light ____ Nautical Miles
When tried Deep ____ Nautical Miles
General Remarks
On the Extent of Repairs or Alterations of the Machinery and Vessel during her Equipment at the Port.

[**207**] *James W. D. Dundas Paper on Proposed Reduction in the Grog Ration*

Admiralty, Private and Confidential
12 February 1849

I beg to submit to the Board of Admiralty the following proposition respecting the allowance of Spirits issued to the Officers, Seamen, and Marines, of the Royal Navy, together with Extracts [*sic*] from the Letters of many Officers of experience,[2] shewing their opinion on the subject. The present allowance of Spirits is much too large; and this fact is, I regret to say, fully borne out by the list of Punishments in the Navy for three years past.
The number of Punishments were –

	For drunkenness only	For various other Offences	Total
In 1846	517	560	1077
1847	405	428	833
1848	527	526	1053

I propose that the pay of every Officer and Man shall be increased 3s. per month, and that half only, of the present allowance of Spirits shall be issued to them. All persons under 18 years of age not to be allowed any Spirits or additional pay.

If this measure were carried out, a period should be fixed, from and after which date, all Ships Commissioned should come under this new regulation, and their Officers and men receive 3s. a month additional, with half the present allowance of Spirits.

[1]Milne added: 'Indicator Cards, originals, are to be attached to this Return; taken on the occasions of the trials "Light" and "Deep," from each Engine, Top and Bottom'.

Cards are likewise to be sent, showing the Performance of the Engines on each of the grades of Expansion.

A List of the Spare Gear actually put on Board is also to be appended, certified to have been tried in place.'

[2]Not included in this edition.

The estimated expense of this alteration at the present price of Rum would be, for the number of Men voted for 1849–50, 40,000 (after deducting Marines on shore, and Boys) and also taking into account the saving of Spirits, (the price of Rum being 1s 4d. per gallon) about £38,000 per ann.; however, as it would not come into operation for the whole Fleet at once, but gradually become general in about three years, the cost would be for the first year about £13,000; for the second, £26,000; and for the third year the sum of £38,000, as already mentioned.[1]

[208] *Milne Minute on the Report of the Committee Appointed to Consider the Expediency of Reducing the Allowance of Spirits Issued to the Seamen of the Fleet*

[Admiralty, 1849]

With reference to the Report of the Committee appointed to consider the expediency of reducing the allowance of spirits issued to the seamen of [the] Fleet[,] I beg to submit my opinions on the various proposals which have been submitted to the Board, in the summary at the end of the report.

1st [:] That the present allowance of spirits or wine be reduced by one half.

In my former opinions which I have given on this subject[,] I had always considered that the cause of drunkenness in our ships was owing to the abuse[,] and not the use of the daily allowance, and after having read the evidence before the Committee which was given by all the P. Officers, Seamen, and Marines, I am bound to say I am confirmed in that opinion, but I was not prepared for the statements that were made[,] nor was I aware of the fact, That [*sic*] in many ships the Cooks of the Messes were allowed to have the whole evenings allowance of their Messes for their own personal use, and that this system has been the cause not only of much drunkenness and irregularity[,] but

[1]Dundas's proposal generated a Committee, which issued a report, which in turn generated the Milne Minute which follows. See *Hansard's Parliamentary Debates*, 3rd ser., vol. 109 (1850), cols. 707–8. In his speech introducing the Navy Estimates in 1850, Sir Francis Baring made reference to the subject and committee. No such report, however, appears in the *Parliamentary Papers*, suggesting that the House was content with the Admiralty's proposed solution to the question. As the subsequent Milne Minute reveals, the Committee recommended that the Grog Ration be halved and the men's pay increased by way of compensation. These proposals and others were subsequently adopted. See *The Times* (London), 26 March 1850, p. 5 for details, and R. Taylor, 'Manning the Royal Navy', pt. 1, p. 309 for a modern gloss.

from it has arisen most of the Punishments in the Service. It appears to me that this system can alone have originated from the issue of the Grog and Tea at the same period of the Evening, and that a preference has been given by the men to the Tea as a supper meal [*sic*]; – The Grog has therefore been considered as a secondary article[,] and from thence had arisen the custom of the Cooks of the Messes getting the whole allowance.

If this view is correct[,] and I am inclined to this opinion from the evidence, I should consider it a most advisable and beneficial measure to reduce the allowance of spirits by one half[,] and to adopt the second recommendation of the Committee, That [*sic*] the remaining portion should be issued at Dinner time.

It will be observed that statements were made by those men who had served in Merchant vessels, That [*sic*] in bad weather and especially after much fatigue the crew's [*sic*] of these vessels were allowed a Cup of Hot Coffee at night, and in some others a small glass of Spirits. The Coffee or Tea can be easily procured in these vessels where the crews are small, but what is to be done in our ships[,] where our crews are numerous and where it would be impossible to give them either Coffee or Tea[?] I should adopt of my own accord [an] order[:] under circumstances of great fatigue and where the men of [*sic*] have been exposed to the wet[, that they be issued] a small wine glass of Spirits before going to their Hammocks, and I should allow the regulation to be adopted at the <u>discretion</u> of the Captain in the same manner as it is now left to the discretion and judgment of the Master of all Merchant vessels[,] with reference to the issue of spirits.

3. That Admirals[,] Captains[, &] Wardroom Officers shall not receive any payment for the half ration of spirits taken from them.

There can be no objection to this proposal[.] These officers cannot expect that they should received [*sic*] the same amount of compensation as the seamen, when they obtain their wine & groceries duty free[,] a privilege only granted within the last few years.

4. That Mates, Second Masters, Ass[istant] Surgeons & Clerks shall receive compensation as the saving prices [*sic*] for the half allowance of spirits to be received.

I entirely concur.

[5.] That Mid.[,] Cadets and Boys who do not receive a ration of spirits be paid a compensation equal to the saving price of the whole allowance.

This proposal of course implies these officers are to have no spirits and no wine. I should be inclined to recommend the issue of wine to these officers at the expense of [the] Govt.[,] and to allow the saving price of the whole allowance to go towards the Expense. I am not an advocate for the cold water system entirely[,] but consider a couple of glasses of wine to the youngsters a beneficial measure. The Regulations of Service allow every person serving ¼ of spirits or 1 Pint of wine. as [*sic*] ½ the allowance of spirits is to be done away with[,] reduce the allowance of wine in the same proportion[,] and allow it to be supplied from the Vict[uallin]g Yards to the Youngsters in the same way as Medical comforts[,] viz in 3 doz cases, and no other wine to be allowed in the Mess. Should the Board entertain this submission, it should be dealt with separately and embrace some other regulations with regard to the Expense of the Mid[s] messes.

6. That Warrant officers[,] working P[etty] officers, AB, Ord[inar]y Seamen, Non Com[missione]d Officers & Privates of Marines shall receive for their half allowance a compensation payment in money of 3/6 per calendar month[.]

I think this measure is a liberal one and will prove beneficial not only to the Seamen but likewise to the discipline of the Fleet, not that it will entirely prevent drunkenness[,] altho it may[,] by the reduction of the allowance of Grog[,] for which this is the substitute, be the means of checking it at sea, but it will not check the evil of smuggling from the shore.

7. That 2nd Class Ord[inar]y Seamen and Landsmen be allowed 2/8 pr day pr calendar month[.]

I entirely agree to this.

8. That men wishing to give up the reduced allowance shall receive a further compensation equal to the saving price for such period as they may think proper.

I see no objection whatever to this proposal.

9. That no raw spirits be issued to anyone except under special circumstances at the discretion of the Captain.

I would refer to what I have stated with reference to the 2d proposal.

10. That in case of persisting drunkenness a deduction or discontinuance be made for a time in the compensation allowance.

I think this proposal will lead to much confusion in the accounts and I am of opinion the compensation allowance should not be kept distinct . . . but should be blended with a new scale of pay which will be made out founded on the compensation money and alteration in the Calendar month. I should recommend a power being granted to the Captain to make the Messes drink their Grog at the Tub[,] in case of persisting drunkenness.

11. That the monthly allowance to the men out of their growing [*sic*] wages be limited to 12/– pr month.

I have long been of opinion that the scale of Monthly Money was much too liberal with reference to the money drawn by the men on Foreign Stations, and that the allotment to their families at Home was much too small to support them. I would therefore recommend an amended form to be adopted[,] and limit the highest amount to be paid abroad to 12/– pr month.

11 [*sic*][.] That the Police on board H.M. Ships be put on a better footing.

This is rather an extensive subject and would embrace[,] according to the Evidence of those examined and who proposed it[,] the formation of a separate and distinct Corp[s]. I do not consider it possible or feasible[,] & at all events it would cause a considerable expense to be incurred and[,] in my opinion[,] without any beneficial result. The men now employed are generally old Marine pensioners who have completed 21 years servitude[,] and if care is taken to obtain men of Good Character[,] many will be found anxious to serve & capable of discharging their duty in a satisfactory manner.

12. That the seamen and Marines shall be at liberty to make a larger allotment for the maintenance of their families viz £1–1–6 pr. month for an AB[.]

This is an admirable recommendation and will be of much advantage.

13. That the Admiralty Circular to the Fleet of the 21 July 1846[,] respecting provisions[,] to be brought under review for the purpose of a more satisfactory adjustment of the scale.

This recommendation embraces a very extensive field and must lead the Board to consider the whole Scheme of Naval Victualling as Est[a]b[lishe]d by the Queens Regulations, and this is certainly the most fit opportunity to make any improvement which may be required. It is advisable on that account to consider the allowance of each article of provisions and to consider whether it is in all respects sufficient, and draw a comparative return [of] that allowance and the quantity issued by the Merchant Marine[.]

Bread, allowance 7 lbs pr man [per week]. I am not aware of any complaint in the service that the allowance of Bread is too small, altho I observe in the Evidence such a sentiment is made [*sic*]. In the Merchant Service there is not generally any fixed allowance[;] they are allowed to eat as much as they like[,] provided there is no <u>waste</u>[,] but they are never paid for any savings unless put on a short allowance[.] By some returns I have obtained from Mercantile houses in Liverpool[,] I observe ¾ lb of Bread pr Man is fixed for the daily allowance and[,] under these circumstances[,] I do not think any alteration should be made in [the] present allowance of Bread.

Spirits[:]

To be reduced one half[,] as proposed by the Committee.

Beef[:]

The following is the allowance of Beef in different employments.

Royal Navy	¾ lb pr man
United States Navy	1 lb
Green & Wigram ships	1.10 lb.
Liverpool ships	1½
West & E India Trade	1½

This is a very great difference . . . [1]

[**209**] *Milne Proposal on Reporting Courts Martial Verdicts*

[Admiralty, 1849][2]

It has often occurred to me with reference to the Discipline of the Fleet, that so little attention has been paid to the sentences of Courts Martial[.] These Courts M[artial] are held on all grades of officers & men on the different Home[,] as well as Foreign Stations. The sentence is passed[,] sent home to the Admiralty and there matter rests[.] That a Court Martial has been held is scarcely known except to those who have been present in the Harbour[,] or perhaps thro the medium of the Public Press. Being therefore strongly of opinion that[,] if the sentences of Naval Courts Martial were publicly circulated throughout the Fleet and read to the respective ships Companies, That [*sic*] it would prove highly beneficial to the Service and its discipline, I beg to submit to the Board, the propriety of their issuing the following Instructions on the Subject.

Whenever a Court Martial is held at any of the Home Ports and a sentence pronounced convicting a person of charges which may have been preferred ag[ains]t him, a Copy of the Charges with the Sentence of such Court Martial will be transmitted from the Admiralty to each of the Commander's [*sic*] in Chief of such ports[,] as well as to those on Foreign Stations, who are[,] on the receipt of the same[,] to direct a Copy to be placed in the public order Book and copied by the respective ships[,] and the said charges and sentence are to be publicly read on the quarter deck to the respective ships companies by the Captain of the Ship [*sic*].

[1]Here the minute ends. On the scale of provisioning, see Milne's minute of 26 April 1850, printed in John Hattendorf et al. (eds), *British Naval Documents 1204–1960* (Navy Records Society, 1993), document 390, pp. 655–7.

[2]An undated paper to which Milne later added '1848–49'.

When a Court Martial is held on a Foreign Station, The [*sic*] Comdr in Chief of said station is to circulate the charges & sentence of such Court M[artial,] agreeably to the former Article[,] to the respective Captains of HMS under his command and[,] on the receipt of such sentence at the Admiralty[,] a Copy will be forwarded to all other Commander's [*sic*] in Chief for circulation and publicity[,] as before directed[.]

[**210**] *Milne Report on HMS* Plumper[1]

[Admiralty, *c.*1849]

Opinion on *Plumper* for Lord Auckland
Her qualities as a Sea Boat are good[,] altho she pitches heavily and deep, but she is a dry, stiff vessel and possesses great buoyancy.
She stows 3 months provisions with difficulty, but her stowage for Stores is lamentably deficient. She has no Sail Binns [*sic*], no place for Rope, and no Hempen Cable on board & her Estab[lishmen]t of Stores is less than a 16 Gun Brig.
Her Armament is not too heavy for her, as she is reported to carry it well and does not strain, but she is so narrow that she cannot fight her Broadside guns.
She cannot berth her Ships Co[mpany]. The space allotted to them is miserably small & confined. There is not room to hang up more than 56 Hammocks without using the space over the Engine room and the Engine room passages for that purpose[,] and when the Steam is up, it is impossible for the men to Sleep there. In consequence of the confined space on the Lower deck[,] the men are obliged to sleep on the Deck or where they best can.
The officers are wretchedly off[.] Their chests (Mates & Mids) are over the Boilers, their clothes are in consequence entirely [?destroyed] with [*sic*] the Heat, and as their Hammocks are hung up in the same locality[,] they are unable to sleep when the fires are lighted. I never witnessed so miserable a place to put officers in.
The Complement of 110 is not more than enough for the Guns. It is much too large for the accommodation[,] and yet it is not large enough for the Masts & Yards[,] and for them should be increased to 130 and [*sic*: 'but'] for the space allotted to accommodation[,] reduced to between 80 & 90.
The Engine Room[,] &c has taken up the largest space in the Ship, and thereby reduced the stowage and accommodation. She is in conse-

[1]Screw Steam Sloop.

quence a Steamer of an Aux[iliar]y power [*sic*], intended to [*sic*] for war purposes, without sufficient space to fight her Guns or space below to accommodate her crew.

I should recommend her present Broadside Guns to be landed and 32 P. carronades to be substituted.

[**211**] *Milne to Napier*

Admiralty
6 April 1849

My dear Sir Charles

I should have written you by yesterday's post[,] had not Adml Dundas done so before he left Town for Devonshire[,] where he is to be for the next week or ten days, but his letter you would not receive[,] as I observe your departure from Devonport[1] last evening in Sir W Gages letter [*sic*][.]

I intended to have run down to Portsmouth on your arrival[,] but I am afraid I will be unable to do so now unless Lord John Hay remains in Town, which is at present a matter of doubt, but if I can get away I will be at Portsmouth tomorrow evening & remain until Sunday night[,] but it must depend on Lord John's movements. We have no news here of much interest[,] altho Sir W Parker's despatches received this morning mention the Sicilians are determined to fight it out with the Neapolitans and will not accept any terms.[2] It will be a severe struggle[,] as I hear the Sicilians are well prepared.

I was in hopes of seeing Henderson[3] but as yet have been unsuccessful. He was at the [United Service] Club yesterday[,] but whether in Town or not Today I cannot find out[.]

I have written Dacres a line to offer my services if anything is wanted[,] and if I can be of use to you I will be very glad to attend to your wishes . . .

[1]The Channel/Lisbon squadron had returned to Spithead and Napier had been ordered to strike his flag. Gage was then Port Adm. at Devonport.

[2]Revolution had broken out in both Sicily and Naples the previous year, as in much of the rest of Europe. Sicily had subsequently declared its independence and, at the time Milne wrote Napier, the Neapolitan government was preparing an invasion force to re-establish control over the island. On the subsequent campaign see *The Times* (London), 14 April 1849, p. 6; 1 May 1849, p. 6; 3 May 1849, p. 6; 8 May 1849, p. 6; 17 May 1849; p. 6; 18 May 1849, p. 6; 21 May 1849, p. 6; 23 May 1849, p. 6; 1 June 1849, p. 6. Palermo fell to Neapolitan troops on 9 May.

[3]Capt. William H. Henderson.

[**212**] *Napier to Milne*

Merchistoun House, Horndean, Hampshire
12 April 1849

My dear Milne

I am very sorry you could not come to Portsmouth. I have not heard from Admiral Dundas or any one except yourself privately[,] tho' enough of public letters and some of them not very agreeable. I have replied to them. As I do not know the movements of the Admiralty[,] I have only sent them this evening[,] and you will much oblige me by seeing they are brought before the full Board. I will not trouble you with my private opinion. You will see my public ones [*sic*].

St Vincent will be nearly cleared tonight. You have got rid of the smartest ships company I ever saw. Some day the Country will have to repent of their reduction. Knowing as I do the difficulty of getting a squadron in order, I confess it alarms me.

The *Sidon* was paid off[,] for why I do not know[,] except to be replaced by *Arrogant*. She would have gone on two years without any repair. The work of destruction has begun – 5 Engineers and 6 Labourers to pull to pieces an engine that required nothing, and 24 boilermakers employed not to repair Boilers but to examine them, which could be done by two and a few labourers and her own Engineer[,] who knows more than any of them, obliged to look on and say nothing. that [*sic*] is the way your money is spent. Had *Sidon* remained in commission she would have gone on for two years, but now she would be folly to repair[, with] Boilers that do not work up to 350 Horse Power, which you will see by Mr Dinnen's[1] Report.

[**213**] *Ellenborough to Milne*

42 Estor Place, London
26 April 1849

Dear Captain Milne

I am much obliged to you for your Letter & am much pleased to hear that young Villiers was so attentive to his duties while he had the advantage of being under your command.

[1]John Dinnen (d. 1866). Inspector of Machinery, 1847–66.

[214] *Milne to Baring*

Inveresk, Musselburgh
2 July 1849

My dear Sir Francis

I have delayed answering your letter of the 29 until this morning[,] as the subject on which you ask my opinion requires a good deal of consideration. I will freely state my views and opinions on the matter[,] because I have seen a good deal of our foreign yards[,] & I am inclined to think that Lord Dundonalds statement[,] 'That there is a large unnecessary Expense' is a mere vague assertion, very often made without knowing anything of the detail of the Establishments or being aware of the circumstances of the Case. The Expense of our Foreign Yards may be subdivided into several heads[,] and by considering each separately we may be enabled to form an opinion whether it is possible to obtain a reduction or not.

(1) The Establishment of the Yards in officers, workmen & other parties including any hired men[.]

(2) The expense incurred in the Dock yard for the Establishment itself independent of the Director of Works Department[.]

(3) The Establishment of Stores including spars, sails, rope and all Naval Stores for the Fleet[.]

(4) New Works.

(1) The returns in officers which are periodically sent home should be carefully considered and the duties of each individual should be carefully considered and[,] on the comparison of duties with other Yards, it may be seen whether any reduction can be made[.] If the returns do not fully explain what duties are performed[,] a return might be ordered from each yard, stating each individual[,] his duties, when entered, age &c[,] & how long employed each day[,] with amount of pay. By having this return[,] a revision of the Est[a]b[lishmen]t might be done with great facility.

(2) The Accounts in the Storekeepers Office will show the charge for repairs, extra issue of stores &c[,] &[,] if gone over with care and attention[,] any extra expense will [become apparent] . . . [1]

[1]The rest of the draft is missing.

[**215**] *Napier to Milne*

Merchistoun House, Horndean, Hampshire
13 December 1849

My dear Milne

My letter with its enclosures will be at the Board tomorrow. I think if Sir Francis Baring has any feeling he will be ashamed of himself.[1] I hope justice will be rendered to me. I am unwilling to make a noise[,] but I do not deserve to be crushed by the caprices of one man.

I am sure you will[,] as far as you can, see justice done to me, and I will write to you that you may know my letter is there, that it will not be burked[,] which I know is sometimes done.

Pray let '*Sidon*' have *Dauntless*'s galley.

[**216**] *Milne to Napier*

Admiralty
20 January 1850

My dear Sir Charles

I should have answered your letter before this[,] but delayed doing so until I heard of yesterday's trial. I see by the papers of this morning she attained a greater degree of speed than you expected[,] and by these trials she appears to have done remarkably well.[2] I should have liked to have been on board, but it was quite out of the question my leaving Town during this week.

[1]Probably relative to Napier's having been relieved of the Channel/Lisbon Squadron command.

[2]This refers to the trial of the Napier-designed paddle steam frigate *Sidon*, which made an average speed of 9.356 knots over six runs in Stokes Bay, with Napier himself observing. See *The Times* (London), 19 January, p. 5.

[**217**] *Milne Draft Paper on Naval Measures to be taken in Case of War*[1]

[Admiralty
*c.*1850]

Home Station
Should events unfortunately arise which may lead to Hostilities[,] it becomes absolutely necessary for the Board to preconsider what steps should be taken with reference to the Fleet for Offensive[,] as well as Defensive[,] Operations. With this view[,] I will assume that the nation with which we will most likely be engaged in hostilities is France and that, that nation will first declare war with England or[,] by her threatening preparations of a warlike character, may render it necessary for this country to demand explanation for her warlike proceedings, and[,] if no satisfactory reason is assigned[,] then it might become the duty of this Country to arm in self-defence, or to act on the offensive[.] If war should be inevitable[,] there can be no doubt that France will put forth all her energies[,] and will attempt as secretly as possible to put in execution the favourite scheme of Invasion of this country, and[,] as offensive operations are always more successful and invariably more decisive in their effects than those of a defensive character[,] and to carry war into an Enemy[']s Country is far more likely to lead to favourable results and to the defeat of that Enemy, It [*sic*] would become absolutely necessary on the part of the Admiralty to have one or more Squadrons ready to blockade the Enemys ships in their own ports, for we ought to assume that her secret preparations will not be made in one port only[,] but in most[,] if not all[,] of the following[:]
Lorient[,] Brest[,] Cherbourgh [*sic*][,] Morlais[,][2] Havre[,] Dunkirk[, &] St. Malo[,] From whence Separate Squadrons would Depart at such periods of time as would admit of their forming a junction at such a point of Rendezvous[,] as would ensure a descent on some locality of the Coast of England. at [*sic*] the Sametime [*sic*][,] one or more faints [*sic*: 'feints'] would no doubt be made on parts of the Coast[,] so as to blind [i.e., cover] the Main Operations[,] then to burn and destroy whatever is most essential to the power and interest of the Country. The Coal Ports of Wales, Pembroke, Liverpool, Bristol, Devonport [&]

[1]Milne later pencilled in at the top 'about 1850'. This, however, is the only means of dating this paper and it may well have been produced later, although the reference to screw ships of the line and their envisioned use only for home defence suggests that it must pre-date the Crimean War.

[2]Morlaix.

Portsmouth are possible points open to the attack of an Enemy Squadron Commanded by an officer of Energy and Enterprise.
The Warlike force thus destined for this invasion of England must[,] if possible[,] be met on our part by offensive operations[,] before it reaches the English Shore. it [*sic*] must be blockaded[,] if possible[,] in its own ports[.] It is there the Blow [*sic*] must be struck[,] for if once the Enemys Squadron get fairly to Sea and evades our force[,] there cannot be a doubt that the chances of Invasion or of depredations on the Coast are rendered more certain.[1]
Paper B. . . . any armament on so large a scale as would be required for the invasion of this Country could not be prepared with that secrecy which it has been assumed may be done. To attempt the Invasion of this Country[,] not less than 40,000 Men would be required[;] at least it is probable it would not be attempted with a less number[,] and besides this number of men, there is [*sic*] the Munitions of War, for such a number.

The largest steamers of France cannot carry more than 2000 men with their crew's [*sic*], and if this number of men is to be embarked in each it will[,] of course[,] require 24 such Steamers. If they will only carry 1400 Men[,] it will require 28 Steamers. to [*sic*] this must be added a further number of Steam Vessels for Horses, Stores, Provisions and other Munitions of War, amounting to at least 12 other Vessels, so that as the least Estimate independent of a Convoy Squadron of other Vessels[,] probably requiring 6 to 8 Steamers[,] there would be 40 Steamers required to embark 40,000. I therefore very much doubt such an Armament can be prepared in Secret.[2]

Viewing therefore the subject in the light of an intended attack on the part of France[,] and supposing the Arrangements which that country may secretly make[,] there may not be but [a] few days for our preparations. What means then has the Admiralty at its disposal to meet such a supposed contingency[?]

[1]Milne added a marginal note, but it is clearly superseded by 'Paper B.', which has been inserted in the text at this point. It is not wholly clear, however, where exactly Milne intended this section or Paper B to fit into the text of the memorandum. The marginal note reads: 'of which however there exists great doubt because an armament of so vast a scale as would be required could not be prepared with any degree of secrecy. If 50,000 men are to be landed, and I think we cannot assume a less number[,] It will require 25 Steam Vessels each carry[ing] 2000 men with their munitions of war, or 37 Steamers carrying each 1500 besides the convoy's [*sic*] which must necessarily accompany [them].'

[2]Here 'Paper B' ends, the gist being since the French could not amass a sufficiently large force for a full-scale invasion in secret (secrecy being vital to any such plan's success) then they would have to settle for a more modest force, and hence an attack/depredation/raid, rather than a full-scale invasion.

We have[,] in the accompanying Sheet A[,][1] a number of Ships of the Line and heavy Frigates in a state of advance[d readiness][:] Their Holds Stowed, Their Gun Carriages & Shot on board, Their Masts, Rigging, Sails and part of their Stores in the Dock Yards[,] but not one of these ships are of any use whatever in the contingency I have assumed. Ships of the Line are useless for checking the rapid movements of a Steam Squadron. No Officer will ever think of using them under such circumstances. They would be a drag on any operation[,] and to get them ready for Service would require no less than 19,000 Seamen and 5600 Marines to complete their crews. Even the Ships of the Line in the Home Ports which are in Commission and partially manned would require at least 3,650 Seamen and 500 Marines to complete[,] & even when they are manned[,] unless fitted with the screw[,] they could only be of service for local defence. They must therefore be discarded from all consideration on the first breaking out [*sic*] of a war with France. Steam power alone can be of service under such circumstances[,] and what Vessels have we ready – that is ordinary or advanced, Rigged & Armed[,] ready to receive men[?] For this statement see Sheet A[,] Where [*sic*] it will be seen that we have 13 Frigates[,] 17 Sloops & 6 smaller Vessels[,] requiring 5,500 Seamen and 1000 Marines to render them effective, exclusive of the officers[,] to meet those of France[,] which would most probably be divided between the ports I have before named. Assuming that these Steam Vessels are manned and ready for sea, I should feel some difficulty as a Member of the Board in directing their Sailing Orders to be made out, but offensive operations are indisputably necessary. Then to what ports are they to be ordered? are [*sic*] they to be divided? all [*sic*] this must depend on 'Secret Information' to be derived from Authentic Sources, not from vague reports perhaps circulated to mislead[,] but to whatever direction or Ports this Squadron is ordered[,] it must be Commanded by an energetic officer[,] if possible acquainted with the Coast of France[,] who will not fail if circumstances will admit to carry destruction into the Enemys Squadron[.] 'All will depend on this, and if ever war comes I believe this must be our policy.'[2]

These offensive operations however, must not leave the Coast of England without Inshore steam Squadrons[,] with steam up and ready to proceed to any point where attack may be expected[,] and here again we require 'Information'[.] we have no Telegraphs on our Shore[,] no lookouts from the Hills, nothing organized or contemplated, the Coast

[1]Missing from this draft.
[2]It is not clear why he chose to put this statement in quotations.

Guard Stations are within sight of each other[,] yet there is no means of Communication[.] 2 year's [*sic*] ago steps were taken to Establish a Telegraph between Ports[mouth] & Plymouth thro the C[oast] G[uard] Stations, but the Coast Guard Departt raised objections[,] and so a good and important object[,] which in time of war would be of National import for giving intelligence to the nearest Electric Telegraph Station[,] fell to the ground[.]

These inshore Squadrons should be formed[,] one at Devonport, one at Portsmouth and on[e] in the Downs[,] with every preparation made and steam up . . . ready for any Emergency which may arise[,] but at the present moment we have not a sufficient number of Vessels capable of forming any Squadron[,] as most [of] our Steam Vessels are on Foreign Stations Viz.

	Frigates	Sloops
Medt	4	4
Africa	1	6
W. Indies	1	5
Brazils	1	2–2 [*sic*]
Cape	–	1
India	–	5

It would therefore appear to be necessary either to increase the number of our steamers or to recall those from Foreign Stations for the duties of Home defence.

No doubt the Screw Ships of the Line would form a strong defensive Squadron on our own Coast, but[1] . . . Having glanced at the steps required for Home defence, we must at the Sametime [*sic*] view those Colonies which form so bright a feature in the English Crown, to which assistance must be sent to defend them from attack[,] for no sooner will the Gov. of France have determined in their own minds to declare war with England than they will send out Squadrons of Heavy Frigates and smaller vessels[,] probably assisted by a few Steamers[,] but their use of Paddle W. Steamers must be limited by the [lack of] means of obtaining Coal[,] and I therefore doubt any active squadron being composed of P W Steam Vessels. Their operation will be chiefly confined to Stations where coal can be obtained[,] to destroy our Trade, destroy our Foreign Colonies[,] and cast as much ruin on them as their Force will admit . . . [2]

[1]It is not certain that the following material goes here. The sentence which ends 'Coast, but . . . ' is at the end of a folio. No other document could possibly fit after it with the exception of the following.

[2]Here the draft ends.

[**218**] *James W. D. Dundas Memorandum on the State of the Flag List*

Admiralty, Confidential
14 August 1850

There appears to be a general feeling both in Parliament and out of it, that a revision of the Flag List should take place, and that those alone who are eligible for Service should be retained on the List, which number should be limited to 110.

I therefore beg to submit to the Board of Admiralty, that the Active List should in future consists [*sic*] as follows: –

1 Admiral of the Fleet
21 Admirals, 7 of each Flag[1]
33 Vice Admirals, 11 of each Flag
45 Rear Admirals, 15 of each Flag
Total 100

At present the List contains 151 Flag Officers, 39 of whom are not eligible to serve, and although they rise in rank, [they] cannot receive higher [half] pay than 25s. per day.

To carry out the proposed reduction to 100, I should recommend that these 39 Officers be removed to a separate List, and in [the] future, when a vacancy occurs on the Flag List, the Senior Captain, if eligible from Sea Service, (agreeable to the Queen's Regulations, Page 8, Section 2.) should be placed on the Active List, but if he has not the necessary qualification, that he should be placed on the Retired List, to rise to the rank of Vice and Full Admiral the same as if he had stood on the Active List, but restricted as at present to the pay of 25s. per day.

In the divisions of the Admirals who are eligible, it will be observed . . . that there are 7 Full and 5 Rear Admirals more than the proposed limited List of 100. I should therefore propose that one Captain only should be advanced to the rank of Rear Admiral, when three vacancies occur on the Active Flag List, until the number be brought down to the Establishment of 100; promotion then to be carried on as at present, viz. – one Captain for every vacancy on the Flag List.

By such an arrangement, the recommendation of the Select Committee of the House of Commons in 1848, limiting the Active Flag List to

[1]Milne inserted in the margin: '6=18', meaning he thought the requisite number under each flag colour – Red, White, and Blue – should be six, rather than seven; likewise, he favoured 30 Vice-Admirals, 10 of each colour, rather than 31, but preferred 51 Rear-Admirals (17 of each colour) on the Active List, rather than 45.

100, would be carried out. At this number it should always be kept up, and the Retirement List limited to 50; but if by any vacancy on the Active Flag List a Captain, eligible for such rank, shall be promoted, who, may be junior to an Officer not eligible for the Active List, then the latter is to be removed from the List of Captains to the Retired List of Rear Admirals, but is only to receive the pay of Captain until there are vacancies on the List of 50.

As no Officer would be passed over, but would rise to the rank of Vice Admiral and Full Admiral as if he remained on the Active List, I should hope the whole Service would approve of the measure, and there can be no doubt that the Flag List would be more efficient, and less expensive to the country.

[**219**] *Bowles Memorandum on the State of the Flag List*[1]

Admiralty
4 February 1846

In a former paper on the subject of Retirement, delivered to Lord Haddington, I stated, at some length, my own ideas with respect to the question now under consideration, and suggested as the best and most popular mode of proceeding, (as well as the least expensive) a promotion to the rank of Rear Admiral of a sufficient number of Captains, to obviate the great difficulty at present felt, (and particularly dwelt on in Mr. Sidney Herbert's[2] original suggestion) of finding competent Officers for important commands; but I strongly recommended at the same time, the reverting to the former practice of the Service, and placing on a '<u>Retired List</u>,' all Officers whose seniority would include them in the proposed promotion, but whose services do not entitle them to any further consideration.

The proposition to promote, for <u>Rank only</u>, and without any immediate increase of pay,[3] is[,] however[,] worthy of a careful consideration, and might perhaps (under some obvious modifications to render it more palatable and satisfactory, by holding out at least a distant hope of

[1]This paper and the following one were composed when Bowles was Third Naval Lord, but was printed along with that by Dundas. For Milne's views on the subject, see [**222**].

[2]Sidney Herbert, first Baron Herbert of Lea (1810–61). Secretary to the Admiralty, 1841–45; Secretary at War, 1856–46; Secretary of State for Home Affairs, 1855; Secretary of State for the Colonies, 1855; Secretary of State for War, 1859–61.

[3]Bowles added 'this was an idea of Lord Ellenborough's thrown out in a paper to which this is a reply'.

advantage) enable the Admiralty to command the services of a very sufficient number of effective Flag Officers for all present purposes.

I will suppose, for instance, that the promotion extends to the first 250 Captains on the list, they would be divided into three classes: –

The First, consisting of Officers of acknowledged good character and service, who from age and health are fully competent for commands afloat.

The Second, of those who are from various reasons determined not to go to sea again, and –

The Third, of those who have either never served, or are now from age and infirmity unable to do so, in future.

To the First Class every possible encouragement should be given, while to the second, little consideration is called for, as well as to the first division of the third; and the last, must stand chiefly on their own merits and former claims.

If the number of paid Flag Officers was fixed at 200, and the first class of the contemplated promotion placed on it, as vacancies occur, while the remainder were transferred to a Retired List, with a pay to be increased with a reference to former character and services [*sic*], at the rate of from £1. a day to something higher, in strong cases, I am of opinion, a satisfactory result will be obtained at a much smaller expense, and with at least equal advantages to the Country, than that originally contemplated.

[**220**] *Bowles Memorandum on Promotion by Selection*

Admiralty
March 1846

Having on two former occasions stated at considerable length my own views with respect to the best mode of effecting the contemplated naval retirement, it will be more convenient to annex copies of those papers, and to apply myself at present to the discussion of the proposition which is contained in a 'Memorandum on Promotion to the Flag',[1] which I have this day received, and in which it is contemplated to select, in future, one third of the Captains advanced to the rank of Admiral, while the remaining two-third shall be promoted as heretofore by Seniority.

It is unnecessary to remark, that this proposition involves an entire departure from the system which has prevailed in the British Navy for

[1]Not included among Milne's papers.

nearly a century and a half, and must tend to place the Officers much more at the mercy of the Government of the day than they have ever been since 1718; thus depriving them of the right to advancement by Seniority (provided always that their own conduct did not disentitle them to it) which they, as well as the Army, have hitherto considered the 'Magna Charta' [*sic*] of both Services.

I am fully aware of the prerogative of the Crown, but this is an abstract principle which it appears unnecessary to discuss on the present occasion, and which I apprehend will always be brought forward with caution and discretion, and especially where it is opposed by regulations or customs of long standing.

I will pass therefore to consideration of the case as it stands at this moment.

It will be seen by *Hansard's Parliamentary Debates* . . . that by an Order in Council, dated in the year 1718, and addressed to the Board of Admiralty, they are directed to proceed in the promotion of Officers to the rank of Admiral, according to the Seniority of such Officers on the List of Captains, regard only being had to their being duly qualified for the Rank to which they should be promoted.

This order was in all probability framed for the express purpose of preventing abuses, previously existing.

In 1703 we find Sir G. Rooke offering his resignation of the command of the Channel Squadron, because his own Captain of the Fleet had been passed over, and a Junior Officer promoted.

Commodore Graves, under similar circumstances, resigned his Commission; and many other instances might be adduced of the like nature.

It was probably with a view of reconciling the Navy to any occasional deviation from the rule of Seniority, that a Retirement, with the rank of Rear Admiral, was established in 1747, for Captains not eligible or qualified for active Service, and from that period very few departures from the rule of Seniority appear to have occurred.

The attempt of Lord Howe in 1787 to promote 16 Captains, while he passed over 40 Senior to them, was most vehemently opposed in Parliament, and led both to his own resignation a few months afterwards, and also to the promotion of almost all the Officers thus passed over by him.

The principle of Seniority was still further recognized by His late Majesty [William IV] when Lord High Admiral, in his Regulations with respect to Flag Promotions, and even more decidedly by the late Naval and Military Commission, at whose recommendation above 60 Retired Rear Admirals were taken from the separate list on which they had always stood, under the Order in Council of 1747, and placed, according to their original seniority, amongst the effective Flag Officers, for the avowed purpose of gratifying their feelings, and sparing them the mortification of standing below those junior to themselves in the service.

The rule of promotion by Seniority having therefore existed since 1718, and having been rigidly adhered to for the last half century, the question naturally arises, whether it is just or expedient to depart from it on the present occasion, and to excite the strongest feelings of alarm and discontent amongst those veteran Officers, who, having already passed through the painful ordeals of three successive selections, and until now considered themselves beyond the reach of favour or injustice during the remainder of their professional career, suddenly discover, that the prerogative of the Crown is to be exercised against them, and that they are menaced with a danger destructive to all their future prospects. I suppose no Officer has ever attained the rank of Captain without experiencing the strongest and liveliest emotions of pleasure at the conviction that he was at last (after perhaps many years of anxiety, disappointment and mortification) firmly established in his profession; and thenceforward no one could pass over his head; but what will be his sensations [*sic*] when he hears that 'selection' may again be resorted to against him, and that if an unjust and unscrupulous Government should be in power, personal or political motives or dislikes may endanger all his fondest and dearest hopes?

I am aware that strong and stringent regulations may be proposed, which for the moment, and while the Government of the country is in the hands of upright and honourable men, may apparently guard this exercise of the prerogative from abuse; but I have very little doubt, that if an Administration, actuated by the same principles of political exclusion, which so remarkably distinguished the last,[1] found this principle of selection established, a very short time would suffice to prove, that a most dangerous and destructive power had been placed in their hands. I should also remark, that the difficulty of selecting Officers from amongst a large number, who, during so long an interval of peace, have had but few opportunities of distinguishing themselves, offers another very strong objection to the proposed departure from established regulations.

I am fully persuaded, that any Government undertaking this invidious and dangerous task, would, when it was too late to recede, find itself exposed to the most injurious suspicions and imputations, be-

[1]A telling indication that political partisanship still ran strong among senior officers; Bowles' strictures were directed toward Melbourne's 1835–41 administration.

cause there are so few Officers of any very acknowledged or remarkable merits or services, that the justice or propriety of every selection would become the subject of bitter controversy and animadversions, and motives be assigned for those preferences which it would be extremely difficult to refute satisfactorily.

All these important considerations induce me to deprecate most earnestly the adoption of the contemplated measure, and to express my strong and decided opinion, that all the objects of Her Majesty's Government can have in view may be accomplished by safer and more ordinary means.

[**221**] *Bowles to Milne*

Confidential
17 November 1850

My dear Milne

You have a little time to think, which is not easy to do amidst the bother & bustle of the Ad[miralt]y.

There are two points which demand consideration –

1. The reserve of seamen.
2. The Admirals List[.]

it [*sic*] is respecting the latter I write at present.

You have the H of Commons proposition,[1] & have probably seen that of Ad Dundas.

To the first my objection is that it would check promotion and encumber the list with officers still older than at present. If[,] with 150 Ads[,] I find it difficult to place my hands on 20 fit for service in the different grades, with one hundred vacancies the case will be worse[,] and[,] as by their recommendation the process of cutting down is by only promoting one captain for three deaths[,] I should not for some time (nay many years) promote above 4 per annum and the Captains . . . [2]

[1]The Government brought in a Supplementary Estimate for the retirement of Naval Officers. See *Hansard*, 3rd ser., vol. 116 (1851), cols. 579–83 and vol. 117 (1851), cols. 642–65.

[2]The rest of the letter was not preserved by Milne.

[**222**] *Milne Paper on Promotion, Retirement, and the Flag List*[1]

[Admiralty, 1850]

Proposal of the House of Commons[:]
Admirals[:]
1. To reduce the List of Admirals to 100. This recommendation of the H[ouse] of C[ommons] will no doubt be forced on the Admi[ra]lty[,] nor can I see any ground on which the Admi[ra]lty can defend the maintaining of 150 Admirals.
2. To put all officers not qualified on a Separate List. These officers were formerly on a retired List and were removed from that List by a Committee of the H[ouse] of C[ommons] in 1840. It is therefore only going back to what was formerly Estab[lishe]d.
3. The reduction to take place by promoting <u>one</u> Captain for three vacancies. Taking the 39 retired Admirals from the List would leave 111 Admirals[.] the average deaths are about 9 p[er] a[nnum.] therefore[,] it would take more than a year to reduce the List, during which time the Captains will be advancing in age.
4. In 3 vacancies or rather promotions, 2 to be advanced by Seniority 1 by Selection. I think the measure inexpedient[,] more especially in peace, when there is no necessity of exercising the prerogative of the Crown. In war it would be different. Merit would then shew itself and meet its reward.

[1]An undated paper. At a later date Milne pencilled in '1850'. This is undoubtedly accurate; the preceding documents clearly establish the time-frame. The subsequent Board decision is found in MLN/152/7 [4]: offprint of a supplementary estimate to Parliament: 'An estimate of the sum required to be voted to defray the Charge of the Retirement of an additional number of Admirals, Captains, Commanders, and Lieutenants of the Royal Navy, in the year ending 31 March 1852.' The policies adopted were to:
1) Establish ten Good Service Pensions (to be funded at £1,500 per annum, that is, £150 per officer).
2) Keep open the retired lists of Captains, Commanders, and Lieutenants and increase the funds available for retired Pay.
3) Mandatorily retire Flag Officers who had not served in that capacity, thus reversing the Order in Council of 1840.
4) Create ten Retired Service Pensions.
5) Reduce the number of captains to 350, by keeping open the retirement of 1846.
6) Reduce the list of Commanders to 450, by increasing the number of Commanders who could retire as Captains to 100.
7) Place on permanent half-pay all Commanders who had not served afloat, or in packet or revenue service for 20 years, or who were physically incapable of service, and by continuing from 'time to time to remove such officers from the active list to permanent half-pay'.
8) Reduce the number of Lieutenants to 1,200, through a variety of means.
Thus the Active Lists would (it was hoped) consist of 100 Admirals; 350 Captains; 450 Commanders; and 1,200 Lieutenants.

Admiral Dundas's proposals[:]
1. To reduce the Active List to 100, By [*sic*] removal of the 39 admirals who are not Eligible to Serve – to a separate List as formerly.
2. Retired List to be re-estab[lishe]d[,] but those on it to advance in Rank, but only to have 25s/p Day.
3. One promotion for 3 vacancies until the List is reduced to 100.
Admiral Dundas's plan is but little diff[eren]t from that proposed by the H[ouse] of C[ommons][,] Except [*sic*] by granting increase of Rank to the retired admirals
Sir Francis Barings proposal[:]
1. To remove the 39 Admirals now on the Active List who have not served to a Retired List as formerly.
2. To establish a Separate or individual List for all those Admirals who are 75 Years of Age[,] to be in all respects the same as to honours &c as those on the Active List.
3. To limit the Active List to 75[.]
This measure forms the basis of all the other recommendations[,] but the H[ouse] of C[ommons] in 1840 put all those men on the Active List from what was considered the Hardship [*sic*] of their case. It appears to me a revision of the Regulations as to the time to be served to entitle an officer to gain his Flag might be considered[,] so as to reduce that time. few [*sic*] people can now serve their time.
This retirement was first Estab[lishe]d [in] 1747, most probably to provide for those captains who were ineligible to be promoted to the active [Flag] List.
If this measure is carried out we will have[:]
The Active List
Redundant List
The Old Retired List
The Retirement of 1847.
The present number of officers on the Admirals List[,] viz. 150[,] is no doubt more than what is required for the Naval Service[,] even in time of War, and I consider it is impossible to continue that number on the List of the Navy. Something must be done[,] more especially after the recommendation of the Committee of the House of Commons, and I believe it to be most true what has been stated by Sir F. Baring, That [*sic*] if the Board of Admiralty do not act, it will be forced on them – and the H[ouse] of C[ommons] will reduce the List.

Admitting that 100 Admirals are sufficient for the wants of the Service, what fair means have the Board for reducing the List from the present [number] of 150 to 100, whilst the claims of officers are considered with fairness and justice[?]

We must first of all remove from the Active List all those Admirals who[,] by the Order in Council of Aug[us]t 1840, were placed upon it, from the Yellow or Retired List[,] which contained the names of those officers who had not served the regulated [*sic*] time to obtain their Flag under the Order in Council of June 1827. This may be looked upon as a harsh measure[,] the more especially after the investigation and report of the Committee of the H[ouse] of Commons in 1840, but there is no feasible mode of dealing with the Admirals List which presents less objection, and it is to be recollected it is the removal from the Active List, of officers who were not qualified to serve, and it is carrying out a measure recommended by the H[ouse] of C[ommons] in 1848.

This removal of about 39 officers will reduce the List of Admirals to 111.

Sir F. Baring[,] in his paper[,] recommends that 10 Good Service or retiring Pensions should be Established of about £150[,] to go to 10 of the above officers to retire from the Active List, by which the List will become reduced to the fixed number of 100.

Admiral Dundas[,] in his submission[,] wishes the List to be reduced from 111 by a promotion of one Captain, when three deaths take place on the Admirals List. This measure would for a period of nearly two years check the current of promotion, and render those Captains now looking for advancement[1] more aged that they now are, and would to a certain extent increase the evil it is wished to remove.

Altho I do not see any objection to Sir F. B.['s] proposal[,] which will be a temporary measure and will reduce the List, Yet [*sic*] I do not think[,] so far as the efficiency of the List of Admirals is considered[,] we will be a bit further advanced. The difficulty of obtaining Admirals efficient for service remains the Same. The List is one which bears on it the names of our most distinguished officers who[,] thro a life of arduous and distinguished Service[,] have grown old in its service [*sic*], and have risen to the highest rank in the profession[,] but most of whom are now incapable of discharging with satisfaction [*sic*] those duties which the service requires.

What is to be done?

My own opinion is that we must adopt some new regulation, some sweeping measure, which will place the Admirals List on an efficient footing, and the only means of carrying this out is by the limit of age,[2] and reestablishing the qualification for Captains becoming eligible for their Flags, either as fixed in 1827, or modified, by which those Cap-

[1]Milne himself included, of course.

[2]Mandatory age retirement would not be extended to the Flag List until 1870.

tains who have not served will be placed on a <u>Retired List</u>. I admit there are difficulties to be overcome[,] not only in the carrying out of this Regulation[,] but likewise in the opposition to a measure which is a new feature in the Naval Service. I however believe we must be all agreed that the First Step to be taken is to reduce the present List by removing to a separate or retired List all those officers who were ineligible under the order in Council of June 1827.

This then is the first measure, viz.

To remove those officers who have not served as Captains sufficient time under the Order in Council of June 1827, to be qualified for their Flags, but to permit all such on the retired List to rise by Seniority to the respective ranks of Vice & Full Admiral[,] but with the pay only of Rear Admiral, and to be eligible to receive the Good Service Pensions.

2nd. To place on a non effective List[,] all Admirals who are above or may attain the age of 70, allowing them likewise to rise in Rank and Pay according to their seniority and standing on the List, and to be allowed to receive the Good Service Pension.

This will remove about 60 Officers[.]

3[.] To fix the number of Admirals at 60, viz. 12 Full, 18 Vice & 30 Rear.

4. The Future [*sic*] promotion from the Captains list to take place on each vacancy, either caused by an officers attaining the age of 70[,] or by death, but no officer to be eligible unless he [has] served a certain period as a Captain[,] as Estab[lishe]d by the O[rder] in C[ouncil] of June 1827 or a modification of that Order.

The Admirals List will then be as follows[:]

At present	150	
Removed non effective	39	
Do. by [being] over age	59	
[total]	98	<u>98</u>
[leaves]		52
To promote from the Capt List		8
[total]		60

The mean average Ages [*sic*] of the Admirals[,] when 60 would be on the list [*sic*][,] would be

		Years	M[onths]
Full Admirals	12	65	7
Vice Admirals	18	66	–
Rear Admirals	30	63	3

Average yearly deaths 5.

If this scheme[,] which I admit is a strong and sweeping one[,] should be adopted[,] we should most probably have the following promotion to the Flag.

In 1852 =	by 5 deaths
In 1853 =	5 Do.
In 1854 =	5 Do.
" 1855 =	6 Do.
" 1856 =	6 Do. & 30 removal [*sic*] from age
" 1857 =	5 Do.
" 1858 =	5 Do. & 30 removal from Age [which would] bring Flag down to the Captains of 1829.
" 1859 =	
" 1860 =	
" 1861 =	

The qualification for the Admirals Flag has always been a source[,] not only of difficulty[,] but complaint by officers[,] and it was so strongly represented in 1840, That [*sic*] the regulation of restriction was abolished. The following are the Order[s] in Council which were[,] at various times[,] promulgated on this question.

3 June 1747}	Captains qualified provided they had served in any war &c.
8 March 1771}	Captains qualified provided they had served in any war &c.
19 Decr 1804}	Captains qualified provided they had served in any war &c.
30 June 1827	This last Order fixed the period a Captain was to Command a rated ship[,] viz. 4 years in War[,] 6 years in peace[,] or 5 years in War or Peace[.]

This regulation I consider too stringent[,] & [it] Excluded [*sic*] many officers <u>who</u> were unable to obtain employment[.] I should be inclined to reduce the periods to 3[,] 4 & 5 years.

The Captain[s] List now consists of about 500 officers, a number larger than required for the service of the Country[,] more especially in time of Peace.

	Y.	M.
The average ages of the First 100 in 1850 was	56	11
Second 100	56	2
Third 100	51	3
Fourth 100	50	3
Fifth 100	46	0

This number of officers should be reduced to 350[,] or at most 400.

How is this to be done?
The Admiralty cannot compel an officer to retire, nor can promotion be entirely stopped[;] it is now limited to one in three.
The only outlet is by means of the Retirement promulgated in 1847, which has already removed ____ officers from the List, but with the present regulation of 20 years standing and 55 years of Age[,] there will be no person on the List who can accept it. for [*sic*] instance[,] 20 years standing in 1851 refers to those officers promoted in 1831. there [*sic*] are only 7 officers on that years List, and and [*sic*] the Same [*sic*] number in 1832, and it is more than probable that not above 2 or 3 officers will accept the offer, Whereas [*sic*] on the head of the List there are many officers who ought to have taken it[,] not having served[,] but who looked forward to their being placed on the Active List of Admirals because the regulation requiring servitude for the Admirals List had be[en] done away with. The top of the List is therefore encumbered with inefficient officers & who[,] having refused the Retirement when offered to them, cannot now accept unless a new regulation is adopted.
The Commander's [*sic*] List consists of about 840. This number is by no means required for the Service and ought to be reduced.
The only boon held out to these Officers is the Rank of retired captain to 50 of the Senior[,] with [the] half pay of a junior Captain & a pension of £75 pr. A[nnum] to their widows – This 50 being independent of the above 840.
I am of opinion this retirement should be increased[,] and 100 officers added to the List under the Same regulation & allowances.

Lieutenants.
This List now contains about 2,200 names.
The retirements allowed to Lieutenants are.
1. The Rank of Retired Commander to 100 of the Senior[,] with lowest Half pay of a Commander[,] formerly 4/ pr Day but now 8/6 pr day.
2nd. By Order in Council of Nov 1830[,] the (300) Senior Lieutenants on the Half pay of the highest rate[,] viz. 7s/ pr Day[,] were allowed the Rank of Commander[,] without any increase of pay. There are now about 219 Officers in this position[,] the remainder of the 300 being on the Lieutenants List at 7s/ pr Day. It would be a very great boon to old Lieuts to extend the provisions to another 100 of those officers whom come under the First regulation.

[**223**] *Milne Proposal to Establish an Admiralty Library*

Admiralty
26 June 1851

I have repeatedly urged the propriety of having a Library at the Admiralty[.] we have at present many valuable Books at Whitehall, in the Board Room at Somerset House, and in the Principal Officers rooms. These should be collected & arranged[,] and Adm Berkeleys room fitted with proper shelves, and again Admiral Beaufort has a large collection of [accounts of] Voyages and Travels[.] all these should be centred in <u>one</u> Adm[ira]lty collection, & we should add yearly to it[,] & whoever would undertake it will deserve well of the Board. I strong[ly] urge it, as a measure of public [?utility.]

[**224**] *Milne Proposal on Instruction and Examination of Officers in Steam Engineering*

Admiralty
September 1851

In 1849 the Board issued a Circular[1] with reference to the Examination of officers who study steam at the Factories of Woolwich and Ports[mou]th. This had reference to the few Lieuts, Comdrs & Captains who took advantage of the permission granted to attend the above Estab[lishmen]ts. We have at the present moment a large number of Steam Vessels in Commission[,] giving employment to a number of Junior Officers of the Fleet, most of whom will no doubt become steam officers in future years, yet no steps have been taken to direct their attention to the subject of the Steam Engine, even when serving on board steam vessels. We have our examination in seamanship & Navigation, and the general introduction of Steam power into the Navy calls for some notice being taken, to <u>instruct</u> our rising officers in the construction, working and application of Steam Engines and Boilers[.] viewing this as a matter of importance to the Naval Service, I would submit to the Board the propriety of taking the following steps on the subject.

1st[:] That an order shall be issued[,] directing that all officers serving on board HM Ships having steam power are to be instructed by the Senior Engineer on board, in the principles[,] construction & working of the Steam Engine & Boilers.

[1] 'No 57', Milne noted in the margin.

2d[:] That after the 1 of March 1852[,] when Mid[shipmen] or other officers are examined in Seamanship for Rank[,] they shall likewise be examined by the passing Captains, or by a Senior Engineer in their presence[,] on the principles[,] construction & working of Steam Engines & Boilers, provided such officer has at any time served for a period of 6 months on board any of HM Ship having steam power, and are to certify the same on the passing Certificate.
3d[:] All Cadets[,] Mid[shipmen], [&] Masters Ass[istan]ts who have served in steam vessels are to be questioned as to the amount of their Steam knowledge, when they pass their periodical examinations.[1]

[**225**] *Milne Draft Circular for the Education and Examination of Officers in Steam Engineering*

Admiralty
20 October 1851

My Lords Commissioners of the Admiralty desire that all subordinate officers except Clerks, serving on board HM Ships having steam power[,] are to be instructed by the Senior Engineer on board in the knowledge of the component parts of the Engine & Boilers and the practice of working the Machinery, as it is their Lordships intention at some future period to institute an examination on the above subject when officers come forward to pass their final examinations for Rank[.] Any officer now serving, on giving in his name to the Comdr in Chief or Senior officer may[,] on coming forward for final examination[,] be examined on the above subjects, should he desire it and[,] if found competent, the same is to be entered on his passing certificate[,] where the letter S will be attached to his name on the List of the Navy.

Comdrs in Chief are[,] in such cases[,] to give the requisite orders for examination and nominate a Senior Engineer officer to attend on the day of Examination[,] should the passing [*sic*] Captains require his services.[2]

[1]This memorandum clearly predates the draft circular below, [**225**].
[2]The subsequent circular enclosed, No. 94, 30 October 1851, follows Milne's wording almost exactly. See ADM1/5610.

[226] *Board Minutes on Milne's Draft Circular for the Education and Examination of Officers in Steam Engineering*

[Admiralty
October 1851]

[Subject:] Proposal that all officers serving in steamers should be instructed by the Senior Engineer on board in the principles &c of the Steam engines[,] & that young officers should be examined as to their knowledge of the Steam Engine &c.

[Sir Francis Baring:] From every station[,] letters mark the progress of steamers for the performance of all services, and the time[,] I think[,] is not far off when every officer must have steam knowledge. It seems to me that Capt Milne's proposals are worthy of consideration[,] and he should look them over with the observations of his colleagues . . .

[James Whitley Deans Dundas:] I would give every officer, Mate, & 2d Master an opportunity of passing an Examination for Steam . . .

[Houston Stewart:] It is desirable that <u>all</u> our officers should possess a competent degree of practical seamanship, it is not possible that they <u>all</u> should possess a practical & efficient knowledge of the principles of Steam Engines.

[Maurice Frederick Fitzhardinge Berkeley:] I agree in much of Admiral Stewart's minute. Every encouragement should be given to officers who study and make themselves masters of the Practical working of Engines, and all officers who have so qualified themselves by the means now at their disposal should be selected for service in steamers in preference to all others.

[William Cowper[1]:] I concur with Captain Milne as to the importance of enabling young officers on board steamers to study steam, but the difficulties are considerable from the want of time[,] & the inducement to neglect other portions of study still more necessary to be pursued at that period . . .

[1]William Francis Cowper (1811–88). Civil Lord of the Admiralty, 1846–52, 1852–55; Undersecretary of State at the Home Department, 1855; President of the Board of Health, 1855–57; Vice-President of the Education Committee of the Privy Council, 1857–58; Vice-President of the Board of Trade, 1859–60; Commissioner of Works and Buildings, 1861–66.

[**227**] *Milne Memorandum on Education and Examination of Officers in Steam Engineering*

[Admiralty
October 1851]

On a perusal of the minutes by my Colleagues[,] I observe a general admission that a knowledge of Steam ought to be obtained by all officers.

The Boatswain instructs the youngsters for an hour or so during the day in practical Rigging[,] and there appears to me no practical or other difficulty for the same youngsters having half an hour's instruction in the Engine Room by the Engineer[,] precisely in the same manner as with the Boatswain[,] but as there appears an objection to any Examination, which after all is the principle object to enforce a knowledge of the subject[,] I have no objection to limiting my submission to an order directing that junior officers in Steam vessels are to make themselves acquainted with the principle of working the Steam Engine.[1]

[**228**] *Milne Paper on Coaling Steamships*[2]

Admiralty
3 November 1851

The question of Coal Depots is one of much importance[,] not to be lightly dealt with, as the daily increasing application of Steam Power to HM Ships renders it necessary to take the most expedient steps[,] not only as to present time, but for the future supply of Coal in case of hostilities, so that all classes of Ships from <u>Steamers</u> to <u>Ships of the Line</u> may in times of Emergency [*sic*] be able to take on board whatever supplies they may require with the least possible delay. The question for the Boards consideration appear to me to divide itself into <u>two</u> separate subjects.

1st. The position of Coal Depots in each Harbour.

2ndly[.] The means by which Coal is to [be] put into store, and subsequently put on board Steam Vessels.

In considering the first subject, It [*sic*] must be recollected, That [*sic*] it is not the Steamer fitting out, or under a permanent refit in Harbour, which will require a speedy supply of Coal, but it will be

[1]Perhaps this is why both the draft and the finished circular too allude only to the intention of establishing an examination at a future date.

[2]Fragmentary rough drafts of this paper can be found in MLN/154 [2].

Steamers making passages, blockading, or Cruizing. They will require to be constantly replenished, altho not in want of any other supplies.

Again[,] Steam Vessels may be under a hasty refit to replace a lost spar, and during such refit must be alongside a Dock Yard Wharf, When [*sic*] it would be advisable to fill up with Coal. Again[,] Steam Vessels will most probably be sent into Port for a Store of Provisions, to replenish a Cruizing Squadron, or for conveyance to a Foreign Station, when it would also be requisite to replenish her [*sic*] Coal.

These several considerations of Vessels employed on active Service, naturally points out [*sic*] that there should be more than one Depot in all our Harbours, not only to save the transporting of the Vessel from the Wharves where she may be refitting, or taking in provisions, but to admit of Several Steam vessels being enabled to obtain Coal at the Sametime [*sic*][.] if we are to have only one Depot, it must be constructed with Wharves [*sic*] of sufficient frontage or extent to admit of several Steam Vessels coaling & being at the same Wharf, and with sufficient depth of water along side, to admit of all classes of Steam Vessels being afloat at low water.

Practically speaking, I am fully convinced that it would be most advantageous for the Service in every respect, to have several Depots in Each Harbour, placed so as to admit of several Steam Vessels coaling when either under refit, or taking in Provisions, and that[,] in coming to an arrangement on this point[,] we must consider the local circumstances of Each port. we [*sic*] must also consider that[,] in the Event of Hostilities[,] our Harbours can never be permitted to be encumbered with Steam Vessels, merely requiring Coal. This is often felt as an inconvenience at the present time, and it has been suggested to have the present floating Depots moved into Plymouth Sound, as well as those at Portsmouth to the Mother Bank, and should ever hostilities take place[,] several such Depots as *Malabar*, or Frigates capable of containing at least 1500 Tons of Coal will be absolutely necessary for the efficiency of the Service; no harbour depots could furnish supplies to vessels under such circumstances[.] take[,] for instance, Ships of the Line. They should never come into Plymouth Harbour and[,] what is more[,] they could not get into Portsmouth Harbour, on account of their draft of water. Therefore[,] Coal Depots[,] either in the Sound at Ply[mou]th, at the Mother Bank, or Cowes or Haslar[,] or inside Calshot Castle at Portsmouth will be necessary.

Moreover[,] in any one fixed Depot, should the Coals take fire, the whole store would be destroyed, and the Service paralyzed.

I therefore feel deeply impressed with the necessity of having several small Depots in each Harbour for the reasons I have given[,] and that such an arrangement will prove the most practical, and efficient, [&] will save labour, time & expense.

With reference to the Second subject[,] of the means to be adopted for placing Coal in store and afterwards on board Steam Vessels.

We should in the first instance have Coaling Hatches in the decks of all our Steam Vessels (leaving the present round Man holes in the centre of such Hatches)[,] as they will or ought to be screwed down to the Beam, when not required to be opened for Coaling.

Wherever Steam power is already fixed and at work in our Establishments[,] we should endeavour to run a shaft or endless chain from such Engine to the Wharf[,] and there we ought to fix [*sic*: 'place'] our small Depots, capable of containing about 1000 Tons. by [*sic*] such an arrangement expense will be saved and efficiency in Coaling obtained.

When Steam power cannot be applied from a fixed engine in the Establishment[,] I think it would be expedient to fix a Small Engine, or to adopt the Hydraulic Crane to the purpose of working the cranes &c by means of a Reservoir at an Elevation, and to which Elevation water could always be pumped by one of the fixed engines in the Estabt. This plan is simple and inexpensive, but a severe winter might freeze the water in the pipes, unless protected[,] or the means taken up for heating the water adapted to the working of the Machinery.

In the larger floating Depots[,] some of our Small obsolete Engines might be fitted, but in doing this I think we ought to obtain information, by sending one of our Engineer Officers to report on Machinery now in operation for this purpose, under nearly similar circumstances as required by us[,] which is [*sic*] different from those large Establishments which daily supply Coal as an Article of Trade.

I have affixed to this paper some plans proposed and adopted by Mr Blyth, C.E.[,] who is now constructing Machinery for clearing Colliers, and there is a machine now in use in The [*sic*] Thames, and capable of being moved from Ship to Ship for the same purpose. Those machines as most applicable to our wants should be reported on[.]

Having stated the foregoing opinions[,] I will now submit my views with reference to Each Port.

Woolwich[:]

Here we do not require either a very large supply or the means of Coaling with haste. Colliers can always be obtained to come alongside with Coal[,] and except with the future trial of a Moveable Engine for clearing the Vessel, I see no necessity for any pressing change in the Coal Depot[.]

Chatham[:]

At the present time this is not a Steam Yard[,] and I see no urgent necessity for any new Depot.

Sheerness[:]

May be considered as a port to which Steam Vessels would resort for a Supply of Coal instead of going to Woolwich or Chatham[.] it was from this last Yard the floating Depot was removed to Sheerness. It is the only means of coaling at the present moment, and any pressure for the services of Steam Vessels would render it necessary to make some arrangement at this Port[.]

A depot might be established in the Yard adjoining the Wharf where vessels might obtain Coal for a few hours on a rising Tide, and for a few hour's [*sic*] ebb, but the prevailing westerly winds is [*sic*] very disadvantageous to such an arrangement. Screw Ships of the Line or Large class Steamers could not coal [at all,] however[,] at this Depot[,] and the only alternative would be add[itiona]l floating Depots. These[,] again[,] in case of Hostilities[,] would be required at or beyond the Nore.

Dover Harbour[,] in case of hostilities[,] would become a Depot for Coals.

Portsmouth[:]

This[,] being one of the principal steam Harbours[,] will require several Depots.

1st. One in or at the Steam Basin[.] This should be on the Wharf[,] so that the Coal may be at once landed on the outside sea wall & transferred to a store[.] I was of opinion the Arches under Frederick Battery at the East End of the new ground would have answered this purpose[,] but it is inconvenient except as a reserve store, requiring great labour and consequent expense in moving the Coal from the Collier[,] and heaping it by manual Labour. This Coal Depot at the Basin should be situated as to allow the Coal being raised to a store at considerable height[,] by which means no further hoisting up may be required[,] but the coal to be shot down into any Steam Vessel. The application of Steam power should be considered.

2d. I am still of opinion a Steam store of at least 800 to 1000 Tons should be Estab[lishe]d on the Wharf as proposed by Mr Fincham[.] The objections raised ag[ains]t it I do not consider sufficiently strong to justify suspension of a proposal which is to [im]prove one of the most efficient & serviceable Depots in the Harbour[.]

3d. A Coal Depot should be Estab[lishe]d at the Royal Clarence [Victualling] Yard[,] not only for the convenience of Coaling Steam Vessels, but It [*sic*] is most probable that[,] in the Event of War, the Coal coasting trade will be almost entirely suspended, [or] freights & insurance will rise[,] which will enable the Railroads to carry cheaper than Vessels. Such being likely to occur, the Rail to Ports[mouth] & Gosport will deposit Coal in our Estab[lishmen]ts. The plan for running out a Wharf from the C[larence] Yard is the only practical mode of gaining the end in view, and carrying it out to Deep water with sufficient frontage for several Steam V[essels] laying alongside at the sametime [*sic*] would then assist the Tide. The submission has been [made] to carry the wharf down to the South Side of the present passage into the C[larence] Yard. I should have thought that if Rat Island could have been made a Depot, it would have been advantageous in saving expense, in having solid ground for either Coal, or placing machinery to work the Cranes &c, and it would be advantageous to remove the Coaling vessels away from the Entrance of the Harbour, or from that part of it which has always been the position for Large Ships ready for sea, but whether above or below[,] a Coal Depot ought to be constructed[.]

4th. Floating Depots will likewise be required[.] at present the *Malabar* and *Maidstone* answer the purpose, but in case of their removal to the outer Anchorage their places will have to be supplied.

5th. It would be expedient in case of war to have other Depots[,] and the places most suited for such purpose are those wharves in all our Yards where Ships of the Line can be [brought] alongside at all times of the Tide[.] in Ports[mouth] Har[bour] There [*sic*] are 3 besides the Wharf already recommended for a Depot. Therefore[,] in future arrangements this should be considered.

Portland[,] in case of war[,] will be a coaling station.

Dartmouth also.

Plymouth[:]

Our present Depots are the *Druid* and another Frigate, and at the port much is required.

Keyham.

1st. There should be a Depot in the working Basin in such a position as to admit of the application of Steam Power. This will require consideration[.] it ought to be near the Sea Wall to save labour & expense in removal from the Colliers[,] and[,] if the depth of water will admit[,] to allow Steamers to coal when alongside the Sea Wall.

[2nd] There are 4 Wharves in the Dock Yard where Ships of the Line can remain alongside at Low water[.] on one or more of these wharves there ought to be a Depot of Coal, to be worked by machinery from one of the fixed engines of the Yard.

3. There ought to be a Coal Depot at the Royal William [Victualling] Yard[.] There is every facility for carrying this out with little expense

and at the sametime [*sic*] with advantage. The Hyd[raulic] Crane[,] I believe[,] could be efficiently applied to work the Machinery. There should be a branch Railway from the Clarence Yard to Mill Bay[,] where a Wharf should be constructed.
4. Larger Floating Depots are required. those [*sic*] now in use are too small and unfit for any pressure of Steam Vessels.

[229] *Baring to Milne*

Stratton, Confidential
[November 1851]

My dear Milne

I saw Mr Rendal[1] on Saturday & had a talk with him about coaling. Told him that I thought it would be of advantage if a civil engineer were to consider the subject in a general view and give us ideas of a general character. That I did not think a detail engineer who was good for the mere machinery was just the person for this part of the work[,] but [rather] one who could take a comprehensive view of the whole question.

He told me that he thought it one of the most important questions for the future[,] and that we were most wise in looking forward . . . That he should be glad to give me any assistance privately or professionally and for detail . . . he would refer me to the best men.

We agreed therefore that he should have the papers confidentially, read them over and then tell me what he thought he could do.

Your very good memo raises the great question, and sketches the course which it should pursue. the [*sic*] rest is detail, of the greatest importance no doubt[,] but in the application of the principle to the several ports & stations [*sic*]. I think therefore he should have your memo[,] if you have no objection[,] and the papers on which it is made[,] together with such of the other papers which you think may be of service to him.

Will you forward them to him[?]

[1]Probably civil engineer James Meadows Rendel (1799–1856), who had designed the packet and refuge harbour at Holyhead and the refuge harbour at Portland for the Navy during the 1840s.

[**230**] *Milne to Baring on French Naval Preparations*

Admiralty, Confidential
December, 1851

During the last few year's [*sic*] the French Govt[,] by means of their Steamers of War[,] have [*sic*] been moving large Bodies of Troops[,] fully equipped for military operations[,] from the port of Toulon to and from the coast of Algeria, and likewise to the Coast of Italy[.] Their vessels of the 1st Class[,] of 450 Horses Power, and about 2000 Tons admeasurement [*sic*][,] are capable of conveying[,] during short voyages[,] from 1100 to 1400 men, but the greatest number ever conveyed by one Steamer, was by the *Montezuma*, viz. From Grau[1] to Port Vendre,[2] 1818 Troops exclusive of her crew of 195, making in all 2013 persons for a voyage of 3½ days, and From [*sic*] Toulon to Cevita [*sic*] Vecchia[,] 1781 Troops[,] 10 Horses and a quantity of 'Material' in about 30 hours. Therefore[,] what has been done, in such cases, may be done again, provided the weather is moderate and fine, otherwise such a feat is impossible.

I believe the following table will give a very just and fair result of the capabilities of Steamers of War for the Conveyance of Troops for Military operations, but in all such cases much must depend on the season of the year and the state of the weather, as the Troops must be exposed on Deck[,] and the length of the voyage with these number's [*sic*] should not exceed from 2 to 3 days.[3]

Conveyance of Troops by Steam vessels of the French Navy
1st Class Steamers:
Tonnage 1500 to 2000 Tons. 400 to 650-H Power [can carry]

Infantry	1100 to 1400
Cavalry	800
Horses	80
Speed	9 knots
No. in French Navy	26

2d Class: Tonnage 1000 to 1600 Tons, 200 to 400 H Power

Infantry	800 to 1000
Cavalry	600
Horses	50
Speed	8 knots

[1]Le Grau de Roi, on the Gulf de Lion.
[2]Port Vendres, near the Franco-Spanish border in the Mediterranean.
[3]Milne noted in the margin: 'this Table is in addition to the Crew baggage & material from the number of men.'

No. in French Navy	32

3rd Class[:] Tonnage: 800 to 1100 Tons, 120 to 250 H Power

Infantry	500 to 750
Cavalry	400
Horses	30
Speed	7 knots
No. in French Navy	40

The above number's [*sic*] can only be considered as approximate, as a great deal must depend on the fittings[,] viz. Size of Engine Room, [&] quantity of Stores on board of Each Vessel. No doubt more men may be squeezed into a vessel for a special purpose or on an emergency, but for more than 48 hours I believe it would not be prudent to expose men on deck for a longer period [*sic*], but for pressing service a 1st Class steamer may with difficulty & risk convey 1700 men.

2d Class	1200
3d Class	900

[**231**] *Milne to Baring*

Admiralty
4 February [1852]

My dear Sir Francis

I enclose you a few notes relative to measures which have been adopted by this Board of Admiralty for the benefit of the Seamen of the Fleet. I feel assured[,] whatever may be the result of this session[,] & should circumstances remove you & this Board from this Establishment, it will always be a most pleasing reflection to think so very much has been done to benefit those who will always be the main stay [*sic*] of our country[,] & I could also give you a Return[,] if you should wish it[,] of the very large improvements which have been carried out under your auspices relative to the material and Establishments of our ships.

These improvements are not known to the Public & few are aware how much has been done, not only with reference to very large reductions in Expense, but to place our Establishments at home & abroad on more systematic footing, & to improve the whole field of the naval service.

I deeply regret there should have been so very shameful an outcry against the Admiralty,[1] knowing that it is undeserved, & at this moment

[1]Public and press criticism of Admiralty administration was frequent and strident in early 1852 on a number of issues. It was alleged that troops had been sent to the Cape of Good Hope in response to the Kaffir War in transports lacking sufficient provisions for the

our stock of stores on hand & the whole Material of the Navy is on a better footing[,] and our Store houses more complete[,] than at any previous period since 1828, &[,] as the Storekeeper General[1] has stated to me, 'If more money was given for Stores I really do not know how we could spend it, we are so complete' . . .

Measures introduced by the Present Board of Admiralty for the benefit of the Seamen of the Fleet[:]

[1] The Prize Proclamation altered so as to give a larger share of the Prize to Seamen.

[2] Extending the benefit to seamen when paid off from their ship[,] so as to give them 2 months leave of absence if they choose to remain in the service[,] & to join any Flag Ship in England, & if they should not return, they could not be considered as deserters or lose any time of servitude.

[3] The introduction of the Good Conduct Badges & extra pay of 1d pr day to all men of very good conduct having 5 years servitude, 2d pr day after 10 years[,] & 3d pr day after 15 years, all persons having the Badge not being liable to Corporal Punishment.

[4] Increase of ratings of Petty Officers to the ships of the line & 4th Rates, with gratuities for good conduct after 3 years service to the most exemplary Petty Officers on being paid off.

[5] The price of the Clothing issued from Naval Stores for the benefit of the Seamen reduced, & the duty taken off soap so as to reduce its price on board all H.M. Ships

[6] Regulations adopted to facilitate the payment of Seamens wages in London, & also facilities given for remittance of their money when paid two months advance.

voyage and that in one case they had been embarked in an unhealthy vessel. Equally notorious, the Board was roundly lambasted for having contracted with a firm named Goldner for canned meat. Much of that which was delivered was unfit for consumption, containing offal and animal excrement. This matter, indeed, generated a Parliamentary demand for information. See 'Date and Terms of the Contract entered into with Goldner and others for Preserved Meat for the Navy; Quantities issued and returned into Store as Unfit for Use; Supplies issued for the Arctic Voyage under Captain Austin; Complaints made of the State of Salt Provision issued to ships on the West India Station during the year 1851; and the Contract Prices for Beef and Pork for the years 1848, 1849, 1850, and 1851', *Parliamentary Papers*, 1852, vol. XXX, p. 317. For press criticism, see *The Times* (London), 10 January 1852, p. 4 (from Napier); 23 January 1852, p. 5; 24 January 1852, p. 5; 28 January 1852, p. 4 (leading article); 31 January 1852, p. 4 (leading article).

As the Naval Lord superintending Victualling Contracts, Milne himself was target of criticism. Milne was defended in Parliament by his former colleague Sir Maurice Berkeley after the Whigs fell from power in February 1852 (*Hansard*, 3rd ser., vol. 119 [1852], col. 1436).

[1]Robert Dundas, later fourth Viscount Melville (1803–86). Deputy Comptroller of the Navy, 1830; Storekeeper-General, 1832–69.

[7] Reduction of the allowance of spirits with a considerable increase to their pay. The Establishment of a fixed day pay, increase of Salt Meat Provisions, Introduction [*sic*] of Mustard & Pepper into the service[,] & other advantages.
[8] The preserved meats[:] 16 oz allowed to the lb[,] instead of 14 oz.
[9] The Petty Officers of H.M.S. *Excellent* directed to inspect the articles of Clothing in store at Portsmouth[,] & to report whether any improvement could be made[,] or whether they have any wish for improved description &[,] if so[,] to forward Returns &c.
[10] Extension of the Regulations for the entry of Seamen into the Dockyards &[,] when absent on duty[,] provision made for payment of their wages to their families[,] & other advantages.
[11] Regulations for the examination of all invalids, or Seamen, or Marines claiming pensions at Portsmouth, Plymouth, Chatham & Woolwich[,] or in London[,] as convenient to the men[,] so as to render it unnecessary to appear in London as formerly[,] by which very serious inconvenience & expense to the Seamen was incurred.
[12] The establishment of Naval Apprentices in the service & their instruction in all the duties of Seamen.
[13] A Defaulters Book established in all H.M. Ships as a check on the secondary Punishments inflicted, a measure highly beneficial to the discipline of the Navy & advantageous to the Seamen.

I may safely assert that no Board of Admiralty has carried out so many real[,] practical measures for the benefit of the naval service as the present Board, & with the exception of giving an increase of monthly money to stationary ships in the Home Ports, & that I have no doubt about, I cannot see <u>any one measure</u> which could be taken towards further improvement or benefit for the Seamen. They are perfectly aware of the . . . pains which have been taken by the Admiralty[,] & they feel that their individual benefit and improvement has been consulted [*sic*] by the measures which have been brought forward & carried out by the Board[.]

[**232**] *Cockburn to Milne*

Highbeech, Essex
24 February 1852

My dear Captain Milne

It has afforded me much pleasure[,] both on public & private account, to learn from you that the Duke of Northumberland is to have the benefit of your assistance at his new Board of Admiralty, which will[,] in my opinion[,] prove a most efficient one, if the health of my friend Hyde Parker with stand the fag of his portion of it.

You acted[,] I think[,] with much considerate delicacy in communicating with Lord John Russell (who first placed you in office) previous to sending your assenting reply to the Duke.

I hope His Grace's example on this point will be followed hereafter, for it must be advantageous for one of a removing Board to remain[,] to afford information on pressing events to the newcomers.

[**233**] *Ogle to Milne*

Torquay
29 February 1852

My dear Capt Milne

I sincerely congratulate you on the compliment paid to you in the offer of continuing a Lord of the Admiralty, and I am sure the Country will derive Benefit from your accepting it. Some time ago I expressed to my Friend Sir George Cockburn the great services you had rendered to the Country, by opening all the Contracts, and that you were now thoroughly acquainted with all the Business at Somerset House[,] which would occupy any one officer two years to acquire the Knowledge [*sic*]: that you worked cordially with Mr Grant[,][1] and you were equally well acquainted with the State of the Dock Yards: Sir G. Cockburn said 'I think that I shall be consulted when there is a Change of Administration and will certainly recommend Capt Milne's Continuance in office . . . '

[**234**] *Milne Opinion on Report of Committee on Pay and Emoluments of Pursers and Paymasters*[2]

[Admiralty
March 1852]

The report of the Committee on the Pay and Emoluments of Pay[maste]rs & Pursers recommends these officers being placed on a fixed Salary[,]

[1]Sir Thomas Tassell Grant, K.C.B. (1795–1859). Comptroller of Victualling, 1850–58.

[2]This memorandum was generated by the 'Report of the Committee of Officers appointed by the Admiralty to inquire into the system of keeping the Victualling Accounts of Her Majesty's Ships, with the view of providing a better mode of remunerating the Paymasters and Pursers in charge of the Victualling Stores.' For the report itself, see *Parliamentary Papers*, 1852, vol. XXX, p. 323.

and I am of opinion this recommendation should be adopted, but with reference to the amount of the future Salary, I think we must weigh the matter well before we adopt so Liberal a Scale. The Pay[masters]s & Pursers former position as to pay was that of a warrant officer, and it was only in the year 1814 that they were first granted Half pay[,] which was fixed for the first 100 at 5s, the next 200 at 4s, and the remainder at 3s. this [*sic*] has been subsequently increased to 7s 6s & 5s[,] with a retirement for 29 officers at the Top of the List at 8/6 pr Day[.] The position of this grade of officer has therefore been materially improved since the peace. It is now recommended by the Committee that they should give fixed Salaries and a large increase to their present Half pay, as pr. the Scale annexed to the report.

This recommendation is based on the present emoluments or income obtained by Pursers from the amount of <u>Extra</u> & other Credits obtained on passing on their accounts. It must[,] however[,] be observed that these <u>Extra</u> Credits could never have been obtained if the provisions had been properly and faithfully issued to the men[,] or paid for if not opened, or the pay[masters] & pursers acted fairly to the Govt in the receipt of provisions from Contractors. The evidence given before the Committee confirms this opinion[,] and I therefore consider these officers who have such <u>Extra Credits</u> are not entitled to them. The Book of Form's [*sic*] for Pursers allude[s] to Extra Credits[,] and Examples are given of the mode of calculation[,] yet it never could be contemplated that Extra Credits were to be made by irregular and improper means. The former Instructions directed 'that all <u>Extraordinary Credits</u> were to be Explained,' and it does seem strange that these words should have been omitted in the last Instructions. I therefore consider these <u>Extra Credits</u> cannot by any means be looked upon as a part of these officers just Emoluments, and in considering the amount of their future Salary, they should be entirely put aside. Again, the fair and legitimate allowance of a 10th of all provisions to a pay[maste]r or purser admits of his obtaining a Salary of about £750 pr. Annum [when appointed] to a Ship of the Line, and with Slop & Tobacco percentage and pay[,] made up about £1100 for vict[uallin]g 1000 men.

but [*sic*] when these regulations were fixed the List of Purser's [*sic*] was large and they had fewer opportunities of Employment than at the present time. This circumstance therefore must also be considered in fixing the amount [of] future Salary. The accompanying Table exhibits the present amount of pay in the respective rates to the various grades of officers and what the Committee propose to give to Pursers.

Rank	1 Rate	2 Rate	3 Rate	4 Rate	5 Rate	6 Rate	Sloop
	£	£	£	£	£	£	£
Captains	701	601	601	500	400	400	301
If Flag Ship	500	500	500	500	[additional]		
Commanders	301	301	301	301			301
1 Lieut	201	201	201	201	201	201	182
Master	213	213	213	182	182	182	182
Surgeon	328	to	200				
Purser	500	450	400	350	300	250	200 to 150

With £ 50 in add[itio]n to [Pursers in] Flag Ships[.]

Let a fair comparison be made of the responsibilities of the respective officers with those of the Purser. The Captain[,] as Flag Captain in a First Rate[,] with all the responsibility & anxiety of a Squadron[,] to have £50 less pay than the purser.
The Lieut[,] in charge of the watch at night[,] to whose care and judgement [*sic*] the safety of the ship & crew depend[,] to have £350 less than the purser.
The master intrusted with the Navigation & pilotage[,] and the supervision of all the Ships Stores, Rigging Sails &c[,] nearly equal in value to the provisions[,] and to whom the charge of those provisions are [*sic*] intrusted in their Stowage in the hold[,] to have £287 less than the purser, who has no anxieties[,] no cares[,] and will have little or no responsibility. These facts speak for themselves. I cannot see the justice or the propriety of this. Either the Executive officers are paid too little (and I know this to be the fact[,] for no Captain can take command of a Ship & pay his expense with his pay) or the purser will be paid too much.

It may be said that the Pay[masters] & Pursers have been making larger incomes than the Salary now proposed to give them, if so I consider it is the duty of the Board to amend those regulations which permitted such large and unnecessary incomes to be granted, far above the position and duties[,] as well as responsibilities[,] of the parties. This might and ought to be corrected by making regulations for all future purser's [*sic*] who may be placed on the List. Again, The [*sic*] Pay[masters] & Pursers[,] in their Evidence[,] have stated their inability to explain how their Extra Credits are obtained and that their Stewards are the parties who conduct their pursing duties. The Committee recommend that Stewards should now be made 1 Class P[etty] officers and have salaries up to £80 pr. Annum. They are to become the servants of the Crown[,] not of the Pursers[,] and they will be neither more or [*sic*] less than the persons who will henceforth perform the purser's duty[,] and the Pursers position[,] with high Salary[,] and better paid than his Captain[,] will hold a sinecure position and a lucrative appointment[.] I therefore am of opinion some responsibility as to the safe custody and proper issue of the provisions should be thrown on the purser and he should be held responsible[,] and I do not think such higher salaries should be given. My own opinion is that the Purser should be divided into three classes[,] viz

1,2 &3d Rates – £350
4,5,6 Rates – £200
Small 6th & Sloops – [no figure given]

It appears to me the report should be considered and discussed at the Board[.] it is not possible to enter into the consideration of all XXI recommendations in writing[,] but the subject must be very attentively considered and weighed before any orders are given. I may be wrong in my objections to the amount of pay[,] but I have considered it with much attention[,] & see no reason to alter my opinion[.]

[**235**] *Board Minutes on Regulations relating to Paymasters of the Navy*

Admiralty
12 March 1852

[The Duke of Northumberland:] Rates should be the Regulation[,] not Classes.

[Hyde Parker:] I am of opinion that rates would be preferable to Classes for the Paymasters of the Navy.

[Phipps Hornby[1]:] Approved[,] & that Rates be substituted for the Classes recommended by the Committee.

[Thomas Herbert[2]:] I entirely concur in the desirableness of remunerating Pursers by fixed rates of pay instead of Emoluments, and the

[1]Phipps Hornby, C.B., K.C.B. (1785–1867). Entered, 1797; Lt, 1804; Cmdr, 1806; Capt., 1810; Rear-Adm., 1846; Vice-Adm., 1854; Adm., 1858; Naval Lord of the Admiralty, 1852.

[2]Sir Thomas Herbert, K.C.B. (1793–1861). Entered, 1803; Lt, 1809; Cmdr, 1814; Capt., 1822; Rear-Adm., 1852; Vice-Adm., 1858; M.P., 1852–57, Naval Lord of the Admiralty, 1852.

enclosed regulations seem to me well calculated to carry out the object. It will be advisable to fix a period from which [*sic*] they should take effect. The dividing of the Pursers into Classes as proposed by the Committee is[,] I think[,] open to objections in practical point of view, therefore I prefer the scheme attached hereto.

[Arthur Duncombe[1]:] Read[.]

[Milne:] These regulations have been drawn up with great care. They do not entirely meet the views of the Committee[.] Their classification of 10 Pay[masters] for First Rates, 20 for Second Rates, &c[,] was so likely to lead to difficulty in the selection of Officers for ships, that it would have proved a continual clog [*sic*] on the Admiralty. The system of Classes has therefore been changed to rates of ships for appointments & pay. The Half Pay recommended by the Committee was[,] for the first 10 [Paymasters,] 12/6 pr day[,] and so in proportion as in the regulations now drawn up . . .

[Augustus Stafford[2]:] Read[,] Naval Question[.]

[**236**] *Milne Memorandum on the Search for Sir John Franklin's Arctic Expedition*

Admiralty
27 March 1852

With reference to the communication from M Cresswell[3] [*sic*] urging on the Board the advantage of sending supplies[,] to be placed in Depot at Melville Island, I think the subject should be considered with reference to the intended search to be undertaken by the expedition about to leave England under the Command of Sir E. Belcher.[4] This expedition was recommended by a Committee of officers, who were called to-

[1]Arthur Duncombe (1806–89). Entered, 1819; Lt, 1826; Cmdr, 1828; Capt., 1834; Rear-Adm. (Ret.), 1856; Vice-Adm. (Ret.), 1863. M.P., 1830, 1835–51, 1851–68; Naval Lord of the Admiralty, 1852.

[2]Augustus Stafford O'Brien (1811–57). M.P., 1841–57; Secretary to the Admiralty, 1852.

[3]Cresswell was, according to Clowes, father of one of the officers on HMS *Investigator*, Lt Samuel Gurney Cresswell. Cresswell senior urged the Admiralty to search for HMS *Investigator* and *Enterprize*, two vessels sent in 1850 in search of Franklin, in the seas around Melville Island.

[4]Sir Edward Belcher, Kt., C.B., K.C.B., F.R.A.S., F.G.S. (1799–1877). Entered, 1810; Lt, 1818; Cmdr, 1829; Capt., 1841; Rear-Adm., 1861; Vice-Adm., 1866; Adm. (Ret.), 1872.

gether to report on the 'results of the late Expeditions, and what benefit would be expected from further search' and in the 12th clause of that report they state their opinion 'that another Expedition should be sent from England, consisting of the same ships which composed Capt. Austin's division, viz. 2 sailing ships and 2 steamers, with orders to proceed to Beechey Island, and to consider that Harbour (beyond which we think one sailing ship and one steamer should <u>on no</u> account be taken) as the base of future operations'[.]

Such being the decided opinion of the Committee on whose report and recommendation Sir E. Belcher's Expedition is fitted out, it was the opinion of the late Board of Admiralty that the recommendation of that Committee should be acted on, and that one sailing ship and one steamer should remain at Beechey Island, whilst one sailing ship and one steamer should proceed thro Wellington Strait, and I have every reason to believe that this arrangement would have been Enforced [*sic*] in the Instructions to be given to Sir E. Belcher.

Since the original order was giving for commissioning the ships now fitting out, viz., the two sailing ships and two steamers, the *North Star* has been added to the Expedition, to accompany the other ships to Beechey Island, instead of a Transport as on former occasions[,] proceeding to Disco with Stores & Fuel. It therefore appears to me that the view taken by the Committee of retaining 'one of the sailing ships and one of the steamers' for the Crews of the other exploring ships to fall back upon in case of their loss, may be departed from '<u>provided the *North Star* should reach Beechey Island</u>'[,] and that it would not be necessary to retain the steamer in reserve at that Island[,] but that she might be employed in conveying a depot of <u>Stores</u> & <u>Provisions</u> to Melville Island should the state of the Ice permit, wintering there, and pushing forward land parties to the westd and to Banks Land, but returning to Beechey Island on the breaking up of the Ice in the following season – altho this is a departure from the general rule 'of not allowing any single vessel to proceed alone'[,] yet there does not appear much objection[,] considering the distance is within the reach of parties travelling on the Ice, but as the *North Star* is fully competent to convey all the Crews of the other ships to England in case of accident, there appears no objection to push on the other sailing vessel from Beechey Island to a spot somewhere between Melville Island and Beechey Island[,] and [to] advance the Steamer to the Westward from Her [*sic*]. The result would be[:]

In Depot at Beechey Island, '*North Star*'[.]
Thro Wellington Straits, 'one Sailing Ship[,] one Steamer'[.]

Halfway to Melville Island[,] 'one Sailing Ship'[.]
Towards or at Melville Island[,] one Steamer[.]

Such an arrangement[,] I am of opinion[,] would embrace every object which is of importance[,] not only as regards Sir J. Franklin, but also as regards the chance of any of Capt. Collinsons[1] party reaching Melville Island[.]
It appears to me Sir E. Belcher should render the Steam Launch now at Port Leopold available for his Expedition[.][2]

[**237**] *Milne Draft Memorandum on Admiralty Priorities*[3]

Admiralty
*c.*March 1852

The following appear to be present subjects which would require attention[:]

1. The necessity of having our Steam Ships ready for Immediate Service[.]
2. Selection of Officers for their Command[.]
3. Sufficient number of Men in reserve to man them[.]
4. The recall of the Lisbon Squadron[.]
5. The means of obtaining authentic Information, and the Estab[lishmen]t of [a] Coast Telegraph[.]
6. Increase[d] supply of coal required[.]
7. Arrangement for Coal being sent to Blockading Squadrons[.] for this purpose colliers or small Frigates to take coal would be necessary.
8. 3 dispatch vessels of great speed required at each of our ports[.]
9. The arming of private steam vessels.[4]
10. The preparation of Steam Gun Boats carrying one or more heavy Guns with small draft of Water.

[1]Richard Collinson, C.B., K.C.B. (1811–83). Entered, 1823; Lt, 1835; Cmdr, 1842; Capt., 1842; Rear-Adm., 1862; Vice-Adm., 1869, Adm. (Ret.), 1875. Collinson commanded the expedition sent out in *Investigator* and *Enterprize*.

[2]For the Reports and Statements laid before the Admiralty and its instructions to Collinson, see *Parliamentary Papers*, 1850, vol. XXXV, 175. For Austin's instructions, see ibid., p. 345. For those to Belcher, see ibid., 1852, vol. L, p. 935.

[3]This list appears to have been drawn up to instruct the Duke of Northumberland's Board, none of whom, Milne excepted, had served at the Admiralty previously, as to the subjects most needful of Board attention.

[4]This recommendation did not pan out. See below, no [**251**] for Milne's minute on an Admiralty Committee Report on the subject.

[238] *Milne to Northumberland on Manning the Navy (Draft)*[1]

Admiralty
27 March 1852

Several paper have been before the Board on the subject of obtaining men for the Navy, viz. one from Sir T Cochrane,[2] another from Capt Plunkett,[3] the Bill brought into Parliament by Sir C[harles] N[apier][4] with regard to Bounties, and there are numerous Pamphlets published by Naval officers and Speeches made in Parliament, all holding out the necessity either for a Standing Navy, a Reserve, [or] a speedy mode of Manning the Fleet[,] &c &c. These various schemes are no doubt important[,] but none of the authors or Orators give any plan how these important measures are to be carried out[,] and the subject of the [*sic*] Manning of the navy requires great consideration[.] In giving my views on the above papers[,] it is necessary to go largely into the Subject and endeavour to consider it in all its Bearings.

We have at this moment what may be considered a Standing Navy so far as relates to the actual numbers of men employed, that is we have a Vote from Parliament[,] which is only sufficient to man those ships required for the Foreign Stations and the Guard Ships at Home[,] for 39,000 Men, composed as follows –
26,000 Seamen[,] 2000 Boys[,] and 5700 Marines afloat[.]
5,300 Marines on Shore or in Reserve.
So long as no change is made in that vote[,] it may be considered to a certain extent a standing Navy. it [*sic*] is a fixed number of men voted by Parliament for Naval Service[,] not to be changed. These men enter voluntary [*sic*] for a particular ship, for her Commission[,] but may be retained for 5 years, under the provisions of the 5&6 William[,] 4 Chap. 25[,] and may even be retained beyond that period should their services be required[,] by add[itiona]l wages being granted equal to ¼ of their [regular] pay. a [*sic*] long established custom has fixed the period of a

[1]At the top, in pencil, he later added ‘paper on Manning the Navy given to the Duke of North[umberlan]d’. An earlier draft of this letter can be found in MLN/153/1 [4] Rough Notes of paper on manning, holograph.

[2]Sir Thomas John Cochrane, Kt., C.B., K.C.B., C.G.B. (1789–1872). Entered, 1796; Lt, 1805; Cmdr, 1805; Capt., 1806; Rear-Adm., 1841; Vice-Adm., 1850; Adm., 1856; Adm. of the Fleet, 1865.

[3]Edward Plunkett, sixteenth Baron Dunsany of Dunsany Castle (1808–89). Entered, 1823; Lt, 1834; Cmdr, 1840; Capt., 1846; Rear-Adm. (Res.), 1864; Vice-Adm. (Res.), 1871; Adm. (Res.), 1877.

[4]Napier’s bill to amend the Seamen’s Enlistment Act was introduced on 27 April 1847 and withdrawn on 12 May after debate on its second reading. See *Hansard*, 3rd ser., vol. 92 (1847), cols. 10–13, 723–9.

Ships Commission at about 3 years – at the end of which time the men look forward to be[ing] paid off. proposals [*sic*] have been recommended for extending the time of a Seaman's servitude in the Navy from 5 Years to a longer period[,] say 10–[,] 12– or 15 years &c.[,] so that compulsory Service may be obtained by drafting men from one ship to another the same as Marines from Barracks, but before adopting this course we must look at the Seaman's position as regards his social state with other persons serving under the Crown[,] viz. the Soldier and the Marine, both of whom are entered for a period of 12 years. Take[,] for instance[,] the Marine who serves his time afloat with his companion the sailor, he is, we will suppose[,] in the same ship, entered on the same day, and to leave the Same [*sic*] day on their return to Ports[mou]th. The Marine goes to his Barrack[,] which is his home[,] [at] which he at once enters on all the advantages, he has 'his leave,' his daily going out of barracks, his family around him, the comforts and advantages of social life, and there he remains in the pay of the Govt provided with every reasonable comfort, until the time arrives for his turn for Embarkation. His companion the sailor is paid off, he has left his Ship which was his home, he is now a free agent on Shore, to do what he likes[,] and is no longer belonging to the Navy, unless he volunteers for the Flag Ship under Admi[ra]lty Circular No. 59, by which he obtains leave[,] retaining his pay whilst absent. he [*sic*] is not compelled to go on shore or leave the service[.] If the Seaman was entered for[,] say 14 years[,] the same as the Marine [*sic*], where is [*sic*] he to go when his ship is paid off[?] It is proposed, to a Flag or Ordinary Guard ship, a floating Barrack[.] If so[,] he is in a worse position than the Marine, he is debarred all those social comforts and advantages which the Marine enjoys at his barracks. The sailor will have none of the shore advantages, he will still have the same daily drudgery of a Ships routine from 5 am, Holystoning Decks, Scrubbing Hammocks, daily drill[,] &c. to go thro, and is never the master of his own wants or wishes, he is on the waters for 12 years[,] deprived of all those associations which are the best attributes of our Nature. It is from this very cause that Men of the best characters and the most Efficient Seamen eagerly seek service in the Coast Guard[,] and many enter the Navy for the very object of ultimately getting into that service[.] again[,] they willingly enter as Seamen Riggers in the Dock Yards under the Ad[miralty] Regul[ation] [of] May 48[,] at those ports where their families reside[,] solely with the view of being with them and having a run on shore. They will enter for the ordinary as part of their Complement[,] as the next best thing to the D[ock]yard[,] and in those ships it is the Custom to give one half the Ships Company leave of absence every night[,] without this few would enter, but they will not go on board the Harbour Ships for general service. The Marine again has other advantages[;] [he] is more of a Machine than the Seaman[:] his duties are more certain and more defined, the discipline of the Corps in [*sic*: 'is'] less irksome and more on a fixed system. The sailor is under no system, every Captain has his own views, his own mode of punishment, his own Black List. The Sailor of Good Conduct in one ship may fall into error in another, he may be punished for an offense in one ship, which may not [have been] considered irregular in his last ship[.] he is therefore always in doubt[,] always in uncertainly, and consequently prefers selecting his ship by asking his former shipmates respecting the Captains & officers[,] than [to] enter for G[enera]l Service to be sent to that very ship which cannot get men to volunteer from [having] a bad name. This leads me to doubt any man entering for an extended period of time[,] unless further inducements are held out for him to do so, viz. by progressive increase of pay[,] as is done with the men of the *Excellent*, but in doing this the same advantages must also be given to such men as are enjoyed by the crew of the *Excellent*, viz. remaining a considerable time in harbour before being again sent to Sea[,] and leave of absence[.] The advocates for a Standing Navy consider the Admi[ra]lty would[,] by entering men for a longer period of time[,] have the means of Manning a certain number of Vessels on any emergency. This I cannot comprehend. If 39,000 are employed[,] as at present[,] of which about 33,000 are afloat . . . thus [the] men are all employed[.] They must be serving as [in the] past[,] [as] complements of Ships [in commission]. How are the reserve Steamers to be manned without taking from some ship already in Commission and recalling such Ships [*sic*] from Foreign Stations[?] The Lisbon Squadron is properly speaking the Channel Squadron[,] forming a part of the Vote of Seamen. Therefore[,] if any Steamers are required on a moment[s notice] there are no means of manning them in a hurry without turning over the Men from the Channel Squadron or some other Ships. If the Flag & Ordinary Guard Ships at the ports are filled up with their full compl[emen]t and kept as a reserve to man Steamers on an Emergency, it will be necessary to pay off and reduce the number of Ships now in Commission, or obtain an increased vote for men from Parliament[.] you will then have Flag & Ordinary Guard Ships full[y] manned, The [*sic*] men idle in Harbour, little or nothing to do, too much of the Shore, no practical experience, they would become useless, and therefore it appears to be better policy to keep up a Channel Squadron and have them always moving about, gaining practical knowledge & experience[,] both for officers & men[,] than have men idle in the Guard Ships[.] The True Reserve independent[,] of the above Squadron[,] is the Coast Guard[,] which might be advantageously increased. The Marines [and] The Seamen Riggers might also be increased[,] as they are a useful body of men[,] ready for any emergency. Again[,] the Advocates for a standing Navy have never yet pointed out how ships are to be relieved on Foreign Stations. If the full vote of men is employed, and of course they must be serving in ships[,] and a Ship of the Line has to be relieved[,] say in India[,] or a Frigate at Halifax, [how] are men to be obtained to commission ships for the relief of these Ships[,] and where are they to come from[?] The Standing Navy cannot give them the men [who] are already serving in Ships. Therefore[,] to send reliefs out you must of necessity pay off some other ship or transfer men from one ship to another[,] which is not possible[,] or enter more men than in actual case the vote allowed[, in which case] an excess will take place, and to reduce this, men must be discharged, that is Ships paid off, to seek Employment else where – as is done at this very time.

I now come to the question of Manning the Fleet. The cry is, the Ships cannot get manned why dont [*sic*] the Admi[ra]lty devise some plan[?] take the case of the *Rodney* at Portsmouth. this [*sic*] Ship has been sometime in Commission – but the *Winchester* has since commiss[ione]d, and is picking up men, and[,] as I said before[,] the sailor looks who is to be his Captain and to his individual comfort, before he selects his Ship – he therefore prefers the *Winchester* to the *Rodney*[,] and for the same reason he would prefer a Brig to the *Winchester* if one was Commiss[ione]d.[1]

2nd[,] It [*sic*] has been recommended that our Seamen might be entered for the same period as the Marines are[,] viz. 14 years. That corps is a standing force[:] they do not select their ships but go where ordered. There is in Barracks a reserve of about 5000 men. There are afloat about 6000 men. To bring this arrangement to bear [for seamen] would require to have at Home[,] borne on a Ships Books (in Barracks afloat)[,] a sufficient number of men waiting for ships being Commissioned so as

[1]There follows a section that Milne subsequently crossed out in this draft. It reads: ‘France obtains her men from her sea faring population[;] she drafts them as required. and the only mode of our obtaining men would be to adopt a Ballot from the Seafaring population of this Country. In war I fully believe it is the only true way to obtain Seamen. The Country has a right to the services of her population when required. Her seafaring population ought to be forthcoming when wanted, the Country has a right to them[,] and it is the duty of this Board to prepare such measures for Establishing a Naval Ballot as may ensure sufficient men when the defence of the Country requires their services[.] the sooner an Act is passed, the sooner will the mercantile seamen be used and accustomed [to it] & their minds made up to such a measure. I do not believe it would be unpopular.’

to relieve the Men in Commission on Foreign Stations. If we have 24,000 men serving in Ships abroad, and these men are to be relieved every 3 Years, 21,000 men must be held in reserve[,] ready to relieve the same number afloat (during the 3 years)[,] but if ⅓ are to be relieved each year[,] then 7,000 men will be necessary to have in readiness[,] that is in depot, in reserve, which number[,] taken on present arrangements[,] must be over and above the Vote for men granted by Parliament, Unless [*sic*] a reserve System is pursued, and the number of men on Foreign Stations so reduced in number as to obtain from them a reserve in depot at Home[,] which must be Equal to about ⅓ of the men employed abroad. Whatever system is adopted or recommended[,] it must come to this. To be enabled to send reliefs to Foreign Stations, to Commission ships for any service on any Emerg[en]cy at Home[,] there must be a depot of men the same as a depot of Marines in Barracks – and the number to be so retained in depot, if the Ships are to be relieved every 3 years[,] will be equal to ⅓d of the number of men in Commission which are to be relieved, and this never can be carried out with men entering for a short period of 5 years.

An experienced Admiral has said 'man the Guard Ship at each port with her full complement of 1000 men. Employ these in the Dock Yards,' discharge labourer's [*sic*][,] and let the Seamen of the above Ship then do the labourers duty. all [*sic*] this looks well on paper[.]
A Seaman will not do a Labourer's duty, he will not turn from his own peculiar habits[.] Where there is Rigging to be fitted, a Ship Rigged, moved or docked, he will do his duty, he will not [however] Sweep [*sic*] the yard, carry Timber, attend the Iron Mills, copper stores, attend on the Shipwrights, [or] carry mud out of the docks[,] this has been proved by the S[eamen] Riggers refusing to do this duty[,] and if he would, he is no longer the trained Seamen at the Guns, and in service afloat[,] gaining experience & practical knowledge. Such a system would entirely fail, but admitting 1000 men are so employed, and it is necessary to send a Ship to sea, where is the power to compel these men to leave the Ship of their choice and go to another[?] they enter for the Ship. You my force them no doubt, and sudden emergency may render it necessary, but these men have not entered for G[enera]l Service.

Taking a review of the whole case[,] it is my opinion that no change of any importance can be made with reference to the mode of entry of Seamen without entirely remodelling the whole system of Entry[,] Pay & Pension & Bounties[.] to do this will require very serious attention and so much time it cannot be given by the Members of the Board, but I think it would be a desirable measure to have a Committee of the Most

Experienced officers to consider this whole question, but it is one for the Cabinet as well as the Admi[ra]lty to consider[,] and the Committee should have some person on it acquainted with the working of the Admi[ra]lty as relates to the Manning of the Fleet, Votes, pay &c.

It is said . . . The only means of gaining men for continuous service will be by a progressive increase of pay [and] Pensions at [i.e., for] shorter periods [of service], but then comes the question[:] will Parliament sanction the Expense[?] a Depot of Seamen at Home as a means of Gaining reliefs abroad will be a large increase to the Vote for Seamen of about one third.

I think it injudicious to have men in Guard Ships doing nothing.

If a standing Navy is estab[lishe]d by entering men for a long period of time, a Reserve of Seamen in Floating Barracks will be necessary[,] equal to ⅓ of the Seamen in Commission. They will be idle in Harbour. These men would be better Employed in sea going ships[,] viz. in the Channel Squadron[,] gaining practical knowledge & experience.

Seamen will not enter for longer servitude unless inducements are held out to them by increase of Pay.

No compelling means of Manning the Fleet can be established[,] except by Balloting from the Sea faring population of the Country.

To keep within an Estab[lishe]d number of men allowed by Parliament[,] the entry of Boys must be restricted[,] or more Boys would grow up to be Men than [would] Men [be] discharged from the Service by Death &c[,] and unless these entries are regulated there will be an increasing Navy.

The great evils of our Service and [the] causes [of] dislike to it are [*sic*] that there is no fixed system of Punishments[.][1]

There is too much Exercise and drill both at Guns & Sails[.]

There is a want of relaxation to [*sic*] the men[,] and not sufficient leave of absence given[.]

The increase of Marines would be an expedient Measure[;] they are a good reserve, they are trained to the Guns and part of a Seamans duty[;] those that serve in small vessels are excellent seamen and go aloft.

The Seamen Riggers might be increased with advantage. They are a picked body of men, but are not under Martial Law.

[1]He added in pencil, in what appears to be an aged, crabbed hand, 'I took up this question of Punishments and Estab[lishe]d Standing Regulations[:] See Circular of Oct 1854'. See [**264–5**].

[**239**] *Milne Opinion on Marine Savings Banks*

Admiralty
9 June 1852

The formation of Marine Saving Banks would cause a large increase of business to the Acc[ountan]t General's Departt[,] nor [*sic*] does there appear to be the same necessity for a Marine Saving Bank, at a fixed locality at the Branches of the Several Divisions[,] as in [an Army] Regiment[,] which is constantly moving about with no fixed place of residence. The Marines[,] being at a fixed residence[,] . . . can always remit their money or place it in the Local Saving Banks[.]
Every Encouragement should be given to the Men; the Rules for the Local Saving Banks should be printed and a Copy given to each man[,] & the Commanding officers of the Marines at the Depots should have a box to receive the Money[,] grant the receipts[,] & invest the Money for them. I may mention that in the new Pursery Instructions it is proposed to have a Strong Box in each ship for the deposit of Money[.]

[**240**] *Milne Draft Instructions for a Committee to Consider Manning HM Ships*

[Admiralty
July 1852]

A Committee &c

To consider the present mode by which seamen are obtained for the Naval service, so far as relates to entering the crews for HM Ships when put in commission.
1. Whether it is possible to introduce into the Naval Service any system by which HM Ships could be more speedily manned, either by entering men for a longer period of time, and thereby retaining them in Reserve until required for active service, and[,] if so[,] how far this could be most satisfactorily carried out, or whether any other arrangement or plan could be adopted by which this great object could be obtained, and thereby place at the disposal of the Board of Admiralty immediate means of manning HM Ships, either in whole or in part[,] when they may see fit.
2. That in case of any sudden emergency arising calling for a Naval Armament, and an increased number of Seamen to man HM Ships, what would be the best means for obtaining such seamen for the defence of the Country[,] & what mode of proceeding should be adopted.

With the view of giving these most important subjects the best consideration, The [*sic*] various plans &c[,] which have at different times been submitted to the Board of Admiralty[,] are forwarded to the Committee, who are authorized by their Lordships to call any witnesses whom they may wish to examine, and to send for all paper's [*sic*] or other documents they may wish to consider[,] and my Lords request their attention, to all Acts of Parliament now in force, relative to Bounty, Prize Proclamations, Rates of Pay, Pensions, entries of Riggers in the Dock Yards, Coast Guard, &c[,] or any other orders now in force, and whether any addition or modification of the same can be made so as to establish a system of manning the Navy, an object most essential & important.[1]

[**241**] *Northumberland Draft Instructions to a Committee to Consider the Case of Seamen of the Navy*[2]

[Admiralty
July 1852]

Entrance of Boys[:]
Care must be taken only to enter healthy & well grown boys. Orphans of Seamen & Marines[,] Sons of d[itt]o d[itt]o [&] of Coast Guard to be preferred.
Period of Service to be Considered[.]
Seamen when entered, Period of Service to be considered [*sic*][.]
To consider how far it would be advisable to make a routine of service for Seamen[,] Say [*sic*] 3 years on Foreign Stations [&] time for leave of absence on returning to England. Then [a] term of Service in Coast Guard or [as] Seamen Riggers[,] or other Harbour duty.
How far it would be advisable to order all seamen[,] after [their] term of Harbour &c[,] to Flag Ships for General Service[,] with permission to Volunteer for any ships.
Gunnery Ships[:]
Present regulations to be well considered.
& [*sic*] how far it will be possible to retain the Best Seamen & Best Seamen Gunners in the Service by Good Conduct Pay & Badges granted[,] or by reduced Pensions for a shorter term of service [*sic*].
How far it will be advisable to endeavour to retain Seamen after a course [*sic*] of service & Pension[,] as a 'Reserve'[.]

[1]First Naval Lord Hyde Parker also initialled this draft.
[2]These appear to have been the result of Milne's earlier letter to the Duke of Northumberland on the subject, [**238**].

How far it will be possible to employ the Plan of [Reserve] Voted by Parliament of £36,000 a year[,] by Lt Brown[1] of the Register Office in forming a system of Reserve.

How far a Coast Militia of Fishermen & Seaportmen [*sic*] on the plan of the present Militia Bill[,] namely by Volunteers[,] will be [?probably successful][.]

Retirement In [*sic*] Greenwich Hospital to be well considered[,] with a view to making it directly a Reward for good Service & good Conduct[,] & a Comfortable retirement to old & wounded seamen.

Acts of Parlt[:]

Especially Bounty act to be repealed.

[**242**] *Instructions to the Committee on Manning*[2]

Admiralty
13 July 1852

The Lords Commissioners of the Admiralty[,] having had under their consideration the present system for entering the crews of HM Ships [and] manning HM Ships[,] and[,] being desirous of having this important subject more fully considered[,] with the view of ascertaining whether more efficient measures might not be adopted with advantage to the Service[,] and at the same time improve the position of the Petty officers and seamen of the Fleet, have determined[,] with that object[,] to appoint a Committee of experienced officers to investigate and consider this question in all its bearings.

My Lords have been pleased to select you[3] to fill the responsible situation of Chairman of the said Committee[,] which will consist of the following Members,[4] and I am to request you will take upon yourself the office of Chairman accordingly.

[1]John Hoskins Brown (*c*.1793–1864). Entered, 1805; Lt, 1814; Cmdr, 1858; Registrar-Gen. of Seamen. Brown's scheme for a Naval Reserve was recommended by the 1858–59 Royal Commission on Manning and implemented in August 1859. See R. Taylor, 'Manning the Royal Navy', pt. 2, *Mariner's Mirror*, 45, no. 1 (1959), p. 54.

[2]This draft, in Milne's hand, clearly incorporated some of Northumberland's suggestions, especially those relative to entry and training of Boys.

[3]Vice-Adm. Sir William Parker.

[4]No names are included in this draft. The Committee consisted of, in addition to Parker, Rear-Adm. Arthur Fanshawe and Capts Richard Saunders Dundas, Peter Richards, and John Shepherd. For a printed copy of the instructions, see 'Copies of a Correspondence between the Board of Treasury and the Board of Admiralty, on the subject of the Manning of the Royal Navy, together with Copies of a Report of a Committee of Naval Officers, and of Her Majesty's Order in Council relating thereto', *Parliamentary Papers*, 1852–53, vol. LX, pp. 15–16.

The principal points to which the Committee will have to direct their attention are as follows –
First, The [*sic*] present system and the present arrangements for the Entry & training of Boys and Seamen for HM Ships, and the terms or period of servitude for which they are respectively entered, and whether it would be advantageous and tend to the benefit of the Naval Service, to extend the period of time for which they are now entered.
Second, The possibility of adopting any measures by which the Services of Boys and Seamen could be permanently retained to the Country[,] as is the case with the Marines[,] instead of their being paid off and discharged from the Navy after limited Service [as] at present, and thereby to ensure to the Admi[ra]lty the means of at once manning those ships which are put in Commission[,] either for the General Service of the Navy[,] or for the relief of those on Foreign Stations; in such a case a period of Service abroad might be followed by a period of Service at Home, either in the Coast Guard, the Dock Yards or in the Home Ports[,] & whether by the adoption of any such measures[,] a Reserve of Seamen might not at the sametime [*sic*] be organized and retained in the Home Ports.
Third[,] To consider[,] in the Event of any sudden armament being ordered and a large body of Seamen being required for the defence of the Country (The Naval Service)[,] what measures could be best adopted to obtain the requisite number for that purpose, from what source they are to be obtained [*sic*], & what measures should <u>now</u> be taken to ensure this object being speedily attained in the time of war [*sic*][.]
With the view of giving these subjects the most full and attentive consideration[,] my Lords request the attention of the Committee to various proposals which have been at different periods been submitted to them, and also to all regulations now in force relative to the Entry and training of Boys & Seamen, and to all Acts of Parliament, for Pay, Prize Money & Bounties[,] and also all other regulations and Institutions relative to Petty Officers, Seamen Gunners, the award of Good Conduct Badges and Pensions – the regulations for admission of Seamen into the Coast Guard and [into the] Dock Yards of Seaman Riggers and[,] lastly[,] the Entry and support of Seamen into [*sic*] Greenwich Hospital &c.[,] with the view of so modifying[,] amending[,] altering[,] or extending them as they may consider most expedient in any recommendation they may see fit to submit[.] My Lords do not deem it advisable to limit the Committee in their Enquiry & proceedings by any definite Instructions[,] but in the consideration of so important a Subject, embracing as it does not only the raising & retaining [of] Seamen for the Fleet, but also defence of

the Country on any sudden Emerg[en]cy, to leave the whole subject in their hands[,] with full authority to call for and examine all persons & papers [&] to submit[,] after full & careful deliberation[,] such recommendations as[,] in their opinion[,] may conduce to effect the important object their Lordships have in mind, by the most efficient manner for raising & retaining Seamen for Manning the Fleet[,] & raising Seamen for the defence of the Country.

[**243**] *Milne Draft Circular on Naval Account Keeping*

Admiralty
18 July 1852

My Lords desire the attention of the Comdrs in Chief Abroad to the importance of a return being made to them of Store officers who neglect to send home their Accounts at the proper period, and[,] when they find any neglect of their Lordships instruction on this subject[,] and the Accounts have not been transmitted[,] that they should immediately order a Board of Officers to examine and inspect that officers accounts & report the same for their Lordships information.

[**244**] *Milne Instructions on the Board's Duties During Visitation to the Dockyards*

[Admiralty
July 1852]

The accompanying paper's [*sic*] give a general sketch of the duties of the Board at the visitation to the Ports.

The subject which will require most attention will be the reports made to the Board by the Sup[erinten]d[en]ts of the Yard[s], relative to the proposed 'New Works and improvements in the Yards,' To [*sic*] consider what is to be done, & may be essentially necessary. Then with reference to the Expense to be taken in the Navy Estimates for the rest [of the present] or succeeding Session.

The visitation of the Board should not be only with reference to the present State of the Yards and Stores, but to remedy any irregularities which may exist, and to improve the general working of the Establishments. The Sup[erinten]d[en]ts can alone state what should or may be required to be done, and to recommend, and with that object He should be asked to give any suggestions. if [*sic*] none[,] it will be satisfactory to know That [*sic*] no improvements can be made.

The state of the advanced ships requires consideration[.] many of them have had their Holds stowed for years & have never been cleared out[,] which would cause sickness on board if put in Commission.

[**245**] *Milne Instructions on the Board of Admiralty's Visitation to the Dockyards*

Admiralty
July 1852

Visitation to the Ports, July 1852
Deptford[:]
1st[,] The Dockyard, [&] Sup[erinten]d[en]ts office in the Vic[tuallin]g Yard. To inspect the Stores, Ships Buildings, The new Works in Progress, [&] depository of Old Stores[.] To muster the officers and men at ½ past eleven[,] and to give them the usual Half Holiday[,] which is done at all the Estab[lishmen]ts[.]
2nd Vic[tuallin]g Yard[:]
To inspect the Stores, first going to the Superintendants [*sic*] Office to see plan of the Yard &c.
To inspect the Salt provision Stores, The Rum Vats, the Mills, the Slop Stores, The Medical department for Medical Stores, the Cooperage.
To consider the new alterations in progress and submission from the Superintendant relative to the Dock & Vic[tuallin]g yard[s].
The Establishment of officers and work people to be mustered & to have their half Holiday on a subsequent day.

Chatham[:]
Superintendants office to see the plan of the Yard.
To muster the officers and work people[,] to give the usual Half Holiday on a subsequent day[,] to be fixed by the Superintendant.
To Inspect the Ships Building[,] The Store Houses, Rope Machinery, Sail Loft, Smitheries, Foundry, Saw Mills, Store of Timber, & Hemp[,] also Copper & Iron.
New Improvements & proposed alterations[,] also representations from the Sup[erinten]d[en]t of the Yard to be considered.
The Ordinary Guard Ship to be mustered[,] with the warrant officers.
Marine Barracks. The Marines to be inspected on parade. Their Barrack rooms & schools to be visited[.] The officers to be introduced.
The (Naval Hospital)[,] or rather[,] the Marine Infirmary forming the Naval Hospital to be visited and the wards inspected.

Woolwich[:]
Superintendants office, to see plan of yard.
To muster the officers & workpeople [*sic*] at ½ past eleven, on their going to Dinner. The usual Half Holiday to be given on a future day.
The Yard to be inspected. The Saw Mills, process of Burnettizing[1] Timber, the Store Houses, Sail Loft, Rigging Loft, Smitheries, Timber Store, [&] Ships building[.] The Factory & all its dependencies of Stores, Boiler Shops, &c, [&] Ships in the Hands of the Factory.
The submission from the Sup[erinten]d[en]t to be considered.
The Marines to be inspected in the Barrack Yard. Officers introduced[.]
The Infirmary[,] Schools and Barracks to be inspected.
The *Fisgard*[,] with her small compl[emen]t & few warrant officers[,] has never been mustered.

Sheerness[:]
Sup[erintenden]ts Office[.]
The plans of Yard & submissions from Sup[erinten]d[en]t[.]
To muster the officers & workpeople at 11:30, Half Holiday on a subsequent day. Inspect the Stores, Sail Loft, Rigging Loft[,] Ships Building[,] Smitheries &c[,] and go round the Yard.
Commander in Chief[’s] House[,] generally at 2 oclock.
Buildings outside the Yard.
Muster Flag ship[,] also the Ordinary[,] including the Warrant officers & Engineers.
Visit some of the Ships in Ordinary (This never has been done for want of time)[.]

Portsmouth[:]
George Hotel
The Day for 1st Lords Levée to be fixed[,] also days for visiting the Marine Barracks[,] The *Victory*[,] Ships in Ordinary & Hospital.
First Day[:]
Dockyard Sup[erinten]d[en]ts office with reference to plans of the Yard and his submission for New Works &c.
Muster the yard on any day at 11:30, usual half Holiday.
Inspection of the Yard. Ships Building[,] Store Houses, Ropery, Saw Mills, Smitheries, Sail Loft, Chain Cable Store, Watering Island, Boat House, [&] Planing Machine[.]

[1]Application of a fluid for preserving timber, canvas, and other materials prone to rot, patented by Sir William Burnett, M.D., F.R.S., K.C.B. (1779–1861). Burnett was Physician-General of the Navy 1832–55, although the title was changed in 1841 to Inspector-General of Naval Hospitals and Fleets and again in 1844 to Director-General of the Medical Department of the Navy.

Factory & Works, new ground[.]
Coal Depots[.]
Second Day[:] probably 1st Lord['s] Levée, other members of the Board to complete the Dock Yard Inspection.
Muster *Victory* & Ordinary[,] unless the 1st Lord wishes to be present
After the Levée[,] inspect the Ships in Ordinary & Steam Reserve also the Naval Hospital.
3[d] Day[:]
The Royal Clarence Yard. Sup[erinten]d[en]ts office for plan of Yard and Submissions[.]
Muster the Officers & Work people[,] the usual Half Holiday.
Inspect the Stores & State of Provisions[,] The Slop Clothing, Bakery and Machinery.
Marine Barracks at Forton[.]
[Inspect] Marines in the Barrack Yard[,] The rooms &c[,] Gun Drill &c[,] Introduced to Officers, Schools[.]
4th Day[:]
Ships at Spithead or other duties with the Sup[erinten]d[en]t of Dock Yard. Schools in the Yard. Royal Naval College[.]
The Board have generally dined with the Admiral, Sup[erinten]d[en]t of the Yard, & [Marine] General[,] and have given one Dinner to the Officers.

Devonport[:]
Royal Hotel, 4 Days
The days for the 1st Lords Levees [*sic*] to be fixed[, also for] visitation to the Hospital[,] Vic[tuallin]g Yard &c.
Dock Yard, Sup[erinten]d[en]ts office for view of plans, submissions &c[.][1]

[**246**] *Milne Draft Minute to the George Hotel, Portsmouth and Royal Hotel, Devonport*

Admiralty
13 July 1852

A private note to be written to the proprietors of the George Hotel at Ports[mouth] & Royal Hotel Devonp[or]t[,] requesting their attention to the very extravagant charges in their respective Bills for the Board of Admiralty on their visitation to the above ports, That [*sic*] the Board do

[1]Here the draft ends.

not wish to make any complaint of those Bills that are now paid, but with reference to the future, they cannot pass over or allow such very large[,] and what they must consider to be exorbitant[,] claims in their Accounts. They wish to say that there appears not the least necessity for ordering expensive items from London. They wish to have plain substantial Dinners, and there does not exist any necessity for the profusion of articles which are generally placed on the Table.

The Charges for Carriages[,] and also to the Waiters[,] Chambermaids &c require to be considered[,] and that on the next visitation the Board expect that this representation will meet with attention.

[**247**] *Milne Draft Board Minute on Royal Marine Savings Banks*

Admiralty
13 October 1852

The Lords Commissioners of the Admiralty[,] with the view of affording facilities to The Royal Marines of depositing their Pay in Savings Banks for the benefit of themselves and families, have considered [it] expedient to adopt the following –

That the Local Saving Banks in the vicinity of the Divisions are to be considered the Banks for the deposit of the Money belonging to the Marines[.]

That a Ledger be opened in each Division for the purpose of Entering the Mens Names with the amount of the Deposits.

That the Marine who wishes to make any deposit in or withdraw money from the Bank shall make the same known to his immediate commanding officer, who[,] on reporting the same to the Commandant[,] will order the Divisional Paymaster to receive the same[,] the name to be entered in the Books & the Money forthwith deposited in or withdrawn out of the Bank.

With the above object of their Lordships[,] The [*sic*] Deputy Acc[ountant] General is to draw up Regulations for the above purpose.

It is not intended that these Accounts should be sent to the Acc[ountan]t General of the Navy, but to be considered as a Divisional Transaction – The [*sic*] Ledgers and other accounts being audited Quarterly by a Board of Officers.[1]

[1]This memorandum suggests that Milne's recommendations in [**239**] were followed. Across the memorandum is the note: '13 October Approved[;] Directions to the Dep [Accountant] Genl to take the necessary steps accordingly. JB' [probably John Henry Briggs]. Addendum, in Milne's hand: 'The Regulations of the Local Saving Banks to be obtained and to be communicated with on the subject.'

[**248**] *Milne to Stafford*

Admiralty, Private
22 October 1852

Dear Stafford

I have given the subject of manning the ships of the Mercantile Service every consideration, and I am of opinion it would be a most dangerous measure to admit a larger proportion of Foreign seamen into English vessels than at present allowed by law. English seamen must be maintained[,] and to allow English ships to be navigated by Foreign Seamen would be a fatal blow to the Naval Service should war unfortunately break out and seamen be required to man our ships[,] for to the Merchant Service we must look for Seamen.

I understand that even now there exists a scarcity of seamen from the late relaxation of the law relative to Apprentices.

[**249**] *Milne to Northumberland on Mechanization of Dockyard Workshops*

Admiralty
20 November 1852

My Lord Duke

I am anxious to direct your attention to the necessity for some definite steps being taken for the progressive improvement of the workshops in our Dock Yards. This I feel to be the more necessary[,] for unless the subject is earnestly taken up by yourself or brought before the Board and some one member deputized to take charge and superintend the details, I feel assured nothing will be done. Year after year will roll on as has already been the case, with the same antiquated system of workmanship in full operation, and the Establishments conducted at an Expense and on a system not at all creditable in the present age of Mechanical improvement. I may mention to your Grace that the Dock Yards[,] so far as relate to their internal arrangements[,] and improvements in the Workshops, are not under the supervision of any one member of this Board. no [*sic*] one looks into their working, because it is no ones duty, and you must be aware it is in the Dock Yards the large amount of Naval money yearly voted by Parliament is sunk.

In 1848 Sir H[enry] Ward[,] then Secretary to the Admiralty[,] took up this subject, after having with Sir B. Walker, Mr. Bromley and myself[,] been engaged on a Committee of Enquiry and Revision of our Establishment. His removal from the Admiralty and the subsequent death of Col Irvine[,][1] the then Director of Works[,] put a stop to contemplative measures which were intended to be gradually carried out, but with new appointments and the subsequent changes which have taken place[,] those intentions have fallen to the ground. I feel most anxious this subject should be revived, and that steps should be taken for the introduction of Machinery. There in our Joiners shops[,] everything in some goods is done entirely by Hand, whereas by a small expenditure of money with some very trivial arrangements, the work might be done by machinery[,] at an immense saving of time and expense. Your Grace may perhaps ask, by whom these arrangements are to be made[?] my answer is, that the Director of Works Department is the one more immediately concerned with this really important subject[,] but the Director of Works himself is working in the dark. I might say he is comparatively ignorant of the views and wishes of the Board, and is without the aid and support of any one individual member of it, from whose practical knowledge of Naval affairs (which must always be a prominent feature in Dock Yard Arrangements) he might receive[,] in many instances[,] assistance and direction with reference to his duties. The Director of Works is in the same position as the Storekeeper General or Comp[trolle]r of Victualling[,] both of whose Departments are superintended by a Member of the Board[,] and so ought the Director of Works. If your Grace should consider it necessary to take any steps on this subject[,] I would propose, That [*sic*] one or more Members of the Board[,] the Surveyor of the Navy & the Director of Works should visit each Dock Yard, consult with the Sup[erinten]d[en]t and principal officers[,] investigate the arrangements, and[,] by the aid of proper person's [*sic*] from private Establishments[,] endeavour to put the Yards on the most improved system that can be devised[,] and I feel assured the result will prove to be advantageous to the public service.

[1]Col. Augustus Irvine, C.B., Director of Works in the late 1840s.

[**250**] *Milne Paper on the Home Naval Force and the Distribution of Men and Ships*[1]

Admiralty
December 1852

Parliament having granted a Sup[plementar]y Vote of 5000 Seamen and 1500 Marines for Naval Service at Home,[2] it becomes necessary to consider how this force is to be distributed and employed, – To [*sic*] do this[,] the present system established in the Home Ports must be considered, with reference to any available force and the Manning of those ships which are at present held ready for Service.

In 1848 the Crews of the Flagships and the Ordinary Guard Ships were reduced to as low a number as possible consistent with the proper care of the Ships, and the discharge of the Harbour duties, and the residue of the men taken from these ships[,] with some additional, and a party of Marines[,] were put into a Ship of the Line at Each [*sic*] of the Ports, viz. Sheerness, Portsmouth and Devonport, such as the *Queen* and *London* at this moment, and the reason for having adopted this arrangement was that the Crews of the Flag and Ordinary Guard Ships, were too large for the harbour duties to be performed, and therefore kept in pay [a number of idle men], who would be more serviceable in a Ship of the Line kept ready for sea. Another plan was adopted in 1845 or 6, which was to have the Flag Ships and Ordinary Guard Ships [as] sea going ships, full manned and ready for sea. Such was the case at Devonport in 1847 when the *Queen* and *Caledonia* were both sent to sea and attached to Sir C. Napiers Squadron. What was the result[?] the Comdr in Chief at Devonport had no Flagship, and the Ordinary had neither Captain[,] Officers[,] or Crew to take charge of the Ships. It was to remedy the difficulties of these different plans, that the arrangements of 1848 were adopted. It must be always considered, that in any arrangement for the distribution of Efficient Ships in the Harbour, that the Admiral must have a Flagship or Depot ship for Harbour duties, and the Ships in Ordinary must be guarded and taken care of, and it is

[1]Much of this paper duplicates a draft found in MLN/142/1 [3]. Milne pencilled in on the back: 'Channel Squadron & Home Ports & State of the Navy 1852.'

[2]For details of this vote, see John Beeler, '"A Whig Private Secretary is itself fatal": Benjamin Disraeli, Lord Derby, Party Politics, and Naval Administration, 1852', in Todd Larson and Michael Shirley (eds), *Splendidly Victorian: Essays in Nineteenth- and Twentieth-Century British History in Honour of Walter L. Arnstein* (Aldershot, Hants., 2001), pp. 117–18. For Parliamentary debate on the Supplementary Estimate for the additional sailors and marines, see *Hansard*, 3rd ser., vol. 123 (1852–53), cols. 997–1015.

therefore indispensable, that proper ships should be set apart for these duties[,] be it peace or war.

It has been stated in Parliament that 5 Sail of the Line and 5 Steamers are to be stationed at Portsmouth, 4 Sail of the Line & 4 Steamers at Devonport [&] 3 Frigates and 3 Steamers at Sheerness.[1] This Force will require about 9,400 men[.] It is obvious[,] therefore[,] that unless the Lisbon Squadron & other ships are added to the Force allowed by the Supplemental Vote, the above number of ships could not be manned.

In the accompanying Sheets, for Port[smouth], Devonport and Sheerness, I have drawn out a scheme for the distribution of three Squadrons. In them I have given an increase of men to the present Flag and Ordinary Guard Ships, which will be more economical than putting them into ships in Commission, and this course will prove equally efficient[,] as these men will be ready to man a certain number of reserved steamers should any emergency arise. The Ships ready for sea service are given in Sheet A, or a number of ships of equal force[,] viz. 7 Sail of the Line, 3 Block Ships, 5 Large Frigates, 10 Steamers – with crews amounting to 11,035 men – and there will remain in Harbour, 4 Sail of the Line partly manned, and with sufficient men to complete 3 of them for effective service[,] or to man 9 Steamers from the Reserves.

What will be difficult to decide is, how are these ships to be employed? As they are specially fitted for Home Defence[,] they cannot be sent from the Channel as a whole Squadron[,] altho detachments of them may be so, and this only in the summer months, for it must not be forgotten, that the Wear & Tear of such a Squadron will amount to at least £50,000 a year in stores alone, and in Coal [to] probably not less than 700 tons pr. Day when under steam alone[,] or about £350 – independent of other expenses – which will probably be at least £100. The whole of this question is one of great importance, requiring a good deal of consideration and arrangement[,] and should be for the Board to decide.

Portsmouth[:]
Present Force Employed[:]

	Men
Victory	215
Supern[umerar]y	230
Neptune	482
Blenheim	320
Sup[ernumerar]y	180

[1]For the Government's intentions regarding the Supplementary Grant, see *Hansard*, 3rd ser., vol. 123 (1852), col. 1005.

Excellent	695
Total	2122

Proposed Force. Those in Red Ink [bold] Sea going ships[; an 'x' denotes a ship in commission:]

	Men
Victory	450
Sup[ernumerar]y	230
Neptune	650
Blenheim	**550**
Sup[ernumerar]y	180
Excellent	695
Harbour [total]	2755
D. of Wellington	**1,100**
Prince Regent	**820x**
Rodney	**820x**
Sans Pareil	**700x**
Imperiuse	**500**
Sidon	**330**
Furious	**330**
Encounter	**175x**
Termagant	**300x**
For above ships	**5075**
In commission at present	2815
Spithead	2260
Harbour	2755
Proposed Force	5015
now	2122
Increase of men at Portsmouth	2893

Note[:]

By this arrangement[,] the Extra men put into the *V[ictoria] & N[eptune]*, with add[itiona]l Marines & Seamen Riggers would man, 3 more reserve steamers[,] and the men of the *Excellent* would man [an]other 2, or the Extra men in *Victory*[,] with Seamen Riggers[,] would man the *Neptune*.

Portsmouth by this will have[:]

For Sea	5 Sail Line
	1 Frigate
	4 Steamers

& [*sic*] disposable men to man 5 Steamers or 2 Steamers and one First Rate[.]

Devonport[:]
Present Force Employed[:]

	Men
Impregnable	209
Supernumeraries	209
St George	493
Edin[bur]gh	444
Hogue	360
Supernumeraries	140
Total	1855

Proposed Force, those in Red Ink [bold] ready for sea[:]

	Men
Impregnable	400
Supernumeraries	209
St George	650
Edinburgh	**550**
Hogue	**550**
Sup[ernumerar]y do.	140
Harbour	2499
Queen	**950x–450**[1]
Agamemnon	**820x–600**
London	**820x–450**
Vulture	**200**
Magicienne	**200**
Cruizer	**160**
Another St[eame]r	**200**
For above ships	3350[2]
In Commission at present	1500
In Sound	1850
Harbour	2499
[total]	4349[3]
Harbour	1855
Increase at this Port	2494

[1]The ships with two figures would be in commission with reduced crews; the first number being the full complement, the second being the peacetime harbour establishment.

[2]This figure is based on the full, rather than the reduced, complements in *Queen*, *Agamemnon*, and *London*.

[3]This total comprises the number in ships in the Sound and the proposed Harbour complement, but not those currently in commission.

Note[:]
The number of men added to the *Impregnable* and *St George* will man[,] with the Seamen Riggers[,] 3 Steamers from the Reserve, or will complete the *St George* for sea.
Devonport by this plan will have[:]

For Sea	5 Sail of the Line
	4 Steamers

And men ready for 3 other Steamers or 1 Ship of the Line (*St George*)

Sheerness[:]
Present Force Employed[:]

	Men
Waterloo	202
Monarch	310
Boscawen	318
Horatio	320
Sup[ernumerar]y	120
Total	1160[1]

Proposed Force. Those in Red Ink [bold] ready for sea[:]

	men
Waterloo	450
Monarch	500
Boscawen	400
Horatio	**320**
Sup[ernumerar]y	130
Harbour	1800
Leander	**500x**
Amphion	**320**
Arrogant	**450x**
A Steamer	**200**
Do	**200**
Tartarus	**67**
For above ships	1737
In commission at Present	1017
For Nore	720
Harbour	1800
[total]	2520
former force	1160

[1]Should be 1,280; Milne may have neglected to include the 120 supernumeraries.

Increase at Sheerness 1380[1]

Note[:]

The add[itiona]l men to the Guard Ships[,] with the few Seamen Riggers at Sheerness[,] and Marines from Chatham or Woolwich[,] would man 3 Steamers from the reserve or complete the crew of the *Waterloo*. Sheerness by this plan will have[:]

For Sea 3 Frigates
3 Steamers

and sufficient men to man 3 Steamers from the Reserve or 1 Ship of the Line.[2]

[**251**] *Milne Opinion on Report No. 1 of the Committee on Arming Mail Contract Steam-Packets*[3]

Admiralty
10 December 1852

This report on the qualities of the Packet Steamers at Southampton at once shew the vast difference between Vessels constructed for War purposes, which have to carry enormous weights of Armament & Stores, and those constructed for Speed, and for the conveyance of passengers only[,] and how totally inadequate these packet steamers are for being armed. 8 only [*sic*] are stated to be capable of carrying guns, and to do this alterations of considerable Extent must be made which would cost about £800 per Vessel[,]

What steps are to be taken[?]

Are these Vessels to be fitted for Guns or are they not[?]

If so at what expense[?]

Are the Gun's [*sic*] to be ordered with the proper amount of Ammunition &c[?]

Are the new Steamers to be altered to carry Guns when in process of Building[?]

Will the companies consent to have their ships altered & Hatchways[,] placed so as to admit of Guns being fitted[?] If so[,] the accommodation for passengers will be inferior to what it is at present[.]

[1]The increase was actually 1,360 men, rather than 1,380.

[2]List A, which follows, is a compilation of the previous three lists.

[3]The report is found in ADM1/5614, 15 November 1851. It was subsequently printed in the *Parliamentary Papers*, 61 (1852–53), pp. 383–99. On the subject of arming merchant steamships during the 1840s and 1850s, see John Beeler, 'Plowshares into Swords: The Royal Navy and Merchant Marine Auxiliaries in the Late Nineteenth Century', in Greg Kennedy (ed.), *The Merchant Marine in International Affairs, 1850–1950* (London, 2000), pp. 5–17.

Are Iron Steamers to be built[?]
I have ever looked upon the Arming of these Vessels for purposes of War as visionary[,] altho they might be employed as Troop Ships or Gun Boats and[,] if emp[loye]d by Govt[,] the Foreign Mail Service would either cease or be discouraged[,] but the Board having carried the subject of inspection of these Vessels so far, It [*sic*] must now be decided what further steps are to be taken.
Steam Vessels built in private yards are totally unfit on every essential point for war purposes, and those who are constantly crying [*sic*] up private builders & private Estab[lishmen]ts had better read this report. Our own Departments and Dock Yards have more sound practical knowledge both in building & in steam for War purposes & for efficiency than all the private Establishments in the Kingdom, where they know nothing of the requirements absolutely necessary for Vessels of war.

[**252**] *Milne Draft Board Minute to the Surveyor of the Navy*

Admiralty
11 December 1852

With reference to the conversation held at the Board this day with the Surveyor of the Navy, Mr Watts[1] & Mr Lloyd[,][2] the professional officers of the Surveyor[s] Depart[,] on the fittings of the *Duke of Wellington* and other Ships; The [*sic*] Surveyor of the Navy is to give directions that Mr Watts and Lloyd should visit the above ship in company with Mr Abthell[,][3] the Master Ship[wrigh]t and Mr Murray[,][4] the Chief Engineer of Portsmouth Dock Yard[,] whilst her Engines are fitting, as my Lords are anxious that the Machinery and Ship be thoroughly inspected, so that any proposed or necessary improvement[,] either in the machinery, mode of fitting or in the internal arrangements of the Ship may at once be made, so as to prevent future alteration or the risk of failure[.]
It is also the Especial [*sic*] wish of the Board that when the Surveyor is unable to visit the ports in person, that the professional officers of his Department who are sent for the purpose of inspecting the fitting of Engines, or on other duties, should freely communicate with the Yard officers on all matters of detail which may be connected with work executing under their directions, so that any accidental oversight may

[1]Isaac Watts, Chief Constructor of the Navy.
[2]Thomas Lloyd, Chief Engineer of the Navy.
[3]John Abthell, Master Shipwright, Portsmouth Dockyard.
[4]Andrew Murray, Chief Engineer, Portsmouth Dockyard.

be immediately corrected and arrangements which may appear to be necessary[,] or an improvement may be at once considered and adopted[,] if approved by the Surveyor, as it may be the means of preventing subsequent alterations or future expense or failure, In [*sic*] all cases the Surveyor keeping the Board informed on these points[,] as it is their Lordships anxious wish to have these most responsible duties carried out with the fullest consideration in sufficient time to prevent any error being accidentally committed[,] and to prevent animadversions on the breaking down or failure of any of HM Ships.

[**253**] *Milne Draft Board Minute on Dockyard Economy*

Admiralty, Confidential
14 December 1852

Write to the Superintendants [*sic*] of the Home Ports[,] acquaint them my Lords are anxious that some further[,] as well as more strict[,] supervision should be exercised in the respective Dock Yards, in regard to the various fittings on board HM Ships during their building or repair, both in the Master Ship[wrigh]t and Engineering Departments, with the express view of having every ship[,] when in the hands of the Dockyard[,] rendered as efficient as circumstances will admit, and likewise as a check on all unauthorized as well as unnecessary alterations and consequent expense. My Lords are fully aware that these various subjects receive the anxious attention of the Surveyor of the Navy and his Depart. at Somerset House, and that periodical inspections[,] either by himself or professional officers from his office are made, but even with all the care and attention which can be given to the very complicated detail in the arrangements of Steam Machinery and the adaptation of ships to Steam purposes, some fittings bearing on essential points may be accidentally overlooked[,] or those ordered to be made may[,] on personal examination of the ship[,] be found to be not only inconvenient but unnecessary[.] It is therefore the desire of their Lordships That [*sic*] as Superintendant of the Dock Yard[,] acting on behalf of the Admiralty in all works carrying on in the Establishments, That [*sic*] you should take a personal interest in the foregoing subjects, and[,] during your inspections of all works[,] especially on board HM Ships, that you should enquire of the professional officers specially in charge of the execution of the details, whom my Lords consider as the responsible parties for their proper execution, if they observe any omission in the plans, or anything at all objectionable[,] either in principle or in detail[,] which may have been inadvertently overlooked[,] so that by immediate representation[,] any error or omission may at once be remedied[.] My Lords are led to these expressions of their views from unsatisfactory results which have taken place in the Machinery[,] as well as in the fittings[,] of some ships after having left the Dock Yards[,] and from officers having stated that their representations have not met with attention. It is to put a check on these various circumstances[,] and to prevent error's [*sic*] being overlooked[,] that my Lords require your supervision[,] and they deem it essential, That [*sic*] whenever a ship is paid off or under repair in the Dock Y[ar]d of which you are Sup[erinten]d[en]t[,] you should call upon the Captain to state in writing any proposals he may have to make with reference to the improvement of the ship, machinery[,] or spars &c[,] or to represent anything found to be wrong[,] and you are then to send the professional officer on Board to report thereon[,] so that the Surveyor of the Navy['s] attention may be called to any recommendations when the ship is under repair[,] and form his instructions thereon[,] and[,] as in the fittings of Steam Vessels[,] it is absolutely necessary some Naval Officer of experience should advise on the requisite arrangements[,] you are at liberty to order the Captain of the Steam Reserve to attend and give his professional advice whenever required or when you may consider it necessary . . .

[**254**] *Napier to Milne*

Merchistoun House, Horndean, Hampshire
31 December 1852

My dear Milne

The Duke of Northumberland took a step in the right direction and left you in office. Sir James Graham has taken two steps and kept you and Parker. I told you they would have nothing to do with me. I am taboo by all parties, but nevertheless I am glad to see my suggestions generally, tho' tardily[,] adopted. The Government is strong if they agree[,] which I doubt.

[**255**] *Milne Memorandum on Entry of Men into the Dockyards*[1]

Admiralty, Confidential
14 January 1853

The appointment of Artificers and Labourer's [*sic*] and other persons to the Dock Yards and Civil Establishments, has been vested in the First Secretary of the Admiralty. It has formed a part of his duty in the distribution of the Board business, to be exercised by him[,] not as a private source of patronage of his own[,] but as the patronage of the Admiralty, for all appointments are made in the name of the Board . . . for which they become answerable [*sic*]. This patronage therefore ought to be exercised solely for the benefit and advantage of the Public Service. It was with this view that printed regulations were issued in Feb. 1847[,] pointing out a system of entry and promotion for all persons entered as Artificers and[,] if honestly carried out[,] ought to check any undue influence of political interest working to the disadvantage of those men who have been told [to] look to merit alone for their advancement in the public service. There can be no doubt that the Treasury exercises a powerful sway in these appointments, and that the Secretary of the Admiralty, is forced by that influence to exercise the patronage intrusted to him more or less politically for the support of whatever Government may be in office[,] and so long as the men in the yards have the power of exercising the elective franchise, so long will they continue to exert that influence for the purpose of their own personal promotion[,] or to obtain nominations in the Establishments[,] and even if they were deprived of the franchise[,] their families & friends would still continue to exert the same political influence[,] altho that influence would be much limited & personal interference by <u>votes</u> would be entirely avoided[.] I do not therefore think it is possible altogether to exclude political influence from exerting a certain sway in the Dock Yards[,] but this should be confined to the first nominations or entries. if [*sic*] any Superintendant of a Yard[,] or even any other party[,] should ask for the entry of an Artificer[,] and men must be entered on some recommendation[,] It [*sic*] is not possible to refuse this privilege to the Member of the County or Borough. Therefore[,] so far as <u>first</u> entries of men into the Yards, there is no reason to say to the M.P. [']we

[1]Milne added afterwards 'Copy of a Paper given to Sir J Graham when he came into office in 1853' and that this paper was the foundation for the subsequent Order in Council on the subject. For the situation regarding Dockyard entries and promotions which prompted Milne to compose this memorandum, see Beeler, '"A Whig Private Secretary is itself fatal,"' pp. 111–15, 119–20, 123–4.

cannot attend to Yours trulys recommendations,['] but this influence ought not to exclude a fair portion of the entries being given to other applicants. The greatest care[,] however[,] should be taken that[,] in the exercise of this patronage, that all persons recommended for entry are in every respect deserving and fit to the Service[,] both by character and capability as workmen. The Service demands that this should be. A man[,] once entered in the Yard[,] should rise by his own Merit and ability alone, and if the Board order of Feb. 1847 is adhered to, with strictness, this will be the case, but if political influence is to be secretly exercised in the recommendations for promotions, There is neither justice to the deserving, nor can the Superintendant carry on his duty, or exercise that control over the Establishment under his charge which is expected from him. he [*sic*] will find his recommendations set aside, The deserving man past [*sic*] over, and he will be undermined in his just selection and recommendation of men for advancement, by secret representations sent by correspondents in his own Yard direct to the Admiralty[,] or the equally strong influence of a political Committee in the Borough[,] who exercise thro the Member of Parliament every possible means to obtain the appointment of their own friends[,] and the result is the Superintendant finds himself a complete Cypher in the Yard, or perhaps receives a public rebuke from the Admiralty[,] because in the honest exercise of his duty he has put forward the most deserving & fit man for the Service, but has not recommended the political supporter of the Government candidate, who may have been secretly recommended by some artificer in his own Yard, or the political committee outside the walls.

To remedy some of the existing evils[,] I would recommend the following to be adopted, engrafted [*sic*] on the Board Minute of Feb 1847[,] but assuming that any new regulations [are] sanctioned by the Board[,] what hold [*sic*] have the Board for their being honestly carried out, or that on a change of Government, a new Board may not countermand these very regulations[?] What one Admiralty orders another may change[.]

Proposals[:]

I would most strongly urge that the Surveyor of the Navy should be again directed to resume his supervision of the Establishment of Men in the Yards[,] and that no vacancies should be filled up unless he states it is requisite[.] That the Estab[lishmen]t should be completed, and therefore that the Monthly report of vacancies should be sent to him[,] and that he should submit the vacancies to be filled up. In Sept 1849 the returns from the Dock Yards were ordered to go direct to him for the purpose of submitting to the Board what app[ointmen]ts should be made. in [*sic*] 1852 this was countermanded[,] & since that period the Surveyor has not exercised any control over the Establishments in which so large a sum of money is expended in wages[,] and for which he is responsible.

Apprentices – Add to the present regulation[:] That no apprentices are on any account whatever to be entered in the Yards[,] except in the month of January in Each [*sic*] year, and then only after the public Examination has been held, and the relative position of the Candidates reported. One half the entries to be those who stand at the Head of the Examination Sheet, The [*sic*] Other Half to be selected by the Board from the remainder on that General List, whose parents have most claim to their son's entry by servitude or character.

Artificers

I have stated that I do not see the possibility of excluding from the entries into the Dock Yards, The [*sic*] recommendations of the Members of Parliament, but to ensure that properly qualified Candidates are entered[,] I would recommend that for each vacancy, 3 names should be sent to the Superintendant, that these 3 Candidates should be examined in his presence by the professional officers of the Yard, and afterwards by the Surgeon, and the most qualified candidate[,] by ability[,] character & constitution admitted, and if any candidate should be reported unfit for the service, on no account whatever should that party be ordered to be entered, without the special authority of the Board being taken.

Labourers

The general appearance of the present Labourers in the Yards is unsatisfactory. They are small men, or poor in constitution, or worn out people, the result of indiscriminate entry by Authority. I would recommend men being selected from several candidates[,] as in the case of artificers, or to place the whole responsibility of their admission in the hands of the Superintendant and hold him responsible.

Promotions

The advancement of men in the yards should be from merit alone, and the Superintendant should be held responsible that the present regulations are faithfully enforced[,] and no person whatever should be promoted without the written report of the Superintendant, The Surveyor, and the professional officers of the Yard, that the person recommended is the most eligible[,] and in all respects fitted for promotion, and[,] as the advancement is not patronage, but the reward of Merit, these promotions should be vested in the Senior Members of the Board superintending the Dock Yards, who should submit them to the Board before being ordered[.]

Extra Men in the Yards

I believe it to be a common custom to enter men by the influence of patronage[,] direct at once to the Establishment from out door applicants, instead of selecting the most efficient men from those employed on Extra [*sic*][.] These men[,] if fit[,] should have the first chance of being placed on the Establishment. I would therefore recommend that this course should be adopted.

I would further suggest that these regulations be added to . . . those of 1847[,] and the whole reprinted after revision By [*sic*] the Board, and some measures adopted[,] either by Order in Council or otherwise[,] to prevent any further deviation from them[,] and to prevent succeeding Boards altering them. It would appear also to be expedient to have a Monthly statement placed before the Board of all promotions in or appointments to the Yards . . . [1]

The appointment of Police men should be very carefully watched, considering the very high trust which must be reposed in them, the many opportunities for plundering the valuable stores[,] and therefore the absolute . . . necessity for having honest steady men, The Sup[erinten]d[en]t should therefore be consulted[,] & the Character of the Applicant should be thoroughly investigated, and no person should be appointed to a Yard who has resided [in] or belongs to the same neighbourhood[.]

[1]Milne's papers also contain an undated minute (MLN/155/1 [19]) on the subject, in his hand, bearing his, Saunders Dundas's, and William Cowper's initials:

> The Board having placed in our Hands the revision of the Dock Yard Circular Regulations of Feb 1847 for the Entry and Promotion of Artificers &c in H.M. Dock Yards[,] with the view of revising an amending the same, so as to render the system more efficient and less liable to be changed, we have to state that we have complied with the wishes of the Board[,] and The [*sic*] amended Regulations are now enclosed and ready for issue to the Yards, so soon as they are confirmed by Her Majesty in Council.
>
> We Beg [*sic*] further to submit that[,] as the Promotions in the Dockyards and other Estabts are founded on the ability and character of Individuals[,] and not a source of Patronage[,] we are of opinion These [*sic*] Promotions should be vested with the Member of the Board who superintends the Dock Yards and other Estbts[,] and by them should be submitted to the Board for confirmations, and as the appointments of all First Entries to the Establishments is the patronage of the Board of Admiralty, that these appointments should be vested in the Hands of the First Secretary[,] & being of opinion that it is essential for the safety of the Dock Yards that only men of good character should be admitted[,] we strongly recommend a man's character & previous conduct, should be ascertained before entry into these Estabt[,] & that henceforth the Form printed in the Appendix to the enclosed Regulations [not here] should be filled [out] for all persons who are recommended to the Board for appointments[,] and that a Copy thereof should be sent to the Yard where the party is nominated for examination.

See also 'Order issued by the Admiralty in 1855, regulating appointments in H.M. Dockyards,' *Parliamentary Papers*, 1856, vol. XLI, p. 107.

[**256**] *Milne Opinion on the Report of the Committee Appointed to Consider Manning the Navy*[1]

[Admiralty
March 1853]

Submitted[:]

That an attempt be made to enter men for a period of ten years.
That increase of Pay should be given as recommended by Committee[:]

	[increase]	Pay to be
2d Class Ord[inar]y	1d pr Day	1/0
Ordinary	2 "	1/2
AB.	3	1/7
Leading Seamen	"	1/9
2nd Class P[etty] Officer	3	1/11 to 1/10 [*sic*]
1 Class P[etty] Officer	3	2/0 to 2/3[2]

also [*sic*] to be allowed Pensions[,] to count from the Age of 18 years instead of 20.[3]

Preference to be given to the above men to [join the] Coast Guard and Seamen Riggers[,] and for Promotion to Warrant Officers[.] Not considered necessary to give the Bounty . . . during Peace[.]

Men now in the Service to be allowed to enter for 10 years[,] with increase of Pay, provided they have not served or completed 15 years time.

All Long Service men to form the Standing Navy [&] to be allowed to wear a small star on the sleeves of Jacket.

The sons of all such men to be allowed to enter the Navy without payment of 40s.

[1]The Manning Committee Report is dated 13 March 1853. This is Milne's gloss and comments on the report, which is itself found in 'Copies of a Correspondence between the Board of Treasury and the Board of Admiralty, on the subject of the Manning of the Royal Navy, together with Copies of a Report of a Committee of Naval Officers, and of Her Majesty's Order in Council relating thereto', *Parliamentary Papers*, 1852–53, vol. LX, pp. 9–57.

[2]In the margin Milne noted: 'See sheet A [follows below] Increase of Pay £112,400 for the whole Navy[,] 17,744 Blue Jackets as voted 1853–54'. An Order in Council implementing continuous service was issued on 1 April 1853, and an Act of Parliament followed. See 'Bill to make better provision concerning the entry and service of seamen, and otherwise to amend the Laws concerning Her Majesty's Navy', *Parliamentary Papers*, 1853–53, vol. III, pp. 307–15. This became law as Act LXIX, 16th & 17th Vic. See also the Admiralty Circular, No. 121 of 14 June 1853, printed in Hattendorf et al., *British Naval Documents 1204–1960*, document 417, pp. 708–14.

[3]Hitherto pensions were earned by 21 years' service, but only time subsequent to the sailors' twentieth birthday was counted toward it. The committee recommended that the age be lowered to 18.

When paid off from ships[, they] will be granted six weeks or two months leave as may be required, may be sent free to any out Port they may wish, but liable to be app[ointe]d to such ships as the Admiralty may determine[,] as in the case of all ranks of officers.

These men to be granted every facility of immediate allotment to their families[,] and an increased amount of allotment[,] equal to their increase of Pay, benefit of Savings Banks, &c.

After ten years of continued [*sic*] Service being completed[,] to grant 1d pr Day in add[itiona]l to their former pay.

The Leading Seamen [designation] only to be granted under the conditions of 10 years continuous service to[,] wear the[1] as a Badge[,] & the 2d Class Petty Officers in future to assume the Crown [Badge,] & [both] to be free from Corp[ora]l Punishment.

Long Service men to be selected for Petty Officers in preference to others.

2d Class Petty Officers & Corporals of Marines should have the present gratuity of £7 . . . increased to £10[,] as in the Army, to whom it was increased a few years ago[.]

The Pay, Pension & other Regulations of all other men who do not wish to enter for 10 years, to remain in every respect as at present.

Boys to be entered for 10 years[,] and when rated[,] to have all the advantages given to the seamen for 10 year's [*sic*] entry.

The recommendations of the Committee to be adopted in principle[,] so far as relates to the entry of these Boys.

The Pensions for Long Service men to count from 18 [years of age,] But [*sic*] in all other respects the Pensions to remain as at present.

The Certificates for Long Service men to be Light Blue instead of White.

Petty Officers[:]

To give the new Ratings as proposed by the Committee[.][2]

Long Service Petty officers to carry their ratings from ship to ship or [awarded] an advance of Ratings [*sic*][,] if found qualified for them.

As Petty officers are men selected for the ratings in consequence of exemplary conduct as well as ability, It [*sic*] appears to be a very doubtful measure to give the foregoing [a] large increase of Pay and also Badge [good conduct] Pay. The men selected for P[etty] Officers

[1]He drew a picture of an anchor.

[2]Clause 77 of the Report recommended the creation of a new class of Chief Petty Officer, comprising the Provost Marshal or Master at Arms, Chief Gunner's Mate, Chief Boatswain's Mate, Admiral's Coxwain, Chief Captain of the Forecastle, Chief Quartermaster, Chief Carpenter's Mate, Seaman's Schoolmaster, Ship's Steward, and Ship's Cook.

have been rewarded for good conduct by promotion, but the gratuities now given to them might be somewhat increased to give a boon to this class.

Present scale of gratuities

No [of] Petty		in	£7	£5	Proposed	
1 C	2C					
49	29	1&2 Rates	4	3	6	4
44	23	3 rates	4	3	5	4
35	13	4 Rates	3	3	5	3
32	12	5 Rates	2	1	4	2
30	11	6 rates	2	1	4	2
34	9	Steamers 1&2 C	2	1	4	2
32	5	" 3 Class	1	1	3	1
22	6	Sloops	1	1	3	1
10	4	Small Vess	0	1	1	1

This increase[,] if granted[,] would cost about £1100 pr. Annum[.][1]

Clauses 82, 83, 84 of the Report to be left open, & not any order's [*sic*] given[,] except so far that care is to be taken that only properly qualified men are advanced to P[etty] O[fficer] ratings.

Warrant Officers[:]

The proposed increase of Pay to the Warrant Officers is as follows –

1 Class Sea Pay	£25.17.1
2 Class "	£23.18
3 Class "	£22.16.3

The proposal not to grant the widows pension[,] but to increase the pay to purchase an annuity for £25 pr A. appears expedient. The annual amount of premium will be £7 to £8. The above increase of Pay is very large[,] and appears capable of reduction. If an average of £20 was added to present pay it would be an ample provision[.] There are 883 Warrant officers in the Service[,] an increase of £20 to the Pay will be[,] for 590 Warrant officers on Sea Service[,] would be [*sic*] £11800.

There are 294 Warrant officers for Harbour Service[.] That number[,] at an average increase of £15[,] would be £4,420[,] or together £16,220[.]

[1]This table refers to the gratuities paid to Petty Officers: 'as an encouragement to deserving Petty Officers, we propose that an increase should be made, as follows, in the number who are eligible to be recommended for Good Conduct Gratuities when ships are paid off.' The four righthand columns refer to the numbers of men presently receiving such gratuities and the inceased number proposed. This was not among the Committee's recommendations (indeed, it advocated discontinuing paying-off gratuities), first appearing as part of a set of recommendations forwarded to the Treasury on 21 March 1853. Milne himself seems to have been responsible for devising it as an alternative to issuing Good Conduct Warrants to Petty Officers. See the Order in Council of 1 April 1853, printed in *Parliamentary Papers*, 1852–53, vol. LX, p. 53.

Men ought to serve afloat by term[,] and not by selection.

Coast Guard[:]

The Entry of men to be after 10 year's [*sic*] servitude from the Age of 18, also [as regards] entry of Seamen Riggers, preference [is to be given] to Long Service Men [*sic*].

Pension to be extended to the Chief & Commission Boatmen [*sic*].

To be allowed to wear badges[,] if gained in service afloat.

Excellent[:]

The views of the Committee to be carried out respecting 2 Classes and the curtailing of the drill.

Prize Proclamation[:]

There appear's [*sic*] little to be gained by alterations with regard to the Rank of some of the Petty Officers.

The Act 5&6 Will IV, Chap 24 to be altered and amended as enclosed with new clauses &c.

[**257**] *Milne Calculations on the Cost of Implementing the Committee on Manning's Recommendations*[1]

[Admiralty
March 1853]

The whole strength of the Navy on 1 March = 27,744 Blue Jackets[,] of these 7000 P. Officers[:]

Petty Officers	7000	3d pr day	£31,775
AB	13,830	3d	£62,760
Ord[inar]y	5,186	2d	£15,330
2d Class Ord[inar]y	728	1d	£2,555
Total	26,744		£112,420

The whole expense would amount to £112,420[,] if the whole Navy was on the new system for 10 year's [*sic*] servitude[.]

If the above could be modified to the following[,] the difference of Expense would be as below[:]

Petty Officers	7000	3d	£31.775
AB	13830	2d	£41.853
Ord[inar]y	5186	1½	£11.498
2d Class Ord[inar]y	1728	1	£2555
			£87,681[2]

[1]This is the 'Sheet A', referred to in footnote 2 on p. 350.

[2]The Government decided to adopt the Manning Committee's recommendation of 1d. per day to second-class Ordinary Seamen, 2d. per day to Ordinary Seamen, and 3d. per day to Abs and Petty Officers. See *Hansard*, 3rd ser., vol. 129 (1853), col. 746.

[**258**] *Graham Minute on Admiralty Oversight of the Dockyards, Victualling Yards, and Work Shops*

Admiralty
23 March 1853

It is desirable to bring the internal arrangements of the Dock Yards and Victualling Yards, more especially the Work Shops, under the immediate Control and Supervision of the Board.

It appears to me, that they should be visited more frequently. Some member of the Board from Time to Time [*sic*] ought to investigate[,] on the Spot[,] the mode, in which the Public Money is here so largely expended, in the hope of ascertaining whether any additional checks on improvident outlay might be devised, and whether[,] by the use of improved Machinery or otherwise, better and more economical arrangements might not be effected.

My belief is that manual Labor [*sic*] might be superseded largely by Machinery in the Dock Yards with great advantage.

I suggest therefore that Captain Milne be requested to visit the Yards, in company with the Surveyor of the Navy and the Director of Works, that all officers, when presence or assistance may require, be directed to attend them, and that[,] after conferring with the Superintendants, they shall present to the Board a separate Report on Each yard, setting forth its State and Condition, together with the Recommendations which[,] after full enquiry[,] they may suggest for consideration.

[**259**] *Milne Draft Orders to Inglefield*[1]

Admiralty
15 April 1853

The Lords C[ommissioners] of the Admiralty[,] having appointed you to the Command of HMS *Phoenix* for the purpose of proceeding to Beechey Island in Lancaster Sound to communicate with Sir E Belcher or the ships under his Command[,] it is their Lords directions [*sic*] that[,] so soon as the ship under your Command is in all respects ready, and the *Braedalbane* Transport which is to accompany you is loaded with Coals & other Stores, That [*sic*] you proceed to sea and make the best of your way to the beforementioned Island. in [*sic*] the

[1]Edward Augustus Inglefield, C.B., K.C.B. (1820–94). Entered, 1832; Lt, 1842; Cmdr, 1845; Capt., 1853; Rear-Adm., 1869; Vice-Adm., 1875; Adm., 1879. For the version issued to Inglefield, see *Parliamentary Papers*, 1852–53, vol. LX, p. 121.

execution of this service[,] you will use your utmost exertion to expedite your passage and afford every aid and assistance to the Transport, so as to reach Beechey Island at the earliest possible period. The most essential duty on your arrival there will be at once to clear the Transport of the Coals and Stores[,] and no delay whatever is to take place. relays [*sic*] of men are to be employed. The Stores are to be landed on the Island or put on Board the *N*[*orth*] *Star*[,] as may be considered most advisable, and according to the circumstances of the case. on [*sic*] the Transport being cleared, she is[,] without a moments delay[,] to be directed to proceed to England, and your most especial duty[,] or that of the Senior officer present[,] will be to carry out these orders.

Part of the Stores on board the *Phoenix* may also to be landed [*sic*] or placed on board the *N*[*orth*] *Star*[,] except what may be required for the return passage to England and[,] having obtained all possible information from Sir E. Belcher or the Senior officer at Beechey Island with reference to the Expeditions and the discoveries which may have been made[,] and exchanged any officers or men whose state of health &c may render it necessary that they should return to England, you are immediately to proceed to sea [to] return to Woolwich with all possible dispatch[,] taking the utmost care that your delay at Beechey Island is not extended to such a period as may risk the ship being frozen in for the winter.

Should the state of the sea in Baffins Bay be such as to render it doubtful whether you will be able to make your passage across it to Lancaster Sound during this summer, it is their Lords most positive direction that you are on no account whatever to run the risk of either the *Phoenix* or [the] Transport being frozen in and detained during the winter of 1853–54[,] and If [*sic*] you should consider there is a chance of such being the case[,] you are immediately to send the Transport to Woolwich and also return with the ship under your command[.] But if you should get thro Baffins Bay and find Lancaster Sound closed[,] you are to endeavour to Land the Stores[,] Coal &c at or near Cape Warrender from thence you will send the Transport to England and endeavour to communicate with Beechey Island by sending overland &c[.]

You are distinctly to understand that the principal & chief object of your orders is to communicate with Beechey Island for the purpose of landing Stores & obtaining information[,] and from thence to return direct to England. you [*sic*] are therefore on no account whatever to deviate in any manner from this object, but to use every possible exertion to carry out their Lordships instructions with the utmost dispatch and to use every caution to prevent the ships being detained by the Ice[.][1]

[**260**] *Milne Draft Orders to Belcher*

Admiralty
15 April 1853

The Lords C[ommissioners] of the Admiralty having dispatched HMS *Phoenix* under the Command of Comdr Inglefield[,] with the *Braedalbane* Transport[,] to Beechey Island for the purpose of replenishing the ships under your Command with Stores and Provisions, In [*sic*] case your supplies have been so far reduced by the Depot formed at Melville Island and the various caches on the Coast, as to prevent the search for Sir J[ohn] F[ranklin] being continued during this Summer and the winter of 1853–54[,] should your experience during the past season[,] and the information you may have gained[,] determine you to pursue such further search[,] which my Lords are anxious no want of supplies should check whilst there is a prospect of affording relief to our missing countrymen[.]

Their Lordships are aware how impossible it is for them to send out any definite Instructions with reference to your future proceedings when they are ignorant of the position in which you may now be placed[,] or whether any traces of the missing exp[edition] may have been found during last Autumn or the Spring of this year[,] and what steps you have considered it most expedient to adopt in furtherance of their former orders. But if no trace of Sir J. Franklin has been found in Wellington Channell [*sic*][,] and if it should appear that by the extended search that you may have made in that quarter, That [*sic*] the missing ships did not proceed in that direction, and if Cap Kellett[2] should have reached Melville Island[,] as directed by his Instructions[,] and his land expeditions should also have failed in finding any trace of

[1]The subsequent printed orders followed Milne's wording and instructions very closely, the only significant deviations being the decision to send out another store ship to serve as a store at Disco Island, and the addition to the final clause: 'But should the season prove to be a very open one, and on your return from Beechey Island, you should have an opportunity of examining the coast in the vicinity of Cape Walsingham, we do not object to your doing so, but on no account are you to risk the safety of the Ship, or your being detained, as you must positively return to England this season.' They also gave Inglefield instructions to be delivered to Belcher or the Senior Naval officer at Beechey Island. The final draft is dated 11 May 1853 and bears the names of Graham, Hyde Parker, Maurice Berkeley, Richard Saunders Dundas, and Milne.

[2]Henry Kellett, C.B., K.C.B. (1806–75). Entered, 1822; Lt, 1828; Cmdr, 1841; Capt., 1842; Rear-Adm., 1862; Vice-Adm., 1868. Kellett commanded HMS *Resolute* in the Franklin search expedition under Belcher.

the missing ships, It [*sic*] does not appear to their Lordships that there is any other direction in which any prospect of their discovery can be expected[.] In such a contingency as this[,] and if such should be your opinion after mature consideration with the Senior Officers under your Command[,] there appear's [*sic*] no other course left but to abandon further search[,] as every accessible part of the shores of the polar Sea within Lancaster Sound will have been visited without a trace of the missing ships, except their station in 1845 & 46 at Beechey Island.

In case you should have found traces of the Expedition[,] it will be your duty to follow up that trace [*sic*], but in doing this you must exercise extreme caution[,] so as not to lose your means of communication with Beechey Island[,] nor are you to endanger your Ship or to proceed beyond reasonable limits, for the safety of your own Crews must be your first care. We place every confidence in your judgment[,] and feel assured you will act with discretion in . . . whatever situation you may be placed[,] and we therefore leave it [to] you either to abandon the Expedition altogether if you see no further steps can be taken[,] or to send such of the ships back to England as you may not require[,] Keeping [*sic*] us informed of your views and intended proceedings[,] That [*sic*] every aid may be given to you next season[.]

But before your departure from the Polar Seas should you adopt that course[,] There [*sic*] appears one subject deserving of very grave consideration and that is the position of Caps Collinson and McClure.[1] Should they be compelled by circumstances to abandon their ships, The [*sic*] crews may possibly attempt to reach Melville Island, and having had this in view when you left England, we directed a Depot of Prov[isions] to be formed at that Island. If they reach that position, They [*sic*] will Endeavour to make their way [to] Beechey Island or Port Leopold. It will therefore be your duty[,] in case of your not considering it necessary to prosecute further search and to give up the Expedtn & return to England[,] to form a Depot on Beechey I[slan]d of Coal[,] Provisions[,] Clothing & Stores, and also to have one of your ships there but without <u>Crews</u> [*sic*] so that Cap Collinson or McClure may have the means of returning to England. but [*sic*] should it be practicable to place the ship in a more advanced position between Melville & Beechey Island it would be expedient to do so[,] but this is a point on which you can form a better judgment that their Lordships[,] whose anxious wish it is to Establish the best possible arrangement to

[1]Sir Robert John Le Mesurier McClure, Kt., C.B. (1807–73). Entered, 1824; Lt, 1837; Cmdr, 1849; Capt., 1850; Rear-Adm., 1867; Vice-Adm. (Ret.), 1873.

give succour and support to the Crews of those ships who may be compelled to seek refuge in the direction they pointed out[.][1]

[**261**] *Milne Report on the Application of Machinery in Devonport Dockyard*[2]

[Admiralty
1853]

As requested by the Board, I proceeded to Devonport on the 21 of last month and remained there until the evening of the 25th in communication with Commodore Seymour[3] and the Yard officers with reference to any Alterations or improvements which they considered it necessary to propose for the benefit of the Dock Yard.

The paper marked A which accompanies this[4] contains various proposals from the Master Shipwrights Department, and to save repetition I have made notations in Red Ink on these various suggestions on which Commodore Seymour has expressed his concerns. It will be observed . . . several considerable works have been postponed[,] as will be seen by reference to the submission viz No 2,3,4 (8) 26, but there does not appear to exist any necessity for so large an outlay of Public Money, and what is recommended is in reality not at present necessary. The Extension of the Building Slips[,] No 8[,] may be questionable[,] for if Frigates of the 4th Rate & under are to be built at Devonport[,] the present slips appear to me to be well adapted for the purpose without an Extension of them as proposed[,] but it is necessary[,] on account of the increased length of Ships of the Line[,] to increase the length of the slips for that class of ship[,] but this question I must leave. This I leave for the decision of the Board in consultation with the Surveyor. The various other subjects mentioned in paper A are more or less of importance [*sic*] and steps should be taken to carry out the views of the professional officers.

[1]Again, the printed version (MLN/159/1 [6]) followed Milne's text closely, although some alterations of content were made: a ship was to be left with or without crew as Belcher deemed, and details on the depot and keeping it safe from bears and other animals were included. It was dated 11 May 1853 and signed by the whole board.

[2]This may to be the report requested by Graham above in [**258**], although if so it seems that Milne made the investigation by himself, rather than with Baldwin Walker and the Director of Works.

[3]Michael Seymour, K.C.B., G.C.B. (1802–87). Entered, 1813; Lt, 1819; Cmdr, 1822; Capt., 1826; Rear-Adm., 1854; Vice-Adm. 1860; Adm., 1864. Seymour was Adm.-Superintendent of Devonport Dockyard 1851–54.

[4]Missing from Milne's papers.

Stores[:] The state of the Store Houses and the Stores in the Yard are most satisfactory and no recommendations or suggestions either to alter or to improve the present arrangements have been made. The Storekeeper[,] however[,] complains of a want of clerical assistance. as [*sic*] this has reference to the state of his office, Books, Accounts &c[,] I have forwarded his letter to the Storekeeper and Acc[ountan]t General for their consideration and report[,] on visiting Devonport [themselves]. Considerable difficulty exists at Devonport in appropriating workmen to repair the returned stores from ships or from Yard Service. These consist of Cables, Shackles, Pumps, Fire Engines, Blocks, Bells, Lamps[,] &c in all about 200 different kinds of articles[,] all of considerable value, and in consequence of no workmen being so appropriated to make the necessary repairs, this large store is on the increase, and the result is a very heavy loss to the Crown[,] for instead of these Articles being repaired and returned into store and again issued, they are deteriorating in value, and new articles have to be purchased and issued instead. It has always been customary for a certain number of Plumbers or Braziers to be constantly employed under the Storekeeper Generals department for this service, independent of the workmen for the Surveyors Depart[,] but in forming the late Estab[lishmen]t of the Dock Yards, this has been overlooked, and the present force of Plumbers & Braziers is barely sufficient to meet the current requirements of yard service for ships repairs[,] much less to spare others. It is therefore absolutely necessary to give a [*sic*] immediate increase to this branch of workmen by at least 4 men[,] to be kept constantly employed on repairs, and not taken therefrom until all these articles are made fit for issue[,] and then they may be employed on other yard duties.

Ropery[:]
Nothing can be more satisfactory than the results obtained by the introduction of steam power into the Rope House at this Yard[.] a large reduction in Labour has taken place[,] at the sametime [*sic*] with a very large increase to the work performed. Last year the Master Ropemaker was sent to Newcastle & Sunderland accompanied by Mr. Giles[,] a Master RN[,] and Mr Hughes[,] Engineer[,] to witness the Spinning of Yarn by machinery[,] as contrasted with the spinning of yarn by hand[,] as now practiced in all our Dock Yards[.] this has for some years past been a subject of dispute, Mr Murray[,] the Chief Engineer at Portsmouth having most strongly urged[,] indeed almost insisted[,] on the necessity of having machinery to spin the yarn if any outlay of money for the improvement [of] the Ropery at Portsmouth was to take place. The result of the visit to Newcastle was most

unsatisfactory as to the spinning of the Yarn by machines[.] The Yarn was irregular in size, coarse[,] and the hemp not fairly laid[,] and it was altogether unsuited to the manufacture of Rope for Naval Service and[,] after a full consideration of all the experiments which have been made[,] I do not consider it would be advisable to alter our present system[,] but to continue to spin the Yarn by hand. When at Newcastle[,] Mr Guard [the Master Ropemaker] observed that the twist of the Rope when making, was worked or thrown in by machinery instead of by manual labour[,] as in our Dock Yards. With very proper zeal for the service and stepping out of the usual backward routine of [a] Dock Yard officer[,] he made a submission to Commodore Seymour to introduce this plan at Devonport Ropery. This the Board sanctioned[,] and the result has been wonderful, as will be seen by the following Table of the manufacture of Rope.

Formerly the Days work by manual Labour was: –

Size of Rope	Number made	Men employed
3	12	8
3½	10	10
4	9	13
5	7	16
6	6	21
7	6	28
8	5	37
13	–	58

Now by the machinery the days work amounts to[:]

Size Rope	No Made	Men employed
3	20	7
3½	20	7
4	15	12
5	12	11
6	12	14
6 [*sic*: 7]	10	21
8	8	28
13	–	38

And with every sized rope[,] the same result has taken place and a further reduction[,] as well as an increased amount of work to be done[,] will follow by allowing Mr Guard about £100 Expenditure to introduce the Fore Twist for Large Rope & cables, the same as he has done for smaller ropes. When he has adopted the application of machinery to both the Fore & Back Twist, He [*sic*] deserves the greatest credit & encouragement of the Board [*sic*].

The Smitheries, & Work Shops, Saw Mills[:]
The state of the workshops in this yard is not satisfactory. The Saw Mills consist of only 2 Frames, one Bench Circular Saw & 2 others for minor purposes. all [*sic*] the other yards have a much larger amount of sawing Power advantageously used for the works of the yard[,] and with economy to the Crown.
The saw's [*sic*] at Devonport are in a Building coloured red in the accompanying Plan,[1] to which there is only one outlet for timber[,] going in & coming out at the same door[,] instead of passing thro the building[,] as in every well regulated Estab[lishmen]t. It is also placed at the E[ast] back end of the Yard.

The engine which drives the saws also drives all the machinery in the Millwrights Shop[,] and when that is in full work[,] there is not sufficient power to drive the saws in a satisfactory manner. It was intended to place the new Planing Machine adjoining these saw Mills[,] also to be driven by the same engine, but I consider this would only [be] sinking money disadvantageously, as it is perfectly evident from what I have just stated that there would not be sufficient power to perform the work. the [*sic*] position of the present Saw Mills is most disadvantageous, being at the extreme east end of the yard[,] away from the locality where timber is stacked. The consequence is [that] it has all to be brought to the Saw Mills & carried back to the building slips. I would strongly urge the Board to convert the Building marked Blue[,] now partly used for Sir W Burnetts Solution[,] and also as a Timber shed . . . [which] is of substantial material & well roofed[,] into a Saw Mill, To [*sic*] contain all the requisite number of sawing frames adapted to the size of the yard, the planing machine[,] turning lathes for Capstans, Blocks[,] & other works of the yard. it [*sic*] would be central as to position of Timber and wants of the yard. The same power would also be employed in applying Sir W. Burnetts solution[,] now in this Building. The Chimney for the Engine is already built[,] but a larger engine[,] say 20 HP[,] will be required, and the Boiler H[ouse] pressure would [also] answer for working the Nasmythe Hammer.

With regard to the Joiners Shop[,] I will in a future report allude to the total want of Machinery in it and the necessity of adopting some system of machines and thusly causing a reduction of Labour & Expense. I may[,] however[,] mention that the power of the engine in driving the Saw Mills when they are transferred to the Building I propose would [also] become applicable to drive machinery in the Joiners shop[.]

[1]Not included with this rough draft.

Coal Stores & Depot[:]
This unfortunate subject has met with my attention,[1] and it is one of great importance. I may mention that at the present time there are 4 floating Depots at this Port capable of holding 4.300 Tons of Coal, Viz[.] *Lavonia* in the Sound [and] *Druid*, *Wye*, *Jupiter* in Hamoaze[,] and also the *Nimrod* ready with Coal in Bags to the amount of 180 Tons[,] ready to be towed into the Sound when required. This amount of Coal is sufficient at the present moment to meet the requirements of the Service during peace, but the store [having been] ordered to be kept up being 6000 Tons[,] it is necessary to provide a plan for 1500 Tons. Keyham being the Steam Yard[,] some depot should exist there, to fill up any vessels in the Basin[.] for this two positions recommend themselves[,] viz[.] the south extreme of the Yard between the Engine House Pumps and the Engine <u>Gates</u>[,] or on the wharf between the two Basins[,] which affords ready means for landing Coals from the River front of the Sea Wall, or putting it on board steam vessels in either the South or N Basins. no [*sic*] doubt this is the most eligible <u>site</u> for work[,] altho somewhat of an Eyesore [*sic*] to the Estab[lishmen]t. The Board[,] on their visitation[,] must decide this question & a corrugated Iron Roof over the Store will be required.

Keyham[:]
The works at this Estab[lishmen]t are so far advanced that the two North Docks are now ready for use[,] and the Director of Works states that he is satisfied with the working of the Cassoons [*sic*: 'Caissons']. Such being the case[,] I would submit to the Board the propriety of giving orders to the Dock Yard to prepare all required Hawsers, Stores &c needed to put the basin & Dock into use at this advanced state of the works[,] and that [as] the various engines for emptying the Docks are at work and the Locks &s are completed[,] amounting in all to nearly 50 [*sic*][,] it is especially necessary some person should be placed in charge of them . . . acquainted with all the details of their filling &c.
Who has been in charge of the works and is acquainted with [them] should be appointed [*sic*]. It will also be requisite to have a detachment of Police under a Serjeant[,] and a <u>Boatswain</u> to be in charge of Docking Gear &c, but at present a Masters Attendant is not necessary[,] and it will become a matter for future consideration what staff of officers may be necessary. My own opinion is that the Establishment should be as limited as possible[,] & that a Master Attendant and other principal officers will not be necessary[.]

[1]See [**228**].

[**262**] *Milne Draft Proposal on Dockyard Efficiency*[1]

Admiralty
16 August 1853

I have to submit to the Board the following note, on matters of detail in the Dock Yards, and recommend that directions should be issued to the Yards.

[1.] In fitting of Rigging for Store, no Futtock Rigging is in future to be cut out, until the ship is ordered to be fitted out, as it optional with the Captain to have Rope or Iron.[2]

[2.] New Rigging now in store which is obsolete[,] or old Half Worn Rigging, neither of which can be brought into use, is to be opened up and remanufactured[,] retaining sufficient for Jury Rigging or for conversion.

[3.] The Store of Anchor's [*sic*] in the Dock Yard is to be separated into Two classes, 1st[,] those fit for service and of established pattern's [*sic*] &c[;] 2d[,] Those of the old Pattern and not fit for service in sea going ships. The same to be reported to the Storekeeper G[enera]l[,] and when Anchors are moved in the Yards, these Classes are to be stowed separate from each other. The Old anchors are to be worked up according to orders of 19 July 1847.

[4.] Fire and Wash Decks [&] Hearles [*sic*] Pumps[,] formerly fixtures in HM Ships[,] are to be immediately repaired, and placed in similar classes of ships as formerly[,] making a submission to the Board to do so in each case.

[5.] When there is an accumulation of Copper[,] mixed metal[,] or Iron articles in the Yards, which are either obsolete or will not be required, it is expedient The [*sic*] Storekeeper should consult with the professional officers as to their disposal, and if not required by them[, transferred] to the Storekeeper G[enera]l[,] that they should be converted.

To prevent such accumulation in future[,] the Superintendants [*sic*] will give special orders that when the professional officers give directions for any article to be made[,] either in the Smitheries, Millwrights Shop, by the Joiners, or other workmen in the Yard, the requisition shall invariably go to the Storekeeper for him to state whether any such articles are in Store, or whether there are any articles which can be converted, as directed by . . . the Dock Yard Instructions.

[1]Hyde Parker added at the top 'Read HP August 17th'.

[2]In the margin beside numbers [1], [2], [3], [4], [5], [6], [7], [8], [9], [10], [11], [12], [14], [15], [16], and [18] Milne noted in red ink 'Order', meaning that it was so ordered.

[6.] When there are any Engineer Stores or other fittings of Steam Vessels which have been landed at a Dock Yard where there is no Factory, and where these articles cannot be again used for such vessels at such Yards[,] they are always to be sent to a Dock Yard where there is a Factory.
[7.] All Iron work made in our Dock Yards ought to bear a private mark for each Yard, that manufactured Iron may in future be traced. I would submit P for Portsmouth, D Devonport[,] M Pembroke[,] W Woolwich, C Chatham, S Sheerness[,] F Deptford[.]
[8.] Sheerness being a fitting yard for all large vessels launched in the Thames and Medway[,] and where all heavy cables &c are kept, It [*sic*] is necessary a Testing machine should be fitted there, in the Store now used for galleys[,] adjoining the Smithery and Cable Store (For Board's inspection)[.]
[9.] The Custom of Marking the Leather Hoses and other Leather articles with the Broad Arrow by the use of copper to be immediately discontinued[,] The [*sic*] leather so marked being eaten into holes[.]
[10.] The Elm Tops or Blocks of Elm of good sound quality[,] not wanted in the yards and fit for making Blocks, are always to be sent to Portsmouth for the manufacture of Blocks, Agreeably to G[enera]l order 5 Nov 1838[.]
[11.] As there is an accumulation of old as well as new castings for Horse [*sic*] Pipes and Riding Bites [*sic*: 'bits'] in some of the Yards, those that are not adapted for the Service are to be reported to the Storekeeper G[enera]l after a survey is held on them, those adapted for service to be brought into use.
[12.] No further demands are to be made for Watch and Half watch Glasses, the future supply is to be confined to ½ Hour and 1 Hour Glasses.
[13.] The Superintendants of the Yards to give positive orders that the Saw Mills at their respective Yards to be kept at Full work, so long as there is wood to be cut, and no work is to be done at the Pitts [*sic*] which can be done at the Mills. Machinery having been established at the Yards at considerable expense, it is the duty of the Professional Officers to see that it is worked on a proper system[,] and to reduce the sawyers as may be found necessary. The work done at the Circular Saws is to be registered.
[14.] Oak Rafters are to be cut at the Circular Saws[.]
[15.] In our Dock Yards there is no fixed system for the Examination of Workmen or labourers who are sent down for entry, each yard follows an arrangement of its own. I would propose that the Surveyor should be called on to fix one regulation for all the Yards, to be printed

and to be promulgated. At Sheerness the Labourers are perfect Boys, and they undergo no trial of their fitness for work.

[16.] In all our establishments it would be a great convenience to the workmen If [*sic*] a Room could be set apart for them to get their Dinner in, instead of their being obliged to go outside the Yard to a public House, or to walk upwards of two miles to their Homes, and the same distance back, by which they are fatigued and unfit for work. Those who reside within a moderate distance would of course go to their own homes.[1]

[17.] In all our Smitheries there ought to be a double handed man [*sic*][,] as is the case in all private establishments, capable of repairing the Furnaces, when out of order, instead of having recourse to the Director of Works Department, causing continued delay.

[18.] With reference to former orders (1818), allowing each officer residing in the Dock Yard a Cart Load of Wood (Chips) every six weeks[,] some general regulation is required. I would propose[:]

'The Cart of Chips allowed to officers every six weeks, is in future to be a Cart of 50 Cubic feet, one half to be chips, the other half small pieces of offal wood[,] fit only for fires[,] and which do not require labour to cut it.'

[**263**] *Milne Draft Board Minute on Dockyard Sawmills and Workmen's Dinner Arrangements*

[Admiralty
1853]

It is their Lordships orders that the Saw Mills at the respective Yards be kept always at full work and none of the Frames to be allowed to be idle, so long as there is work to be performed[,] & no work is to be done at the Pits [*sic*] which can be done at the Mills. if [*sic*] necessary[,] the number of Sawyers must be reduced.

The work done at the Circular saws is to be registered[.]

I believe it would be a very great convenience to the workmen in our establishments, if a room was set apart for them to get their Dinner in, in the Yard, instead of being obliged to go outside either to a public House or to walk one or even 2 or 3 Miles to their own Houses[,] by which they are fatigued and unfit for work in the afternoon.

A Notice might be put up at the Gate of each Yard, for men who wish to remain in the yard to put down their names[,] and by that means to see what number would take advantage of the offer.

[1]Milne added in the margin 'For the consideration of the Board'. See [**263**].

In all our Smitheries there ought to be[,] as in private trade[,] a double handed man, capable of repairing the furnaces when out of order instead of having recourse to the Director of Works Department, causing delay and unnecessary expense.

[**264**] *Milne Draft Circular on Minor Punishments and Seamen's Certificates*[1]

Admiralty
7 October 1853

The attention of my Lords Commissioners of the Admiralty having been directed to the returns of the minor punishments awarded by Officers in command of Her Majesty's ships, have deemed it necessary to issue the following regulations, establishing for the future a more uniform system, defining their nature and duration, which, their Lordships feel confident, when administered with judgment and impartiality, will not only prove advantageous in maintaining the discipline of the Fleet, but[,] by checking offences[,] will tend to promote the comfort of well-conducted men.

The Officer appointed to command of one of Her Majesty's ships, being invested with full authority for establishing discipline and good order, must constantly bear in mind the responsibility of the charge committed to him. It will be his early and particular care to inculcate a constant and zealous attention on the part of the Officers to their respective duties; and as all persons serving under his command will look to him for example and encouragement, he is to make himself acquainted with their characters, that he may be enabled the more readily and impartially to confer advancement on the meritorious, or award punishment to those who are negligent or insubordinate.

It will likewise be his duty to impress upon those deputed to carry out his orders, the necessity of strictly avoiding abusive language and degrading expressions, which tend to irritate the minds of the men, and lead them to commit offences, causing complaints, and subsequent punishment; but whilst upholding the legitimate authority of all the

[1]At the top of the printed Circular (Circular 131; Minor Punishments and Seamen's Certificates), Milne wrote at the top 'Drawn up by Cap Milne when at the Admiralty', a claim substantiated by the following letter from Peter Richards [**265**]. This revision seems to have stemmed from a recommendation made by the Manning Committee: 'we recommend that the whole system of secondary punishments for minor offense be regulated and defined by the Board of Admiralty, so as to establish one general and uniform rule, and that no deviation therefrom be permitted.' See *Parliamentary Papers*, 1852–53, vol. LX, p. 28.

Officers under his command, he is never to fail in checking by timely reproof any tendency to abuse of power, and recommending, by his own example, a firm but conciliatory manner of conducting their duty, by which the respect and confidence of the men will be ensured, and the Officers will gain increased power to prevent and repress irregularities.

As intemperance frequently leads to the commission of offences, and is the cause of serious accidents, the Commanding Officer will feel the necessity of checking it by every means in his power, – occasionally warning the crews of its debasing effects and ulterior consequences, and urging the zealous cooperation and example of the Officers under his command towards subduing this serious evil, with the hope that a vice so derogatory to the honour and character of seamen may no longer degrade the Service. Altercation with a drunken man is in all cases to be avoided; nor is a person under the influence of liquor to be placed in a situation which may cause further excitement, and thereby lead to unconscious violence and insubordination.

Hasty complaints are invariably to be discouraged. When complaints are made, my Lords consider it advisable, whenever the Service and the circumstances of the case will admit, that their investigation should be deferred until the following morning; at which time they should be fully investigated on the quarter-deck, the accuser and accused heard with impartiality; both having a legitimate claim upon the Captain's attention, and an equal right to the just exercise of his authority.

Officers in command must remember that inconsiderate as well as protracted punishments generally lead to discontent, defeat their intended object, and cause distaste to the Service; that the first consideration is the prevention of crime, and that discipline depends not on the severity either in amount or duration of punishment, but on its just administration, by making it commensurate to the offence.

First and second offences, when not of a grave nature, should in most cases be considered with leniency, and the previous character and conduct of the accused should always be taken into account. Admonition, and pointing out to the defaulter where error has been committed, may be the means of checking future misconduct.

The minor and other punishments which are hereby authorized by their Lordships are to be of the following description, which they consider, when judiciously awarded, will be sufficient to check all offences not peremptorily demanding confinement in jail [*sic*], corporal punishment, or trial by court-martial. Their duration is to be fixed when each complaint is investigated, and no punishment is ever to be prolonged 'until further orders.'

1. The offender to drink his grog on the quarter-deck, and to remain standing there, or between two guns, for a limited period, but never exceeding two hours at a time, or four hours in one day, the number of consecutive days not to exceed fourteen.
2. The offender to drink six-water grog on the quarter deck, and to remain standing there, or between two guns, for the above daily periods; and in more aggravated cases of misconduct, with deprivation of smoking, or to perform extra duty, between 7 a.m. and 7 p.m., such as picking oakum, &c., cleaning the head, pump-well, stoning the galley, or performing other similar work, as may be required; stationing at lee sheets and wheel, care being taken to limit the periods of the punishments according to the degree of the offence, but never to exceed in duration twenty-one days.
3. Stoppage of leave to go on shore for breaking leave, but not to exceed three months of harbour time, with or without deduction from pay for time of absence, as authorized by Circular No. 121.
4. Stoppage of grog, for drunkenness; or deduction from pay for persisting drunkenness, as authorized by Circular No. 70, neither of these punishments to exceed thirty days; but if any person is a habitual drunkard, his grog may be entirely stopped, for which payment is to be made.
5. Persons of careless and inattentive habits, with reference to their hammock or bag, may be made to carry them on the shoulder, but not to exceed an hour in the same day; and limited to three days.
6. Stoppage of monthly allowance money, as authorized in Art. 13, page 190, of the Admiralty Instructions.
7. Forfeiture of any indulgences granted to the rest of the ship's company.
8. Deprivation of the good-conduct badge, as authorized by the Circular 46, to be most strictly enforced.
9. Disrating Petty Officers, as authorized in Art, 4, page 94, of the Admiralty Instructions; and Leading Seamen, as authorized in Circular No. 121.

Petty Officers should only be subject to the minor punishments, stated in Nos. 3, 7, 8, and 9; if admonition will not avail with persons so rated, they are unfit for the situations they hold. They should be granted every reasonable indulgence, and treated with consideration. Being placed in situations of trust, they should be made to feel that confidence is placed in them.

10. Extra drills for neglect or inattention at drills only, but never to exceed two hours in one day. Extra guards are never to be ordered except for offences on duty.

11. For want of alacrity or attention aloft or on duty, or slackness in their watch or boats, the officer in command may authorize the officer carrying on duty to cause the performance of any evolution to be repeated in moderation, or extra lee-wheel, extra look-out, or walking the gangway, to be awarded, but these not to exceed two hours, and never to extend beyond the period of the watch.

12. Solitary confinement in a cell, or under a canvas screen. This punishment is never to exceed ten days. In more aggravated causes of misconduct, the delinquent may be put on half allowance of provisions for the whole or a portion of that time, or on a diet of bread and water, for a period not exceeding three days. To be visited every four hours, and once a day by a medical officer.

Men under solitary confinement in a cell, or under a canvas screen, or in irons, are to be deprived for the time of their knives, tobacco, and amusing books. They are to have their beds and bedding, and a sufficient quantity of clothes, and are always to be brought on the quarter-deck to stand abaft the main-mast during morning inspection, or abaft the mizzen-mast at noon, to have their dinners there if the Captain should so direct, and they are to attend Divine Service.

13. Imprisonment in jail under the Act of 10 & 11 Vict. c. 62. Strict care is to be taken to award the period of confinement according to the degree of the offence.

14. Corporal punishment. Except for insubordination or other heinous crime, it can rarely be expedient to inflict corporal punishment for a first offence; but in every instance where its infliction is deemed absolutely necessary for a first offence, the fact and circumstances are to be stated in the warrant, and also in the quarterly returns.

Before corporal punishment is inflicted, or confinement in jail, or in a cell, or under a canvas screen, or a Petty Officer or Leading Seaman disrated, or a person deprived of his good-conduct badge, the warrant for doing so is to be read on the quarter-deck, with the Article of War under which the prisoner is sentenced. Every warrant must bear the signature of the Officer preferring the complaint, in attestation of the fact that such complaint was made by him.

15. Discharge with disgrace, as directed by Art. 5, sec. 1, Chap. II of Admiralty Instructions. As a person discharged with disgrace forfeits all previous service, and will not again be received in the Navy, the Captain of the ship will exercise great caution before making application for his discharge, and not until he has found other sources of punishment unavailing in reclaiming him. If under any circumstances re-admission should be obtained, all servitude and wages subsequent to discharge with disgrace will be forfeited.

16. As it is essential to check inattention or dirty habits in Boys, the custom of punishing them on the hand with a slight cane may be resorted to with moderation in such cases as the Captain may direct.

Men of continued irregular habits and disorderly conduct may be made to mess by themselves until they are reformed, and respectable messes are willing to receive them. And those who are habitually dirty may be mustered in the morning with the boys.

The use of irons is as much as possible to be avoided, recourse to that punishment being had only for security, or mutinous conduct.

All minor punishments, except to prisoners confined to cells or under a canvas screen, are to be suspended on Sundays.

Confinement in coal-bunkers, or other close places is strictly forbidden, and no man is to be deprived of his night's rest as a punishment.

The inconsiderate award of straggling money having led to much abuse, the Officer in command will take care that it is not given unless really necessary, and only in special cases to the Police, or other persons belonging to the ship, whose duty it is to apprehend stragglers; and it is never to exceed in amount the actual merits of the case.

Although the Officer in command of a ship is held responsible for all punishments inflicted on board, as directed in their Lordships Circular Letter of the 26th May 1848, he is not debarred from delegating to the officer next in command the power of awarding minor punishments mentioned in Articles 1, 2, 3, and 4, for a period not exceeding 7 days, or in Article 5, for a period of 3 days, which punishments are to be recorded in the Defaulters Book, and to be submitted at least once a week for the Captain's approval and initials; but the infliction of all minor punishment by other Officers, is strictly forbidden.

The Captain[s] of Her Majesty's ships will direct the Lieutenants, to take special charge of the men belonging to their divisions as ordered by Article 17, sec. 1, Chap. V. of the 'Admiralty Instructions;' it is their duty to make themselves acquainted with their characters and conduct, to aid them as may be required in their duties, and to give them such advice as may be for their advantage. This duty, when carried out in that spirit which its importance deserves, must exert a beneficial influence on the conduct of the men, and prove advantageous to their future welfare.

Their Lordships hope, by holding out every reasonable encouragement to the zealous and deserving, and by a judicious and temperate application of the foregoing minor punishments, the discipline of Her Majesty's ships will be upheld, and the necessity of having recourse to more severe measures may be of rare occurrence. To this end their Lordships rely on the zealous co-operation and exertions of the Officers of the Fleet; and they feel assured that by their personal example in the discharge of the duties confided to them, and by attention to the health, comfort, and improvement of the men, a spirit of cheerfulness and contentment will be promoted throughout Her Majesty's Service.

The several Commanders in Chief will take measures to inquire into the state of discipline of the ships under their command, and see that their Lordships orders have been strictly adhered to; and will regulate a proper system of leave of absence, that the crews of all the ships on their respective stations may enjoy an equal amount of indulgence.

Certificates of Service[1]

In connexion with the subject of punishments on board Her Majesty's ships, my Lords have to call the attention of Officers in command to the characters given by them to seamen on their parchment certificates.

It has come to their Lordships' knowledge that, in some instances, for a minor fault inadvertently committed after a long period of good conduct, the character awarded has been of such a nature as to deprive the seamen [*sic*] of re-entry into Her Majesty's Service, thereby inflicting a severe and permanent punishment for some casual minor offence.

Officers should reflect that the character of a seaman on his certificate is his passport through life; by it he gains promotion or employment, and by it his future pension is affected. It should, therefore, be maturely considered, and decided with strict justice to the individual and to the Service. To this end, the Captain, in filling up the certificate of character, is to take to his assistance the Officer next in command to himself, the Lieutenant of the division to which the man belongs, and such other persons as he may see fit. This should be done on the ship's passage to England, or, in the case of vessels on the Home Station, before being paid off. And when once the character has been fairly awarded and written on the certificate, it is not, under any circumstances, to be altered, nor interlineations or erasures made therein; but any subsequent misconduct is to be awarded according to the custom of the Service, and not by an alteration in the certificate.

The word 'Fair,' which my Lordships consider to mean a passable, and not an objectionable man, and which was not originally intended to imply an indifferent character, having been too often considered by Officers in that sense, and eligible seamen having thereby been refused re-admittance into the Service, their Lordships desire, when seamen present themselves for entry with characters in their last ships marked

[1]Appended to foregoing.

'Fair,' that inquiry be made into their characters in former ships, and if not unsatisfactory, and they are otherwise desirable men for the Service, that the said men be received, to give them an opportunity of re-establishing their 'good' character.

The following scale of character of men is to be adopted in future with any additional notice of very deserving men: –

1. Very good
2. Good
3. Fair or Passable
4. Indifferent
5. Bad

By command of their Lordships
To all Commanders in Chief, Captains, Commanders, and Commanding Officers of Her Majesty's Ships and Vessels.

[**265**] *Richards to Milne*

Chatham, Private
3 September 1853

My dear Milne

My [attention] has been devoted to your paper[,][1] which I have gone over with all the care & attention in my power, & [I] find it[,] as far as my opinion goes, admirably calculated to improve our naval system on a point which has too long stood sadly in want of correction. Officers should know on what they have to rest for the Maintenance of Discipline, & the men what they have to expect if they transgress . . . [2]

On the whole however you have done an immense amount of good by reducing to system that which was before carried out at discretion[,] & not infrequently I fear by men who had no discretion at all. It is possible revision will be required as experience shews the working of the order, but no one can doubt that a foundation here is laid that cannot be shaken or removed.

I fear you may find my observations tedious, but I have offered them as you wished & shall be glad if any are found useful. if [*sic*] not let them go into the Waste Basket.

[1]The foregoing, [**264**].
[2]There follows several pages of suggested minor revisions.

[**266**] *Graham to Milne*

[London], Private
8 November 1853

My dear Capt Milne

. . . I have received the enclosed[1] letter from Admiral Dundas[,] which has greatly annoyed me. I sent for Mr. Grant to come before the Board this morning. It is admitted that Arrack[2] was received as Rum under his Terms of the Contract until the last six months; and even now, no precautions have been taken with respect to the Quality of the Samples, there is no security for inspection on delivery, if the Article be not equal to the Sample: and the mysterious loss of Quantity still goes on at Deptford, while, as Mr. Grant asserts, no equal loss takes place at Gosport.

So also with respect to Slops: Mr. Grant says, that the receiving Officers at Deptford are not competent judges of the Quality of the Articles received; and that an experienced Store Receiver there would be an invaluable Assistant.

I have requested Mr. Grant to prepare in regular form a Submission to the Board on these important Points, and to communicate with you concerning them. Discontent in the Fleet, occasioned by just causes of complaint with respect both to their Grog and their Clothing, is a great annoyance after all the pains, which have been taken, and the expense, which has been incurred.

I am not satisfied that Mr. Grant understands his business; and if he understands it, that he pays due attention. His admissions this morning with respect to his imperfect Check on receipt under Contract by Sample are most unsatisfactory.

[**267**] *Graham to Milne*

[London], Private
14 November 1853

My dear Capt Milne

The French are making immense Efforts to increase their Navy and to apply the [*sic*] Steam Power. We must not lag behind; and I hope, that we

[1]Missing from Milne's papers; presumably he returned it to Graham. From what follows it seems to have referred to Comptroller of Victualling Thomas Grant.

[2]Liquor usually distilled from fermented rice and sugar or from fermented coco-palm sap.

are neither inactive nor indifferent. I return the enclosed letter,[1] which entirely coincides with information derived from other Quarters.

As you will be here so soon, I will not go at length into the question of Deliveries under Contract. It is there that we now fail; and an effective Remedy must be applied. I have obtained from the Treasury Power to appoint a Store Receiver at Deptford Victualling Yard. If we make a good selection of a competent Paymaster for this most important Post, I am sanguine in my belief, that some at least of the existing Defects will be cured.

I shall be glad to have again the benefit of your active assistance and advice, which I value very highly.

[**268**] *Milne Memorandum on Sir John Franklin's Arctic Expedition*

Admiralty, Private
26 December 1853

Eight years and a Half having elapsed since the *Erebus & Terror* left England, It [*sic*] is for the Board to consider what steps should be taken for the removal of Sir J. Franklin and the Officers names from the List of the Navy.

If this is done, timely notice should be given in a proper letter addressed to Lady Franklin with the expressions of the Lords [Commissioners'] sympathy &c[,] having decided on the removal of the Names. The Pay due to all the Parties should be paid to the representatives at the close of this Financial year out of this years votes, but as this involves the payment of £80,000, might it not be necessary to take the opinion of Counsel as to the legality of the Step[.]

If the names are removed[,] the wives of the officers will be entitled to pensions[,] and it will be for the Board also to consider whether any promotion is due to those now in *Erebus & Terror*[,] involving as it does an increase of pension.

[**269**] *Graham Minute on Sir John Franklin's Arctic Expedition*

[Admiralty]
30 December 1853

If any doubt be entertained of the Power of the Board to remove the names from the List and to suspend the accumulation of Pay, it can be

[1]Not preserved with Graham's letter.

fully stated to the Counsel of the Admiralty and his Opinion taken forthwith.

He must also advise, whether the Pay due should be made out in full to the Representatives of the Officers and Men; and whether[,] if they should happily appear to claim their own Pay after such distribution, they would not have a Right to their full . . . Payment without any abatement, altho' the account may have been previously closed with their Representatives.

I cannot recognize the Claim for Promotion with the view of augmenting Pensions . . . Sir John Franklin rose by Seniority, while the Board still hoped, that he might be alive: it would be unseemly at the same time to remove his name from the List, because we believe him to be dead, and to Promote him to the rank of Vice Admiral, that his Wife might obtain a larger Pension. What is true in his Case is equally so in the case of Officers of lower Grade.[1]

[1]A subsequent Minute reads: '[Send to] Solicitor[:] Case to be drawn up & then submitted to the Counsel of the Admiralty as proposed in Memo of Sir J. Graham[,] 30 Decr 53'. Milne's suggestion was adopted. See the 19 January 1854 'Notice Respecting the Officers and Crews of Her Majesty's Ships "*Erebus*" and "*Terror*"', *Parliamentary Papers*, 1854, vol. XLII, p. 339.

PART V

THE RUSSIAN WAR, 1854–55

Milne's multifarious duties as the Board's *de facto* naval staff were substantially curtailed as the crisis with Russia came to a head in early 1854, to be replaced by others of an even more demanding nature.[1] On 9 February the Secretary for War and Colonies, the Duke of Newcastle,[2] requested that the Admiralty 'prepare the means for sending out a large number of troops' to the Black Sea.[3] Simultaneously, the War Office contacted the Comptroller of Victualling, Thomas T. Grant, about provisioning arrangements 'for the whole of that army'. Milne immediately became involved in securing troop transports since, as he told Roebuck's Committee,

> from the large amount of duties that the Comptroller of Victualling and Transport had to perform, it was quite obvious to me that Mr. Grant would be unable to undertake the transport duties, [and] as I was the superintending Lord of that department, I took upon myself the responsibility of making the proper arrangements with regard to the conveyance of the troops, stores, and horses to be sent from this country.

This last was a considerable understatement. Milne not only oversaw arrangements for transport of British forces; he was later ordered to

[1]For a synopsis of the Eastern Crisis of 1853–54 and its escalation to war, see Andrew Lambert, *The Crimean War: British Grand Strategy, 1853–56* (Manchester, 1990), pp. 1–79. Milne himself would have preferred service afloat. He applied for assignment to active duty in 1854 and was evidently offered the post of Flag Captain of the Baltic Squadron by Richard Saunders Dundas the following year, but was both times refused, his presence at the Admiralty being too valuable to spare. See below, Milne to Napier, 12 March 1854, [**283**], and Milne to Pakington, 10 September 1858, [**633**].

[2]Henry Pelham Fiennes Clinton, fifth Duke of Newcastle-under-Lyme, D.C.L. (1811–64). Junior Lord of the Treasury, 1834–35; First Commissioner of Woods and Forests, 1841–46; Chief Secretary of Ireland, 1846; Secretary of State for War and the Colonies, 1852–54; Secretary of State for War, 1854–55; Secretary of State for the Colonies, 1859–64.

[3]'Minutes of Evidence Taken before the Select Committee on the Army before Sebastopol' (generally called the Roebuck Committee, and hereafter cited as such), *Parliamentary Papers*, 1855, vol. IX, pt II, p. 266, question 16,358. This and subsequent quotations, unless otherwise noted, are drawn from testimony to the Committee.

secure conveyance for several thousand French troops bound for both the Baltic and the Black Seas, and 15,000 Piedmontese soldiers bound for the latter theatre. Only in February 1855 was a separate Transport Board re-established, relieving Milne of some of this heavy responsibility, although he remained closely involved in all major transport undertakings for the remainder of the war.[1] Milne's papers for all of 1854 and much of 1855 are not surprisingly dominated by correspondence relating to these tasks.

The first and most intractable problem he faced was securing ships [**278–9**]. As he informed Roebuck's Committee, the Admiralty contacted no less than fifteen steamship firms, but the appeal produced a mere nineteen vessels, only three of which were immediately available.[2] The Board even advertised at Lloyd's (10 February) but the only vessels offered as a result of this appeal were two cattle vessels and the *Great Britain*, which was then homeward bound from Australia.[3] More steamships were chartered piecemeal as they became available during the following months, but at much higher rates than prevailed in peacetime, as owners took advantage of the unprecedented demand.[4] Samuel Cunard,[5] with whom Milne carried on an extensive correspondence [**280**, **285**, **296**, **300**, **302**, **309**, **312**, **314**, **318**, **345**, **377**, **411–12**, **421**, **428**] was more helpful than many, but nonetheless maintained that he could not afford to offer his vessels at a loss [**355**].

As a consequence, the Admiralty was not able to dispatch troops, horses, and supplies at the rate expected by the War Office, even with extensive recourse to sailing vessels. The ramifications of this bottleneck are clearly reflected in the correspondence between Milne, Graham, and Newcastle during February and March 1854 [**270**, **272–7**, **281**, **284**,

[1]As part of his 1832 reform of Admiralty administration, Graham had abolished the old Transport Board. As Superintending Lord of the Victualling and Transport Department, Milne retained supervisory responsibility after the Board's reconstitution. See ibid., questions 16,563–8, p. 283.

[2]Roebuck Committee evidence, *Parliamentary Papers*, 1855, vol. IX, pt II, pp. 270–71, question 16,358.

[3]Ibid.

[4]For specifics, see Milne's testimony in ibid., pp. 292–3, questions 16,376–80, pp. 272–3; 16,679–86, and 'A Return of the Ships engaged as Regular Transports, with the Names (stating whether Steam or Sailing), from the 1st day of January 1854 to the 1st day of January 1855; with the Dates of Engagement, and if still in the Service; the Register Tonnage on which the Freight is calculated; the Rates of Freight, and whether Reduced or Increased since first engaged; the Service performed, with the Quantity of Cargo, Troops, or Stores taken by each; the Length of the Passages; in Steam Ships, the Horse-power and Consumption or Coals or Fuel per Hour', *Parliamentary Papers*, 1854–55, vol. 34, p. 235.

[5]Sir Samuel Cunard, Bt. (1787–1865); cofounder of the British and North American Royal Mail Steam Packet Company (1839).

286–91, **293**].[1] By the end of April, Milne could inform Newcastle that no fewer than 92 ships had been fitted as transports, although the majority of them were sailing vessels [**311**].[2] Still, the results were impressive, given the difficulties initially encountered. Between 9 February and 27 April Milne supervised the dispatch of almost 22,000 officers and men, 2,259 horses, and 171 wagons and guns to the Black Sea, an operation, as he observed to Sir Charles Napier [**307**] of greater magnitude and at a greater distance from Britain than had ever been attempted hitherto.

By 5 June 1854 the number of chartered transports in Admiralty service topped 100 and, thinking that the worst was over, Milne wrote to Newcastle to see if any reduction could be made [**323**].[3] However, this and subsequent attempts to draw down the force and reduce the enormous expense all failed. Indeed, for the next ten months the Admiralty faced a succession of demands for transports which baffled all of Milne's efforts at economy.[4]

The troops had first been dispatched to Malta and were only ordered to Gallipoli in May. The decision to send them to Varna, on the Bulgarian coast was taken by the British Cabinet on 27 May, but the landing there took over a month as there was no suitable harbour and the force had to come ashore across an open beach. By the time the landing was completed, the Russian army had abandoned the siege of Silistria and had, by 25 June, retreated north of the Danube, leaving no rationale for the British and French presence at Varna and Baljik. Only after the Russian evacuation, did the Cabinet officially decided to transfer the Army to the Crimea (28 June), and word of the decision did not reach Lord Raglan[5] until 17 July. Before the move could be made the peninsula had to be reconnoitred. As a consequence, loading some 26,000 British troops onto 52 sailing and 27 steam hired transports at Varna was not carried out until the very end of August and beginning of September. Landing them at Eupatoria began only on 15 September. The same month about 10,000 Turkish

[1]For subsequent letters between Milne and Graham, see [**308**, **315**, **322**, **326**, **357**, **393**, **395**, **409–10**, **416**, **419–20**, **423**, **432**, **453**]. For those between Milne and Newcastle, see [**310–11**, **316–17**, **319**, **323**, **382**, **385**, **397**, **403–4**, **407**, **426**, **434**, **440**, **442**, **446**, **452**, **466**, **474**]. Following his resignation from the Admiralty, Graham wrote several letters to Milne relative to testifying before Roebuck's Committee; see [**520–24**].

[2]See Roebuck Committee evidence, *Parliamentary Papers*, 1855, vol. IX, pt II, pp. 271, 278; questions 16,359, 16,453–60. The first contingent, comprising more than 10,000 officers and troops, sailed between 23 February and 20 March.

[3]See also ibid., p. 281, question 16,529.

[4]See ibid., p. 304, question 16,824.

[5]Fitzroy James Henry Somerset, first Baron Raglan (1788–1855). General; C-in-C of the British Army in the East until his death in June 1855.

troops were also carried from the Danubian Principalities to the Crimea in British transports. Arrangements for all of these movements rested with the Army and Navy chiefs in theatre – in particular Sir Edmund Lyons,[1] second in command of the Black Sea Fleet, and his Flag Captain, William Robert Mends[2] – rather than Milne, but their very occurrence meant that transports, once sent out to the East, tended to remain there.

Quite aside from the expeditionary force's movements to and in the Black Sea, Milne had, from its dispatch, to arrange conveyance for the continuous flow of supplies, replacements, and reinforcements needed to sustain it and by November the Army was demanding additional transports to convey warm clothing and huts to the Black Sea [**403–4**, **407–8**, **423–4**, **427**, **432**, **437–40**, **442**, **445–7**, **452**].[3] Compounding the difficulties faced in carrying out the last task was the immense gale which swept the anchorage and harbour at Balaklava on 14 November [**435**, **449**].

Even as 1854 drew to a close, Milne's labours continued unabated. In mid-November he was ordered to find the means to carry more than 16,000 French soldiers from Marseilles [**411–17**]. During the first three months of 1855 more than 44,000 Turkish troops were transported from various places on the Black Sea coast to Eupatoria in British vessels [**461**], and in February and March Milne had to arrange for carrying the Piedmontese contingent from Genoa and Spezzia to the East [**473**, **489–90**, **497–8**, **500**, **503–7**, **513–18**] and simultaneously meet further demands from the French to carry reinforcements from Toulon [**496–8**, **500**, **502–9**, **513–14**, **517–18**].

If the incessant demands for conveyance to, from, and in the Black Sea were not headache enough, Milne also had to contend with dispatching more than 13,000 French troops to the Baltic during 1854 [**341–4**, **351**, **359**, **363**], in addition to the coal, provisions, and ordnance stores[4] being sent to both theatres on a continuing basis. By April

[1]Edmund, first Baron Lyons of Christchurch, Bt., K.C.H., G.C.B. (Civil and Military) (1790–1858). Entered, 1798; Lt, 1809; Cmdr, 1812; Capt., 1814; Rear-Adm., 1850; Vice-Adm., 1857.

[2]William Robert Mends, K.C.B., G.C.B. (1812–95). Entered, 1825; Lt, 1835; Cmdr, 1846; Capt. 1852; Rear-Adm. (Ret.), 1869; Vice-Adm. (Ret.), 1874; Adm. (Ret.), 1879. Mends was Captain of Lyons' flagship *Agamemnon* and played the principal role in organising the transport of the British Army to Varna and again to the Crimea, for which he earned high commendations from both James Whitley Deans Dundas and Edmund Lyons. See Lambert, *The Crimean War*, p. 115. Mends subsequently served as Director of Transports, 1862–83.

[3]See Roebuck Committee evidence, pp. 280–81, questions 16,581–4.

[4]The term 'ordnance stores' comprehended, in addition to guns and munitions, clothing and medical supplies.

1855 the number of transports under hire had swelled to 216, of which 113 were steamers.[1] So much paperwork was involved in these efforts, that in early July 1854 Milne began copying much of his outgoing correspondence to letter books to assist him in keeping track of details.[2] As a consequence, his papers provide an extraordinarily comprehensive picture of the logistics of early steam-era combined operations.

Beyond Graham, Newcastle, and Cunard, Milne's chief correspondents at home during 1854 were Grant [**333**, **337**, **342**, **350**, **367**, **369–70**, **388–91**, **444–5**, **451**, **474**, **510**, **534**], several steamship firms or their representatives [**345**, **376**, **379**, **413–15**, **422**, **425**, **463**, **465**, **470**], and several Resident Agents of Transports at the major commercial ports, the most important of whom were Captains Horatio Austin [**370**, **427**, **443**] and Robert Craigie[3] [**437–8**, **456**] at Southampton,[4] and Commander Thomas Bevis[5] [**424**, **441**] at Liverpool.[6] He also had occasion to write to George Bohun Martin,[7] Captain-Superintendent at Deptford Dockyard [**348**], and William Fanshawe Martin, Rear-Admiral-Superintendent at Portsmouth Dockyard [**469**]. Through these officers Milne made most of the arrangements for the dispatch of troops, horses, guns, and stores from Britain. His directives to them usually consisted of terse instructions, often communicated via the Comptroller of Victualling, although he wrote a few formal letters to Grant. Of course, Milne had also to coordinate matters with the Army, and thus his correspondence also contains numerous letters to and from not only Newcastle but also several of his subordinates, especially Ordnance Comptroller Sir

[1]'An Abstract of the Services performed by the Transports in conveying Troops, Stores, &c., to the East, from 9th February 1854 to the 27th April 1855', Appendix No. 4 of the Roebuck Committee Report, *Parliamentary Papers*, 1855, vol. IX, pt. III, p. 315.

[2]MLN/169/5: Milne to Michael Seymour, 4 July 1854. Milne wrote at the bottom of this letter: 'I have been obliged to adopt this mode of writing to keep Copies of my letters to Christie and Adl Boxer and several respecting Transports &c[,] as I have much arrangement to make with them.'

[3]Robert Craigie (1800–1873). Entered, 1811; Lt, 1823; Cmdr, 1828; Capt., 1839; Rear-Adm. (Ret.), 1858; Vice-Adm. (Ret.), 1865; Adm. (Ret.), 1870.

[4]Austin served at Southampton until 18 October 1854, when he was appointed Captain-Superintendent of Deptford Dockyard, in which role he continued to play an important part in transport arrangements. Craigie took Austin's place at Southampton when the latter was transferred.

[5]Thomas Bevis (*c*.1785–1868). Entered, 1797; Lt, 1806; Cmdr, 1829; Capt. (Res.), 1858. Bevis had been Superintendent of the Packet Service at Liverpool since 1839 and Resident Transport Agent there since 1843.

[6]Most of the surviving correspondence with the Transport Agents at the outports and with Dockyard Superintendents relates to minor matters such as individual ships' fittings, and has not been included in this collection.

[7]George Bohun Martin, C.B., K.S.L., K.S.A., K.R.G. (*c*.1800–1854). Entered, 1812; Lt, 1821; Cmdr, 1824; Capt., 1828. Martin died 14 October 1854.

Thomas Hastings[1] [**303**, **305–6**, **324–5**], and Assistant Undersecretary for War Colonel Godfrey Charles Mundy [**328**, **366**, **375**, **378**, **396**, **460**].[2] His correspondence with the Army authorities also includes one missive from Lord Raglan [**271**], some addressed simply to Horse Guards [**380**, **431**, **447**], and some interdepartmental correspondence in the War Office [**282**, **408**].

His network of correspondents overseas was similarly comprehensive. The route for transports to and from the East touched at Gibraltar, where Captain George Grey[3] commanded [**353**]; Malta, where Milne's former Admiralty colleague Rear-Admiral Houston Stewart was Superintendent [**294**, **299**, **353**, **361**, **373**, **383**, **430**, **439**, **450**, **458**]; Constantinople, where the Navy's establishment was overseen by Rear-Admiral Edward Boxer[4] [**327**, **339**, **352**, **360**, **365**, **371**, **392**, **398**, **406**, **417**, **436**, **448**]; and finally the Black Sea itself, where Captain Peter Christie[5] served as Chief Agent of Transports [**298**, **320**, **329**, **331**, **336**, **340**, **346**, **356**, **364**, **374**, **384**, **394**, **402**, **429**, **435**, **454**, **457**, **461–2**, **464**, **467**, **471**, **475**, **481**, **483**, **495**, **499**]. His principal correspondents in the Baltic were Commander-in-Chief Sir Charles Napier[6] [**283**, **292**, **295**, **297**, **304**, **307**, **313**, **321**, **330**, **344**, **354–5**, **363**, **381**, **386–7**, **399**] and his Flag Captain, Rear-Admiral Michael Seymour [**341**, **343**, **362**, **368**, **526**].

[1]Sir Thomas Hastings, Kt., C.B., K.C.B. (1790–1870). Entered, 1803; Lt, 1810; Cmdr, 1825; Capt., 1830; Rear-Adm., 1855; Vice-Adm., 1862; Adm. (Ret.), 1866. Captain of HMS *Excellent* (her first), 1832–45; Superintendent, Royal Naval College, Portsmouth, 1839–45; Comptroller of Ordnance Stores and Principal Storekeeper, 1845–55.

[2]Col. Godfrey Charles Mundy (b. 1803). Assistant Undersecretary for War, appointed by Newcastle 16 March 1854.

[3]George Grey (1809–91). Entered, 1822; Lt, 1829; Cmdr, 1831; Capt., 1834; Rear-Adm., 1856; Vice-Adm., 1863; Adm. (Ret.) 1866. Grey was Captain of the port of Gibraltar 1846–56.

[4]Edward Boxer, C.B. (1784–1855). Entered, 1798; Lt, 1807; Cmdr, 1815; Capt., 1823; Rear-Adm., 1853. Boxer had extensive experience with transport arrangements during the Peninsular Campaign, and subsequently served a long stretch as Agent of Transports at Quebec. For the circumstances surrounding his appointment to Constantinople, see Roebuck Committee evidence, *Parliamentary Papers*, 1855, vol. IX, pt. II, p. 279, questions 16,477–87.

[5]Peter Christie (1797–1855). Entered, 1810; Lt, 1820; Cmdr, 1827; Capt., 1841. For the circumstances surrounding his appointment, see both Milne's and Graham's evidence before the Roebuck Committee. Graham testified (vol. IX, pt. III, p. 264, question 21,063): 'I selected Captain Christie on these grounds; I asked Captain Milne, the officer who, with great ability and zeal, had under me managed the transport service, who, he thought, upon the great occasion of so large an armament, was a fit officer to be entrusted with the supreme control, and immediate power over the transports . . . and Captain Milne recommended to me Captain Christie . . . ' Milne's evidence (vol. IX, pt. II, p. 280, questions 504–7) essentially corroborates Graham.

[6]Milne and Napier's friendship seems to have foundered due to the acrimonious relations that developed between Admiral and Admiralty during the autumn, as is suggested in Milne's 29 January 1855 letter to James Stirling [**477**].

Command shake-ups in late 1854 and early 1855 meant that much of Milne's subsequent overseas correspondence was carried on with a new cast of officers. Christie was relieved from his post as Chief Agent for Transports as a consequence of numerous complaints at home, to be replaced by Leopold Heath.[1] Black Sea Commander-in-Chief James Whitley Deans Dundas, to whom Milne had addressed a few letters [**405**, **418**, **433**, **455**], hauled down his flag late in 1854 and was replaced by Lyons [**480**, **484**, **486**, **488**, **492**, **494**, **496**, **503**, **517**, **532**, **536–7**]. Houston Stewart was subsequently (January 1855) dispatched to the Black Sea to fill Lyons' old slot [**478**, **485**, **487**], and Montagu Stopford[2] appointed to replace Stewart at Malta [**472**, **482**, **491**, **497–8**, **504**, **507–8**, **511–14**, **518**]. Edward Boxer was sent from Constantinople to Balaklava late January 1855 in an attempt to improve matters at the latter place, and Frederick Grey[3] became Superintendent at Constantinople [**476**, **493**]. When Boxer died in June 1855, Rear-Admiral Charles Fremantle[4] assumed general oversight of transport operations in the Black Sea [**530**, **533**]. Finally, Milne dispatched several letters to Captains Edward Tatham [**502**, **505–6**, **509**, **531**] and Thomas Brock [**515–16**], who were sent to the western Mediterranean to oversee the transport of French and Sardinian troops in early 1855.

The magnitude of Milne's effort is suggested by statistical returns furnished to Roebuck's Committee in conjunction with his testimony. Between 9 February 1854 and 27 April 1855, transports in the Mediterranean and Black Sea conveyed 3,162 officers and 172,299 men of various nationalities, of which some of the British contingent – ultimately almost 70,000 officers and men – was moved on no fewer than four separate occasions, plus almost 14,000 horses, 42,000 tons of Army and 25,930 tons of Navy provisions, and 38,105 tons of Army and Ordnance Stores.[5]

[1]Sir Leopold George Heath, K.C.B. (1817–1907). Entered, 1831; Lt, 1840; Cmdr, 1847; Capt., 1854; Rear-Adm., 1871; Vice-Adm. (Ret.), 1873; Adm. (Ret.), 1877. Heath superseded Christie in February 1855.

[2]Sir Montagu Stopford, K.C.B. (1798–1868). Entered, 1810; Lt, 1819; Cmdr, 1822; Capt., 1825; Rear-Adm., 1853; Vice-Adm., 1858; Adm., 1863.

[3]Sir Frederick Grey, C.B., K.C.B., G.C.B. (1805–78). Entered, 1819; Lt, 1825; Cmdr, 1827; Capt., 1828; Rear-Adm., 1855; Vice-Adm., 1861; Adm., 1865; First Naval Lord, 1861–66.

[4]Charles Howe Fremantle, K.C.B., G.C.B. (1800–1869). Entered, 1812; Lt, 1819; Cmdr, 1822; Capt., 1826; Rear-Adm., 1854; Vice Adm., 1860; Adm., 1864.

[5]'An Abstract of the Services performed by the Transports in conveying Troops, Stores, &c., to the East, from 9th February 1854 to the 27th April 1855', Appendix No. 4 of the Roebuck Committee Report, *Parliamentary Papers*, 1854–55, vol. IX, pt. III, p. 315. Transports carried in addition, modest amounts of Navy Stores (4,285 tons) and provisions (8,687 tons) from Malta. See also the evidence given by Milne (vol. IX, pt. II, p. 289, questions 16,647–53) and Graham (vol. IX, pt. III, pp. 271–2, question 21,116) to Roebuck's Committee.

Additionally, as Milne informed the Committee, 111,446 tons of coal and 4,176 tons of patent fuel were dispatched to Constantinople and another 69,123 tons of the former and 3,529 of the latter to Malta between 1 February 1854 and 23 April 1855.[1]

Nonetheless, in the furore generated by public outcry at the Army's condition in the Crimea, Milne did not escape scrutiny, especially since the Duke of Newcastle pointedly stated in the House of Lords that the one department at home that had 'most eminently failed' was that under his charge.[2] Thus, Roebuck's Committee subjected him to two lengthy examinations. Milne himself was deprecating of his achievement:

> I carried on the whole of this service, from the first embarkation, for upwards of one year; and I must say, it is rather too heavy an undertaking for any one individual. I endeavoured to carry through that service, to the best of my ability. I believe there was some feeling, not of dissatisfaction, but some feeling that it was not done sufficiently quick to meet the emergencies of the case.[3]

First Lord Graham was less equivocal. When asked if 'the management [of the transport service] under Captain Milne was not efficient', he replied, 'It was far from that; and if Captain Milne could have been spared to devote his attention exclusively to the transport service, I think it would have been more efficiently conducted than by any Board.'[4]

The Committee itself took Graham's lead, rather than Newcastle's. '[C]onsidering the urgent pressure of the public service', stated the Fifth Report, the steps taken to secure transport vessels appeared 'to have been ably performed', and since this duty was 'under the immediate superintendence of Captain Milne', the Report amounted to both a vindication and a considerable compliment, the more so when contrasted to the unflattering verdicts rendered on many other aspects of the war's conduct.[5] The Committee was much more critical regarding the shortcomings in forwarding stores, especially medical supplies,

[1]Ibid., pt. II, p. 282, question 16,453.

[2]See *Hansard*, 3rd ser., vol. 136 (1854–55), cols. 1094–1105. Newcastle's remark, made in the midst of a lengthy debate on the War Department, appears in col. 1099. Milne was so irked by this charge that he wrote personally to the Duke on 31 January 1855 [**479**], asking for specific instances in which the transport service had failed.

[3]'Minutes of Evidence', Roebuck Committee, *Parliamentary Papers*, 1855, vol. IX, pt II, p. 283, question 16,569.

[4]Ibid., pt. III, pp. 282–3, question 21,189. The only reservation Graham expressed about entrusting the transport service to a single person was that 'it is a great trust to have the power, amidst extraordinary temptations, of spending five millions, year by year, without the intervention of any second person', but predicated this statement by explicitly praising 'the spotless honour of Captain Milne'.

[5]Roebuck Committee, fifth Report, *Parliamentary Papers*, 1855, vol. IX, pt. III, p. 374.

warm clothing, and housing, to the East, and was downright condemnatory of the defective arrangements for transporting sick and wounded soldiers from the Crimea to Scutari, but both Milne's and Graham's evidence made clear that the Army was responsible for the latter failure. As to the former, the Committee, which admitted itself 'unable to decide' whether the blame should rest upon Raglan, Newcastle, or Secretary at War Sidney Herbert, implicitly exonerated the Admiralty.[1]

From the perspective of Milne's incoming correspondence, Christie, widely blamed in the press for the disastrous losses in the gale of 14 November 1854 and for the chaos at Balaklava generally, was more sinned against than sinning, although Houston Stewart's lengthy letter of 13 February 1855 [**487**] suggests otherwise.[2] The verdict on Boxer is more ambiguous. Both Milne and Graham were at pains to inform Roebuck's Committee that they received no *official* criticism of his performance, but the latter's decision to transfer him from Constantinople to Sevastopol was explained in terms less than flattering to Boxer.[3] More to the point, Milne's private view, expressed to James Stirling[4] [**477**], implies that he had sought to avoid airing dirty laundry in public when testifying to the Committee. On the other hand, Houston Stewart, especially when commanding at Malta, was a font of valuable intelligence for Milne and appears to have conducted his duties with the energy and the high standards on which the Navy prided itself.

Chief fault for the widely publicised defects of the transport service, according to all naval officers and subsequent commentators, lay with the Army's failure to make adequate transport arrangements between Balaklava and its camp and, to a lesser extent, overcrowding in the harbour itself.[5] True, a more commodious port would probably have saved the vessels lost on 14 November – in particular the *Prince*, a large steamer which had been purchased by the Admiralty and which was carrying much-needed winter clothing – but the same result would have been achieved by providing adequate warehouse space ashore;

[1]Ibid., p. 375. See also Graham's evidence on conveying warm clothing (vol. IX, pt. III, pp. 281–2, questions 21,181–4) and Milne's on the manner in which medical stores were conveyed (vol. IX, pt. II, pp. 276–7, questions 16,429–32) and that regarding hospital ships (vol. IX, pt. II, p. 283, questions 16,553–8).

[2]See also Milne's evidence in ibid., (vol. IX, pt. II, p. 280, question 16,508) and that of Graham (pt. III, pp. 264–5, questions 21,064–82).

[3]For Milne's statements, see ibid., vol. IX, pt. II, p. 279, questions 16,491–7 and p. 317, questions 16,996–17,002; for Graham's see ibid., vol. IX, pt. III, pp. 279–80, questions 21,167–71.

[4]Sir James Stirling, Kt. (1791–1865). Entered, 1803; Lt, 1809; Cmdr, 1812; Capt., 1818; Rear-Adm., 1851; Vice-Adm., 1857; Adm., 1862; Naval Lord of the Admiralty, 1852; C-in-C, East Indies Squadron, 1854–56.

[5]See Milne's testimony in ibid., vol. IX, pt. II, p. 304, questions 16,818–20.

transports were often detained at anchor outside Balaklava, forced to serve as floating storehouses owing to the want of storage space.

Graham's observation that had Milne been able to devote undivided attention to the transport service, the need for a new Board would have been obviated, also suggests that even during the height of the crisis, the latter remained responsible for other aspects of Admiralty business. In late April 1854, for instance, he was assigned to draft instructions for Sir Edward Belcher, commander of one of the Franklin search parties [**301**]. The following October he composed a request to the Hudson Bay Company to follow up on earlier discoveries regarding the lost expedition's fate [**401**]. Throughout 1854 and the first half of 1855 these duties were exceptions, but as affairs in the East calmed down Milne began to resume some of the tasks that had occupied him prior to the war, especially those concerned with personnel matters. Thus he drafted memoranda on the status and retired pay of Commanders [**527**] and on Acting Masters' qualifications [**528**]. After 1855 these and similar issues would again become his primary focus.

[**270**] *Milne to Graham*

Admiralty
3 February 1854

Dear Sir James

The four ships which have been chartered to convey the 62d and 9th Regiments from Ireland to Malta have left the River for Ireland to embark them, but no answer has yet been given to the Owner's [*sic*] whether they are to be taken up as Transports for 6 Months or to remain as taken up, viz. for the performance of the voyage from Ireland to Malta thence to West Indies and Home[.]

The other services as follows have been delayed[:]

The 37th Reg from Ireland to Malta
47th " from Malta to W. Indies
67th " from W. Indies to Canada
71st " from Canada to England

——

The 89th Reg from Ireland to Gibraltar
30th " from Gibr to W. Indies
69th " from W. Indies to N. Brunswick
72nd " from N. Brunswick to England

——

The 14th Reg from Ireland to Gibraltar
17th " from Ireland to Gibraltar
x44th " from Gibr to Bermuda
x56th " from Bermuda to England

xThese two Regiments are 1000 strong[;] all the rest 620[.]

You will observe there is only one Regiment intended for Malta viz. the 37th. Transports could be taken up for 5 or 6 Months to perform this service and[,] if you thought proper[,] could either remain at Malta or perform the Service to the West Indies, or go to Gibraltar to convey any Troops from thence to Malta so as to land them there, if it is intended to move Troops from thence to Malta[.]

The *Simoom* & *Vulcan* will be ready to convey Regiments from this country in about a month or six weeks from this time[.]

[**271**] *Raglan to Milne*

Horse Guards
10 February 1854

My dear Captain Milne

I send you the weight of the Guns, Carriages and ammunition as far as we have been able to make it out, but my impression is that some additions will still be necessary[,] of which I will apprize you as soon as I can.

I think the harness might go in the same Vessels as the Horses but you will know best whether there will be room.

[**272**] *Milne to Newcastle*[1]

Admiralty
*c.*15 February 1854

The Duke of Newcastle may be informed

. . . The *Ripon* & *Manilla* will be ready to Embark 1100 Men including Women & Children on the morning of Saturday next . . . 18th and the Baggage on the previous day.

Orinoco will also be ready [on] the morning of the 18th to Embark the same numbers[.] these [ships will be] at Southampton.

Niagara of [1,825 tons] will be ready to Embark 1100 Men on Saturday m[orning] the 18th[.] The Baggage required to be sent on the previous day.

The *Simoom* will be ready to Embark 1100 men also including Women & Children on the 28th Inst.

and [*sic*] the *Vulcan* will be ready for 780 Men on the 24th Inst.

As soon as the *Himalaya* & *Cambria* arrive they will be prepared, and the *Golden Fleece* will also be got ready[.] These vessels will probably be completed about the 1st March.

[?9] Transports have been [?or]dered for . . . this day . . . the Artillery & Horses[.]

[1]This letter was damaged by fire, thus the gaps in the text.

[**273**] *Graham to Milne*

House of Commons, Private
14 February 1854

My dear Capt Milne

I have received the enclosed note[1] from the D[uke] of Newcastle.

Can you enable me at once to answer it with certainty? or [*sic*] will it be prudent to suspend the answer until tomorrow after the Enquiry?

I have received your note. In present circumstances[,] with immense naval demands impending[,] we must not hamper ourselves unnecessarily with Army Commissariat Service. Why purchase Rum from us when they may go to into the Market and buy on their [own] account?

As for Biscuit and Salt Meat[,] you may sway [*sic*] away with advantage on some of our <u>old</u> stock at Gibraltar and Malta. Mind that this <u>old</u> stock is used on this occasion. As to Casks and Cooperage[,] on no account meddle with any <u>new</u> work: accommodate them as far as possible from your stock on hand, stipulating for <u>ample Payment</u>.

[**274**] *Newcastle to Graham*

Downing Street, Private
9 February 1854

My dear Graham

I send you, in case it may assist Capt Milne, a list of the Steam vessels which I am informed can be provided at the time affixed to each.

Ripon[,] P[eninsular] & O[rient] S[team] [Navigation] C[ompany] for 1500 men[:]

&

Victoria A[ustralian] [and] P[acific] Mail Co[2] for 1500 men[:]

in 10 days or less.

Golden Fleece	2000 men
Peopontis [*sic*]	500 do
Cape of Good Hope	300 do

All belonging to G[eneral] Screw Steam S[hip] Compy[:]

in less than a fortnight[.]

Himalaya P&O S[team] C[ompany] for 3000 men[:]

at the end of the Month[.]

[1]Not among Milne's papers, but certainly relative to providing provisions for troops.

[2]Actually the Australian Royal Mail Steam Navigation Company.

[**275**] *Newcastle to Graham*

Downing Street
14 February 1854

My dear Graham

Will you be so kind as to desire Capt Milne to inform me on what day the transports will be ready to embark the first Brigade – the Guards – of about 2500 men. I should be glad also to know if he can yet ascertain the day when the second batch of transports will be ready.

I am very anxious on this point, because so much admirable spirit has been shewn by the Troops[,] that I should much regret any avoidable inconvenience to them from uncertainty. If the day for the first embarkation can be fixed[,] I will at once apprize Ld Hardinge[1] that orders for marching may be issued to the Regiments.

[**276**] *Milne Memorandum on Embarkation of Troops for the East*

Admiralty
15 February 1854

Embarkation of Troops with Dates[:]

Ships	[Unit]	[No. of men]	[Horses]	[From]	[Date]
Ripon & *Manilla*	1. Guards	1100 Men &c	12 Horses	Southampton	22nd Feb
Orinoco	2. Guards	Do.	12 Horses	Do	22nd
Simoom	3. "	Do.	12 Horses	Portsmouth	28th
Part in *Vulcan* 750 [*sic*]	Rifles	1100	12 Horses	Portsmouth	24th
Golden Fleece	33d	1100	Do.	Dublin	4 March
Cambria	50th	1100	Do.	Dublin	26th Feb
Niagara	28th	1100	Do.	Liverpool	22nd Feb
#	{77th	1000	Do.	Glasgow}	
	4th	1100	Do.	Glasgow}	
Himalaya	93d	1100	Do.	Portsmouth	4 to 6 March

[1]Sir Henry Hardinge, first Viscount Hardinge of Lahore (1785–1856). Secretary at War, 1828–30, 1841–44; Chief Secretary for Ireland, 1830, 1834–35; Governor-Gen. of India, 1844–48; C-in-C, 1852–56.

The arrangements for the 77th & 4th are not completed, and the *Himalaya* not having arrived in England, it is doubtful whether the 4th to 6th of March can be depended upon to a day[.]

[**277**] *Milne List of Steamers Chartered by the Admiralty*

Admiralty
20 February [1854]

List of Steamer's [*sic*] Chartered by the Admiralty[:]

[Ships]	[Sailing Date]	[Men]	[Horses]
Ripon & Manilla	[February] 22d	1100	12 Horses
Orinoco	22d	1100	Do.
Niagara	22d	1100	Do.
Cambria	24th	500	Do.
Vulcan	24th	750	Do.
Himalaya	about 27th	1400	Do.
Emeu	about 28th	800	Do.
Simoom	28	1100	Do.
Golden Fleece	about [March] 4th	1100	Do.
Arabia	about 6	1100	Do.
[Total]		10,350	

It is probable that 2 or 300 men will require special conveyance . . .
These vessels will all cease service at Malta so soon as the Troops are disembarked[,] except *Orinoco*. That vessel on landing Troops at Malta will go to Gibraltar and convey from that place the 44th Reg to Malta[,] where the service will cease.

[**278**] *Admiralty to McIver*[1]

Admiralty
22 February 1854

Do you know if any Steamers are at Liverpool or in the North capable of carrying a large number of Horses to Malta[?]
Immediate

[1]Stewart McIver of the British North American Steam Navigation Company, Liverpool, one of Cunard's partners.

[**279**] *McIver to Cunard*

[Liverpool
23 February 1854]

My dear Sir

The above is [a] copy of a Telegraph which reached Liverpool at about 5 Oclock, but as I was on board the *Niagara* at the time seeing that all was ready for a start in the morning[,] I did not get it until about 6 Oclock[,] too late[,] I fancied[,] to Telegraph. perhaps [*sic*] you will explain this much to the Admiralty & give this reply from me or as much of it as you think fit. There are no steam vessels in Liverpool[,] Screw or Paddle[,] capable of carrying any number of Horses below deck excepting the '*Great Britain*' and three of our own Mediterranean Screw vessels[,] namely the *Taurus*, *Tenerife* & *Karnak*[,] together with the '*Andes*' & '*Alps*'. Messrs Richardson Bros & Co have two screw steamers[,] the *City of Glasgow* & *City of Manchester*[,] which to my mind embrace all of the vessels hailing from Liverpool capable of carrying Horses or Cattle under deck a distance of Two thousand miles[,] & I know of no steamer I would recommend [to] the Admiralty to ship horses on deck unless it were our own North American Paddle Wheel Steamers. Now as for the *Great Britain*[,] I don't know whether Gibbs[,] Bright & Co would charter or not. Mr Bright was at [*sic*] me a week ago or so[,] what I would call nibbling, 'he did not want to offer his vessel' but it was quite plain to me he would like an offer for her, & I told him as plainly[,] if he wanted anything the way to get it[,] or to come to terms at all was to make up his mind and say what it was. Now as for Richardson Bros[,] the state of their own trade is such as to preclude the chance of getting any offer from them[,] & now I come to ourselves. We have our own regular traffic & it is a serious matter to think of disturbing that, but of the Mediterranean fleet[,] the only one they could possibly have for a voyage would be the *Taurus* & I fancy she might arrive in time to go again about the 10th March. The *Andes* & *Alps* they could have up till the end of October [as] soon as they return from this American voyage. These could be beautifully adapted for carrying Horses under deck[,] the very ships in fact for either Horses or Troops.

As for the Clyde[,] the only vessels that I know of that could be available there are the Australian Pacific Companys Screw vessels, but with the exception of the *Kangaroo*[,] none of them will be ready for a long time (Months) and even if they were ready[,] I fancy they would not be inclined to tear down their fine fittings to carry Horses[.] I fancy this would be the Case with even the *Kangaroo*[,] if wanted.

I dont [*sic*] believe there are any fit vessels in the Clyde available now or that could be got ready for months to come[,] even if the parties were willing to charter them[.] It just sums up to this[;] I dont think there is anything in the Clyde[,] & we are ourselves about the only parties in Liverpool who are in a position to render service anything like immediately[,] namely by the *Taurus* & *Andes* & *Alps* [*sic*] on their return from America, but with regard to the *Taurus* I am very loath to take her off her regular trade and would rather not as a matter of choice[.] however[,] I have written you very fully on the subject of *Niagara* & *Cambria* not going more than one other voyage to Malta & with the foregoing before you[,] I am trusting to you making to the Admiralty a full reply to their Telegraph to me of this day, as it will be more easy for you to explain than me to write[.]

[**280**] *Cunard to Milne*

Burlington Hotel, Private
23 February 1854

Dear Capt Milne

I think you have now a list of every available steam ship in the kingdom, suited to your purpose.

If you had rushed into the Market you would have paid £100,000 more than you have paid, without getting any additional Tonnage, besides establishing an extravagant rate of Freight.

Other steam ships will be dropping in, which you may obtain, but not to any great extent.

The Steamers you have already taken up will be back in three weeks and ready to perform another voyage[,] which will be more advantageous than taking up a great steam fleet at once, even if the ships could be obtained.

I dare say it has not escaped your observation that it would be impossible to have a supply of Coal at Malta and other ports in the Mediterranean to meet the demand of so many additional steamers at once.

I will keep you informed of any steamers that may arrive . . .

[**281**] *Milne Memorandum on Conveyance of Troops to the East*

Admiralty
4 March 1854

Troop Service to be Performed[:]
470 Men left out from 33d, 50th & 77th Regiments will be sent in *Melbourne*[,] chartered for four months. This completes the whole of the First Service of Infantry.

Second Service[:]
Drafts to be sent out immediately

[Unit]	[Officers]	[Men]	[Destination]
30th Reg	8 officers	206 men	to Gibraltar
55th Reg	8 officers	206 "	to Gibraltar
41st Reg	8 officers	206 "	to Malta
47th Reg	8 officers	206 "	to Malta
49th Reg	8 officers	206 "	to Malta

No provision has yet been made for sending out the above, but endeavour has been made to send them by the Packets from Southampton & screw vessels from Liverpool.

Regiments required to be sent out [to] and beyond Malta, all 941 strong[:]
1st Batt Royals
7th Foot
19th Foot
23d Foot
88th Foot
95 Foot
Total 6 Regiments[,] 5746 Men[.]
14th Foot 941 Men to Malta
17th Foot 941 do. to Gibraltar
89th Foot 941 do. to Gibraltar
39 Foot 941 do. to Malta
[Total] 3764
Grand total 11,048[,] out of which provision has been made for[:]
470 by *Melbourne*
800 by *Victoria*
[leaving] 10,678

Ships disposable[:]

[Ship]	[Status]	[Capacity]
Magdalena (W.I. Co.)	on arrival in England	941
Victoria	Chartered for 4 Months	800
Cambria	on return from Malta about 25 March	750
Ripon	about 11 April	650
{*Euxine*	about 4 May	600
{*Jason*	about 10 May	941

At present the only available ship is the *Victoria*. I have done nothing with respect to *Euxine* & *Jason*, as the Letter was only received this morning, but as these ships cannot be ready until May[,] I presume they will not be required.

I have endeavoured to Charter the *Great Britain*, but this seems doubtful[,] so that up to the 11 of April I only see the means of conveyance for 3,110 men by steam vessels. This requires consideration?!

The First Division of Horse Transports will be completed on Wednesday night[,] consisting of 6 ships[,] each capable of carrying 50 to 52 Horses.
4 of them will convey the full Troop of Royal Horse Artillery[.]
2 the half of the Reserve Ammunition [*sic*][.]

The other ships are progressing[,] and some of them will be fitted by Messrs Marc, Wigram, and Green to prevent delay.

The *City of Edinb[ur]gh*	1150 Tons	} Paddle Wheel
The *Emperor*	1300 "	
The *Tonning*	800 "	

Have been chartered for 4 Months for the Staff[,] and will convey all officers &c and their 150 Horses . . .

Ships Engaged by the Admiralty

[Ship]	[Terms]
Ripon	to cease on arrival at Malta
Manilla	Do.
Himalaya	Do.
Cambria	Do.
Niagara	Do.
Orinoco	To go to Gib. to convey the 44th to Malta[,] then service to cease
Emeu	chartered 6 Months gone to Malta
Kangaroo	chartered 6 months do.

Melbourne	chartered 6 Months[,] in England
Victoria	chartered 4 Months[,] in England
Golden Fleece	gone to Malta with 4th Reg can be chartered for 4 Months or 6
The City of London *The Emperor* *Tonning*	[all three] for the Staff
Simoom *Vulcan*	to remain at Malta

Note: the *Cambria* can be reengaged[,] *Niagara* No as *Africa* is on shore & *Niagara* will have to take her place.

[282] *Raglan to Hastings*

Great Stanhope Street
9 March 1854

My dear Sir Thomas

I return you Captain Milne's note and the Paper that accompanied it.

I was quite aware of the difficulty[,] not to say impossibility[,] of sending the Artillery and Cavalry horses in Steamers[,] and I wish Captain Milne to understand that I am not one of those who professed to consider the arrangement feasible.

[283] *Milne to Napier*

Admiralty
12 March 1854

My dear Sir Charles

I enclose you some letters which have come for you. now [*sic*] [that] your Flag is up and you are in so high and honourable a Command[,] I must wish you every success and that all may go to your satisfaction is the sincere wish of Yours very truly . . .

I told Sir James this morning I was like to bite my fingers of vexation at not being in the Fleet[,] and I must say I am very sorry for it indeed, instead of the really worrying work here . . .

[**284**] *Milne to Newcastle*

Admiralty
14 March 1854

Write to the Duke of Newcastle and acquaint him[,] with reference to his Letters of the 9th and 28th Feb. and 1 of March[,] directing that steps should be taken for securing the requisite amount of Tonnage for the embarkation of Troops, that My Lords consider it will be satisfactory if they give in detail the arrangements which have been made consequent upon his communications[.]
First with respect to the Letter of the 9th Feb For [*sic*] the embarkation of 10,000 Infantry, 200 Artillery and 1000 Horses[,] to which 500 Cavalry were subsequently added, My Lords immediately chartered the following and they sailed as follows[:]

Ship	Regt	Sailed	From	Arrived Malta
Ripon and *Manilla*}	Guards	23 Feb		
Orinoco	Guards	23 Feb		
Himalaya	93 Regt	26 Feb		
Niagara	28 Regt	23 "		
Cambria	50th Regt	26 "		
HMS *Vulcan*	Rifles	25th Feb		
HMS *Simoom*	Guards	29th Feb.		
Emeu	33 Regt			
Kangaroo	77 Regt	11th March		
Golden Fleece	4 Regt	Now at Devonp[or]t to sail 14th		

The above completes the whole of the 10,000 Infantry[,] with the exception of a small portion of the 33d, 50th & 70th Regt[,] which will be immediately embarked in the *Melbourne*[.]
The services of the *Ripon*, *Manilla Himalaya Niagara* & *Cambria* will cease at Malta[.]
The *Orinoco*[,] after landing the Guards at Malta[,] would [*sic*] proceed to Gibraltar[,] there take on board the 44th and convey them to Malta[,] when the services of that vessel would also cease[.]
The *Simoom* will return to England from Malta for the purpose of embarking other Troops and the following steam vessels[,] having been chartered by the Admiralty for a period of 6 months[,] will remain at Malta for whatever service may be required[:]

Emeu
Kangaroo

Golden Fleece
HMS *Vulcan*
Melbourne

These are capable of carrying for a short voyage about 4000 Troops[,] and in addition to the above there are 4 Sailing Transports now at Malta[,] capable of carrying 1500 men[,] in all 5,500[.]

In regard to the 200 Artillery[,] 1000 Horses[,] and 500 Cavalry for which Tonnage was ordered to be provided[,] the following arrangement has been made.

19 Sailing vessels have already been engaged for the conveyance of the Artillery and the 1000 Horses.

Each ship will contain on an average the following

2 Guns

46 to 58 Non Commissnd & Men

51 Horses, with the regulated number of Guns, Carriages, Waggons [*sic*], spare gear, [&] ammunition, with provisions for 80 days for the men[,] and will have about 5 to 6 months fodder for the Horses if it can be procured.

Most of these ships are fitted[,] and the 1st Division gone to Woolwich [where the horses would be embarked] and their Lordships hope to report tomorrow when the embarkation may take place[.]

The 500 Cavalry will require eleven ships[;] some of these are also fitting both in London and Liverpool[,] and every exertion is being used [*sic*] in preparing the requisite stores[,] which have all to be made in the Dock Yards[,] viz. slings, Halters, Hammocks for the Horses [*sic*] and numerous other articles, and in about 10 days it is expected these vessels will be nearly completed.

By the Letter[s] of the 23rd Feb and the 1 of March the following arrangements were required to be made.

1st

The Depots of the 41st, 47th, 49th Regts[,] each consisting of about 8 officers and 206 Rank and File[,] to be sent to Malta.

Provision has already been made to convey the 41st & 47th by steam from Liverpool on the 17th Inst and provision will likewise be made for the 49th about the 20th.

2d

The Depots of the 30th & 55th Regt[,] each consisting of about 8 officers & 206 Rank & File[,] from Gibraltar[.]

No means have yet been obtained to send these Depots. Neither the Packets from Southampton to Gib[ralta]r or [*sic*] those calling there on their way to Malta can convey them. But arrangements are in progress[.]

3[d]

For the conveyance of the 17th, 39th, & 89th to Gibraltar[,] sailing ships have been chartered and are now fitting[.] on landing these Regt at that place[,] they will embark the 30th & 55th and convey them to Malta, & the 14th Regt will also be forwarded to that Island by sailing ships.

These Transports[,] being engaged for 4 Months[,] will then be at the disposal of the Government for any service which may be required.

Their Lordships have avoided giving any definite Instructions for this preparation[,] or provisioning of ships for the embarkation of the Infantry Regiments[,] amounting in all to about 9,250 Men[,] until they are informed when and where they are to embark, but ships have been provided for the same to the following extent[:]

23 Regt	*Magdalena*	for 941	
7 Regt	*Niagara*	941	on arrival from Malta
95 Regt	*Cambria*	750	Do
88 Regt	*Simoom*	941	Do
19 Regt	*Victoria*	750	

With reference to the D[uke] of N[ewcastle's] Letter of the 11th Inst[,] requiring their Lordships to provide Tonnage for the conveyance to Malta or Turkey for the Add[itiona]l Troops, Artillery & Horses –
viz. Artillery[,] 41 officers, 1020 men, 735 Horses and 86 G[un] Carriages and 1500 Men[, &] Cavalry Soldiers [*sic*] with their Horses.

My Lords[,] before attempting this very large and difficult service[,] would wish to be informed on the following points[:]

First, as 38 Sailing Transports have been chartered in the country for 4 months certain [*sic*] with power of retaining them for longer periods[,] and as there are 4 other's [*sic*] now at Malta under the same conditions, whether the add[itiona]l ships now required[,] namely about 50 in number[,] should be engaged as Transports by the Month, and continued in the service, and to be placed at the disposal of the Comdr in Chief of the Army in the East, making in all about 85 sailing vessels, or whether it would suit the views of the D[uke] of N[ewcastle] that the Admiralty should endeavour to hire these 50 vessels to land the Troops & Horses in the Sea of Marmora or other fixed spot[,] and then their services to cease. If this view of the case should be adopted[,] it would release the Government from the heavy expense of keeping so large a number of Transports on monthly pay, but at the sametime [*sic*] Their Lordships deem it important to point out that if the C in C of the Army should require by circumstances [*sic*] to reembark the whole of the Force[,] which the above 85 Transports will have conveyed from England[,] only 35 fitted Transports will be in attendance with the Force, altho there may be from 6 to 10 other vessels with Stores & Provisions[.]

It is desirable an early answer should be given to their Lordships on [this] subject, as they will either advertize for ships by the month as Transports or advertize for ships to land Troops[,] Horses, Guns &c (at a point if possible to be fixed by the Duke of Newcastle) and there their services to cease.

With respect to the services already performed and the steps taken for the embarkation of the Second Division of the Infantry[,] The Duke of N[ewcastle] will be furnished with a full explanation this afternoon[.]

[**285**] *Cunard to Milne*

Burlington Hotel, London
15 March 1854

Dear Capt Milne

In your statement of the cost to the Government of employing steam ships for the conveyance of Troops, Horses, &c (which in fact could not have been procured in the Kingdom at any price) you have very much understated the expense, for instance the *Niagara* took on board at Malta 630 Tons of coal to bring her back to Liverpool, which was not a ton more that [*sic*] was absolutely necessary. You estimate the quantity at 4000 Tons.

The price of Coal now at Malta is just what the holders of it think proper to charge, say from £4 to £6 per Ton[,] and if you had sent out more steamers they must have remained at Malta until coal could have been imported from England by sailing ships. I have repeatedly heard it said that the Horses should have been sent by steam, this circumstance alone will shew the impossibility of doing so.

[**286**] *Graham to Milne*

House of Commons, Private
16 March 1854

My dear Capt Milne

It is not worth while to notice the use of your name in Mr. Lindsay's letter.[1] It is honourable in you to wish that the praise should be fairly

[1]A letter by shipowner and Radical politician William Shaw Lindsay appeared in *The Times* on 16 March 1854 (p. 8). In it Lindsay praised Milne for 'his untiring zeal and indefatigable labours in sending to sea, in so short a space of time, the most perfect fleet of ships that ever sailed from our ports'.

distributed: still a good share is due to you[,] and I am not sorry to see the debt publickly [*sic*] acknowledged. No one will suspect you of courting this praise: I see no reason why you should repudiate it.

We work so well together, that no jealousies of this kind exist among ourselves.

[**287**] *Milne to Newcastle*

Admiralty
17 March [1854]

Captain Milne presents his complts to the Duke of Newcastle and will be obliged if he will let him know[,] so soon as he may be in a position to do so[,] the arrangements he proposes to make with reference to the Chartering of ships for the conveyance of the Cavalry to the East. Cap[tain] M[ilne] now writes, as no answer has been received to an official Letter on this subject transmitted from the Admiralty a few days ago, and <u>steps</u> for the Chartering of ships (50 in number) are now suspended, and Cap[tain] M[ilne] writes in case any mistake may have occurred[.]

[**288**] *Milne to Newcastle*

Admiralty
20 March 1854

My Lord Duke

I write you a Line to say The [*sic*] 6 Transports with the Horses on Board are now ready for Sea and will sail for Malta at daylight tomorrow morning. I will send you a copy of the Sailing Orders.

[**289**] *Milne to Newcastle*

Admiralty
21 March 1854

On the 16th day of Feby the Admiralty advertized for a Contract for 1500 loads of pressed upland meadow Hay for the use of the 1600 Horses under their Order's [*sic*] for Embarkation. On the day of Treaty [*sic*] only one offer was received[,] for 50 loads[,] which was accepted[.]

Seven parties who were in the habit of supplying Hay for the Island of Ascension were then written to, calling upon them to state what quantity they could deliver and at what price within three weeks. The offers received are only for 600 loads[,] to be delivered at Deptford, and to ensure that the Hay was in all respects fit for the Service, the Board of Ordnance was requested to appoint one or more military officers to inspect the Hay when sent in to the Yard.

The result has been that a large portion of the Hay so delivered under agreement was found to be of inferior quality, especially in the centre of the Bales[,] and it was consequently rejected and thrown back on the hands of the parties who were delivering it.

These rejections have caused great inconvenience to the Service[,] but every precaution has been taken both at Deptford, Southampton, Ply[mou]th, Liverpool & other places to prevent fraud.

[**290**] *Newcastle to Milne*

[Downing Street]
24 March 1854

My dear Captn. Milne

I think if you can come here tomorrow (Friday) at ½ past 2 & meet Lord Raglan & Lord DeRos[1] we can finally settle everything about the Horse-transports – even the <u>number</u> required, which I am anxious not to extend further if we can help it.

I have written to Lds R. and DeR.

[**291**] *Milne to Newcastle*

Admiralty
24 March [1854]

My Lord Duke

I regret my absence last evening prevented me from answering your queries. I now give you the following statement relative to the Transports &c.

1st. There are 19 Ships required for the Embarkation of the Artillery and the 1000 Horses attached thereto. 9 of these ships have the Horses on Board. 6 have sailed, and 3 more will leave Woolwich this afternoon. The remaining 10 ships are in course of preparation and I expect <u>all</u> will be ready to sail from Woolwich before ten day's [*sic*].

[1]William Lennox Lascelles, twentieth Baron De Ros (1797–1874). Quartermaster-General of the Army in the East; invalided home before the Army landed in the Crimea.

2nd. 11 Ships are fitting for the 540 cavalry Horses first ordered to Embark. They are nearly completed[,] and in ten or twelve days will be ready at Southampton & Devonp[or]t.

The above completes the First Service requested by the Duke of Newcastles letter of 9 Feby.

With reference to the Second Embarkment of 2500 Horses (Artillery & Cavalry)[:]

20 Ships have been ordered for Survey[;] about 6 of these are now fitting. The others are in various stages of preparation but I do not expect more than 10 can be ready in less than 14 to 18 days[,] and the other 10 in about 24 days.

To execute this Second Service[,] about 32 ships in addition to the above 20, will be required, but as yet none can be secured[,] as every Ship offered in pursuance of Public advertizement was accepted on Tuesday last. It will be requisite to advertize again for Tenders to be taken in on Tuesday next, but at present there are few ships in England adapted for the service.

If you wish any further information I will call at the Colonial Office at any hour you may name . . .

[**292**] *Napier to Milne*

HMS *Duke of Wellington*
24 March 1854

My Dear Milne

I have sent you [a] public letter. I have not your private letter and I have sent you [a] telegraph and desire the reply.

I received my traps. You are a shabby fellow[:] your supplies are not fit for His Excellency the Commander in Chief of the Baltic Fleet. your [*sic*] cups and saucers are fine[.] your cutlery and your glass is good. your [*sic*] dishes are enough for ten Commanders in Chief[.] I dont want them[.] your [*sic*] plate and linen I don't need, but they are good, but you ought to have Tea Pots[,] Coffee Pots[,] and every thing grand for the *Duke of Wellington*.

I have got through all the difficulties of the Belt and await a clear day to get to Kioge Bay where I can watch the Sound & Belt. When there I shall have 30 sail of the line in front,[1] but I shall go on to Sweaborg where the advance [units] of the Russian Fleet are.

[1]Meaning the Russian Fleet.

I must not press them[,] for they may get out and escape to the North Sea, and if I do, and fight the Cronstadt Fleet[,] I will be an easy prey[,] whether Victor or Vanquished[,] to the Sweiborg [*sic*] Fleet. so [*sic*] the sooner you send me out Reinforcements the better, and you are niggling with asking the men to enter for a year . . . Why dont you come forward with your bounty and proclamation and you will man them[?] If you won't do that, make the present of a suit of Cloath [*sic*] and their bedding[,] that will do some good. do [*sic*] something at all events, and dont [*sic*] let us be driven out of the Baltic as Lord St Vincent was driven out of the Mediterranean.[1]

[**293**] *Milne to Newcastle*

Admiralty
27 March 1854

I write you this note to say that the *Orinoco* has arrived at Southampton from Malta[,] having performed the last service by moving the 44th Reg from Gib[ralta]r to Malta. The W[est] India Company now wish to know if the *Orinoco* will be required for further Troops Service. If not[,] the ship will be docked to get new Paddle Wheels fitted.

If the Troops now under orders for the East are likely to Embark at an early date, the *Orinoco* would be required as we have only provided Steam Transport for 5000 men and the number to Embark will be about 9000[,] but the Company will charge Demurrage at the rate of £100 pr Day for the time the Ships [*sic*] are waiting to Embark the Troops. If you think we should hold the *Orinoco* at the disposal of [the] Government[,] we should inform the Company at once. I will be obliged if you will let me know your wishes.

[**294**] *Houston Stewart to Milne*

Malta
30 March 1854

My dear Milne

I begin this letter with my <u>immediate want</u>[,] which is Instructions for Transport Service & Transport Agents[,] of which not a copy is extant in this Island, I believe. Pray send me out some as fast as you possibly can, <u>one over land if possible</u>.

[1]In 1796, following the Treaty of Ildefonso, by which Spain allied with France.

I have appointed Lt Rundle[1] of *Ceylon* to act as Agent[,] but I can give him no definite laws & Regulations to guide him. My recollections of Transport War work are too distant to enable me to act with confidence in the constantly arising questions & emergencies . . .

I have yours of the 18th & yesterday Evng also yours of the 24th Inst[.]

There have been no coals to purchase here for a considerable time at less than from £4 to £5 per Ton[,] & by purchasing on prior intelligence before the arrival of the Cargoes[.] One or two of the Merchants & Agents for Steam Companies have been able to prevent any Coals coming into the Market, although it was well known that the French Consul & our own Department here would purchase all at anything like a reasonable price, or even an unreasonable one, but £5 is demanded. as [*sic*] the Spaniards say[,] they keep on sending out Coals[,] but in writing to Sir James Graham a day or two ago[,] I suggested one of the large Iron Steamers being chartered or bought[,] before she rec[eive]d fittings for Horses or Troops . . . [be] sent out here with a large quantity of Coals and small expenditure in [*sic*: 'for'] her Voyage, which could follow the Fleet also, and carry lots of Provisions or Stores with exactitude as to time. This mornings mail brings me orders to examine *Emeu* & *Kangaroo* with a view to your purchasing them, & I shall do so carefully, but such a vessel as the *Golden Fleece* is worth them both together.

Sir G. Brown[2] [&] E Boxer arrived yesterday Evng & Sir J. Burgoyne[3] in *Caradoc* this morning. I am going to confabulate with them & with our worthy Governor & General & you shall have a few words after I have seen them.

The *Golden Fleece*[,] if cleared of fittings[,] will bring out 2000 Tons of Coal & her own consumption of about 300 Tons (& less if fair wind) in a ten days voyage, & will carry Troops quite well if necessary, but her present passengers fittings necessarily absorb her stowage for Cargo. She takes 1100 men of Rifles & Sappers & has them now embarked awaiting the embarkation of Sir G Brown.

[1]Joseph Sparkhill Rundle (1815–80). Entered, *c*.1827; Lt, 1839; Cmdr, 1856; Cmdr (Ret.), 1860. Rundle served in HMS *Ceylon*, Receiving Ship at Malta from April 1850 to June 1854 and subsequently as an Agent for Transports Afloat, April 1854 to June 1855.

[2]Lt Gen. Sir George Brown, K.H., K.C.B. (1790–1865). The first British general to reach Turkey.

[3]Field-Marshal Sir John Fox Burgoyne, C.B., K.C.B., G.C.B., D.C.L., Bt., (1782–1871). Inspector-General of Fortifications, 1845–53; sent to the East in 1853 to reconnoitre the geography; returned there in 1854 with Lord Raglan's army.

March 31st

The *Golden Fleece* started at daylight this morning with Sir G. Brown[,] Rifles & Sappers 1100[,] & 20 Horses & one months provisions for the whole, on disembarking. the [*sic*] Captain of the *Golden Fleece* (Stewart) is by no means fit for his present work. he [*sic*] should have a hint from his Master to be more energetic, preserve better order & regularity amongst his officers & himself to put more life into the carrying out of the public service[.] He is a gentlemany man, & dined with me, in order that I might get him to move on[,] but he does not like the service, can scarcely be got to sign a receipt & will do nothing without . . . delays & excuses. Last night he refused to take his ship out because it was dark, & although I urged him he declined the responsibility. I then directed [him] to allow his Attendant, who said there was no risk whatever to do it, but by the time all this was arranged, Genl Brown[,] who had embarked at 2½ pm[,] thought it better (the steam not having been got up) that I should desire the steam to be up at Gunfire & a start made with daylight[,] which has been done. With all this we had no row[,] for Capt Stewart is a mild & gentlemany man[,] but timid[,] slow & tenacious, & his officers do as they like. he [*sic*] refused to sign the receipt for provisions sent off to him for vic[tuallin]g officers[,] because he had not seen them all himself, & he said the number did not correspond with the tally left on board. It now appears no tally whatever was kept. You will understand the worry of such a man in heavy and multifarious work. When he returns I shall deal with him by written memoranda.

With best wishes from me & mine to you and yours.

[P.S.:] The *Wasp* has just come in from Corfu, sent for victuals for the Troops. She will go back immediately with as much Provisions & Stores as she can carry.

[**295**] *Napier to Milne*

HMS *Duke of Wellington*, Kioge Bay
1 April 1854

I have this to say. I anchored at 12 this day in Kioge Bay[,] apparently a good anchorage but rather wild[.] I have just heard that *Boscawen*[,] *Caesar* & *James Watt* . . . are in the Neighbourhood and that French Ships are coming[.] this is all right[.] I shall not move till the English ships come. . . .

You are a curious sett [*sic*] of Gentlemen at the Admiralty, you & the Secretary of State order me to the entrance of the Baltic and you find fault with me in going there.[1]

[**296**] *Cunard to Milne*

Burlington Hotel, London
5 April 1854

Dear Capt Milne

I can place the *Balbec* [*sic*] Steamer at your disposal to take about 1000 Tons Provisions & Stores[.] She can depart from Liverpool for Gallipoli on the morning of the 15th Instant if the Stores are forwarded without delay.

[**297**] *Napier to Milne*

HMS *Duke of Wellington*, Copenhagen
5 April 1854

My Dear Milne

We have had nothing but heavy gales since we came here[,] nevertheless between the teeth I have succeeded in nearly coaling the Fleet. in [*sic*] so doing I have emptied the first batch of Colliers without damage.

The second Batch arrived at Elsinore the other day and I have brought them here. two [*sic*] of them are not to go eastward of Lubeck by Charter [so] they will stay here to complete the ships arriving. the [*sic*] two for Bornholm will stay here also[.] one[,] the *John* [?*Ingo*] was lost on the coast of Jutland. three [*sic*] are not to go north of Gothland by Charter [so] they will go to Faro [Sound] and two will come to the Fleet[,] wherever we are[,] according to Charter.

This you will see will give us seven Colliers containing 2700 tons untouched after sailing from here[,] leaving four to fill up the ships arriving from England.

. . . it is impossible to say how much coal we shall consume as yet[,] for I am checking their flush propensities as much as possible. I think if you begin with starting a Screw Collier once a week[,] beginning on the

[1]See D. Bonner-Smith and A. C. Dewar (eds), *Russian War, 1854 Baltic and Black Sea: Official Correspondence* (1943), pp. 46, 48–9; Lambert, *The Crimean War*, p. 158.

1st of June[,] that will do, as I calculated that you have now 7000 tons on the Road [*sic*].

I have great difficulty about water and I came up here myself to arrange about it[,] and I got the Minister of Marine to lend me water casks and two lighters. Those I have filled and sent down by the steamer[.] the casks will be emptied and so will the steamer, and return for another cargo till we are complete. this [*sic*] you will see is turning the steamer into water tanks [*sic*], and I was ass enough not to think of that for two or three days.

I have had some talk with the Minister of Marine here[,] who knows the Russian Fleet well, and he says I will find them in excellent order and manoeuvre perfectly well and sail in close order. that [*sic*] is more than I can get our own ships to do. I was forced to fire five Guns the other day before I could get Capt Ryder[1] to set his Main sail, and this after reprimanding him both by letter and by the Captain of the Fleet the day before. he [*sic*] is the same gentleman who joined me off the Tagus with his ship unrigged[,] and he does not seem improved.

You had better allow me to make an example[,] either by telling them by Telegraph that they are useless and to go home[,] or authorize me to supersede them[,] or I never will get on. Trying a man would be of no use because his judges would be as bad as himself.

I have at last got a public approval of my conduct [in passing the Belt] which is preferable to a reproof, but I do think the Admiralty ought to express their regret at writing to me as they do[.] it was most discouraging when I was doing my best to fulfill their own orders. I never get the kind letter[s] I used to when last employed, my private letters are not answered[,] and I will write no more.

[P.S.:] Your arrangement with the agent will be very expensive, for instance the Purser of the *Valorous* needs £100[:] he gets it from the agent. To make it clear, we will suffer[;] the exchange is not at par[:] the agent gives him £100, he charges you for . . . agency [i.e., commission] & whatever it be[,] and the Government are charged £165. this [*sic*] is the first time it has happened and it shall be the last unless you order to the contrary.[2] The Pursers will draw their money as before[,] and the agent will be limited to furnishing us with supplies, and I can see we shall have great trouble in controlling him.

[1]Alfred Phillips Ryder, K.C.B. (1820–88). Entered, 1833; Lt, 1841; Cmdr, 1846; Capt., 1848; Rear-Adm., 1866; Vice-Adm., 1872; Adm., 1877; Adm. of the Fleet, 1885. Ryder commanded HMS *Dauntless*.

[2]Either Napier meant that he would prohibit Agents from providing money on account unless the Admiralty overruled him, or he omitted to write ‘not’ between ‘shall’ and ‘be’.

[**298**] *Milne Draft Orders to Christie*

Admiralty
6 April 1854

Having appointed you as Principal Agent of Transports in the Mediterranean, It [*sic*] is their Lordships directions [*sic*] that you proceed in the *Emperor* steamer[,] which has been chartered for the conveyance of Lord Raglans Staff[,] and in which your Pendant is now flying, to Malta, and from thence to Gallipoli[,] which is for the present your Head Quarters.

You are to assume the charge and command of the various steam vessels and Sailing Transports which have been or will hereafter be chartered by the Admiralty for the conveyance of Troops or Military Stores, and you will take care that these vessels are always kept in an efficient state, full manned in accordance with the Charter Party's [*sic*], and at all times ready for service, and that the respective Agents or Masters in Command perform their duty in a proper and attentive manner.

As the Transports have been chartered for the service of the Army, it will be your duty to attend to all requisitions which you may receive from the Commander in Chief or officer in command of the Troops, and to afford every assistance in your power to forward the Military service. with [*sic*] this in view[,] you will correspond direct with him, on all subjects which relate to the embarkation, landing, or movements of Troops or Military Stores by Sea, Keeping [*sic*] us informed of the same[,] and likewise the Naval Commander in Chief in the Med[iterranea]n[,] and[,] if necessary[,] the Rear Ad[miral] Sup[erinten]d[en]t at Malta.

Should the Naval Commander in Chief or Rear Ad[mira]l or other Senior Officer of HM Ships be on the spot where you are employed[,] acting in concert with the Army, it will be necessary that all official correspondence with the Comdr in Chief of the Army should pass thro him[,] that he may be aware of the intended movement of the Troops and that, [he be] enabled to afford all necessary assistance.

You will control the movement of all steam vessels & Transports which are under your orders[,] and you will afford such assistance to the Naval Comdr in Chief or Rear Ad[mira]l Sup[erinten]d[en]t at Malta, as may be necessary for the conveyance of Stores or Provisions when it does not in any manner interfere with military movements, but in all the orders you may give respecting steam vessels[,] you are to inculcate the saving of coal [*sic*] and screw vessels are not to get up their steam unless really necessary for the exigency of the Public Service.

In the List of vessels which have been chartered and with which you will be furnished, there are several attached to the Commissariat Department and placed exclusively under the control of the senior officer of that Depart[men]t[,] & you are not to detain these vessels from this service[,] but you are to afford every aid & assistance to that Depart[men]t which the importance of the service may require.

We have furnished you with Charts of the Mediterranean[,] also with Signal Books of the Fleet and those of Cap Maryatt[,][1] each Transport having a Copy and also the necessary Flags[,] and we have directed you to be supplied with 4 Copies of the Boats Signal Books & Flags[,] with the view of your furnishing them to [the] Army for the purpose of Establishing Stations on the Hills[,] and thereby having the means of communicating with you[.]

Having confided to you this responsible command[,] we place the utmost confidence in your exertions to discharge the duties of your office in a satisfactory manner[,] and to whatever position the Troops may be moved, you are to consider the nearest Harbour as the proper rendezvous for the Transports and as your Head Quarters[,] or such other position as the Commander in Chief of the Army[,] on consultation with you[,] may decide.[2]

[**299**] *Houston Stewart to Milne*

Malta
7 April 1854

My dear Milne

My public letter of proceedings, & my private letter to Richd Dundas will tell you nearly all you can care to know. We are looking hourly for the *Emeu* back from Constantinople[,] where I know she arrived on the 25th Ulto & also for the *Cambria* from England. I hope you will be satisfied with what we have been able to do. The *Emeu* [was] absent & the *Kangaroo* in dock when the order to send forward Troops arrived. The *Vulcan* took Sir G. Brown & all the Rifles except one Company

[1]Captain Frederick Marryat, C.B., F.R.S., F.L.S. (1792–1848). Entered, 1806; Lt, 1812; Cmdr, 1815; Capt., 1825. Marryatt adapted Sir Home Popham's signalling system for use by the merchant marine.

[2]Graham's minute on Milne's Instructions is also found in MLN/156/4: 'Immediate. Approved. Prepare orders accordingly for Cap Christie, & when prepared to send copies to Admirals Dundas & Stewart & to the Duke of Newcastle for their information.'

[which was] put into the *Sir G*[*eorge*] *Pollack* sailing Transport. She also took 200 Sappers & Miners & 20 Horses. 4500 Men are gone up to this date & 3000 more at least will be off within 48 hours hence I trust.

You ask me if I have bought Coals? Not a bit has been in the Market under £5 & even £7 per Ton here for the last 3 weeks. I bought whenever I could[,] but the arrivals were all forestalled & bought . . . [by order of the French Consul] ere I had any chance. The last Cargo I bought was 50/– deliverable in the Bosphorus. that [*sic*] was on the 14th March.

Pray send me out Transport Instructions. the [*sic*] Master of the *Georgiana* has caused trouble & delayed the service by his intemperance.

I most sincerely trust your dear Wife's job is by this time happily over.[1] Pray offer her our affecte good wishes.

. . . The General[2] tells me his reports from the Commissariat office sent to Gallipoli are rather favourable. However to make sure of our gallant fellows having grub[,] I have sent one months provisions on disembarking[,] for every soldier taken up, and if unwanted the Commissariat are to store them at Gallipoli for the use of the Fleet. Only Bread, Beef & Rum & a little Flour are required for Army Rations. Our Master Baker Gibbs[,] who is truly a Master of the Rolls[,] is floored by a Dysentery attack, but I hope a few days quiet will bring him right. He is an invaluable personage just now. So is Clifton.[3] I wish his strength & health were equal to his genl intelligence & devotion to the public weal.

[**300**] *Cunard to Grant*

Burlington Hotel
8 April 1854

We can take from four hundred to five hundred Horses, in the *Andes*, *Alps*, and *Arabia*, from Ireland to Gallipoli, and land them there in about 15 days. the [*sic*] risk would not be equal to the conveyance of the Horses from Ireland to Havre, in small steamers.

We could embark them in a week from this time, and after landing the Horses at Gallipoli[,] the ships could proceed to Marseilles and take other Horses from there.

[1]Euphemia Milne was expecting; the child, a girl, was born on 11 April.
[2]Probably Sir George Brown.
[3]Francis Clifton, Agent Victualler at Malta.

[**301**] *Draft Instructions to Belcher*[1]

Admiralty
[8 April 1854]

Instructions to Captain Sir E. Belcher or the Senior Officer of HM Ships at Beechey Island

My Lords Commissioners of the Admiralty having directed HMS *Phoenix* and *Talbot* under the orders of Captain Inglefield to proceed with Provisions & Stores to Beechey Island, for the purpose of replenishing the Ships and Depots under your orders, they have to acquaint you that by the return of the *Phoenix* from Beechey Island last year they were made aware of the arrival of HMS *Investigator* under the command of Cap McClure at Banks Land, and that part of the crew had been enabled to reach Cap Kelletts station at Melville Island.

In August 1851 Cap Collinson in H.M.S. *Enterprize*, passed the entrance of the Colville River, and their Lordships trust that by information he may have gained from the natives of Prince Alberts Land, as well as from the records deposited by Cap McClure on his passage along that shore, Cap Collinson may have been enabled to reach some position on Banks Land and that[,] having abandoned his ships[,] he may from thence have reached Melville Island or have made known his position to Cap McClure or Kellett.[2]

Their Lordships have to direct your most special attention to affording assistance to Cap Collinson.[3] If he and his Crew are at Baring Island[,][4] they as well as Cap McClure should abandon their ships and[,] with Cap Kellett and his Tender[,] endeavour to reach Beechey Island with the view of their immediate return to England.

If however the crews of these ships are still at Baring Island[,] it will [be] your anxious duty to use every possible exertion to send Provisions[,] Clothing &c to Melville Island, or even to Baring Island if possible to do so.[5]

To give positive instructions to you how you are to act or what steps you are to take is impossible, you must be guided by those varying

[1]Belcher commanded an expedition based at Beechey Island, searching for Sir John Franklin and his men. The instructions were drafted by Milne and undated, although '8 April' was later pencilled in. The printed instructions were dated 28 April 1854.

[2]Milne wrote over this portion of the paper 'See printed orders on this AM'.

[3]The following section has been crossed out.

[4]Subsequently altered to 'Banks Land.'

[5]End of crossed out section.

circumstances which in that climate alone can direct your operations, but our views are[:]
1. If the crews of the *Enterprize* & *Investigator* are at Banks Land[,] they should abandon their ships and every endeavour should be made to get the crews to Beechey Island[,] that they may return to England. In such a case as this and if the crews can be got to Beechey Island, then you are immediately to return to England with the whole of the Ships & the Crews[,] abandoning all further search for the missing expedition unless any circumstances should induce you to believe that your remaining out another year would tend to clear up the fate of our missing countrymen[.]
2. To carry out this it may be necessary to give orders of Cap Kellett to abandon the *Resolute* and *Intrepid* at Melville Island[,] as the state of the ice may prevent those ships returning to Beechey I[slan]d[.]
3. Should no tidings have been heard of Cap Collinson in H.M.S. *Enterprize*, it becomes absolutely necessary to make provision for his safety. For this purpose the Melville Island Depot must be replenished, and it will be necessary for a ship & steam Tender to remain there, also the *North Star* or *Talbot* with a Tender at Beechey Island[,] and at those stations everything which could add to the health [&] comfort of the crew should be deposited, and having done this, It [*sic*] does not appear to their Lordships to be necessary that any of the other ships should remain another year in the polar seas unless you consider further search to be necessary.
These are the views of their Lordships, their great object being to recall the whole of ships or [*sic*] crews named in the margin[1] if it can be done. If not possible to do so[,] they leave it to your judgment and discretion to adopt those measures which you consider most necessary to ensure the <u>safety</u> of Cap Collinson and his Crew and to ensure their speedy return to England.

You must be guided in the Instructions you give by the information you may have received from Melville Island[,] The [*sic*] position of the respective ships under your orders[,] the state of the Depots &c[.] all their Lordships can do is to confide in your judgment[,] and they authorize you to take such steps and give such orders as you may deem necessary for carry[ing] their wishes into effect. They trust however Cap Collinson is safe, and if so, it will be a source of much satisfaction to their Lordships if they find in the

[1]*Assistance* & *Pioneer*, *Resolute* & *Intrepid*, *Enterprize*, *Investigator*, *North Star*, *Phoenix*, *Talbot*.

approaching Autumn that the whole of your ships & crews have arrived in England.[1]

[302] *Cunard to Milne*

[?Burlington Hotel], Private
[*c*.10 April 1854]

Remarks for Capt Milne['s] private reading –

'*Victoria*'[,] being expensively fitted up[,] will only carry a small number of Troops or a small amount of Cargo. If the fittings are removed it would cost ten or twelve hundred pounds to replace them, and the replacement could not be effected, including painting & drying[,] in less than a month. The Charter is £4600 per month and she has already been on pay for three weeks.

The '*Andes*' will carry fifty per cent more cargo, [&] has no fittings to be removed or replaced. I will put her in at £3600 per month for 6 months[.] she is now Coaled and ready for sea[,] no idle time would therefore be paid for.

If required[,] the *Andes* could carry a load of Coal to Gallipoli or the Black Sea in fourteen days and at the same time take a quantity of light Stores or some Troops. She will carry a full Regiment with Camp Equipage &c.

I see the '*Emeu*' is taking coal from Malta to the Black Sea. She will not carry more than half the quantity of the *Andes*, in consequence of being fitted for passengers, and the coal must be much injured by being frequently removed, and it will be required at Malta.

The *Andes* would take the Coal direct from the Mines and deliver it on board the different Men of War in the Black Sea at a less rate that you can now send it out by Sailing vessels, the passage of which is very uncertain[,] and which may compel you to employ Steamers to take the coal from Malta to supply the Fleet as you have now to do[.] She is a fine ship with two Decks 7 feet between the Decks.

[1]Some other hand added in pencil: 'A clause required about the ships not engaging in hostilities.' Milne himself also minuted '[send to] Sir F. Beaufort for any observations AM, 14 April'. The subsequent printed orders vary in wording from the original, though not to a large degree. The organisation was altered, and a few new words added, but it was fundamentally taken from Milne's draft. See 'Instructions issued to commanders of H.M. Ships in the Arctic Expedition,' *Parliamentary Papers*, 1854, vol. XLII, p. 171, and 'Instructions issued from the Admiralty to the Arctic Expedition,' ibid., p. 357.

[**303**] *Hastings to Milne*

Ordnance Department
8 April [1854]

My dear Milne

You have already an application for tonnage for blank ammunition cartridges 3½ tons & for ball cartridges for service at Gallipoli, for 29½ Tons & a supply had been previously forwarded. there [*sic*] is also nearly the same ready for transmission[,] coming from Ireland to Ports[mouth] or Woolwich & it is important that it should be forwarded as soon as may be to Gallipoli. In reference to the points you alluded to[1] I should feel obliged by your pointing out the contradictory applications solely with a view to an arrangement being made to prevent the recurrence of the evil . . .

We shall also . . . settle the amount of the reserve ammunition [and] send you a detail[,] but routine has been lost because we had not store of rifled ammunition & are now making nearly a million a day[.]

[**304**] *Napier to Milne*

HMS *Duke of Wellington*, Copenhagen
9 April 1854

My Dear Milne

. . . Mr Rainals[,][2] who I instantly do not like much because he has showed [*sic*] such symptoms of grabbing[,] tells me that he told Capt Washington[3] that he could supply Newcastle coal delivered here at 22 and 6 to 25 and 6 a ton[,] demurrage if any falling on the Admiralty. Capt Washington told him he was too late, as the Contract was closed. Mr Rainals does not include in that his agency [*sic*: commission][.] I tell you I dont like the man as he endeavours to get every thing into his own hands, but I suppose there can be no roguery about the coals. I will[,] however[,] to test the Market[,] call for Tenders for the supply of Coals, delivered here & at Faro, and I will let you know the price and

[1]No reference to this matter survives in Milne's papers.

[2]Of Rainals, Deacon, and Co., hired by the Admiralty to supply the ships of the Baltic Squadron.

[3]John Washington, F.R.S. (1800–1863). Entered, 1812; Lt, 1821; Cmdr, 1833; Capt., 1842; Rear-Adm., 1862; Deputy Hydrographer, 1853–55; Hydrographer, 1855–62. Washington was dispatched by Sir James Graham in late 1853 to gather information on the state and disposition of the Russian Baltic Fleet and shore defences at Cronstadt, Reval, and Sweaborg.

then you can do as you please. You will remember how much cheaper we got them at Lisbon.

We had another heavy Gale yesterday and *Cressy* parted two cables and went to sea. I dont much like this, and have given an order to Courtenay[1] to use never less than 6 Shackles and[,] if it blows[,] to let go a second anchor before veering. I am nearly complete and shall go to sea the moment the weather settles. I shall send this to a Mr Crozier[,][2] a clerk at Somerset House[,] who will deliver or send it to you. And you had better give me the name and the address of some Admiralty Clerk to whom my letters can be addressed[,] as I believe they are all opened at the various Post Offices said to be in the Pay of Russia . . .

PS You had better give me the names of several Clerks[,] as it will be suspected if large [numbers of] letters are addressed to the same person.

[**305**] *Hastings to Milne*

Ordnance Department
11 April 1854

My dear Milne

Herewith you will receive an official letter from this Board, which will, I hope clear up all doubts about the ball cartridges. Their transmission as they are got ready is most important to the port nearest to the locality where the troops may be [*sic*].

The reason I have asked for the probable time of sailing of the ships you have named, is this. it [*sic*] would enable us to purchase & transmit the ammunition till the last moment [*sic*].

I did not return from Woolwich in time yesterday to write you, but I wish you to understand I have hitherto written privately to you to advise you of army wants. I close now in reference to the ambulances & Hospital Waggons Carts & Medical Stores. There will in all be almost 50 of them & as soon as I can learn what will be about the measurement tonnage, you shall hear privately . . .

The application for tonnage for Coke was made under an impression that it could be obtained from our Contractor, but it appears subsequently he was not bound to deliver at Malta, consequently tenders have been called for. Moreover, the Treasury has not yet determined

[1]This reference is obscure; *Cressy*'s Captain was Richard Laird Warren.

[2]Francis G. Crozier, Third-Class Clerk in the Contingencies and Prize Branch of the Accountant-General's Department.

whether the Coke should be common or oven baked. These difficulties must be expected & all we can do is to strive to work cordially together[.]

[**306**] *Hastings to Milne*

Ordnance Department
11 April [1854]

My dear Milne

Since I wrote to you I have received a note informing us that *Euxine* will sail for Malta & Constantinople on Saturday[.] 15 tons of ball cartridges have been ordered to be sent to Ports[mouth] & 14½ to the *Rajah* at Southampton this day. We have still 50 tons ready &[,] as we hope to make 144,6000 [*sic*] per week, I trust we shall have a portion for all the vessels you have named, *Magaera* & *Simoom* included[.]

[**307**] *Milne to Napier*

Admiralty
13 April 1854

My dear Sir Charles

Thanks for your letter. although [*sic*] you call me a shabby fellow, I sent you everything you asked for[.] what the deuce more do you want[?] as to the Crockery I could not tell what was packed up for you before I received your application. The Telegph I sent to Ports[mouth] was to send you the best of Everything[,] but the Crockery had been previously packed before you left Spithead. Now to business. I am getting uneasy about your Coal, (1) have you enough when we send you 5000 Tons pr Month or will you require more[?] (2) Do you intend to Form [*sic*] a Depot any where [*sic*] on Shore[?] if so we would keep that supplied. I believe Mr Dundas[1] has written to you on these subjects[,] as I had not time to do so.

Now you must keep us informed in due time of your 'wants' in Provisions &c[,] That [*sic*] we make arrangements in time. I have now a Screw Steamer chartered to send out to you when I know your want.

It is a terrible pressure here and I am almost done up. This Troop affair, which is sending out above 25,000 men and 4000 Horses with all the munitions of War and supplying provisions is a large undertaking,

[1]Storekeeper-General Robert Dundas.

and we have never yet carried on a war so far from England. The Horses were to have gone thro France, but this is all changed[.] Luckily we have had fine weather to get thro our work[,] but it is not half over[,] and I do not see my way at all clear to meet the constant requisitions of the Military Departments. The Penmanship of the Comdr in Chief in the Black Sea has always been considered illegible, but It [*sic*] strikes me the Comdr in Chief in the Baltic is going to out do him[.] I hope you will take the hint.

Let me know if I can be of any use to you or send any thing out to you. The Sheerness Tank[1] a better sea Boat than [?*Myrtle*][2] goes out to join you.

Mrs. Milne presented me with a Daughter two evenings ago. She sends her best wishes & all success attend you is the sincere wish of yours very faithfully . . .

[**308**] *Graham to Milne*

Netherby, Private
20 April 1854

My dear Capt Milne

I have appointed Commander Mason[3] according to your desire.

Everything that man can do has been done by you to fit out and dispatch the Transports with the least possible delay. The wonder is, that so much has been done, not that there is some difficulty at the last moment.

Get Lord Cardigan[4] away as soon as you can; he is a most troublesome Customer [*sic*] and I wish him well, as far off as possible.

I wish Admiral Parker[5] would quickly take the vacant Good Service Pension on the Reserved List and voluntarily retire from the Board. It will be painful to me to state to him the necessity of his going.

I shall be at the Board on Monday Morning.

[1]HMS *Hart* or HMS *Hope*.

[2]Tank vessel at Chatham.

[3]George Mason (*c*.1800–1876). Entered, 1813; Lt, 1827; Cmdr, 1853; Capt., 1858; Rear-Adm. (Ret.), 1875. Agent for Transports Afloat, April 1854–February 1855.

[4]James Thomas Brudenel, seventh Earl of Cardigan (1797–1868). Quarrelsome Army officer; Cmdr of the Light Brigade in Maj. Gen. Lord Lucan's cavalry division.

[5]First Naval Lord Adm. Hyde Parker.

[**309**] *Cunard to Milne*

Strictly Private
24 April 1854

Dear Capt Milne

You shall have '*Alps*' instead of '*Balbec*'. She will carry 150 Horses, together with the men and Stores that *Balbec* was to carry[,] and depart at the same time. she [*sic*] will leave Liverpool by the end of next week.

It will be necessary to remove the Saloon from the Deck but all that shall be done within the time. The cost will be trifling[,] it is not [an] expensive fitting.

You shall have *Alps* at the same rate as *Andes*, say £3600 per Month for 4 or 6 months, Govt finding Coal, some short time to be allowed at the end of the term to replace the Saloon &c[,] the cost of which will be trifling.

The *Taurus*, *Tenerife* & *Karnak* are expected at Liverpool about the 1st May, they will each carry 150 Horses. you [*sic*] shall have them all or any of them at £3000 per Month. a [*sic*] Deck must be laid in each of them but we could get the materials ready and a very few days would suffice to send them to sea[.]

Andes[,] *Alps*[,] *Tenerife*[,] *Taurus* & *Karnak* will cost you only three fourths as much as *Golden Fleece*, *Jason*, *Victoria* & others and will do as much work[,] and will be ready for service without being long on pay.

I offered these ships to you formerly but declined pressing them on you lest you should think I was activated solely by interested motives[,] but now that you find *Andes* has taken as many Troops as any of them together with a very large supply of coal[,] I may venture to mention the subject to you in confidence.

[P.S.:] If you entertain this I will make you a formal offer. I'll call on you in a short time

[**310**] *Milne to Newcastle*

Admiralty
27 April 1854

Dear Duke of Newcastle

I send you a precis of the troop service. I do not send the actual return[,] but have brought the whole into one sheet of Paper. If you wish any further explanation I will be ready to attend on you. I have in vain endeavoured to get Steamers for some of the Cavalry Reg[iments] but with the exception of the *Jason* not one has been forthcoming. I asked Mr Cunard if he could send out 300 for me. The enclosed papers[1] will show [*sic*] you the result. 7 ft 4 in only between Deck & Deck, and the H[orse] G[uards] will not be satisfied with less than 8 feet. The Steamer's [*sic*] which we have already in our Service have been entirely engaged with the Infantry and therefore could not be employed on Horse Conveyance at the sametime.

You may be attacked about delay. *Victoria* & *Melbourne* were purposely delayed to carry out stores[,] especially ammunition[.] it would have been culpable to have allowed them to go empty when Ball Cartridge was so much wanted[.]

Our sailing ships have been hasten[ed] in all our power. much [*sic*] has been done[:] no less than about 78 Sailing Transports have been fitted or are fitting since the 15 Feb[.] of these about 50 have sailed, and[,] from the difficulty of getting ships[,] we were obliged to take ships with Cargoes in[,] and there has been a great want of Docks to get the Ship's [*sic*] into. Many of them had to be refitted with Iron Knees & some had to get new masts & large repair. In fact we have drained the Harbours of 1 Class Ships & [have been] obliged to take others.

[**311**] *Milne to Newcastle*

Admiralty
27 April 1854

Abstract of the Accompanying Sheet relative to the Military Service[:]

	Off[icers]	Men	Horses	Waggons
17 Steam vessels have conveyed to Malta between the 23d Feb and 18th April	539	15,625	138	
4 of these vessels have made second trips				
The Staff of Lord Raglan has also been sent out in Steamers	123	478	265	
19 Artillery Transports have sailed from England between the 18th March and 18 April with	43	1090	965	
	and 138 Waggons & Guns			

[1]Not preserved among Milne's letters in the Duke of Newcastle's papers.

6 Transports have received on Board belonging to the 2 Div of Artillery	8	298	295	
	[and] 33 Waggons & Guns			
6 Transports have sailed with the 17th Lancers from Ports[mouth]	8	298	298	
6 Transports have sailed with the 8th Hussars from Plymouth	8	298	298	
6 Transports have sailed with 3 Regts for Gibr	74	2,186	–	
1 Transport with the 14th Reg for Malta	23	747	[–]	
Total Embarked	830	21,119	2259	171

Services in Progress[:]

	Officers	Men	Horses
On the 4th May will sail from Cork for Corfu (Steam)	20	493	2
On the 4th May will sail from Cork for Malta (Steam)	23	637	2
On the 4th May will sail from Ports[mouth] in *Simoom* the 79th Reg	30	936	8
On the 14th May will sail from Ports[mouth] the 42d Reg in the *Hydaspes*[,] now detained by machinery	37	917	12
On the 27 April will sail from Liverpool 6 Transports to embark the 11th Hussars	20	321	300
On or about the 4th May[,] 6 Transports will be at Portsmouth to Embark the 13th Drag[oon] G[uar]ds	20	298	298
6 Transports are almost ready to sail from the Thames for Plymouth to Embark the 6th D[ragoon] G[uards]	20	298	298
6 Ships are also nearly ready at Liverpool to embark the 4th D[ragoon] G[uards] at Dublin	20	298	298
6 Ships are nearly complete at Liverpool to embark the 1st D[ragoon] G[uards]	20	298	298

6 Ships are ordered for survey for the Drag[oon] G[uards] (5th) at Cork[;] it has been attempted to obtain Steamer's [*sic*] for this service but without avail.

On or about the 4th May the *Jason* Steamer will embark Artillery	9	261	231
	and 28 Waggons & Guns		
2 Steamers will embark the Reserve of Artillery including the Battering Train, Heavy Guns &c[.] This about 3 May	17	286	33
	3 Waggons & Guns		
A Transport will embark about 2 May the Spare Horses of Artillery	1	30	48
	6 Waggons & Guns		

When these services are completed the Whole Troop Service will have been executed[.]

3 Steamers and 2 Transports have conveyed from England to the Dardanelles[,] Commissariat Stores[,] about 2300 Tons

Ordnance Stores have also been sent by the Admiralty to the same destination[,] amounting to about 3,100 Tons

92 vessels including steam vessels have been fitted as Transports, at Liverpool & London[,] and to hasten the service private ship building establishments have been employed. The Slings, Hammocks & Halters for Horses and other fittings have been made in H. M. Dock Yards and the Service has been hastened in every way possible and urged forward to meet the requirements of the Public Service and even to do this Ships with Cargoes on board had to be accepted and the requisite number of Ships could not be obtained to meet the requirements of the Public Service. no [*sic*] delay has taken place.

The *Victoria* and *Melbourne* might have embarked the 39th & 35th Regts at an earlier date, but they were purposely detained to convey Stores & Ammunition to the East[.] The *Victoria* took 80 Tons of Ball Cartridge[.]

[**312**] *Cunard to Milne*

Burlington Hotel
1 May 1854

Dear Capt Milne

I am sure you would not think it at all derogatory to your position as a Lord of the Admiralty to request me to go with you, or to be present with you, at any time that you might wish to inspect one of our steamers. I should be able to give you the information you might require and which you could not otherwise obtain correctly.

If Capt Bevis were to consult with Mr McIver in such cases[,] I am sure the service would be beneficial. more [*sic*] than one instance has recently come to my knowledge, in which much inconvenience and annoyance have arisen for want of a little courtesy. Capt Bevis in a note to Mr McIver says it is not necessary that he should consult him at all, whereas in the particular instance to which Capt Bevis alluded[,] he had no right to interfere, the ship was not taken up by [the] Government[:] we had engaged to provide passage for 15 officers. Capt Bevis had no right to fix any precise time that our Steam Tender should take them off. that [*sic*] was our business, not his.

I received a letter on the 28 April from Mr Grant[1] to say that the *British Queen* had been inspected and that there was [*sic*] no provisions or Forage on board. now [*sic*] if Mr McIver had been requested to attend, the requisite information would have been furnished and the necessity of any such report would have been saved. I am not making any complaint against Capt Bevis. you [*sic*] know that I have always spoken of him in the most friendly manner. a [*sic*] kind note from you to him, requesting him to consult with Mr McIver, will do good to the service, and to Capt Bevis also. I shall be very glad to see a good feeling kept between us.

[**313**] *Milne to Napier*

Admiralty
2 May 1854

My dear Sir Charles

I should have written to you before this but I have been laid[,] that is knocked[,] up and confined to Bed for some days, but I am now all

[1]Comptroller of Victualling Thomas Grant.

right again and[,] as you may suppose[,] well employed and more on my hands than I can well get thro. I hope you[r] Coal is in sufficient quantities[.] as to the Smoke it is not to be avoided[:] the demand on the Welch [*sic*] Ports has been so enormous we can scarcely get a Cargo for the Baltic. we [*sic*] have sent 30,000 Tons to the Medn[.] The French have sent out 45,000 and the Egyptian Gov. 28,000[,] all this independent of Steam Companies &c. Let Seymour keep us informed if he wants for more supplies and if he has other demands[.] we see in the papers that a Coal Depot has been formed at Faro [Sound]. if [*sic*] so you must let us know[,] as it may further our arrangements[.] we have entered into a new engagement to allow colliers to go to the Gulf of Bothnia & Finland[,] so I presume bye & bye they will have to go up there to meet you in some harbours on either side of the Gulf[,] where you will no doubt find an Anchorage, and be able to establish a watering place. your small steamers ought to be able to find some place with [a] good anchorage. The *Tyne* sails tomorrow with Provisions[,] also a Chartered Screw Steamer called the *Holyrood*[,] and the *Resistance* will sail with Powder[,] Shot &c[,] also Provisions in about a week. They are ordered to call at Copenhagen for Letters &c[.] we have had a S.W. Gale for some days but it is now clearing which I am glad of[,] as we have many of our Transports to get away[.] 500 Horses have arrived at Malta but we have still a good many to go out. We have reports of the Bombardment of Odessa[,][1] but no particulars[,] altho I have no doubt it is true. Dundas[2] is most infamously abused in the Papers[,] especially the *Morning Advertizer*[,] and the *Morning Herald* has confessed in a leading article the impropriety of attending to correspondents who are biased and abusing officers and have given up the practice[,] so it has reformed.

We are going on here much as usual[.] Hope Johnstone[3] goes to Brazils,[4] Mansel[5] has *Powerful*, *Calcutta* given to James Stopford.[6] Have you tried the Night Coloured Lights which were sent to you[?] Mrs Parker[7] has been very ill but is somewhat better[,] but it is now becoming serious and only a matter of time. You ask the names of the

[1]22 April 1854.

[2]Deans Dundas.

[3]William James Hope Johnstone, K.C.B., G.C.B. (1798–1878). Entered, 1811; Lt, 1818; Cmdr, 1820; Capt., 1823; Rear-Adm., 1853; Vice-Adm., 1858; Adm., 1863.

[4]The South America Station.

[5]George Mansel (*c*.1796–1854). Entered, 1808; Lt, 1821; Cmdr, 1826; Capt., 1840. Appointed to *Powerful*, 1854.

[6]James John Stopford (1817–68). Entered, 1829; Lt, 1837; Cmdr, 1840; Capt., 1841; Rear-Adm., 1861.

[7]Wife of Adm. Sir Hyde Parker.

Clerks[:] address to or put the Letter [*sic*] under cover to Rob Bell Esq[1] or J. H. Houghton[,][2] but if you put a good seal on the letter it will not be opened. Success to you . . .

[**314**] *Cunard to Milne*

Burlington Hotel
4 May 1854

Dear Capt Milne

I have just received a communication from my partner at Liverpool[.]

He says '*Niagara*' can carry two hundred and fifty Horses with safety, and comfortably. I think she can carry a greater number. She is a first class Paddle Wheel Steam ship and will carry Horses with much greater Safety and dispatch than a Screw Steam Ship. *Niagara* has just returned from Constantinople in 12 days after having landed the 88th Regiment.

She could proceed to Quebec, take the Horses on board, and thence to Constantinople direct.

[**315**] *Milne to Graham*

Admiralty
10 May 1854

Dear Sir James

In answer to the Duke of Newcastles note[,] I send a list of Steam Vessels that will remain with the Troops[,] to be employed as the Comdr in Chief and the Naval Officers on the Spot may determine. I also give the number of Sailing Transports to be retained for the Army. I cannot help expressing an opinion that these enquiries may lead to great inconvenience and give information to the enemy that should only be known to those who are carrying on the Public Service.[3]

With reference to the 2d question[,] to lay before the House the details of the expenditure under the head of Freight[;] I do think it

[1]Robert Bell, Second Class Clerk.

[2]J. H. N. Houghton, Senior Clerk.

[3]This letter refers to queries raised in the House of Lords by Lord Ellenborough. The debate on his questions (which were submitted in advance) took place on 10 May 1854. Newcastle followed Milne's line of argument; to answer fully, he asserted 'might be giving a very great advantage to the enemy, while it would have no good effect in this country'. See *Hansard*, 3rd ser., vol. 133 (1854), cols. 128–42.

would be most injudicious to comply with this request. it [*sic*] will lead to all sorts of remarks and suspicions on the part of individual ship owners. it [*sic*] will give rise to unfounded complaints[,] and it will ultimately lead to so many accusations, that I foresee a Committee of Enquiry of the House of Commons. As yet it is impossible for us to give the full particular's [*sic*] of the claims sent in, as Payment of ¾ of the Bills have only been made[,] leaving the other ¼ for enquiry before any final payment is completed. The urgency of the Service has been so great and the means of Transport so limited[,] that it has not been possible to make any previous arrangement as to prices before the Troops [were] embarked[.] we have been obliged to keep a running account with the Steam Companies, and we [are] now endeavouring to come to a close with them. I cannot this evening give the Duke of Newcastle an abstract of the expense &c but I will furnish him with the details tomorrow. It would be a great blessing if Lord Ellenborough had some appointment to keep him from troubling other people.

[**316**] *Milne to Newcastle*

[Admiralty
10 May 1854]

Steam Vessels for Troop Service in the East[:]

Golden Fleece	HMS *Simoom*
Cambria	HMS *Vulcan*
Medway	HMS *Megaera*
Trent	Commissariat Steamers[:]
Victoria	–
Andes	*Sovereign*
Melbourne	*Hope*
Hydaspes	*Albatross*
Tonning	
City of London	
Emperor	
Jason	
Sydney	
Harbinger	

These Steam vessels would be capable of embarking for any emergency 12,000 men . . .

Note[:] the *Emeu* & *Kangaroo* have been discharged, not being very fit.

There are 85 Cavalry Transports and each Transport on an average will carry 150 men in addition to the officers, men & Horses they have conveyed from England.

	Men
Each Ship has carried on an average 50 Men	4,250
150 in each ship in addition	12,750
[Subtotal]	17,000
There are 11 Infantry Transports[,] each of which will carry on an average 500 men	5,500
Total in sailing ships	22,500
on any emergency for a short period of time but take it at 100 men instead of 150[;] it would be[:]	8,500
Each ship had on Board	4,250
11 Infantry Ships	5,500
[Subtotal]	18,250
Steamers	12,000
Provisions for	30,250 men

[**317**] *Milne to Newcastle*

[Admiralty
11 May 1854]

Transports taken up for the Conveyance of Horses for the East[:]

	Men	Horses
19 – Sailing Transports to Convey the 1 Division of the Artillery[,] Horses and Gun Carriages	1087	952
10 – Sailing Transports and 3 – Steam Transports for 2nd Division of Artillery, Battering Train & Guns	1150	735
10 – Sailing Transports for 8th Hussars & 17th Lancers	600	600
18 – Do. for 11th Hussars, 1st & 13th Dragoons	900	900
4 – Steam Transports for Staff of Lord Raglan — Men 350, Horses 136; 6 – Steamers (Mail Packets and Cunards) for remainder of Staff — Men 124, Horses 132	474	268
Services Performed	4211	3455

In Progress[:]

		Men	Horses
15	6 Sailing Transports for 4th Drag[oon] Guards	300	300
	5 Do. for 6th Drag[oon Guards]	300	300
	3 Do. and 1 Steamer (Mail Packet Co.) for 5 Drag[oon Guards]	300	300
[Total]		900	900
85 [Total Ships]			

The 3 latter services are in progress[.] some of the Troops will embark and be despatched in the course of next week, and the *Himalaya*[,] for 5th Dragoons[,] will embark the 22nd inst.

[**318**] *Cunard to Milne*

Burlington Hotel
19 May 1854

Dear Capt Milne

I was very glad to read Sir James Grahams very proper reply in the House last night.[1] You would have very little time to spare for other purposes, if you were bound to give reasons for declining to accept the proposals of every one who may offer a Steam Ship for the Service.

Even if you had accepted the offer for the *Great Britain* your Horses might now be in England, as she broke down a few days after leaving Liverpool and is now under repairs. I enclose you a letter[2] signed by every officer of the 1st Royal to the Commander of the '*Andes*'. This ship landed the Regiment at Gallipoli in 15 days after embarkation. all [*sic*] went well & all [were] perfectly satisfied with the ship and everything on board.

It is a little vexing that such misstatements should find their way into the Public, but it is too bad that Members of both Houses of Parliament should take these statements for fact, when by enquiry at the Admiralty they could get correct information.

Be so good as to return the letter to me. Sir James was not exactly correct in the time occupied. the [*sic*] '*Niagara*' returned from Constantinople to Liverpool in 12 days, '*Andes*' landed her Troops at Gallipoli in 15 days[,] but 18 days may be a fair average.

[1]This had reference to a question put regarding the Admiralty's refusal to charter the *Great Britain*. See ibid., cols. 537–8.

[2]Milne evidently returned this letter to Cunard, as per his request.

[**319**] *Milne to Newcastle*

Admiralty
20 May [1854]

Dear Duke of Newcastle

I did not receive your note until very late last night and was therefore unable to write to you as you wished. I have sent a Telegraph to Southampton to detain the sailing of the *Orinoco*, until after Port Hour tomorrow morning or until the officer in command of the Troops receives a message from you . . .
The officer in command of the *Orinoco* has orders to attend to any Instruction with reference to the Ship's destination, as he may receive from the Officer in Command of the Troops after passing Gibraltar, and having landed the Troops to proceed to Malta and England bringing Home Invalids &c from Gibraltar.

I was informed yesterday by one of the clerks that the destination was Athens[,] and it came from an officer going out in the *Orinoco*. I mention this that you may be aware that these matters are known and do not transpire from this office[.] I was made aware of Gallipoli from the same public source long before anything came from you.

[**320**] *Christie to Milne*

Scutari
24 May 1854

My dear Milne

I hope my returns reach their destination regularly. I shall send one every mail till all the Transports have arrived.

I have got on capitally as yet, and done all with the assistance of one steam tug[,] without which it would have been impossible to have done the Needful [*sic*]. They have raised their price [for the Tug] very much since I arrived here and the time is nearly out. I must have her again, and will make the best bargain I can.

A portion of the Art[i]ll[er]y will move tomorrow or next day. I have made all necessary arrangements, appointed the Steamers & Transports officers & Boats to attend at the embarkation, and shall go up myself to Varna, leaving the Senior Commander [Boxer] here till my return, after that I shall move up & down according to circumstances.

I had anticipated your wishes by supplying each Transport with five weeks Provisions, and they are all pretty well supplied with Water now, altho' I have had great difficulty in getting it. I am in hopes that Admiral Boxer will make better arrangements for getting supplied before he has been here much longer.

I have as hard work as ever I had in my life, but everything goes on cheerily. The Masters of the Transports are generally speaking good, willing men, any disagreements that have been brought before me have arisen generally through the fault of the agents. My plan is to be strict with the Navy, but pamper the Skippers as much as circumstances will allow, and I find it has a good effect.

I have arranged all my Signals and got the Boats fitted with . . . all the necessaries.

The Troop Boats have arrived in Capital time.

I have had more trouble with the *Golden Fleece* than any Steamer in the Fleet, and entirely through the example of the Master[,] who hates the Service he is employed upon, and does nothing without grumbling. Today he told me the crew had no right [*sic*] to go into the Black Sea without extra pay, and that many of them refused to go. I told them that if they refused to go to the Black Sea now and ever showed their faces in England again[,] they would be posted out of the Country, and threatened to turn them all out of the ship and enter a fresh crew. We shall have no more refusals.

All the others are most zealous and anxious to do all in their power for the service.

In hiring Steamers for this Service I would strongly recommend that it should be clearly stipulated that they are to Tow when necessary. Many of them don't like it and some have refused altogether, namely *Golden Fleece Niagara* & *Trent*. Nothing can be done here without towing.

[321] *Milne to Napier*

Admiralty, Private
30 May 1854

My dear Admiral

You will be sorry to hear of the death of Hyde Parker.[1] he [*sic*] was ill for about a week with a cold he caught in his daily journey to and from Ham[,] where his wife was staying on account of her health. This brought on inflammation of the Lungs which very quickly carried him off. there [*sic*] is no doubt he has been breaking [*sic*] for several

[1]26 May 1854.

months[,] but neither he or [*sic*] his friends appear to have been aware of it. we [*sic*] do not know who comes here [in his place].[1] Mrs Parker remains very much in the same state and it is an awful contemplation for the poor family that she also will ere long be taken away from them. we [*sic*] have no news here except the loss of the *Tiger* off Odessa[2] which you must have seen ere this reaches you in the paper's [*sic*]. we [*sic*] only know of the event from the same source. nothing [*sic*] more has been done in the Black Sea since the attack on Odessa, but a Squadron has gone to the Gulf of Circassia[,] probably to destroy the Forts. In this part of the world we are quiet enough, but reports are reaching this country that Silistria has fallen and that the Russian Forces are within 35 miles of Varna.[3] This however requires confirmation. Our Troops, I believe have gone to Varna, and some of the French to Adrianople. I believe one of our Regts has also gone to Greece. I am glad you have got well supplied with Provisions & Stores. *Tyne* and *Resistance* will have joined you ere this, and we only want your demands to send out further supplies, which we will keep up as well as we can. The Coal is now all chartered to go into the Gulphs [*sic*] of Finland and Bothnia and you must therefore order it from Faro[,] where the colliers are all ordered to call [at] your place of Rendezvous. I was in hopes you would have been enabled to secure some safe anchorage up the Gulf [*sic*] of Finland where you could have security and at the sametime [*sic*] be ready for any emergency, but you have more information on these points than I have. The *Holyrood* will return to you in a few days and will[,] I hope[,] take your private supplies[.] I have ordered your wine from Willis to go in her and Chambers at Common Hard to send any moderate quantity of supplies for the Fleet. I am amused and yet vexed about that stupid fellow Ryder. he [*sic*] is certainly no sailor, and I have no doubt there exists a good deal of trial of your patience [*sic*]. with [*sic*] reference to ships keeping station, I think there often exists a good deal of fault in the Flag Ship, more especially when that ship sails well, by keeping <u>too close</u> to the wind; if a Symondite or a ship rigged as a Symondite, and the braces of her yards sharp up. none [*sic*] of the old class [of] ship can hold the same wind. they [*sic*] accordingly chop to leeward and fall out of their stations from no fault of the officers. It is therefore absolutely necessary that the order in the Signal Book for the leading ships to steer 6 points from the

[1]On 1 June, Maurice Berkeley was elevated to First Naval Lord, Saunders Dundas to Second Naval Lord, and Peter Richards appointed Third Naval Lord.

[2]*Tiger* grounded under the batteries at Odessa and was destroyed by Russian gunfire on 12 May 1854.

[3]These reports were erroneous.

wind should be attended to, but I know it is not generally the case[,] and whenever there is a departure from the above rule, it is sure to lead to bad stations.

Excuse the Digression[.]

We have been favored by several rumours from Copenhagen of your having destroyed the Forts at Hango and again repeated last evening [*sic*].[1] 'Secret[:]' it is reported that at Odessa a good many of Moorsom's shells fired from our ships were found without having exploded, there being no powder in them[,] and it is suggested that they were supplied in that state from [the] B[oard] of O[rdnance]. 'This must not be made known,' but in the supply noted [*sic*] to your ships, they may have been supplied Half Filled & Half Empty shells. if [*sic*] so it should be rectified in time.

Wm Gordon[2] goes as Admiral to Sheerness to relieve Adl Percy[3] at the expiration of his time. no [*sic*] other changes that I know of. Talbot[4] is arrived from the Cape and has been transferred to the *Algiers*. Cap Baillie[5] has been appt to the *Marauder*.

We had letters from Dundas yesterday, but nothing new. he [*sic*] gets well on with his French Colleague. it [*sic*] is a difficult duty to perform and you will have it on your hands, but civility and attention will go a great way to soothe any difficulties which may arise.

You must have had severe weather and been most uncomfortable with those confounded fogs, but I really believe the best way is to have the Stream anchor always ready, and when in doubt to down Anchor[.] you will probably have to do this when you get into the Gulf of Finland. we [*sic*] are looking for your sending a Steamer home once a Fortnight. I presume you will immediately do this. Good bye all success attend you and yours, in which my wife joins[.] she is very well and just returned from a recruit [*sic*] of her Health at Brighton. I will write to Seymour. . . .

[P.S.:] Your face is hung up in every shop from 10/– to 1/6 each, but I must say I cannot say much for their beauty or their likeness.

[1]These reports were incorrect; several Russian vessels were seized off Hango on 26 May, but no bombardment took place. See Clowes, *The Royal Navy*, vol. 6, p. 480.

[2]William Gordon (1785–1858). Entered, 1797; Lt, 1804; Cmdr, 1807; Capt., 1810; Rear-Adm., 1841; Vice-Adm., 1854; Naval Lord of the Admiralty, 1841–46.

[3]Josceline Percy, C.B. (1784–1856). Entered, 1797; Lt, 1805; Cmdr, 1806; Capt., 1806; Rear-Adm., 1841; M.P., 1806–20. Percy was C-in-C at the Nore, 1851–54.

[4]Charles Talbot, K.C.B. (*c*.1802–76). Entered, 1815; Lt, 1823, Cmdr, 1827; Capt., 1830; Rear-Adm., 1855; Vice-Adm., 1862; Adm., 1866.

[5]Thomas Baillie (1811–89). Entered, 1827; Lt, 1837; Cmdr, 1841; Capt., 1845; Rear-Adm., 1863; Vice-Adm., 1870; Adm. (Ret.), 1877.

[**322**] *Graham to Milne*

Netherby
[*c*.1] June 1854

My dear Capt Milne

I return Capt Christie's letter, which is on the whole very satisfactory.

The loss of the *Tiger* has evidently been the result of want of ordinary caution. Poor Giffard[1] has paid, however, a heavy Penalty; and the example will be a salutary warning.

I will give you a Somerset House Midshipman's Place, when there is a Vacancy. I have had but one and I gave it to Sir B. Walker.

[**323**] *Milne Draft Board Minute to Newcastle*

Admiralty
5 June 1854

Inform the Duke of Newcastle that my Lords herewith transmit a general List of all vessels which have been chartered by the Admiralty for periods of 4 or 6 months, for the purpose of conveying Troops to the East and for the special service of the Army under the Command of Lord Raglan.

Their Lordships submit this return for the consideration of his Grace[,] with the view of them being informed whether[,] in his opinion[,] it is necessary that the whole of these vessels should be retained in the service of the Government[,] or whether a portion of them might not be paid off at the expiration of the period of their charter or when no longer required for military purposes[.] on this point their Lordships are unable to form an opinion[,] on being unaware of the movements of the Military Force under Lord Raglans command[,] or what number of ships he may deem it necessary to retain for that purpose. They would[,] however[,] instruct for the consideration of his Grace[,] whether it might not be expedient to send this return to Lord Raglan and Rear Ad Boxer for their consideration, with instructions to send to Malta, Gibraltar & England to bring home old & unusable Stores in those vessels which are not absolutely required for military operations, and whose time of charter may have expired[,] and thereby reduce the heavy expense which would otherwise be incurred. If His Grace should enter-

[1]Henry Wells Giffard (*c*.1812–54). Entered, 1824; Lt, 1831; Cmdr, 1838; Capt., 1841. Giffard commanded HMS *Tiger*.

tain the proposal[,] Their Lordships would furnish R.A. Boxer with a return of the Names [*sic*] of those ships which are the most expensive and which it would be expedient to discharge at as early a date as possible.

Abstract now enclosed[1]

Sailing Ships Chartered for the Conveyance of Troops[:]	
Infantry	11 Ships
Artillery	19 "
Artillery	10 [*sic*]
1st Dragoons	6
4th Dragoon	6
6th Dragoons	5
13th Dragoons	6
8th Hussars	5
11th Hussars	6
17th Hussars	5
[Subtotal]	79
Store Ships &c	4
[Total]	83

Steam Vessels chartered for service of Troops in the East[:]	
Commissariat Dept	4 in Number
Staff	3
Battering Train	2
Ambulance Corps	1
To Bring Horses from Tunis &c	1
General Service	10
[Subtotal]	21
1 on Trip [*sic*]	1
[Total]	22

[**324**] *Hastings to Milne*

Ordnance Department
5 June 1854

My dear Milne

I have just received a communication from Colonel Mundy[,] informing me that the Duke of Newcastle wishes that a Company of Artillery should be sent out in the *Taurus* & *Cormorant* with the guns

[1]The detailed list to which Milne referred is missing from this draft.

of position[,] 2 pr batteries[,] & other stores[,] & to be attached to the army under the Command of Lord Raglan.

Information has been sent to Portsmouth to this effect, & I take the earliest opportunity of advising you of the wishes of the Duke of Newcastle on this point.

Colonel Mundy adds 'the guns of position will have to ship at Gallipoli[,] there to await the orders of Lord Raglan. they [*sic*] ought not therefore to be disembarked there, until orders have been secured by the Senior officer at Gallipoli'[.]

[**325**] *Hastings to Milne*

Ordnance Department
5 June 1854

Dear Milne

When will you be at leisure to see me[?]

There is a further demand from the Colonial Office to send out 30 or 34 Ar[tiller]y Horses. I wish to shew you the letter received.

[**326**] *Graham to Milne*

Netherby, Private
6 June 1854

My dear Capt Milne

I return Admiral Price's[1] letter. They will be pretty close on the Traces of *Aurora*, and I have hopes, that they may succeed in capturing her.[2]

The 10th Hussars from India will be a valuable reinforcement to our Cavalry in the East, and every effort should be made to bring them into the Field with the least possible delay. The E. India Company ought to bring them to Suez: you can make arrangements to have Horse Transports ready to receive them at Alexandria. I conclude that Horses can be disembarked at Suez and Shipped at Alexandria: but this point should be made quite certain.

[1]David Price (1790–1854). Entered, 1801; Lt, 1809; Cmdr, 1813; Capt., 1815; Rear-Adm., 1850. C-in-C of the Pacific Station. The letter is not among Milne's papers.

[2]This refers to a Russian cruiser operating in the Pacific. Graham was wrong; Price's squadron cornered two Russian frigates at Petropavlovsk-Kamchatka, in late August, but Price killed himself (30 August) before a planned assault commenced. That assault was repulsed the day after his death.

Pray and be Patient [*sic*] and bring Capt Richards[1] into Harness without delay. I am anxious to relieve you of a portion of the heavy duties, which you have discharged in so exemplary a manner . . .

[**327**] *Milne to Boxer*

Admiralty, Confidential
8 June 1854

Write to Rear Ad Boxer at Constantinople and inform him that it becomes necessary to send from England to you[,] [for] the Army in the East[,] 3700 Infantry, and 250 Horses. for [*sic*] this service the only available steamers in this Country are the *Kangaroo*, *Tonning*, & *Vulcan*, capable of carrying about 2300 Men[,] and as it is inexpedient to charter more steamers if it can be possibly avoided, he may sent [*sic*] to England one or more of the Chartered Steamers now at Constantinople[,] capable of Carrying about 1500 men and 250 Horses, provided he is perfectly satisfied in his own mind that these vessels can be spared from the Service in the East[,] and will not be required by Lord Raglan for any military purpose[.] The *Jason* would convey the Horses and the *Victoria* and *Medway* or *Cambria* about 1500 men, but my Lords will not bind him down by any specific order[,] but leave it to him to send such vessels as can be spared, and whatever course he determines to adopt[,] he is to request the Ambassador at Constantinople to Forward a Telegraph without delay to the F[oreign] Office in London[,] that their Lordships may be aware of the steps he has adopted[,] bearing in mind these vessels will again be at Constantinople by the 1 of August.
The *Himalaya* is not to be considered as a chartered vessel as [she] is merely employed for the voyage to Constantinople and then to return at once to England[,] but may bring home Invalids, Stores &c[.]

[**328**] *Mundy to Milne*

War Office, Confidential
8 June 1854

Sir,

Having laid before the Duke of Newcastle your letter of the 5th instant and its enclosure, I am directed to request you will state to the Lords Commissioners of the Admiralty that His Grace approves their

[1]Peter Richards, the Third Naval Lord.

Lordships proposal that such Vessels as are not absolutely required for military purposes, and whose time of Charter may have expired, shall be sent to Gibraltar and Malta, for the purpose of bringing home unserviceable stores. I am accordingly to request you will move the Lords Commissioners to furnish Admiral Boxer with the Return proposed in your letter and that you will at the same time suggest to their Lordships that advantage might be taken of the opportunity of sending away these ships to bring home in them such invalided, weakly or wounded men of the Army or Navy as the Medical Officers might desire to send home.

His Grace has, on his part, instructed Lord Raglan to do all in his power to carry out the views of the Lords Commissioners, as conveyed in your letter.

[**329**] *Christie to Milne*

Scutari
10 June 1854

My dear Milne

Himalaya has just arrived with the 5th Dragoon Guards on board, after 13 days run. Out of 318 Horses she has lost only two, and one of them was shot. They are all to be landed here, and I shall send her alongside the Wharf where the *Jason* landed hers[,] as soon as it moderates. at [*sic*] present it blows too fresh.

I have sent a full account of the Transports, their distribution &c to the Admiralty, also one to each of the Admirals. I am keeping all the Transports complete with five weeks Provisions and they are all ready for immediate service.

I have a great deal of hard work, and since Admiral Boxer came here it has been considerably increased, as much of my time is taken up communicating to him all that is going on. This he obliges me to do[,] altho' living miles off on the opposite side of the water, and it causes considerable delay & hindrance to the Service, however I shall endeavour to carry on as well as I can. It also adds considerably to the labours of my Secretary.[1]

I am much indebted to Admiral Stewart who has allowed me to keep Lieut. Rundle of the *Ceylon* for a time. He has been of great use in assisting me in arranging the Signals &c.

[1]Charles D. Pritchard (1822–90). Passed Clerk, 1843; Paymaster, 1850; Paymaster-in-Chief (Ret.), 1882.

It will surely not be necessary to keep so many ships after the next Division of the Army is landed at Varna. I shall send you a list, at all events afterwards, for your consideration.

[330] *Milne to Napier*

Admiralty
20 June 1854

My dear Sir Charles

Thanks for your note of the 12th which I received yesterday.[1] I am glad to find you have better weather, and that your wants have been met. I am anxiously looking for your Demands [*sic*] which have never reached this. it [*sic*] would be as well if you would let us have them at least once a month[,] so as to collect the Stores &c together. Your Fleet[,] as well as Dundas's[,] and the Army[,] is a heavy drain on us, and requires us to look well ahead. but [*sic*] your supplies will be sent to you as soon as possible.

It would not have answered to have one or two colliers (Steam) running with Coal. it [*sic*] would not have met your wants[,] and the only safe mode was to have a good supply at Faro and for you to order the colliers whenever you might consider necessary. There is now 8,000 Tons at Faro. we [*sic*] do not know what your ships will consume, and we are therefore obliged to make our own rough estimate here, and we get no estimate from your Fleet of your probable wants. we [*sic*] are therefore obliged to keep the collier going to prevent any disappointment to you. we [*sic*] have heard nothing of *Tyne* or *Resistance*, or *Dauntless*. we [*sic*] authorized the Hire of a Steamer for two or three months to carry you Bullocks from the Agents whenever they may be enabled to get them, so I hope you will be better supplied. The Anchors will be sent out by the first ship. we [*sic*] have nothing new here. The *Colossus* is commissioned by Robinson,[2] *Termagant* by Keith Stewart[.] we are sending out 4000 more Troops to the East and probably 600 more Cavalry[.] it is a very heavy business sending them so far and [being] obliged to send out their Forage (Hay & Oats) for all the Horses[,] there now [*sic*] above 5000[,] as it is not to be obtained in the country. The Expense is awful as there are no return Freights from Constantinople[,] and we are

[1]Not preserved among Milne's papers.

[2]Sir Robert Spencer Robinson, K.C.B. (1809–89). Entered, 1821; Lt, 1830; Cmdr, 1838; Capt., 1840; Rear-Adm., 1860; Vice-Adm., 1866; Adm. (Ret.), 1871; Controller of the Navy, 1861–68; Third Lord and Controller, 1868–71.

obliged to pay for out and Home. I have upwards to 110 sail of vessels as Transports and all on my shoulders besides my other duties. We have only had one casualty viz. the burning of the *Europa*[1] at Sea and loss of Col. Willoughby Moore and 17 men of the 6 Dragoons[,] also 57 Horses. everything [*sic*] else has gone smooth and the loss of Horses not 4 pr cent, those principally [belonging to] the officers, from overfeeding and not [being] fit to be embarked.

We have reports of the retreat of the Russians beyond the Pruth but this requires confirmation, but it strikes me as not at all unlikely, our Troops now being in position between Shumla & Varna[,] The [*sic*] French also at the latter place[,] and this reinforcement to the Turkish Army, will check any advance of the Russians. if [*sic*] they cannot advance what can they do? but [*sic*] either to remain where they are, or retreat. a [*sic*] few days will probably bring us some information. Dundas often writes and says he hopes Napier will be able to do more than I [*sic*] can do in the Black Sea. I[n] fact there is little to be done there except the attack of Anapa[,] which I presume will be done[:] it is the great strong hold on the Circassian Coast.

I have no news in London[:] all is quiet. Gov't [has] been beat several times in the H[ouse] of Commons and certainly very weak there. I believe if there was to be any more outvoting it would lead to a dissolution. Good bye[.] my wife sends her kind regards and best wishes . . .

[P.S.:] As there must be coal at Copenhagen for the ships going backward & forward[,] we are going to keep up a supply of 500 Tons there[.] I think this is necessary.

We should know if the French ships are to have Provisions sent from France[.] we know nothing about supplying them except coal.

[**331**] *Christie to Milne*

Orient, Scutari
20 June 1854

My dear Milne

I am happy to inform you that the whole of the Troops that have entered the Dardanelles will be landed at Varna by the end of this week except [those of] the Depot. The last of the 3d Division will leave Gallipoli on Friday.

[1]The *Europa* burnt at sea en route to Gibraltar on 31 May. The official account of her destruction is found in *The Times* (London), 17 June, p. 9.

I now enclose you a list of ships that may at once be got rid of[,] I think, and I hope you will let me know how they are to be disposed of.[1] Those that are to be kept Admiral Dundas has recommended me to moor in a Bay at the upper end of the Bosphorus. I don't think I can do far wrong in starting a dozen of the worst at once for Malta.

Admiral Boxer has requested that he may have three, the *Bombay* as a [?River] ship, *Canterbury* as a Store ship and the *Gometza* as a scout vessel. He also wishes to have the *Harbinger* as a Passage or Packet vessel to the Black Sea; but this I think a most unnecessary expense when there are two already[,] the *Caradoc & Banshee*, however you will decide on the whole. The Commissariat have also requested to have one, and I have let them have *Sir Geo Pollock* for the present.

Where there are so many vessels together[,] of course[,] there will be some troublesome characters. the [*sic*] punishments allowed by the Law Books are not severe enough to maintain the least discipline. I hope therefore you will take this matter into consideration and ascertain from the Law officers how far I can go. I may possibly have no course [*sic*] to go to, and the trifling fine of a few shillings they care little about.

The [mail] Steamers time is up so I must conclude in haste.

[**332**] *Liddell*[2] *to Milne*

Bodmin
26 June 1854

My dear Sir

Remembering your great kindness to me whilst under your command, and also the warm interest which you have always taken in everything connected with the Naval Service, I am sure you will be gratified to learn that I came out at the head of the batch at the Royal Naval College last week, and have been accordingly recommended for my Lieutenant's commission[.]

Another of your youngsters in the '*St Vincent*', 'Phillimore'[3] and [*sic*] who was also formerly a Naval School boy with me[,] came out

[1]Not preserved among Milne's papers.

[2]William Henry Liddell (*c.*1833–80). Entered, 1846; Lt, 1854; Cmdr, 1863; Capt., 1871.

[3]Henry Bouchier Phillimore, C.B. (d. 1893). Lt, 1854; Cmdr, 1863; Capt., 1864; Rear-Adm., 1880; Vice-Adm. (Ret.), 1887; Adm. (Ret.), 1892.

second in the examination and was highly complimented by Professor Main.[1]

Apologies for taking up a moment of your valuable time.

[**333**] *Milne to Grant*

Admiralty
1 July 1854

Write the P&O Company and inform that H M Government are most anxious to forward to the East another Cavalry Regt in the *Simla*, and with that view request the Company will take steps for putting up the requisite fittings in that ship for 300 Horses[.] Their Lordships have to inform the Co. that the Regt for *Himalaya* will embark at Plymouth[,] and the one in *Simla* at Liverpool and they will be ready in about 10 days[.]

[**334**] *Milne to Berkeley*

Admiralty
1 July 1854

Dear Berkeley

I received your Telegraph this afternoon[.] We all think (Baldwin Walker included) that you overestimate the number of Persons the *St Vincent* will carry.[2] it [*sic*] will not do to have any overcrowding[;] it will cause discontent and sickness in this hot weather. We estimated at the Board that *St* V[*incent*] and *R*[*oyal*] *William* would carry 850 each[,] *Hannibal* and *Algiers* 650 (say 950 and 650)[,] but this we can arrange before the day of Embarkation. I have chartered 2 vessels of 1300 tons and will charter one or two more if possible[,] and they will be fitted with all haste. I hope I have secured the *Prince*[,] the large steamer[:] she will take 1500.

[1]Thomas John Main (1818–85). Professor of Mathematics at the Royal Naval College, Portsmouth, 1851–85.

[2]*St Vincent* was being readied to transport French troops to the Baltic. See below, [**341**, **343**].

[**335**] *Milne to Berkeley*

Admiralty
2 July 1854

Dear Berkeley

There is nothing new in the office but I write a line to say there is a doubt about the French Troops Embarking in the Downs and[,] as application has been made[,] I believe[,] from Cherbourgh [*sic*]. Boulogne is a dry harbour and to Embark 6000 troops there with Baggage will be difficult, so hold on with your orders.

[**336**] *Milne to Christie*

Admiralty, Private
2 July 1854

My dear Christie

Thanks for your letter received by yesterdays Post. I will immediately attend to the question respecting the punishment of Transports Crews. We have no power of Martial Law. I took the opinion of the Solicitor on this some weeks ago. It is very satisfactory to find everything has been so well done in your Department[,] and that all the operations have been attended with so much success. Ad[miral] Boxer does you full credit in a Public letter and says you have been most indefatigable. I had a letter from him yesterday in regard to paying off Transports, but the public letters which have gone out will of course give him full power to deal with the whole question. of [*sic*] course a good deal depends on the intended operations of the Army. This is only known to Lord Raglan and he must decide what he can spare and what he cannot. I may however now mention, that 2 Cavalry Reg[imen]ts are about to embark, one in the *Himalaya* and the other in *Simla*[,] also 6 Infantry Reg[imen]ts . . . [in addition to] the 3,700 men who are going out[,] to be an increase to the present Reg[imen]t[s], 1500 of whom have already gone in *Tonning*[,] *Vulcan* and *Kangaroo*. We are most anxious to hear if *Jason* and 2 other steamers are coming to England[.] if not[,] we will have no means of sending out the Troops, as the only Vessel we can as yet get is *Orinoco* except those above mentioned[.] It is therefore very difficult to see our way in forwarding these add[itiona]l Troops. There is also another Battering Train ready to embark and we have advertised for two steamers to take it out, Tenders [*sic*] to be received on Wednesday next. I almost doubt our being able to secure

Vessels. besides [*sic*] all this movement for [the] Black Sea[,] we have 6000 French Troops to send to the Baltic, for this we have to Employ [*sic*] *St. Vincent*, *R*[*oyal*] *William*, *Hannibal*, *Algiers*[,] some Transports and the *Prince*, sister vessel to *Jason*. All this move[ment] is to be done by [July] 14, but it is hardly possible[.] I have enough on my hands and have been laid up for a few days with downright worry. This further move[ment] of Troops may effect the Discharge of Transports. Lord Raglan is no doubt aware of the intentions as to future operations. I will add a line tomorrow if anything new . . .

[**337**] *Milne to Grant*

Admiralty, Private
2 July 1854

Dear Mr. Grant

I am getting somewhat anxious in regard to our Provisions[,] especially of Salt Meat. The 6000 French Troops to be sent to the Baltic will most probably come upon our supplies. They have 70,000 men in the Black Sea[,] and it is by no means unlikely that if any special conjoint operation goes on that we may be compelled to aid in their daily support[,] and to a considerable extent. It is a contingency we must not entirely overlook. Such being the case[,] you must look to your store of Salt Meat, and I should wish to know what number of months supply you have for our own Force (Naval)[,] including what is now in the Baltic Fleet, and in the Medn and Black Sea. Secondly, what have we for the Army in the East[?] This force will now be increased by 11,000 men[.] Since Commissary Filder's[1] last letter as [of] when he wrote[,] he was not aware of this additional force being sent from England[.] This whole subject is one of much anxiety and it is absolutely necessary to look at it at once, so that if it is necessary, we may make any necessary purchases in our markets before they are swept by the Agents of France. You must also look to other supplies and on no account to allow the Store to get low[.] There will be a heavy Demand on us and the success of our Arms may depend on the arrangements we make. I will be obliged if you will at once look to this, there is no time to be lost . . .

[P.S.:] You must hasten out the Bread to Malta[.]

[1]William Filder (b. 1788); Commissary-General of the Army in the East and one of those most responsible for that force's poor physical condition in late 1854 and early 1855.

[**338**] *Milne to Eden*[1]

Admiralty, Private
3 July 1854

My dear Eden

Thanks for your Letter received on Sat[urda]y last[2] for which I am much obliged. I have often threatened you with a line but I have really had so much on my hands I have little time to attend to my friends in the Black Sea. I have a letter now and then from Dacres[,] but I am afraid he thinks me a shabby fellow that I do not write to him oftener than I do[.] however[,] there is no help for it. War time has brought a heap of work on us and it is no idle time. I thought I had enough on my hands in peace time, it is now become somewhat more anxious and important. I am flattered at your remark about Transports. it [*sic*] has been a heavy and an anxious business. The pressure here was so great[,] and I was thought a Slow Coach because the Horses were not sent sooner [but] it was not to be done[.] we did more than has ever been done before, and I flatter myself there was no delay, but a lot of yelping cur's [*sic*] in the Club [i.e., Parliament] who have no knowledge of the business and [who are] not blessed with much Brains thought they could have done it better, but no more of this part of the show, except to say 2 more Cavalry Regts are going out at once in *Himalaya* & *Simla* and 6 Regts of Infantry, but how they are to go I am blessed if I know[,] for we have got all the steamers in England and there are now none to be got. I have also another Battering Train to ship in 2 Steamers this week but I have none and [am] very doubtful whether I can get any, but we have advertized in the various Ports in England.

There is no naval news. We are run dry in men & officers. downright [*sic*] low water spring tides, so if the war goes on I dont [*sic*] know what we will do. I have had a Screw Steam Transport [*Industry*] ready the last 3 weeks & cannot enter a man. This is sad work[,] when a Vessel of that sort is so much wanted in [the] Black Sea.

The Poor Old Admiral[3] went off very suddenly but we saw much change on [*sic*] him for some months previous to his death. he [*sic*] was [a] worthy[,] good man. how [*sic*] little did we expect he would [not] have survived Mrs. Parker. The poor soul is better again[,] and when

[1]Charles Eden C.B., K.C.B. (1808–78). Entered, *c.*1820; Lt, 1832; Cmdr, 1834; Capt. 1841; Rear-Adm., 1861; Vice-Adm., 1866; Adm. (Ret.), 1873; Naval Lord of the Admiralty, 1859–66. Eden commanded HMS *London* in the Black Sea.

[2]Not preserved among Milne's papers.

[3]Hyde Parker.

free from pain[,] is in good spirits[,] but of course you hear from a better source[.] Berkeley is very well[,] better than I have seen him for years[,] and is going steadily in his business. Richard[s] is hardly in place[.] I have no doubt he will work well[,] but these constant changes are very mischief [*sic*][.] after having had my fingers in so many of the Admiraltys pies during [the last] 6 years and more, I now find as I give them up to new hands, there is a deal of bother[,] and new hands think this is wrong & that is wrong &c &c &c[,] and[,] as to fighting every objection[,] it is impossible as the Junior of [*sic*] the Board[,] where I appear to [be] stuck. Sir J. Graham behaved very handsomely about it[,] but I could not expect he was to accept junior to suit my Book . . .

My wife is very well[,] also her 3 Chicks . . . depend on it you have some tough work before you. Kind regards to Dacres[,] Lushington[1] and other friends.

[**339**] *Milne to Boxer*

Admiralty, Private
3 July 1854

My dear Admiral

I am much obliged to you for your letter which I received on Saturday[2] and I read it to Sir James Graham. I wrote you sometime 10 days ago on the subject of the Transports[,] and you would likewise [have] receive[d] a Public Letter with ours to the Duke of Newcastle[,] and his reply. Not one ship more than was absolutely required has been taken up[,] but having now concentrated the Army at Varna, what is to be done[?] First[:] have means to move the Force wherever it may be wanted[.] Secondly[:] to not keep more ships than will be required for that service. I must now tell you that 2 more Cavalry Regts are about to embark in *Himalaya* and *Simla*, besides 6 Regt of Infantry and store[s,] in addition to the 3700 men going out to augment the present Regiment[s,] part of which have gone in *Tonning*, *Vulcan* and *Kangaroo*, but how I am to get out the others I really do not know[,] as the only ship I can get is the *Orinoco*, for one Reg. how [*sic*] the 5 others are to go I know not. there [*sic*] is hardly one steamer in England, so I am in a fix[,] but we have advertized for Tenders on Wednesday[.] The French are purchasing provisions in in [*sic*] London & Liverpool and

[1]Sir Stephen Lushington, K.C.B., G.C.B. (1803–1879). Entered, 1816; Lt., 1824; Cmdr., 1828; Capt., 1829; Rear-Adm., 1855; Vice-Adm. (Ret.), 1865.

[2]Not preserved among Milne's papers.

sending [them] out in steamers to Varna. I hope Dundas will use as much Fresh Beef as he can get to save our Store of Salt Meat. this [*sic*] was so unexpectedly got up [it] is a very heavy pull on our stores, more especially when the Army is added to the consumers and they must now depend on our store. Bread we are sending out as fast as we can in sailing vessels[,] as we cannot get steam. There is nothing new here[.] we are about to send 6000 French Troops to the Baltic in 4 Sail of the Line[,] some Transports and Steamers. This is something quite new. we [*sic*] are badly off for men and really [there are] none to be procured[.] we are come to a stand still, which is vexatious[,] and I cannot get the *Industry* Screw Steam Transport manned.
We are all very well here.

[**340**] *Christie to Milne*

Orient, Beicos Bay
4 July 1854

My dear Milne

I arrived in the Bosphorus from Varna the day before yesterday and found the *Cormorant* hard & fast on the Englishmans Shoal. I immediately tried her with two Hawsers from the *Emperor* but both went. I then reached close to her and sent Comdr Franklin[1] with all the long boats to get the Chain Cables and Shot out, and to start her water. When this was done we tried her with four Hawsers and brought her off. She is apparently none the worse for it and after getting her Shot and Cables in again[,] I sent her on to Varna.

Lord Raglan has now given his consent to discharge the vessels of which I sent you a list, and I am now getting everything out of them, and expect to start most of them tomorrow. The remaining ships are all in good order and ready for Service with plenty of Provisions & Water. I shall take some of the Horse fittings out of the returning ships[,] as I find some of the roomy ones can carry many more Horses than they brought out, and it is astonishing how the Horses in the Army accumulate.

Lord Raglan tells me he will require to be in readiness[,] Transport for the Head Quarters staff and two Divisional Staffs[,] together with two divisions of the Army with Cavalry & Artillery. now [*sic*] according to my calculations this will require all our steamers, and from 36 to 40

[1]Edward Franklin (*c*.1798–1875). Entered, 1810; Lt, 1825; Cmdr, 1846; Capt., 1857; Rear-Adm. (Ret.), 1875.

Sailing vessels. *Jason Medway* and *Golden Fleece* having gone to England, I ran down to Admiral Dundas from Varna and asked him if he could afford [to spare] two or three war steamers in the event of their being required for the Army[,] and he said he would [*sic*]. I shall have the sailing vessels all ready here, and I have written to Adml Boxer to request he will Coal & Water the steamers, and allow them to proceed to this Anchorage, so that everything may be in readiness at shortest notice.

I have a serious complaint to make against the Master of the *Hydaspes* for deserting two Transports which I had given him charge of[,] with positive orders to tow to Varna, also for leaving a Horse Boat adrift in the Sea of Marmora which Admiral Stewart had ordered him to tow to Scutari. Through his neglect I consider the Nation has been put to the expense of at least four or five hundred pounds in Coals &c[,] besides losing the Services of two steamers for two days. I shall send a full statement of the matter and hope he will not be allowed to escape altogether.

Most of the steamers have behaved well, but I wish to bring to your notice particularly Mr Cape of the *Emperor* and Mr Carziel of the *City of London*; these two men have at all times shown the greatest zeal and activity, and I feel much indebted to them for the vast deal of service they have done in towing &c, and if any little mark of approbation is ever awarded for such service, they are well worthy of it, and it would have its effect.

I have stationed a Commander at Scutari, and one at Varna. The Transports here I have placed in two Divisions, a Commander to each.

The <u>Home</u> Division I have given to Comdr Baynton,[1] who has been very ill[,] poor man. Lieutenants James[2] and Ballard[3] I have thought it necessary to send with these ships[,] also to endeavour to prevent anything like delay on their passage.

The *Trent* has just landed 302 Horses at Varna[,] brought from the neighbourhood of Alexandretta, and Lord Raglan has requested that she may be kept here for the present.

We are very well off for Horse Boats at Varna now. I sent one of the heavy Pontoon Boats received from Malta up there, the other I have moored in this Bay.

[1]Benjamin Baynton (*c.*1789–1854). Entered, 1801; Lt, 1810; Cmdr, 1841. Baynton had served as an Agent of Transports during the 1827 Portugal expedition, and was lost during the gale of 14 November 1854.

[2]Thomas James (*c.*1800–1857). Entered, 1812; Lt, 1821; discharged at his own request following complaints of disobedience from Houston Stewart.

[3]James Boucher Ballard (*c.*1819–1906). Entered, 1831; Lt, 1843; Cmdr, 1856; Cmdr (Ret.), 1860; Capt. (Ret.), 1870.

I have ordered each Transport to keep six weeks Forage on board, and we have a considerable Quantity of Hay & Oats besides. no [*sic*] doubt the Commissariat will be crying out for it before long.

The Russians are in strong force opposite Silistria, and don't seem inclined to retire further at present. I hope the Army will soon bring them to the scratch [*sic*] . . .

P.S. I enclose a Form[1] containing the list of vessels I consider necessary to embark two Divisions with the Staff &c.

[**341**] *Milne to Michael Seymour*

Admiralty
4 July 1854

My dear Seymour

I send you a few lines by this mail[,] which leaves tonight[,] to say what is going on which may be of interest to yourself as well as that of the Admiral[,] to whom I may not have time to write.

We are sending out Provisions in *Tyne*[,] *Holyrood*[,] and also in a hired vessel[.] you must get your provisions when we can spare them[,] and it is better you should have your wants supplied as soon as we can. There is also a private Venture going out to the Fleet and they have asked for 200 Tons of Stores to fill up their vessel[,] which we have consented to give to help them out for the aid of the Officers. Now I believe we will meet all your wants. I have now to tell you that 6000 French Troops are coming out to you for disposal in the French and our ships. They will be taken to the Baltic in *St Vincent*[,] *R*[*oyal*] *William*[,] *Hannibal*[,] *Algiers*, 3 or 4 Transports and in Steamers[.] They are to be ready for Embarkation on [the] 14th and then proceed to the Baltic[,] so you will have a Corps of French Marines on the weather Gangway to inspect. Wonders will never cease. I wish you joy of your lot but I dare say you will find them very agreeable jolly men in their way[,] but it will be a curious sight in an English Ship of War.

We have not a word on Naval matters, Except [*sic*] the Embarkation of 2 more Cavalry Regts and 6 Infantry Do for the East[.] This looks like business[.] More I am unable to say.

We look anxiously for your regular returns of wants[.] your private note rather frightened me in which you said you had only 40 days full provisions, but the official letter says 40 Beef, 40 Pork[,] which I

[1]Not included in this edition.

presume means 80 days in all, which agrees with your former returns. Save all the Salt Meat you can, as there is a terrible pull on it with Army & Navy[.] we have to supply the former with Bread[,] Meat[,] Hay, Oats &c from England[.] this in itself is no easy matter and so great is the pressure I cannot get Steamers to convey what is wanted. I have sent out a French & English Technical Dictionary of Military Phrases for the use of our officers to aid in conjoint operations[.] it may be of much use . . .

[**342**] *Milne to Grant*

Admiralty
5 July 1854

Dear Mr. Grant

The French Troops, 7347 Exclusive of the Staff[,] which number 34[,] and also 106 Horses[,] are to be victualled by us, but for which the French Gov. are to pay[,] but it is necessary to arrange this at once so far as it relates to the expense of each Man and Horse. I wish you therefore to prepare for the Board a Statement of Expense of one mans victualling per Day – putting Bread[,] Beef[,] Cocoa &c all separate, so that the French Govt may see the charge per Man[,] also expense per Day for Horse[.]

Be so good as to get this done at once to send to [the] French Govt.

[**343**] *Milne to Michael Seymour*

Admiralty
10 July 1854

My dear Seymour

I received your letter this morning from off Cronstadt dated 01 but I presume the 28th [of] June,[1] and I now write to say that a large store of provisions is on its way to you[.] are the ships to call at Faro and Baro Sound[?] *Tyne* sailed on Saturday with general supplies and about 1800 Bags of Bread. The *Chieftain* sails today with about the same. The Steamer *Kangaroo* will start with Bread in four days hence, The [*sic*] *Holyrood* in about 7 days and another steamer[,] *City of Norwich*[,] about 4 days hence[,] and the *Rajah* steamer on or about the 17[,] also with about 2000 Bags. each [*sic*] of these vessels will take about the

[1]Not preserved among Milne's papers.

same quantity. The *Hannibal*, *Algiers*[,] *St Vincent* and the *Royal William* are to sail on [the] 14th[.] they are filled with provisions for you to take out before they return Home. The above ships[,] with *Termangant*[,] *Gladiator*[,] *Sphinx* – and the Contract Steamer *Prince*[,] and Six Sailing Transports carry out 9004 French Infantry and 21 Horses. The *Prince* & Transports are to remain with the Fleet[,] and the Troops in the 4 Sail of the Line are to be divided in four Ships. How will they take to Holystoning Decks and lookout on the weather Cap Head[?] I have given up the Department and handed it over to Richards. I can assure you I have enough anxiety on my hands with the Troop business[.] I have now 10,000 men to send to Black Sea and 1000 Horses[.] this is no easy matter as we have chartered every large vessel in England[,] and they are almost all abroad in the Medn[.] you should send a steamer to assist in towing the *Tyne* & *Chieftain*[,] as they are slow and will require help.

Instead of sending your returns of the provisns in the State of Condition abstract, It [*sic*] will be a great convenience to send a separate return of Provisions[,] so that it may go to the Comp[troller] of Vic[tuallin]g. Please to order this[,] say once a fortnight. I find you are to be out of Bread on 6 Augt[,] which makes me very anxious to get your supplies out as fast as possible so as to prevent your going on short allowance. What has become of *Resistance*[?] we have been anxiously looking for her for a long time but no tidings of her. I will close this tomorrow. . . .

July 11th

I have no news for you[.] we are all quiet enough[,] but plenty to do and very anxious about all your proceedings. Cronstadt was no doubt impossible but it will make the Russians crow when they see the Fleet retiring[,] and no doubt they will make a fine story of it.[1] we [*sic*] regret the Cholera in the Fleet[.] this is a serious matter[;] we hear it is very severe at Cronstadt and it is said also in Paris. I am much afraid it will be a severe season[,] and that this awful scourge will spread to this country. we [*sic*] are all alive here but no promotion going on. The Brevet for the Army is the last they are to have[.] I hope we are meeting your wants[,] if not pray let me know. I am anxious about your provisions. My best wishes to all friends . . .

[1]Napier had reconnoitred Cronstadt at the end of June and concluded that it was too strong to attack. See Bonner-Smith and Dewar, *Russian War, 1854*, pp. 85–6.

[**344**] *Milne to Napier*

Admiralty, Private
11 July 1854

My dear Admiral

Altho Sir James and Berkeley may have written to you[,] I send you a few lines by this Evenings Messenger to Dantzic[.] not that I have any news for you from this[.] We got your Letters from off Cronstadt dated 1 July[,] and I have to thank you for the few lines you wrote me.[1] Your survey and inspection of the Entrance and Forts of Cronstadt is very interesting and Evidently [*sic*] [they are] too strong for you to make any attempt. The only thing which appears to me worthy of consideration is an attempt to burn the Town &c by means of Rockets from the North side of the Island. it [*sic*] would require a large number of Small Vessels of light draft of water, but I have no doubt Chads[2] and others will have considered this, and the feasibility of such a plan. It is rather disheartening to go away from before the Enemy's forts, but it is sound discretion to do so. I think Hall[3] made a good escape from the Alland [*sic*] [Islands] and he ran a great risk in what he did. I was surprised to find he had gone there without orders, and Entirely [*sic*] on an Exploration of his own. This is a strange way of carrying on the Service and[,] as you very rightly say, no Commander in Chief can be responsible for his Fleet if every Captain is to act for himself.

We have sent you out Provisions and Stores. *Tyne* has sailed. The *Chieftain* leaves today and 4 steamers will follow in a week. They will call off Faro and Baro Sound for Orders. I have written to the Captain of the Fleet all about them[,] and asked him if possible to give the *Tyne* and *Chieftain* a tow up. The *Kangaroo*, *Holyrood*, *City of Norwich* & *Rajah* are the steamers going out[,] and principally with Bread. Salt Meat will follow. The 9000 French Troops will Embark on [the] 14th in 4 Sail of the Line and 8 Transports[,] one of them the *Prince* Steamer. She is a splendid ship[.] we have offered to purchase her and I may say we have bought the *Himalaya*[.] She carries 370 Horses and men and is now about to start for the Black Sea[.] The Transports going to [the] Baltic will hold more Troops than those they will embark[,] which will

[1]Not copied to Napier's letter book or preserved among Milne's papers.

[2]Henry Ducie Chads; Second-in-Command of the Baltic Fleet.

[3]Sir William Hutcheon Hall, C.B., K.C.B. (*c*.1797–1878). Entered, 1811; Lt, 1841; Cmdr, 1843; Capt., 1844; Rear-Adm., 1863; Vice-Adm. (Ret.) 1869; Adm. (Ret.), 1875. Hall, commanding HMS *Hecla*, had reconnoitred Bomarsund on 22 June in company with HMS *Odin* and *Valorous* and had engaged the Russian fortifications. See Bonner-Smith and Dewar, *Russian War, 1854*, pp. 82–4.

relieve your ships[,] as a Guard of French Troops in each of our Ships will not be very agreeable to Captains or men. We have 10,000 men and about 1000 Horses to send to the Black Sea[.] it is a very heavy and an anxious business[,] causing me very great anxiety[,] and we have to send our Bread and other supplies to the Army. The French Gov. is purchasing Bread for their Army in this Country and all the Bakers in Bristol[,] Hull[,] Glasgow[,] Liverpool[,] London &c are at work for them. I cannot get a Bag of Bread to buy. In fact they are clearing our Country of everything – and we have cleared the Country of Steamers[,] for I cannot get Vessels to send out the Troops.

We have not one word of news for you[.] we are all quiet so far as Naval matters are concerned. There is nothing doing or going to be done that I am aware of. No Breach [in the Government] &c. The Houses of Parliament are going on much as usual[.] it was expected the Session would have closed in a week or a fortnight[,] but there is no[w] no prospect until next month. The Admirals are all well & consequently no promotion. I had a long letter from Sartorius[1] at Lisbon[.] he is growling at not being employed and disappointed you did not apply for him instead of Plumridge.[2] poor [*sic*] man[,] he is always writing complaining letters to me and asking me to urge on Sir James his employment.

My wife sends her kind regards and best wishes to you & with every sincere wish . . .

[P.S.:] We are sorry to hear of the cholera in the Ships (Query[:] is it owing to the water[?]) it is raging at Cronstadt and we hear likewise in Paris, but I believe the Baltic has never been entirely free of it for many years past.

[**345**] *Milne to Cunard*

Admiralty, Confidential
12 July 1854

Dear Mr. Cunard

We are in want of Biscuit for the supply of Malta[.] can you give me any information how we can secure about 500 Tons[?] Do you think[,]

[1]Sir George Rose Sartorius, Kt., K.C.B., G.C.B. (1790–1885). Entered, 1801; Lt, 1808; Cmdr, 1812; Capt., 1814; Rear-Adm., 1849; Vice-Adm., 1856; Adm., 1861; Adm. of the Fleet, 1869.

[2]Sir James Hanway Plumridge, K.C.B. (1787–1863). Entered, 1799; Lt, 1806; Cmdr, 1814; Capt., 1822; Rear-Adm., 1852; Vice-Adm., 1857; M.P., 1841–47. Third-in-Command of the Baltic Fleet.

if we cannot get it in England[,] you could get us the above quantity shipped from Boston or New York in one ship[?] will you call and see me about this[?]

[**346**] *Milne to Christie*

Admiralty, Private
13 July 1854

My dear Christie

I write you a line by this Messenger[,] altho I have little information to give you, but at the sametime [*sic*] I will give you the contemplated movements of Troops &c.

Himalaya will carry out the Scotch Greys[.] She will leave Southampt. on 15th for Liverpool[,] and will sail from there for the East about the 19th. The *Simla*[,] with a Cavalry Regt[,] will sail from Plymouth on the 13th[.] The *Orinoco* will sail today with 1 Batt[alion] of Rifles and 2 companies of [the] 68th[.] The *Avon* will sail next week with a regt. The *Colombo* on Tuesday next with [the] 34th[.] The *Medway* will receive on Board a Battering Train in conjunction with the *Australia*. The *Jason* will carry out remount Horses and the *Golden Fleece* a Regt and a Half[.] these two last ships have not yet arrived, but [are] daily expected. This is all I have to say as to Troops. The *Industry*[,] Steam Transport[,] is to sail next week full of Bread for Varna[.] She belongs to us. The *Sea Nymph* also goes out full of Bread and all the Steam Transports will be filled up with as much as they can stow. all [*sic*] this [is for] for Army service[.] we have purchased *Himalaya* and also the *Prince*[,] sister vessel to the *Golden Fleece*, 2691 Tons. I am glad you are sending home some of the ships as they are not wanted with you[,] but all depends on this[,] of which I am no judge[,] on what Lord Raglan may require.

We have nothing going on here[;] all exceedingly dull &c . . .

[P.S.:] You must have plenty of work on your hands[.]

[**347**] *Milne to the General Screw Steamship Company*

Admiralty
15 July 1854

Write to the Secretary of the General Screw S[hip] Coy and inform it is Their Lordships wish, that they should take steps[,] in accordance with previous verbal communication[,] to complete the officers and crews of the *Prince* in the same manner as if the ship was in their Service. Their Lordships trust they will use every caution in the selection of officers of experience and trust, and that the crew will consist of steady men. When the crew is complete, it is requested that a list of the officers & men may be transmitted to this office with the amount of monthly pay which is to be paid to them, which Their Lordships request the Company will defray and[,] on application for the same, it will be immediately repaid.

It is hoped that the officer to be placed in Command is a person in whom the Company have entire confidence, as the charge is one of great responsibility[,] considering the number of Troops to be Embarked, and the special service on which the ship is to be employed.

[**348**] *Milne to George Bohun Martin*

[Admiralty
17 July 1854]

Captain Martin is to report if the *Australia* is in that state to admit of her proceeding to Woolwich to complete her coal and to take on Board part of the Battering Train. The *Medway* is intended to take a portion[,] but the *Australia* [is] to be [the] principal ship for this Service[.] It is necessary every exertion should be used to load these ships[,] & Capt Martin is therefore to give the necessary orders[.] Messrs Somes[1] having removed the internal fittings of the *Australia*[,] [they] may be employed to put up any required fittings[.]

[**349**] *Milne to Greene*[2]

Admiralty
17 July 1854

The Director of Works is to take immediate steps to bring the Electric Teleg[rap]h into operation at once with Deptford & Woolwich & to report on which day this can be done[.]

[1]Messrs. Somes Brothers, Shipowners.
[2]Director of Works Col. Godfrey Thomas Greene.

[**350**] *Milne to Grant*

[Admiralty
17 July 1854]

Write to Comp V[ictualling] and order the *Jason* to proceed at once or as soon as ready to Woolwich[,] there to receive on Board Capt Townsends Battery with Guns Horses & and also about 60 remount Horses for the Cavalry.
[copies to:] A[ccountant] g[eneral,] Capt Martin[,] B of Ordnance
The 100 Artillery remount Horses will not go in this ship[.]

[**351**] *Milne to Lefebvre*[1]

Admiralty
17 July 1854

Dear Capt Le Febvre

I write you a line to say I hope the *Prince* steamer will be with you early tomorrow and that she will be found in a serviceable state. it [*sic*] has been a hurried business to get her ready[,] but I hope all will go well. Be so good as to inform the Agent Comdr[,] Steane[,][2] that he must be very cautious and keep a good look out for the safety of the ship, and to take care the French Troops are properly looked after[.] I wish you to impress this upon the other Agents[,] and where there are no agents[,] to the Masters of the Ships[.] we ought to have had an Agent in each Vessel[,] but it was not possible to get officers, and several who have been appointed have declined to join from ill health &c[.] You must take care that the Masters of the Transports have proper sailing orders[,] and have it made quite clear to them how they are to proceed. They should go thro the Sound instead of the Belt if they do not draw too much water[.] By Telegraph from Dover we hear the *Termag[an]t* has broken down and [the] damage will not be rectified [in] under 18 hours[.] I am much afraid she will be unable to proceed[.] In the distribution of the Troops in the Transports[,] it will be found they will carry more troops than what has been [previously] allotted to them, and all were to be accommodated <u>below</u>[.] now with ¼th on

[1]Nicholas Lefebvre (*c*.1799–1884). Entered, 1811; Lt, 1826; Cmdr, 1838; Capt., 1853; Rear-Adm. (Ret.), 1869; Vice-Adm. (Ret.), 1876; Adm. (Ret.), 1880. Attached to *Victory* to supervise Transports, 1854.

[2]John Steane (*c*.1795–1857). Entered, 1807; Lt, 1815; Cmdr, 1841; Capt. (Res.), 1856.

Deck you can not put more on Board. In case of any difficulty for want of an Agent in any of these Transports[,] you may put in any officer who may be on the ship[,] such as a Master or 2nd Master[,] if you consider it necessary[,] or even a lieutenant[.] I write this to you as I presume you are senior officer[.] if not hand this over to him, and if anything is wanted, let us know[.] also make a return of the proceedings that we may know what is going on[.]

[352] *Milne to Boxer*

Admiralty, Private
18 July 1854

My dear Admiral

As the Messenger leaves this today for Constantinople[,] I write you a few lines to say what are our movements here in regard to military operations.

The *Himalaya* takes out the Scotch Greys, but cannot leave Liverpool for a week on account of the Tides. The *Simla* sails tomorrow from Ply[mou]th with a Cavalry Regt. The *Orinoco* has sailed with the Rifles and 2 Coy of [the] 68[th] Reg. The *Colombo* and *Avon* with Regts will sail in a few days. *Medway* and the *Australia* take the Battering Train. The *Jason* takes a Battery of Field Artillery with 60 remount Horses for the Cavalry. This is all we have done as yet, and it will be necessary for you to send home some of the steamers which are going out. this [*sic*] however will depend on the operations which may be undertaken, and of course if absolutely necessary the vessels will be required to be detained. we [*sic*] have made a purchase of *Himalaya* and also of the *Prince*, sister ship to *Jason*, but for Baltic service. We are sending out Bread as fast as we can[,] but Genl Filder must be cautious not to issue more than can be help[ed], until we get the store replenished, and if the Army should want, you must let them have some of the Navy store. The Troop ships are so full we could not get any Bread on Board of them. we [*sic*] are forwarding supplies as fast as ever we can, but it is difficult[,] as the French are now in our market for all they want for their Troops at Varna, viz. Bread, Beef[,] Pork &c[,] and our Department having to purchase everything required for our Troops makes it a very heavy duty to be carried out. I am glad some of the Transports are coming home, but be cautious not to cripple the Army in case of active operations[,] and you must not trust too much to Dundas Fleet or his Steamers. We have sent a circular around calling upon the Ships owners to reduce their charge to 20/ per Ton. we [*sic*] are now getting ships at that price for the Baltic Service. We have sent 9000 French Troops to the Baltic[.] they sailed on Sunday and also yesterday. I went over to Calais to see them Embark. You will see the report from Portsmouth D[ock]yard on the Coals you sent home. They are reported to be inferior to Newcastle[,] but about the same average as some of the inland pits, but I have no doubt they will be better when the seams are properly worked[,] and they are taken more distant from the surface. Adl Henderson[1] died on his passage from Brazils. This promotion gives Lushington the G[ood] S[ervice] P[ension]. and Baldwin Walker the A[ide] D[e] C[amp]. we [*sic*] have no Naval news whatever[;] all quiet and really nothing doing. Anxious to get our ships manned but there are really no men to be got. The *Industry* Steam Store Ship is gone out to you. She is manned in the same manner as the Dock Yard Lighters and the men sign[ed] articles[.] it was the only way to get her away from this. We cannot send out any more Flat Boats. if [*sic*] necessary you will have to purchase and fit Flat Boats at your Headquarters.

[**353**] *Milne to Houston Stewart and George Grey*

Admiralty
18 July 1854

Inform Rear Adl H[ouston] Stewart at Malta and Capt Grey at Gibraltar that several of the Transports now in the Bosphorus have been ordered to call at Malta & Gib[ralta]r on their way to England to be discharged from the Service, but to call at their respective Ports to load with any old Ordnance Naval or Other Stores for England. They are to hasten the Vessels and on no account to allow them to be unnecessarily detained[.]

[**354**] *Milne to Napier*

Admiralty
18 July 1854

My dear Admiral

Thanks for your last letter received a few days ago. I have not much news for you. We are sending you Bread and other Provisions by *Tyne* and *Chieftain*[,] also by *Screw* Steamers. some [*sic*] of these have sailed

[1]William Wilmot Henderson, C.B., K.H. (*c*.1787–1854). Entered, 1799; Lt, 1804; Cmdr, 1809; Capt., 1815; Rear-Adm., 1850.

in the *Kangaroo* and *City of Norwich*[.] *Rajah* will go tomorrow and *Holyrood* on Thursday and a vessel called the *Nimrod* is loading[.] she will become a Transport for Troops when cleared of Provisions. Sir J. Graham just told me to provide Transports for all the Troops now in the 4 Sail of the Line[.] This will be done forthwith. I hope we have completed you in all Eatables up to Nov. 1st. We had a Telegraph from the House of Rainals Deacon and Co.[,] our Agents[,] to say he was coming over here to ask [for] an interview. This I presume relates to your stopping the supplies from him[.]

Capt Chads[1] I hear is to be app[ointe]d as Principal Agent of Transports in the Baltic in charge of all the private vessels. this [*sic*] is better than nothing and will give him something to do. he [*sic*] will have about 15 ships.

Adl Henderson is dead, which makes Martin of *Nile*.[2] Mundy[3] goes out in *Holyrood* to supersede him. Lushington got the G.S.P. and Baldwin Walker the A.D.C. There is no other news whatever. at [*sic*] last we have some warm weather and some indication of Summer. I hope you will get your wine by *Holyrood*[.] I told Willis to send it to Deptford. My wife sends her best wishes . . .

[**355**] *Milne to Napier*[4]

Admiralty
19 July 1854

My dear Sir Charles

We have been considering your Letters and the proceedings of Mr. Rainals with regard to the supply of Bullocks, and we have expressed our disapproval to him from his inattention in sending you such large supplies at once[.] no doubt it has been over done[,] but it does not appear he was acting by any selfish motive. his [*sic*] object was to furnish your Fleet with Fresh Beef and for this purpose he was appointed agent. If he has exceeded your orders he is much to blame, [but] at the sametime [*sic*] he produces an order from you to keep you

[1]Henry Chads, K.C.B. (1819–1906). Entered, 1833; Lt, 1841; Cmdr, 1845; Capt., 1848; Rear-Adm., 1856; Vice-Adm., 1872; Adm., 1877.

[2]Henry Byam Martin C.B., KC.B. (1803–65). Entered, 1816; Lt, 1823; Cmdr, 1825; Capt., 1827; Rear-Adm., 1854; Vice-Adm., 1860; Adm., 1864. Martin was promoted into the vacancy on the Flag List and thus had to give up the captaincy of HMS *Nile*.

[3]George Rodney Mundy, C.B., K.C.B., G.C.B. (1805–84). Entered, 1818; Lt, 1826; Cmdr, 1828; Capt., 1837; Rear-Adm., 1857; Vice-Adm., 1863; Adm., 1869.

[4]A Board Minute to the same effect as this letter was also drafted by Milne on 19 July.

supplied and to hire a steamer[.] This he referred to us by Telegraph from Elsinore, and we approved of the Vessel being chartered, at £1200 per month. The owners would only let their Vessel for 3 months and we have to reject her unless they agreed to 2 months[,] which they at last consented to do. We are paying a much higher rate for all our Steam Vessels – some of them up to £3 per Ton and the average £2.5, and we cannot help ourselves[,] and I know the owners are making that money in other trades. We pay Mr Cunard for his *Andes* £3000 p. month[;] in 3 weeks he cleared by a Sister Vessel £5,300. I was endeavouring to beat Cunard down when he produced me the above. It is surprising what Money is now made by Steam Vessels[.] the *Rajah* going out to you with Bread will get £2.10 pr Ton for the period she is absent from England[.] we have given every attention to your representation, but we do not think we would be justified in rejecting M Rainals. he [*sic*] ought to be kept in check[,] and on no account allowed to act independently, but having been appointed agent and [having] made arrangements under the order and authority of the Board, we feel bound to retain his services so long as he acts with honesty. It is a difficult duty to perform when the Fleet is so distant, and some allowance must be made for this. We know nothing of Mr Rainals[,] but he was strongly recommended by Mr. Buchanan[,] the Minister at Copenhagen. If he has written instructions to send either 200 or whatever number of Bullocks are required per week[,] and to send a cargo once a Fortnight[,] it appears to me the proceedings of M R[ainals] will be subject to a proper check.

I write this in haste if possible to save the *Holyrood*[,] which sails in the morning[,] and you ought to know our decision[.]

[**356**] *Christie to Milne*

Orient, Beicos
20 July 1854

My dear Milne

I am happy to think that *Jason*, *Golden Fleece* and *Medway* would get to England just about the right time for you. What a pity it is that everything can't be done by steam, it would be such a saving of time and expense too in the long run.

What the Army is to do now I do not know, but I should hope an attempt upon the Crimea will be the next step. I intend [on] going to Varna tomorrow[,] when I shall perhaps find out from Lord Raglan something about it and prepare accordingly.

I have got the Transports in two very snug Bays opposite to each other, immediately above Beicos Bay, and all ready with 6 weeks of everything on board.

There are very few of them supplied with Fire Engines. I think they should each have one. Some have very bad hawsers, the consequence is they frequently snap when being towed. I have just issued an order for each vessel to furnish herself with two good ones.

If nothing more is to be done this season, I should think a good many more of the Sailing vessels might be paid off. I have fitted several of the large Liverpool ships with from 30 to 50 more stalls than they carried from England. They have plenty of height on the main deck particularly for the Horses of this country.

I send a Return of all the Transports and a small Sketch which will give you some idea of the position of the Ships here.[1] it [*sic*] is done by Lt. Rundle an officer who has been of considerable use to me. I consider that from this Anchorage we can get, with the assistance of the steamers, a sufficient number of ships to Varna in 16 hours to embark a Division of the Army.

I appoint two vessels for each steamer to be in constant readiness, and hope soon to have to start them.[2]

[**357**] *Graham to Milne*

[London], Private
20 July 1854

My dear Capt Milne
. . . Consider, when we meet Tomorrow, whether[,] with a view to continued naval and military operations in the Black Sea[,] we can prudently ask for a diminution of the means of Transport by Steam in that Quarter at the present moment.

[**358**] *Milne to Dacres*

Admiralty
21 July 1854

My dear Dacres
Thanks for your Letter received by yesterdays mail. I am glad to find you are progressing in more ways than one[,] and that your chief has

[1]Neither document is preserved among Milne's papers.
[2]Meaning that he had arranged for each steamer to tow two sailing vessels.

given you something to do[,] and in the execution you have given satisfaction[.][1] your Cruise and proceedings are interesting and it must have been a satisfactory service to have been selected to execute. I am sorry however you give so bad an account of your Ship. it [*sic*] is much to be regretted but it was an Experiment of Small power in that class [of] ship and[,] had the Engines been good[,] would have proved satisfactory[;] as it is the faulty Engines has [*sic*] upset the whole affair[.] our ulterior measures have proved much more satisfactory[,] and there has hardly been a single cause of complaint in all the new Ships, much to the Credit of the Engines as well as to Walker[,][2] whose merits are great and he has done much for the benefit of the service [*sic*]. I think myself wonders have been done here[,] and if any impartial person will review what has been done for the Service in the last 7 years it must be admitted we have not neglected our duty or the Service. I have had my humble share in the work and my various colleagues have done their duty. My last work in the Conveyance of Troops &c[,] as well as the Munitions of War[,] has not been an easy one, but amidst all the conflicting opinions and all the nonsense that has been said and written[,] I see nothing to regret and nothing to change. not [*sic*] a Man or Horse or Ton of Stores has left this Country without my own personal arrangement and in all that has been Effected we have only had one accident and that the *Europa*. I think this is saying a great deal, considering the number of Men sent and the distance to be conveyed. Sir J. Graham behaved most handsomely to me in the House and far beyond my merits.[3] There was a time I took a more prominent lead here, but since fresh working men as Dundas[4] & Richards have been here I have given up a good deal to them, but 3 years ago I was doing all the Chief work of detail[.]

There is not much on the Table now[;] we are Endeavouring to form a Home reserve of 12 Sail of the Line to meet any contingency in any of the Fleets[,] but we do not get men[:] it is very sad but there is no help for it. You will see [of] the death of Admiral Henderson on his passage home from Brazils. Lushington gets the G.S.P and Baldwin

[1]It is unclear to what Milne referred; Dacres' ship had participated in the attack on Odessa, but that had taken place almost three months earlier.

[2]Surveyor of the Navy Baldwin Walker.

[3]Milne was referring to a speech by Graham of 5 May 1854, when the Government brought forward a Supplementary Estimate to cover the costs of the war. Graham stated: 'I may name in particular the services of my hon. and gallant Friend the Member for Gloucester (Adm. Berkeley) and Captain Milne, whose efforts – almost undivided efforts – have been given to that vast work, and without which it would have been impossible to send out such a vast fleet in such a short period of time.'

[4]Richard Saunders Dundas.

Walker the A.D.C. You say I ought to get the Civil Order,[1] but I say no; I have never looked forward to any Mark for my work here and I do not expect any such honour. I have done my duty faithfully and honestly[,] and I suspect people think I have been sufficiently rewarded by being allowed to remain here. I take things as they come. I neither ask or expect, but jog on the best way I can[,] and never leave the office. I believe no one ever worked more assiduously than I have done, but I will say no more on the subject. I hear your Chief[2] is very tired of his Command and anxious to be relieved when his time expires, this is the report but I know nothing officially. It has never been mooted here, nor in case of relief who is to assume the command. This is not an easy question[:] when any one takes up the List he will find it so. Martin comes home from the *Nile*, and from [*sic*] which I hear he is plenty sick of it, but the old Admiral[3] thought he would have retained his Flag in the Baltic. People sometimes expect too much, and I think this is [such] a case. Thompson[4] has been up in town staying here for a week and his pretty little wife with him. I endeavoured to get him a Dock Yard, but Sir J. G. I suspect has no intention of doing anything for him[.] it [*sic*] strikes me, Thompson does not stand well with the 1 Lord. I have done all I can and perhaps more than was prudent on my part. Noble[5] I saw at Dover[;] he has an appointment there as Sup[erinten]d[en]t of Pilots which gives him about £200 per A[nnum] and he appears pleased at having got it.

In Political matters there is nothing new. people [*sic*] are beginning to grumble at the Expense of the War, and in the H[ouse] of C[ommons] there is to be a Vote for a Credit in aid, during the recess, which the opposition intend to seize on as a subject of attack and worry [the Government][,] but nothing will be made of it. no [*sic*] doubt the Ministry are weak, but they are working the House of Commons with Lord Derby's tools, and had the Session to be continued [*sic*] it is by no means unlikely that a dissolution would have taken place[,] and it will come to that before this Govt can work well[.]

Must now close this with best wishes from my Wife & self and Believe me my dear Dacres
always very sincerely yours

[P.S.:] My 3 Chicks are all thriving.

[1]Of the Bath (K.C.B.).

[2]Deans Dundas.

[3]Probably a reference to Henry Byam Martin's father, Thomas Byam Martin.

[4]Probably Milne's old captain, Sir Thomas Raikes Trigg Thompson.

[5]Probably Jeffrey Wheelock Noble (*c.*1804–65). Entered, 1816; Lt, 1826; Cmdr, 1841; Capt., 1846.

[**359**] *Milne Draft Orders to Henry Chads*

Admiralty
22 July 1854

Orders to Captain Chads to proceed as soon as possible on Board the chartered Steam Vessel *Prince*[,] now at the Downs[,] and take charge as Principal agent of Transports in the Baltic[,] assuming the control and command of all the Hired Transports employed in the conveyance of Troops or Military Stores[.]

He is to obey all orders he may receive from Vice Adl Sir Charles Napier or other [of] his Superior officers and[,] as the Transports have been chartered for the conveyance of French Troops, he is to Exercise [*sic*] the utmost caution in keeping up a cordial understanding with their officers and men[,] affording on all occasions [*sic*] every possible assistance on board the different ships[,] and taking care that they are properly attended to in regard to their Provisions, water, &c[.]

He is to attend to any requisitions or wishes of the officer in Command of the French Troops[,] and afford him every aid in his power[,] bearing in mind that the Transports under his charge are specially chartered to the conveyance of the French Troops[,] and to be attached to that force[.]

[**360**] *Milne to Boxer*

Admiralty
22 July 1854

My dear Admiral

Thanks for your Letter of the 10th of June which I only received a few days ago[.] Where it has been on its travels I know not, but I think in looking over it, you ought to have put July[.] Such I believe is the case. I have no news for you since my last[.] The Steam Store Ship *Industry* is now at Devonport loading with Bread and will be at your disposal as a Collier. We will also send out another[,] the *Supply*[.] They are 650 Tons and are manned as Dock Yard Lighters[,] and I hope this may work well[,] but it is requiring a New [*sic*] system.

As to the discharge of Transports[,] I am glad you have been enabled to make the reduction you have[.] The *Simla*, *Avon*, [&] *Colombo*, should return to England unless there is any urgent cause to detain them. This I do not know, and it can only be known to the Chiefs in the Black Sea. I am not in a position to deal with it here. you [*sic*] must therefore be guided by Events. The *Jason* has come home[,] also *Golden Fleece*[,] which vessel has on board a large quantity of Bread and other provisions which would have been better had it been landed at Constantinople or Varna[,] as we are finding out at a heavy Expense. The *Harbinger* we intend to keep in the Service at a reduced rate of hire for carrying Bread and Provisions to Malta, but I hope H Stewart has sent her to Barcelona for Mules. If you have not[,] send down the *Trent* or *Tonning*. The Service is urgent and we have no Vessel in England for the Emergency.

We have a report here of the death of Capt Parker[1] of *Firebrand*, we hope this is not true, but it is reported in the papers from Malta and by *Harbinger* from Constantinople. His Friends are in a sad state about it but we have no information to give them.

I am glad you have arranged about the Coals but it strikes me if we are to pay 10/ [shillings] Royalty to the Sultan he has made a good bargain. This is the price of Coal in England at the Pits [*sic*] mouth.

Good bye with best wishes . . .

[**361**] *Milne to Houston Stewart*

Admiralty
24 July 1854

My dear Admiral

I write you a few lines by this Mail of the 24th[,] not that I have much information for you. All deeply regret to hear of the death of Capt Hyde Parker. this [*sic*] information was in the *Morning Chronicle* of Saturday last and caused the greatest anxiety to his Friends. today [*sic*] we have it confirmed by the *Times* and his funeral having taken place on the 17th at Constantinople. this [*sic*] is a most sad and melancholy event and the poor family will be again thrown into sad distress. Poor Mrs Parker[,] what a time for her. She lingers on, one day better and then free from all pain. I heard she was in the Drawing Room a few days ago, but the disease itself goes on progressively increasing[,] but at a slow rate; we hear or rather see in the *Times* that Dundas promoted your son[2] into *Firebrand*[;] this must be most satisfactory to you and with all my heart I wish you joy.

[1]Hyde Parker (1824–54). Entered, *c*.1835; Lt, 1844; Cmdr, 1846. Parker, the son of Milne's late colleague on the Board, was killed on 7 July 1854, while assaulting Russian fortifications at the Sulina mouth of the Danube.

[2]William Houston Stewart, C.B., K.C.B., G.C.B. (1821–1901). Entered, 1835; Lt, 1842; Cmdr, 1848; Capt., 1854; Rear-Adm., 1870; Vice-Adm., 1876; Adm., 1881; Controller of the Navy, 1872–82. Houston Stewart was promoted from HMS *Modeste* into *Firebrand* following the younger Hyde Parker's death.

We have not a word of news here and we are rubbing on the best way we can and[,] I think[,] progressing. If we had about 3000 men in hand it would be a god send, but at present we get on very slowly in manning our Ships. The *Simla*, *Avon*, *Colombo*, [and] *Orinoco* have sailed, *Medway*, [and] *Australia*, with Battering Train will soon follow, also *Jason* with a Field Battery and *Himalaya* with 370 Horses will leave Liverpool on Wednesday. You know perhaps we have bought her for £130,000, and the *Prince*[,] sister vessel to *Golden Fleece*[,] for £105,000.

The *Himalaya* will pay her own expenses before the war ends, of which there appears to be no seeing the end[.]

The *Sea Nymph* is going out with 2500 Bags of Bread[.] She is a Screw [*sic*] and will go on to Varna. I propose loading the *Harbinger* when she comes Home, unless you have sent her to Barcelona or given her some other job, which I rather expect you may have done. I have got her charge [for] Hire reduced 10/ per Ton per Month. not [*sic*] a word on news in Naval Matters[:] all quiet, Napier is at the Alland [*sic*] Islands or thereabouts; Berkeley is in better health than I have ever seen him and is going on very well here.

With best wishes[,] in which my wife joins . . .

[**362**] *Milne to Michael Seymour*

Admiralty, Private
25 July 1854

My dear Seymour

I ought to have written you a line by the *Holyrood*[,] but I had not time to do so, but wrote to the Admiral in regard to Messrs Rainals Deacon & Co[.] now [*sic*] between ourselves I think the Admiral has been somewhat hasty in the dismissal of the Agent. There is nothing proved of a fraudulent or other improper proceeding on his part and we cannot act with Injustice [*sic*] towards him, no sooner had he got his sub Agents appointed and all his arrangements made than he is at once dismissed. This cant [*sic*] be. I do not see in the correspondence that he has ever received any specific instructions as to the number of Bullocks he was to supply. he [*sic*] talks of having been directed verbally to keep up supplies of Fresh Beef for 40,000 Men, and he does not appear to have had any specific order or directions how to proceed or what to do. This may not be correct[,] but I see a strong order for him to keep the Fleet supplied without specifying number of Bullocks.

I hope there is no feeling in favour of the Paymaster of the *D*[*uke*] *of W*[*ellingon*],[1] to the prejudice of Mr Rainals, of whom I know nothing, but we must be just and not do an injury where it is undeserved. We have sent M Rainals letter to Sir C[harles] this day with directions to continue his services and to make Demands on him for what he may require. Bread and other Provisions we have ordered to be sent out and the Ships of the Line on coming Home will fill you up before they leave you.

Poor young Hyde Parker we hear was shot at the Sulina mouth[,] at least so we hear [*sic*]. We only know it by the Papers but expect the Mail tomorrow. This is a sad blow to the afflicted family[.] we have no other news.

[**363**] *Milne to Napier*

Admiralty
28 July 1854

Write to Sir C Napier and inform him that the Transports now fitting at Deptford for the purpose of receiving on Board the French Troops now on Board the English Ships of War in the Baltic, will proceed from England to Faro Sound for further orders[,] and he is to give orders as to their future proceedings.

[**364**] *Milne to Christie*

Admiralty
29 July 1854

My dear Captain Christie

I write you a few lines by this E[ve]n[in]gs Messenger to mention Events &c as to the Transports.

1st[.] We have obtained a reduction in the Charter of the Sailing Transports to 20/ pr Ton, and also some of the Steamers to 40/[,] which will make a large saving in expense.

2. The paying off of some of the Ships will likewise add to the reduction and I presume those ordered have already left Constantinople. The *Palmyra* is a very expensive ship[.] The owners have not behaved well[,] and I wish her sent home as soon as possible so as to pay her off at the end of 4 months. if [*sic*] necessary I would rather you would keep some other ship in her place if this is necessary [*sic*].

[1]John Marks (d. 1871). Paymaster, 1814.

Admiral Boxer must be cautious not to reduce too much, because if any contemplated movement is intended[,] it will become absolutely necessary for Transports to be ready and the more so as the add[itiona]l number of Troops are being sent out. This question requires very grave and serious consideration[,] for too much reliance must not be placed on Admiral Dundas cooperation[.] Therefore be cautious in your proceedings on this point.

The *Avon*, *Colombo*, *Jason* [&] *Simla* have sailed[,] also *Himalaya*. *Jason*[,] I believe[,] went this morning, *Medway* and *Australia* will go next week with the Battering Train[,] and an Add[itiona]l Co of Artillery. *Golden Fleece* was to take out the 46th[,] but the ship is in dock and will not be ready until the 5 or 6th[,] owing to the screw bearings having been damaged[,] and this again owing to a towing Hawser having got round the screw. if [*sic*] so we cannot put the ship out of Pay. you [*sic*] will be called on to report on this. The *Jason* must come back to us at once[,] as we have another Field Battery to go out in Her [*sic*]. *Himalaya* would answer the purpose if she is not required. I may however say this[:] that the *Orinoco*, *Simla*, *Avon* should come back[,] if not required in the Black Sea[,] to be delivered to their owners. *Jason* or *Himalaya* we want for a Field Battery and we also want 2 or 3 Steamers such as *Simoom*[,] *Vulcan* or *Victoria* to carry out 2 Regiments or Drafts. If these ships cannot be spared[,] we should be informed by Telegraph, but I will put this in official shape at once.

We are sending out large supplies of Bread and I hope to get away 3 Screw vessels next week or so.

We have nothing new here[;] we are in much anxiety to get all our work properly done. we [*sic*] regret the death of young Parker, he has shewn himself to be a gallant fellow and more worthy of a better end . . .

[**365**] *Milne to Boxer*

Admiralty
29 July 1854

My dear Admiral

I write you a few lines by this Evenings Messenger[.] I have also written to Cap Christie. The *Avon*[,] *Himalaya*, *Orinoco*, *Colombo* and *Jason* have sailed. The *Golden Fleece* will go about 6th [Aug.,] The [*sic*] *Medway* and *Australia* next week. we [*sic*] have therefore nothing left for our other Troops which are to go out[.] we have 4000 Infantry or nearly that number[,] and 1 Field Battery with remount Horses[,] in all about 260. We therefore want 4 Steamers home independent of those going out or gone out[,] as already mentioned in this note, also the *Jason* and *Himalaya* for Horses. Now we do not expect you can spare any of the Steamers now with you, and you may not be able to spare the *Avon*, *Colombo*, *Orinoco* or *Simla*, but of this I am ignorant. if [*sic*] they come home and you cannot spare 4 others[,] they will have to go back again[.] if you send the others and the above vessels they will be delivered up to their owners. Whatever you decide on upon consultation with Lord Raglan[,] you <u>must</u> let us know by Telegh, but your last one which I understand you sent respecting the vessels coming home never reached this at all.

Be cautious about your reduction of ships[,] altho I am glad to see a reduction, you must be cautious and do not go too far. I do not think you should place too much reliance on Ad. Dundas Fleet, it may be sent to other parts of the Coast and not be able to render much assistance for the Conveyance of Troops. recollect [*sic*] we are sending out <u>bodies</u> of Men & large supplies of Stores and the Steamers which conveyed them are not remaining with them. We have got the owners of ships to reduce their Freight to 20/ pr Ton instead of £1.5 to £1.12. The *Palmyra* is a dear ship[.] I want her sent Home as the owners have not behaved well[.] keep another ship in her place[.] Lord Raglan must have a <u>voice</u> in all the Transports [arrangements]. he [*sic*] is the Servt of [the] Govt and he know[s] what may be wanted. he [*sic*] must be consulted. if [*sic*] our Troops go to the Crimea and there are no <u>Transports</u>[,] it will be a serious business[,] therefore be on <u>your guard</u>.

[P.S.:] we [*sic*] have no news here[.] we [are] all quiet. we hear that a heavy firing was heard near the Alland [*sic*] [Islands.] I think Napier has had a shy [*sic*] at the Forts & Islands.

[366] *Milne to Mundy*

Admiralty
31 July 1854

My dear Col Mundy

I have just now received your Letter respecting Tonnage for 200 Horses, from Gibraltar[.] I have not taken any steps nor could I attempt to do so, until you sent [*sic*] me some specific information. If the Horses were ready, we would stop one of the ships returning from the East at Gib[ralta]r and Embark [*sic*] the Horses[,] but it is not possible to do this until we know more on the subject. If 200 Artillerymen are required to go to Gibraltar[,] let me have something official to go on and I will endeavour to send them out by small Detachments[.] *Medway* and *Australia* have been hastened and I hope will be off in a day or two[.]

Resistance sailed for Barbadoes yesterday and went direct[,] as I understood the Duke [of Newcastle] was anxious about the 26th Reg[.] we will make provision for Bermuda by some other vessel. It is most difficult to meet every contingency at once[,] but I hope all matters are in a fair way of being carried out. I have sent to Portsmouth & Plymouth to send out & recall the *Resistance* if we can find her.

[**367**] *Milne to Grant*

Admiralty
1 August 1854

Write immediately to the owners of the *Australia* and inform that there are no officers or crew on Board this ship[,] That [*sic*] the public service is delayed in consequence[,] and that the ship will not be considered in Pay unless the proper officers and crew are on Board to assist in Coaling and preparing the ship for immediate service, and urgent immediate attention [must] be given to the Subject, as the ship must proceed without the least delay[.]

[**368**] *Milne to Michael Seymour*

Admiralty
1 August 1854

My dear Seymour

Thanks for your letter of the 21 which I received two days ago. I have literally no news for you. we [*sic*] have sent out all your supplies[,] you are now in clover and full up to the middle of October. The *City of Norwich* was only sent for the run out to the Baltic – also the *Kangaroo* and *Rajah*. The *Nicholai* is for 2 months certain and I hope the Demands [*sic*] will be regularly sent to the Agent[,] stating what supplies are required. It would never have done to have thrown over our Agent without there had been [*sic*] sufficient cause, which we could not find out that there was [*sic*][.]

The *Nimrod* has sailed[.] She takes out provisions[,] and when she is unloaded the ship becomes a Transport for French Troops. Another sails from Deptford tomorrow[.] She is empty[.] 4 will sail on the 6th and the others will follow immediately after[.] Stopford[1] goes out as Captain of the Fleet to Black Sea and Eden[2] will Take [*sic*] the . . . [Dockyard] in your absence.[3] There has been some not very agreeable business on board *Britannia* and matters are not quite satisfactory there, but this is between ourselves. Give my kind regards to the Chief [Napier][.] he must be a good deal worried at this time and also very anxious. take [*sic*] care the Russian Fleet does not come out. I really think they will. it [*sic*] will require a sharp look out and to be prepared for such an emergency.

[P.S.:] I would be glad to meet your wishes about your Sisters Son[,] but I am afraid I cannot hold out any hope[.] I am in debt and several candidates coming forward that I cannot set aside, and Eden also Sir J Stirling owe me each one[,] and they have none to give me. I have been done[.] if any increase of Entries takes place I will not forget you[.]

[**369**] *Milne to Grant*

Admiralty
4 August 1854

Dear Mr Grant

I have a note last evening [*sic*] from Capt Martin at Deptford to say the *Minden* Transport is ready for Sea. as [*sic*] one of those now fitting out must go to Calais to Embark some French Troops and stores[,] be so goods as to send to Deptford the following orders. Orders to be sent to Deptford to order the *Minden* Transport[,] so soon as in all respects ready[,] to proceed to Calais roads, there to receive on board 200 French Troops and Stores and[,] having received the same on board[,] to proceed to Faro Sound for further orders, calling at Copenhagen to communicate with H.M. Minister.

If an Agent has joined Deptford Yard[,] he is to be put on Board the *Minden* and Captain Martin is to take care, that Hammocks[,] Blankets & Mess utensils have been put on Board the Ship[,] and the Master or Agent is to be warned to shew every attention to the French Troops[,] and make every possible arrangement for their comfort[,]

[1]Montagu Stopford.

[2]Henry Eden (1798–1888). Entered, 1811; Lt, 1817; Cmdr, 1821; Capt., 1827; Rear-Adm., 1854; Vice-Adm., 1861; Adm., 1864; Naval Lord of the Admiralty, 1855–58.

[3]Seymour was Rear-Adm. Superintendent of Devonport Dockyard; when he was dispatched to the Baltic, Montagu Stopford was temporarily appointed to fill the post, and when that officer was sent to the Black Sea, Henry Eden deputized for him.

which is especially required owing to their being unacquainted with the English language and to the Customs & mode of provisioning in English ships.

Comdr Herrick[1] will be at Dover to attend to the Embarkation and the Agent or Master is to attend to his orders.

[**370**] *Milne to Grant and Austin*

Admiralty
5 August 1854

Sailing orders for the *Harbinger* to receive on Board Lt. General Sir G. Cathcart[2] and Staff[,] consisting of 10 officers including the G[enera]l, also Rear Ad Stopford and his Secy[, &] 16 to 18 Servants, 23 to 25 Horses. also [*sic*] whatever stores she can stow and which have been sent from the Ordnance Dept[,] and to proceed to Malta & Constantinople with all possible expedition.

[P.S.:] Send Copy to Night to Capt Austin with the Names of all the officers & he is to appropriate the Cabins.

[**371**] *Milne to Boxer*

Admiralty
8 August 1854

My dear Admiral

I write a line to say, That The [*sic*] *Industry*[,] H Majestys Steam Store ship[,] has sailed full of Bread, also the *Sea Nymph* (Screw) and the *Cottingham*[.] both of these have Bread and the 1st vessel passengers. It is intended for the *Cottingham* to come home[,] so as to take out more Bread[.] if she reaches Constantinople[,] please to transfer the Bread to your stores and send her back as soon as you can[.] It is not at all unlikely that Houston Stewart will land the Bread from her at Malta and send her Home from thence, and[,] if so[,] *Sea Nymph* must go back to Malta and bring up Bread from thence, also the *Industry*[,] if not otherwise required. The *Harbinger*[,] which sails tomorrow with Sir G Cathcart & Suite, also Admiral Stopford as Captain of the Fleet[,]

[1]Edward Herrick (*c*.1793–1862). Entered, 1805; Lt, 1815; Cmdr; 1849; Capt., 1855, Capt. (Ret.), 1860. Herrick was attached to HMS *Waterloo,* flagship at Sheerness, for packet service at Dover.

[2]Sir George Cathcart, K.C.B. (1794–1854).

must likewise come to England[,] as by Her [*sic*] and *Cottingham* I intend to keep up the supply of Provisions required for the Army. it [*sic*] is therefore necessary they should return as soon as possible, and I will be obliged if you will order this.

We have no news here. I was glad to hear the Transports were all ready. The *Golden Fleece* will not get away until Friday next.

[P.S.:] All eyes are directed from this to the Crimea, I mean the public, but it will be a heavy undertaking[.]

[**372**] *Milne to Napier*

Admiralty
8 August 1854

My dear Admiral

Thanks for your Letters of the 28 and 30 July which I received yesterday. I regret there has been any misunderstanding with Messrs Rainals[,] Deacon & Co, but I really believe they acted for the best[,] and without any intention of acting improperly. I must say I do not think they had sufficient information to guide them. I saw him [Rainals] here and he told me he was verbally directed to provide Bullocks for <u>40,000</u> men[,] and this was the reason he sent so large a supply. He has had a <u>setting</u> down [on] this and we have again written to him[,] informing him with the statement of Mr Markes[1] and the directions he received from him, and we have ordered him to be more cautious in future. it [*sic*] would not have been quite fair to have given him up altogether[,] after having appointed 45 sub Agents and having declined a great deal of private business at their House at Elsinore.

The French Troops are victualled by us so long as they are in our Transports[,] and are therefore to be supplied with Fresh Beef the same as our own people. When landed they will have to take some supplies with them, and it was understood that they were to fall on their own resources[,] but we have never got any <u>definite</u> information from the French Govt on this subject. I think it would be expedient for you to write to the French Admiral & General on this subject and come to some clear understanding, at the sametime [*sic*] there will be no objection to furnish them with Bullocks and Vegetables[,] so long as an Account is kept of the same, in order to raise a claim for repayment from the French Govt.

[1]John Marks.

There is no objection to your sending to [Elsinore] for Bullock[s,] giving Messrs Rainals notice of your intention.

I will write you again on Tuesday week[,] relative to provisions for the French[,] as I cannot see Sir J Graham to know what was the understanding with himself and the French Gov[,] as he is ill in Bed and has been for the last 3 days.

Your Warm Clothing is all in hand and will be sent out in a few days. I do not know anything else that you require. we [*sic*] have not a word of news. Parliament is to be up on [the] 15th[.]

[**373**] *Milne to Houston Stewart*

Admiralty
9 August 1854

My dear Admiral

I write you a few lines by this Evenings Mail with reference to 3 Vessels, The [*sic*] *Industry*[,] our own Screw Transport, The [*sic*] *Sea Nymphe* [*sic*] and the *Cottingham*[.] all three have bread on board for the East, but I do not exactly know whether it is indispensable that all the 3 Cargoes should go to the Black Sea. If not necessary[,] I am anxious that the *Cottingham* on her arrival at Malta[,] to land her Cargo there[,] and from there return to Devonport for another Cargo, by which means we will have a Vessel running between England and Malta[,] and by means of *Sea Nymphe*, *Industry* and others [a link from Malta to the Black Sea.][1] The *Cottingham* sails today[.] she has also a few passengers on board[,] but they could wait at Malta if this ship is sent Home. The *Harbinger* sails this evng from South[ampton] with Sir G Cathcart & Staff[,] also Stopford as Captain of the Fleet[,] & I have written to Boxer to send her to England as soon as he can to forward out Bread &c. The *Golden Fleece* will leave Cork for the East with the 21st about the 15 or 16th[,] and the *Mauritius* will leave South[ampto]n with the 34th for Corfu[,] and from thence take a Reg to Turkey. The *Australia* with the remainder of the Battering Train will get away today or tomorrow[.] This exhausts all our means of sending out reinforcements[,] but I have still 3000 men to get away and also another Field Battery with Horses &c. I hope you are better[.] I was glad to see your hand writing [*sic*] on some notes[,] altho I did not hear from you myself.

[1]Milne seems to have dropped a line here, but this would appear to have been his intent, based on the information in his letter of 8 August to Boxer, [**371**].

The Iron[1] goes out in *Golden Fleece*[,] so take care it is taken out of her on her arrival. we [*sic*] have no news from [the] Baltic, but we hear of some measures being adopted at the Alland [*sic*] Islands. Also reports from the Black Sea [*sic*] which looks like business, but it [*sic*] the Steamer getting out of Sevastopol is a disagreeable business,[2] and will cause Dundas much annoyance.

[**374**] *Christie to Milne*

Orient, Beicos Bay
10 August 1854

My dear Milne

We are all alive here in hopes of something being done soon. I am sending all the Transports up to Baljik as fast as possible[,] and am happy to say have got nearly the whole of them there without towing. I am now anxious to collect the Steamers and get them filled with water[,] coals & Provisions so that the whole may be on the spot and ready for anything that may be required.

There are plenty of steamers and ships to transport the Army. All the sailing ships are well outfitted with Provisions[,] Water & Forage.

Sir Edmund Lyons has been here for a few days and done a great deal of good[,] particularly in hurrying the Boats for Stages. He got the Dockyard at Constantinople well supplied with Plank and we shall have as many Boats as will be required for the Army immediately.

Sir Geo Brown[,] Sir E Lyons & myself[,] assisted by Capt Mends of *Agamemnon*[,] met on board that ship three days ago to consult & arrange a plan for embarking & transporting the Army, and I have submitted a form of a plan, a copy of which I enclose that you may be fully informed of what we are about.[3] It has been submitted to Lord Raglan[,] and will probably be adopted. You will see that we have ample means to accomplish all that is required. *Cornwall* is rather a smaller ship than I bargained for, but I have placed *Bombay* in her Division to make up for her deficiency. I only wish they were all embarked & under weigh[.] I should have no fear for the result, but I fear delay.

[1]This reference is obscure; in a subsequent letter to Houston Stewart [**383**] Milne refers to the 'iron and rivets' on *Golden Fleece*, suggesting that this might have been for repairing ships at Malta.

[2]Milne was probably referring to the steam frigate *Vladimir*, which escaped from Sebastopol in late July, sank several Turkish vessels, and captured two. See Clowes, vol. 6, p. 407.

[3]Not preserved among Milne's papers.

I shall start for Baljik myself tomorrow or next day[,] if I can get the steamers up from Constantinople, so that I may appoint the officers of Divisions &c &c and have everything in readiness in my department.

I hope you will excuse this hurried letter . . .

[**375**] *Mundy to Milne*

War Office
11 August 1854

My dear Milne

The D. of Newcastle will be disappointed & so will Ld Raglan (under existing intention at the seat of war) if the Sappers & Miners are detained. They ought to have precedence over all other kinds of Force[.]

[**376**] *Milne to the General Screw Steamship Company*

Admiralty
11 August 1854

Inform them [their] Lordships received a Telegraph last evening from Southampton[,] stating that the *Mauritius* was not capable of conveying more than about 420 men under cover. As this vessel[,] when offered to the Gov[,] was understood to be able to carry a Reg of 1000 Men, their Lordships have to call the immediate attention of the Company to this circumstance and expect they will take such measures by the removal of some of the Internal fittings as will enable accommodation to be obtained for the Troops to be embarked.

They are further informed that the ship will never be able to carry more than 860 Rank & File[,] but their Lordships expect the Company will give immediate Instructions on this subject[.]

[**377**] *Milne to Cunard*

Admiralty
11 August 1854

Write to Mr Cunard and request to know if he can convey at an early date 80 Sappers to Constantinople with 7 or 8 officers and their Tools[,] probably about 20 to 30 Tons[.]

[**378**] *Mundy to Milne*

War Office, London
14 August 1854

Dear Captain Milne

The Duke of Newcastle is very desirous that the party of Engr Officers & Sappers from England and ditto from Corfu should precede Infantry.

He has therefore desired the H[orse] G[uar]ds to deduct from the 34th Regt so many officers & men as will leave room for the Engrs from here, and from the 57th Regt at Corfu so many as will give access for the Corfu Engrs, for '*Mauritius*.'

The H[orse] G[uar]ds and Ordnance have been requested to communicate with the Admiralty on the subject.

[**379**] *Milne to the Peninsular and Orient Steamship Company*

Admiralty
15 August 1854

Immediate
Write to the Peninsular & Ol Co and inform [them] the *Rajah* has been ordered from Ports[mou]th to Southampton[.] request to know if that ship is going to Constantinople[,] if so[,] whether she can convey 70 Sappers & miners[,] also about 14 officers and 11 Horses with a small proportion of Stores[.]

[**380**] *Milne to Horse Guards*

Admiralty
15 August 1854

Write to the Horse Guards and[,] with reference to their former application for conveying the various Drafts to complete the different Regiments in the East, request to know whether it is the intention that these various Drafts should still be forwarded to this destination[.]

[**381**] *Milne to Napier*

Admiralty, Private
15 August 1854

My dear Sir Charles

My wife sends you two pictures of Yourself and in the cases something for breakfast on your marauding expeditions[.] I hope they may prove acceptable. I have nothing very new for you, but in this Evenings *Globe*, There [*sic*] is a most disagreeable Telegph that on the 4th Inst. a portion of the Russian Fleet out of Sebastopol arrived off Odessa[,] no doubt to Embark Troops[.][1] This[,] if true[,] is a most serious business. Take care of your Russian Fleets that they dont move. It is really very serious if they were to get out [*sic*], and do all sorts of mischief.

[P.S.:] We are most anxious to hear from you[.]

[**382**] *Milne to Newcastle*

Admiralty, Private
17 August 1854

Dear Duke of Newcastle

I was obliged to go to Woolwich last Evg[,] or I would have called on you at your office in accordance with the wishes of Sir J Graham, who mentioned to me some days ago, that there was an intention to bring Home some Troops from Canada[,] and that arrangement would have to be made so soon as the official communication was received from the War Depart.

I may mention that the season is now advancing[,] and to send ships from England to Quebec is running considerable risk of their being detained all winter in the St. Lawrence, and it will therefore require some early decision on the subject. If ships cannot proceed from England, the Authorities at Quebec might endeavour to secure vessels at that place, but these vessels would have Cargoes on Board[,] and could only bring home small detachments.

The Mail leaves London for North America tomorrow Evening[.] The two Parcels for your son[2] were sent to Deptford and will be forwarded by the *Holyrood*[.]

[1]The report was erroneous.
[2]Arthur Pelham Clinton (1840–70).

[**383**] *Milne to Houston Stewart*

Admiralty
18 August 1854

My dear Admiral

Thanks for your Letter of the 12th received this morning[.][1] I am glad to find you are yourself again[,] but be cautious and dont [*sic*] overwork yourself. The Iron & Rivets sailed from Cork yesterday by *Golden Fleece*. The Towing Hawsers . . . will be sent out and it has been already ordered.

The *Mauritius* will Embark the Sappers & Miners with a portion of the 34th Reg for Corfu and will sail on Tuesday. The *Supply*[,] our own Screw Transport[,] is loading for Varna and will sail in a week[.] she has all ordnance stores. we have no other Steam Transports preparing and I have nothing further fitting out.

We have endeavoured to get the sailing ships reduced in price and a good many have come down, others [however] refuse[,] so that if any ship so reduced in price is at Malta[,] we have requested you to send them back to Boxer, that he may send home the high priced ships & we have advertized for others in England [*sic*][.] I think we will have a reduction by so doing. All are absent from this [office] except myself, Hamilton & Osborne[,][2] the Board being at Portsmouth on the visitation.

The *Trent* I hear has gone to Varna with the Mules[.] when she returns she is to go to Gibraltar for 100 Horses[,] & then to Barcelona for more mules[.] will you keep this in mind and order it[?] an order however will go out by this Evenings mail[.]

The Cholera is spreading here a good <u>Deal</u>. Cap Richd Rowley[3] died of it this morning . . . My youngest Child I thought would have died yesterday with something of that kind, having been ill for 14 days[,] but by aid of Brandy it was revived and is better today and[,] I am happy to say[,] out of danger[.]

We have no news from [the] Baltic[.] Bomarsund is <u>invested</u> but we have no news of any attack[.][4]

[1]Not preserved among Milne's papers.

[2]Ralph Bernal Osborne (1811–82). M.P., 1841–59, 1859–65, 1866–68, 1870–74; Secretary to the Admiralty, 1852–58.

[3]Richard Freeman Rowley (1806–54). Entered, 1819; Lt, 1825; Cmdr, 1827; Capt., 1830.

[4]For the operations at Bomarsund, see Clowes, vol. 6, pp. 419–28, and Bonner-Smith and Dewar, *Russian War, 1854*, pp. 10–13, 93–103.

[**384**] *Christie to Milne*

City of London, Baljik
19 August 1854

My dear Captain

Your will no doubt have heard how severely the Men of War have suffered from Cholera, and will[,] I dare say[,] be anxious to hear about the Transports. I am thankful to say that they have been most mercifully visited [*sic*]. out [*sic*] of 50 Steamers & Transports[,] here there have been only 20 fatal cases. The vessels which suffered were six sailing ships, they were anchored near each other and pretty close in shore. the [*sic*] rest are all quite healthy. I have moved the infected ships out, and ordered the whole to spring their Broadsides to the breeze, and some to start out to sea for a day or two.

They are all perfectly fit for any service.

Britannia is in a sad state. I have been obliged to give up five spare Transports to receive her crew, in order that the ship may be thoroughly cleaned. This I grudge exceedingly, but it cannot be helped. Tents on shore might have answered fully as well, and kept the Transports pure.

I dined with the Admiral[1] yesterday, he is wonderfully well, but of course much distressed at losing so many fine fellows. He can easily make up for it by taking hands out of some of the sailing Frigates. I hope we shall then make a dash at Sevastopol.

I have just arranged the Transports in five Divisions[,] agreeably to the Form I enclosed in my last letter, which was approved of, and as soon as the Steamers arrive from England we shall be ready to start on any Service that may be ordered.

Poor Capt Smith[2] of *Simoom* is dead after a few hours illness.

Pray excuse a hurried note as I am just going down to Varna.

[**385**] *Milne to Newcastle*

Admiralty
21 August [1854]

A Telegraph was received last evening from Al Boxer [dated] 14th Aug[,] stating he was not able under the aspect of affairs in the Black Sea[,] to send Home any of the Steam Transports. I was looking forward to 2 or 3 being sent to England to convey the Drafts of Regiments

[1]Deans Dundas.
[2]Henry Smith (*c*.1798–1854). Entered, 1810; Lt, 1822; Cmdr, 1841; Capt., 1846.

now waiting[,] in all about 2000 men[,] the 9 pr Field Battery[,] and the 46 Reg.[,] but I presume I must now look round and endeavour to Charter nine Steamer's [*sic*]. if [*sic*] this is your wish[,] I would be glad to be informed.

[P.S.:] Orders were sent to Canada and Halifax in regard to the Troops coming to England[.]

[**386**] *Milne to Napier*

Admiralty
22 August 1854

My dear Admiral
I write you a hurried line by this Evenings messenger to offer you my sincere good wishes and congratulations on the Capture [*sic*] of Bomarsund, and at the success of the operations under your Command. It is a most satisfactory result and one which will be considered as such by the English Public[,] who are anxious for some great Event. I hope the allied Forces will be equally successful at Sevastopol[,] where I hear they are now going.

My poor wife is in sad distress[:] her Baby is very very ill and I am much afraid there is but little hope for it[,] but whilst life there is always some expectation of a favorable change [*sic*]. Agnew[1] arrived here last night and he went down to Sir J Graham at Cowes this morning. Your Letters will be in this Evenings *Gazette*.

[**387**] *Milne to Napier*

Admiralty
27 August 1854

My dear Sir Charles
I write you a line by Cap Nugent[2] who returns this Evening with Lord Clarendons[3] Letter respecting the Alland Islands and Forts

[1]John De Courcy Andrew Agnew (1819–1916). Entered, 1834; Lt, 1843; Cmdr, 1854; Capt. (Ret.), 1870. Agnew was Napier's Flag Lt in the Baltic and had arrived in Britain carrying the dispatches relative to Bomarsund. See Bonner-Smith and Dewar, *Russian War, 1854*, p. 12.

[2]Presumably a War or Foreign Office functionary.

[3]George William Frederick Villiers, fourth Earl of Clarendon and fourth Baron Hyde (1800–1870). Lord Privy Seal, 1839–41; President of the Board of Trade, 1846–47; Lord Lt of Ireland, 1847–52; Foreign Secretary, 1853–58; 1868–70; Chancellor of the Duchy of Lancaster, 1865–66.

Bomarsund. you [*sic*] will see that future proceedings depend on the answer the General Barguay de Hilliers[1] [*sic*] will receive from the Government of Sweden[,] and that you are to be guided by that answer.[2]

Sir J. Graham returns to Town tomorrow[,] and as the Messenger will leave this on Tuesday[,] you will probably hear from him by that opportunity.

There is nothing new here except a Telegph from Varna dated the 17th[,] which mentions that Cholera was subsiding in the Army, but increasing in the French Fleet. we [*sic*] know nothing of the Troops having embarked for the Crimea . . .

I am the only person in Town[.]

[**388**] *Milne to Grant*

Inveresk, Musselburgh
9 September 1854

Dear Mr Grant

I received your note and I am glad to find the arrangements of the Rooms of the Office will be for the advantage of the different Departments. I am most anxious about the Transport accounts and the outstanding Claims. This should be at once put in hand[,] and with all the possible strength of the office as it will not do, [*sic*] to delay the payments of claims that are due.

I find from a Note from Mr LeFevre[3] that more of the owners have now reduced the charge for their Ships. It will be necessary[,] if all abroad are reduced[,] to pay off some of those now coming home and probably already arrived. Please to look at the State of these ships[,] for we must not have more ships that we may actually require[,] and had all the owners reduced[,] then it would not have been necessary to have taken up the 5 ships we did[.]

I sent forward your paper in regard to Deptford to Sir J. Graham and some measures will have to be immediately adopted; Deptford[,] with its present Force of officers and Buildings[,] is not able to perform what is required. The idea of an inner Basin where the Mast Pond is, is a good one, and would be a great advantage to the Establishment.

[1]Achille Baraguay d'Hilliers (1795–1878). Commander of the French military forces sent to the Baltic.

[2]The British hoped that the success at Bomarsund would encourage Sweden to join their alliance. It did not. See Lambert, *The Crimean War*, pp. 181–2.

[3]Probably Nicholas Lefebvre, one of the Transport Agents.

We have most charming weather here and the Harvest most abundant[.] My little Girl is daily improving[.]

[**389**] *Milne to Grant*

Inveresk, Musselburgh
11 September [1854]

Dear Mr Grant

. . . In regard to Steam Transport[s,] it is right to have advertised[,] and thus to have tested the Market, but I doubt whether any vessels will be offered[.] I think [that] if you do not receive offers[,] you can get assistance from Mr Cunard and the P&O Co. You might send out the *Holyrood*[,] and I think you should submit to the Board that any of HM Ships going out should take Provisions to Malta or Constantinople[.] Nothing new from this[.]

[**390**] *Milne to Grant*

Inveresk, Musselburgh
13 September 1854

Dear Mr Grant

I have received a note from the Captain of the Fleet in the Black Sea,[1] which I have now sent to Captain Richards[,] and he will forward it to you, as it contains information about Provisions & the *Nimrod* Transport. As that vessel is going on to Stockholm for repair, I think the owners should be informed, that they may take the necessary Steps, as we are not bound to do so. The sooner this is done the better[,] if it is the legal course for us to pursue. It strikes me from what Admiral [Michael] Seymour says, that you can spare the *Holyrood* from the Baltic Service, but before doing so you should mention it to the Board[.]

[1]Montagu Stopford.

[**391**] *Milne to Grant*

Inveresk, Musselburgh
16 September 1854

Dear Mr Grant

Thanks for your Letter and all the Information which it contains[.][1] I write to mention, that as the *Prince* Steamer will soon be in England from the Baltic[,] she could be sent to the Black Sea and to recall [*sic*] one of the Hired Vessels. But before she goes there she will require a good overhaul and a New Capstan[,] which is now at Deptford Yard. I think it might be as well to give Ad Boxer a hint about Mr. Moubray[2] keeping up the supplies and making all demands in time. I have accordingly made a minute which I enclose to you & you can name it [*sic*] to Capn Richards & the Board . . .
I will be anxious to hear what has been decided at Deptford[.] I hope the Machine has been put up for cleaning the wheat[.]

[**392**] *Milne to Boxer*

Inveresk, Musselburgh
16 September [1854]

Write to Admiral Boxer and acquaint[,] as it is necessary that early information should be obtained in regard to all Supplies required at Constantinople, he is to make the same known to Mr Moubray and to direct him to keep the wants of the Fleet as well as the Army in view[,] so that every arrangement may be made at Malta or in England as early as possible for the purpose of sending out all requisite supplies[.]

[1]Not preserved among Milne's papers.

[2]George Henry Moubray (1810–86). Passed Clerk, 1831; Paymaster, 1847; Paymaster-in-Chief, 1870. Borne on HMS *Britannia*'s books as an additional paymaster for particular service; he earned much praise for his work with Boxer at Constantinople, and was appointed Paymaster to the Royal Yacht *Victoria and Albert* in recognition of his service; Paymaster on *Victoria and Albert*, 1856–62; Agent Victualler and Storekeeper, Malta Dockyard, 1862–70. See below, Wood to Milne, [**578**].

[**393**] *Graham to Milne*

Admiralty, Private
21 September 1854

My dear Capt Milne

I have just placed the letters from Adls Stewart and Boxer in the hands of Capt Richards, who has undertaken to give the necessary orders with respect to the various demands. Some of their Requisitions have been met by Supplies already sent in anticipation, and measures have been taken to render the Hospital Establishment at Malta more effective.

The landing of the Army in the Crimea will bring this conflict in the East to an early and decisive Issue.[1] If happily Sebastopol is taken, our difficulties in the Black Sea will be greatly diminished. In a short time our exact position in that Quarter will be developped [*sic*]; and we shall see more clearly what our arrangements for the Winter must be. In the mean time[,] we must send out constantly both Biscuit and Salt Meat. The *Prince* is fitting out for an immediate Voyage to the Black Sea. It will be necessary, I believe, to put her under a Pendant and to man her from the Fleet.

I see no immediate necessity for breaking up your Holidays and for calling in your assistance here; tho we never get on so well in your absence. Your services for the last six months have been invaluable . . .

[**394**] *Christie to Milne*

Melbourne, off Balaklava
27 September 1854

My dear Milne

We have had such a very great deal to do that I have not had a moment to write[,] even to you. I am happy to inform you that the Transports, with the exception of one or two repairing damages, are all ready for Service[,] and with a sufficient supply of Provisions & Water for three weeks[,] should the Army reembark. By dint of great economy[,] I have made the Coal spin [*sic*] out wonderfully, but I begin to long for a Collier or two.

The landing of the Troops was most successful, almost without a casualty. not [*sic*] a shot was fired at us. The Cholera however has been

[1]This belief of Graham's is addressed in Lambert, *The Crimean War*, p. 141.

making sad havoc. I have already sent 8 or 9 vessels to the Bosphorus with them [i.e., the sick] and the wounded[,] and two more are filling fast. I had placed a number of the ships in Eupatoria Bay[,] where there is tolerable shelter except from the S.W., but I have been obliged to get a number of them down to be in readiness to receive the Sick & Wounded.

On the whole, the Ships & Masters have given me great satisfaction. The Crews I have[,] at times[,] had a good deal of trouble with[,] in consequence of having no power to punish them in an effectual manner. Some of the agents are zealous useful men, but many are quite worn out. I never had so much anxiety and hard work in my life before, but I am most thankful that everything has gone on so successfully, and that the Army have been abundantly supplied with everything, and have wanted for nothing afloat. The working of the Transport men is very trying to the patience of one who has been accustomed to the pace of a Man of War, but I think myself very fortunate to have got so much extra work out of them, considering the wording of their Charter Duties. Most naval men know nothing of the difficulties of the Transport Service.

The Battle of Alma[1] would [*sic*] cheer the people in England, and let them see that we have not been idle. We took possession of this place yesterday, and I brought up the Siege Train this morning. It is now being landed, and I trust Sebastopol [*sic*] will very soon be ours. All hands will go at it with a regular good will.

[**395**] *Graham to Milne*

Balmoral, Private
5 October 1854

My dear Capt Milne

I have shown to Capt Richards your answer[2] to my letter and he agrees entirely with you in opinion.

If[,] therefore[,] the Miller at Deptford be unequal to the adequate discharge of his duties, at all cost he must be removed, for the loss, which may arise from his ignorance or neglect, is almost incalculable. When you return to London you must put this branch of the Victualling to rights. I am afraid that Martin with his greatest zeal and best intentions, wants method and controlling power. He stands, however, further

[1]20 September 1854.
[2]Milne evidently did not copy this letter.

for Promotion, and his tenure of this present appointment cannot be long. Could you make enquiries about a Master Miller from the Private Trade, who would suit our purpose? I am quite resolved, that this Deptford Mill shall be rendered really efficient under the direction of an able Master Miller[,] bred to the business in the best school, and I believe that training to be [found] in Scotland, with a Scotch education.

I remain here till Monday. I shall return to London before the end of next week. We are still anxious to know for certain, that Sebastopol has fallen. I am sanguine in my hopes. It will place a great force at our immediate disposal. Napier, I am afraid, will end in doing nothing. He has had his opportunity: and neither he nor the Nation will henceforth have reason to complain, that he has not been trusted with a great command.

[**396**] *Mundy to Milne*

War Office, Immediate and Confidential
13 October 1854

Sir

I am directed by the Duke of Newcastle to request that you will move the Lords Commissioners of the Admiralty to send instructions to Rear Admiral Boxer by the messenger who will leave London this evening for Constantinople, to ascertain from General Lord Raglan whether, after sending home certain large Transport steamers for the conveyance of Drafts of Regiments to the seat of War, his Lordship can spare any others for a limited time.

If such should be the case, His Grace requests that their Lordships will further instruct the Rear Admiral that he will be at liberty to place at the disposal of General Canrobert,[1] the Commander of the French Army, three or four Steamers to convey reinforcements to the Army under his command from Marseilles, but expressly upon the condition that they shall not be detained longer than is absolutely necessary for the double voyage [*sic*], and the embarkation of the Troops.

[1]François-Antoine Certain Canrobert (1809–95). C-in-C of French troops in the Crimea following the death of Gen. Armand St Arnaud on 20 September 1854.

[**397**] *Milne to Newcastle*

Admiralty
23 October [1854]

Steam Transports preparing to Convey Troops to the Crimea

Ship	Number			From	Will Sail
Jura	1200	men &	off	Cork	28th Oct
Queen of South	780	do	do	Portsmouth	2nd Nov
Cleopatra	700	do	do	Portsmouth	5th Nov
Ottawa	500	do	do	Portsmouth	8th Nov
Robt Lowe	600	do	do	–	12th Nov
Brandon	600	do	do	–	14th Nov
Charity	500	do	do	Doubtful[.]	ship not yet arrived from Quebec[.] Another Steamer will be offered to the Admiralty & will be ready in 3 weeks[.]
Total	4780				

[P.S.:] The above is the probable time of sailing[;] a day less or more may take place.

[**398**] *Milne to Boxer*

Admiralty
23 October 1854

My dear Admiral

I have to thank you for several Letters which I have not answered[,] as I have been absent from the Admiralty on leave[,] and I would not write in case of others writing from this[,] and thereby we might have been a[t] cross purposes[.]

I am glad you have retained your health and all goes well with you amid the Sickness which has so unfortunately prevailed. I have little news from this, it is from the East we look for news.

The only thing I have to tell you is the Fate [*sic*] of Franklin. his [*sic*] star, Silver Spoons &c have been found at the Entrance of [the] Back or G[rea]t Fish River, where the Esquimaux found the Bodies of about 40 people, and they were seen in the same year 1850 marching over the Ice from the North[.]

I write in haste to save post. I hear some reports of the Accounts of the Storekeeper at Constantinople falling into arrear[s] and that matters are not working well. if [*sic*] this is so[,] it may as well have your attention to be directed to this, but this is private.

[**399**] *Milne to Napier*

Admiralty
24 October 1854

My dear Sir Charles

I have been absent from this for some weeks past and enjoying the Highlands of Scotland instead of my den at the Adm[iralt]y[,] and my absence must be my excuse for not having written to you for sometime past. I only returned on Sunday. I have to thank [you] for several Letters[,][1] and I have been turning over in my mind how we can deal with the remarks you made on Minor Punishments, but if Captains will not make honest returns[,] it is in vain to give orders, for they will in some way or [an]other be avoided. I will however see what can be done. Your Letters [*sic*] about Provisions were received last night, but as far as I have yet been able to make out[,] your Fleet will be provisioned to the 10th of Decr[.] The *Holyrood* will have reached you long ere this, The [*sic*] *Rhadamanthus* sailed two or three days ago[,] and the *Gottenburgh* [*sic*] went off[,] I believe[,] yesterday Evg., but the best arrangement must be made on the spot to fill up [the] Flying Squadron[,] as we have not sent any vessel to Faro, and no other vessels than the three I have named are preparing for the Baltic. it [*sic*] is a pity so much provisions [*sic*] were allowed to come home in Grey's Squadron[2] and the Transports, as we reckoned that you would have taken everything out of them. Having been here only 2 days[,] I have not got into the thread of <u>what</u> is going on, and I think the Newspaper's [*sic*] give all information[.] with the exception of the news of the fate of Franklin having been decided there is really nothing new. The Bodies of his Party were found at or near the Entrance of the Back or the Great Fish River[,] and the Esquimaux saw them travelling in that direction from the North early in 1850. I send you a chart with all the new discoveries. we [*sic*] have nothing from abroad. I hear the Batteries were <u>not</u> opened on Sebastopol on the 15th[.] This comes by Telegh.

[1]Not preserved among Milne's papers.

[2]Frederick Grey, in HMS *Hannibal*, had escorted a convoy carrying Russian prisoners of war to Britain, following the capture of Bomarsund.

My wife is in Berwickshire & begged when I wrote you to send her best wishes and many thanks for your most sympathy [*sic*] about her Child[,] which is now quite well . . .

[**400**] *Milne to British Consul at Marseilles*

Admiralty
24 October 1854

To inform the Master of the *City of London* Steamer that as soon as the French Troops are on board[,] and also Lt Col Fraser of the Royal Marines[,] who is on his way from England, He [*sic*] is to proceed to Sea and make the best of his way to Balaclava in the Crimea[,] reporting before sailing the number of Troops on board[.]

[**401**] *Milne Draft Instructions to the Hudson's Bay Company*

Admiralty
27 October 1854

Inform the Hudson's Bay Company that my Lords[,] having taken into consideration the important information which has been brought to this Country by Dr Rae,[1] respecting the unfortunate fate of a part of Sir John Franklins expedition[,] consisting of about 40 persons out of a Crew of 134 Men, who[,] by the statements given to him by the Esquimaux[,] are said to have been seen travelling from the North along the western shore of King Williams Land[,] and to have subsequently perished at or near Cape Sir C Ogle[,] at the entrance of the Back or Gt Fish River in the spring of 1850; the Silver plate[,] the Badge of the Order of Hanover belonging to Sir J. Franklin, and other Articles the property of the officers of HMS *Erebus* & *Terror*, obtained by D Rae from the Natives of the dreary region about King Williams Land, appears to confirm this unfortunate intelligence of their fate.
My Lords deem it to be their duty that[,] having thus obtained this important information, which fixes the locality where a portion of our long lost countrymen have met their melancholy fate, that immediate steps should be adopted to trace this information to its source and[,] if possible[,] to gain some further knowledge of all the facts, by a personal inspection of the locality, and[,] if possible[,] to obtain from

[1]John Rae, Arctic explorer (1813–93). See *DNB*, XVI, p. 595 for particulars of this expedition.

those Esquimaux who saw the Party travelling on the ice, such information as they can give in regard to their proceedings, and to secure from them by barter, all articles of plate, Books &c as can be obtained with the view of throwing further light on the proceedings of that expedition, The [*sic*] fate of the remainder of the Crew, The [*sic*] position of the ships, and[,] as there can be no doubt that a record would have been kept of their proceedings[,] even to the last days of their existence[,] if possible to obtain it.

Their Lordships on this occasion[,] and to carry out their Instructions, have to appeal to the well known liberality of the Hudsons Bay Company, and have to request their aid and assistance in this undertaking of difficulty and danger, by asking them to organize[,] at the expense of the Government[,] an Expedition to the Great Slave Lake, and from thence to proceed by the Back or Gt Fish River to the Sea during the approaching season of 1855. My Lords would wish to confide the whole detail and the Command of this expedition to the officers serving under the Hudson Bay Coy[,] whose well known ability, energy and decision in travelling over the dreary regions of the North would meet with the entire confidence of the Government.

If the Hudsons Bay Coy[,] on considering these views of their Lordships, will concur in the request, they would wish every possible means to be adopted as early as possible to carry out this expedition during the approaching season of 1855, with the view of the exploring party returning from the Entrance of the River in that year, but if[,] from the state of the Ice, a backward season, or other cause, no information could be obtained in 1855, then it would seem advisable that the expedition[,] having wintered at the nearest Port to the Sea[,] should again return to complete the search in the Season of 1856.

But there is still another subject connected with the Polar regions, which has likewise engaged the anxious consideration of their Lordships and in regard to which they must also request the aid of the Hudson Bay Coy.

That subject is the safety of Cap Collinson and the Crew of HMS *Enterprize*[.] My Lords are aware by the records deposited by that officer on the 27th Aug. 1852, which is the last information they have of his proceedings, That [*sic*] he intended to pursue an Easterly course in the *Enterprize* between Prince Albert and Woolaston Land. My Lords have reason to believe that a barrier will be found in that direction, and that that officer will be compelled to retrace his steps or to abandon His [*sic*] ships. under [*sic*] those circumstances[,] my Lords look to the Mackenzie River for his relief, and they are informed by an officer who communicated with Cap Collinson on his leaving England, That [*sic*] in case of finding such barrier he was recommended to fall back on the Mackenzie. Such being the case[,] and The Hudson Bay Co having at the request of their Lordships sent supplies to the various Ports on that River, They [*sic*] would now request the Company to organize an Expedition at the expense of HM Government[,] to be sent to the mouth of the Mackenzie River, and to follow the Coast to the Eastward to afford assistance to Cap Collinsons party[,] and to leave supplies & notices on the Coast giving information of the manner in which they should proceed in order to obtain succour & assistance in case they abandon their ship or[,] in case of falling in with that officer[,] to desire him to abandon the *Enterprize* and return to England.[1]

[**402**] *Christie to Milne*

Melbourne, off Balaklava
28 October 1854

My dear Milne

I have just received a letter from the Admiralty signed by Capt Hamilton[,] directing me to transmit my letters through Admiral Boxer. This must surely be a mistake. Admiral Boxer is at Constantinople and I am at the Crimea with Admiral Dundas & Admiral Lyons. After leaving the Bosphorus I considered that I had no more to do with Adml Boxer, except demanding supplies for the Transports. This will give me five different Departments to communicate with[,] and God knows I have enough of harassing business to go through without adding more. My Instructions tell me clearly to correspond direct with Head Quarters, and to keep the Commander in Chief and the Admiralty acquainted with all proceedings.

Will you kindly explain this matter to me.

I fear we have been making little impression upon Sebastopol the last ten days, although an immense quantity of Powder & Shot has been expended upon it. The Russians are becoming more bold and made a serious attack two days ago, drove the Turks from their Batteries capturing the guns, charged through the Scots Greys[,] and were only prevented from entering Balaclava by the 93d, which Regt turned them.[2] A charge was afterwards made by the light division of Cavalry headed by Lord Cardigan, in which we suffered a severe loss by [*sic*] the Russian Artillery, 600 Horses killed. In fact they gained a victory.

[1]Collinson and the *Enterprize* returned safely to Britain in late 1854.

[2]On this action and the subsequent charge of the Light Brigade, see Christopher Hibbert, *The Destruction of Lord Raglan* (Boston, 1961), pp. 129–53.

Yesterday they again attacked near Sebastopol, but on this occasion they got the worst of it, having about 400 killed & wounded.

I have been very anxious about the Transports, and have got all out of the Harbour except those absolutely necessary for supplies, and to carry the Sick and Wounded. There is very deep water but good holding ground, 35 to 38 f[atho]m.

At Katcha there is also good holding ground and 10 & 12 f[atho]m water, but Admiral Dundas does not like that Anchorage. He prefers the distant Anchorage of Eupatoria, where I have got most of them anchored, and am filling up their six weeks Provisions as fast as I can get it from Constantinople.

There is still a good deal of sickness amongst the Troops, and I am sorry to say Scurvy has begun to show itself. I have sent to Constantinople for a large supply of vegetables at the request of Lord Raglan, which I hope may have good effect.

The Transports are all ready for service, full of Water most of them, and plenty of Provisions to carry the Army back.

Himalaya will have to go home I fear[.] The ships shaft in the after bearing is defective and she leaks abaft[,] making about 2½ feet water pr. day. I have requested Admiral Dundas to have her Surveyed on her return from Varna. Her Master and Crew are also constantly grumbling at being kept. They however do their business well. She might take home 1500 Invalids and bring out two fresh Regiments.

We have had no bad weather yet, but we cannot expect to be much longer without trying our ground tackle. I shall get the ships into as snug berths as circumstances will allow.

[**403**] *Milne to Newcastle*

Admiralty
1 November [1854]

My dear Duke

I write a line to say that all Medical Comforts for the East demanded previous to the 12th of October have been sent out. Those demanded on the 12th of Octr and on the 24th are partly shipped and I hope will sail next week.

I have seen Dr. Smith[1] and I will arrange with him a more expeditious arrangement for obtaining the Army supplies[.] He ought to make

[1]Dr Sir Andrew Smith, K.C.B. (1797–1872). Dir-Gen. of the Army Medical Department.

his own purchases and we will pay on obtaining his signature to [*sic*] the Bills. it [*sic*] will save a great deal of trouble and be more satisfactory to both Departments.

[**404**] *Milne to Newcastle*

Admiralty
2 November 1854

Dear Duke of Newcastle

I have written to the Ordnance to endeavour to obtain some definite information in regard to the Amount of Stores required to be shipped to the East. it [*sic*] may be difficult to give this, but at any rate we should have some information to guide us. we [*sic*] have provided for all the requisitions we have received. we [*sic*] have now obtained space for 150 Tons in the *Rajah*[,] to sail from Southampton on the 15th. we [*sic*] have Chartered the *Adelaide* for 500 Troops or perhaps 600, and she will take about 700 Tons of Stores, but will not be ready for three weeks. Anything that is urgent should go in the *Rajah*. I will keep a lookout to hasten all that is urgent, but the Military Department must keep us informed. I should think it would be requisite to hasten out Powder[,] Shot & Shell, but this you know better than I do.

[**405**] *Milne to James W. D. Dundas*

Admiralty
3 November 1854

Write to Adl Dundas and acquaint him that such of the Sailing Transports as are not required to be retained for the Military Service are to be sent to England[,] conferring with Lord Raglan on the Subject, The most expensive ships being selected for this purpose in accordance with returns already sent to Cap Christie[.]
Copy to Ad Boxer

[**406**] *Milne to Boxer*

Admiralty
3 November 1854

My dear Admiral

I write you a few lines by this Evenings Mail and there are one or two points which will require your attention.

We wish to have a return from Mr Moubray of the Quantity of Provisions at Constantinople for Army and Naval Service. we [*sic*] are without such a return as [*sic*: and] we are consequently in the Dark of the wants of the Army[,] and as we are [those] who supply the provisions[,] we are anxious for all and every information on the subject. we [*sic*] have therefore ordered a return to be sent home every 14 days.

In the papers it was mentioned that considerable delay took place by the unnecessary detention of the Steam Transports at Constan[tino]ple[,] and that one vessel was there for Eleven days and could get no orders &c. I have no doubt this was an exaggeration[,] but please to let me have an answer on this point. The *Taurus* Steamer in July was kept 17 days at Scutari to land some Guns & Stores, and I believe we have had claims for Demurrage in consequence. I think this requires some enquiry and Comdr Boys[1] had something to do with it. This question has been raised by the Duke of Newcastle[,] & from what I heard[,] it was stated to be neglect on the part of some of our Agents[,] but if you can give any information I will be obliged[.] We are anxious to get home some of the Expensive Sailing Transports and if you can[,] with the sanction of Lord Raglan, hasten their departure[,] pray do so. We are sending out all descriptions of Provisions as fast as we can, but I hope orders will be given to get as much Fresh Beef as possible[,] so as to save the Salt [meat,] which is scarce and dear.

No news here, we are most anxious for news from Crimea, nothing authentic from thence since the 13th Octr[.]

Plumridge has just arrived in London with best wishes[.]

[1]William Boys (*c*.1813–79). Entered, *c*.1825; Lt, 1835; Cmdr, 1846; Capt. (Res.), 1858; Rear-Adm. (Ret.), 1875. Agent for Transports afloat, 1841–44, 1845–46.

[**407**] *Milne to Newcastle*

Admiralty
5 November 1854

The '*Robt Lowe*' steamer will sail this week from Deptford & Portsmouth[.]
The *Cleopatra* steamer from Cork sails Tuesday[.]
The *Ottawa* steamer sails from Portsmouth, Wednesday[.]
The *Brandon* steamer from Deptford will sail in about 8 to 10 days[.]
The *Adelaide* steamer will sail in about 3 weeks.
all [*sic*] the above [sail] with Troops & Stores[.]
6 Sailing Transports will sail in 4 or 5 days, from Deptford full of Provisions & Stores[.]

[**408**] *Ramsay*[1] *to Roberts*[2]

War Office, Private
9 November 1854

My dear Roberts

Will you have the kindness to tell the Duke of Newcastle that I lost no time in going to the Admiralty, but I did not find Captain Milne. I wrote him a note stating what his Grace had said on the subject and I enclose his answer[3] which if I am allowed to observe is very unsatisfactory. the [*sic*] Admiralty should not promise what they cannot perform. They promised to give us eighty tons[,] & they should have made such arrangements to prevent the *Ottawa* from being overloaded at Liverpool.

I wish you would state to the Duke of Newcastle that Messrs Howell & Hayter[,] the great Army packers[,] have proposed to Charter a vessel themselves & if the Government would consent to this we should be independent of the Admiralty.

[1]George D. Ramsay, Private Secretary to Secretary at War Sidney Herbert.

[2]H. Roberts, Temporary Assistant Undersecretary for War, appointed by the Duke of Newcastle when the War and Colonial Offices were separated in June 1854.

[3]Not preserved among Newcastle's papers, but possibly relative to carrying warm clothing to the Crimea.

[**409**] *Milne to Graham*

Admiralty
11 November 1854

There are at present in the Black Sea 34 Steam vessels[,] including 4 which have sailed from England[,] and 4 others are on the point of sailing[,] and[,] deducting 4 of those which are attached to the Commissariat Dept.[,] There [*sic*] remain 34 steam vessels available for the embarkation of Troops[.] these will easily receive <u>21,500</u> men.

There are in the Black Sea at this time 97 Sailing vessels[,] independent of about 15 others on the voyage out full of Provisions[.] These 97 vessels could embark with perfect ease no less than 35,000 men if required to do so, but if some should be absent &c[,] it may be assumed that there are means of receiving on board Sailing Transports 30,000 men excluding Horses . . .

By Steam Transports	21,500	
By Sailing Transports	30,000	
Total	51,500	
By ships of War and Steam Transports of War	13,390	
	64,890	
Total means of Transport of Troops in Black Sea		64,890[1]

[**410**] *Milne to Graham*

Admiralty
11 November [1854] 3:30 p.m.

Dear Sir James

I have made a mistake in the number of Sailing Transports. I assumed it at 95, but it will hardly average that number[.] we have only 65 in the Enclosed return[2] but by this time we will have probably 10 to 15 more at Constantinople[,] making in all say about 75[,] but the calculation I gave you will not be much reduced[,] as I assumed too low an average[,] viz. 350 soldiers for each ship. This ought to be 400 men at least and 75×400 = 30,000 men

[1]This memorandum also contains a more detailed breakdown of the numbers carried by steamers and ships of war but not sailing transports, which is not included in this collection.

[2]There is no copy of this return in Milne's papers.

I feel confident of this[.]

[P.S.:] nothing [*sic*] from Glasgow[.][1]

[411] *Cunard to Milne*

Howchins Hotel[, ?London]
11 November 1854

Dear Capt Milne

You shall have one or perhaps two Steamers of the first class. I sent a telegraph Message to Liverpool to commence coaling immediately & to take a large supply on Board[.] I have rec[eive]d an answer to say that the coaling is going on[.] Are we to find provisions for the troops[?] Give me your orders.

I shall go to Liverpool to night[.] We have a new steam ship at Glasgow[,] the *Etna* of 2300 Tons. I think I can get her ready for sea in a few days by working night and day. She is 8 feet between decks[:] no finer ship in the Kingdom for Horses or Troops[.] If you desire I will commence fitting her to day by Telegraph Message. she [*sic*] is the sister ship to the *Jura*. I'll be with you shortly . . .

[P.S,:] The *Alps* is loaded at Liverpool and leaves for Havre in the morning[,] from whence she is to proceed to New York[,] but I have given direction that she shall not go to New York and shall be at your disposal on Wednesday next at Havre[,] to proceed to any place you may order, either in England or to Toulon direct from Havre[.]

[412] *Milne to Cunard*

Admiralty
11 November [1854], 4:00 p.m.

Dear Sir

I have this moment seen Sir J Graham in regard to the Transport of Troops from Toulon to the Crimea[,] and he has requested we communicate to you the great anxiety that exists for at once sending out these reinforcements. I will therefore be obliged if you will give immediate Instructions for the following arrangements being made[,] which I believe will be almost in accordance with your letter to me[.]

The *Etna* to proceed to Dublin to embark the 90th Regt.

[1]That is, no news of any available steamers.

The *Alps* to proceed to Toulon to embark as many Troops as she can carry[,] say 900 to 1000, and another First Class Steamer to proceed to the same port also to embark 1000 men[.] I will further be obliged if you will order provisions and other Stores for this Service[,] but Hammocks will be supplied from the Dock Yards[,] and the French Govt will be requested to provide Blankets.

I may say the Emergency is urgent and the Board feels assured that[,] under such circumstances[,] your well known zeal may be depended on for these vessels being at Toulon at the Earliest possible day.

[**413**] *Milne to Allen*[1]

Admiralty
11 November [1854], 4:00 p.m.

Dear Sir

Since I saw you I have communicated with Sir James Graham[,] and he begs me to express to yourself and the Directors of the Company[,] the necessity for active measures being taken to send out reinforcements from Toulon to the Crimea with the least possible delay. Such being the case[,] I beg you will place the *Candia* at the disposal of the Government and give directions for that ship being victualled to carry 1200 men or more from Toulon to the Crimea.

We also wish the Services of the *Nubia* and *Ripon* for the same Service and[,] as time is urgent[,] I have to request that not a moment may be lost in directing these ships to be at Toulon at the very earliest day it is possible, The [*sic*] Company to find provisions and other Stores, the Gov. finding Hammocks[,] and the French Gov. providing Blankets.

I will be ready to afford any further information you may wish, but time is of [greatest] importance[.]

[**414**] *Milne to Chappell*[2]

Admiralty
11 November [1854] 4:30 p.m.

Dear Sir

There is an urgent necessity for sending out reinforcements to the Crimea[,] and I will therefore be obliged if you will place the *Thames*

[1]Of the P&O Company.
[2]Of the Royal Mail Steam Packet Company.

at the disposal of the Government to convey 1200 men from Toulon to the Crimea[,] and that this ship should proceed there at the very Earliest [*sic*] possible Day . . .

[**415**] *Milne to Ellis*[1]

Admiralty
11 November 1854

Dear Sir

As soon as *Indiana* arrives I beg you will Coal and Provision her with all possible haste, that not a moment may be lost in sending her to Toulon . . .

[**416**] *Milne to* [*?Graham*]

Admiralty
11 November [1854]

The following steam vessels will be ready as follows[:][2]

1. *Indiana* sailed [*sic*] from England on the 18th [will] be at Toulon 26th	1300 Soldiers
2. *Thames* do. do.	1200 [soldiers]
3. Another steamer to be [at] Toulon on the 26th	1000 [soldiers]

Say 3.500 men to embark at Toulon about the 27 Nov [and] 1500 about the 16th Decr[.]
The above I may say are almost certain[.]
Other arrangements making for a further number[.]

	nautical miles
Portsmouth to Gibraltar	1172
Gibraltar to Toulon	748
[subtotal]	1920
Toulon to Balaklava	1730
Total Distance	3650

[1]Of the General Screw Steamship Shipping Company.
[2]Milne wrote in the margin 'these ships will arrive in England about the 14th'.

[**417**] *Milne to Boxer*

Admiralty
13 November 1854

My dear Admiral

I write you a line by this Evenings Mail to say we are sending out Stores &c as fast as we can[:] by this I mean provisions. Several sailing vessels have gone and I hope others will follow this week. I may also mention the following arrangements[:] The [*sic*] *Manilla* Screw will sail on Thursday full of Army Clothing. Some has also gone out in the *Ottawa*[,] and 80 Tons in HMS *Curacoa*[.] The *Rajah* sails on the 15th and has on board Naval & Army Medical Stores[.] The *Brandon* will sail this week and has on board Lancaster [gun] projectiles[,] also stores of various kinds.

The *Alps*, *Candia*[,] *Thames*[, &] R*ipon* will proceed this week[,] all to embark French Troops for the Crimea, the *Europa* will Embark the 90th Reg on Saturday for the same destination[,] and one or two more Steamers will follow for French Troops. we [*sic*] have also two small Screw Steamers about to load with other Stores for the Black Sea, and we are to send forward one million pounds of Biscuit every month. to [*sic*] do this we must have Steamers back, but I will send orders out on this subject by the next mail[.] The *Hannibal* sails for the Black Sea tomorrow and it is likely the *Royal Albert* will soon follow[.]

Mrs Hyde Parker died on Friday[,] a happy release to her long continued sufferings.

[**418**] *Milne to James W. D. Dundas*

Admiralty
14 November 1854

Write to Vice Admiral Dundas and inform him my Lords have sent to the Black Sea in the Steam Ship *Robt Lowe*, 12 large and 12 small Iron Cylinders with Galvanic Apparatus & wires for the purpose of blowing up the sunken ships at the Entrance of Sebastopol[,] should circumstances require or admit of this being done[.] Mr Deane the experienced Submarine Surveyor and Engineer[,] with an assistant[,] has been sent out in the *Robt Lowe* with 2 men, and also an officer of the Royal Engineers[,] who has been instructed in the mode of Exploding the Cylinders and who is in charge of the Party[.]

[**419**] *Milne to* [*?Graham*]

Admiralty
14 November [1854]

Mr Samuel Bright from Liverpool
Called here to state that the *Great Britain* steamer will probably arrive in England from Australia about the 15th to 20th of Decr and he wished to know[:]
1st[,] If the Government would be inclined to purchase the Ship[.]
2d[,] If they would not purchase[,] whether the Government would be inclined to Charter her for a period of 6 Months[,] certain terms to be afterwards agreed upon[.]

He said he asked the above information as the French Government were anxious to Charter Steam Vessels and have made [an] offer for 6 months.

[**420**] *Graham to Milne*

Windsor Castle, Private
14 November 1854

My dear Capt Milne

Mr. Herbert[1] has placed in my hands the enclosed private letter from Lord De Ros. I am disposed to believe, that Admiral Boxer does stand in need of some assistance from subordinates: and if[,] during the approaching Winter[,] there be a large assemblage of Troops and Transports at Constantinople, it may be well to consider, whether an increase of his Establishment would not be a prudent measure.

I do not understand the comments of Lord De Ros on the fittings of the Horse Transports. I have always heard that on board the Screw Steamers they are most successful; and that the loss of Horses on this long Voyage had been been [*sic*] unusually small.

The loss, which he did sustain, was in the Black Sea on a short Voyage in sailing Transports: but that was in a Gale of Wind, when the Vessels were nearly swamped.

We shall want a Steamer capable of carrying 800 men to Corfu, there to land the 800, and to proceed with another Regiment from thence to the East. You must not interfere with the promised Toulon arrange-

[1]Sidney Herbert, Secretary of War. The letter to which Graham referred is not preserved among Milne's papers.

ments, but you must obtain this extra Steam Conveyance for the Corps Detachments as soon as possible.

I shall be at the Admiralty in the morning. What have you done about the Admiralty Houses?

I do not believe that the Treasury will object to the hiring of a second House in Spring Garden Terrace; and if you and Capt Richards can be there accommodated and will consent to go there, the whole matter may be well and easily settled.[1]

[**421**] *Cunard to Milne*

Howchins Hotel, London
15 November 1854

Dear Capt Milne

I send you a telegraph about removing Berths in the *Alps*. She has just been fitted up to carry 800 passengers from Havre to New York. The accommodations will of course occupy a deal of Room[,] and as the object is to carry as many Troops as possible, I have not hesitated, but ordered the Berths to be removed. it [*sic*] cannot be helped. you [*sic*] must only allow us a week at the end of the Service to replace the Berths[,] and to paint & clean the *Alps* & *Europa*, in the same way as it is arranged in the agreement for the *Taurus*[.] be so good as to make a note of this that it may not be forgotten.

I hope the Hammocks and Bedding may be ready at Liverpool for the *Europa*[,] that she may not be delayed . . .

From Toulon [to the Crimea] is only a short distance[;] *Alps* will take a great many Troops[.] it will be of no consequence if they are crowded.

[**422**] *Milne to Ellis*

Admiralty, Private
17 November 1854

My dear Sir

The Admiralty is in want of some other Steam Vessels for the speedy conveyance of reinforcements to the Crimea[,] and I have been informed that your Company has a vessel daily expected from Australia[.] May I request you to inform me if this is the case and[,] if so[,] the

[1]Graham was trying to arrange for government-owned housing for Milne and Richards closer to the Admiralty than their private dwellings.

Admiralty will be prepared to charter as such vessel for a period of 3 months certain [*sic*] on the same conditions as those vessels now belonging to the Company and in Government Employ[.]

Perhaps you will kindly inform me on this subject with the name and Tonnage of the vessel and when it may be expected, that the ship can Embark Troops[.]

[**423**] *Milne to Graham*

Admiralty
[17 November 1854]

Prince & *Faith* Steamers sailed in the end of Sept & Octr and took out the following[:]
87 Tons Ball Cartridge
7 Tons of Ammunition
50½ Tons Ammunition
70 Tons Shot & Shell
29¼ Tons of Cartridges
34 Tons of filled Cartridges
15 Tons of Shot
15 Tons of filled Cartridges

By HMS *Supply* [was sent out] end August[:]
54 Tons Shot & Shell

On the way out in *Alipore* and *Blake*[:]
56 Tons of filled Shells
25 Tons of Ball Cartridges

Manilla will sail Sunday[:]
132 Tons filled Shells
36 Tons of small Ammunition
160 [tons] Army Clothing
19 Tons filled Cartridges

Robt Lowe will sail early in the week[:]
19 Tons of Combustibles
57 Tons of filled Shells

Holyrood is loading with[:]
169 Tons of Ammunition
10 Tons Shot & Shells

[**424**] *Milne to Bevis*

Admiralty
18 November [1854]

We want to send out to the Black Sea, a Cargo of Wood plank for building Huts &c. Make enquiry if any ships are ready loaded at Liverpool and what could be done to meet this requirement[.]

[**425**] *Milne to Laird*[1]

Admiralty
18 November [1854]

Write to Mr Laird and request to be informed if[,] in Tendering the Steam ship *Imperatriz* to the Government, any derangement will be occasioned to the Postal arrangement for the Conveyance of the Brazil Mails – if that vessel should be accepted; and to state[,] should the *Imperatriz* be so withdrawn[,] what arrangement is to be made for the conveyance of the mails[.]

[**426**] *Milne to Newcastle*

Admiralty
18 November [1854]

Write to the Duke of Newcastle and inform him the following steam ships will be prepared for the Embarkation of Troops on the days mentioned against each[,] and request to be informed to what Regiments he wishes the preference of Embarkation to be given[.]

[Vessel]	[To Sail From]	[On]
HMS *Royal Albert*	Ports[mou]th	25 Nov
HMS *Dauntless*	Ports[mou]th	21 Nov
Niagara	Liverpool	23 "
Charity	Thames	24 "
Tamar	Southampton	23 "
Clyde	Greenock	2 Dec

[1]Of the South American and General Steam Navigation Company.

[**427**] *Milne to Austin*[1]

Admiralty
18 November 1854

It is wished to send out Plank and Lumber to the Black Sea. let [*sic*] Enquiry be made in the Docks if there are any ships that may be loaded with the same, which could be sent out[.] it is for building Huts[.]

[**428**] *Milne to Cunard*

[Admiralty
18 November 1854][2]

Write to Mr Cunard and inform him, it is necessary for the purpose of conveying Troops to the Crimea[,] withdraw two of the North America Mail Steam Packets. my [*sic*] Lords therefore request that the *Niagara* and *Arabia* may be prepared with all possible haste for this service[,] and that he will inform their Lordships what arrangement he proposes to make for the Conveyance of the Mails[.]

[**429**] *Milne to Christie*

Admiralty
18 November 1854

My dear Cap Christie

I write you a line by this Evgs Mail to let you know what we are doing in regard to Troops &c going from England[,] as there is much in hand and you should have notice.

We have sent *Alps*, *Candia*[,] *Thames* [&] *Ripon* to Toulon to Embark 4200 French Troops[.] These ships have all gone 3 days ago from England. The *Nubia* and *Indiana* will follow in a few days for the same destination and they will embark about 2,300 more. in [*sic*] all we have promised them to move 8000 men[.]

The *Europa* embarks today the 90th Reg at Dublin and goes direct to the Crimea[.] we have also 4 other Steamers from the Mail Service, The [*sic*] *Tamar*, *Niagara* and *Arabia*[.][3] The two former will each

[1]Horatio Austin had, by this point, been transferred to Deptford.

[2]Both the entry preceding this one and that following bear the date 18 November, leaving little doubt as to the date of this one, although Milne did not note it.

[3]Milne stated four but listed only three.

bring up a reg[iment] from Gib[raltar] and I hope will leave England on the 24th, taking out a Reg[iment] to Gib[raltar] and then the Gib[ralta]r regiment on to [the] Crimea. *Arabia* will perhaps go to Toulon. The *Royal Albert* will embark 700 Guards on [the] 25th. *Dauntless* will embark 300 R[oyal] Artillery on the 21st. The *Manilla* Steamer sails tomorrow with 160 Tons of Army Clothg and also a large quantity of Ammunition[.] The *Holyrood* is also loading with Shot[,] Shell &c. The *Robt Lowe* will sail on Thursday with Troops[,] also full of Powder &c[,] also large Cylinders for blowing up the ships sunk at Sebastopol. The *Brandon* has sailed with Clothing[,] Bread &c[,] & *Ottawa* is well on her voyage. We are going to send out two ship loads of plank for building Huts[.] they will sail probably on [the] 23rd and 2500 Tons of <u>Huts</u> will be ready in a fortnight[,] but we find difficulty in getting Steam ships for all this service.

Provisions we [are] also sending forward as fast as possible. We are sorry to hear about *Himalaya*[.] I only hope she will come home that we may get her into Dock &c[.] You must have an increased amount of duty & responsibility on your hands[,] but it must be satisfactory to you that all has gone on so well[.] our anxiety is great in regard to the Events in the East[.] we have just heard of the sad loss of Cathcart &c[.][1] it is very dreadful to think of the awful loss of life[.]

[**430**] *Milne to Houston Stewart*[2]

Admiralty
18 November [1854]

My dear Admiral

I drop you a line and [*sic*] to let you know what is going on in the line of Transports & Troops[,] in which you take so active and admirable a part. Your Telegh was received about Shot & Shell. The *Europa* which Embarked the 90th Reg today takes out the . . . Cartridges . . . and the *Holyrood* is loading with Shot[,] Shell[,] Powder &c. The *Manilla* is ready for sea with 160 Tons of warm Army Clothing and filled up with ammunition. The *Rajah* has sailed with Stores, Bread[,] Clothing &c.

The *Alps*, *Candia*, *Thames* and *Ripon* have sailed for Toulon to take on board 4200 French Troops[.] we have promised to Embark (Independent of any you are to send for) 8000[,] and to do this *Arabia* & *Indiana*[,] with another ship[,] will follow.

[1]Gen. Cathcart was killed at the Battle of Inkerman, 5 November 1854.
[2]A similar letter was sent to Boxer at Constantinople.

The *Dauntless* sails on Wednesday with 300 Artillery[,] and the *Royal Albert* on 25 [Nov] will take out 700 of the Guards[.] The *Niagara* and *Tamar* will each take a Reg. next week to Gibr[altar] and from thence will each take a Reg. to Crimea[.] other vessels will follow but [are] not yet arranged. Provisions we are pouring out[,] and I have now to provide steam [vessels] for 2500 Tons of Huts and Stoves to warm them[,] and we will send on 2 ships full of Plank for the same purpose. I dont [*sic*] think I have any more news.
Yrs.[1] *R Lowe* will sail on Wednesday. The *Brandon* on Monday all [*sic*] with Troops. I hope we will be enabled to supply every want[,] but it is an awful pull on the Transport and Vict[uall]ing Depart at Somerset House. As yet we have done well and I dont despair. We are most anxious for further news from the East[.] we hear by Letters [&] by the Papers from Crimea to 7 Nov. The loss of Poor Cathcart is very sad.

Poor Mrs Hyde Parker died without the least pain, from Inflammation of the Lungs caught by sleeping at an open window to relieve the pain and difficulty of breathing of [*sic*] the throat. Sir J Graham bids me to say he is unable to write to you tonight but begs me to say he is most pleased with all your valuable arrangements. I congratulate you on your sons gallant conduct & the high position he took in *Firebrand*[.][2] his 1st L is made a Comdr,[3] with some other promotions for the 17th. good bye [*sic*] our kindest regards . . . [4]

[**431**] *Milne to Horse Guards*

Admiralty
20 November [1854]

Inform the Horse Guards that the *Tamar* at Southampton and the *Niagara* at Liverpool will soon be ready to Embark a Reg for Gibraltar on the 24th Inst[,] and from Gibraltar will each convey a Reg. to the Crimea. request [*sic*] to know [from] whence these two Regiments are to Embark[?]

[1]Milne evidently started to finish the letter, but then thought of something else to add.

[2]William Houston Stewart's vessel, HMS *Firebrand*, had played a prominent role during the allied naval assault on Sebastopol (17 October 1854) by towing the sailing ship-of-the-line, HMS *London*, into action.

[3]William Gore Jones.

[4]A letter containing much the same information on vessels bound for the east was also sent to Boxer.

[**432**] *Milne to Graham*

Admiralty
*c.*21 November 1854[1]

My dear Sir James

We have not been able to obtain the Cargo of Deals[.][2] on enquiry they were found to be 2½ and 3 Inches thick, and therefore unfit for the purpose for which they were required, & they cannot be obtained unless they are regularly sawn [*sic*] to the thickness required[,] which should not [exceed] one inch[,] otherwise they will split in the carriage on exposure to the weather. were [*sic*] any steps to be taken for Deals of this thickness[,] nothing can [*sic*] be shipped under a fortnight at the soonest.

The Huts are[,] I understand[,] to be ready in that time and to the extent of 4000 Tons[,] as specified in an Ordnance Letter which came this Evening, but how we are to obtain 4000 Tons of Steam conveyance (which will actually require 6000 Tons . . .) I cannot at present make out[.] we have advertized . . . for the conveyance of [?6000] Tons to the Crimea by Steamer, but I [am] afraid it will produce little or no result.

[**433**] *Milne to James W. D. Dundas*

[Admiralty
21 November 1854][3]

Write to V.A. Dundas and inform him my Lords deem it to be absolutely necessary that steps should be immediately taken to send to England some of the Steam Transports now in the Black Sea, in exchange for those on their passage from England to the Crimea, as in order to meet the exigencies of the public service in the transmission of Troops[,] my Lords have been obliged to withdraw several Steam Vessels from the Packet Service, thereby causing derangement in the Postal connection with the W.I. & North American Colonies.
The steamers now on their passage from England and conveying Troops are the *Jura*, *Queen of the S*[*outh*], *Cleopatra*, *Ottawa*, *Alps*, *Thames*, *Candia*, *Ripon*, *Moravia*, *Europa* & they will be followed by the *Niagara*,

[1]Date not visible owing to fire damage.

[2]Planks.

[3]Milne wrote at the top 'Let these letters be written & let me see them before being forwarded.' The subsequent minute to Dundas reads: 'Immediate 22 Nov. Write as amended & send . . . '

Arabian, *Nubia*, *Adelaide*[,] *Charity*[,] *Clyde*, *Imperatrice*[,] *R*[*obert*] *Lowe* and *Brandon*. Besides these[,] there are a number of Smaller Class Vessels[,] such as the *Cottingham*, *Faith*, *Lion*, *Manilla*, *Holyrood*, [&] *Gottenburgh* employed in the Transport of Stores[.]

The withdrawal of this large amount of Steam Tonnage[,] independent [of] and in addition to those Steam Ships already in the Black Sea, as per the enclosed return[1] has drained The [*sic*] source from whence these ships were obtained[,] and unless vessels [are] at once sent to England to take out further reinforcements of Troops or supplies & Stores[,] my Lords will be unable to obtain Steam V[essels] to meet these requirements of the P[ostal] Service[.] He is therefore immediately to place himself in communication with Lord Raglan and make this arrangement, if possible, with his consent.

[**434**] *Milne to Newcastle*

Admiralty
21 November 1854

Enclose this Letter to the Duke of Newcastle and inform my Lords consider it necessary that this communication should be immediately sent to V.A. Dundas, and that His Grace may be aware how great is the pressure on the steam companies[,] and how difficult it may be to procure further steam vessels for sending out reinforcements[,] & the necessity for some of the vessels now in the Black Sea being sent to England

The following extract from a letter from the P&O Co has this day be[en] received[:]

The withdrawal of so many of the Companys vessels for the service of the War, having prevented and being likely to prevent for sometime to come[,] the reinforcement of the Companys Fleet in the India Sea [*sic*] branches of the postal service, The [*sic*] Directors have no resource left for maintaining the East India and China postal communications uninterrupted except that of withdrawing the two vessels now employed in the Bimonthly postal service between Ceylon[,] Singapore and Australia[,] and placing them on the China[,] Calcutta and Suez and Bombay and Aden Lines. They therefore propose to withdraw the two vessels immediately.[2]

[1]Not preserved among Milne's papers.

[2]Milne added 'Let these letters be written & let me see them before being forwarded'. The minute on this letter reads: 'Immediate 2 Nov . . . ' Presumably Milne meant '21 November'.

[**435**] *Christie to Milne*

Melbourne, off Balaklava
23 November 1854

My dear Milne

I fear several of my letters would be too late [*sic*] for the last Mail[,] owing to the severity of the weather, but no doubt you will have heard before this of the heavy loss we sustained in the tremendous gale of the 14th. I was in the *Melbourne* and only saved her by cutting away the Masts. Nos. 5, 40, 63, and 82[1] were dashed to attoms [*sic*] close to us[,] as well as five Commissnd vessels. The *Prince* was wrecked in a heavy thick squall. when [*sic*] it cleared away there was not a vestige of her to be seen.

I trust this gale will prove the utter absurdity of keeping Sailing Transports in the Black Sea in the winter, beyond what are absolutely necessary. If I had my will I would have sent three dozen of them home two months ago. Twelve Sailing vessels[,] with the steam power we have[,] would be ample. I have sent in a list to the Admiral of the vessels I think we can spare[,] and of those I wish to keep, and I trust I shall be enabled to send them either to England or the Bosphorus. If Admiral Boxer can only arrange to Coal the Steamers rapidly enough at Constantinople[,] there will be very little use for the Sail[in]g vessels, particularly if we have not to assist the French & Turks quite so much as we have lately been obliged to do.

There is great dissatisfaction amongst the Transports, in consequence of no arrangements having been made for them to get their letters. There is a regular Post Office established for the Army and the letters are delivered in due time and the proper Postage charged, but the unfortunate Transports seldom get a letter[,] and when they do double Postage is charged. Can this be remedied?

I shall try [to see] what Lord Raglan can do, and if you will be so kind as to lend a helping hand[,] you will confer a great favor on the Service. The Transports are surely entitled to the same privileges as the Army while they are employed with them.

There has been little fighting since the 5th. I have just got a hint to send Steamers for about 10,000 Turkish Troops from Varna. We have plenty of Coal at present, but shall want some more before long.

[1]Namely, *Resolute*, *Kenilworth*, *Wild Wave*, and *Rip Van Winkle*.

[**436**] *Milne to Boxer*

Admiralty
26 November [1854], 6:00 p.m.

My dear Admiral

Thanks for your last Letter[,] and I am always glad to hear from you on matters at Constantinople & that all goes on well. We are well aware you are hard hard [*sic*] pressed and so we are here and doing all we can to keep up the Supply[,] which must be done at all cost[.] There are a number of Sailing Ships on their way out, full of all sorts of provisions &c[,] which we trust will arrive safe. my [*sic*] last [letter] would give you an Account of the Steamers with Troops &c. The *Royal Albert* has gone with 1300[,] besides 800 of her own crew[.] The *Dauntless*[,] has also sailed and the *Indiana*. *Nubia* [sails] for Marseilles and *Arabia* will go in 3 days for the same destination. The *Rob Lowe* has sailed from this for Constantinople[,] also the *Holyrood* & *Manilla* with Ordnance Stores and warm Clothing. The Steamers of 500 tons[,] about ten of them[,] will begin to load the Huts tomorrow and I hope they will soon get away[.]

we [*sic*] are in great anxiety about the gale in the Black Sea, we do not know details but hear the *Prince* is lost[,] also 8 of the Transports. we [*sic*] are most anxious for news and we are afraid it will be of the loss of life &c.

Something has been said here[,] and Parties have been attempting to impute blame to our Reports[,] at the want of arrangements at Constan[tino]ple[,] in Sending Ships to the Black Sea having stores on board for Scutari[,] and that these stores have not been allowed to be landed, and also that the Custom House has been filled with Stores [*sic*], which should never have gone there. Just enquire into this and let me know, that I may have an Answer[.]

I enclose [to] you a note from the master of the *Supply*, which does not say much for the attention of your subordinates, who have been app[ointe]d to take charge of these matters. We do not get any return or Information about the State of the Stores at Constan[tino]ple. Some few lines to give us an idea of what is wanted would be useful. We have no news here[.] all we now care about comes from your quarter.

[**437**] *Milne to Craigie*

Admiralty
27 November 1854

The *Cumberland* & *William Hutt* Steamers have been ordered to Portsmouth to embark the Wooden Houses for the Crimea[.] Their loading must be hastened, and the arrival of all Vessels chartered by Gov. as Transports for Troops or Stores are to be reported by Telegraph[.]

[**438**] *Milne to Craigie*

Admiralty
28 November [1854]

The Admiralty have Chartered the *Norman*[,] Screw Steamer[,] now at Southampton. She is to load with the Wooden Huts now at Southampton. It is important this should be done with all haste. 2 more steamers are under orders[.]

[**439**] *Milne to Houston Stewart*

Admiralty
29 November [1854]

My dear Admiral

I have not much news for you but I write you a line to let you know what is going forward in regard to Military Service[.]

Tamar & *Niagara* sailed some days ago for Gib[raltar,] then to Crimea with two Regiments.

Indiana [&] *Nubia* [have] gone two days hence[.]

The *Rob Lowe* has also sailed as [have] *Royal Albert* and *Dauntless*[,] with 1300 Troops in former and 350 in later [*sic*]. *Holyrood* with Shot &c [&] *Manilla* with Warm Clothing [have also sailed]. Some other vessels will follow in a few days and there is a large Fleet of sailing vessels on their way out full of provisions &c[.]

We tremble for the news from [the] B[lack] Sea[.] we hear the *Prince* is lost[,] also 8 or 10 other Transports, but we want authentic information[.] when it comes I am afraid it will be very serious. The whole state of the affairs in the East is the cause of <u>greatest anxiety</u> and must prove so for many months. The Wooden Huts will begin loading tomorrow[.] Send up Plank if you can[,] to make Huts for our Marines &

Blue Jackets[,] also warm Clothing for them[.] if any is to be bought in Malta[,] it would be as well to prepare some Drawers[,] Shirts &c[,] but you can judge of this [yourself.] we will send off some in about a fortnight, but anything sent up [by you] might prove welcome.

Rum we are sending out[.] There is on the Sea [*sic*] a Store for our Army for 100 days[,] if no losses. We have chartered 12 or 14 Small Steamers to carry the Huts. if [*sic*] you send Plank[,] try to send some old Canvass[*sic*][,] Nails &c[.] We have not provided Huts for our people[,] so try & meet this want. Sir James has no time to write you this day[.] he says it would be a good thing to purchase some 'Gregoes'[,][1] which the Greeks wear[.] is that the name[?]

[**440**] *Newcastle to Milne*

Downing Street
1 December 1854

My dear Capt Milne

Only 50 tons out of 237 of Buffalo skins have yet been embarked.

Will you endeavour to obtain a preference for this cargo in the vessels which are sailing[,] as it is very important to the comfort of the Army.

Sir James Graham leads me to hope you have now at liberty a second steamer for the battery train. I shall be very glad if the [loading] can be pushed on.

[**441**] *Milne to Bevis*

Admiralty
1 December [1854]

When will the *Imperatrice* [*sic*] be ready to receive Troops[?] are preparations making[?] she will Embark a Reg[,] 650 Rank & File[,] at Cork and may perhaps take 150 more men[.]

[1]Grego: 'A coarse jacket with a hood, worn in the Levant.' *Oxford Universal Dictionary*, 1955 edn, p. 830.

[**442**] *Milne to Newcastle*

[Admiralty
4 December 1854]

Norman sailed with 100 Huts & Stores[.]
The *Metropolitan*[,] *Cosmopolitan & Cumberland* will sail on Tuesday also with Huts[.] The two former have also Shot & Warm Clothing[.]
The *Magdalena* will sail with the 18 Reg on Saturday[,] and one million of Minie Cartridges[.]
The *Charity* will sail from Ports[mouth] on Wednesday. She has ammunition and about 450 men Detachments [*sic*][.]
A Steamer will sail from Portsmouth about Saturday with a further supply of Minie ammunition and warm Clothing.
and [*sic*] 4 more Steamers will sail with Huts if they are ready.

The *Adelaide* is loading with a large quantity of Stores & would go direct to Crimea if the D. of Newcastle will withdraw the 82 Reg. from that ship[,] which she was intended to convey to Corfu[.]

She might then take out Artillery if any is ready[,] say 300 men at least[,] or even 500.

[**443**] *Milne to Austin*[1]

Admiralty
4 December [1854]

There are Stores sent to Deptford for officers in Crimea from Fortnum & Mason[.] a selection of Cases is to be made[,] and say about 10 Tons to go in Every Steamer loading at Dept[ford]. This to be reported[,] and special orders given to Masters of Vessels[.]

[**444**] *Milne to Grant*

Admiralty
4 December [1854]

Write to Messrs Fortnum & Mason & inform their Lordships understand a large number of Cases have been sent to Deptford without any addresses or List of Contents. request [*sic*] they will inform what List of articles have been sent[,] and that[,] to prevent confusion[,] some

[1]Milne also instructed that a copy of this memorandum be sent to the Comptroller of Victualling.

person should call at the Ad[mira]lty to arrange the detail [*sic*] of the Embarkation & see Cap Milne on this subject[.]

[**445**] *Milne to Grant*

Admiralty
5 December [1854]

HMS *Malacca* has been ordered to receive on board warm Clothing for the Crimea[.] Let Mr. Howell[1] be informed & request to send to Woolwich Dock Yard early on Thursday Evg[,] and to continue such supply until ordered not to send any more[.] [She] may take 40 to 50 Tons[.]

[**446**] *Milne to Newcastle*

Admiralty
5 December [1854]

Write to D[uke] of Newcastle[:] inform [him] the *Adelaide* Steamer is now loading at Deptford with ordnance and other Stores for the East. it [*sic*] was ordered that this ship should convey the 82 Reg to Corfu and one of the Regts from thence to Crimea, but as Stores are urgently wanted in the East[,] their Lordships would wish to know whether the *Adelaide* should still go to Corfu or direct to Crimea[,] to which place she can convey nearly 600 men. an [*sic*] early decision is requested on this subject[.]

[**447**] *Milne to Horse Guards*

Admiralty
6 December 1854

Write to the Horse Guards and inform that under special circumstances[,] in order to hasten the delivery of Ammunition and Stores in the Crimea[,] the *Adelaide* will not convey the 82 Reg to Corfu[,] but that [that] ship will go direct to the Black Sea & take the Draft of the 34 Reg[,] also some Artillery[,] officers & men[.]

[1]Thomas Howell; Dir-Gen. of Contracts, Ordnance Department.

[**448**] *Milne to Boxer*

Admiralty
8 December 1854

My dear Admiral

The Messenger leaves this a day sooner that usual[.] I write you my usual note to give you any information. We have all been much distressed and annoyed at the serious losses in the Black Sea[,] and the damage done to our ships and Transports, but there is no contending ag[ains]t such fearful Gales[,] and of so sudden a nature[.] we are[,] however[,] without any detail as to the facts connected with the Ships sunk[,] and why the *Prince* had not landed her cargo[,] and at her being at anchor outside instead of in the Harbour. The same applies to several other ships which have Stores on board. We have ordered Admiral Dundas to have full enquiry made into all the Circumstances [*sic*], also why the Stores for Scutari were not landed in passing. I think you must adopt some regulations in regard to this[,] and endeavour to land stores at Constantinople intend[ed] for that place before the Ships are sent [further.] we [*sic*] are not aware what orders have been given in regard to the charge of ships at Balaclava[.] this is a matter of detail which should have been organized on the spot[.]

The *Magdalena* sails tomorrow morning with the 18 Reg[,] also a supply of Ball Cartridge[,] Minie and Smooth[,] about one million of each[.]

The *Norman*, *Metropolitan*[,] *Hetton*[,] *Cosmopolitan* and *Cumberland* have sailed with about 90 Huts in each[.] The *Charity* with warm clothing[,] also *Gottenburg* [*sic*] have gone[,] the former from Ports[mouth] and the latter this Evg from Deptford[.] others will follow as soon as possible. The *Firefly*[,] with the Third [*sic*] of a Battering Train[,] also goes tomorrow[.]

We have no news here of any moment[.] all [are] looking to affairs in the East. Sir C. Napiers Squadron is on its way home with all his Squadron[,] as all in the Gulf of Finland is frozen up.

Provisions &c are flowing out[,] and we are now called on to form a large reserve at Constan[tino]ple for any Service. You ought to fill up your Flag Lieutenancy, it has been noticed here.

[**449**] *Milne to Christie*

Admiralty
8 December 1854

My dear Cap Christie

The Letters containing the news from the Black Sea and giving information of the losses of the Transports, arrived here a few days ago and caused us great regret[.] it is a most serious and lamentable loss, but still more serious from depriving our Army of the Stores and Clothing[.] this has caused here very great anxiety[,] and we are endeavring [*sic*] all in our power to send out other supplies. The Letters from Admiral Dundas give us no facts or information[,] which is to be regretted[.] we only know the Ships are lost[,] not a word said about Stores &c[,] and why *Prince* was not cleared after being 8 days at or off the Harbour of Balaclava[,] and why she was not in Harbour. We cannot make out this and it is a pity Cap Dacres did not give us some information[,] and if any of the Crews were saved[.]

We have ordered Ad Dundas to have full Enquiry made into all the circumstances. I presume you have[,] in concert with Ad Dundas[,] made every arrangement of the unloading of ships and put some one in charge at Balaclava. we [*sic*] hear that the stores sent in ships are often never landed[,] and that the *Golden Fleece* has now on board a large quantity of Powder she shipped in England, That [*sic*] Scutari stores have never been landed from the ships as they passed the Bosphorus[,] but all [*sic*: 'are'] carried on to the Crimea[.] These things may be incorrect, but if correct some supervision must be Enacted [*sic*] to check this. I have written to Boxer about it[.]

The *Magdalena* with the 18th Reg and 40 Tons of warm Clothing and 1 million of Minie and 1 Million of Smooth Ball Cartridges sail[s] tomorrow. The *Charity* with Stores, Warm Clothing and drafts sailed two days ago[.] The *Metropolitan*, *Cosmopolitan*[,] *Norman*[,] *Hetton* & *Cumberland*[,] all Steamers of about 500 Tons[,] have sailed with about 90 Huts Each. The *Gottenburg* [*sic*] sails tomorrow with Warm Clothing[,] also *Sydney Hall* with Provisions &c.[,] and several other vessels are now loading. The *Firefly* sails tomorrow with the Third [*sic*] of a Battering Train[,] another to load on Monday. in [*sic*] fact we are doing all we can to meet the enormous demands[,] but we have nearly swept all the Steamers from the Home Ports[,] and there is no end to the daily wants of the various departments. we [*sic*] hope to hear from you in a day or two[,] as we are very anxious for detailed news.

We have nothing going on here of any moment but what you will see in the public papers[.] the engrossing subject is the Crimea[.]

[**450**] *Milne to Houston Stewart*

Admiralty
8 December 1854

My dear Admiral

I write you a few lines to say what we are doing that you may be aware of what you may expect at Malta.

Charity with Stores, Warm Clothing & detachments for Crimea sailed two days ago.

Cumberland[,] *Norman*[,] *Metropolitan*[,] *Cosmopolitan* [&] *Hetton* have all sailed with about 90 Huts in each [and] others are loading. The *Magdalena* sails with [the] 18 Reg at Daylight [*sic*]. The *Gottenburgh* will go tomorrow with warm Clothing, the *Firefly* with third [*sic*] of a Battering Train goes tonight. The *Adelaide* is loading[.] There are 130 Men[,] and some of the 71[st Regiment] and some Ball Cartridge to go from Corfu[.] if you had [*sic*] any vessel[,] you could send there to take them up[.] [?Ward[1]] had to take up a private steamer called the *Danube* but we stopped it here[,] as the owners were most shamefully Exorbitant [*sic*] in their demands[,] and we thought it very likely that a Steamer would be sent from the B[lack] Sea to take the 71 Reg to Crimea[.] if you can send any small vessels to Corfu it might be as well to do so. The *Adelaide* was intended to go to Corfu with the 82d Reg but the pressure for stores in the Crimea is so great she will now go direct[ly] there[,] calling at Malta, and we must endeavour to send the 82d by some other means. all [*sic*] our Steamers are gone to Marseilles for the French Troops[.] *Neptune* & *St George* are coming to you each with a Regiment[,] and they have also Ordnance Stores[,] and you are to take from these ships anything and everything you may wish or want.

We are anxious to hear from you and any news about Steamers &c[.] This Gale in the Black Sea has caused us serious distress and inconvenience.

[1]It is not clear to whom Milne was referring.

[**451**] *Milne to Grant*

Admiralty
9 December [1854]

Dear Mr Grant

I hear that the various Insurance Companies have raised their rate of Insurance on Vessels going to the Black Sea[,] and we will not be able to get Steamers at 50/ per Ton and[,] as we had to pay 55/ yesterday, you had better send to Mr [?Baughan[1]] and ask him to offer any vessels at that price[,] as we now require several vessels as soon as possible[,] Screw vessels in preference to Paddle vessels[.]

[**452**] *Milne to Newcastle*

Admiralty
12 December 1854

Dear Duke of Newcastle

I write this line to say that Huts for 11,500 men have left this country in Steamers. [Huts] for 3200 will sail this week[.]

[**453**] *Milne to Graham*

Admiralty
14 December 1854

Sir James Graham

The large number of Steam Transports which have lately been send [*sic*] from this Country with English[,] or for the purpose of embarking French Troops, in addition to those which have for some months past been employed in the Black Sea[,] and the number of small steam vessels now conveying Huts to the Crimea, renders it expedient that some instructions should be given to Admiral Dundas as to the future disposal of those vessels.

According to the accompanying return[2] there are no less than 80 Steam Vessels now employed[.] of these about 30 are conveying Huts,

[1]One of the clerks in the Transport Branch of the Victualling Department.

[2]The return is not included in this edition. For such information, see 'Return of the Ships engaged as Regular Transports, with the Names (stating whether Steam or Sailing), from the 1st day of January 1854 to the 1st day of January 1855 . . . ', *Parliamentary Papers*, 1855, vol. XXXIV, pp. 229–35.

Ammunition and Stores[,] and when these have landed their respective cargoes, what is to be done with them?

I would submit whether it would not be expedient to send out instructions to Admiral Dundas to take this whole question into consideration, and to come to a decision on the following[:]

1st[.] That he is to organize an arrangement for keeping up a constant communication by steam vessels with Constantinople and the Crimea[,] and to select a certain number of the best adapted steam vessels for this purpose[,] making every allowance for any special service which may be required in retaining[,] if necessary[,] a certain number in the harbour of Balaclava.

2d[.] To select a certain number of vessels to keep up the communication between Constantinople & Malta[,] and for the service of towing vessels in the Bosphorus.

Having provided satisfactorily for these two services[,] he is to consider if any additional vessels will be required for the Commissariat Dept or for the conveyance of Coal or Wood from Constantinople[,] Sinope or other ports, and[,] having met all these requirements, he is to send to England all other vessels not absolutely required for service in the East [and] he order That [*sic*] these vessels may again resume the Postal Communication (& selecting such vessels for return to England as will be required for this purpose)[,] and the other vessels which may then be sent to England will be either paid off or again employed in keeping up the supplies required to be sent from England[,][1] and[,] as a considerable number of Sailing Transports have left England with Stores or have arrived in the Black Sea since[,] he command several of these vessels which were originally chartered to be sent to England[.] he is to continue to reduce the number of these vessels from time to time by sending Home those which are the most expensive and least efficient[.][2]

[1]The remainder of this paragraph was written in the margin; it appears to have been an additional clause to the memorandum and has thus been inserted as such.

[2]Graham initialled the memorandum on 15 December and minuted: 'I approve of this Proposal: but the Order to the Commander in Chief in the Black Sea must be made contingent on the previous consent of Lord Raglan. A copy of this order should be sent to the Duke of Newcastle.'

[**454**] *Milne to Christie*

Admiralty
15 December 1854

My dear Cap Christie

I am not aware that I have very much to say to you since my last Letter. we [*sic*] have received your public Letter of the 18th in regard to the loss of Transports and the *Prince*[,] but you say nothing about her Stores[,] or if any had been landed. if [*sic*] you would add any remarks to your return of the Vessels it would be satisfactory[,] as we rather complain of a want of information which we glean by reference to the paper's [*sic*] or from private Letters sent to us for perusal. We have sanctioned the return of the Sailing vessels mentioned in your public Letter[,] but it did not require our Sanction, for I believe we have always sent [*sic*: 'given'] full power to send home those ships which were not required for service in the East[.] an order will probably go tonight to send Home Steamer's [*sic*][,] as there appears to be an unnecessary number in the Black Sea. The order goes to Ad Dundas to consult with Lord Raglan before this is done[,] and the Admiral will be told 1st, to organize an arrangement to keep up Communication between Constantinople and the Crimea by selecting such a number of Steam Vessels as are best adapted for this service, 2d[,] to select a certain number of Steamers to keep up the Communication between Constantinople & Malta and for towing in the Bosphorus. 3[rd,] to see if more Steamers are required for the Commissariat[,] and then to send to England all other vessels not absolutely required[,] especially those withdrawn from the Mail Service[,] so that it may be resumed[.] The vessels coming home will either be paid off or sent out with Stores. I hope these orders will go tonight.

Then again we are sending out more Transports and others which are high freighted [*sic*] should be immediately sent to England. You can shew this to Admiral Dundas. it [*sic*] is not necessary to encur [*sic*] more expense than is absolutely necessary.

Malacca will sail in a day or two with 120 Artillery Men & warm clothing[.] She is at Spithead. Cap Farquhar[1] [has] gone to Hospital with a broken leg. it [*sic*] blows hard from SW.

We have nothing new here but a number of Ships loading for the East.

[1]Sir Arthur Farquhar, K.C.B. (1815–1908). Entered, 1829; Lt, 1840; Cmdr, 1844; Capt., 1849; Rear-Adm., 1866; Vice-Adm., 1873; Adm., 1878.

[**455**] *Milne to James W. D. Dundas*

Admiralty
15 December 1854

My dear Admiral

Thanks for your letter of the 27th[,] and I am glad to find you keep up in all your anxious duties. I now write you a few lines in regard to an order gone out about the Steam Transports. it [*sic*] is[,] I believe[,] so clear that it will explain itself. It is of course important that the Mail Service should be returned as soon as practicable & that all the Mail Steamers should return home. We therefore hope this may be done as soon as possible with the consent of Lord Raglan[.] we have no less than 5 large vessels coming forward here[,] of which the *Great Britain* is one, so we are provided for sending out Troops for the next 2 or 3 months.

Sailing Transports are going out and some of those now in the Black Sea and at the higher rates of Charter should come home as soon as possible[,] and they should be ordered off without waiting for sanction from this.

The *Malacca* is at Spithead with 100 Artillerymen on board and warm clothing for Navy men on shore. there [*sic*] are other vessels following with all sorts of Ordnance and other Stores, Huts &c[,] but we have strong SW Gales which is [*sic*] much against our proceedings [*sic*]. We are inundated with demands for transport of Stores for the East. as [*sic*] yet we have managed to keep up the supplies[,] but it is a very heavy business and if our Army is to be increased I am afraid we will experience some difficulty, but it must be done[.] I know I never get one moments peace and I am all anxiety on the subject [*sic*]. I have been here no less than 7 years this month, & not been idle – or much absent.

We are all well at Home[.] Ad M[1] not strong and is now at Brighton for change of air[.]

Good bye and every [?divine] wish attend you . . .

[P.S.:] I think *St Jean d'Acre* will be the first ship ready[,] and will join you with 500 Troops[.]

[1]Milne may have been referring to First Naval Lord Maurice Berkeley.

[**456**] *Craigie to Milne*

Southampton
15 December 1854

My dear Capt Milne

Having observed a letter in the '*Times*' from an officer in the Crimea, complaining that many of the Packages sent out from this Port, had not reached their destination, I felt it to be my duty to make some enquiry upon the subject.

[The] Admiralty Agent of the '*Arabia*,' states that all the Packages he took out for the Black Sea, and which he landed at Malta on the 14th Novr, were still there on his return from Alexandria, on the 20th Novr, besides a great many others previously landed from England.

Mr. Borley, a Merchant in Southampton, also states that Packages sent by him, & others, 2 or 3 Months ago, for Sir Ed. Lyons[,] had not been received when he last heard from the Admiral.

There is doubtless some good reason for those Articles not being sent on to the Crimea, but as their detention at Malta has defeated the Kind [*sic*] intentions of the Ad[miralt]y, I have thought it right to bring the matter before you.

PS I am happy to hear that 'the speedy departure of the Huts had given great satisfaction'[.]

[**457**] *Milne to Christie*

Admiralty
18 December 1854

My dear Cap Christie

I have written these few lines privately to you[,] to say there is much said in higher quarters in London in regard to the discomforts of the Army[,] and the officers never having received their baggage since they left Varna[.] can you let me know how all this is[,] and why they have been left in this state. We hear very sad tales of wretchedness and misery in consequence[,] and people are ever ready to impute blame[.] it does appear to be unfortunate that such should be the case[.] The *Times* correspondent in todays paper is very severe on all the arrangements at Balaclava & the want of proper command, that there is no system or arrangement[.][1] I must say, this is no part of our duty to enter

[1]*The Times* (London), 18 December 1854, p. 8. William Howard Russell's dispatch of 25 November, printed therein, stated: 'Will it be credited, that with all our naval officers

into all these details but[,] as far as you are concerned[,] endeavour to put matters right[.]

Ad Boxer has been ordered up to take charge at Balaclava and the Ad and Lord Raglan are to come to some definite arrangement in the regard to the mode of keeping up the supplies from Constantinople. Some system must be adopted and ought to have been long ago, but my opinion has been given here that Balaclava is so small it will not afford space to discharge the various vessels that daily arrive with Stores, but every exertion must be used [*sic*] to press matters forward in every way possible.

I write in haste to save the Mail. The *St Jean d'Acre* will sail for [the] Black Sea with 600 Troops about the New Year and *Adelaide* will get away this week.

[**458**] *Milne to Houston Stewart*

Admiralty
18 December 1854

My dear Admiral

Thanks for yours of the 11th[1] and for the full information you give, but do not distress your own Stores for Provisions for the Army[,] as we are sending out Enormous supplies direct from England to the Crimea[:] 1¼ million lbs of Bread every month and 50,000 gallons of Rum. you [*sic*] are quite right to purchase the Rum at Malta[.] do so again if you have the chance[,] as we are hard put to it here [to obtain] the quantity we want and the price is rising to 3.9 per gallon . . . There is very great confusion at Balaclava[,] and I am afraid it will be worse for want of local arrangements[.] it is too bad that all was not put on a proper footing when it could have been easily done. Ad Boxer is ordered up to Balaclava and [Montagu] Stopford is to be the senior officer at Constantinople. He wont [*sic*] like this but it has been ordered.

I hope no Boxes or Parcels for the East have been left at Malta[.] Just ask the question and send any to their destinations by the first opportunity. *St Jean d'Acre* will get away with 600 Troops about the

in Balaklava with nothing else to do . . . there is no more care taken for the vessels in Balaklava than if they were colliers in a gale off Newcastle? Ships come in and anchor where they like, do what they like, go out when they like, and are permitted to perform whatever vagaries they like, in accordance with the old rule of "higgledy-piggledy, rough and tumble," combined with "happy go lucky."'

[1]Not preserved among Milne's papers.

New Year. I cannot get the 52d [Regiment] away for 3 weeks at least, but if you send a Steamer to Corfu I hope [the Transport Agent there] will not detain the 71st until the 82nd arrives. There are also Stores there to go East. I have sent for a new Master for the *Esk* and we gave that order for *Cambria* to be sent home, in accordance with your agreement[.]

Bye the Bye[,] let Beds be supplied to the ships bringing home the Sick and Wounded[,] it is necessary to do [so]. please [*sic*] to look after this[.] It would [not] do to have any complaint about this. you [*sic*] had better have the opinion of the military authorities on this subject. I see some trouble me writing about it[.]

I am afraid there is much bad feeling getting up in the East[.]

My wife sends kind regards[.]

[P.S.:] Hore[1] is promoted[.]

[**459**] *Boys[2] to Milne*

8 Northumberland Street, Strand
22 December [1854][3]

Sir

In reply to your enquiry on the subject of the heavy baggage belonging to the officers of the Army serving in the Crimea[,] I have the honour to state that it was the general practice of the Officers[,] on arrival at Varna[,] to leave their heavy baggage on board the various Transports that brought them out, in charge of the Masters of the Transports, some expressing a wish to the Divisional Comdr or Lieut that it should be permitted to remain altogether on board, others requesting it might be forwarded to Constantinople or landed in the store at Varna.

As it was impossible the Army could embark in the same ships that conveyed them from England, on the Invasion of the Crimea, a further quantity of baggage was left on board the various Transports, and as the exigencies of the service constantly required these ships at a distance from Balaklava[,] the baggage was not accessible until the cold weather set in in November, when Capt Christie sent the *Tonning* from Balaklava to me, at Eupatoria with 40 Serjeants and orders to collect the baggage

[1]George Edward Hore (1823–71). Entered, *c*.1836; Lt, 1846; Cmdr, 1854; Capt., 1860.

[2]William Boys, Transport Service Agent.

[3]This letter was filed among Milne's papers along with that from Peter Christie, 8 January [1855], on the same subject. See [**464**] below.

in the various Transports under my charge, place it on board the *Tonning* and send her on to the Katcha for the same purpose. these [*sic*] orders were duly executed and she arrived in safety at Balaklava before the Gale of the 14th November[.]

Any further information that I can afford I shall be most happy to do so . . .

[**460**] *Milne to Mundy*

Admiralty, Private
22 December [1854]

My dear Mundy

The orders Ad H Stewart has at Malta is [*sic*] to send all the Steamers which arrive there from the East to Marseilles to embark French Troops[,] and I am told this order will not be altered without official authority from the War Department[,] and if any Horses are to be sent out we ought to look ahead and order home all the large Steamer's [*sic*] which are fitted for Horses, *Himalaya*, *Simla*, *Jason*, but this is not to be done unless we have official application made to this Board.

You must therefore look well ahead to prevent the delay which must follow[.]

[**461**] *Christie to Milne*

Orient, off Balaklava
1 January 1855

My dear Milne

That fearful Gale threw everything into confusion here for a time, even the mails appear to have gone wrong. I only received your letter of the 8th this morning.

The '*Prince*' was no doubt the most grievous loss, but I do not think the Army have suffered one bit in consequence. the [*sic*] abundant supplies that have been rolling in here since have well made up for it. The day the *Prince* arrived here it was beautifully fine and the water perfectly smooth. She stood in, chose her own anchorage, but now her cables were clinched. I dont [*sic*] know [the particulars but] at all events they were not sufficiently secured[,] for she lost one anchor after the other, the cables running completely out. She stood out for the night and the following morning being still fine, hung on by the '*Jason*' till she had landed her Troops and got another Anchor ready.

I[,] being outside myself in '*Melbourne*[,]' was most anxious to get the *Prince* into Harbour, and sent an officer three different times to the Senior Naval Officer to request that she might be allowed to go in, but the object being at that time to have as few vessels in Harbour as possible[,] she was not allowed.

On the morning of the Gale the *Prince's* steam was up in good time, but the Sea rose and became so heavy that she soon began to drive, when she cut away her masts, and the survivors state that the mizzen rigging fouled her screw before she struck. Nothing was saved from any of the vessels wrecked here, as they were literally dashed to attoms [*sic*]. The Men of War Transports saved a great quantity at Katcha and Eupatoria.

The Guns & Powder on board the *Golden Fleece* are the Circassian Equipment she brought out from England. After writing and trying by every means to get rid of it[,] it was decided on the 24th Novr that it should all be landed at Scutari, but now it appears they have no room for it there and will not receive it. Adml Boxer told the Captain to let it remain on board, she accordingly arrived here yesterday with it still remaining.

I suffer no vessel to leave this till they have cleared out everything from her.

This is perhaps the most wretched place you can possibly imagine. There are no Stores [i.e., store houses], not even a shed to place anything in, consequently Powder, Bread, and quantities of Stores of every description are a good deal exposed and can only be secured by Tarpaulins. This of course prevents the vessels from clearing so rapidly as they otherwise would. I make the Transports clear out their own ships. They embark all the Sick (and a very great number that has been), Land [*sic*] the regiments and when there is any heavy work, I apply to the Senior Naval Officer, who is always ready and willing to assist in Boats and hands.

To show you the critical state of affairs here about the 27th October last I enclose you a copy of a letter I received from the Quarter Master General,[1] in answer to one I wrote relative to securing the Magazine

[1]Sir Richard Airey, first Baron Airey, K.C.B., G.C.B. (1803–81). That letter reads:

My dear Sir

It is quite in accordance with Lord Raglans views that you should get all the Transports not required, out of Balaklava Harbour, and that Magazine ships should be anchored as you propose.

It is only as a precautionary measure that these arrangements are suggested. We only prepare for an eventuality which may never come off. perhaps we may not change the place for landing our supplies at all. (MLN/156/1 [11/5]: Airey to Christie [copy], 27 October 1854)

Ships and clearing the Harbour as much as possible. Of course I only send it for your own information.

Tents, Warm Clothing &c have been landed in great abundance, and I have sent a supply of twenty good Carpenters and twenty or thirty men to assist in putting them [*sic*] up.

Your note of the 15th I have this moment received and [I] am very glad my letters of the 18th have arrived.

There was nothing landed from the *Prince* but the Troops and some of the Baggage.

I have just had a serious job given to me[,] viz. the transporting of Omar Pachas Army[,] 40,000 strong[,] from Varna to Eupatoria. I have already sent over about 11,000[,] and I trust I shall not do very wrong if I take one trip out of some of the splendid vessels that are bringing the French Troops out before sending them home. They will carry upwards of 2000 Turks each.

The '*Thames*' I should like to keep out here[,] and send the '*Medway*' home in her room.

Wishing you & Mrs Milne every happiness and many happy returns of the season[.]

[**462**] *Milne to Christie*

Admiralty, Private
4 January 1855

My dear Cap Christie

I have nothing very particular to say and therefore did not write you by the last two mails, but I now write you in regard to the Transports and the Complaints which are made here of want of arrangement in the landing of Stores & Provisions. it [*sic*] is said in some private letters, that the Troops are half starved for want of the provisions being sent up from Constantinople[,] and that vessels are detained there for days without any orders. This of course is under Admiral Boxer[,] and he will have to answer this, but it is reported, that there is a want of steamers, and that the Principal Agent of Transports appropriated one of the largest and best steamers to himself[,] and that that vessel does nothing whatever, instead of being employed in the conveyance of Troops or Stores[.] I hope this may not be the case[.] Again[,] it is said there is no arrangement in the Harbour of Balaclava in regard to the Transports discharging their cargoes, and that everything is in perfect confusion. The routine of the discharge of Transports [rests] no doubt with you, but the arrangement of the Harbour rests with the Senior

N[aval] Officer[,] and it is surprising that on our first taking possession of Balaclava[,] wharves were not constructed and some system arranged in regard to the unloading of vessels and the receipt of Stores. It is[,] however[,] to be regretted that all these complaints are made[,] and the more so if true; they may be without foundation but we are entirely ignorant of any detailed information either from the Admiral[,] the Senior Officer at Balaclava[,] or yourself. We are in perfect ignorance of all matters of detail. We have never had a suggestion made to us or a request made. We have seen no correspondence between the Naval authorities and the Military in Command [*sic*], and therefore all these complaints may be without foundation[.] at the sametime [*sic*], these matters are publicly talked of here, which is most disagreeable, as we have not the means of contradicting them.

It is also mentioned that vessels never deliver their <u>Cargoes at all</u> at <u>Balaclava</u>, but are sent back full, or [with a] portion of [their] cargoes on board[.] that this is the case, I mentioned to you in a former letter. This state of things has obliged Sir J. Graham to write to the Commander in Chief[,] and steps will be immediately taken on this[,] but it is no part of our duty to have to enter into the detail of all the local duties of the Harbours at Balaclava and Constantinople[.] this is left to the officer to whom the Admiralty have confided the various commands, but it would be a sad affair, if the failure of the Army and their misfortunes, should be caused by what is stated[,] viz. the neglect of the Naval departments[.]

I write you thus fully[,] that you may turn these matters over in your mind[,] and that I may hear from [you] in regard thereto that I may be in a position to contradict or answer these disagreeable statements which are forwarded on [*sic*] letters from officers on the spot, which we are now unable to do for want of any information.

I trust you keep a register of all vessels, their arrival, their cargoes, when delivered, to whom, &c. There should be such a register. you [*sic*] ought to have an agent of the Transports in Balaclava Harbour to attend to the Transport detail[,] or even two [agents] if necessary. you [*sic*] have only to order this, in concert with the Admiral or Senior N[aval] Officer[.] I hear there are no boats to land stores. what [*sic*] has become of all [the] Flat Boats from England and Malta[?]

However[,] I will say no more on the subject, but I am afraid it will become the source of much dissatisfaction if no organization has been established[,] and do not keep a steamer for your own private convenience if the service of such steamer is otherwise required. you [*sic*] must go to one of the sailing Transports or ships in Balaclava. We supplied you with signals[,] some should be established at the entrance of the Harbour to prevent ships coming in of [*sic*: to] the Harbour if full, and these signals[,] 4 or 5[,] should be communicated to each vessel as she passed [*sic*] Constantinople or[,] if sent here[,] we could have given them to each ship as she left England.

If you have any wants you should let us know in a public letter[,] but I am not aware of a single request of any kind and we therefore assumed all was going on well. I trust it is, but be on your guard, look into matters yourself[.] we have done everything here to meet the emergency of war and we only hope those details so necessary have been worked out by those in Command[.]

I write in haste . . .

[**463**] *Milne to the Peninsular and Orient Steamship Company*

Admiralty
5 January 1855

Write to the Pen[insular] & O[riental] Com[pan]y and inform that if the *Rajah* Steamer is not required by the Co.[,] their Lordships will be prepared to Charter her for 3 months at 50/ pr Ton on the new measurement[,] and request to know if they have any large steam vessels which they can place at the disposal of the Admi[ral]ty for the conveyance of Troops or Stores[.]

[**464**] *Christie to Milne*[1]

Orient, off Balaklava
8 January 1855

My dear Milne

I have received your note of the 18th Ult. When the Army landed in the Crimea[,] all the Baggage & Knapsacks were left on board the ships. Afterwards[,] of course[,] the vessels were dispersed in various directions, many went down to the Bosphorus with Sick & Wounded, others to Eupatoria, Katcha, &c. When we got to Balaklava[,] the Troops were allowed to get their Knapsacks and the officers their Baggage. They were procured for them as soon as possible by sending steamers round to collect from the different vessels, and they were delivered at Balaklava. Those officers who wished to have their Bag-

[1]This letter has a cover around it with Milne's note 'Cap. Christie[,] Baggage[,] *Golden Fleece*[,] Charcoal'.

gage, Portmanteaus &c got them, but many preferred leaving them on board the Transports.

When the cold weather began to set in, there was another outcry for the Portmanteaus & Baggage. They were again collected. Non Com[missione]d officers were sent to collect what the officers required[,] and every effort was made to get the Baggage to Balaklava. Of course[,] some were not accommodated so soon as others and if some officers did not receive their Portmanteaus so soon as they expected, of course there would be more said about it than if a thousand knapsacks had been missing. There was considerable difficulty with the officers. Some wished to leave their Baggage on board altogether. Many left their things without any address upon them, of course they could not expect to find them in a hurry. Generally speaking[,] it was the officers own fault if he did not get his Baggage.

With regard to the arrangements in Balaklava Harbour, When [*sic*] I first came here I wrote to Admiral Dundas about the placing of the ships, recommending a guard boat &c &c[,] but he wrote me in reply that he did not wish his arrangements to be interfered with. since [*sic*] that I have never had anything to do with the placing [of] the ships.

The Harbour is very small[,] and unless strict attention is paid to placing the vessels they soon get into confusion, foul their anchors &c[,] which causes great loss of time when they are wanted to sail again. The Harbour Master has been changed too often. A proper person should have been appointed at first, and he should have remained there throughout.

We are very busy landing the Huts warm clothing &c., but they get them away very slowly. The poor Horses are fearfully reduced, and the roads are very bad.

I hope you will not allow the Papers to attack one so unjustly.[1] The owners of the *Resolute*[,] I suppose[,] imagine that is was all my fault that the vessel was lost, not knowing the uncertainty of our position at that time, and everything that goes wrong at Balaklava the *Times* correspondent[2] would lead people to suppose was partly my fault, whereas I have nothing atall [*sic*] to do with it. I refused him a passage for a Horse once and probably he has not forgotten it.

[1]This may be a reference to Russell's dispatch of 25 November, in which he stated '. . . the order and regularity which prevail in the French marine [at Kamiesch Bay] are in the most painful contrast to the confusion and disorganization of our own transport and mercantile marine service. Captain Christie avers that our merchant captains won't attend to him.'

[2]William Howard Russell.

[**465**] *Milne to Neatheson and Company*

Admiralty
8 January 1855

Write to Messrs Neatheson & Co[,] Lombard St[,] and request to be informed if the Steam Vessels *Lancefield* and [?*Firey*] *Cross* belong to them and[,] if so[,] whether they would be prepared[,] should their services be required[,] to Charter them to the Govt for Transport Service . . .
Write also with regard to the Steam Ship *Glasgow* to the Secretary of the Glasgow & New York Packet Co . . .
Write also to Richardson Brothers thro Cap Bevis in regard to the *City of Baltimore* . . .

[**466**] *Milne to Newcastle*

Admiralty
8 January 1855

Acquaint the Duke of Newcastle that the following List of Steam Vessels have been chartered by the Adm[iralt]y and are now in England[,] also a List of Vessels coming home from the Black Sea for repair[,] and request to know for what service they are respectively to be appropriated[.]

Canadian[,] 1800 Tons[,] now ready for Troops and ordered from Liverpool to Portsmouth[.]
The *Empador*[,][1] 1700 Tons[,] now ready to be fitted at Liverpool[.]
The *Himalaya* is fitted for Horses and is now at Southampton[.]
The *Great Britain*[,] expected from Australia, at Liverpool[.]
The *Candia*[,] 2200 Tons[,] fitted for Troops[,] coming Home for repairs to South[ampton.]
The *Avon*[,] 2069 Tons[,] also fitted for Troops[,] coming Home for repairs to Southampton[.]

[P.S.:] The *Croesus*[,] 2000 Tons[,] will be ready about the 20th for Detachments and the *Bahiana*[,] 700 [tons,] is now ready at Liverpool [a]waiting the Embarkation of the 82d Reg[.][2]

[1]Milne probably meant *Imperador*.
[2]Sir James Graham initialled this memorandum on 9 January.

[**467**] *Milne to Christie*

Admiralty
15 January 1855

My dear Cap Christie

I write you a few hurried lines by this Evenings Mail to say that I have just received yours of the 1st of January[,] and I am glad I have heard from you as it affords explanations in regard to some matters which have been talked of here. Your note I have given to Sir J. Graham and he intends to take it to the Cabinet. I suspect some dissatisfaction has been expressed in regard to the loss of the ships[,] and that you are to blame. this [*sic*] is surmised on my part, but your note may help to disabuse any impression which may have been adopted by those in power here.

You ought to keep us informed of all requisitions from Lord Raglan or other persons[.] we ought to know what is going on[,] for instance the removal of the ships from Balaclava, [&] the moving of the Turkish Army[.] these orders or requisitions to you should come to us for our information[,] and unless you do so, we are quite ignorant of all that goes on. Therefore take the hint and keep us informed of everything. it [*sic*] <u>is really important</u> for your own <u>sake</u> as well as for the service.

I will now privately tell you what has been said here[,] and if you have made a mistake[,] why it cannot be helped. it [*sic*] is this[:] 'That Cap Christie instead of ordering the Turkish Troops to Eupatoria as requested, ordered them to Balaclava'. If this is untrue[,] I would wish to contradict it[,] and on your own Account [*sic*], be very careful of your doings, and some what [*sic*] cautious, as any mistake or inadvertence will be sure to be laid hold of and complaint made[,] so just keep your Eyes open and keep this to yourself[.]

Dont sent [*sic*] home any Agents of Transports[.] keep them[,] if fit[,] to any service required of them . . .

[P.S.:] We hear the Plank sent for Huts was floating about the Harbour of Balaclava[.] you must appeal to Sir E Lyons for any advice or assistance[.]

[468] *Stirling to Milne*

HMS *Winchester*, Hong Kong
17 January 1855

My dear Milne

Although I am not quite ready to send you an official Report as to what we are doing about the Naval Yard here, I trouble you with a line to say that[,] having got possession of the premises about a month ago[,] I set the Colonial architect to work to survey the Buildings and [to] give an Estimate of such Repairs as would make them available for 2 or 3 years for our purposes, and finding accordingly that for about £300 or £400 being laid out[,] I could make an effectual and respectable provision for storing the things, I caused a Contract to be made. One of the larger buildings has been in consequence repaired[,] and Captn Wilson[1] with a party of men from this ship is busily employed in removing the stores from West Point[,] the Ordnance barracks[,] and Fletchers warehouse to our own Premises . . . I am well satisfied with the job so far, and you will have[,] when completed[,] a respectable Depot yard for all our purposes for the next 3 or 4 years or until you decide upon what buildings you will erect.

In the meanwhile[,] you may now send out the Stores which have been demanded[,] as they can be well housed and cared for. You have a very good man here in Commander Parker,[2] who[,] with my small assistance to help him[,] never makes any difficulty. I hope you will not begrudge the expense of £300 or £400 I have put you to for repairs[,] considering that there was no time to lose to get this done . . .

We hear nothing whatever of the Russian Ships.[3] I suppose they are frozen up some where . . . and will not be heard of before the warm season sets in.

I have been ailing for the last month or six weeks but am now better again. I much fear however that I and this climate are not very good friends[,] and I begin to think I should be better off with a subordinate Flag in the Baltic or Channel than with the Chief command here[,] even with £2000 a year.

[1]Thomas Wilson (1811–94). Entered, 1828; Lt, 1839; Cmdr, 1843; Capt., 1853; Rear-Adm., 1869; Vice-Adm. (Ret.), 1875; Adm. (Ret.), 1879. Wilson commanded HMS *Winchester* in 1854.

[2]Charles Parker (d. 1859). Lt, 1820; Cmdr, 1829; Capt. (Res.), 1858. Naval Officer in Charge of Stores at Hong Kong.

[3]Those at Petropalovsk-Kamchatka.

I think the rebels are going to take Canton before long.[1] I am going up there in a few days[,] and hope to be there at the change of [?ownership] in the City. We must do our best to take care of the Tea Ships there . . .

I return your thanks for your agreeable note of the 25 October . . .

[**469**] *Milne to William Fanshawe Martin*

Admiralty
18 January [1855]

The *Canadian* has been ordered into Harbour at Portsmouth and is substituted for the *Croesus*[,] as that ship cannot be ready for 10 days, at least[.] write to the Horse Guards and inform[,] but she will not be able to Embark more than <u>950 to 1000</u> men.

[**470**] *Milne to the West India Company*

Admiralty
19 January [1855]

Immediate
Write to the West India Co and inform [that,] in preparing the *Severn* for the Embarkation of Troops[,] my Lords request that the ship may be so prepared as to form a Hospital Ship, and[,] if the Co have no objection[,] that Mr Revelt [*sic*][,] Cap of the *Tamar*[,] should be permitted to superintend the arrangements.[2]

[**471**] *Christie to Milne*

Orient, off Balaklava
19 January 1855

My dear Milne

I have just seen an Article in the *Times* from the 3d Mate of the '*Resolute*' against me, which I enclose.[3] It is quite contrary to the truth, because I met the Master of the *Resolute* at all times in the kindest manner, and I always found him a most attentive, good man. He did

[1]Stirling was referring to the T'ai P'ing Rebellion (1850–64). He was wrong, as events turned out; the rebels were repelled in 1855.

[2]Milne also instructed Grant to inform Robert Craigie at Southampton.

[3]Not preserved among Milne's papers.

express to me his dislike of the outside anchorage and I told him how anxious I was[,] not only to get his ship into the Harbour, but all the others, and that it was my intention to get them in as soon as circumstances would admit of it.

It is very annoying when one is working his heart out for the Army and his Country, that the Editor of a Paper should suffer such a letter to be inserted without ascertaining whether it is true or false. These vessels [i.e., ammunition ships] were anchored outside the Harbour, it being absolutely necessary for the safety of the Army, and was sanctioned by the Commander in Chief, as at that time it was by no means certain that we should be able to hold Balaklava, and I divided the Magazine Ships two outside and two in, and went out myself in the *Melbourne* and anchored amongst them.

I have no time to Battle with Newspapers[,] but I do hope the Admiralty will not suffer this article to pass unnoticed[,] and if you will be kind enough to assist me I shall be exceedingly obliged.[1]

I have nothing to do with the placing of the ships in Balaklava, that is left entirely to the Harbour Master. I assist him as much as I can and have created a Flag Staff for the purpose of keeping the Transports out by Signal, till he is ready for them.

The Army is suffering fearfully from sickness, and the Hospitals in the Bosphorus are so crowded[,] Admiral Boxer writes me the sick are obliged to remain on board the Steamers. This impedes our progress in embarking the Turkish Army from Varna very much, as those vessels had orders to Coal at Constantinople and proceed on that service with all despatch.

[**472**] *Milne to Stopford*

Admiralty
19 January 1855

My dear Stopford

I write you a line in explanation of an order which goes out this Evng in regard to the Transports. The order is to detain the Sailing Ships at Malta which are ordered to England. these [*sic*] are intended to go to Genoa to embark Sardinian Troops and[,] if it is necessary[,] these ships should be completed in their fittings as soon as possible. They

[1]No official statement was issued by the Admiralty, but Graham gave a strong defence of Christie's actions in his testimony to the Roebuck Committee. See *Parliamentary Papers*, 1855, vol. IX, pt II, p. 260, questions 21,062–71.

will also have to be provisioned and prepared for the embarkation of Horses, probably slings Halters &c will be required[,] but this can only be known when you get the ships at Malta. I[t] may not be necessary to detain absolutely every one, as some may be loaded with Stores for England. Let us know what you may want or wish and we will be ready to meet your wants & wishes[.]

[**473**] *Milne to Grant*

Admiralty
22 January [1855]

Give notice at Sh[i]py[ar]ds, also Liverpool[,] Bristol[,] Hull [&] Glasgow[:]
That the Admiralty is prepared to receive offers of steamers above 400 Tons for Transports in the Conveyance of Troops and Stores.
and [*sic*] for a steamer of about 500 Tons to convey Medical Stores to Scutari. Vessels requested to be offered by the month for 3 months certain[,] or by the voyage[.]

[**474**] *Milne to Newcastle*

Admiralty
22 January [1855]

Inform the Duke of Newcastle that my Lords have been enabled to Charter the *Etna* of 2200 Tons[,] which vessel has been withdrawn from the French Govt owing to some dispute with the owners in regard to the Charter party[.]

This ship is now ready for sea at Liverpool[,] and has great height between decks for the conveyance of Horses, if all the internal fittings are removed.

The *Great Britain* is expected at Liverpool to day, which ship was chartered some weeks ago[,] and a new ship[,] the *Indian*[,] 1800 Tons[,] may be ready in about five weeks.

Their Lordships request to know for which service these ships are to be prepared, also the *Empador* [*sic*] & *Cambria*, which ship has returned from the Medn and is now under repair[.]

[**475**] *Christie to Milne*

Orient, off Balaklava
22 January 1855

My dear Milne

I have just received yours of the 4th, and am much annoyed and astonished at the reports you have heard.

I am accused of keeping one of the best steamers for my own use, whereas I have been almost constantly on board a sailing vessel, and have changed my ship six different times in order that the Service might not suffer, and I am now, and have been for a considerable time in the *Orient* sailing ship, now full of Stores.[1]

The Transports land their Cargoes regularly as they arrive at the proper Wharves, and I am not aware that any vessel was sent to sea with any part of her Cargo left, except the *Himalaya* with a small quantity of charcoal, which was left [on board] rather than detain her outside the Harbour.

There are plenty of steamers sent from this to Constantinople, their detention there I of course have nothing to do with[,] but I believe Adml Boxer has considerable difficulty in finding hands to coal.

The cause of the Troops suffering from want of Provisions &c is the difficulty of getting them up from Balaklava to the Camp, there being so few Horses, Mules or Waggons, and the roads so bad.

The arrangements in the Harbour I do not interfere with, but assist the Harbour Master in every way I can. I erected a Flag staff at the entrance of the Harbour some considerable time ago, and established signals, and no Transport is allowed to enter the Port till the established signal is hoisted with her Pendant. I also suggested the propriety of rowing guard regularly.

The cause of the *Times* Correspondent's report relative to the vessels running in 'Helter Skelter' &c[,] was in consequence of some Colliers and Private vessels running in one day in a fresh breeze, not knowing the Signals, and causing some damage to the ships in Port. this [*sic*] he happened to witness[,] I believe.

Many of the large [flat] Boats suffered in the severe Gale of the 14th Novr at Eupatoria and Varna. They were placed in charge of the Senior Naval Officer. If six more large flat boats were sent out from England, they would be of great use in landing Provisions & Stores.

[1]Christie's earlier letters largely support this claim, although he was for a time on board the steamship *Melbourne*.

I have four Agents here, one superintends the embarkation of the Sick, another boards all the vessels directly they come in and brings me a report of what they have on board, which I transmit immediately to Headquarters, the third attends to the disembarking of Troops and the unloading of the vessels[,] and the fourth I have ordered to Superintend a large party of Carpenters and seamen which I have sent to erect Huts, Stables &c for the Army.

I do all in my power to expedite the Service, and to assist the Army, and I trust that the reports that fly about will not be listened to as gospel.

[**476**] *Milne to Grey*[1]

Admiralty
25 January 1855

My dear Grey

First of all let me congratulate you on obtaining your Flag[,] and long may you live to enjoy the Rank and Position which it confers, but it is no easy matter in these days to get ahead, and more especially in your present position, where I am much afraid there is sad Chaos of Confusion [*sic*], so at least it is reported by all and everyone who comes home. I send you a specimen of the difficulties &c and the Complaints which come to us.[2] All this you will have to put right.

There are several Transports doing nothing in the Bosphorus[.] they have been there for months[.] It strikes me it would be much better for [*sic*: 'to'] form a Naval Est[ablishmen]t on shore by hiring Stores [houses] if they could be got[,] even somewhere above Constantinople . . . and thusly get no [*sic*: 'rid'] of the Transport Depots. I merely mention this as a hint for your consideration.

We send you all Bills of Lading or lists of private Boxes &c[,] which are embarked in England[.] will you forward a Copy on to the Senior N[aval] Officer or Transport Agent at Balaclava so that those poor people in the Crimea may get their things, but I am afraid Balaclava will remain a dead Lock [*sic*] from the Enormous quantity of things sent there[.] Employ your officers and men in any way you may see fit so as[,] if possible[,] to get things put through. You might make use of [?*Alipore*] in any way you wish[,] only say so to Sir E. Lyons.

[1]Frederick Grey, who replaced Boxer at Constantinople.
[2]Not included in this copy of Milne's letter.

I am fitting *Severn* as an Hosp[ital] Ship[.] She will sail in about 10 days and will run between Balaclava & Scutari. I hear a new Hospital is forming at Smyrna. Lord J. Russell has resigned,[1] so I presume there will be a break up of the Ministry this day.

[**477**] *Milne to Stirling*

Brighton
29 January 1855

My dear Sir James

Thanks for a very agreeable and pleasant letter[,][2] which I received from you about a month ago[,] and I rejoice to find you were [*sic*] well and going on pleasantly on the station. Your visit to Japan is much applauded here[,] and you have proved yourself a <u>Sterling diplomat</u>[.] Your recommendations have all been attended to[,] and a Screw Yacht will be obtained as soon as possible, but at present time there is great pressure on the Dock Yards to meet the requirements of the Baltic[.] Our late Comdr in Chief[,] Sir C Napier[,] has struck his Flag and is more <u>rabid</u> than ever. he [*sic*] is violent against this Board and all our doings, but he is an unmanageable man and [there is] really no dealing with him. Every one of his letters have been impertinent from the day he left England, and all his correspondence is evidently written for the Eye [*sic*] of the Public. all [*sic*] this is very much to be regretted. In his last public letter he alludes at [*sic*] not having been again [invited] ashore to <u>Windsor</u> (the first note he did not receive in time)[,] which he attributes to the First Lord. He also says when <u>his life is written</u>, and if the correspondence is allowed to remain without his calling for public Enquiry [*sic*][,] he might be considered a <u>Coward</u>[.] What think you of all this[?] He has been to Cobden and some other MPs to get the correspondence moved for in the House, but as yet no one will take it up. I now hear that Sir C[harles] wants to insult Sir J. Graham and at the Lord Mayors Dinner on the 5th intends to let out.[3] In fact our old Chief is as wild as ever, and he intends to have a flare up, by any means that he can. The

[1]Russell, the Secretary for War, resigned following John Arthur Roebuck's motion of censure was introduced on 23 January 1855. The Government subsequently followed suit when the motion passed 305–148 on the 29th.

[2]Not preserved among Milne's papers.

[3]Napier's speech is printed in Bonner-Smith and Dewar, *Russian War, 1854*, pp. 24–8. The official correspondence between Napier and the Admiralty was printed for the Cabinet in January 1854.

state of affairs in the East is most awful[,] which you will see in the papers, but perhaps made really more than what it is. The whole fault rests with the Army people [for] not having made a road from Balaclava to the Camp. There is everything in the Har[bour] but nothing can be got up except by manual labour. What is to be said of all this, no one can predict[.] we are having all sorts of rows in the House of Common's [*sic*] and today there is to be a change[,] but by next mail you will see the result[,] which will be decided on Monday next by a division in the House of Commons.

In Naval Matters we have nothing new. *Nankin* & *Esk* are to join you as soon as possible. I would [have] a Screw frigate sent also but this cannot be done. Nothing is yet arranged who is to Command the Baltic Fleet, but Napier or Chads or perhaps Plumridge, but I have no idea who will be the man. Berkeley is anxious for it, but I very much doubt whether he will be the man. he [*sic*] is much changed and broken.

. . . Your visit to Japan must have been a most interesting one, and you certainly managed it most admirably[.] The ratification I believe goes out by the next mail[.][1]

. . . Houston Stewart has gone as 2d in Command in [the] Black Sea[.] Stopford gets Malta, Boxer goes from Constantinople[,] where he has caused much confusion & no system [*sic*] to Balaclava[,] and F[rederick] Grey hoists his Flag in *Queen* in the Bosphorus. C[harles] Graham[2] & C[harles] Eden have come home invalided[,] also Carnegie.[3] Ad [James] Dundas we expect in ten days. he [*sic*] also has his back up[,] and is not pleased with our board [*sic*] because we suspended his own appoint[ment] of Master of the Fleet, Deputy Inspector of Hospital & a Comdr from Half Pay at Malta to Command the *Ceylon*. now [*sic*] Dundas ought to have known better than to make these appoint[men]ts without the knowledge or sanction of the Board. had [*sic*] he asked for them[,] they would have been done, but he put in his own people[,] which looked rather a job.

I write this at Brighton[,] having run down with my wife for 24 [hours] fresh air[,] but go back this morning[.] now I dont [*sic*] think I have any more to say. we [*sic*] rub on at the Board much as usual, but the work has been much increased and I have had a great pressure for [*sic*: 'from'] the Transport Department. We have now 102 Steam Trans-

[1]Of the trade treaty with Japan, signed in October 1854.

[2]Sir James Graham's brother Charles.

[3]Swynfen Thomas Carnegie, C.B. (1813–79). Entered, 1826; Lt, 1832; Cmdr, 1838; Capt., 1845; Rear-Adm., 1863; Vice-Adm., 1870; Adm. (Ret.), 1876; Naval Lord of the Admiralty, 1859.

ports employed, also 112 Sailing Ships[.] we are moving 35,000 Turks to Eupatoria, have moved 16,000 French from Marseilles to [the] Crimea, have now to move 15,000 Piedmontese from Genoa to Crimea, 12,000 Foreign Legion to D[itt]o[,] and 6000 Horses from England. our [*sic*] work has been enormous. 107,000 Tons of Stores to Black Sea [*sic*][.]

[**478**] *Milne to Houston Stewart*

Brighton
29 January 1855

My dear Admiral

I congratulate you on your having obtained the promotion as 2d in Command[, for] which you have so much wished, and I hope and trust all will go well with you[,] and that you have everything as you could wish [*sic*], but also I regret your have [*sic*] left Malta. Your energy and zeal and foresight has [*sic*] been the means of preventing many complaints from the Army departments, but your thorough knowledge of all that has passed may[,] I trust[,] be the means of putting all to rights at Constantinople and in the Crimea. It is no time to stand upon ceremony when the safety of the Army is at stake. but [*sic*] why this is[,] no one at present seems to know. I cannot attribute any blame to the Admiralty[,] the Transport or Vict[uallin]g Department[s]. we [*sic*] have done all in our power to meet the views[,] wishes and demands of the War department. we [*sic*] may not have been sufficiently quick in meeting their requisitions, but it was not possible to secure steam vessels at a moments notice, and I am not aware that the Army have been in want from this cause. The Evil has been in the want of management on Shore in the Crimea, [&] The [*sic*] neglect in not making a proper road, but you will be able to judge of that & why & wherefore when you are on the Spot. There is an awful feeling in England on the subject and if the H[ouse] of C[ommons] carry the Vote tonight for a Committee of Enquiry[,] the Govt resigns, but I presume will be reformed with Lord Palmerston as War Minister[.] I will be anxious to hear your opinion of matters. Sir J. Graham gave me your last letter and an Engineer will be selected from Portsmouth to go to Malta. I am writing this at Brighton on [the] 28th[,] as I have come down here to see my Children who are located [*sic*] here for a month for sea air. My wife sends her kind regards and best wishes[,] and begs me again to thank you for the charming oranges which you sent her by *Himalaya*[,] which she enjoyed very much.

I presume you know D. Hay[1] has been appointed your Flag Captain[.]
All success attend you. . . .

[**479**] *Milne to Newcastle*

Admiralty
31 January 1855

Dear Duke of Newcastle
I regret being compelled by a sense of justice to my own character and conduct, to write these few lines, with reference to the statement made by your Grace of Monday evening in the House of Lords, in which you so strongly condemn the Transport system. Personally, I feel obliged for the flattering manner in which you mentioned my name. I consciously feel that I have endeavoured all in my power to meet the incessant and difficult requirements of the War Department, and to carry out to the best of my ability what was required of me[,] and which has been the source of continued anxiety ever since the commencement of the War.

Your Grace may well conceive that I cannot but feel distressed and annoyed, that you should have considered it necessary to pass so sweeping a public censure on the Transport Department, when you stated 'that that Department had more eminently failed and broken down than any other part of our system as far as the home departments are concerned.' What has led you to this condemnation I know not. My object in writing you is not to cavil about words or to find fault, but to ask you for my own justification, what are the circumstances which have given you so much dissatisfaction. I am entirely ignorant of any complaint having been made either by yourself or other Departments either at Home or Abroad. no [*sic*] hint has ever been given that things were going wrong, no suggestions have ever been proposed or alterations recommended[,] and you must be aware that in any communications I used to have with your Grace some months ago, I was always most ready and anxious to afford you every explanation in my power, and at all time ready to meet your wishes, any suggestion, any proposal from you, any recommendation would have met with my immediate attention. My whole anxiety has been to do what was right. I was therefore perfectly taken by surprise when I

[1]Sir John Charles Dalrymple Hay, Bt., C.B., K.C.B., F.R.S., D.C.L. (1821–1912). Entered, 1834; Lt, 1845; Cmdr, 1846; Capt., 1850; Rear-Adm. (Ret.), 1870; Vice-Adm. (Ret.), 1873; Adm. (Ret.), 1878; M.P., 1862–65, 1866–80, 1880–85; Naval Lord of the Admiralty, 1866–68.

read the statement your Grace made in the House of Lords, and it would be not only satisfactory[,] but an act of justice to me, to know what you consider to be wrong, for it is never too late to correct an error or remedy a defeat [*sic*].

It may be said that Stores sent from this country urgently wanted for the Army have not been delivered. This does not rest with the Departments at Home, for I may state that in the enormous consignments of Naval and Army provisions and stores from this country[,] and which have been consigned under the sole and direct control of the Naval Department, not one accident or one mistake that I am aware of has occurred. The Bills of Lading have been signed by the Master of each ship, by which he became the responsible Storekeeper for the period these provisions or stores were on board his ship, and his receipts from the party to whom they were consigned were the proof of delivery, and on which payment for Freight is made. In regard to Ordnance Stores[,] the Admiralty only provides the ship or the portion of a ship as may be required. The Ordnance then acts for itself, loads, consigns, delivers. The Naval Department is ignorant of everything, until payment for Freight is claimed after delivery, and this is not paid until the Ordnance transmits a receipt from their Agent.

Whatever may have occurred in the non delivery of stores at Balaclava, I must say I am under the impression that the fault does not lie with the Transport Department[,] but with the authorities on shore[,] whose duty it is to receive Stores, because I have been repeatedly told that the Masters of Transports who are the Storekeepers of the Stores during transit, could not get anyone either to receive the Stores or grant receipts. It is well known how limited the Harbour of Balaclava is, how still more limited the shore is for landing Stores, and how numerous have been the vessels sent from this country, I may say daily loading at Deptford, Woolwich, Portsmouth and Devonport, all to be concentrated in one small spot 410 yards long by 210 yards wide. all [*sic*] the vessels have to be discharged, after discharge to be ballasted [&] to be coaled and watered. This requires time and space, but I will say no more, but express my regret at having taken up your time, but under the feelings of annoyance I trust that you will consider it reasonable . . .

[**480**] *Milne to Lyons*

Admiralty
2 February 1855

Enclose this[1] to Sir E Lyons and request he will direct enquiry to be made into the facts as stated[,] and if he has not already done so[,] He [*sic*] is to order one of the Agents of Transports to be stationed in Balaclava Harbour to visit each ship on her arrival and sailing, to obtain from the Master a List of the Stores on Board[,] to examine her Hold, and to enter in a Book what Cargo or Stores she has in [her]. he [*sic*] is not to detain any Bills of Lading which may be addressed to the Military Authorities[,] but to see that they are delivered to the proper Departments, and he is to exercise a special supervision over each ship[,] and to take care that no such irregularities are allowed to take place[,] which from statements made[,] both public & private[,] would seem to be the case.[2]

[**481**] *Christie to Milne*

Orient, off Balaklava
2 February 1855

My dear Milne

I have received your letter of the 15th Jany and am very sorry to think that any one should be impressed with the idea that I was to blame in any way for the loss of the ships at Balaklava. I have sent Sir Edmund Lyons, for the information of the Lords of the Admiralty, a full account of that unfortunate occurrence, which I trust will show that I was in no way to blame.

It is a strange thing, but neither before nor since that storm have we had a breeze that a ship could not have been at that anchorage in perfect safety. I made sure that the Commander in Chief had reported all that took place. I sent him a full report directly after the 14th Novr.

It is quite true that one of the steam vessels came from Varna with Turks to Balaklava instead of Eupatoria, and the cause of it was this, my clerk in making out the order for the vessel wrote Balaklava instead of Eupatoria[,] and I, equally to blame, read it in a hurry and signed it

[1]An extract from *The Times* of 23 January 1855, headed 'Chaos at Balaklava & containing the Story of the Boots & Shoes'.

[2]This memorandum was initialled by Sir James Graham on 2 February. Milne then added: '2 Feb, Immediate To go tonight'.

without discovering the mistake, however, this only caused the loss of about an hours time, for when the ship arrived I ordered her off to Eupatoria immediately, and reported the circumstance to Lord Raglan.

You mention that you have heard that Planks for Huts have been seen floating about the Harbour. In landing such a large quantity of Plank in all sorts of Boats, I have no doubt that a few may have slipped into the water, but I will answer for it, that not one has been lost. I have an officer stationed on shore and two afloat when they are being landed, and I am there as much as possible myself. All molehills appear to be turned into mountains at home.

We have landed about 26,000 Turks at Eupatoria with upwards to two months Provisions, and I should think if the weather keeps fine, the whole army will be landed there by the end of next week. I only wish we had 20,000 French & English with them.

The Russians made a sortie yesterday morning against the French. The latter lost some officers and a considerable number of men, several taken prisoners. What the Russian loss was remains uncertain. There is no doubt that the two Gd Dukes have returned to Sebastopol.[1]

Our Troops look warm & comfortable now. they [*sic*] have [an] abundance of warm clothing, a great number of Huts & Stables have been put up, and the Commissariat have six weeks Provisions in Store. the [*sic*] only thing they are short of is Forage, and we know there are vessels with Hay and Oats no great distance off. The small Hut steamers I am sending down to the Bosphorus for Forage, Coal and firewood to assist the Commissariat[,] also Bullocks & Sheep. I met Sir Edmund Lyons some days ago, and we agreed to send a number of the larger Steamers[,] as well as sailing vessels[,] home immediately, as you will see by my last return to the Admiralty.

I am sorry to tell you that I have embarked in Steam Transports for Scutari no less that 7941 Sick since the 1st December last, and there are 200 more coming down today, but on the whole Sickness in the Army is on the decrease.

I have just received a requisition for vessels to bring up about 1500 Mules from Candia & other places. this [*sic*] I will do with the three Horse steamers, *Trent*, *Jason* & *Simla*, towing the *Harkaway*[,] *Arabia* and another sailing vessel.

I am very much obliged to you for all the kind hints you give me[,] and hope you will continue to do so.

[1]Russian Grand Dukes Michael and Nicholas.

[**482**] *Milne to Stopford*

Admiralty
2 February [1855]

My dear Stopford

I write you a hurried line and have a request to make to prevent the many vexations which arrive aboard vessels passing Scutari and Constantinople and not landing their stores. Be so good as to give an order to every vessel proceeding to the Black Sea[,] to land the Stores at Scutari or Constantinople & not carry them on to the Black Sea. Please to enforce this . . .

[**483**] *Christie to Milne*

Orient, off Balaklava
5 February 1855

My dear Milne

I send you a few lines by the Post which is just about to start.

Sir Edmund Lyons has just sent me a letter requesting me to countermand all the Steamers I had ordered home[,] as they may be required to convey Sardinian Troops here from Genoa or Spezzia, and to send him a list of vessels I think available for this service.

I enclose you a Duplicate of what I have sent.[1] You will see there are a considerable number of smaller Steamers, Hut vessels &c[,] which will be very useful here for the Army. All that can be dispensed with after the hurry is over shall be sent home.

The Forage was getting very low with the Commissariat [*sic*], but I am happy to say two Sailing vessels arrived this morning with a large supply.

I have a good deal of trouble with the *Simla*'s Crew. Their time is up that they entered for [*sic*], and they refuse to go [on] any more trips, but wish to insist upon going home, however I think I shall get it arranged [*sic*].

The weather has been very favorable for embarking the Turkish Troops, and I am in hopes the whole Army will soon be got over. Another Horse Transport Steamer would be of great use just now, we miss *Himalaya* a good deal.

[1]Not included in this edition.

[**484**] *Milne to Lyons*

Admiralty
6 February 1855

Acquaint Sir E. Lyons, that the Chartered Steamer *Severn* has been fitted out with Bedplaces and other accommodation for the conveyance of Sick & Wounded men from the Crimea to Scutari or other Military Hospitals, That [*sic*] Medical comforts have been put on board[,] also Medical Stores in charge of the Surgeon of that Ship, who has been granted a salary at the rate of £100 pr annum for such charge[,] and to afford assistance to the sick, but not to take medical charge, he is therefore to give orders that when Military Invalids are embarked[,] that it will be necessary for Medical officers and Attendants to be embarked with the Sick Men.

In regard to the numerous Steam vessels which have been sent to the Black Sea from England, it is most desirable that immediate attention should be given to their being discharged of their cargoes so that they may be immediately sent to England without delay, The [*sic*] detention of these vessels being attended with a very heavy expense[,] and their services are urgently required in England to return with Stores, if they are not absolutely required in the Black Sea[.]

[**485**] *Milne to Houston Stewart*

Admiralty
7 February 1855

My dear Admiral

I have not written to you for sometime or since you left the sphere of your usefulness[,] but I believe you have gone to another more important sphere[,] where I trust you may be enabled to do much good. It [is] on the state of affairs in the East I now drop you a line. I am in sad distress at the awful expense of the Transport Department[,] and people are beginning to call out and blame me. I have done all I can to keep down the audacious [*sic*] claims but it is to no avail. There is combination in the Market[,] and the French are paying 62/6 to 65/. per Ton for steamers and we have held to 50/. on large ships. we [*sic*] cannot therefore get a hope [*sic*] or prospect of reduction. The sums are enormous. This is enhanced by vessels being kept in the East. Do look at this and [see] if you can get some of these steamers sent home. This I know must depend on what may be wanted to be performed in the

Black Sea, and I can not judge of that, but we have sent out about 30 steamers in the last two months and surely they are not all wanted[?] we have drained all England and no more vessels can be obtained until they are built, and yet we have about 4000 Tons of stores coming in <u>every week</u> to be sent to the <u>Crimea</u>. This is an awful pull on the Department, and unless vessels are sent home we cannot meet it. I will be very much obliged if you will look round[,] and with your usual activity and knowledge of all that has been done, endeavour to place matters in proper working order. Steamers laying idle are ruinous to everyone. Sailing ships are bad enough.

We are in a sad mess here[;] no Ministry for some days[,] but I believe the Peelites or a part of them will join Lord Palmerston to-day[.][1] it is an awful crisis and the *Times* articles are perfectly <u>Revolutionary</u>. for [*sic*] the last two days they have been stirring up the people of the Country to monster meetings, and to take things into their own hands. It is quite awful to see this, and if Lord P[almerston's] government does not stand[,] which many say it cannot[,] God only knows what is to follow. I do not write about the steamers to Sir E Lyons, but privately to you[,] so that you can give any hint or say nothing. Sir E[dmund] has enough on his hands[,] and I presume[,] as Second in Command[,] you will have to attend to these matters all [*sic*: as] well.

[**486**] *Lyons to Milne*

HMS *Agamemnon*, off Sevastopol
10 February 1855

My dear Milne

We have Telegraphic accounts from Varna of the Queen having sent for Ld Derby on the 29th, Inst[.] I submit our hopes that no such misfortune as a change at the Adm[iral]ty can have taken place at this juncture, when all you do inspires confidence here in everyone from the highest to the lowest. Come what may[,] I trust that you will remain at the Board.

Now for Transports Coals &c[.]

We have already done something with our transports in bringing some 25000 of firm Turkish Troops and Provisions for them[,] in so

[1]For the political crisis, see Lambert, *The Crimean War*, p. 202. Palmerston's Ministry was formed on 8 February, after Lords Derby and Lansdowne and Lord John Russell had each failed to form a government.

short a time at this season of the year[,] when at the exposed place of Embarkation & Disembarkation[,] there are but few days in a month that either is possible. But we must strain every nerve to get it done[,] so as to have the means of bringing the Sardinian Troops here, and . . . I think we shall have done the busiest part of our work here in time to have the Steam Transports maybe at Genoa or Spezzia in the beginning of April, if you wish it, to bring 15000 [Sardinian] Troops, but not much more than 250 or 300 horses, for if we are to have a spring campaign here[,] we shall have enough to do with our horse transports in bringing Mules and other means of Transport for our own Army. Perhaps I might continue to bring here[,] from Ibryzia or Varna[,] the Artillery horses, but certainly not the Cavalry Horses with the means I now possess. I will, however, by the next mail send you a list of the Transports, both the Steam & Sailing ones. The *Simla* I have kept here to make two trips for Varna for Omar Pasha at the particular request of L. Raglan[,] who is naturally anxious to give him the means of cutting off the supplies . . . to Sebastopol by the [?Post] road . . .

[**487**] *Houston Stewart to Milne*

HMS *Hannibal*, off Sevastopol, Private
13 February 1855

My dear Milne

I hope that this letter will find <u>you</u> still at the post of labour and usefulness[,] which you have so ably filled, and nothing grieves me more in the political news which has reached us than the possibility of the present most efficient Board & its <u>most able</u> head being arrested in their career of patriotic & powerful exertion on behalf of the Country & its Naval Service.

I however still hope that Sir James Graham may remain, as I can hardly think Lord Derby will be rash enough to attempt the responsibility for Government at such a critical moment in public affairs. Still[,] there are many men who will be ready to go to him, now that the question of Protection is for ever laid at rest.[1] I truly hope that such useful working men as <u>yourself</u> and <u>Richards</u>[,] who are <u>not Partisans</u>[,] may, under any circumstances be induced to remain, & keep your strong & able shoulders at the wheel.

[1]The Conservative Party, of which Derby was leader 1846–68, had split with Prime Minister Sir Robert Peel over the latter's decision to abandon agricultural protection in 1846. The Conservatives subsequently dropped Protectionism during Derby's brief 1852 minority ministry.

Your letter of the 29th Inst reached me yesterday morning by *Banshee*, and I need not assure you how deeply I feel your kind approval of my past work & your warm good wishes for my success in my present line of duty.

I arrived here only on Saturday last in the *Spiteful*, and I found Sir Edmund still in *Agamemnon*[,] but he shifts into *Royal Albert* tomorrow or next day. She is moored carefully in Kazatch [*sic*] Bay & the *Rodney* also, whilst the *Hannibal*, *Agamemnon*, *P*[*rince*]*ss Royal*, *Algiers* & *St J. d'Acre* are at single anchor with a long scope of Cable (160 f[atho]ms in from 35 to 40 fms) outside & leaving Sevastopol well open [*sic*]. Our topmasts are struck & lashed[,] so as to carry close reefed sails[,] & one boiler is left warm &[,] as weather becomes fresher[,] a 2d or 3d is lighted. It would be wild work in a Sailing Vessel, but the Screw makes all safe. I have not yet had a chance of going on shore. The day after I arrived (Sunday) it blew & snowed (or as Adl Boxer would wish it, 'it blowed & snowed') so as to set the ship a rolling, in a way that made many cast up their accounts & cost some crockery. But it did not last long. Yesterday was fine in the morning & all the Captains dined with Sir Edmund[,] but we were all forced to sleep there & I have only just now got on board again. This will shew you that it is roughish & uncertain work, but I do not think it nearly so anxious as it used to be off Brest & Rochefort blockading in the last war, for there were no screws & the Gales lasted much longer than[,] happily[,] they ever do in these Seas.

Each ship has discretionary permission to slip & put to sea if thought desirable. Sir Edmund is well, in good spirits & working very hard; he is unwilling to go into the Bay[,] but finds it impossible to carry on the necessary intercourse with the French Navy[,] & Army & with our own People on shore from this exposed Anchorage.

I brought Sir G. Brown up with men in *Spiteful* & yesterday[;] he went from *Agamemnon* to his Camp[,] saw Lord Raglan[,] who rode with him along the whole line to his own Division, and I am very thankful to say that the General[,] although by no means a sanguine man, thinks there is decided improvement in the appearance of things in general. Indeed[,] from all I have been able to learn[,] I do not think things are now so bad as they are supposed to be at home, altho' they certainly have been very bad. The improvement seems to have taken place within the last 3 or 4 weeks, Although [*sic*] I cannot understand that matters have ever been in such a wretched state as has been represented, and most assuredly all the well informed seem to agree in saying that much more blame has been cast upon People[,] both at home & out here[,] than what either has deserved.

Upon one subject I shall say no more than to remark to you confidentially that I think it most fortunate for the public interests & for his own, that our Friend Dundas has retired. Indeed it is to be regretted that he did not do so long ago. You know my friendship for him, & you will easily believe that it grieves me to write this, but to you & to Sir James Graham only I would state it.

I am sorry to say that already there are 2 Courts Martial, but not from any breach of discipline here but in England. The first is a Mate of the *P[rince]ss Royal* for breaking his arrest before the ship left England. This is to come off on board this ship day after tomorrow, & until they are over, I fear I shall not be able to get to Balaklava. Talking of Courts Martial, What [*sic*] could be the reason for sending Pasley[1] into the *Agamemnon* instead of the *Hannibal*, the former fitted for a flag[,] for Courts Martial &c[,] & this ship having every thing to alter & prepare[?] It seemed so simple that the 2d in Command should succeed to the 2d Flagship. I don't say this in disparagement of the *Hannibal*[,] but simply looking to the convenience of the public service.

Boxer is at Balaklava & is very busy, but[,] poor old fellow[,] he has got himself such a name for bad arrangements & bad language & indecorous bearing, that I fear he will not recover his proper position & authority, especially with the Army & Masters of Transports. However I have always thought him a valuable & zealous officer[,] & I hope to be useful to him in venturing a gentle hint or two when I get hold of him.

Christie seems to be universally condemned as quite incompetent to his work [*sic*]. Honourable, zealous & gentleman like, but slow, without energy, memory or tact. Heath seems to have given satisfaction & to have done a good deal toward reform, but the Naval arrangements at Balaklava are not the blamable, inefficient things as represented. On the contrary, but [*sic*] it is the Army Staff, the Commissariat & Ordnance Subordinates. Indeed[,] the Staff of Head Quarters seems to be condemned as useless and inefficient by general consent, especially the Adjutant General.[2] now [*sic*] for this it is not possible to avoid holding the Comdr in Chief responsible &[,] although he very chivalrously defends his staff & takes responsibility on his own shoulders, yet the deduction is inevitable that if his staff be unsatisfactory[,] it is the Comdr in Chief's fault for not bettering it.

Brown's arrival has done much good & given a fillip[,] & indeed it is a fine spirited thing, his joining again so soon, when 19 men out of 20

[1]Sir Thomas Sabine Pasley, Bt. (1804–84). Entered, 1817; Lt, 1824; Cmdr, 1828; Capt., 1831; Rear-Adm., 1856; Vice-Adm., 1863; Adm., 1866.

[2]Major-General J. B. B. Estcourt.

would have lingered on at Malta, or even have gone to England.[1] He is a right good[,] honest, gallant Soldier & will always set a good example[,] I am confident[,] & I think myself fortunate in having had the opportunity of our voyage up from Malta together to make his acquaintance so thoroughly as I have done.

I was much concerned to learn by your letter & also from O'Brien[2] that Sir James Graham was seriously indisposed. I beg of you to offer him my best & most grateful regards[,] & the expression of my ardent hope that his health may very speedily be all right again[,] & the Country have the benefit of his invaluable Services in this hour of need.

There is no want of Provisions at the Commissariat just now, & all the men have warm clothing[.] There are Huts enough up for the Hospital wants & they are getting them up for the men[,] the difficulty still being the Road or rather no Road, but the Navvies are pushing on & the Rail Road does progress. It seems generally thought that the worst of the winter is now over, and that the French[,] having taken a considerable portion of the defence of the Right [*sic*], has relieved our men to a great degree & thus made a valuable improvement[,] for all agree in saying that over-work & consequent inability to cook victuals, & later rest, added in some degree to want of proper shelter & clothing[,] has caused all the mischief & specially that dreadful dysentery.

Genl Brown & I visited the Hospitals at Scutari & certainly a dismal sight it was, but as to comfort & attendance, I do not think there was any fault to be found, considering the numbers. Utensils seemed most to be required[,] such as night stools &c[,] & certainly it will be desirable[,] if it were possible[,] to have softer beds than what the mattresses stuffed with straw are [*sic*]. The numerous cases of dysentery make it impossible that any great number of those now in Hospital at Scutari will ever rejoin the ranks of our Army in the Crimea.

I saw Grey for 2 days at Constantinople. He has plenty to do, & a difficult task. It is such a mess of confusion & bustle, combined with want of knowledge of language & people, but I hope he will not scruple to cling to Lord Stratford[,][3] who is quite willing to be clung to, & he is omniscient [*sic*] & all difficulties will be overcome with his cordial intervention, but the invitation should come from him. Whether Grey will be politic enough to see the prudence of this course I somewhat

[1]Brown had been wounded in the chest and left arm during a Russian attack on the allied position on 5 November 1854.

[2]Capt. Henry Higgins Donatus O'Brien, R.A., Sir James Graham's Private Secretary.

[3]Stratford Canning, first Viscount Stratford de Redcliffe (1786–1880). British Ambassador to the Sublime Porte.

doubt, but to be really useful & to succeed in carrying on his public Interest [*sic*] at Stamboul, this should be his course. The 2 Archdukes have returned to Sevastopol & an attack upon our Forces has been talked of, but no movement of any consequence has been observed. An Assault is also talked of at no distant date, but with what probability I cannot say. The French say they have 80.000 Troops of all arms. Perhaps 60.000 effective would be nearer the truth. We have not less than 14, or 15,000 & Genl Brown says the fellows look well & cheery, & very picturesque[,] many of them in their different sorts & descriptions of Garments.

If we have men enough to protect our Works[,] & allow a sufficient force to march out & attack the enemy, I should have more confidence, than in the result of an assault upon a place such as Sevastopol now is, & with the North Batteries still in their progression.

And now my dear Fellow I have written you a long yarn, you must not place too much confidence in either the facts or opinions I have written, as I am much too ignorant & too short a time here, to be able to offer you anything to be relied upon. Meantime[,] with love to your Wife & little ones, & cordial regards to all my old friends at the Admiralty . . .

P.S. The premonitions from the French[,] made known yesterday[,] diffused much joy & gave life & spirit all round.[1]

One word on Naval matters. I do not see what we can do. I need hardly say that Sir Edmund is keen, keen to lend a hand, should an assault be determined on, but so far as I can as yet judge, little or nothing could be affected by the ships. This is humiliating[,] but it is nevertheless true, and I hope you will believe that I am not the man to dissuade my Chief or hold back myself, if there be a chance for Naval Work.

As to running over the sunken ships & Booms[,] the scheme is wild[,] & I scruple not to say utterly impracticable, nor do I see what the ship could do[,] supposing one or two or even more to get over the succession of impediments. The Batteries are so high that even with the after trucks off[,] the ships guns could not elevate so as to touch the batteries above them. What then could they do? so [*sic*] long as the Batteries on the North side were all in the hands of the Enemies? but [*sic*] I am convinced that no ship[,] whether impelled by steam or wind or both[,] could succeed in forcing herself over the successive impediments & the rigging of the sunken ships[,] together with all sorts of

[1]Perhaps a reference to the reinforcements being sent out.

entanglements purposely & most carefully placed there, would inevitably & immediately choke & disable the screw. You will get officers & men to volunteer for anything, but I hold him to be an unfit Chief to do what all cool reason & calculation shewed to be not merely a forlorn, but an absolutely desperate hope, for supposing the obstacles passed, the ships must inevitably be sunk in the course of a few minutes from plunging Batteries[,] to which they could not return an effective shot.

I daresay this opinion of mine may disappoint some of the sanguine, but I believe that even Harry Keppel[1] & Clarence Paget,[2] now they are here, fully share it. Sir Edmund & I talked it over yesterday[,] & are perfectly at one on the subject. Pray let me hear from you now & then[.] You will have no cause to regret my departure from Malta now, because Stopford will exert himself[,] & he will be assisted by Comdr Hore[,] who knows what is wanted & how to proceed right well.
Once more, farewell . . .
Will you tell [Peter] Richards[,] with my cordial regards[,] that the Tailor has fitted me famously & that the things he sent out arrived at Malta the day before I quitted it, & are just the very thing that I wanted here[,] & an unspeakable comfort. Many thanks to him for his kind care in executing my commission so very well.

I daresay John Dalrymple Hay will have left England ere this reaches you, but should he not have done so, pray let him know that my Coxswain rating is vacant[,] & that if he can bring me out the proper sort of man for it, I shall be very glad[,] & I shall keep the rating open till Hay's arrival.

Leicester Keppel[,][3] Midshipman now in *Bellerophon*[,] to be applied for to fill a vacancy in *Hannibal*. I should be very glad if this can be complied with & the youngster sent out. He is Harry Keppel's nephew.

[P.P.S.:] The naval Brigade have few very few on the sick list & those chiefly colds[.]

[1]Sir Henry Keppel, C.B., K.C.B., G.C.B. (1809–1904). Entered, 1822; Lt, 1829; Cmdr, 1833; Capt., 1837; Rear-Adm., 1857; Vice-Adm., 1861; Adm., 1869; Adm. of the Fleet, 1877.

[2]Lord Clarence Edward Paget, C.B. K.C.B., G.C.B. (1811–95). Entered, 1823; Lt, 1831; Cmdr, 1834; Capt., 1839; Rear-Adm., 1858; Vice-Adm., 1865; Adm., 1870; M.P., 1847–52, 1857–66; Secretary to the Admiralty, 1859–66.

[3]Leicester Keppel (1837–1917). Entered, 1850; Lt, 1859; Cmdr, 1869; Capt., 1880; Rear-Adm. (Ret.), 1895.

[**488**] *Lyons to Milne*

HMS *Agamemnon*, off Sevastopol
13 February 1855

My dear Milne

With reference to my scrawl by the last Mail[,] I now send you a Return of the Transports that will be available for bringing over the Piedmontese Troops.[1] You will see that we shall have plenty of Steam Transports for more than the 15000 men, but for 252 Horses only unless we should be able to spare the *Simla*, which I hope will be possible, tho' I cannot engage to do so, for we must take special care that our own Army has the means of bringing Mules &c for the spring campaign.

Of the sailing Horse Transports, of which I also enclose a Return[,][2] we may be able to send eight or ten[,] which could bring about 500 Horses. Each of those vessels can bring, besides the Horses, two Light Guns and all their appurtenances, together with the men to man them. Some three of those vessels can take on board a complete Battery of six guns. It seems then that I may engage to bring the Infantry–/15000/[,] Two or three Batteries of Artillery[,] and 250 Staff Horses – but not any more than 320 Cavalry Horses[,] even if the *Simla* should be disposable.

All I know of this matter is by a private letter from Sir James Graham[,] so I cannot write officially upon it . . .

[**489**] *Milne to Panmure*[3]

Admiralty
14 February 1855

Write to the Secy for War and inform him my Lords deem it expedient at the present juncture to place before him a concise statement in regard to the Transport Service[,] that he may be aware of the arrangements which have already been made[,] and the measures which have been adopted to carry out that Service to meet the requisitions of the War and other depart[ment]s.

[1]Not preserved among Milne's papers.

[2]This, too, is not preserved among Milne's papers.

[3]Fox Maule, later Maule-Ramsay, second Baron Panmure and later eleventh Earl of Dalhousie (1801–74). Undersecretary of State for Home Affairs, 1835–41; Vice-President of the Board of Trade, 1841; Secretary at War, 1846–52; President of the Board of Control, 1852; Lord Privy Seal, Scotland, 1853–74; Secretary of State for War, 1855–58.

In regard to the services required to be executed by the Admiralty in the Conveyance of Troops & Stores from this country, Information [*sic*] is given to the Admiralty from the War Department from time to time of the numbers & destinations of the various troops required to be moved, and from the Horse Guards their Lordships receive more detailed information with reference to the actual number of officers, Rank & File[,] Horses & Baggage to be embarked[,] and the Port of embarkation.

For the transmission of Ordnance Stores from this country[,] no requisition is specially forwarded from the War Depart, but daily applications are made upon the Admiralty from the Ordnance for the means of conveyance of such Stores to the East or other places, but when the Royal Artillery is to be embarked[,] or a Battering Train, then the Admiralty receives intimation from the War Dept[,] followed by more detailed information from the Ordnance[,] in the same manner as is given from the H[orse] Guards.

Provisions for the Army in the East are provided by the Naval Department and forwarded to their destination upon requisitions from the Secretary for War.

Medical Stores & Warm Clothing are likewise forwarded by the Admiralty from this Country[,] on requisitions from the Ordnance and these articles have been considered under the charge of Messrs Howell & Hayter[,] the Army Packers[,] and are shipped by them in communication with the Admiralty.

For all these various services the Admiralty has to provide the means of Conveyance[,] and it has been intimated that all Stores going to the Eastward of Malta must be conveyed in Steam Vessels.

The whole arrangement and control of the Transport Service in the Medn & Black Sea has been left to the supervision and orders of the Military & Naval Commanders in Chief[.] They were and are empowered to appropriate the ships for any service they might require [of] them[,] and they have been repeatedly urged to send home all such vessels as are not required for service in the East[,] with the view of having these vessels available in England for further Troop service[,] or to be paid off if not otherwise required & thereby to save unnecessary expense.

The enclosed printed form[,][1] giving an abstract of the services performed by the Transports during the last year[,] will give the Secy for a [*sic*] War a general idea of the services performed from England in

[1]Not preserved among Milne's papers. For a similar enumeration, see 'A Return of the Number of Transports employed in carrying Troops or Munitions of every Description for War in the East, between the 1st day of October 1853 and the 1st day of March 1855, inclusive', *Parliamentary Papers* 1854–55, vol. XXXIV, pp. 279–97.

regard to the embarkation of British Troops & Stores[,] and from Calais & Marseilles in regard to French Troops.

The services performed by the steamers and sailing vessels in the Black Sea, since the landing of the Army in the Crimea have been as follows. Conveying the French Cavalry from Borgos & Varna to the Crimea, Conveying Stores, Provisions, Coal, Wood, Warm Clothing, Horses, Cattle, Vegetables and all descriptions of supplies from Constantinople and other ports of the Black Sea to the Crimea[,] conveying sick and wounded[,] keeping up communication with Malta for Troops & Stores, with Marseilles for French Troops[,] with various ports in the Medn for Horses & Mules, and a large number of steamers are now employed in conveying Turkish Troops from Varna to Eupatoria, and the Naval C in C has become bound to the Turkish Govt to appropriate 400 tons of steam vessels to keep that army supplied with provisions from the Bosphorus.

The Sailing Transports are employed as Store & Powder ships and as Depot & Hospital Ships.

This is a concise view of the services which have been and are now being performed by the Transports in the East.

With reference to future embarkation of Troops, their Lordships were informed by the Secy for War on the 26th Jany that, in the course of next financial year[,] the following service would have to be executed by the conveyance of these Troops and Stores to the East.

10,000 Foreign Legion
15,500 Piedmontese Troops
7 or 8 Regiments of Militia
Drafts to reinforce 40 Battalions
6000 Horses
Stores to supply an Army of 50,000 men & 20,000 Tons of Ordnance Stores.

It was intimated that[,] as the Railway thro France would be completed to Marseilles in the course of the Month of February, that the Horses might proceed by Railway and be embarked at Marseilles.

Their Lordships obtained some information of Marseilles in regard to this contemplated embarkation of Horses at that Port, a Copy of which was transmitted to the Secy for War on the 3rd Inst[,] and on the 5th their L[or]dships requested some information in regard to the very large service which the Admiralty would be called on to perform in the transmission of the Troops & Horses from this country[,] as mentioned in the Secretary of [*sic*] War['s] letter of the 26th of Jany.

Their Lordships deem it their duty to draw the attention of the Secy for War to this very important and anxious question. The service to be performed is one of vast extent[,] and it is by no means an easy matter to arrange its complicated detail[,] or to find the means of Transport for so very large a force[,] more especially 6000 Horses[,] & early concert of measures for this purpose will be necessary[.]

In the transmission of Stores from the Ordnance Dept[,] difficulties more or less have invariably occurred ever since the commencement of the war[.] those have resulted from the very heavy & pressing demands for early conveyance[,] and to meet these there has been very great difficulty in procuring an adequate number of steam vessels. To illustrate this[,] and to point out to the Secy for War how vast are the requirements of that Department alone, their Lordships have to mention that the week ending Jany 15 brought in requisitions for 2908 Tons[,] the next week 4723 Tons, the next 3621 Tons[,] the next 4898 Tons[,] making in four weeks a total of 16,150 Tons[,] of which only 6,763 Tons have been able to be sent. In the same period of time[,] their Lordships were called on to provide conveyance for about 3000 men to the East, the whole of the service to be performed by steam vessels, and the Stores to be conveyed no less than 3,500 Tons.

Their Lordships are most anxious to meet every wish of the War and other Departments with the least possible delay[,] and to do all in their power to forward the wants of the Public Service, but it is at times impracticable to obtain steam vessels at the moment they are required[,] which must cause unavoidable delay, and it does appear to their Lordships to be necessary as well as expedient to employ small fast sailing ships to convey the stores which are not urgently required[,] as at this moment there are nearly 10,000 Tons of Stores awaiting conveyance to the East & their Lordships have only 3 [steam] vessels appropriated for about 1000 Tons[.]

The Steam vessels which their Lordships have lately chartered[,] and which are now fitting for the conveyance of Troops from England are the following[:]

The *Great Britain* for 1500 Infantry
The *Himalaya* for about 370 Horses
The *Etna* for 170 Horses
The *Niagara* for 850 Infantry
The *Cambria* for 850 Infantry
The *Candia* for 1000 Infantry
The *Hydaspes* for 800 Infantry
The *Indian* either for 100 Horses or 900 Infantry

The *Emperador* [*sic*] and *Croesus* have sailed for Malta with 1000 Troops in each and will return to England about the middle of March.

Several vessels are also ordered to return to England from the Black Sea[,] they will become available for Troop service as soon as they can refit & repair. My Lords beg to inform the Secy of [*sic*] War, that these are the only available vessels at the command of the Admiralty[,] and it is probable they will not be ready for embarkation of Troops under three weeks. There are two or three vessels offered to the Govt at the very exorbitant sum of 60s. per Ton per month,[1] a sum which[,] however[,] is even exceeded by the agents of the French Govt, but my Lords have declined to charter large vessels at this rate & have continually endeavoured to keep down the rates of hire to the sum of 50s.[,] altho really forced by necessity to pay 55s.[,] and they are not prepared to make a further advance to 60s, Unless [*sic*] the Secretary for War deems it necessary to Charter more vessels, as he only is cognizant of what Troops are to be embarked, and whether under the circumstances the high rate of 60s. should be paid.
Their Lordships herewith enclose a List of all steam vessels now chartered by the Admiralty[,][2] and Sir E Lyons[,] in concert with Lord Raglan[,] has instructions to send to England those vessels not required for service in the East[.]

[**490**] *Milne Memorandum on Communications with the War Office and Impending Transport Arrangements*[3]

Admiralty
17 February 1855

Letter written to Secy for War 5 Feb, asking information in regard to Military Service. 'No answer'[.][4]
No information until the 15 & 16 Feb has been received at the Admiralty[,] and then only by a private conversation with Lord P[anmure] in regard to the Transport of the Horses & Troops contained in the enclosed notes, with the exception of the General Letters of the War Dept on the Estimates for the ensuing year.

[1]'2 Belgian 1 English' Milne noted in the margin.

[2]Not included in this edition.

[3]It is not clear for whom these memoranda were composed, although the opening paragraph suggests that Milne either compiled the information to inform the Board of Admiralty of the difficulties in dealing with the War Office, or to inform new Secretary of State for War, Lord Panmure, of the difficulties encountered at the Admiralty in its communications with his department.

[4]It is not clear why Milne chose to use quotation marks around the words 'No answer.'

No 1[:]
Horses for the East from England[,] say 2000 Horses

Himalaya	370 Horses
Etna	180 "
[Total]	550

Sail	about 1st March
At Crimea	22nd March
Back in England	16th April
Again in Crimea	10th May

550 Horses landed in Crimea 22 March, 550 10th May, 1100 Total

Indian	120 Horses
Cambria	100
[Total]	220

Sail	13th March
In Crimea	8th April
In England,	1 May
In Crimea	25 May

220 Landed 8th April, 220 Landed 25th May[,] 440 Total[.]
Note, This [*sic*] only provides for 1540 Horses, out of 2000. No other Steam Vessels are available in England.

No. 2[:]
Horse Sailing Transports
Last year about 4500 Horses were sent to the East in 84 Sailing Transports, Each [*sic*] Ship carrying about 52 Horses.

If the 500 Horses to make up the remainder of the 2000 are to go out immediately, 10 Sailing ships ought to be immediately chartered.

10 Ships at 50 Horses	500
5 pr C[ent] Loss	50
[Total remaining]	450

25 to 30 Days to fit,	
Embark and Sail	20th March
Arrive at Malta 26 Days	16th April
Detention	20th April
Passage to Crimea 16 Days	7th May

Therefore[,] ships at once fitted will not arrive in Crimea before 7th May[.]
If a larger number of Horses than the 2000 now mentioned are to go to the East[,] Immediate [*sic*] steps should be taken to fit out sailing ships[,] but are the Horses to go thro France[?]
A larger amount of Forage should be hastened to the East[.]
No Information in regard to this service [has been received] at the Admiralty[.]

No 3[:]
Piedmontese Contingent
15,500 Men, will require[,] if to be embarked at once[,] 20 Steamers[.]
2000 Horses at 50 each ship will require 40 sailing ships[.]
Guns & Waggons & Material, Probably 4 Ships[.]
Note[:] to embark in March[,] 2 Steamers might now take out 2 Militia Regiments to Corfu & then proceed to Malta & Genoa.
orders [*sic*] will be required to be sent to Malta to detain some of the Steamers & Sailing ships now coming Home, but defective Steamers to come to England.
Sir E Lyons has orders to send for the above force, but he has not sufficient ships[.]

No 4[:]
Embarkation of Horses at Alexandria for the Crimea[.]
Nothing whatever known on the subject at the Admiralty.

No. 5[:]
Military Service from England
Steamer's [*sic*] available for Troops[:]

Great Britain	1500 Men
A Bremen Ship	800 "
Do Do	800 "
Candia	1000 "
Calcutta	900 "
Croesus } *Imperador* }	Will return from Mediterranean [and will carry between them] 1800

If steamers come home from Malta they will carry out Troops and go to Genoa[.]

[**491**] *Milne to Stopford*

Admiralty
19 February 1855

My dear Stopford

I write you a line in regard to the Transports. an [*sic*] order goes out tonight to detain Steamers & sailing vessels, but if the former are defective[,] to send them home[,] and some of the large & clumsy sailing Transports to return to England. From what I hear the Genoese contingent may be ordered to embark in March[.]

[**492**] *Milne to Lyons*

Admiralty
21 February 1855

Write to Sir E Lyons and inform him it is of the utmost importance that the various steamers sent to the Crimea with Stores should be immediately unloaded instead of being detained for weeks with their cargoes on board. request [*sic*] he will give orders on this subject and[,] if necessary[,] communicate with the Military Authorities[,] as it is most important & absolutely necessary that these steam ships should again return to England with the least possible delay[.]

[**493**] *Milne to Frederick Grey*

[Admiralty
c.27 February 1855]

My dear Grey

I have to thank you for your several notes which I have from time to time received[1] and as far as possible we have endeavoured to meet your wishes in regard to Tugs. The *Oberon* has been ordered out[,] the *Medusa* is preparing[,] and we have purchased a small one[,] and I hope this week we will have secured two others, all of them with the exception of one for Gibraltar will be sent to the Bosphorus. Your Brother[2] is calling out for one, as the *Hecla* has been on shore and is now unfit for service. A Telegraph was sent to you on Saturday afternoon[,] to direct all available steamers to be immediately sent to Malta. This is owing to the Government having been called upon by France to assist in sending up more French Troops from Marseilles with all possible haste[,] viz. 10000 Infantry & 3000 Horses. This the Government has expressed a wish to do, and it is with this in view that every available steamer is urgently wanted. When these vessels arrive at Malta[,] there will be orders there to send most of them to Genoa & a certain number to Marseilles[.] The ships from England now about to sail will[,] I believe[,] be ordered to Marseilles instead of returning to England as intended, viz. the *Great Britain*, *Calcutta*, *Croesus*, *Imperador* and some other. it [*sic*] is[,] however[,] not yet arranged but will be today[.] there is also the *Himalaya*[,] *Indian*[,] *Etna* [&] *Cambria* going to Scutari with Horses[.] they also were to have come home, but

[1]Not preserved among Milne's papers.
[2]George Grey at Gibraltar.

this again may be changed. The Cabinet will decide today, but I must say we are undertaking too much[,] and more than we can perform. I regret this[,] and it is now too far advanced in the season. all [*sic*] this ought to have been settled two months ago, but even up to this moment I [do not] know what are the intentions of the Govt. It is too bad and very serious. Sir E Lyons has orders to send to Alexandria to bring up the 10th Hussars 600 strong, but I very much doubt his having the means at his command.

I have been most anxious to get Transports[,] both Steam & Sailing[,] sent to England. orders [*sic*] have been repeatedly sent, but without avail and I have urged this as much as possible in private letters. I trust Sir E Lyons and yourself will force them home if not required for the public service. We have bad news from the Cape[.] it is feared the Caffres[1] are again on the move[.]

[**494**] *Lyons to Milne*

HMS *Royal Albert*, off Sebastopol, Private
27 February 1855

My dear Milne

I congratulate you on rising into [*sic*] such importance as to be an object of attack.[2] Better to be unjustly abused than to be over praised. It is certainly very unjust to find fault with you with regard to the Transports, for you have done wonders[,] for which you deserve the thanks of the Country. As to the number of Transports, if the War should continue[,] you may have to find more & more, and at an increased expense too, for the Emperor of the French, finding that he can obtain loans without difficulty, & that the success of the Expedition is something like a Dynastical consideration for him, is resolved to have what he wants at any price, and he will bid against you in the Steam Market. Within the last ten days, fearless of the ghost of Louis XIV[,] he has, to the horror of the Bourbonites, employed the First Boat [*sic*] of that name to bring up Hay from Algiers.

When shall we ever be able to send Transports home from hence? No sooner do we determine to do so than something occurs to prevent it.

[1]Kaffirs.

[2]This remark may have been in reference to a speech by M.P. Austen Henry Layard on 19 February. Although he did not mention Milne by name, Layard's claim that 'hon. Members [had] risen over and over again in this House to complain of the utter confusion which existed in [the transport service] and the almost helpless condition of the transport system' certainly criticised Milne by implication. See *Hansard* 3rd ser., vol. 136, col. 1517.

When second in Command[,] I urged Lord Raglan and Admiral Dundas to send a vast number home[,] and obtained their consent & many more were actually dispatched[,] but they were stopped at Malta to carry French Troops from Marseilles to the Crimea.

When Commander in Chief myself[,] I ordered another batch to be sent home at a great saving to the Govt, but I had hardly done so when I was called upon to transport 40000 Turkish Troops with all possible expedition from Bulgaria to Eupatoria . . . and I suppose I was right in acquiescing, for the announcement of my having done so crossed an Order [*sic*] from the Admiralty to that effect.

Still[,] by putting my shoulder to the wheel and by being ably seconded, I had made such progress that I should have been able to send home a great many Steamers next month, but lo and behold out comes an order to me to send to Italy for 15000 Troops, Horses, Artillery &c &c[,] and probably before the Ink [*sic*] of this letter is dry[,] I shall be ordered to send to Egypt for the 10th Hussars, and why not for the Elite of the Egyptian Army[?]

Now all this is very nice and proper and nothing more than the natural consequences of War.

England and France have together entered into this struggle with Russia: France contributes largely by Troops, and she may reasonably expect England to do all she can by Sea. Our Government have apparently recognized this principle[,] & acts upon it, and if John Bull is not willing to pay his share of the expenses of the War[,] he must withdraw from it; but <u>that</u> he won't[.] He is too fine a fellow to do anything of the sort. He will go on grumbling[,] fighting & paying to the last.

[**495**] *Christie to Milne*

Orient, off Balaklava
5 March 1855

My dear Milne

Many thanks for your kind note of the 16th.[1] Although a Court Martial is at all times a formidable thing, still on this occasion I feel such confidence of success I rather rejoice at it, as it will, I am in hopes, prove to the Admiralty and the Public the rectitude of all my proceedings. I was as innocent of the loss of the *Prince* and *Resolute* as a Babe in its Cradle. No officer could do more than I did in my endeavour to place them in safety. I only wanted a Tug and leave for them to enter the Harbour to

[1]Milne did not copy this missive in his letterbook.

accomplish this. After the *Prince* arrived on the 8th Novr[,] there were four days before the Gale on the 14th in which she might have gone in. There was nothing of greater importance in my opinion going on at the time. There was plenty of room in the Harbour, two Tugs, two Line of Battle ships and several other men of war present, yet with all this force at command if necessary[,] my earnest request was not attended to, and this ship with her <u>one anchor</u> and valuable cargo was allowed to remain outside. I[,] of course[,] did not order her to Sea with one anchor as I expected her to be taken in every hour, and I knew it was of great consequence to the Army that the Warm Clothing should be landed as soon as possible[,] as well as the rest of the cargo. I am afraid poor Dacres will never forgive himself for this.[1]

The weather has been fine for some days now, which has dried up the Country & Roads famously. The Railway is getting on rapidly[,] and is now conveying goods out about two miles towards the Camp. The number of Sick is diminishing as the Season advances[,] and everything is improving, but I cannot see any likelihood of Sebastopol falling yet.

Our Transports have landed about 38000 Turks at Eupatoria with a good supply of Provisions and 2000 Cavalry.

Our Army has a good supply of everything except reinforcements.

[P.S.:] Capt Heath has not yet arrived.

[**496**] *Milne to Lyons*

Admiralty
5 March 1855

My dear Sir Edmund

I am much obliged to you for your last note with the returns of the Transp[or]t[s][,] which I received a few days ago. I do hope you will send to Malta any vessel you can possibly spare, as we are most anxious to get steam as well as sailing Vessels sent to England[.] we are inclined to think that they get stowed away[,] and require a good deal of looking up, but I will now explain what is now intended here. I believe[,] on a sudden request of the French Government three days ago[,] I was sent for by the Cabinet in order to explain what Steam vessels we had which could go to Marseilles for 10,000 French Troops and 3000 Horses. My answer was the production of your return in regard to the Piedmontese contingent. They are not however satisfied with this, and

[1]Sydney Dacres was Harbour Master at the time of the gale and *Prince*'s loss. Someone, presumably Milne, circled this line of Christie's letter.

think more vessels could be spared from the Black Sea. A telegraph was sent on Saturday to you and also to Admiral Grey at Constantinople to send any available steamers fit for Troops to Malta[.] When they get there, orders will be in waiting [*sic*] to send a certain number for the Piedmontese contingent[,] and some to Marseilles[,] but this will be decided today, also if those vessels now leaving England for Malta & Corfu are to return to England or go to Marseilles[,] viz. the *Great Britain*, *Croesus*, *Calcutta*, [&] *Emperador* [*sic*]. The *Himalaya*[,] *Indian*[,] *Etna* & *Cambria* are to Embark Horses and are to go to Scutari[.] it is not yet decided whether they are [then] to go to Marseilles or follow the orders to return Home. I must say we are undertaking more than we can execute[,] and both the Turkish service and this French service was [*sic*] quite unknown to me, and is really an arduous service in itself, but we must do our best. then [*sic*] you have orders to send for the 10th Hussars[,] 600 strong[,] from Alexandria, all this is very serious and the executive in the Cabinet do not appear to be aware of the greatness of the undertakings and the vast amount of vessels which are required. Again[,] I hear we are to Victual the Piedmontese Troops[,] but of this we have never been informed. I asked the question at the Cabinet[,] as no increase of the army supplies have [*sic*] been sent out[.] I have been in a state of the very greatest anxiety ever since the New Year[,] in regard to which services were contemplated by the Govt. we [*sic*] wrote on the 5 Feb to the War Depart to say we were quite in the dark[.] we requested information[,] but have never received any answer even to this day[.] You will imagine how anxious I now am when the Cabinet wish to undertake to carry 10000 French Troops and 3000 Horses. the [*sic*] Horses I believe to be impossible, the Infantry doubtful[,] and if we do carry the Infantry we entirely neglect our own Service from England. But do send to Malta every Steamer you do not want, Large and small[,] are all urgently wanted at Home[.] we have cleared England of steam vessels but have some building[.] as to small vessels[,] they are not to be had. We have some thousands of Tons of Stores wanting to go to the East but not a Steamer to be got to put them into. We are sending Tugs for the Bosphorus[,] viz. the *Oberon* and *Medusa*[,] and we have purchased 2 or 3 others[,] but one of the above will be required at Gibraltar[,] as *Hecla* is unfit for service.

We have ordered Stopford at Malta not to be sending on Provisions[,] as we want to get up a Store for 30.000 men there. There is a large Naval Store at Constantinople and this might[1] . . . and the Army in

[1]Milne appears to have missed copying a page to his letterbook, as the text skips abruptly in the transition from one page to the next.

case of [?men], but in regard to the details of provisioning the Army and other duties in the Black Sea[,] we are in the Dark [*sic*][,] and it is as well we should be[,] as it would never do for us to interfere in there [*sic*] local arrangement[.] we send out Army Provisions on the War Office['s] requisition, further than that we are ignorant, and it has been a heavy business to meet the enormous demands, which of course must now be increased, but of which we have no notice. I am afraid our friend Boxer gives sad offense by his loose language &c – [1]

[**497**] *Milne to Stopford*

Admiralty
5 March 1855

Dear Stopford

This letter is one of importance and on which you will have to act. it [*sic*] embraces the embarkation of the Piedmontese contingent[,] and also Troops for [*sic*: 'from'] Marseilles, and we stand as follows – Sir E Lyons and Grey were telegraphed on Saturday to send to Malta every available Steamer for carrying Troops or Horses to Malta. It is with the view of a certain number going to Genoa for the 15,500 Piedmontese contingent[,] viz. 15,000 Infantry and 2000 Horses. now [*sic*] it happens that the Sardinian Gov wont [*sic*] hear of sailing ships for Horses[;] they would be offended if we did[,] and we must endeavour to meet their wishes. now [*sic*] the List of Steamers which Sir E Lyons was to send for the Piedmontese is enclosed,[2] but it is approximate[ly] for 19,800 men[,] which is too many[.] you must therefore fit up two[,] three or four ships selected from that return for Horses[,] so that we may be enabled to send them to Genoa[,] or you may fit up any other Steamers[.] Sir E Lyons will perhaps send other vessels from the Black Sea if he can spare them[,] in which case they are to go to Marseilles for French Troops as soon as possible[,] and the Sailing Transports must all be detained by you, refitted for Horses with all haste[,] and sent off to Marseilles as soon as possible[.] You are to do this. Fit 4 or even 5 Transport Steamer's [*sic*] for Horses with all possible haste[,] and to carry as many as possible[,] as was done with *Trent*, also prepare the Steamers for Infantry to go to Genoa. they [*sic*] should carry Horses[,] as many as they can carry [*sic*][,] and these will require to be at Genoa about the 26th of this month.[3] having [*sic*] provided for this service[,]

[1]Milne's letterbook text ended here; possibly the subsequent page was not copied.
[2]Not included with this copy of the letter.
[3]Milne here inserted in pencil: 'but I will write you again about this'.

all [remaining] disposable steamer's [*sic*] must go to Marseilles for French Troops[,] and send the sailing ships there for Horses as soon as possible[.] you will hear again from me by next mail, but as of this no orders are sent out[.]

We expect the *Emperador* [*sic*] and *Croesus* in England. *Calcutta* has sailed for Corfu[.] she will be ordered to Marseilles[,] therefore stop her at Malta after she lands her Reg at Corfu[.]

[**498**] *Milne to Stopford*

Admiralty
*c.*10 March 1855

With reference to their Lordships last order of the 9th March[,] directing the 21 steamers (amongst which the *Adelaide* should have been included) to proceed to Spezzia for the Piedmontese contingent[,] & to fit 4 of those vessels for the Embarkation of Horses, that my Lords have directed Sir E Lyons to send to Malta such other steam vessels as can be spared from service in the Black Sea[,] and on the arrival of these vessels[,] he [Stopford] is to send them to Marseilles for the purpose of embarking French Troops for the Black Sea.

The Rear Admiral is further to send to Spezzia any of the Sailing Horse Transports for Piedmontese Horses[,] and not to Marseilles [&] to send an agent of Transports in them[.] Their Lordships have directed a Captain to proceed from England to that port[,] & the Rear Admiral is to write to the Consul at Spezzia or Genoa & keep him informed of the movements of ships[.]

[**499**] *Christie to Milne*

Orient, off Balaklava
12 March 1855

My dear Milne

No doubt you are aware of the false and outrageous attack Mr. Layard thought proper to make upon me in the House of Commons on the 22d Feby last.[1] If you approve of the letter which I enclose[,]

[1]Austen Henry Layard, D.C.L. (1817–94). M.P., 1852–57, 1860–70; Undersecretary of State for Foreign Affairs, 1852, 1861–66; Chief Commissioner of Works and Buildings, 1869–70. Layard's speech was actually made on 19 February. See *Hansard*, 3rd ser., vol. 136, cols. 1514–30. With reference to Christie, Layard said: 'Who is at the head of the transports at Balaklava? Captain Christie, an old gentleman of upward of 60

perhaps you will be so kind as to give it to Sir James Graham[1] and endeavour to get Mr. Layard's statements contradicted. They are utterly false from beginning to end, as almost every one out here can prove, and when such attacks are made[,] an officer can only look to the Admiralty for protection.

Captain Heath has not yet made his appearance, but I shall start homewards directly he does, and you will do me a great favor if you will allow and order my Secretary[,] Mr Pritchard[,] to accompany me. He will be very necessary to me, and he has no desire to remain out.

I have made over eight of the Hut Steamers to the Commissariat to carry Cattle, Provisions &c, and I cannot get either Lord Raglan or Sir E Lyons to decide what should be done with the others. I want to send them to England after selecting enough for the use of the Army.

Everything here looks very different since the dry weather came on. We have got the Wharves much improved, and the Railway is becoming very useful.

I find I must conclude to save [*sic*] this Mail.[2]

[**500**] *Milne to Wood*[3]

Admiralty
14 March [1855]

List of Steam vessels from England to Corfu and Malta, which are afterwards to proceed to Marseilles for French Troops[:]

	No of Troops	Horses	Probable arrival at Marseilles
Calcutta	800	10	6 April
Great Britain	1500	15	4th April
Croesus	1100	12	12 April
Hansa	850	12	16th April
Arabia	800	12	16 April
Totals	5050	61	

years of age – a gallant gentleman, no doubt; but probably cannot leave his ship after dark for fear of a catarrh, which might endanger his existence. I know that he was often five or six days without being able to land at Balaklava. Are you surprised, then, that Balaklava harbour should be in the state it was . . . ' (col. 1522).

[1]Presumably Milne followed Christie's instructions and the enclosed letter was forwarded to Graham.

[2]This was evidently Christie's last letter to Milne. He died on 1 May 1855 at Malta, prior even to the Court Martial which he seemed confident would exonerate him.

[3]Sir Charles Wood, who became First Lord on 8 March 1855.

These numbers may perhaps be very slightly increased, on inspection of the vessels by the French Authorities[.]
Several Steam vessels have likewise been ordered to Marseilles from the Black Sea, if they can be spared, and if so, it is probable they will be enabled to embark about 5.000 Men and 40 Horses, and they may be expected at Marseilles about the 14th to 20 April[.]
Admiralty List of the Steam Transports destined for the embarkation of the Piedmontese Contingent[:]

Four of these vessels will be fitted for the Embarkation of Horses and they will probably carry 640 Horses. other [*sic*] Horse ships[,] it is expected[,] will be sent from the Black Sea for a further number of about 560[,] making together 1200 Horses[.]

The Ships will probably be at Spezzia about the 10 of April[.]

Ships	Tonnage	Men	Horses
Golden Fleece	–	1200	12
Andes	1440	900	12
Tynemouth	1364	900	12
Columbo	1864	1000	12
Medway	1800	1000	12
Queen of South	1825	1000	12
Cleopatra	1452	800	12
Ottawa	1274	600	12
Europa	1772	1000	12
Thames	1889	1000	12
Niagara	1008	750	12
Hydaspes	1871	900	12
Charity	1240	650	12
Indiana	2364	1200	12
Magdalena	2943	1300	12
Adelaide	1859	900	12
Imperador	1739	900	12
Ripon	1926	900	12
Emeu	1660	750	12
Taurus	–	900	12
Jura	–	1200	12
Approximate Number of Troops		19,750	252

A nominal List of Transports from the Black Sea that can be sent to Marseilles and on what day they may be expected[:]

No exact return can be given[,] as these ships may be in various parts of the Black Sea[,] but some of them will no doubt be sent to Malta to [a]wait orders.

	Men	Horses
Robt Lowe for	900	10
Clyde	600	–
Prompt	300	–
Canadian	700	10
Rajah	300	4
Nubia	1100	12
Alps	700	10
Bahiana	900	10
Simoom	900	8
Vulcan	700	8
Magaera	650	4
[Total]	7750	76

Note[:] it is probable Sir E. Lyons will be able to spare some of these vessels and [*sic*] capable of Embarking 4000 Men and 40 Horses[,] and they would reach Marseilles about the 12 to 15 April.

A Nominal List of Transports at Home and what day they would probably reach Marseilles.

These vessels are all under orders for Corfu and Malta and to return to England for other Troops[.]

If their destination is altered[,] they could go to Marseilles[,] but it will cause great delay and inconvenience in regard to the Conveyance of Troops from England.

	[Men]	[Horses]
Great Britain	1500	12
Calcutta	750	10
Croesus	1100	12
Hansa	800	12
Emperador [*sic*]	900	12
Arabia	900	–
[Total]	5,050	58

Could be at Marseilles from 2nd to 15th April if orders are given in time.

Steam Horse Transports[:]

These ships are all under orders for Scutari with Horses[,] and to return Home for others. They could go to Marseilles[,] if ordered[,] but it will cause great delay in sending out Horses from England.

	Men	Horses
Etna	150	170
Indian	110	120
Cambria	100	100
[Total]	360	390

Himalaya goes to Genoa from Scutari. These ships could be at Marseilles about [the] middle of April.

A Nominal Return of the Sailing Transports[:]

No Nominal return can be given, as many of the ships ordered to England have not put into Malta[.] all those which have put in there have been stopped and fitted for Horses and ordered to Marseilles.

About 10 to 15 vessels may be detained[,] and would carry 500 to 600 Horses.

[**501**] *Milne to Wood*

[Admiralty
March 1855]

Ordnance and Medical Stores sent to the East

March 1854	1,517 Tons
April "	1996
May "	1328
June "	2476
July "	1753
Aug "	869
Sept "	1057
Octr "	939
Nov "	12,646
Dec "	15,659
Jany [1855]	10,677
Feb "	2,513
[Total]	54,139 Tons[1]
Army Provs in Addition	31,562 Tons
[Grand Total]	85,701 Tons
Provisions sent Monthly	2,500 Tons for Army

[1]The monthly figures actually total 53,430 tons; the grand total, therefore, should be 84,992 tons, rather than 85,701.

Number of English Troops Embarked[,] including French [*sic*][:]

Officers	3433	80,000 [approx.]	
Men	76,545		
W[omen] &C[hildren]	1930		
Horses		5994	Deaths among 5248 Horses only 147
Waggons		86	
Huts		1026	

Turkish Troops Embarked[:]

37,700 Men
3,248 Horses
12½ Artillery Batteries

Besides an immense amount of Provisions[,] Camp Equipage[,] Forage[,] Ammunition & Stores of Wood &c.
French Troops from Marseilles – From 5, to 10,000 Men.

[**502**] *Milne to Tatham*

Admiralty
15 March 1855

My dear Sir

I write you a few lines to let you know the arrangements which have been made in regard to further embarkation of F[rench] Troops from Marseilles for the Crimea. The following ships have sailed or are about to sail for Corfu & Malta and[,] instead of returning to England[,] they will got to Marseilles and will probably be there at the dates I have mentioned.

	[To Carry]		[At] Marseilles
Calcutta	950 men	10 Horses	6 April
Great Britain	1500 "	15 "	4 April
Croesus	1100 "	12 "	12 April
Hansa	850 "	12 "	16 April
Arabia	800 "	12 "	16 April

This makes 5,050 men and 61 Horses[.] it is probable[,] however[,] that you may be enabled to give some slight increase to this, and it is advisable to do so if possible[,] and to get the ships away as fast as possible.
Besides this[,] Sir E Lyons has been ordered to send as many spare Steamer's [*sic*] as possible from the Black Sea to Malta (independent of

31 specially ordered for the Piedmontese contingent) and Ad Stopford is to send these to Marseilles. We consider it possible that steamers for a further number of 5000 men & 40 Horses may be sent[.] if so[,] you must get them sent on as soon as you can. This is all the information I have to give you. The French Gov have been informed and have been furnished with a Copy of the Ships Names &c. I think with French Troops[,] and the urgency of the service[,] as well as the shortness of the voyage[,] that the numbers in each ship might be increased[.] this you must look to and arrange.

[**503**] *Lyons to Milne*

HMS *Royal Albert*, off Sebastopol, Private
20 March 1855

My dear Milne

I have just received your letter of the 5th Inst suggesting that as many Transports as possible should be sent to Malta. My official letters to the Board of the 10th & 13th Inst No 191 & 201, with their enclosures, will have shown you that I anticipated your wishes not only on that point[,] but also by directing Stopford to be prepared for an order from the Board to fit some of them for Horses.

I am by no means surprised at the anxious desire of the Cabinet to comply with the request of the Emperor of the French[,] that more Troops and Horses may be conveyed from Marseilles to the Crimea in our Transports, and, as you justly say, we must do our best, but there must be a limit to our undertakings or we shall break down & be reprimanded for not fulfilling our engagements.

It is evident that what I have to do is pack off any Transports that can be dispensed with here to Malta, and that I will endeavour to do, but I must take care to keep enough for the indispensable services of our own Army[,] as well as for bringing the 10th Hussars from Alexandria. Grey will give you notice of the departure of the vessels from the Bosphorus and Stopford will take care to announce to you their arrival at Malta, and you [have] my strong . . . [assurance] that not a moment shall be lost in coaling & expediting them here, nor will I fail to do all in my power to induce my French colleague to clear out the Transports as soon as possible after their arrival. They have in Kamich [Kamiesch] Bay & this Bay more than Fifty English Transport vessels in demurrage at this moment[,] some of which have been three[,] four & five Months[,] but they cannot land their Cargoes for want of Store Houses . . .

[504] *Milne to Stopford*

Admiralty
24 March 1855

My dear Stopford

I write you a line to say we has [*sic*] this morning received your Letters which mention the return of the *Mary Ann* to Malta. as [*sic*] we have promised the French this vessel[,] she should go to Marseilles or[,] if she has gone to Genoa[,] we must send them another in lieu of her. The *Edendale* you have no doubt sent to Genoa[,] and also any other sailing Transports which may have arrived at Malta[.] It is our wish that all such vessels should go to Genoa for the Horses[,] as our means of embarking them in Steamer's [*sic*] will not meet their wants.

The *Himalaya* goes to Genoa for Horses. The *Etna*, *Cambria* [&] *Arabia*[,] all fitted for Horses[,] will return to England for more. The *Great Britain*, *Croesus*, [&] *Hansa*, will go to Marseilles as ordered[.] The *Resistance* sailed for Malta yesterday[.] she might go up to [the] Bosphorus if you want[,] or Home[,] but orders will be sent.

Your public letter for your family to come out is only signed in Pencil[,] and no date filled in[.] When you wish them to come out, send home another Letter[,] in case I am unable to find out what date you wanted put in.

We have nothing new here[,] all worried to death, vexed & annoyed[,] at least I am[,] and would wish myself well out of this[.]

[505] *Milne to Tatham*

Admiralty
27 March [1855]

Write to Admiral Stopford to send *Himalaya* to Genoa for Horses.[1]
Croesus [&] *Great Britain* to go to Marseilles.
Etna & *Indian* to England[.]

[1]It was quicker to contact Stopford at Malta by telegraphing Marseilles and sending a message from thence by sea than it was to dispatch one by ship from Britain.

[**506**] *Milne to Tatham*

Admiralty
31 March [1855]

Write to Admiral Stopford that he is not to send any of the Vessels which are specially intended for Genoa to Marseilles[.]

[**507**] *Milne to Stopford*

Admiralty
2 April 1855

My dear Stopford

I am much afraid there is some misunderstanding in regard to the Steamers[,] which may lead to some difficulty. I will therefore state what was wanted.

1. There was a List of 21 Steamers which were specially appropriated for the Piedmontese contingent[.] these 21 vessels would carry 19500 men[,] and as the contingent was only 15500[,] we wanted you to fit 3 or 4 of these steamers to carry Genoese [*sic*] Horses[,] as I mentioned to you in my letter of the 5th March that the Sardinian Gov objected to sailing ships.

2d[.] All steam vessels not appropriated for the Piedmontese contingent and sent down from the Black Sea were to go to Marseilles for French Troops.

3d[.] The vessels sent from England with Troops to Malta & Corfu were all to go to Marseilles[.]

4th[.] The *Himalaya*, *Indian*, *Cambria*[,] *Etna* [&] *Arabia*[,] being all Horses [*sic*] ships for Scutari[,] were all to return to England with the exception of the *Himalaya*[,] which ship was to go to Genoa.

Now with reference to the Piedmontese ships[,] we find one of them[,] the *Colomba*[1] has been sent to Marseilles instead of Genoa, which may[,] however[,] have been caused by some local arrangement of your own. I Enclose a List of these 21 Ships [A], also a list of the others for your guidance[.][2]

Since writing this[,] we have heard from Admiral Grey[,] and he thinks some of the 21 Steamers for the Genoese service may not get down for more than a fortnight[,] which may cause some delay. Our object however is for you to send steam vessels for the Genoese, both

[1]Milne probably meant *Columbo*.
[2]Neither list included in this copy.

Infantry and cavalry. The next service is to send disposable or available vessels to Marseilles, and we must have you do this as best you can and as you may judge best under the circumstances.

The *Holyrood*, *Albatross* & *Cormorant* were ordered Home on account of some difficulty in regard to their Payment[.] if any of these are fit for Horses[,] you may detain them & send them on to Genoa[.] the *Great Britain* you will have out again immediately & she will land Troops at Malta & go to Marseilles[.]

We hear the *Simla* & *Jason* and some other of the Horse ships are so foul that they ought to be docked[.] this cannot be done except in England[.] Admiral Grey has been told by this mail that he may substitute the *Etna* or *Indiana* for these ships and send the others to England.

You can do so likewise if you think it necessary[.]

The *Alma* will sail on the 6th to 8th [*sic*] for the Crimea with 1400 men[.]

We have a Telegh from Lord Raglan to day to send out another Battering Train and more 32 Pdr Shot[.] You should send some up if you have them.

Dacres arrived yesterday[.] Your wifes passage has all been arranged[,] as you will hear[:] 3 1st Class & 3 2d Class [accommodations] by Steamer on [the] 20th[.]

[**508**] *Milne to Stopford*

[Admiralty
c.5 April 1855]

He is to direct all Steam Vessels proceeding to Marseilles for French Troops to call at Toulon & to communicate with the Guard Ship at the entrance to that Port for instructions[,] whether they are to enter the Port of Toulon for Troops or proceed to Marseilles . . .
Inform Cap Tatham at Marseilles

[**509**] *Milne to Tatham*

Admiralty
6 April [1855]

Write to Admiral Stopford [at] Malta, to send to Marseilles two Steamers for French Troops[,] to take the place of *Great Britain*, and another to take the place of *Alps*.

[**510**] *Graham to Milne*

Netherby, Private
6 April 1855

My dear Capt Milne

There is a small Parcel of Cheroots,[1] I am sorry to say, from Stocken in Gracechurch St., which I wish to be sent to my Boy[2] on board the *St Jean d'Acre*.

I have told Stocken to send the Parcel to you at the Admiralty; and I will be greatly obliged if you will forward it for me, hoping that you will not be contaminated by the touch of the abominable thing . . .

[**511**] *Milne to Stopford*

Admiralty
8 April [1855]

HMS *Resistance* having been sent from England with Troops for Malta[, she] may be ordered on [to] the Bosphorus[,] if the Rear Ad considers [it] necessary to convey Troops or Stores.

Inform Sir E Lyons & Ad Grey and[,] if detained in the Bosphorus or Black Sea[,] a Large Hired sailing Transport should be sent to England in her place.

[**512**] *Milne to Stopford*

Admiralty
8 April [1855]

To enquire on the arrival of the *Tynemouth* at Malta[,] if the Stores (Guns &c) sent from England in that ship were landed at Malta on her first arrival there, and[,] if not[,] he is to call on the Master of that Vessel to explain his reasons for not having landed them, as consigned by the B[oard] of Ordnance.

He is to give strict orders to the officer who boards all transports to make enquiry both on arrival & before sailing, that they have landed all stores intended for Malta, & that they do not proceed to England with any Stores on board which were intended for Malta or the East. With this view[,] he is to establish a Boarding Book[,] in which it is to be

[1]A type of cigar.
[2]James Stanley Graham (1836–73).

stated in a proper columns [*sic*] whether any stores are on Board &c, It [*sic*] having been stated that from the neglect of the Masters of Vessels[,] stores sent from England for the use of the Army have been brought back to England without [having] been delivered to the parties to whom they were consigned . . .
Copy to Ad Grey[,] Bosphorus for his information & guidance[.]

[**513**] *Milne to Stopford*

Admiralty, London
9 April 1855

Inform Rear Admiral Stopford that it is of the utmost importance that the steam vessels for the Embarkation of the Piedmontese contingent should proceed to Genoa with all possible dispatch and their Lordships trust he has already ordered them to their destination. It is also important that no delay should take place in sending steam vessels to Marseilles to embark French Troops to the Crimea. The *Calcutta*, *Canadian*, *Colombo* and *Clyde* have already embarked about 2500. The same number are now waiting for vessels from Malta, for part of which the *Great Britain* was expected, but as she has returned to England, he must immediately dispatch 2 vessels to Marseilles to embark the Troops she would have taken (viz. 1500), also another steamer in lieu of the *Alps*[,] detained in England for a portion of a Battering Train[,] and Their Lordships expect that the *Croesus* & *Hansa* will also proceed for French Troops and not be diverted from that service, but if he has given other orders, then it will be necessary for other vessels to be sent to Marseilles in their place.

The Rear Ad is to report when he received the order of the 9th of March from the Transport Board[,] ordering *Gt Britain* to Marseilles[.]

[**514**] *Milne to Stopford*

Admiralty
9 April 1855

My dear Stopford

We hear from Sir E Lyons and Grey that the *Simoom* & *Vulcan*[,] with some other steamers[,] have been sent to Malta from the Black Sea[.] we hope this is the case[,] as we are very anxious in regard to the embarkation of the Genoese as well as the French Troops[,] and we trust to your having sent forward the steamers as fast as possible. The Emperor of the French complains we have not forwarded steam vessels to Marseilles for his Troops in accordance with our promise to take the place of 3 sail of the line which he had appropriated for Troops, but had[,] at our request[,] had [*sic*] withdrawn from that service in order to send them to the Baltic[,] and we were to embark those troops for him, and this in add[itio]n to 5000 others. The sending Home [*sic*] [of] the *Great Britain* was unfortunate[,] as we wrote you on the 9th of March to send her to Marseilles[,] and we cannot make out why you did not act on that Letter. We sent a Telegh to you to send 2 vessels in lieu of the *Alps*, we trust you may have done this, as we must keep faith with our allies, and you must send [them] to Marseilles if you have not already done so. we [*sic*] have already embarked about 2500. we [*sic*] ought immediately to embark 2500 more[,] and to follow that up as soon as possible with about the same number. There has been some confusion in regard to the ships to go to both ports [i.e., Genoa and Marseilles], as they were unwisely named by name to the respective Governments[,] and the detention of some of them in the Black Sea and breaking down of others, has caused each Govt to think we have made some error.

It is a heavy pressure on all the Departments[,] and you no doubt find it equally so at Malta, but know our wishes and you must work it out with as much haste as you can[.]

We have no news here. The *Arabia* has sailed with Horses. The *Alma* ought to have gone as [well] today but will be delayed. The *Gt Britain* I hope will get away this week.

I will add to this if there is anything new in the Evening[.]

[**515**] *Milne to Brock*[1]

Admiralty
10 April [1855]

Acquaint Cap Brock in reply to His [*sic*] Letter of the 6 April[,] that there will be no objection to his making arrangements for the purchase of Coal at Genoa at the Price stated[,] altho it is somewhat high[,] and he is therefore to endeavour to obtain a reduction in price[.]

The steam vessels should go direct to Constantinople for further orders from Rear Ad Grey, and it seems advisable that each steam vessel should tow a Sailing Transport with Horses, if he should consider this necessary, the great object being to hasten the Embarkation of the Troops and their departure for the East[.]

[1]Thomas Saumarez Brock, C.B. (*c*.1802–73). Entered, 1815; Lt, 1827; Cmdr, 1842; Capt., 1850; Rear-Adm. (Ret.), 1867. Brock was Transport Service Agent at Genoa.

The names and accounts of the vessels at Genoa[,] their sailing & number of Troops & Horses Embarked [*sic*][,] all to be immediately reported to their Lordships

[516] *Milne to Brock*

Admiralty
10 April [1855]

Dear Cap Brock

I received your Letter this morning and you will receive an official answer. The Price of the Coal is very high and it ought not to exceed 45 to 48 shillings. The best plan would be for you to make an agreement by contract to supply all such Coal as may be required on your demand[,] & from time to time[,] and at a fixed price for a period of say one[,] two[,] or three months[,] and if the Parties do not give [*sic*: 'sell'] it at a moderate rate[,] the Ships will coal at Malta[.]

Let us have a daily return of the ships arrived and the number of Troops & Horses Embarked[.] if you want any speedy answer from us use the Telegraph[.]

[517] *Milne to Lyons*

Admiralty
12 April [1855]

So soon as the Steamers have landed the Piedmontese contingent[,] these vessels are to return to Malta to complete the embarkation of that force[,] or to proceed to Marseilles for French Troops[,] if it should be necessary[,] the Comdr in Chief retaining such as may be necessary for any special service in the Black Sea . . .
Inform Rear Ad Grey & Stopford

[518] *Milne to Stopford*

Admiralty
25 April 1855

My dear Stopford

Thanks for all your Letters[,] which I have been unable to answer as I have been absent for a few days. all [*sic*] your arrangements are right and well done[,] and the ships arriving at Marseilles is putting matters right with the French[.] we must take up more than 10,000 of their men[,] and you must therefore send steamers for them. they [*sic*] have sent another demand for 6000 more and[,] I believe[,] 3000 Horses[,] but we have not dealt with this yet. We have telegraphed to Sir E Lyons to send us the *Simla* & *Jason* to England[,] as well as any other Horse Steam Transport[s] requiring refit. We have about 900 Horses due waiting [*sic*] and upwards of 1000 appropriated to ships[,] and I hear another 1000 are to go, so that at present we have no means of sending out about 1900. This is an anxious question[.] we have just received a Telegh from Lyons dated yesterday 24th[.] This is quick work[.]

We have no news here[,] the conference have [*sic*] failed so it is all war war [war].[1]

Cap Brock sent to say he wanted transport for 1000 Horses & 360 waggons[,] as the sailing ships had been withdrawn[.] I dont know what this means[.] you may have to send him more aid[,] but I presume you will hear from him[.]

I was very glad to be of use to Mrs Stopford in arranging her passage &c[.] always write me if I can be of any use to you[.]

[**519**] *George F. Seymour[2] to Milne*

5 May 1855

My dear Milne

I am glad to hear you have decided against the Desk[,] for I plan & hope you may be destined to do good service on the Deck when the Board can spare you from those [duties] you are at present executing, & when you go afloat you will carry an unusual stock of administrative experience with you.[3]

I think [Sir Thomas] Hastings evidence[4] shows that placing Civilians at the Head of the War Department & their management of detailed work [*sic*] without that requisite [experience] has only put the old

[1]The Vienna Conference, which continued fitfully until June.

[2]Sir George Francis Seymour, C.B., G.C.H., K.C.B., G.C.B. (1787–1870). Entered, 1797; Lt, 1804; Cmdr, 1806; Capt., 1806; Rear-Adm., 1841; Vice-Adm., 1850; Adm., 1857; Adm. of the Fleet, 1866; Naval Lord of the Admiralty, 1841–44.

[3]Seymour must have heard a rumour that Milne was soon to leave the Board of Admiralty.

[4]To Roebuck's Committee, perhaps with reference to Hastings' 'statement as to the powers of the Master-General [of the Ordnance] having been exercised by the Minister for War' (Question 19,047). The whole of Hastings' evidence occupies Questions 18,096–19,169.

Machinery out of gear (imperfect as it may have been) at a time when system was unusually required.

We are indebted however to the newspapers for that as well as for other mistakes[,] on which they now try to work additional mischief by charging faults elsewhere[.]

Dont take the trouble of replying . . .

[**520**] *Graham to Milne*

Grosvenor Place, Private
8 May 1855

My dear Capt Milne

I have read your Evidence[1] and have made some notes on it. It is quite accurate to the best of my knowledge and recollection, and appears to me a conclusive defence of the Admiralty.

I suppose that I shall be summoned before the [Roebuck] Committee; but as yet they have said nothing to me on the subject.

If I am summoned[,] I shall ask you to call on me that I may refresh my memory, before I make my appearance.

The state of the Board of Ordnance is now transparent. This and the Medical Department[,] together with Sir C. Trevelyan's follies,[2] have been the abundant sources of Many Blunders and Omissions.

[**521**] *Graham to Milne*

Grosvenor Place, Private
8 May 1855

My dear Capt Milne

I hear that Sir Thomas Hastings has left on the [Roebuck] Committee an unfavorable [*sic*] impression, at our Expense, with respect to the supply of Tonnage for warm Clothing at the close of last summer. He says that this Requisition was sent to us in August and that the Shipment was not provided till October [*sic*]. You were absent at that moment; but I have no doubt, that some explanation can be given. Was the Requisition marked 'urgent'; or was it even once repeated?

[1]Milne was examined by the Committee on 27 and 30 April 1855.

[2]Sir Charles Edward Trevelyan (1807–86). Asst Secretary to the Treasury, 1840–59. Trevelyan had oversight of the Commissary arrangements for the Army in the East, that department being under the Treasury's auspices.

If not, considering the Shipment previously made in the *Prince*, was it not believed, that this Clothing might rightly form part of a 'mixed Cargo'; and that delay, longer than had been intended, was the Consequence [*sic*]?

Have the kindness to let me know the Explanation [*sic*], which I am to give, if any Question be put to me on this point.

In Questions 16,854–16,855 you are asked respecting delay in coaling steamers last Autumn at Constantinople. Would you have the kindness to cause strict Enquiry [*sic*] to be made, whether there are any such complaints in Office? and [*sic*] let me know the result. I should also like to see any Despatches from Admiral Boxer in the Bosphorus, in which he states the inadequacy of the means at his disposal, and asks for assistance, and likewise the Answers [*sic*] given to such complaints, and an account of the means taken to supply the alleged deficiencies. The dates on both sides are important. Much will depend on the Evidence, which Admiral Dundas may give, as to the course to be taken by me before the Committee . . .

[**522**] *Graham to Milne*

Grosvenor Place, Private
10 May 1855

My dear Capt Milne

I will not trouble you to call here today; for I wish to see the Evidence to be given by Admiral Dundas, before I consult you further. I do not expect to go before the Committee until Monday; and in the mean time we shall have ample leisure and opportunities both for consultation and the removal of misapprehensions.

Your statement as to the Clothing is clear and quite conclusive. Do not overlook the points, which I mentioned, respecting Coaling in the Bosphorus, and the requisitions of Admiral Boxer for additional assistance.

[**523**] *Graham to Milne*

Grosvenor Place, Private
10 May 1855

My dear Capt Milne

I have a copy of the Evidence of Admiral Dundas; and I am summoned to appear before the Committee on Monday next. I should like to see you tomorrow morning at any hour, which may be most convenient to you.

I wish that you would previously ascertain from Capt Washington the precise date, when we sent out the Vice Consul of Kertch to the Black Sea, on his return to England from the Crimea via Petersburgh [*sic*]: and if Capt Washington has a Copy of the Deposition of this Vice Consul, which he took down in writing at my desire[,] and which was sent to Lord Raglan and to Al Dundas, I should like to have the use of it.

[524] *Graham to Milne*

Grosvenor Place, Private
16 May 1855

My dear Capt Milne

I have received the enclosed letter and documents from Sir Thomas Hastings.[1]

I propose to return to him the Documents and to say, that my Evidence was in strict conformity with his official Requisitions, which are on Record and which I had verified; and that any answer or comments which he may wish to make, must be addressed by himself to the Chairman of the Committee.

I know nothing of letters, which may have been passed between Clerks in the two Departments. Reliance on them shares the vice of the past system. It is not even now pretended, that any urgency for the despatch of 'Warm Clothing' to the East was notified to us [*sic*].

I do not wish to enter into a Controversy with Sir Thomas Hastings. Let me know, if you approve of my proposed answer: if not, suggest what you think best.

[525] *Milne to Wood*

Admiralty
15 June 1855

No. of Transports now Employed 15 June 1855[:]

Steamers	No.	Approximate Tonnage
Government Vessels	10	16000
Chartered Do.	130	143,000

[1]These documents were evidently returned to Graham.

Sailing Vessels[:]		
Government Vessels	1	1100
Chartered Do.	96	78,000

The Tonnage is only approximate.

[**526**] *Michael Seymour to Milne*

HMS *Exmouth*, near Cronstadt
7 July 1855

My dear Milne

My recent accident[1] has left me, for a time, mainly dependent for news, on others[.] Hall,[2] however, kindly reads to me the contents of . . . [the] Papers. Amongst the latest received, is one containing a copy of the 'Report of Roebuck's Committee' and I cannot conceal from you, the glow of real satisfaction, with which I listened to the high acknowledgements it contains, of your most able administration, of the Admiralty department, of our Transport Service, the duties of which, all admitted to have been enormous in extent, and involving interests of the greatest possible national importance. It is therefore with a feeling of sincere pleasure, that I congratulate you, on this public expression of the Nation's appreciation of the great services you have rendered to your country.

On Baltic affairs I do not enter, for little belongs to them, that is at all encouraging[,] and you probably are fully informed on the relative position of Russia and ourselves in the near vicinity of Cronstadt Waters.

The effects of my recent accidents are I am happy to say subsiding[.] Whether the full restoration of my left Eye sight [*sic*] will be permitted[,] time only will show. My right is quite un-impaired. A few days will I trust emancipate me from my Cabin & Stern Walk. I hope you are quite well 'at home', & remain most sincerely yours . . .

[1]Seymour was wounded when a small Russian mine retrieved off Cronstadt exploded as he was examining it. He lost sight in his left eye as a consequence.

[2]Sir William King Hall, C.B., K.C.B. (1816–1886). Entered, 1829; Lt, 1841; Cmdr, 1848; Capt., 1853; Rear-Adm., 1869; Vice-Adm., 1875; Adm., 1879. King Hall was Seymour's Flag Captain in HMS *Exmouth*.

[**527**] *Milne Memorandum on Commanders' Memorial*

Admiralty
19 July 1855

Commanders Memorial[:]
There are 3 claims put forward in the Memorial of the Commanders which they have submitted for the consideration of the Board.
1st[:] That they have only two grades of Half Pay, and they request the higher rate of the Half Pay[,] viz. 10/. per day[,] to be granted to a greater number than the present 150 from the Top of the List.
The List of Commander's [*sic*] consists of 549 Officers[,] to be reduced hereafter by the regulations of June 1851 to 450, and[,] as it may be assumed that the 250 Commanders at the Top of the List will never be selected for promotion to the active list of Captains, I see nothing to prevent the increase of Half Pay to be extended to 250 officers from the Top of the List[,] instead of 150, or to place the Commanders List on 3 Grades of Half Pay, as follows[:]

	S[hillings]	d [pence]
The first 150	10	0
The next 100	9	0
The remainder	8	6

but [*sic*] this would not grant so great a boon to those old officers.
2d[:] They complain of the Regulation which limits the Age of Entry into the Coast Guard to 45.
I am of opinion that this is a very severe regulation upon this class of officers, but few officers who have attained this Age [*sic*] can expect promotion to the Rank of Captain[.] they are[,] therefore[,] at the early age of 45, already entirely excluded from active service, and have nothing to look forward to, but to continue on Half Pay, and to pass the remainder of their days in idleness & disappointment. So long as the service of the Crown does not suffer[,] I think it is the duty of the Admiralty to provide service for Officers of the Fleet, and I certainly am of opinion that the Coast Guard service would not suffer if Commanders were appointed up to the age of 50 or even 52, when there are officers now serving as Lieutenants some years in advance of 60.
3d[:] They allude to their unequal Retirement compared with the Rank of Captains, Masters, Paymrs &c[.] It must be noticed, that Masters, Surgeons & Paymasters have peculiar & independent Ranks of their own, and it is only a few of each in these Ranks that can rise to the comparative High Rank & High Pay, in the same manner as the Lieu-

tenant rises to the Rank of Captain and Admiral. Therefore[,] Commanders cannot draw a fair comparison between their claims & those of the above civil officers.
No doubt[,] in regard to Masters, Surgeons & Paymasters[,] as the number of these officers on their respective lists is so much smaller in number than the List of Lieutenants, they have a more certain prospect of advancement to the Higher Rates of Pay than Lieutenants.
I think it would be a great boon to the Commanders[,] and an act of justice, to extend the List of the Reserved Captains which was established in June 1851. There are a large number of deserving Commander's [*sic*] who have seen good service and who have an equitable claim for advancement. I think this List should be 100 instead of 50 and I see no reason why the List of the Senior Commander's [*sic*] [elevated] to the Rank of Retired Captain should not be extended to 150 instead of 100.
The measures I would therefore recommend, would be as follows.
1. Extend the 100 Commanders who retire to the Retired Captains Rank from the Top of the List from 100 to 150 [*sic*]. This would reduce the Commanders List by 50. This is an extension of Orders in Council of 1840 and June 1851[.][1]
2. Increase the Reserved List of Captains (of June 1851) from 50 to 100. This will also reduce the Commanders List 50. This is an extension of Order in Council of June 1851. This might be extended to Lieutenant [to be promoted] to the Rank of [Retired] Comdr.
3. Give the first 150 of the Commanders from the Top of the List

	s[hillings]	d [pence]
	10	0
The next 100	9	0
The Remainder	8	6
or	s	d
Give the first 250	10	0
The Remainder	8	6

4. Extend the age for appointment to the Coast Guard to 50 years of Age instead of 45.
I believe this would give great satisfaction and it would afford the opportunity of promoting some old and deserving officers.
It is not possible to give the Commanders who retire more than 10/6 per day[,] being the lowest rate of Captains Half Pay, unless the same boon

[1]This alteration, and Milne's recommendation to increase the Reserved List of Captains, were duly enacted by an Order in Council of 30 January 1856.

was given to the Retired Lieutenants who get the lowest rate of Commanders Half Pay.[1]

The Memorialists draw the contrast between their own Half pay and that of Captains[,] who go on the Retired List with an addition of 5/6 to their Half Pay, but as this addition[,] when added to the scale of their Half Pay[,] does not bring it up to the Lowest rate of H Pay of the next Rank[,] namely Rear Admiral[,] the Commanders have no right to complain[;] it is rather an argument that the Rates of Captains Half Pay is not enough for the rank they hold.[2]

[**528**] *Milne Draft Circular on Acting Masters*

Admiralty
20 July 1855

The Exigencies of the Service having induced their Lordships to admit into the Navy[,] with the rating of Act[in]g 2d Master[,] persons from the Merchant service who have served not less than four years at sea, my Lords direct that these officers be considered eligible for examination for the confirmed rank of Second Master[,] when they shall have completed the term of six years at sea[,] reckoning their time served in the Merchant Service in accordance with . . . the Queens Regulations, and the time served by those officers in the rating of Masters Ass[t]s or Acting 2d Masters may be allowed to reckon as time served as inferior [*sic*] mate. The seniority of these officers for the confirmed Rank of Second Master will be allowed from the date of their passing in Seamanship, subject to the usual conditions of their repassing at the R.N. College and Trinity House within the regulated period.

[**529**] *Milne to Wood*

Admiralty
27 July 1855

Provisions to be sent out to Crimea at the Request of the Secretary for War, by Letter of July 1855[:]

[1]The following addendum was written in red ink.

[2]An Order in Council promulgated on 30 January 1856 provided that more than 100 Commanders be promoted (on 1 April) to the rank of Retired Captain. As per Milne's suggestion, a similar clause allowed additional Lieutenants to retire with the rank of Commander.

Bread	1,320,000	lbs
Rum	60,000	Gall
Salt Meat	950,000	lbs
Sugar	325,000	lbs
Rice	270,000	lbs
Tea	14,500	lbs
Coffee ground	59,000	lbs
Tons measurement	3,390	Tons

This quantity every month[.]

[**530**] *Milne to Fremantle*

Admiralty
28 July 1855

My dear Fremantle

It is probable that by this time you will have arrived at the scene of your labours[,] and that you will have received orders which were sent from this in regard to all Transports being placed under your charge[,] and that the Commissariat vessels are no longer to be independent of Naval control. Such being the case[,] I send you these few lines which will put you in possession of the views which may be of use to you[.] at the beginning of the war the demand for steam vessels was in excess of the supply and prices rose to a very high rate[,] more especially when[,] in Novr last[,] such large supplies of Warm Clothing had to be hurried out to the Crimea. Matters have changed[,] and the small class of steamers have fallen in price to 25/ to 30/ per Ton per month. The P&O Comy and also W India have also [*sic*] come down to 45/ per Ton[,] and sailing ships to 16/ per Ton[.] these are facts for your guidance and consideration.

I send you herewith a List of the Transports Steam & Sailing now employed,[1] but it does not contain the names of those lately engaged[,] as we have got them at reduced rates[.] My object in sending you the return is to point out the high Priced [*sic*] vessels which should be sent home, and to retain or substitute those of the reduced rate of Freight, now on their way out. In the course of Monday we will endeavour to get some reduction in the vessels now in the Black Sea[,] and if they reduce [*sic*][,] you will be furnished with a List so that you may know what vessels to retain.

[1]Milne did not copy the list to his letterbook.

We have endeavoured ever since last year to get some reduction in the Number of Vessels in the Black Sea. Month after month we have urged this[,] and no doubt a good deal has been done, but we still think reduction might take place[,] provided the efficiency of the service is not interfered with[,] of which those in the Black Sea are no doubt the best judges of what vessels are actually required [*sic*][.]

It appears to me that the first matter for consideration is, what vessels are permanently wanted[,] 1st Steamers[,] 2d Sailing ships

In regard to Steamer's [*sic*], some law should be at once established not to keep them loaded[,] doing nothing in Balaclava. if [*sic*] this could be done[,] it would release a number of vessels from the service. Again[,] it is said the Vessels more specially under Commissariat control waste their time in constant delay wherever they are sent, and do not do half the work that they should do. how [*sic*] is this to be remedied[?] Either by examination of their Log Book[s,] & if found loitering[,] to inflict a fine or by[,] if possible[,] putting an agent or supercargo on board.

Now in regard to sailing ships. Do get sent home the ships Chartered above 20/ per Ton[.] This was ordered in Sep last[,] but there are still several hanging on in the Black Sea, and are all there now engaged. [This is] absolutely required[.] this is a Military as well as a reduction question.

Large Transports (Steam) not required in B[lack] Sea should either be sent to England or Malta[,] acquainting us by Telegraph [*sic*][,] and then we can send order[s] about them to Stopford.

We want to establish a weekly communication by steam from England & from [the] Crimea[,] via a vessel to sail from each place on every Saturday[.] this will take 16 vessels of good power & speed and 2 spare vessels[,] making in all 18 vessels for this one service. So [*sic*] that if you can arrange this with Sir E Lyons (to whom I have not written but who will exercise chief control)[,] there is no reason why you should not begin whenever you can do so[.] The ship[s] should bring home invalids[.] Since the Transport Board was formed I have ceased to meddle in these matters, but I think you should know what we think here, that you may be aware of our views[,] and you can act on them or otherwise as you may see requisite[.]

The accompanying List of vessels &c give[s] you full information which are the expensive ships &c. Mr Cunards ships we hope to get down in Sep to 45/–[.]

No news here. let [*sic*] me hear from you when you have any wants . . . It strikes me & is worthy of your consideration whether we should not purchase one two or three of the Sailing Transports as Depot ships. Why should not the *Acbar* & *Mariner* be so emp[loye]d[?]

[**531**] *Milne to Tatham*

Admiralty
2 August [1855]

Inform Rear Ad Stopford that he is to send to Marseilles for French Troops, 2 of the Steam Transports which may arrive at that place from the Black Sea.

[**532**] *Lyons to Milne*

HMS *Royal Albert*, off Sevastopol, Private
18 [August] 1855

My dear Milne

Fremantle has sent to me your letter to him of the 28th July on the subject of the Transport Service, and I need hardly say that I have read it with interest and attention, for I feel to the furthest extent the importance of a matter which involves a monstrous Expenditure as well as the efficiency of the Crimean Expedition, on which the result of the War so much depends.

You say 'We have endeavoured ever since last year to get some reduction in the number of Vessels in the Black Sea, month after month we have argued this and no doubt a good deal has been done, but we still think reduction might take place provided the efficiency of the service is not interfered with &c.'

Now let us look at the matter fairly in the face. It is quite true that you have from time to time argued the reduction you now speak of, but on every occasion the Board (very naturally & properly I admit) covered its own responsibility by adding 'provided the efficiency &c' & or some such saving clause, and the Instructions have been immediately followed by orders to send French[,] Sardinian or Turkish Troops. Nor could it be otherwise when unexpected demands [were] arising, and if Connections [*sic*] with Foreign Governments came upon you, but then you should not forget that your sudden and fresh orders to find means for Transporting large bodies of Troops, Horses, Artillery & what not, nullified the preceding ones for reduction, and put me to my wits end to carry out your wishes.

To say nothing of the past, let us calmly look at the present state of the case: on my return from Kertch it appeared to me that the time had arrived when a reduction might be again attempted on an extended scale and with prudence, and I informed the Secretary of the Admiralty by Telegraph on the 26th of June that nineteen first class Steamers were on their way home, and shortly afterwards I sent the '*Europa*'[,] '*Great Britain*['] and others also to England, and here let me observe that all these were in addition to a gradual reduction which for several months had been in progress. In three weeks from that time[,] I received an order by Telegraph to sail to Marseilles immediately for 15,000 French Troops, to accomplish which I was obliged to send to Balaclava and Constantinople to stop Steamers on their way home, and yet on the 28th July you write to Fremantle still arguing for reduction: Well [*sic*], before your letter arrived I received a fresh order to convey Omar Pasha and his Troops from the Crimea to Asia, and to bring Gamal Hussain and his Turkish Contingent from the Bosphorus to Eupatoria. Now all of these . . . calls upon us are in the nature of things[,] and inseparable from such warfare as we are engaged in, & I am far from complaining in the least degree of these things, but let me ask you if they are compatible with systematic reduction?

Again, you say to Fremantle 'Do get sent home the Ships chartered at 20s per Ton. This was ordered in September last but there are still several hanging on in the Black Sea.' Now I really do not think that I deserve this record [*sic*: 'reproof'] against me any more than the other, for on several occasions I have ordered these Vessels to England[,] when in consequence of subsequent orders from the Admiralty[,] they have been stopped at Malta. Some have returned two or three times in this way.

I am the last man in the world to make a difficulty – nor am I conscious of having made one in this or any other subject, but when you console yourself for the want of reduction by writing lamentations at my expense[,] it is but fair that I should state to you what has really occurred.

I am very sorry that I have failed in my endeavours to conduct this part of my duty with satisfaction to you who who [*sic*: 'who have'] undertaken the whole question so well & taken so much interest in it for the benefit of the public service, and I have no doubt of my having made many mistakes, but they have not been cursed by any want of a conscientious discharge of my duty to the best of my humble abilities.

It is just possible the transport of the Turkish Army last winter might not have been concluded with the success stated in my letters No 479 & 480 of this year[,] if I had not given the subject my constant & anxious attention night and day, thinking how each change of wind & weather might affect the different places of embarkation and disembarkation[,] & keeping up a constant correspondence with all concerned in the operation. Everyone here said that I had undertaken [a task] which could not be done in the winter months, that Vessels & Lives must inevitably be lost &c &c &c, but by pushing our shoulders to the wheel and leaving as little as possible to chance, we, through the blessing of Providence, pulled through . . .

Believe me my dear Milne, altho you have not a very exalted opinion of my administrative talents, that I am a very great admirer of your zeal & ability . . .

P.S. I have omitted to state that one of your orders to send home transports was simultaneous with an urgent request from the Ambassador at Constantinople to bring his delectable Bashi Bazooks from all points of Asia Minor, & the Turkish Contingent from Bessarabia & elsewhere. Those extraneous demands I complied with, & whilst I, poor goose that I was, thought I was acquiring some little credit for being able to do so, I was in reality incurring discredit for not realizing reductions . . .

[**533**] *Milne to Fremantle*

Inveresk and Edinburgh
[*c.*1 September 1855]

My dear Fremantle

I regret to find by a letter which I have received from Sir E Lyons[,] that he has unfortunately taken serious offense at my letter to you[,] and considers I have cast a reflection on his administration of the Transport service. nothing [*sic*] could or would be further from my mind than to have written any one word which should have caused him annoyance. I have too much respect and regard for him to do anything of the kind[,] and regret that in my zeal for the public good[,] and with the view of giving you some general information[,] that I should have thus inadvertently wounded his feelings. I have written to him by this mail, which I hope may put matters right. he [*sic*] says I wrote to this effect[:] Do get sent home some of the ships chartered at 20/[.] now my letter was above 20/[,] and I alluded to 5 or 6 ships at high rates which we have been endeavouring to get home, as the owners most positively refused to lower their prices. two [*sic*] of these I think were in the Bosphorus[,] the others in the Black Sea, and these very vessels were brought forward in the House of C[ommons] as an example of the maladministration of the Admiralty. So there is some excuse for my writing as I did [*sic*], but I never contemplated given offense to Sir E Lyons[,] or that I should have in any manner cast a reflection on him. It is quite the reverse[,] for I have always expressed how much we are indebted to him for what he has done. You may as well take an opportunity of mentioning my regret to him[,] as I should deeply regret having caused him the least annoyance. God knows I have endeavoured to steer clear of all such vexations and no one is more careful than myself in these matters.

I am absent from the Admiralty and I have therefore no news for you. in [*sic*] fact there is nothing of any moment going on so far as relates to our service. We look for news from [the] Crimea. I am very much obliged for your two letters[1] and I will endeavour all in my power to aid you in your Exertion[s.] the duties are no doubt most arduous[,] and will be more so as the Season [*sic*] advances. What you are to do I know not with all the vast supplies which are pouring out of this country[.] how you are to get them to the Front [*sic*] will be a matter of great difficulty, unless matters come to a crisis before the month of Nov.

The First Lord & Berkeley are on their visitations to the Ports, Richards & Eden[2] in Town, and I will be[,] on my return south in a few days, ready for work again[.]

[**534**] *Milne to Grant*

Inveresk, Musselburgh
8 September 1855

Dear Mr Grant

I received your note this afternoon on my return here and I regret to find the *Lion* is not required for the service of the Army. The question is what is now to be done with her[?] She might be attached to the Black Sea Fleet, but if not to be used for that service[,] but kept in England[,] Her [*sic*] Master & Crew &c should be paid off. Perhaps you will mention this to Admiral Richards, as I am not writing to him today. I regret the state of the Salt Meat[,] and the apparent neglect which has been shown at Haulbowline by the Inspecting officers. If meat is to be received[,] then no doubt it will be absolutely necessary to have a larger staff of officers there, and to take more stringent measures for the future, but even this is not any reason why neglect should have occurred as it evidently has done[.] The Supply for next season I see is limited[,] and it would perhaps be advisable not to give up receiving at

[1]Not preserved among Milne's papers.
[2]Second Naval Lord Henry Eden.

Haulbowline entirely[,] but to limit the supply to that place. However[,] I leave you to consider this and to say what you deem most convenient for the service.

The Curing at the Home Yards might be given up for this year[.] if so, some men retained in the yards should be discharged[.]

Your submission in regard to the Clarence Yard I have sent to the Board for the Portsmouth Inspection. I entirely concur with you in everything[,] with the exception of restoring the Masters of Trades[.] I doubt whether we should do this[.] I leave it to the Board as a matter for their decision. The[1] . . . it is only giving the present men a new title and more pay, and not bringing in a superior set of men. In regard to the Transports[,] some increase of the Estab[lishmen]t should be made[,] but I see no place where the duties can be carried on except at the Clarence Yard. This I have also left for investigation by the Board[.] I wish Mr Jameison[2] could be recalled to his own duties & someone else sent to Haulbowline[.] could this be done[?] I return you the Salt Meat papers with this[,] but I see no answer from the War Dep. if [*sic*] none[,] you should request the Board to urge a reply to their former letter of Augt the 3d.

I have no news for you from this.

I return the Papers in reference to the Railway at Deptford. I see Ad Richards has made a minute on the paper and you had better see him upon the subject[.] an interview with the Railway people would be desirable. I believe there is some very great error between us & them, in regard to the measurement & price. I think they mean 20 Bags of Bread[,] or 1 Ton brought for 12/– to Gosport[.] You pay 7/6 per Ton in sailing vessel[s] for 6 Bags of Bread[,] which is one Ton measurement[,] or you would pay 25/– for the Ton weight of Bread[,] which by Rail would be carried for 12/6. The Railway people mean 1 Ton weight[,] be it Bread[,] Beef[,] Hops[,] or Beds[,] for 12/6[,] and not measurement. if [*sic*] I am right[,] and I believe I am[,] the Railway is much the cheapest. An interview would put this right. depend [*sic*] on it. There is Error [*sic*] somewhere[.]

[1]A sentence seems to be missing here.

[2]Thomas E. Jamieson, Storekeeper at the Royal Victoria Victualling Yard, Deptford, who had been sent to Hawlbowline to deal with problems in that yard. See below, Milne to Sartorius, 16 November 1855, [**547**].

[535] *Fremantle to Lyons*

HMS *Leander*, off Balaklava
17 September 1855

My dear Sir Edmund

I have received your note respecting the number of Transports in the Bosphorus. I was in hopes that it was decided not to move the Turkish Contingent, so long as things remain in their unsettled state. I agree with you that we must be prepared to meet any demand made upon us. The land Transports Corps this morning requested <u>immediate</u> Transport for 1800 animals, 600 drivers and probably 200 camels from Sinope to Balaclava, in the <u>event</u> of the Army taking the field. Now[,] as I cannot act upon chances, I requested Captain Heath to go to Head Quarters and take General Simpson's[1] orders on the subject. I know that Col McMurdo[2] has more animals here than men to look after them, and mules are daily arriving for this Corps. Captain Johnson[3] of the *Transit* states that some of his machinery is left behind at Malta. I have ordered him to join your Flag and to receive your orders.

The *Leander*'s are returned rather rough. I hope when they have officers to look after them that they will fall into their places. I sadly want an active Captain. The *Wasp* is preparing for departure[.] I shall miss Commander Lloyd,[4] he took charge of the Police of the Harbour which he conducted well. In the event of the other men of war being removed, I should require one vessel Expressly [*sic*] for that Service, to manage the Merchant Seamen, be a Prison ship, and for the Police of the Harbour, to live on board[,] also to protect the valley.

On Captain Heath's return from Head Quarters he informs me that General Simpson thinks it desirable that every assistance should be given to the Land Transport Corps, in the event of the Army taking the Field. I have therefore sent *Oneida* and *Kangaroo* to Sinope[,] to be followed by the *Cambria* and *Veloz*. I did not send the *Transit* for the reasons stated in my official letter.

[1]Sir James Simpson (1792–1868). General, sent to the Crimea as Chief of Staff in February 1855; he succeeded Lord Raglan as C-in-C of the Army before Sebastopol on that officer's death in June 1855.

[2]Colonel W. M. G. M. McMurdo, Dir-Gen. of Transports in the Crimea.

[3]Charles Richardson Johnson (*c.*1814–82). Entered, 1834; Lt, 1840; Cmdr, 1847; Capt., 1856; Rear-Adm., 1874; Vice-Adm. (Ret.), 1879.

[4]Probably Edward Alexander Tylden Lloyd (c. 1821–?). Entered, 1833; Lt, 1842.

[**536**] *Lyons to Milne*

HMS *Royal Albert*, off Sevastopol, Private
18 [September] 1855

My dear Milne

I cannot be sorry that I wrote as I did to you[,] since it has led to your writing so frank, agreeable, and satisfactory an answer.

[**537**] *Milne to Lyons*

Admiralty
18 September [1855]

The three Battalions of Turkish Troops are to go to Batoum[.] Can Transport be found for them and how soon[?]

PART VI

THE ADMIRALTY, 1855–59

By the autumn of 1855, the Board of Admiralty had largely resumed its peacetime routine, which meant that matters related to the Service's ongoing *matériel* and personnel transformation again became Milne's principal concerns. The Russian War had shown that although important first steps had been taken with regard to manning the fleet, much remained to be done, especially by way of creating a numerous reserve, so that ships could be fitted out and sent to sea quickly, thus avoiding the problems which had plagued the 1854 armament. One perceived expedient for augmenting the pool of seamen at the Navy's disposal was to transfer the Coast Guard from Treasury to Admiralty control, and in the autumn of 1856 First Lord Sir Charles Wood and his colleagues began to contemplate the steps necessary to assuming direction of the force.[1] This generated a substantial correspondence [**572**, **574**, **580–81**, **583–7**, **591–2**, **599**] between Milne and Wood, as the latter preferred to work from home when Parliament was not sitting. Milne saw several problems with the scheme, and indeed composed a memorandum which Wood probably did not see, questioning whether it would actually enhance naval preparedness [**579**]. Beyond that fundamental doubt, he had objections to Wood's preference that the Comptrollership of the Coast Guard be a civilian post, for, as he repeatedly stressed, the moment a Coast Guard vessel was commissioned, the Comptroller would be unable to issue orders to it, and the Board would become the *de facto* executive agency of the service, with deleterious consequences for both administrative efficiency and rational command structure.

At the same time the Board was wrestling with the ramifications of overseeing the Coast Guard, it was also pondering officers' education. Their concern was focused, first, on the standards for admitting and instructing naval cadets and midshipmen, and, second, on the curriculum for mid-career officers studying at the Royal Naval College. In October 1855, on Wood's request, Milne wrote to the Reverend George Fisher, Principal of the Greenwich School for naval apprentices, asking

[1]On the Coast Guard, see R. Taylor, 'Manning the Royal Navy: The Reform of the Recruiting System, 1852–1862', *Mariner's Mirror*, 45, no. 1 (1959), pp. 46–7.

for suggested revisions in the entry exam for cadets, the existing test being insufficiently rigorous to ensure that unqualified candidates were turned away [**538**]. A month later, Milne privately addressed Sir Thomas Maitland, Captain of the Gunnery School HMS *Excellent*, suggesting alterations in the examination for Lieutenant which would, he hoped, encourage thinking rather than rote memorisation [**544**]. It was lamentable, he stated bluntly, that future enlisted men in the Greenwich school were better educated than those who would later command them. The following month he drafted instructions formally to alter the Lieutenants' examination to contain practical and theoretical questions on navigation [**549**], in April 1856 he wrote to Robert Harris, Captain of the Training Ship HMS *Illustrious* (established 1854) on the educational regimen he envisioned on board that vessel [**560**], and in July, with more demanding examinations in place for both aspiring cadets and Lieutenants, argued to the rest of the Board that it was necessary to consider the increased accommodation required on board to house cadets and faculty,[1] and to consider how midshipmen's instruction might be improved after leaving the Training Ship [**568**].[2] During the subsequent autumn, as they were dealing with the Coast Guard's transfer, Milne and Wood both devoted much thought to the regulations for entry of Cadets, the former being especially concerned that the path from entry to Lieutenant be systematised as much as possible, so that all midshipmen would be able to qualify for their commission at 19 or 20 years of age [**573**, **577**, **582**, **596–8**, **600–2**].

In late 1857 Milne brought the question of continuing education for officers at the Royal Naval College, Portsmouth, to the Board's attention, with the object of expanding the curriculum to provide students with a better-rounded education [**613**]. To this end he recommended that a committee be appointed to consider the existing system of instruction at the College and to suggest ways in which it might be improved. The following February the Board agreed, named a Committee consisting of Rear-Admiral James Hope, Thomas Main, and Joseph Woolley,[3] and delegated Milne to draft its Instructions [**617**]. The Com-

[1]The ultimate remedy was, in 1859, to create a larger Cadet Training establishment, HMS *Britannia*.

[2]See also Milne's memorandum on instruction of Naval Cadets, 9 July 1857, [**610**], and Harris to Milne, 25 November 1856, printed in Hattendorf et al., (eds), *British Naval Documents 1204–1906*, document 419, pp. 715–16.

[3]Revd Joseph Woolley (1817–89). Mathematician and naval architect, appointed Principal of the School of Naval Construction at Portsmouth Dockyard, 1848. Among Woolley's pupils were future Directors of Naval Construction Sir Edward Reed and Sir

mittee's report, issued in June 1859, was summarised by Milne [**659**] and accompanied by a set of confidential recommendations by Hope [**660**].

Nor were enlisted personnel forgotten. In May 1858, First Naval Lord William Fanshawe Martin[1] proposed several changes to the Continuous Service system that Milne had played a significant role in forwarding during 1852–53. Milne himself deprecated any substantial alterations in the regulations [**624**] and the Board subsequently followed his lead [**625**]. In late 1856 Milne and Portsmouth Commander-in-Chief George Francis Seymour corresponded on the subject of providing sailors with clothing, rather than having them pay for it from the Paymaster's store of 'slop clothing,' a reform that was duly enacted the following year [**593–4**]. As an ancillary to furnishing men with uniforms, in April 1859 Milne drafted a Board request to have straw hats manufactured at Malta, as an experiment, for servicemen [**656**].[2] In October 1858 he also composed a minute urging that additional pay be given to seamen who qualified as Captains of Guns [**636**].

These boons were designed to ameliorate continuing problems in attracting men to the Service, but did not address fundamental causes. In a series of memoranda on the state of the Navy drafted by the Board in 1858, First Lord Sir John Pakington[3] [**619**], Milne [**622**], Third Naval Lord James Robert Drummond[4] [**623**], Second Naval Lord Richard Saunders Dundas [**626**], Civil Lord Algernon, Lord Louvaine[5] [**627**], and Fanshawe Martin [**629**], all lamented the inadequate means at the Service's disposal for manning the Fleet in the event of war. Milne,

Nathaniel Barnaby. Upon the School's closure in 1853, Woolley served as Admiralty Inspector of Schools. He subsequently played a major role in founding the Institution of Naval Architects in 1860 and served on Committees appointed to report on the designs of ships of war (Lord Dufferin's Committee, 1871–72) and the stability of HMS *Inflexible* (1877).

[1]William Fanshawe Martin, Bt., K.C.B., G.C.B. (1801–95). Entered, 1813; Lt, 1820; Cmdr, 1823; Capt., 1824; Rear-Adm., 1853; Vice-Adm., 1858; Adm., 1863; First Naval Lord, 1858–59.

[2]In MLN/145/5: 'Measures brought forward by Captain Milne when a Member of the Board of Admiralty, from December 1847', nd, Milne claimed responsibility for having 'Obtain[ed] sinatt [*sic*] and straw from Jamaica and Havannah for making Straw Hats for the Petty Officers and Seamen, also at Malta.'

[3]Sir John Pakington, 1st Baron Hampton, Bt. (1799–1880). Sec. of State for War and Colonies, 1852; First Lord of Admiralty, 1858–59, 1866–67; Sec. of State for War, 1867–68.

[4]James Robert Drummond, C.B., K.C.B., G.C.B. (1812–95). Entered, *c*.1824; Lt, 1832; Cmdr, 1838; Capt., 1846; Rear-Adm., 1864; Vice-Adm., 1870; Adm., 187; Naval Lord of the Admiralty, 1858–59, 1861–66.

[5]Algernon George Percy, Lord Louvaine, later sixth Duke of Northumberland (1810–99). Civil Lord of the Admiralty, 1858–59; Vice-President of the Board of Trade, 1859; Lord Privy Seal, 1878–80.

indeed, devoted several paragraphs of his paper to the questions, put by Queen Victoria, 'What are the resources of England in point of seamen, and to what extent are those resources organized and available in case of war?' He also addressed the subject in a memorandum of March 1858 to Pakington [**620**] on providing reliefs for vessels stationed overseas, alluding to the case of HMS *Marlborough*, which vessel was delayed in harbour for 129 days following her commissioning, owing to want of men.[1] Of such gravity, indeed, was the problem that in June 1858, following Sir Charles Napier's motion for an inquiry into manning, Victoria appointed a Royal Commission to consider the subject.[2] In its Report (February 1859), the Commission recommended the establishment of a proper Naval Reserve, in which merchant seamen would enrol, be paid a modest retainer, and be subject to naval service for annual training cruises and in the event of an emergency.[3] Derby, Pakington, and the Conservatives were out of office in June 1859, before they could enact these proposals, but the succeeding Palmerston government duly created the Royal Naval Reserve that August.[4]

As long as Wood was First Lord, Milne's activities chiefly related to personnel matters, as they had prior to the Russian War. When Pakington succeeded Wood, however, questions relating to the size and nature of the battlefleet, the navies of rivals, the building policy to be pursued, and the logistics of steam-era naval warfare became, for the first time, Milne's principal concern. Part of the reason for this change in emphasis was owing to Pakington himself, who, probably influenced by the Naval Lords, was deeply alarmed by the balance of naval power between Britain and France. Upon coming to office in March 1858, Pakington composed the (confidential and highly critical) memorandum on the state of the Navy mentioned above, probably for the Cabinet's information. This assessment prompted Queen Victoria to solicit the rest of the Board's opinions on a series of questions relating to the Navy's *matériel* and personnel, in turn generating the memoranda by Milne, Drummond, Saunders Dundas, Lord Louvaine, and Fanshawe

[1]The incident was of sufficient notoriety to warrant mention in Clowes, *The Royal Navy*, vol. 7, p. 18.

[2]See Taylor, 'Manning the Royal Navy', pt. 2, pp. 48–49. For the Report itself, see 'Report of the Commissioners appointed to inquire into the best means for Manning the Navy, with Minutes of Evidence and Appendix', *Parliamentary Papers*, 1859, vol. VI, p. 1.

[3]Taylor, 'Manning the Royal Navy', pt. 2, p. 54. The scheme originated with Cmdr J. H. Brown, Registrar of Seamen.

[4]Although out of office, too, Milne nonetheless composed a memorandum on the government's August 1859 Bill to establish a Naval Reserve [**666**].

Martin also referred to above, and one by Admiralty Political Secretary Henry T. L. Corry[1] [**630**], all of them as alarmist as Pakington's. Almost simultaneously, Milne composed another paper on Surveyor Baldwin Walker's proposal to increase the pace of shipbuilding [**628**], and in July 1858 drafted a Board Minute supporting the Surveyor [**631**]. The following November, their fears of Napoleon III's apparent challenge to British naval supremacy – including the construction of sea-going ironclads – were, if anything, even greater than a few months previously, and Fanshawe Martin [**644**], Saunders Dundas [**645**], Milne [**646**], and Corry [**647**] composed still another round of memoranda on Walker's programme, probably as a preliminary to drafting the Navy Estimates for 1859–60. In short, the entire Board was obsessed with the French threat.[2]

Only Milne, however, seems to have given much thought to how the battlefleet was to be kept supplied with coal in the event of war. In February 1859, apparently of his own volition, he solicited answers from the Crown's legal advisors on a series of questions about British access to coal in neutral ports during wartime [**657**]. The subsequent opinion [**658**] appears to have confirmed his fear that the Navy would likely be denied the use of such supplies, and prompted him, as he was on the verge of leaving office in June, to urge Saunders Dundas, the incoming First Naval Lord, to take up the subject [**664**]. Again, his views and actions are at odds with the widely-held myth of Admiralty conservatism and hostility to steam power. So far from resisting technological progress, Milne recognised the crucial logistical basis for steam-era imperial defence – a world-wide network of defended coaling stations – and, in so doing, anticipated by almost a decade the argu-

[1]Henry Thomas Lowry Corry (1803–73). M.P., 1825–73; Civil Lord of the Admiralty, 1841–45; Secretary to the Admiralty, 1845–46, 1858–59; First Lord of the Admiralty, 1867–68.

[2]This fear was neither surprising nor wholly unwarranted; the years 1858–63 witnessed the most sustained challenge to the Royal Navy's supremacy between 1815 and 1900. On the naval scare of those years, see, C. I. Hamilton, *Anglo-French Naval Rivalry, 1840–1870* (Oxford, 1994). The dramatic increase in the Navy Estimates caused largely by the Fleet's technological transformation also prompted Derby to appoint a Committee, consisting of Corry, Treasury Undersecretary George Hamilton, Navy Accountant-General Richard Bromley, and W. G. Anderson, to investigate and report on the causes for the increase. A copy of the Report, which was confidential, is found in Milne's papers, MLN/142/4 [1]: *Confidential Report on the Navy Estimates, 1852&1858 Addressed to the Right Hon. the Earl of Derby, 6 January 1859*. An expurgated version was subsequently presented to Parliament. See 'Report of a Committee appointed by the Treasury to inquire into the Navy Estimates, from 1852 to 1858, and into the comparative state of the Navies of England and France', *Parliamentary Papers*, 1859, vol. XIV, p. 703.

ments of John Charles Ready Colomb, generally regarded as the pioneering theorist on the subject.[1]

Beyond these major issues, Milne also had to deal with a welter of matters which, although of lesser long-term importance, nonetheless demanded prompt attention. Thus he had, in late 1855 and early 1856, to confront problems emanating from careless oversight in the Haulbowline Victualling Yard which resulted in a large-scale condemnation of salt pork cured and packed there [**534**, **547–8**, **554**, **558**], initiate inquiry and propose remedies for theft and malfeasance in the Dockyards [**637**, **638**, **641**, **650**, **652–3**], contend with ongoing tasks associated with the Transport Service, including the establishment of uniform regulations for Troopship accommodations [**539–41**, **543**, **546**, **551–2**, **555–7**, **563–7**, **571**, **605–8**],[2] and take steps to curb extravagance in subordinate officers' messes [**559**], along with several other subjects. For that matter, when, in September 1856, instability in Naples prompted the dispatch of a British Squadron to that city, Milne, the only Board member in London, found himself undertaking the First Naval Lord's duties, corresponding with Wood on the composition and commander of the force to be sent [**569–72**, **574–6**].

Finally, two situations concerning Milne personally surfaced in 1858–59, both of them relative to recognition for his long service at the Admiralty. In September 1858, Derby's Conservative government nominated retired Comptroller of Victualling, Sir Thomas Grant, and Accountant-General, Sir Richard Madox Bromley, for the Civil K.C.B., while overlooking Milne, who had not only supervised Grant during his entire tenure at Somerset House (1850–58), but had taken on the bulk of his duties relating to Transports during the Russian War. Milne, moreover, had served in the Navy's administration longer than either man, and although he was normally reticent in advancing his claims, this slight prompted him to protest forcefully to Pakington [**633**]. He was not alone; both Sir Edmund Lyons (now Lord Lyons) and Sir

[1]John Charles Ready Colomb, R.M.A. (1838–1909). Colomb's *The Protection of Our Commerce and Distribution of our Naval Forces considered* (London, 1867) is typically credited as the first systematic enunciation of steam-era imperial defence strategy. On the evolution of that strategy, see Donald M. Schurman, *Imperial Defence, 1868–1887*, ed. John Beeler (London, 2000).

[2]In MLN/145/5, 'Measures brought forward by Captain Milne when a Member of the Board of Admiralty, from December 1847', nd, Milne claimed to have 'Proposed and carried out the system of Troop Service in H.M. Troopships; formerly only a Table supplied and a few seats; nothing else whatever; no Bedding, no Crockery; the Troops had to unpack all their own Plate, Crockery, Glass; they had no Bedding allowed, no Cabin Fittings; now they are furnished with Bedding, Linen, Crockery, Glass, Steward, and Cook. No greater boon was ever given to the Army on my special and sole recommendation.'

Charles Wood took up Milne's cause, the former stressing his indispensable services during the war [**632**], and the latter the fundamental injustice of Pakington's and Derby's failure to reward Milne while honouring two less-deserving civil servants [**635**]. Pakington's defence – that it was not for him to reward service performed for previous naval administrations – was, Wood charged, inconsistent and unconvincing, since Bromley had already received the C.B. and had done nothing during Pakington's tenure at the Admiralty to warrant further recognition. The Conservatives' subsequent decision in mid-November to Gazette Milne with the K.C.B., as he had requested, suggests that Wood's arguments carried weight; indeed, Pakington's position appears so weak, logically, as to suggest that he realised he had made a mistake but was loath to admit it, and instead allowed enough time to pass before reversing his stance to avoid the implication of a *mea culpa*. Whatever the case, Milne had his reward, and must have felt satisfaction at having his efforts publicly acknowledged. Moreover, he had reached the Flag List the previous January, and he and his wife were raising four young children. Life had been good to him, both professionally and personally.

The following June, when Derby's government fell, Milne, then suffering a bout of ill health, decided that he had had enough of naval administration for the time being, and left the Admiralty, after almost a dozen years on the Board. As he prepared to leave office, numerous acquaintances and colleagues, ranging from old friend and commanding officer Sir William Bowles [**662**] to Admiralty clerk Robert Bell [**665**], wrote to Milne, thanking him for his service and assistance over the years, and expressing regret at his impending departure.[1] He had, however, no intention of ending his career at age 53, and in September 1859, in response to new First Lord the Duke of Somerset's[2] offer of active duty, requested that, as a further reward for his administrative service, he be considered for command of the North America and West Indies Station [**667**]. The Duke initially replied [**668**] that Milne's name would be put forward for that post, but made no promise of compliance with his wish. Milne's former Admiralty colleague, Richard Saunders Dundas, was now First Naval Lord, and

[1]Upon his retirement in 1857, Admiralty Permanent Secretary Thomas Phinn also thanked Milne for his willing assistance [**609**]. MLN/166/2 contains several testimonials written in 1859 in addition to those included in this volume.

[2]Edward Adolphus Seymour, twelfth Duke of Somerset, (1804–85). Junior Lord of the Treasury, 1835–39; Secretary of the Board of Control, 1839–41; Home Department Undersecretary, 1841; First Commissioner of Works, 1851–52; First Lord of the Admiralty, 1859–65.

clearly supported his candidacy [**669**]. Whether due to Dundas' advocacy, his own deliberations, or other factors, in October Somerset submitted Milne's name to the Queen and received her approval [**670**]. When he learned of Milne's appointment, Pakington wrote to congratulate him [**672**], presciently suggesting that he would eventually return to the Admiralty.

[**538**] *Milne to Fisher*[1]

Admiralty
29 October [1855]

Dear Mr Fisher

Sir C Wood is anxious to have your opinion in regard to what examination a lad from 14 to 15 years of age should undergo on his entry into the service[.] he wishes to make this as near the standard of the Greenwich Schools as possible, but of course this can only be approximate, as in any such examination it must depend upon the course of Education which is pursued in the Schools of England[,] and not by what is taught in the Schools at G[reenwic]h, and[,] as Boys are selected for Cadets from all Great Britain, the examination must be based on a fair average of what is taught in such schools[.] at the sametime [*sic*] when nominated he would give them two months to prepare for their Examination[,] and therefore some higher standard or some special questions might be introduced for which they would have[2] . . . our present limit of age is 12 to 14 and the Examination you will find in the Navy List[,] which is far too low a standard. will [*sic*] you kindly consider this and Sir C. Wood would be glad to see you on Wednesday at 11 oclock[.]

[**539**] *Milne to Fremantle*

Admiralty
29 October 1855

We are anxious to get Home the Steam Transports *Cleopatra*[,] *Australian* [&] *Sydney*[.] arrange this if you possibly can and[,] in selecting the screw store ships for service[,] keep those at the lowest rates, sending the others home when they can be spared[.]

[**540**] *Milne to Fremantle, Frederick Grey, and Stopford*

Admiralty
2 November [1855]

Write to Rear Admiral[s] Fremantle[,] Grey and Stopford and acquaint that it would be very advantageous to the Transport Service, if[,] in the fortnightly returns to the Transport Dep[,] if a notation was made [*sic*]

[1]Revd George Fisher, M.A., Principal and Chaplain of Greenwich School.
[2]There may be a sentence or more missing here.

how each vessel has performed her duties to the Service[,] and request in future that a notation may be made against the name of each vessel such a[s] 'very good'[,] 'good', satisfactory [*sic*] or otherwise[.] it will enable the Transport Director to retain the services of good vessels & pay off others.

[**541**] *Milne Minute on a War Office Proposal to alter the System of Transporting Ordnance Stores*

Admiralty
2 November [1855]

There appears no objection to carry[ing] out the proposal of the Secy for War. it [*sic*] is however an alteration of a system which has been in force for more than 50 year's [*sic*] and I am not aware that it has proved disadvantageous to the Service. It will be necessary that the Admiralty Dept superintending the stowage of Cargoes should [be] in communication with some person at the Ordnance at Woolwich well acquainted with shipping[,] the Navigation of the River, and with the stowage of Cargoes, for unless there is, some misunderstanding will inevitably take place.

On the requisition of the War Dept[,] conveyance will be requested for a certain amount of Tonnage[,] say 500 Tons to Malta. The ship will be obtained and sent off [to] the Arsenal[.] the Transport Officers at Deptford will inform the Woolwich authorities that the vessel has arrived for 500 Tons of Stores[,] in accordance with a requisition dated ______, and request the stores may be sent up alongside [*sic*] the ship. now [*sic*] comes the [question:] who decides what is to be embarked first; our naval officers are unacquainted with the component parts of a Battering Train or Carts . . . and all the complicated details of Ordnance shipments. the [*sic*] whole arrangement of the embarkation of these various items must rest with the Ordnance dept.[,] and they also had [charge of] the stowage in the ships, but as this is to be changed, it appears to me to be necessary that the Ordnance should have some one person with whom our Superintendant [*sic*] of Transport duties at Woolwich can be in constant daily communication, that they may work together in the embarkation & proper stowage of Cargoes[.]

[**542**] *Milne to Richard Saunders Dundas*[1]

Admiralty
5 November 1855

Request him to state on enquiry from the ships of the Squadron under his Command, whether the ships have been properly supplied with Fresh Provisions[,] and if Messrs Rainals & Deacon have given satisfaction in the discharge of their duties as Agents to the Admiralty[.]

[**543**] *Milne to Lyons*

Admiralty
6 November 1855

The Sardinian Government have requested that two steamers may be sent to Genoa for the purpose of Conveying stores to their Army in the Crimea[.] Endeavour to arrange this.

[**544**] *Milne to Maitland*[2]

Admiralty
12 November 1855

My dear Maitland

I have always taken a good deal of Interest in matters connected with the Examination of officers &c[,] and have at various times been the mean's [*sic*] of introducing new matter into the College Sheet, and I have been looking over some of those for the last year or so[,] and I [*sic*: 'it'] strikes me they are somewhat meagre in practical questions on Astronomy[.] This I think should be avoided, but what I want to draw your attention to is the Introduction [*sic*] of a series of questions for officers to state the Theory of Astronomy &c[,] and to shew that they are acquainted with the principles on which they are working[.] I dont [*sic*] consider that so much advantage is to follow to the Individual who is to pass [*sic*], as to [the] publicity that such questions are to be put & answered. it [*sic*] will cause officers to investigate and to study the Theory of the questions instead of learning like Parrots. It strikes me it will do much good.

[1]C-in-C, Baltic Squadron.
[2]Sir Thomas Maitland.

The questions I would propose are not numerous, but I add the following[:]

Describe what are the powerful currents of the Ocean and the directions in which they run – or
Describe the Florida stream from whence it arises & where it ends.
Describe the principal [*sic*] of the Artificial Horizon & how angles are obtained[,] & why double the angle is obtained[.]
Describe the Trade winds. how [*sic*] they blow[,] with their limits[.]
Describe what is the Local alteration & how it is formed[.]
Describe the mode of Surveying a Harbour[.]
Suppose a ship on shore on a Rock in sight of land[.] how will you find the ships position[?]
Describe how a chart is made and what steps are necessary[.]
Shew by figure that by having the [?Angle] & Declination[,] the Latitude is obtained on the Meridian[.]
D[itt]o for the Pole* [star] – above[,] also [?return] this Pole.
Explain the correction for Dip & what it is.
Describe how a Log Line is marked for a 14 second glass.
Subdivide the Arc of a Sextant of ten degrees and into 20 and 10 Seconds on a vernier[.]
Explain the principle of the Barometre[.]

These may be multiplied in every variety of way[,] and many practical questions put, which would make our officers <u>think</u>. What say you to this[?] It can do no harm and do much good[.] I wish you saw the Examination of the Greenwich Boys and attended to see their charts &c[.] it [*sic*] is lamentable to think how superior in Education they are to our officers[.]

[**545**] *Milne to Cochrane*

Admiralty
13 November 1855

Inform [him that] my Lords have ordered Split pease to be issued for from 14 to 21 days issue[,] to be supplied to HMS *Hastings*[,] *Hawke* and *Russell* from the Royal Clarence Yard as an experiment. he [*sic*] is to give orders to the Captains of these ships to have their split peas issued to the Crews of these ships the proportion to be ⅔ the allowance of the present issue of the Common Peas[.] after full trial of these Split Peas[,] the Captains are to report whether they prefer them as an Article of General issue or whether they prefer the Common Peas as are now issued[.]

[**546**] *Milne Instructions to Transport Department*

Admiralty
15 November [1855]

Transport Dept to prepare a return of the different voyages performed by Different Steam Transports between Malta and England & England and Malta[,] so as to contrast the expense of the several vessels[.]

Niagara	Paddle	*Gt Britain*	Screw
Orinoco	"	*Bahania*	"
Ripon	"	*Resolute*	"
Europa	"	*Robt Lowe*	"
Thames	"	*Tynemouth*	"
Cambria	"	*Imperatriz*	"
Germania	"	*Jura*	"
Hansa	"	*Harbinger*	"
Arabia	"	*Alps*	"

Giving the Horse Power and average consumption of Coal[,] taking it at 10 lbs per H Power per Day.

[**547**] *Milne to Sartorius*

Admiralty
16 November 1855

Write to Sir George Sartorius and direct him to acquaint Mr Ede[,][1] the Naval & Victualling Storekeeper at Haulbowline, that my Lords have received a report from the Comp[troller] of Vict[uallin]g that a large quantity of Salt Pork, as per the enclosed return[,] has been condemned at the Victualling Establishments named therein and[,] as this meat was issued by him at Haulbowline, to call his attention to the circumstances and the causes which have led to this condemnation. he [*sic*] is to report fully under what circumstances he allowed such inferior and defective meat to pass inspection[,] and to be received into Store when[,] from his personal experience in the receipt

[1]Edward Ede, Agent Victualler and Naval Storekeeper at Cork.

of Meat at Deptford[,] he should have been aware it was unfit for the Service[.]

[**548**] *Milne to Austin*

Admiralty
17 November 1855

Captain Austin to direct Mr Jamieson[,] the Store Receiver[,] to report to the Board his opinion of the condition of the Salt Pork examined by him at the Several Ports, where he has been employed on survey[.] To state with reference to the Enclosed return whether he is of opinion that the causes of Condemnation existed prior to the final receipt of the Meat, or from any other circumstance[,] and he is to inform the Board what causes have[,] in his opinion[,] . . . led to the heavy condemnations[.]

[**549**] *Milne Draft Instructions for Maitland*

Admiralty
10 December [1855]

Inform Sir Thos Maitland that my Lords have had under consideration the Examination which officers are now required to pass for the Rank of Lieutenants [*sic*] and Masters, and as the College Sheet does not contain any questions which bear on the Theory of Navigation, or in regard to the currents of the Ocean, or the prevailing winds in different parts of the Globe, or as a test of the knowledge which officers may have attained of the more practical part of their professional knowledge as Navigators & Surveyors, My Lords direct that henceforth every College Sheet shall contain in the first page at least three questions on these subjects as [*sic*: and] also on[:]
Drawing Charts[.]
Ships position on Charts[.]
Defining position of Shoals when a ship is on shore[.]
Explaining by Figure the theory of finding the Latitude on the Meridian, by Star or Sun.
Explaining Dip of Horizon[.]
Explaining Artificial Horizon[.]
and [*sic*] many other theoretical questions contained in every Book of Navigation[,] and with which the officers [entrusted] with the Navigation of HM Ships ought to be acquainted[.]

[**550**] *Milne Memorandum on Chaplains' Pay*

Admiralty
23 December 1855

The Pay of Chaplains is now fixed at £161.4.2 pr A[nnum,] being £21 less than Lieutenants and Masters. I think it would be injudicious to raise the Pay of the Chaplain[s] to the same rate as the Executive and working officers of the Fleet. It would cause general discontent[.] I think the executive officers would immediately claim an increase of Pay. When the relative duties of these officers are considered and their responsibilities compared, I must say that I think the Chaplains have no great Claim [*sic*]. I see no reason why the Pay should not be increased to £182.10 after 6 years service at Sea[,] that is[,] employed afloat.

The half Pay was fixed by Order in Council of 1812. This might be increased or altered so as to give Half Pay previous to 8 years service [*sic*][,] as no one can at present obtain it until the party has served 8 years at sea.

I think it might be as follows[:] after 3 years service 3/6[,] after 5 years service 4/–[,] and after 8 years at 5/– per day. The scale proposed by Mr Baring[1] is a very fair one[,] but care must be taken that these officers do not become a burden after 4 years service on the Half Pay List and refuse to serve. This will be the case unless guarded against.

The Rank to Chaplains [*sic*] presents difficulties[:] if given to them in the Wardroom[,] it could not be refused to others[,] and it would cause difficulties to arise which had better be avoided[.]

The Chaplain General I think is unnecessary and would not tend to any benefit[.] this appointment was done away with by Order in Council in 1815 . . .

[1]Probably Thomas George Baring, later second Baron and first Earl Northbrook (1826–1904). Civil Lord of the Admiralty, 1857–58; Under-Secretary of State for India, 1859–64; Under-Secretary of State for Home Affairs, 1864–66; Parliamentary Secretary to the Admiralty, 1866; Under-Secretary of State for War, 1868–72; Viceroy of India, 1876–77; First Lord of the Admiralty, 1880–85. Baring was Wood's Private Secretary March 1855–March 1857.

[**551**] *Milne to Frederick Grey*

Admiralty
27 December [1855]

We are paying off most of the Steamers coming home[.] let us know which Steamers you will require from England – *Transit*, *Emperador* [*sic*], *Thames*, *Indiana*, *Perseverance* [are] going out.

[**552**] *Milne to Gibbon*[1]

Admiralty
2 January 1856

Cap Milne present his Compliments to Mr Gibbon[,] and has taken the liberty of writing to him confidentially in order to obtain any information he may be disposed to give him in regard to the Transport Service at Ports[mouth]. Cap Milne has heard it rumoured that unnecessary expense is taking place[,] and this money might be saved to Govt [*sic*] by some more judicious arrangements at Ports[mouth], and[,] as Cap M[ilne] has heard Mr Gibbons name mentioned[,] he would be much obliged if he could give him a private hint on the subject[,] as he is most anxious to do all in his power to place matters on a proper footing and prevent all unnecessary expense and[,] having this object in view[,] he trusts Mr Gibbon will excuse him from taking the liberty of addressing him on the subject[.]

[**553**] *Milne to Frederick Grey and Fremantle*

Admiralty
15 January 1856

Send to England as soon as possible all Horse Transports which can be spared. they [*sic*] will return to the East with Horses. others [*sic*] are leaving England this month[.]

[1]George T. Gibbon, Master. Admiralty Agent on Board Contract Mail Steam Vessels.

[554] *Milne to Austin*

Admiralty
*c.*1 February 1856

Write to Captain Austin at Deptford inform him that my Lords have already transmitted to him[,] for the information and guidance of the professional officers of the Yard, Scientific and professional opinion on the Measly [*sic*] Pork which has been sent into the Victualling Yards by Contractors[,] as neither himself or [*sic*] the Members of the Committee who met at Haulbowline to enquire into the receipt of Salt Pork at that Establishment, could have been aware of the unwholesome nature of the meat. My Lords have every reason to suppose that the Committee would have reported such meat to be unfit for issue to the seamen of the Fleet[,] instead of reporting that the Committee [*sic*] were unable to satisfy themselves that what was termed 'Measle' in Salt Pork[,] in this case is a disease[,] or that such meat is unwholesome or unfit for issue in the Fleet[.] My Lords[,] on a review of the foregoing opinions of the professional person's [*sic*] who have been consulted[,] consider that the professional officers at Deptford & Plymouth Vic[tuallin]g Yards were fully justified in rejecting such meat as unfit for HM Service[,] and this meat having previously passed the inspection of the officers at Haulbowline clearly shews that there existed a want of proper care and attention in the examination of the meat, a fact fully established by the present almost daily rejection of Pork from the reason that such meat was rejected at Portsmouth and Plymouth [*sic*].

My Lords have directed a Copy of this Letter to be sent to [the] Rear Ad at Queenstown for the information of the other Members of the Committee[.]

Send also to Mr Ede and to inform him that had he exercised a more strict inspection no such meat should have been received which was subsequently condemned at Ports[mouth] & Plymouth[.]

[555] *Milne to Tulloch*[1]

Admiralty, Private
7 February 1856

Dear Col. Tulloch

Not being personally acquainted with Sir John McNeill[,][2] altho perhaps I ought to be[,] I write you a private note not by any means to complain[,] far from it [*sic*], but merely to point out a remark in your report about the Huts and to explain the facts. you [*sic*] mention in your report that the Huts were ready in a short period of time, but considerable difficulty arose in obtaining transport[,] so that the first cargo did not arrive in Balaclava until the 25 Decr. now [*sic*] the facts are the following[:] the ordnance requisition for 5600 Tons of Huts reached the Admiralty on the 24 Nov. On the 30th Nov [the] Admiralty wrote [the] Duke of Newcastle [of] a Steamer detained at Southampton for want of Huts. After the 24 Nov the Steamers had to be procured[,] no doubt a difficulty for it was so, and we had to get the Steamers from the regular coal trade for the purpose[,] vessels which could only carry a few days coal[.] however

2 Sailed on 6 Decr with 170 Huts
2 Sailed on 8&9th Decr with 180 Do
4 Sailed on 10&11 Dec with 254 Do
1 Sailed on 15th with 90 Do
1 Sailed on 21 " with 90 Do
1 Sailed on 31 " with 90 Do

There was much difficulty[,] no doubt[,] in getting Steam Transports after the 12 of Decr because we had exhausted the market, but there was really no delay in shipping the first Huts, and even on 30 Nov the Transports were [ready] before the Huts[.]

I merely write this to make you aware of the real facts of the case. I have no other object[.]

[1]Sir Alexander Murray Tulloch, K.C.B. (1803–64). Tulloch, with Sir John McNeill, was sent to the Crimea to examine the Army Commissariat. For their Report, see 'Report of the Commission of Inquiry into the supplies of the British Army in the Crimea, with the Evidence annexed', *Parliamentary Papers*, 1856, vol. XX, p. 1.

[2]Sir John McNeill, D.C.L. (1795–1883). Diplomat; sent to the Crimea in early 1855 with Tulloch to report on the commissariat department and on the reasons for delay in unloading and distributing food and stores to the troops.

[**556**] *Tulloch to Milne*

War Office
8 February 1856

My Dear Captain Milne

It was to the difficulty generally of providing transport for the Huts, that Sir John and I referred, rather than to the first Ship [*sic*] or ships, though in looking at the paragraph, it might perhaps bear the construction you appear anxious should not be put upon it.

No one knows better than I do, the exertions you made to procure transport, for you will perhaps recollect that I was one of the Committee for the construction of the huts, and participated with you in all the difficulties which appeared likely to arise for want of it. It was the impression this left upon me which led me to frame the paragraph you refer to for the approval of my colleagues, but the fact of one vessel having been ready before the huts came down, would not[,] I think[,] affect the statement we have made in so general a way, & which was intended only to be taken in that light. Had I thought the volumes would have been so much read, I would have probably weighed each paragraph more carefully.

So far as the huts are concerned[,] however[,] it was perhaps an advantage rather than otherwise that they did not arrive sooner[,] for when there was no means of transport[,] they only created embarrassment by crowding the harbour & wharf with materials which could not be carried further[,] as explained by us in the Report.

[**557**] *Milne Instructions to Superintendents of Transports*

Admiralty
15 February [1856]

Orders to Adls Stopford – Malta
Grey – Constantinople
Fremantle – Balaclava
Transport Dept – Portsmouth
Genoa
Marseilles
Gibraltar
Liverpool
Southampton
Woolwich

Deptford
Plymouth

Directing that on the arrival of every Transport[,] the Log Book of the vessel is to be strictly examined to ascertain whether there has been any unnecessary expenditure of Coal, any delay in [*sic*: from] not carrying sufficient sail[,] or any detention in consequence of not steering a direct course[,] or from any other cause, and to report any apparent delay or neglect to their Lordships[,] in order that the expense caused thereby may be charged ag[ains]t the Hire of the Ship[.]

Acq Transport Directors[.]

[**558**] *Milne to* [*?Curgenven*][1]

Admiralty, Private
27 February 1856

Dear Sir

I have seen your note of the 20th to Mr Grant[,] and I have read it with much satisfaction[,] and you may be assured you will have full support in the execution of your duties[.] we regret what has taken place in regard to the inspection of the Salt Meat at Haulbowline[,] and it is certainly not at all creditable to a government Estab[lishmen]t to find what has been passed at Haulbowline should be found unfit for the Service at an other [*sic*] Port. all [*sic*] we require is for officers to do their duty with strict impartiality to Govt and to Contractors. This Dept can have no other wish[,] no other object, and you may rest assured that every officer will have the assistance and support of the Admiralty in the discharge of the duties entrusted to them. I have been anxious that officers should make their wishes known[,] and I will say to you as I have ever done to others, write and let me know your wishes & wants[,] whenever any improvement can be made or an error rectified. it [*sic*] is our wish that it should be so. we [*sic*] act for the public good and the benefit of the Service. you [*sic*] have been specially selected for Haulbowline[.] I trust you will do your duty honestly and fearlessly and keep the Board informed officially on all matters which require their attention . . .

Let me hear from you whenever you deem it necessary[.]

[1]Richard Curgenven, Secretary to Henry D. Chads, Flag-Officer, Queenstown. Milne's letter does not state to whom it was addressed, but Curgenven appears the most likely recipient; he was appointed to the secretaryship on 20 February 1856, whereas Chads and the rest of HMS *Hogue*'s officers had commissions dated 1 April or later. Additionally, Edward Ede remained Agent Victualler at Haulbowline, so whomever Milne was writing to was to exercise oversight and control over Ede.

[559] *Milne Draft Board Order on Officers' Messes*

Admiralty
4 March [1856]

My Lords Commissioners of the Admiralty have to call the attention of the Captains and Commanders of HMS to Clause 6 Sect 11 Chap V of the Admiralty Instructions in regard to the measures to be adopted to prevent an extravagant mode of living in the Subordinate officers messes. As my Lords have reason to believe that sufficient check has not been exercised in some of HM Ships to prevent such extravagance[,] my Lords direct that in future the Mess amount of the Mates and subordinate messes be subjected to inspection, by a Lieut. & Paymaster of the ship[,] and be submitted to the Captain for his approval or otherwise[,] and this inspection is to take place at the close of each quarter[,] and in the report to the Captain the Names of all officers who have not paid their mess is to be stated[,] and also all outstanding liabilities[,] and the Captains & Commdrs of HM Ships are to fix the amount of Expense money and monthly Payments on such a scale as they may see fit & proper[,] and the circumstances of the ship & station may require[.]

[560] *Milne to Harris*[1]

Admiralty, Private
15 March 1856

Dear Cap Harris

We have measures in hand relative to the Cadets and their future Examinations[,] and I think it as well to let you know what is going on, that you may be able to think over the matter in private[.]

1[.] cadets [*sic*] will henceforth be entered between the ages of 13 and 15. They will[,] on entry[,] be sent into Training Ships for 6 to 9 Months. After this they will pass out and [there will] also [be] an Examination after 2 years from entry[,] for the Rank of Mids[,] as at present. They will then pass again [*sic*] at 18 months further service[,] taking the place of the present 2 years Examination[,] and [they will] have to serve 18 months more before they can pass the final Examinations; in all to serve 5 years and[,] being 19 years of age[,] they will be eligible for the Rank of Lieut[.]

[1]Robert Harris (1809–65). Entered, 1822; Lt, 1833; Cmdr, 1841; Capt., 1849. Harris was Captain of HMS *Illustrious*, the Training Ship for naval cadets.

Now[,] the various examinations from entry and also the intermediate ones and the final one at the College are all to be remodelled and improved. a [*sic*] Committee will meet on Monday week to do this, but I want you to consider the Scheme for the Training Ships –
1. They must be grounded in the First principles of Navigation and practical Astronomy, use of Instruments, but this only to a certain extent in the forenoon[.]
2. The afternoon must be devoted to Seamanship[,] but you must fix a regular course from the manufacture of Rope to the Fittings at the Truck – I am of opinion the Cutlass & Small Arm exercise should be given to drill the Boys into shape &c[,] but I would not give much of the Gun drill.

I have strongly recommended Evening Lectures[,] which will be carried out, on Navigation, Astronomy, Signals, Rigging, use of Globes, Charts, &c. The Boys must have occupation in the Evenings and this is the best[;] it will open their minds and interest. Think over the Scheme &c[.] Say nothing about all this[.]

[**561**] *Milne Draft Board Order on Courts Martial Procedure*

Admiralty
20 March [1856]

My Lords Commissioners of the Admiralty desire that[,] on the occasion of Courts Martial being held on officers for the loss of a ship or for running a ship on shore, the following circumstances are invariably to be enquired into[:]
1. The Log Book is to be produced[,] and investigation is to be made whether the Courses steered and distance's [*sic*] run are correctly inserted.
2. Whether the position of the ship was accurately ascertained at the previous noon[,] or at any subsequent period.
3. The Master of the Ship on board of which the C[ourt] M[artial] is held[,] or some other responsible officer[,] is to be directed to work up the ships position from the previous noon or subsequent observations[,] until she went on shore. This is to be read off the Chart by which the ship was navigated[,] and is to be transcribed with the Minutes of the C[ourt] M[artial] and likewise a Copy of the Log for 48 hours before the ship struck[.]

[**562**] *Wood to Milne*

En route to Devonport
5 April 1856

Dear Captain Milne

. . . It is mortifying to find how completely the Russians have done us in the Pacific. They beat us when we attacked them[,] & concealed their ships & their force when we looked for them.[1]

I dont quite understand their able communication from the Baltic to the Pacific[,] unless they can go along the northern coast & up one of the Siberian rivers.

I have had a copy made of the information & find it curious.

I am a little alarmed by Cherbourg, 9 basins big enough to hold several ships of the line & with 50 feet depth of water at the lowest tide, 4 docks single, & 2 double out of one basin (not yet finished but to be completed in two years) & one out of the other [*sic*]. We cannot produce as many large docks altogether.

[**563**] *Milne to Houston Stewart*

Admiralty
23 April 1856

Write to Ad Sir H Stewart at Malta, and inform him that HMS *Himalaya*, *Vulcan* and *Perseverance* have been ordered to Malta to follow his orders. Admiral Fremantle has been directed by telegraph to embark in HMS *Resolute* & *Simoom*[,] part of the Troops intended for Halifax and Canada, and he is to send the remainder to Malta to be embarked in HMS *Himalaya* and *Vulcan*.

The total number of men to be embarked consists of 4000 men of the 9th, 17th, 39th, 62d [&] 63d Regts.

The *Himalaya* should carry one of the Halifax Regiments and the portion of another for the same place, and[,] as the fine season has commenced[,] ¼ of the Troops are to be upon Deck.

[1]Wood was referring to the Russian vessels *Aurora* and *Dwina*. Following the failed assault on Petropavlovsk-Kamchatski of 31 August 1854 and another on 4 September, British and French forces withdrew. In the spring of 1855 a small British squadron renewed the blockade of the port, but during a snowstorm on 17 April the entire garrison of the town was evacuated by the Russian warships and several merchantmen, which escaped up the Amur River, where shallow water prevented the British from pursuing them.

These ships are to call at Gibraltar for Coal[,] with which they are to fill up as much as they can stow and[,] in making the voyage across the Atlantic[,] every care is to be taken to make the Coals last during the voyage by using only 2 Boilers or using sail only when there is a fair wind.

The Rear Ad is to give orders for their being supplied with No[rth] A[tlantic] Charts at Gibraltar and[,] on landing the Troops at Halifax and Quebec[,] they are to bring home any Troops or Stores and proceed to Ports[mouth] for further orders.

The Ships under orders for Quebec[,] if short of Coal[,] may put into Halifax or Sydney[,] Cape Breton to complete the same[.]

[**564**] *Milne to Houston Stewart*

Admiralty
28 April [1856]

On arrival of *Perseverance* at Malta[,] she is to be ordered to the Crimea and to be at the disposal of Rear Admiral Fremantle for the Embarkation of Troops[.]

[**565**] *Milne Draft Memorandum to the Judge Advocate General, Board of General Officers*[1]

Admiralty
12 May 1856

Sir

With reference to my Evidence before the Board of General Officers at Chelsea on the 6th Inst[,] and to the question which was put to me respecting several Horse Transports said to have been short of Forage when conveying the Cavalry from Varna to Gea [*sic*] Fort in Sept 1854, I beg to acquaint you for the information of the Board of General officers[,] That [*sic*] after full inquiry I cannot find that any complaint was ever made to the Admiralty of any such deficiency[,] nor was I ever aware of any such circumstance having occurred until it was men-

[1]The Board of General Officers had been appointed by the Army in response to the complaints of many high-ranking officers in the Crimea who had been criticised in Tulloch and McNeill's Report. For their findings, see 'Report of the Board of General Officers appointed to inquire into the statements contained in the reports of Sir John M'Neill and Colonel Tulloch, and the evidence taken by them, animadverting upon the conduct of certain officers on the general staff, and others in the Army; with Minutes of Evidence and Appendix', *Parliamentary Papers*, 1856, vol. XXI, p. 1.

tioned. I enclose for the information of the Board a series of Letters[1] which passed between the Board of Admiralty and the Treasury on the subject of the supply of Hay for service in the East[,] by which it will be seen that the Admiralty first raised the question of the supply of Hay on the 17th Feb 1854.

The Horse Transports which sailed from England took out as much as they could possible [*sic*] carry[,] and many vessels were likewise sent from England entirely loaded with Forage. This[,] I have reason to believe[,] was landed at Scutari [&] Varna[,] and in an order dated the 25 June 1854 of Captain Christie[,] who was in command of the Transports[,] a Copy of which is sent with the series of paper's [*sic*] No 2[,] it will be seen that six weeks forage & provisions were to be retained on board of Every [*sic*] Transport so that they might be ready for any immediate service. Amongst these paper's [*sic*] will likewise be found several requisitions In [*sic*] July & Augt 1854 from the Commissariat Dept for a supply of spare Forage from the Transports[.] It appear's [*sic*] therefore[,] to be most probable that when some of the last Transports arrived at Varna from the Medtn immediately previous to the Embarkation of Horses for the Crimea[,] that the spare stock may have been exhausted by the supplies thus furnished to the Shore. The death[s] of Rear Ad Boxer and Cap. Christie[,] and the absence of other officers who were at Varna in Sept 1854 has precluded me at this distance of time from obtaining authentic information[,] but a Letter has been addressed to the owner's [*sic*] of the *Simla*[,] requesting information and under what circumstances so small a supply as only eight Days forage was said to be on board.

I have the honour herewith to forward[:]

1. The Instructions for an Agent of Transports[.]
2. Do. for a Master of a Transport[.]
3. Regulations in Chartering Ships[.]

[**566**] *Milne to Panmure*

Admiralty
5 June 1856

Write to the Secretary for War and inform[,] with reference to his letter of the 2d Inst enclosing one from General Codrington[2] of the 17 of

[1]Not copied to Milne's letterbook.

[2]Sir William John Codrington, K.C.B., G.C.B. (1804–84). Cmdr of a Brigade of the Light Division in the Crimea. Codrington was the son of Adm. Sir Edward Codrington and brother to Sir Henry John Codrington.

May, That [*sic*] the following is the state of the Embarkation of the English Troops in the Crimea and Scutari, as far as it can at present be made out, and altho not so accurate as could be wished[,] for want of the returns not having had time to arrive[,] it may be considered a very close approximation thereto. My Lords have added a statement of the arrangements which have been ordered for the further Embarkation of the Army[.] They also state that nearly the whole of the Sardinian Troops & Horses have been conveyed to Ibryzia, and a considerable number of the Turkish contingent have been landed at Constantinople from Kertch.

General Statement of the Troops in the Crimea & Scutari By a return from the War Office of 12 May[:]

there were in the Crimea at the end of April	53,326
Addl Army Works Corp, say	5000
[approx. total]	58,000
Deduct embarked from Crimea up to 1 June	17,000
Total [remaining]	41,000
Of these[,] 3000 Artillery will come [home] with the Horses	3000
Troops to Embark in Crimea in Infantry Ships	38,000
Troops still to be embarked at Scutari	11,000
Will come [home] in Horse ships [*sic*]	2000
Grand Total	47,000
Provision made for Infantry alone	51,000

Statement relative to the Embarkation of the English Troops in the Crimea & Scutari[:]

Embarked from the Crimea up to the 15 of May & passed Constantinople[,] including the Regiments for Canada[,] Corfu & Gibraltar, Army Work Corps,

Invalids, &c	7000
Embarked from Crimea between the 15th of May and 1 of June	10,000
[Total]	17,000
Embarked from Scutari up to the 15 May	4,226

The following number of men will be embarked as nearly as possible as follows: –

Between the 1st and 20th of June[:]

In Steam Transports	9,000
In H.M. Ships of the Medn Fleet	7,500
In H.M. *Rodney*, *London*, *Belleisle*, *Resistance*	2,500
Total	19,000

Between the 20th June & 10th July[:]

In Steam Transports	6,700

May be others for [*sic*]	2,300
In 10 Sail of the Line sent from England	9,000
Total	18,000
Between 10th and 31st July[:]	
In Steam Transports	5,000
In Sailing Transports sent out	9,000
[Total]	14,000
Grand Total	51,000

The foregoing is independent of vessels which have been chartered in the East and vessels which are now employed in moving the Turkish Contingent from Kertch, also Cattle & Store ships, all of which will be available for Troops.
So that it may be assumed there will be[,] between the 1 of June and 31 of July[,] sufficient Tonnage for 55,000 Men.

[**567**] *Yorke*[1] *to Milne*

Horse Guards
14 July 1856

My dear Captain Milne

Lord Panmure has approved of one regiment of Infantry, one Battery of Artillery and one Company of Sappers & Miners being embarked in this country at once for the Cape.[2] The Regiment will be the 80th Foot, but Returns will be called for this bearing the numbers to embark.

Could the Company of Sappers & Miners be embarked in the *Geyser*? The order for this Company to be held in readiness will be only given this evening.

The arrangements with respect to the other two Regiments for the Cape that has [*sic*] been approved by his Lordship is as follows.

The 3d Battn Rifle Brigade to be embarked at Portsmouth or Southampton for Gibraltar and the 96th Regt at Dublin for Gibraltar. The Steamers which take these Regiments to Gibraltar will receive on Board at that station the 13th & 89th Regiments[,] each 800 men[,] & convey them to the Cape.

This will cause some short delay but[,] as one Regt[,] the Artillery & Sappers & Miners proceed at once from this Country, it is not

[1]Major Gen. Sir Charles Yorke, K.C.B., G.C.B. (1790–1880). Military Secretary, 1854–60.

[2]The dispatch of these troops coincided with the creation of the colony of Natal, separate from Cape Colony, and with famine and unrest among the Kaffirs.

considered of any great importance[,] but it is the only way in which this force can be sent out at the present moment with justice to the troops,
The 80th Regt[,] being in the Northern District[,] shall be embarked at Liverpool.

[**568**] *Milne Minute on Naval Education*[1]

Admiralty
29 July 1856

Circulate for any observations &c of the Members of the Board[:]
When this [new scheme for admission of naval cadets] is adopted[,] with any modifications which may be proposed, The [*sic*] staff of the Training Ships &c will have to be considered[.]
1. Are the present ships fit for the purpose of receiving the Cadets[?]
There will probably be 25 entered in October
25 in January
25 in April. at [*sic*] this time[,] 25 or a certain portion will pass out[,] say 15 out of 25. this [*sic*] will leave 60 Cadets in the Training ship[.] for this a larger ship than *Illustrious* will be required for School Room's [*sic*], Mess Place, officer Cabins &c[.] The accommodation is as follows[:]

1. The Poop Cabin – for the Captain
2. The Ward Room – for the officers of the ship
3. The Gunroom – for the officers and Cadets but not enough for more than 20.

No place for School Rooms &c[.]
The staff of Instructors will have to be for each ship (Ports[mouth] & Devonp[or]t)[:]

1. Naval Instructor

2 or 3 Assistants

1. French Master

1. Drawing Master combined with some other duties.

For Mess of Cadets, There [*sic*] will be required[:]

1. Steward

2. Under Do [understewards]

2. Cooks

[1]This paper accompanied a report on naval education for Cadets, followed by minutes from Wood, Berkeley, and Milne, Richards and Eden. This particular minute refers to a circular regarding the entry of Naval Cadets.

In the foregoing circular[1] we have gained an increased age[,] as we must admit that a Boy from 12 to 13 was [*sic*] too young to go to sea. With this increased age we obtain a higher standard of examination[.] We have six months instruction in the Training ship[,] which will be a good foundation for the youngsters, and we have a higher standard of examination when passing for Lieutenant. But I am afraid we have not made any advance in any general instruction between leaving the Training ship and the final examination, all this remains as at present. It strikes me some more defined Instructions to the Naval Instructors must be issued.

[**569**] *Milne to Wood*

Admiralty
10 September 1856

My dear Sir Charles

Mr Hammond[2] has just been with me[,] in Ad Eden and Richards absence[,] and was very anxious that Instructions should be sent out to Malta by this Evenings Mail to prepare two or three sail of the line and as many steam Frigates to join an equal force of the French at some appointed rendezvous[,] and to proceed from thence to Naples.[3]

Mr Hammond left the enclosed papers for me to send to you[,] which please to return to him. I could not act on Mr Hammonds wish without reference to you, more especially as a Telegraph can be sent to the Consul at Marseilles to be sent on to Stopford at Malta by the same Mail Steamer which will convey tonight Mail from Marseilles to Malta.

I am not aware what ships are at Malta, but the *Hannibal* might be stopped if she has not passed, and Lord Lyons might be Telegraphed to at Constantinople.

Mr Hammond was not aware whether the ships were to be in the Command of an English or a French Officer, but the orders to be given to the English Senior officer would be to protect British Interest in the absence of civil agents.

[1]'Memorandum – Naval cadets – Midshipmen, Regulations for Entry, Examination, &c, July 1856'.

[2]Edmund, first Baron Hammond (1802–90). Permanent Undersecretary of State for Foreign Affairs, 1854–73.

[3]The Anglo-French intervention at Naples was prompted by the misrule of Neapolitan King Ferdinand II (1830–59), in particular maltreatment of political prisoners and the resumption of political trials despite British and French objections. On British actions, see 'Correspondence relative to Naples', *Parliamentary Papers* 1857, vol. XXXVIII, pp. 100–103.

I find *Majestic* has gone to Vourla Bay[1] under sail.

Will you say what is to be done and what orders are to be sent out by Telegraph. Mr Hammond had not time to send a public letter but will do so.

Eden has gone out of town for 48 Hours, Richards is laid up with a swollen foot but carries on in his own House . . . .

nothing [*sic*] yet decided about the [?Gunners] going to the Cape.

We have only the *Urgent* and *Vulcan* fit for service[;] the others are all in the Hands of the Engineers. *Perseverance* goes to the Indies to perform the removal of the Black Troops.

I will send a messenger to meet the Express Train on its arrival in London at 4 PM tomorrow in case you should send up any parcel in charge of the Guard[.]

A Steamer might be sent to Admiral Dundas to order the *Conqueror* on to Malta.

Cressy is ready for Sea at Spithead but 50 short of Compl[emen]t.

[**570**] *Milne to Wood*

Admiralty
10 September 1856, 6:30 p.m.

My dear Sir Charles

Since writing to you my Former [*sic*] letter[,] Mr Hammond has been again to me[,] after having seen Lord Palmerston[,] who wished me to write you to say Lord Lyons should on no account leave the Bosphorus[.]

The 2 ships under Admiral Dundas would answer every purpose if they could be sent there (to Medtn). I presume he means with Admiral Dundas and[,] if thought necessary[,] another Ship of the Line could be sent from England. *Cressy* is ready with the exception of her crew, requiring about 50 men.

[**571**] *Milne to Wood*

Admiralty
11 September 1856

Dear Sir Charles

I find the Transport Board was appointed by a warrant from the Admiralty and not by an Act of Parliament, and it was constituted for a

[1]On the east coast of Turkey.

period not exceeding six months after the ratification of a Treaty of Peace. The Peace was signed at Paris on the 30th of March last[,] consequently the Transport Board would cease on the 30th of this month[.]

I find the Vote for the Board, salaries &c, has been taken for the whole financial year.

After reading the report sent to you by Cap Craigie[,] a copy of which he sent to me, I do not think it will be possible to reduce the Number of Directors until the End of the Year, as there is still a good deal of detail matters [*sic*] which requires their attention, and owing to the large number of accounts to be examined[,] the office itself cannot be reduced to a Peace Estab[lishmen]t until after March next[,] if then. It appear's [*sic*] to me it would be advisable to renew the warrant for six months longer, that is up to the end of the financial year, and in the meantime to reduce from time to time as it may be found possible to do so. If you approve of this course[,] a Letter should perhaps be sent to the Treasury stating the case and what you propose to do.

There is nothing new here. This evening the *Dido* is in the entrance to the Channel having been spoken [to] by a Steamer.

Richards has written to you about Cap Nias[1] and Mr Triscott.[2] It appears now absolutely necessary to have some public investigation[.] Matters cannot go on any longer as they are. I really believe Mr Triscott is somewhat wrong in the head[,] and have always had that idea. I have seen Mr Moubray[3] from Constantinople and [am] much pleased with his manner &c. he [*sic*] asked me to aid him with you about the Clarence Yard[,] but I pointed out to him his position as a Pay[maste]r of 1841 was not more to his advantage[,] and he is to reconsider his application[.] he appear's [*sic*] a very superior man and he has done his work well.

I have received your letter and have recalled *Cressy*'s former orders for her to proceed to sea when ready and to join Ad. Dundas off the

[1]Joseph Nias, C.B., K.C.B. (*c*.1795–1879). Entered, 1807; Lt, 1820; Cmdr, 1827; Capt., 1835; Rear-Adm., 1857; Vice-Adm., 1863; Adm. (Ret.), 1867; Superintendent of the Royal William Victualling Yard.

[2]Samuel Triscott, Storekeeper at the Royal William Victualling Yard. The sole surviving information on this dispute appears to be the Admiralty Digest, ADM12/625, which states that Nias sent four letters of complaint about Triscott on 6, 9, 10, and 15 September 1856, and that Triscott supplied counterstatements. Additionally, Triscott's brother, a merchant captain, complained 'that Captain Nias had refused him permission to land' at the yard quay. The 'Board . . . received these papers with much regret' and appointed a Committee consisting of Sir William Parker, Henry Ducie Chads, and William Fanshawe Martin to inquire 'into each officer's conduct.' For subsequent letters on the matter, see [**572**, **574**, **591**]

[3]Paymaster George Moubray.

Tagus[,] Vigo[,] or Cadiz and deliver to him the orders which would be enclosed[,] and your letter.

The orders to Dundas are to proceed to Gib[ralta]r to complete Coal[,] Water & Provisions[,] as a Mail leaves Southampton for Gib[ralta]r on 16th & 19th, which will enable Lord P[almerston] to arrange a rendezvous[,] if necessary[,] or orders the ships to Naples or Malta as may be wished. I have teleghd to Malta to detain 3 Steam Frigates or Sloops at that place until further orders.

[**572**] *Milne to Wood*

Admiralty
12 September 1856

Dear Sir Charles

I enclose you some remarks about the Coast Guard.[1]

I received your note about Cap Hope.[2] The *Cressy* has sailed this afternoon and would have gone this morning had not her orders been recalled. She may be some days in finding Admiral Dundas[,] and they may not get to Gibraltar before the packet[,] which leaves this on the morning of the 17th, by which time the F.O. may have fixed something definite with the French in regard to a rendezvous. I think it is as well that Dundas should go. a [*sic*] Rear Admiral with his Flag will have more weight than a senior officer[,] and as Hope has gone to Vourla[,] he would probably not have been in time. The French ships are ready.

There is no news of any sort about naval matters. Cap Nias has sent up a very extraordinary letter. He says he was accosted in the Vict[uallin]g Yard by a Gentleman who saluted him which he returned. The Gentleman offered him a note. Cap Nias['s] answer was if you will come to my office I will transact any business there you may have, and walked on. he [*sic*] looked round to see whether the Stranger was following when he called [']Captain Sir you are the greatest brute I ever met with[',] which he repeated several times. This Stranger is a Dr Budd[3] of Plymouth. This is all we know, but I presume we will have Dr Budds version of this business tomorrow.

I send you a proof of the regulations for the Coast Guard Men[.]

[1]Not preserved with this copy.

[2]James Hope.

[3]See ADM12/625. Nias reported 'that he turned Dr. Budd out of the Yard for calling him "a Brute" without the slightest provocation.' Budd, in turn, complained 'that Capt Nias treated him in the most discourteous manner' and requested an enquiry. The matter was referred to the Committee already investigating the Nias–Triscott affair.

[**573**] *Milne to Wood*

Admiralty
15 September 1856

Dear Sir Charles

I have again gone over the paper's [*sic*] relating to the proposed Regulations of the Cadets, and I have read Cap Mends[1] letter which you sent me last week. It clearly points out[,] and with perfect truth and accuracy, how little is to be expected or gained by Cadets in general education when serving afloat.

We all admit that the Greenwich Boy's [*sic*] are better instructed and have higher attainments than the Cadets entering, and this is owing to their having passed five years in an Estab[lishmen]t peculiarly adapted for giving instruction.

We also admit that the entry of Cadets between the Ages of 12 and 13 is far too young and some think that 15 is too old.

Assuming that 14 is the Age which would satisfy all the old officers as the fair time for entry[,] and that they should go into Sea going ships as soon after that as possible, It [*sic*] remains for us to decide what is to be done.

The Greenwich Boy leaves the Estab[lishmen]t at 15 year's [*sic*] of Age, having been entered there between the ages of 10 and 11.

Now I see no prospect of ever our being enabled to obtain any fair standard of Naval Education, unless a Naval School or College is established for this purpose, to receive Boys on nomination at the age of 10[,] and to pass them out at 14, into Sea Going ships.

Now are you prepared to do this[?] I do not think the expense will be large, but there are objections which may be urged against it, and I know Sir Francis Baring objected to the reestab[lishmen]t of the College.

Now[,] failing the reestablishment of the College[,] what can be done next[?] If the Age is extended to 15, The [*sic*] Board appears to object to reducing the time to be served by a Midshipman from the present rule of 6 years to the intended new rule of 5 Year's [*sic*], because he would not have time to gain sufficient experience in Seamanship, which previously required 6 years; but as Cadets were formerly entered at 13[,] 6 years service brought them to 19 years of age, but the Boy entering at 15 and serving 6 years would make him 21. Consequently[,] instead of reducing the Age of Captain's &c[,] it would[,] by

[1]William Robert Mends.

making 6 years as the period of service, be increasing their age before they could be promoted, which is an evil to be avoided.

Perhaps the best Plan would be to fix the Age between 13 and 14½[, and] modify the proposed new Regulations for entry, which are generally thought to be rather high.

To reconsider the whole Circular[,] and to modify where it is thought to be rather too stringent, and to issue it, retaining the Cadets 6 months in the Training Ship, and giving every reasonable assistance in sea going ships [*sic*]. I really do not see what more can be done.

The Captains of ships must be specially directed to take all requisite steps and to afford every assistance to the Naval Instructors & to enforce the Admiralty Orders.

[**574**] *Milne to Wood*

Admiralty
15 September [1856]

Dear Sir Charles

I have no doubt of Cap J Hopes judgment[,] and I think he would be a good reasonable man to be Senior Officer, he has also experience, but an Admiral would carry more weight, unless you gave Cap Hope a Blue Pendt. I certainly have a good opinion of him. Warren[1] is also a good man. I have made enquiry about Captain Sparke Thompson.[2] I find I do not know him. Cap Eden does and served with him[,] or rather together, he says he is a good man[,] a perfect Gentleman[,] and a very fair officer, and he has a very good opinion of him. This is all I can find out concerning him.

I send you the enclosed[3] which has just come in from the Printer[;] the other papers I will send tomorrow[.] I have added the share's [*sic*] of Prizes captured to it. Some department ought to send a circular to say what is going to be done. The Treasury I presume should do it[,] as the Treasury I suppose will order the Transfer [*sic*] to the Admiralty[.] The Admiralty cannot do it as the Coast Guard is not yet under us.

This point has occurred to me. suppose [*sic*] a man has entered for continuous service for 10 years[.] is he to be allowed to join the Coast

[1]Probably Richard Laird Warren (*c*. 1810–1875). Entered, 1822; Lt, 1829; Cmdr, 1833; Capt., 1839; Rear-Adm., 1858; Vice-Adm., 1865; Adm. 1870.

[2]Thomas Sparke Thompson (*c*.1799–1873). Entered, 1811; Lt, 1824; Cmdr, 1832; Capt., 1846; Rear-Adm., 1864; Vice-Adm. (Ret.), 1871.

[3]Not included among Milne's papers, but certainly relative to the impending transfer of the Coast Guard to Admiralty jurisdiction.

Guard before the 10 years expire[?] I should say 'yes' but this will have to be decided.

The Surgeon of *Dido* has written for a Court Martial on the two Lieutenants for unofficer like conduct connected with the mess amounts we have ordered.

Codrington[1] has been here this [day] complaining of the extravagance and debts of his midshipmans mess[,] which he only found out as the ship was being paid off[.] I suspect before we can stop all of this mess business and the extravagance &c that is going on[,] we must try some officers by Court Martial[,] and unless some such measure is taken[,] officers will do as they like, and they will think the Admiralty care nothing about the matter.

Nias's business is a very serious one. Mr Phinn[2] was very anxious for a Civilian to be on the Inquiry and I gave him my views, as Eden and Richards were inclined to adopt his recommendation, but I said then as I now do, that if a civilian was placed on such an Inquiry with two Admirals, it was [*sic*] the first time that such an order was given. In the case of differences between Cap Supdt Nicholas[3] and Dr Rae[4] at the Naval Hospital at Ply[mou]th in 1849–50, Sir W. Gage and two other (naval officers) [*sic*] were ordered to make the inquiry[,] and Sir Wm Burnett[5] was ordered to be present to assist the Board of Officers if they should require it [*sic*][.] I thought on this occasion Mr Grant[,] as Compt of V[ictualling,] might be ordered to attend in the same manner . . .

[**575**] *Milne to Saunders Dundas*

Admiralty, Private
19 September 1856

My dear Dundas

Your orders have gone by mail of this Evening for you to proceed from Gibraltar to Ajaccio in Corsica, with *Duke of Wellington*[,] *Conqueror* and Gun Boats, dispatching one Gun Boat to wait at Marseilles

[1]Sir Henry John Codrington, C.B., K.C.B. (1808–1877). Entered, 1823; Lt., 1829; Cmdr, 1831; Capt., 1836; Rear-Adm., 1857; Vice-Adm., 1863; Adm., 1867.

[2]Thomas Phinn (1814–66). M.P., 1852–55; Counsel for the Admiralty, 1854–55; Admiralty Permanent Secretary 1855–57.

[3]John Toup Nicholas (or Nicolas), C.B., K.H., K.F.M. (1788–1851). Entered, 1797; Lt, 1805; Cmdr, 1809; Capt., 1815; Rear-Adm., 1850. Nicholas was Superintendent of the Royal William Victualling Yard 1847–50.

[4]James Rae, M.D.

[5]The Navy's Medical Dir-Gen.

for any orders which may be sent for your leaving Ajaccio &c, as the French are only to have 2 sail of the line and 2 or 3 Frigates. The *Cressy* is to go on to Malta to follow the orders of Lord Lyons and Stopford has orders to send you a couple of Steamers to meet you at Ajaccio, which place you are on no account to leave without further orders from this. Ajaccio is the rendezvous fixed by the French and you will most probably find French ships there[.] The Instructions under which you will have to act at Naples are not yet fixed[,] but I dare say will be some days hence[,] and you will receive them via Marseilles. we [*sic*] have no news for you from this. you [*sic*] will have to make demands on Malta for what you may want.
Sir C Wood[,] Berkeley and Eden out of Town[.] Richards was laid up with a sore foot but is now all right again and at work[.]

[**576**] *Milne to Stopford*

Admiralty, Confidential
19 September 1856

My dear Stopford

You received a Telegh some days ago to stop 3 Steam Frigates or Sloops at Malta until further orders. I may mention to you confidentially that they were intended for a Squadron of Naples [*sic*]. Dundas with *Duke of Wellington*[,] *Conqueror* and 3 Gun Boats is now ordered from Gibraltar to Ajaccio in Corsica, there to wait [for] further orders from this. you [*sic*] will now receive orders to send 2 Steam frigates or Sloops to join him at that place. we [*sic*] hope you have <u>2</u> vessels[.] if not[,] you must endeavour to find them, as we are to send to Ajaccio and subsequently to Naples the same amount of force as the French[.] keep this entirely to yourself but have the vessels you send complete.

Cressy is ordered to Malta to be dispatched from Dundas as <u>now</u>[,] only 2 Sail of the Line are required[.] there is nothing more to add[.] the third steamer will not be required to be detained at Malta[.]

Sir C Wood[,] Berkeley and Eden are out of Town[.] I therefore write you & him[1] [un]officially from this[,] that you may be aware what is going on[.] Dundas is told to make any demands on you[.] He will no doubt want <u>Coal</u> &c[.]

[1]Saunders Dundas.

[**577**] *Milne to Wood*

Admiralty
6 October 1856

I have been giving a good deal of consideration to the Cadet question, since you last spoke to me on the subject. you [*sic*] then appeared to me to be in favor of a Training Ship as a substitute for a College, on board of which the Cadet should be one year[.] If you adhere to this view, it strikes me it somewhat modifies the proposed regulation of increasing the age from 14 to 15.

I think the starting point for establishing the new regulations would be to fix a rule, 'That Cadets should go into sea going ships not later than 15 years of Age.' I think this is a fair age for their going into such ships. If more advanced[,] it might be objectionable their being in Harbour &c[,] and having after wards [*sic*] so short a period of actual sea-life.

Assuming this rule as one which is fixed, and that the Cadet is to be one year in the Training Ship, it is obvious he must be entered at 14 and the nomination be given between 13 & 14[,] allowing say 3 months for his appearance at the College after receiving his nomination.

This changes the whole feature of the Circular, and until the Age of entry is fixed and the period of time in the Training Ship, nothing further can be done. Pray do not answer this[.] I merely write the new view, which presents itself.

I do not see any reason why an examination of Lieutenants to the Rank of Comdr should not be established[.]

[**578**] *Wood to Milne*

Hickleton
7 October 1856

Dear Captain Milne

I do not know what the practice is, as to appointing a paymaster to the [Royal] Yacht. I should name Moubray at once & unless it is usual to send 3 names to the Queen[,] I would write to her recommending Moubray. They ought to know in the private office . . . Will you let me know if you agree as to Moubray, & tell me at the same time, what is usual as to submitting name[s:] a name [*sic*] or more names to HM.

I think at any rate a short E [*sic*] breakwater will be necessary at Alderney.

Thanks for your note on Cadetships. There will be several alterations in the Circular. I send you Sir F Baring's last view for perusal.[1]

[579] *Milne Memorandum on Transferral of the Coast Guard*

[October 1856]

The Coast Guard is at present the only available Naval reserve of seamen, and so far as the limited number of men embarked during the war[,] viz about 2,200 men, It [*sic*] was found that they were of much value from their steady conduct and experience.

The Admiralty ought to adopt every available measure for Extending [*sic*] this force and keeping it efficient.

1. The number of men in the Coast Guard should be increased by not less than 1000 men.

2d[.] None but seamen from the Navy or seafaring men should be allowed in the force.

3d. Officers and men should be inspected every year and those unfit by Age or other causes should be pensioned or otherwise removed.

I believe I am correct in saying that the Admiralty experienced no difficulty in obtaining the men from the Coast Guard when they were required in 1854, and the men are compelled by the Act 17. Vic chap. 73 to serve when required[.]

If the Admiralty can under the present regulations easily obtain the services of the Coast Guard men when they are wanted? If these men whilst in the Coast Guard are trained to the Guns? If all inefficient men are annually withdrawn and efficient men entered to fill up vacancies[?] [Then] I do not see what object is to be gained by any transfer of that force to the Admiralty, which would burden the department with the whole duties connected with that Force and the protection of the Revenue.

The Coast Guard is a force created for the protection of the revenue, it is therefore attached to the Revenue Department, with a proviso of being withdrawn for Naval Service when specially required.

If I assume that this force is transferred to the Admiralty and the men borne on Ships Books what is gained[?]

1. Do we obtain any more advantage for securing the services of the men[?]

None, because that is already secured by Act of Parliament[.]

2. Would the discipline and efficiency of the men be improved[?]

[1]Not preserved in Milne's papers.

I think not.

I must acknowledge I do not see my way to any advantage by a transfer of [the] duties to the Admiralty. The Coast Guard regulations in regard to Duties, Pay, Allowances, Pensions &c are well defined. If this is so, why not leave matters in principle as present[?]

We get the men when we want them.

We do not interfere with the detail duties of another Depart[men]t of the Crown[.]

We reap all the advantages of the Coast Guard when we require them [*sic*], without any of the trouble of having to perform the duties of the Department.

But I think the Force ought to be increased and efficient men alone retained . . .

[**580**] *Milne to Wood*

Admiralty, Private
7 October 1856

Dear Sir Charles

I am afraid you will think me troublesome and that I am raising difficulties &c[,] but it is not so. It is right I should point out matters of detail which will require your careful consideration before you go further in the Coast Guard business, and before you commission any of the ships[.] The moment the Pendants are hoisted there will at once arise questions to be settled and it appears to me more advisable that these should be decided before hand [*sic*].

I enclose some rules &c.

I don't see my way at all clear, or what shape the correspondence is to take when the ships are commissioned. As it stands at present, the Comp[trolle]r General can go on, but when the Pendants are up his position is changed[:] he will no longer have any power. I write this in entire ignorance of what is intended[,] but now[,] as Eden has brought the Coast Guard Instructions to revise[,] I am in a difficulty not knowing what to decide or how to word the regulation.

[581] *Milne Memorandum on Proposed Coast Guard Regulations*

[Admiralty
7 October 1856]

Coast Guard
The Comp[troller] G[enera]l [of the Coast Guard] and his Depart[ment] are both civil officers [*sic*], having no authority or power over any of HM Ships in commission[.]
The Coast Guard Ships will be in all respects as any of HM Ships in Commission[,] also the Revenue vessels[.]
Therefore[,] so soon as any of HM Ships for the Coast Guard are Commissioned and Coast Guard Men put on the Ships Books[,] the Comp[trolle]r General can exercise no authority whatever over them.
The former Coast Blockade was under the orders of the Commander[s] in Chief at Portsmouth & Chatham[.]
Let me assume that a ship is put in Commission at Portsmouth. The Captain & Ship will be fitted out under the orders of the Admiral. She sails[,] say for Newhaven. when [*sic*] she is there, under whose orders is she to be[?] From whom will he [the Captain] receive the numerous orders about the discipline, Pay [*sic*], provisions, savings on men, stores &c[,] and to whom are demands for stores to be sent for approval[?]

The Comp[trolle]r G[enera]l can exercise no authority whatever. He is a civilian. If the Admiralty is to do this, it will be bringing detail duty on the office which is the duty of an Admiral at the out Ports, and it will be making the Admiralty into an executive department[.]

The Coast Guard being in Commission, it would appear to be necessary that the Comp[trolle]r General should also be in Commission.

The Transport Board could not give any orders to the Sup[erinten]d[en]ts of the Yards or any of HM Troop Ships in Commission, in all such cases that Board had to make a submission to the Admiralty that such & such orders should be given[.]

This was seldom required[,] as there were few Troop Ships in Commission, but as the whole Coast Guard will be in Commission[,] the same form for conducting its duties could not be carried out.

The Surveyor of the Navy can deal with questions of the Dock Yards and their Civil Establishments, but he cannot give an order in reference to a ship in commission; so it is with the Comp[trolle]r G[enera]l of the Coast Guard[;] he can order &c &c[,] so long as it is a Civil Estab[lishmen]t[,] but put the Coast Guard in Commission and the Comp[trolle]r G[enera]l has no longer any power[.]

The Head of the Coast Guard must be in London[;] if he goes away his second in Command ought to be Senior to the Captains of the Districts, or else a junior officer will be commanding a senior.[1]

[**582**] *Milne to Wood*

Admiralty
9 October 1856

Dear Sir Charles

I return you Sir F. Baring's Letter with many thanks[.]

How would it answer to have the Entries &c as follows[:]

1. Appointments made between the Ages of 13 & 14[,] to be appointed to the Training Ship for one year.

2. Appointments made between 14 & 15 to be to seagoing ships. The Examination between 14 & 15 to be a higher standard than for those entered between 13 & 14.

[**583**] *Wood to Milne*

Hickleton
9 October 1856

Dear Captain Milne

I was aware that there would be some difficulty about the points on which you have written to me relative to the Coast Guard, but I confess I thought they had been difficulties <u>of detail</u> only. Indeed[,] I thought that I had had some conversation with you on the subject & that you had agreed that the difficulties were of detail only. Berkeley has always been for an Admiral with his flag flying, & I am inclined to think that if we are to raise so completely a novel & independent organization[,] there are advantages in having a flag officer. But I am averse to giving it such an organization, in the first instance at any rate[,] & in peace [time]. The duties are so entirely civil at present & the force is of so mixed a character[,] & it will be necessary to watch it so closely in the beginning[,] that I prefer its being if possible under the Admiralty. My notion was that all the ships with all their complements would be placed under the Commanders in Chief of the respective stations, with orders to them not to interfere in carrying on the Coast Guard duties. For all such purposes [there would be] no Courts Martial[,] he [*sic*]

[1]There is no evidence that Wood saw this memorandum.

would be under the Civil [code]. With regard to the questions you mention [regarding] pay[,] provisions[,] &c, I really do not know to what extent they go, or whether there could be any difficulty in their going thro' the Commander in Chief. I have always understood that the Surveying Service was on this footing, that the discipline &c was under the Civil [authorities,] but that the surveying duty was carried on under directions from the Civilian Hydrographer. The Comptroller General would act somewhat as the Hydrographer does, somewhat as the Surveyor does in relation to the Superintendents[,] who have flags or pendants flying. You can say much better than I can whether the practical difficulties of this course are insuperable.

The second course is for the Adm[iralt]y to give orders on the report of the C[omptroller] General in such matter as cannot be done properly by the C[ommande]rs in Chief. This throws detail upon them, unless standing orders can be given. The practicality of this would depend very much on the number & nature of the orders to be given, & of that I cannot . . . here form an opinion.

If Cap Eden & yourself do not see your way, I am afraid I cannot help you. He knows the nature of the orders for ships in commission. If you cannot adopt a practice of the Surveying Service or Transport Service to the C[oast] Guard, I am afraid I must give up the point. But it certainly will in my opinion be unfortunate. It renders it necessary to have a Comptroller & Deputy Comptroller, Admirals or Senior Captains. I don't know how a junior flag officer could command in a military sense, ships in [*sic*] different stations under different C[ommande]rs in Chief. The Admiral of the Coast Guard[,] flag flying[,] could be under the C in C of Portsmouth as to 2 ships, under [the] C in C. of Devonport for 4 or 5, & so on. I do not see that giving him his flag would obviate all difficulties. It would <u>change</u> them, but try that scheme, & I think you will find strong objections to it, c.f. If [*sic*] the Ad[miralt]y sends an order to the Admiral of the C[oast] G[uard], is it to go through the Port Admirals according to the ships or to which it relates [*sic*]? Or is [it] to go to him in London[,] irrespective of the station of the ships? Is he to summon Courts Martial of C[oast] guard officers only? Or is a ship to be ordered to Portsmouth or Devonport to have a trial? There are no doubt difficulties in all cases, & so there must be in an anomalous service; as it is & must be. But if the difficulties are not very formidable indeed [as] in the Civilian Establishment of the Comptroller General – I prefer it. You say the Coast Blockade was under the C in Ch. I suppose they did not give orders regarding the civil duties of the prevention of smuggling. Who gave them? But it affords a precedent I suppose.

I have written at greater length than I intended & may have made mistakes from ignorance, but I think you will understand what I mean & wish so far as my knowledge goes.

[**584**] *Milne Memorandum on Transferring the Coast Guard to Admiralty Control*[1]

[Admiralty
October 1856]

Coast Guard
First Plan
[Plan:] Captain Eden as Comp[trolle]r General[,] holding a Civil appointment as at present.
[Milne:] The Comp[trolle]r G[enera]l as a civilian will be unable to give any order to any officers or men in Commission. He will have to make submissions to the Admiralty for orders to be given.

[Plan:] All the Coast Guard Ships to be under the direct orders of the Admiralty as ships employed on Special Service. To hoist the Red Ensign and Pendant[,] and not to be under the orders of the Commanders in Chief of the Stations.
[Milne:] It will be necessary to establish a Coast Guard Office at Whitehall for the purpose of carrying out the detail of the Coast Guard Service, and not only with reference to the Ships, but also to give those orders &c formerly carried out by the Board of Customs[,] see accompanying paper A[.][2] If this should be, All [*sic*] Letters, Returns, Correspondence, and references would be sent direct to the Secr[etar]y of the Admiralty with 'Coast Guard' on the left corner of the envelope[.]
As these ships will be under Martial Law, the whole arrangement in regard to them must be under one of the Senior [Lords] of the Board. Orders would be given to the Captains of ships and districts direct from the Admiralty, but these would[,] in the first Instance[,] be in the shape of submissions from the Compt[trolle]r General[,] or Letters would be previously referred to him for answer's [*sic*], to be carried out by an Admiralty Order.
The Admirals at the out Ports would [have to] be made acquainted with any orders given for the movement of a ship from one Port to another

[1]Milne filled out the system as proposed in one column, and followed with his critique of each point in red ink in the other. There is no evidence that Wood saw this memorandum.

[2]Not included with this copy.

within his [*sic*] Command, as with [regard to] the discharge of men from any of his Ships to the Coast Guard &c.

[Plan:] At present the Comp[trolle]r General appoints all officers and men to Coast Guard Station, removes them as he sees fit, Issues [*sic*] orders to the Coast Guard.
[Milne:] The Comptroller General could not appoint, as the officers will now be required to <u>have commissions</u> made out at <u>Whitehall</u> for particular ships, but he might <u>submit</u> for approval of the Board.

[Plan:] The Inspecting Commanders of Stations, report to the Comp[trolle]r General everything connected with the <u>district</u> under his charge, also all wrecks, seizures, conduct of officers & men, men absent or sick, State of Buildings & Boats, Stores, Reserve Vessels [&c]. He approves of the Pay Lists of the Men for the Collectors of Customs[,] Keep's [*sic*] a contingent account for each quarter of [*sic*: for] special expenses, Portage, &c.
[Milne:] The Inspecting Commanders will have to send these returns to the Captains of the District, for Transmission to the Sec[retar]y of the Admiralty for the Comp[trolle]r General.

[Plan:] New appointment of a Captain of a District may include several Inspecting Commanders
What are to be his duties[?]
1. Captain of the Guard Ship
2. Cap of the Coast Volunteers
3. As Captain of the District to receive all reports of the Inspecting Commanders and transmit them to the Admiralty[,] to inspect the district under his orders, & to report to the Board.
[Milne:] This will be doing a [*sic*] duty now performed by the Inspecting Commander[s,] for if the Captain is appointed to a district, this must become his duty.

[Plan:] The visitation of the Comp[trolle]r General to the Coast Guard Districts is now enforced for the purpose of inspecting the officers and men, state of the Buildings &c.
[Milne:] The Comp[trolle]r General as a civilian would be in a false position if he visited HM Ships in Commission in the districts.

Second Plan
[Plan:] The Comp[trolle]r General of the Coast Guard to have a Commission as a Commodore and to be checked for Service in London.
[Milne:] Might be borne on one of the Guard Ships of the Coast Guards Book, and his Pendant struck, but he cannot hoist it again in any ship

except the one for which he holds a Commission[,] unless he has a Commission as a Commodore of [the] 1st Class.

[Plan:] All ships to be under the direct orders of the Admiralty as ships employed on Special Service[.] To hoist the Red ensign and Pendant[,] and not to be under the orders of the Commanders in Chief[,] or to be under the orders of the Commodore in Command of the Coast Guard for all matters of detail duty.
[Milne:] If this plan should be adopted[,] there must be a special office at Whitehall and the details of the Coast Guard Service will have to be worked out and be superintended by a Senior Member of the Board.

[Plan:] All letters, returns, correspondence to be sent to the Comptr[oller] General of the Coast Guard, who will submit to the Admiralty all matters which are connected with Discipline[,] discharges of officers & men and which are not Coast Guard detail[.]
All correspondence connected with the Coast Volunteers to be sent to the Admiralty[.]

[**585**] *Wood to Milne*

Hickleton
[*c.*10 October 1856]

Dear Capt Milne
. . . How is the Surveying Service done? All matters [there] go on without rub. . . . I shall be very sorry if we must have a Naval officer in commission to [rule] it [the Coast Guard] . . .

[**586**] *Wood to Milne*

Hickleton
12 October 1856

Dear Capt Milne
I see that we shall not get forward with the C[oast] Guard by correspondence, so I will come up on Tuesday evening. do [*sic*] be ready for work on Wednesday.

I write to Berkeley to meet me, so that we shall have a full Board.

I am sorry that you find so much difficulty. I certainly had not anticipated so much. I am very unwilling, I confess[,] to have an Admiral or Commodore over all the Coast of the United Kingdom, but it may be necessary.

[587] *Wood to Milne*

21 October 1856

Dear Captain Milne

I have suggested several alterations in the Instructions.

The Captains[,] I think[,] should have all ordinary matters go through them, or else they will be passed by & not have the proper authority or responsibility over the officers & men ashore.

The Adm[iralt]y must[,] I think[,] appoint to the ship & district, of course on the representation of the Comptroller . . . moving from one station to another of a different district involves a commission to a different ship. This sh[oul]d be done by the Adm[iralt]y, allowing [that movement] within the district sh[oul]d be [the] responsibility of the C[omptroller] general.

Nothing else occurs to me . . .

[588] *Milne to Wood*

Admiralty
21 October [1856]

Dear Sir Charles

I send you herewith the Articles of War. No one whose duty it is to deal with the subject has ever taken the trouble to have them corrected with reference to Acts of Parliament which have passed. I have revised them and added the necessary notes of explanation[,] so that any officer who reads them on the 1st of each month to the Ships [Company] may read the 'Law as it is' and not 'as it was', and as supplied to him by the Admi[ra]lty[.]

The Gentlemen at the head[s] of [the] important Branches of this office take no interest whatever in what goes on[,] and there is a want of system in all these matters which is quite lamentable to witness. When any regulation is ordered by the Board[,] it should be the duty of the Branch to see that everything connected with that order is carried out in all its various ramifications, but there is no such regulation, everything is left to chance or the lottery of any member of the Board doing these Gentlemen's duty. however [*sic*] I send to you what I would submit should be printed . . .

It is better to do this than to have to revise and consolidate the Articles of War[.]

[589] *Wood to Milne*

Hickleton
27 October 1856

Dear Captain Milne

I do not quite understand what is done with the Articles of War, & what is supplied to Officers. to [*sic*] enable me to come to a conclusion on your paper, I think I require conversation with you . . . Will you keep the papers till I come up[?] I think I see an improvement if I am right in my notions.

[590] *Wood to Milne*

Hickleton
29 October 1856

Dear Captain Milne

It seems to me that the best mode of dealing with the Revenue Cutter men will be to repay [i.e., refund] to men under 10 years service the sum they have paid to the superannuation fund[,] & then to give them [the] choice of discharge or going under the new arrangement.[1]

& [*sic*] with regard to men above 10 years service, to transfer them to the land service, so that we may get all men afloat on the Naval condition of service.

What do you & Eden say to these schemes?

[591] *Milne to Wood*

Admiralty
4 November [1856]

Dear Sir Charles

I hope I may be enabled to send you tomorrow a detailed return of all the complaints which are made against the Coast Guard regulation. Some are trivial, but there are others very difficult to deal with. It will never answer to place the present Coastguard [*sic*] men in a worse position than they are at present.

[1]This sentence deals again with the Coast Guard transferral question, specifically what to do with men serving according to Revenue Cutter standards, when they were brought under a different system.

I do not see how you can in any manner deprive them of any advantages which they possess.

For instance[,] the Widows pension and benefit to their Children on the death of the Parent by [*sic*] the Service. This Extents [*sic*: extends] to all men in the Coast Guard Service ashore or afloat. Again[,] it will be impossible to take from any man even one penny per Day and say to him [']you are to serve for a less sum of money than what you have hitherto received.['] If this is the case[,] what is to be done with the Men[?] are to they to be borne on Ships Books at their former rate of Pay, or are we to compromise with the men and say, we give you less pay but we give you lodgings free of rent[?] If this is to be so[,] we must make a separate agreement with each man now serving, and ask him to say whether he will agree to the new arrangement or not. These are matters requiring very serious consideration, for much harm may be done if matters are not made clear.

There are two Regiments[,] I hear[,] to go to [the] West Indies and then to come home. I will let you know what should be done about Troop Ships. There is also[,] I believe[,] a Regiment for Mauritius and China. we [*sic*] have only *Vulcan* & *Urgent* ready[,] and with so many Troop Ships belonging to the Service not in commission (*Simoom*, *Transit*, *Assistance* [&] *Himalaya*)[,] it will not do to be chartering vessels. The *Simoom* will be ready about 15 Nov. *Resolute* & *Assistance*[,] I am afraid[,] have not accommodation for a Commander and a Staff of Lieuts &c[,] unless they have a Poop built on them, but if they were commanded by a Master then they have enough space &c. The question is should they be a Commanders or a Masters Command[?] If the former[,] a Poop must be built and no delay should take place in doing so.

I am glad you are to be up on [the] 10th but I hope you will go to the Lord Mayor's Dinner[,] as except myself there is no one going from the Admiralty[.]

I believe the Nias enquiry closed today[.][1]

[1]The Court of Enquiry papers appear not to have been preserved, but Nias's service record in ADM196/6 states that on 8 November the 'Board considers that it is not desirable for the good of the Public Service that he [Nias] should continue any longer in the position of Capt Supt & suspended him accordingly.' The Board had earlier (1852) stated 'their strong disapprobation' at Nias's 'highly disrespectful conduct to his Commander in Chief, in direct violation of the Articles of War.'

[**592**] *Wood to Milne*

Hickleton
9 November 1856

Dear Captain Milne

Do not let the printed instructions for C[oast] guard be seen till we have gone carefully over them again. We cannot be too careful. As to the complaints & grumbling[,] it [*sic*] was sure to come. everybody [*sic*] wishes to retain all they have, & to get as much more as they can.

It may however be wise not to mix up the old men with the new ones. The new men clearly can have no cause of complaint. We ought[,] therefore[, to] compose a district entirely of non-seafaring men, & new entries. However[,] it will be time enough to discuss these matters when we meet. I shall be up on the 10th sharing the Lord Mayors dinner on that day. . . .

[**593**] *George F. Seymour to Milne*

Portsmouth
19 November 1856

My dear Capt Milne

I will set about revising Cochrane's[1] orders as the days shorten[,] but I do not think any one out of the Admiralty could make a full digest of the Admiralty's orders in a satisfactory manner, so I shall confine myself to what will tend to carry those out which relate to the Port duties, with reference[,] when necessary[,] to the circulars.

I am afraid Sir Baldwin[2] will not get much more out of the *Shannon* under steam than was obtained yesterday[,] and I am sorry the opportunity has not been taken of trying her sailing qualities with the *Raleigh*[,] which form so great an ingredient in her Probable [*sic*] advantages[.] 11 [knots] is a good rate[,] & if we expect faster steaming with Capacity [*sic*] I suspect we must go to the length and sharpness of the *Persia* or such ship.

[1]Sir Thomas Cochrane, the preceding C-in-C at Portsmouth.
[2]Baldwin Walker, Surveyor of the Navy.

[594] *George F. Seymour to Milne*

Portsmouth
20 November 1856

My dear Capt Milne

A small Committee here about the Clothing might not terminate a question which the officers who were appointed for the purpose at the Admiralty in the spring did not settle.[1] If it was desired to take the opinions of the officers in Command of ships at the Ports[,] there would be a precedent for asking Votes[,] as I remember when at the Admiralty about 1842 . . . that the Admirals at the Ports were directed (at Sir G Cockburns suggestion) to collect the Captains opinions as to each of certain articles.

About dress[,] I should be in favour of Blue Cloth Frocks of No 1 Cloth and Trowsers [*sic*] of No 2[.] The Badges look well on the former and in the *Flying Fish* and[,] I think[,] the *Cormorant*[,] the men had them of this material and looked remarkably well[,] as do some of the Boats Crews of other ships. Frocks of inferior material change colour & soon look ill[,] and when you have Jackets [of inferior material] there are rarely half a dozen alike or which fit the men[,] & they are oftener sold than frocks.

But selling is the great obstacle[,] and I do not see how it can be effectually remedied legally unless the Clothes belong to the man himself.

It is to be wished that the Men were allowed a suit of Clothes annually[,] and that the material might be made [?peculiar] or marked[,] and the job be illegal as in the Army[.][2] It will come to that at last[,] but the expense will make it objectionable to financiers[,][3] & it will not be feasible unless an increase of pay was under consideration[,] & then the Boon [*sic*] might take that shape.

Berkeley was over here today to see a Gun Boat hauled up but[,] as they were not ready[,] he went to see the *Bellerophon*[,] the new hull of which he quite approved.

[1]The Admiralty was considering reforming the system by which men were supplied with 'slop clothing'. At this point there was no standard uniform, men had to purchase their materials, and were often tempted to trade them for inferior goods ashore and pocket the difference.

[2]Seymour was suggesting that 1) the navy provide each enlisted man with a uniform *gratis* (one suit per year), and 2) that it be made of a distinctive material or marked in such fashion that it could not be duplicated by tailors onshore. This reform was duly enacted the following year, along with the adoption of uniform dress. See R. Taylor, 'Manning the Royal Navy: The Reform of the Recruiting System, 1852–1862,' *Mariner's Mirror*, 45, no. 1 (1959), p. 50, esp. n. 1.

[3]That is, the Treasury.

Adml Martin cannot arrange for the *Shannon* to be docked before next Thursday[.]

[**595**] *Gage to Milne*

Pharston, Bury St. Edmunds
18 [December] 1856

My dear Milne

As I know you pass this dreary period of the year far from home, I hope you will kindly accept my little tribute of regards for old acquaintance sake, in the shape of a Christmas Turkey which I shall forward by a train from this station tomorrow[,] which should arrive at the Admiralty on Saturday[.]

With my best regards to Mrs Milne . . .

[PS:] Is Nias [*sic*] to be relieved[?] If he be I think you and your Colleagues will also be relieved[.][1]

[**596**] *Milne Minute on Proposed Circular for Admission and Education of Naval Cadets*[2]

Admiralty
19 December 1856

The Circular enclosed is now framed to admit Cadets between the Ages of 13 and 15.

None who are examined at the College between the Ages of 13 and 14 will be appointed to the Training Ship for one year[.]

None who are examined between the ages of 14 and 15 will be at once appointed to Sea Going Ships. These gentlemen will pass a higher examination than those who enter between the Ages of 13 and 14[.]

When the circular was first drawn up[,] it was intended that all Cadets were to go to the Training Ship, but this would have kept Boys from 15 to 16 in Portsmouth Harbour, which was no doubt objectionable[.]

[1]Nias had already been relieved; see [**591**] and note 1 on p. 652.

[2]This memorandum was written in reference to 'Circular respecting Naval Cadets and Midshipmen'. It is clear from this collection of papers that Milne was in charge of revising the regulations for entry and examination; there is a great volume of correspondence to him from various officers he consulted in the revision. His summary memorandum explaining the proposed alterations, is reproduced here. ADM1/5676 also contains a copy of the new regulations, with Milne's annotation on it.

I must acknowledge there has been some difficulty in so arranging the future examinations of these Boys[,] as to place them as near as possible on a par with each other. to [*sic*] do so when there is a difference of age is impossible, but we must make such an arrangement as may be clearly understood and the sametime [*sic*] make each Cadet as near as practicable on par with the others[.]

I have drawn two proposals[,] No 1 making all the Cadets serve 18 months with that rating in <u>Sea Going Ships</u>. The other No. 2[,] I fix the age for passing for Mid. at the age of <u>16</u>[.] I incline to the plan <u>No. 1</u> as more just to those Cadets who have not had the advantage of the Training Ship.

To qualify for the Rank of Lieutenant he must have served <u>5</u> years at sea and be 19 years of age.

(1)	Training Ship		Seagoing Ship	
	1	2	3	4
	y/m	y/m	y/m	y/m
Suppose 4 Boys are appointed at the ages of	13	13/8	14	14/8
They will pass at the College	13/3	13/11	14/3	14/11
Go to Training Ship	13/3	13/11	–	–
Will go to Sea Going Ships as Cadets	14/3	14/11	14/3	14/11
Each Cadet must serve 18 months in a sea going ship where he is to pass for Mid at the age of	15/9	16/5	15/9	16/5
Each Mid must serve 18 Months before he can pass his intermediate examination at the age of	17/3	17/11	17/3	17/11
Each Candidate will be obliged to serve from the date of this examination[,] the time which he requires to complete for the rank of Lieutenant from the day on which he should have passed his intermediate examination. This he should do at the age of	19/–	19/–	19/3	19/11
Each officer would serve as Cadet	1/6	1/6	1/6	1/6
As Mid 1 [before intermediate exam]	1/6	1/6	1/6	1/6
2 [after intermediate exam]	1/9	1/1	2/–	2/–
In sea going ships	4/9	4/1	5	5
Allow time in Training ship	–/3	–/11		
[Total]	5	5	5	5

(2)	Training Ship		Seagoing Ship	
	1	2	3	4
	y/m	y/m	y/m	y/m
Suppose 4 Boys are appointed at the ages of	13	13/8	14	14/8
They will pass at the College	13/3	13/11	14/3	14/11
In Training Ship	1/–	1/–	–	–
Will be appointed to Sea Going Ships	14/3	14/11	14/3	14/11
There they are to serve as cadets until they 16 years of age when they may pass for Mid.	16	16	16	16
Then to serve 18 months[,] when they may pass the intermediate Examn at the age of	17/6	17/6	17/6	17/6
Each Candidate will then be required to serve from the date of this examination[,] that time to complete for the rank of Lieut. which was required when he had completed his first 18 Months as Mid[.] he would then pass for Lt. at the age of	19/–	19/–	19/3	19/11
Training Ship	1	1	–	–
Each officer would serve as Cadet	1/9	1/1	1/9	1/1
As Mid 1 [before intermediate exam] 2 [after intermediate exam]	3/–	3/–	3/–	3/–

The Circular has been framed on the plan of No 1.
I would be glad if any Member of the Board would point out anything that seems to be objectionable[.] If the Cadet was only to serve <u>one year</u> in a sea going [ship,] the Boy who enters above the age of 14 could not be qualified in the examination to pass for Mid.

[**597**] *Milne to Wood*

Admiralty
21 December 1856

Dear Sir Charles

I ought to have written to you last Evg about the Service of the Cadets, but was obliged to be absent during the afternoon.

The reason why they are now made to serve 18 months was to place those who enter under 14 and those who enter above it on a par with each other[,] and I was afraid the Boy who entered above 14 and who had to pass for Midshipman could not get up his examination in a sea going ship in <u>one</u> year. I admit it is somewhat hard on the Boys in the Training Ship, but I considered they were under instruction from the age of <u>13 to 14</u> on board the Training Ship, whilst those from 14 to 15 were under instruction on <u>shore</u>[.]

The one year as Cadet would no doubt be better for those Boys who come from the Training Ship[,] as with the time in that ship and the <u>one</u> years cadet time[,] they would be <u>two</u> years in the service, but if this be adopted for them it must likewise be adopted for the older Boys

	Training Ship				Sea Going Ship			
	y[ear]	m[onth]	y[ear]	m[onth]	y[ear]	m[onth]	y[ear]	m[onth]
	13	3	13	11	14	3	14	11
T ship	1	–	1	–	–	–	–	–
Cadet	1	–	1	–	1	–	1	–
[Age]	15	3	15	11	15	3	15	11

I made it 6 months later in each case. I see no objection to alter it to <u>One Year</u>[,] and at one time it was so made out, but it is giving the Older Boys who go to sea going ships but little experience, and it is reducing the present regulation <u>one year</u>[,] as those Cadets who <u>were entered</u> above 14 will have to serve <u>two years as Cadets</u>. It must not be forgotten that the Service as Cadet and Midshipman has been reduced from <u>6</u> years to <u>5</u>[,] and that <u>18</u> months out of <u>five</u> years is not too large a proportion of time to ask a Cadet to serve. However[,] I am not wedded to 18 months if you think it should be reduced.

[**598**] *Milne to Wood*

Admiralty
31 December 1856

Dear Sir Charles

I again send you a copy of the Cadet Circular, which will require explanation[.]

1. A Boy now enters the Service between 12 and 14 and has to serve 6 years[.]

The Boy of 12 has therefore to serve 7 years until 19 years of age[.]

The Boy of 13 has to serve 6 years until 19 years Do.

The Boy of 14 has to serve 6 years & will be <u>20</u> years[.]

This must be kept in view in regard to the New Regulations[.]

Applying this to the Boy who enters at[:]
13 and he[,] by serving 6 years[,] would be 19 years of age[.]
14 and he[,] by serving 6 years[,] would be 20[.]
15 and he would be 21[.]

This advanced age of 21 was a disadvantage to the new arrangement. it [*sic*] would also prove more generally disadvantageous in the new scheme than the old[,] as more Boys would no doubt be entered at or above 14 than formerly[.] consequently[,] if they were to serve 6 years[,] most of the Midshipmen on passing for Lieutenant would be about or above 20 years old and even 21.

To remedy this[,] it was proposed that the future service under the new system should be 5 years instead of 6.

I now start with the Five Year's [*sic*], but the Candidate before passing for Lieutenant must be 19 years of Age as formerly.

The Boy of[:]
13 – would complete his time (supposing there was no Training Ship) at 18 years of age[,] but must go on serving until 19 years of age.
14 at 19[,] and the Boy of 15 at 20.

Therefore so far as these 3 Boys are on the same conditions as to age for qualification for passing for Lieut as the 3 Boys of 12–13–14 on the old system of 6 years.

Now comes the difficulty[:]
1. Are the Boys who go to the Training Ship to count that time or not[?]
2. The Boy who goes direct into a sea going ship on his passing at College will have to serve as follows.

At 14.3 into a sea going ship, 18 months as a Cadet, 18 months to the Intermediate Examination[,] and 2 years more to complete 5 years service[.] he will be 19.3 years of age[.] again 14.9 into sea going ship[,] 18 months Cadet, 18 months to the Intermediate Examination 2 years to make up 5 years service[,] and he will be 20 years of Age.

So that these Boys[,] by serving only 5 years[,] will not be older when passing for Lieutenant than the Boys who had to serve 6 years under the Old Regulation, but there will no doubt be more of them [*sic*].

I may here state, that in framing the Circular as it now is, I wanted to make all those Cadets who passed at the College between 13 and 14 to be able to pass for Lieutenant at one age viz. 19. to [*sic*] do this[,] some of the Training Ships time was allowed to count[,] but I doubt whether such time should be allowed, because the Boy who enters between 14 and 15 and goes direct to sea is at school to qualify himself for the service[.]

The Boy 13 to 14 is in the Training Ship at School at Govt expense to qualify for the service.

Now let me give the Boys servitude as follows in the Training Ship[:]

	y[ear]	m[onth]		y[ear]	m[onth]
Joins Training Ship at	13	3	again	13	9
Joins Sea Going Ship at	14	3		14	9
Serves 18 months	15	9		16	3
Serves 18 months to I[ntermediate].Ex[am].	17	3		17	9
If he has to serve 2 years[,] as the Boy who goes direct to sea[,] this Boy will not be eligible for Lieutenant until he is	19	3		19	9

This rule would make the Boys from the Training Ship and those who go direct to sea on exactly the same footing. Each would begin the Service from their appointments to sea going ships as cadets, but there is a <u>disadvantage</u>[:] that none of these Boys can be qualified for the Rank of Lieutenant until they are the following ages, but which correspond directly with those who enter into sea going ships directly from the shore[:]

Enter Training Ship	Enter Sea Going Ship	Pass for Lieut.
13.3	14.3	19.3
13.6	14.6	19.6
13.9	14.9	19.9

If this stands good as the Rule[,] the Clause VIII must come out and one general regulation introduced instead of the two separate articles of Clause XIII[,] in which case it would run thus[:]

The Seatime [*sic*] of a Cadet and Midshipman is to commence from the date of his appointment to a Sea Going Ship as a Cadet and[,] having served 18 months as provided for in Article X[,] and also 18 months under Article XII[,] and having completed 3 years and six months with the rating of Midshipman[,] and being at least 19 years of age[,] he will be qualified to pass &c.

But if these Boys are to <u>have</u> part of the Training Ship time [count,] Clause VIII will have to be modified by stating[:]

Such part of the time in the Training Ship will be allowed to count as in 'X' Clause XIII[.]

This would only be allowed to permit those officers from the Training Ship passing at one Age viz. 19.

The whole difficulty occurs in this[:]

Is any of the cadets time in the Training Ship to Count[?]

If not[,] the regulation can be made quite clear.

If it is to count[,] Clause XIII explains it.

But as it would [be] hard to keep a Boy in the Training Ship for the whole 12 months[,] he might[,] if he likes[,] pass out and if so[,] he will gain advantage by being sooner rated as a Cadet in a sea going ship[,] provided he is 14 years of age. This would be an inducement for the Boys to study and get to sea.

[**599**] *Wood to Milne*

Hickleton
1 January 1857

Dear Cap Milne

I have returned the C[oast] guard paper to Berkeley with an amended minute for crews' appointment. I sent one up yesterday naming the *Fisgard*[,][1] but I directed Mr Bedford[2] to take it to Berkeley to see that it was right, so I hope he has corrected it.

I will study your N[aval] C[adet] circular this afternoon . . .

[**600**] *Wood to Milne*

Hickleton
2 January 1857

Dear Captain Milne

I send you a Cadet paper altered as I think it should run.

I agree with you that the time in the training ship[,] beyond a short period of 3 months[,] should not count, & I cannot see why a youth of 15 should not learn practical rigging &c[,] before he goes to sea. Therefore[,] I think all cadets should go to a training ship for a short time to learn this. Give 3 months time to all for the training ship. the [*sic*] lad of 15 will then pass at 20[, &] the lad of 14 at 19, which will leave them in the same position as now, i.e., [as] the lad of medium age passes at the present time.

[It] was 13 + 6 = 19

[It will] henceforth [be] 14 + 5 = 19

[1]Commodore's Flagship at Woolwich Dockyard. Wood probably meant that he had named *Fisgard* – whose ship's book bore numerous supernumerary officers for detached duties – as the Comptroller of the Coast Guard's nominal flagship.

[2]Henry Charles Grosvenor Bedford, Third Class Clerk.

The paragraph about indifferent conduct should apply to both classes, & to make this clear I think that the paragraphs about Lads under 14 should all be under VI[.]
Those as to lads above 14 shd be under VII[.]
The rule about indifferent conduct should be VIII[.]
& the allowance of time IX.

I have not marked it so, in order to avoid confusion, and I am not sure whether you will agree with me as to sending all to the training ship, tho' I am more & more inclined to it since I wrote yesterday.
I have altered XII to suit this view . . .
The long sentences of XIII sh[oul]d be broken for the sake of clearness.

[**601**] *Milne to Wood*

Admiralty
6 January [1857]

Dear Sir Charles

I have just come back from my few days absence, and should have written you before this about the Cadet Circular, but have really been so puzzled that I could not do so.

You mention that the Elder Boys[,] viz. those above 14[,] should go to the Training Ship for 3 Months. I am afraid this short period will do no good, and you also say that they could count 3 Months Training Ship Time. There is no difficulty in regard to these Lads time[,] their case is quite clear. They will be required to serve 5 years in a sea going ship[.]
14 + 5 would bring this Boy to 19 (B)
15 + 5 would bring this Boy to 20
There can be no objection this arrangement[.] it is simple and clear[.]
It is the Boy in the Training Ship whose case requires consideration[,] I mean those Boys of more advanced age.

y[ear]	m[onth]	T[raining] S[hip]		Sea Time		Age
13	3	+ 1	+	5	=	19.3 (D)
13	6	+ 1	+	5	=	19.6
13	9	+ 1	+	5	=	19.9
13	11	+ 1	+	5	=	19.11
14	0	+ 1	+	5	=	20 (A) This is an extreme case

You will see that the Boy A[,] who enters the Training Ship at 14[,] cannot pass until he is 20[,] whereas the Boy B[,] who goes direct to sea[,] can pass at 19. In the same manner[,] all the Boys in the Training Ship will be placed at a disadvantage with B, as none of them can pass at 19, unless some of the Training Ships Time is allowed to count.

I believe it will be right to establish the rule that all must serve 5 years in sea going ships[,] 1 [year] 6 [months] as cadet and 3.6 as Mid[,] assuming this is fixed and final.

We have now only to define some rule by which a certain portion of Time [*sic*] may be given in the Training Ship[.]

There are two ways of doing this[:]

1. By allowing an Average fixed time. The Boy only requires 3 months but A wants 12. say [*sic*] 6 months to be allowed to all who pass thro the Training Ship.

2. Do not keep the Boys the whole 12 months in the Training Ship, but have an Examination at 6 and 9 Months, and allow any Boy to pass out if he can. The gain to him will be his getting into a sea going ship at an earlier age & therefore after serving 5 years he will be earlier qualified: – suppose[:]

14 passed at the 6 months [Examination], serves 5 years, passes = 19.6
" passes at the 9 " , serves 5 years, passes = 19.9

Still this Boy [*sic*] is not on the same equality as the Boy of 14 who goes direct to sea[.]

or make it a sliding scale[.]

Any Boy who passes at the 6 months examination will be allowed to count 9 [or] (12) months time[.] At the 9 months [count] 6 [or] (9) months[;] at the 12 months examination [count] 3 [or] (6) months only[.]

This would be a great incentive to learn and get to Sea, and it would give the benefit of time to those who would work[.]

If we could only define some general rule for the Time [*sic*] to be allowed in the Training Ship[,] the difficulty would be got over.

I write in haste[.]

I have not done anything further with the Circular until the above is decided[.] An Order in Council will be required[.]

[**602**] *Milne to Wood*

Admiralty
7 January [1857]

Dear Sir Charles

I wont [*sic*] say any more about the Cadet question at present[,] except that some of the Time [*sic*] in the Training Ship will have to count as part of the 5 years [sea time]. You will see in the enclosed[1] that such a Regulation was in force at the College.

I have some papers to send you respecting the Store Receiver appointment[.] I do not think it will be necessary to fill it up. There will be nothing for him to do for a year or more[,] and even then I am of opinion that the receipt of all Stores should take place at Deptford. I was also averse to the receipt of Clothing &c at Deptford and the Clarence Yard. The result has been that Articles have been received at the Clarence Yard and the same Articles rejected at Deptford.

I believe the proper course will be to have only one Store Receiver at Deptford[,] with a proper staff, but I will send you the Papers.

There is nothing new here.

[**603**] *Milne Memorandum on the Authority to Hold Courts Martial*[2]

Admiralty
12 February 1857

Looking at the wording of the Clauses of the Articles of War, I consider the Admiralty has power and should grant warrants to officers in Command of Stations and Squadrons to hold Courts Martial[,] altho they are not Commanders in Chief.

The case of Commander's [*sic*] in Chief is clear and is an Every day business. The Admiralty grant warrants to them to Hold [*sic*] Courts Martial as in Mediterranean, Brazils, N. America &c[.]

The Senior officers at the Cape[,] Coast of Africa[, &] Lisbon Squadron are cases[,] in my opinion[,] of officers Commanding in Chief. They are the chief officers in Command of these stations or squadrons, and ought[,] in my opinion[,] to have Admiralty authority to hold Courts Martial. It never could be the intention to give to one Officer in Command of a station of 6 ships authority to Hold [*sic*] Courts Martial and to withhold that power from the Senior Officer of 12 ships on another station[,] in which the Discipline of the Service has equally to be maintained[.] There are many instances where such authority has been given.

2. I see no reason why some scale of punishment should not be made known to the Comdrs in Chief. it [*sic*] would be more advisable to issue such a scale than for the Admiralty to admit of the constant remission of the sentences of C. Martial, which must ultimately prove disadvantageous to the discipline of the Fleet.

[1]The Regulations for the Naval College.

[2]A virtually identical draft can be found in MLN/116/3/1.

[**604**] *Wood Minute on the Authority to Hold Courts Martial*

Admiralty
[February 1857]

My Lords are clearly of opinion that a commission to hold Courts Martial ought to be issued to every officer sent to a foreign station[,] & commanding in Chief any fleet or squadron of ships of war on such station, whether he has or has not a commission of Commander of [*sic*] Chief[,] authorizing him to appoint to death vacancies &c[.]
My Lords are equally of opinion that a commission to hold courts martial may be issued to any officer commanding [in] Chief [of] any fleet or squadron of ships of war, tho' not commanding in chief on a foreign station, but that it must rest with the Lords Com[missioner]s of the Admiralty to determine in each case whether such commission to hold courts martial shall or shall not be issued to such officers . . .

[**605**] *George F. Seymour to Milne*

Portsmouth
21 February 1857

Dear Milne

The Admiralty Instructions and the different explanatory directions relative to Troop ships have formed at Portsmouth the guides when their Commanders require information[,] but no systematic plan has been issued here.

To save trouble in writing out the Admiralty letters which have been sent here[,] I transmit [them] open herewith, and also a Printed order for the regulation of the Military onboard the *Urgent*[,] which Commander Phillips[1] has found useful & which appears to [meet] the purpose[.]

I have shown your proposed Report of Inspection to Admiral Martin[,] and agree with him that it will be desirable that it should include a report of the Ventilation and if windsails are fitted[,] and also whether the Troops & Ships Companies Beads [*sic*] &c are in order, and also the Closets and Washing Places need attention on such occasions, & he adds a question of whether the ladder ways are sufficient . . .

[1]Commander Charles G. Phillips.

[606] *George F. Seymour to Milne*

Portsmouth
28 February 1857

Dear Milne

I meant to have sent back the proof sheets of the proposed Regulations for Troop ships[,][1] which you paid me the compliment of sending me with such observations as occurred to me[,] which are partly the result of some conversation with Captain Phillips of the *Urgent*, but recollecting that Von Donop[,][2] late of the *Vulcan*[,] who appeared to me to understand the management of a Trooper better than any one I have met[,] I took the liberty of sending him in confidence the paper[,] inviting his remarks on the items & especially those on which you had marked 'Query'[.]

Van Dorop was at Ryde[,] however[,] so I shall not be able to recover the paper or gain any remarks he may have to offer untill [*sic*] tomorrow[,] when I will return it.

In the mean time [*sic*][,] I may say that I think some of Phillips remarks are worth your attention viz . . .
He would limit the paymasters responsibility to the Bath linen[,] Crockery[,] Glass & furniture . . .
That the Steward should give security . . .
That the choice & selection of wines & provisions should be left to the Steward . . .
He thinks that the Cook . . . to be underpaid & that he should have 30 [shillings?][,] which the Man [i.e., Cook] in the yards has . . .
Supper objectionable[,] as the fires ought to be out by 7 PM[,] besides the Servants having to clean every thing used at a late hour[,] and Phillips thinks that the Steward could hardly afford another meal[,] & that a bread & cheese luncheon should be substituted for Supper . . .

I suppose supper is allowed in Hired Troop ships when the Cooks & Stewards have been inured to perpetual entry of Passengers, but even in the Cunard Packets few supped, as the Tea . . . [included] some solids.

The Steward[,] by the New Regulations[,] is allowed to draw provisions[,] so I suppose is entitled to savings[,] as in other ships[,] for what is not drawn.

I should think it would be useful to number the soldiers hammocks by Companies A & so many numbers & B so many . . .

[1]These draft regulations seem not to have been preserved by Milne.
[2]Edward Pelham Brenton Von Donop (1811–90). Entered, 1827; Lt, 1838; Cmdr, 1849; Capt., 1855; Rear-Adm. (Ret.), 1873; Vice-Adm. (Ret.), 1878.

Dress[1]

I regret that the jacket has been decided upon for the Mens uniform[,] but as it is[,] I hope it will look well & be comfortable.

Only two sizes of Buttons are mentioned in the regulations[,] those of 7⁄10 of an inch in dia[mete]r for the Jacket and 1½ inch for the Pea Jacket, but an intermediate size has been sent down[,] of 1 inch[,] which may make some confusion with the other two[,] & its purpose does not appear.

I think the Hats will not do for general wear[,] and that it would be better to have the general use of caps allowed when ordered [*sic*][,] both ashore and at sea[,] as it is permitted to the officers when not in dress uniform, & therefore that a pen might be usefully drawn in the 9th regulation across the words [']at night & at sea['].

The Warrant officers of the *St Vincent* & most in the *Excellent* have addressed a memorial to the Board[,] asking for frock Coats, being jealous of the Engineers I presume. It will increase their Dress Expenses.

I shall transmit the Memorials . . . that no obstacle should be offered to Representations to the Board[,] & I wish always to show respect to the class which I think requires to be kept up as much as possible[,] and in more important particulars than in Coats Tails & Skirts[.]

[**607**] *George F. Seymour to Milne*

Portsmouth
4 March 1857

Dear Milne

I return one of the Printed forms for Troop Ships with some notes in pencil which Capt Van Donop has added[.][2]

The Regulations in their present shape appear to me judicious[,] except that I think No. 7 assigns to the Paymaster a too minute duty over the Steward, as to be carried out it would require them to go to market together[.] He might[,] I think[,] be directed to examine the vouchers for the Stewards Payments[,] & I think that would be better than having the whole of No 7 out[,] which Capt V[on] D[orop's] remark goes [on] to recommend[.]

[1]See also Seymour's earlier letter of 20 November 1856, [**594**] on this subject.
[2]Not preserved among Milne's papers.

I think you and I must be the only people corresponding on such dull matters at this exciting time, but political crises[1] never advance professional objects & I wish they were more rare.

[608] *Milne to Panmure*

Admiralty
14 March [1857]

Dear Lord Panmure

You wished to have some data respecting passages to the Cape[,] China[2] &c[;] I send you the following[:]

The distance from England to Madeira is 1250 miles and [from there] to the Cape de Verds 2,300[,] and from the Cape de Verds to the Cape is 4.900 miles.

The average quantity of coal stowed by steam vessels is about 12 days[,] and at full steaming the vessel will average about 190 miles a day. The 12 days coal will therefore carry her about 2380 miles. If she has experienced unfavourable weather[,] she will therefore have to coal at Madeira, and again at the Cape de Verds.

From the Cape de Verds to the Cape is 4900 miles. The Coals will therefore not carry her this distance, and if she went to Sierra Leone or Ascension it would be the same. In this passage[,] the steamer is placed at a disadvantage with the sailing ship unless she can lift her screw and is a full rigged ship with a proper spread of canvas. The steamer is also detained at Madeira and St Vincent [in the Cape Verde Islands] to replenish coal[,] whilst the sailing ship is progressing on her voyage.

The <u>full</u> powered Screw Packets to the Cape[,] calling at Sierra Leone[,] could not face the Easterly Trade Wind, but had to make to the Southward into Latitude 25S[,] and they reached the Cape on an average of 40 days.

In the present contract the auxiliary powered vessels were to have made the passage in 31 days[,] but some have exceeded 50 days.

Sailing vessels have made it in 47 days[,] but the average may be taken at 60 days.

I assume that HM Troop Ships which lift the Screw[,] by steaming and sailing[,] may reach the Cape in 53 to 56 days, where they will be

[1]Palmerston's government had just lost a division on Richard Cobden's resolution condemning 'the violent measures resorted to at Canton in the late affair of the *Arrow*'.

[2]The government was anxious to send forces to China for the Second Opium War.

detained to coal at least 4 days, so that there will be scarcely any difference between the Steamer and Sailing ship.

From the Cape to Mauritius is 2550 Miles. The steamer must go there to coal, and from thence to Singapore is 3.500 miles. The steamer cannot reach this with her Coal and will therefore have to sail part of the way, or will have to go to Ceylon for further supplies and from there to Singapore to Coal again. 4 days at each place will give the sailing ship about 12 days progress, and[,] with the SW Monsoon blowing from April to Oct[,] will carry her well on her voyage.

A sailing ship just sailed with Ordnance Stores for Hong Kong made the passage last year in 88 days.

The following is an approximate Table of the passages to China &c.[:]

	days
Steamer to Cape de Verds	13
Coaling	4
Steaming towards Cape	18
sailing do.	18
Arrive at Cape	53
Coaling	4
To Mauritius	14
detention [for coaling]	4
[arrive at Mauritius]	75
To Singapore Steaming	18
Sailing	6
Coaling	4
To Singapore	103
To Hong Kong	8
[Total]	111
Sailing ship to the Cape	60
detention	3
To Hong Kong with SW Monsoon	40
Days	103

It may be said that in this long voyage[,] there can be but little difference between steam and sailing vessels.

By the foregoing it is very doubtful whether it is necessary to go to the great expense of Chartering Steam vessels[,] when they will carry less than sailing vessels of the same tonnage. If there are sufficient steam vessels in China to tow sailing transports[,] I think the sailing vessels are more advantageous for the Govt than steamers.

[**609**] *Phinn to Milne*

Admiralty
7 May [1857]

Dear Cap. Milne

I cannot part the Admiralty without offering my best thanks for the kind aid you have ever afforded me in the discharge of my duties.

Necessarily ignorant as every civilian must be of professional details[,] it is of the greatest advantage for the Second Secretary to be able to have recourse to one who is so thoroughly served [*sic*] in all the usages of his profession as yourself.

I am sure I can honestly say that I have never sought your assistance without finding it most readily given, in the midst of all the perplexing cases with which you have been ever surrounded.

I trust you will be long able to devote yourself to the public service, & that it may long reap the advantage of your efforts.

I trust you will also thank Mrs. Milne on my behalf & accept my thanks yourself for much social kindness, & agreeable intercourse in private.

[**610**] *Milne Memorandum on Instruction of Naval Cadets*

Admiralty
9 July 1857

The Cadets[,] on passing their examination for entry into the service at the R. N. College[,] will then proceed to the *Illustrious* and be entered on her Books and be granted 14 days leave. They are to be furnished with a list of such articles of Clothing & Books as the Capt of the *Illustrious* may consider necessary, to be brought on board on their return from leave.

The Course of Instruction by the sanction in Circular No 288 is to be fixed by 'The P[rincipal] Naval Instructor in conjunction with the Cap of *Illustrious*,' [&] further terms are to be arranged for study as well as for exercises in small arms and Rigging.

Arrangements are to be made for obtaining the services of a French and Drawing Master[,] either by the month or quarter as may be found convenient, but no permanent arrangement is to be made.

So soon as the Cap of the *Illustrious* has made all arrangements in regard to the future course of study[,] Mess &c[,] he is to submit them for the consideration and approval of their Lordships.

[**611**] *Wood to Milne*

Windsor Castle
22 October 1857

Dear Milne

I have had a long visit with the Prince[1] this morning as to the returns from the ports.

Pray go carefully into the matter with Martin.[2] There are some points which I cannot explain, but it clearly requires very careful examination.

He [Prince Albert] has a great wish to have an efficient ship in each port, but the main question is the time it will require to put all the ships at home into a proper state for keeping them [ready] for going to sea.

[Work] out if you can what the amount of deterioration is, incurred by having a ship in commission in the harbour, beyond that of having her in 2nd class steam reserve.

[**612**] *Milne Draft Board Instructions to Commanders-in-Chief on Ship Inspections*

Admiralty
14 November 1857

Acquaint Comdrs in Chief[:]
That in several instances my Lords have observed that HM Ships returning to England from abroad have not been mustered and inspected by the Cmdrs in Chief on the Stations, or even by a senior officer and[,] as my Lords attach much importance to this duty[,] they desire that the Comdrs in Chief are invariably to muster and inspect the ships under their Command.
First, on arrival on the Station[.] Second[:] Once in each year between the months of March & July[,] or as soon afterwards as the service will admit. Third[:] Before quitting the station.
Reports of Inspections are to be transmitted in form No 126 late 189, which my Lords desire may be carefully filled up[.][3]

[1]Prince Albert, the Prince Consort.
[2]William Fanshawe Martin, Rear-Adm. Superintendent of Portsmouth Dockyard.
[3]The subsequent Board Order (also in ADM1/5698, Box 1) closely followed Milne's draft.

[**613**] *Milne Memorandum on Naval Education*[1]

Admiralty
28 November 1857

The Enclosed papers were called for more than a year ago with the view of bringing before the Board, the course of study pursued at the Naval College at Portsmouth. I have reason to believe that no system of Instruction is followed out at that Estab[lishmen]t, and that each officer who goes there only studies that which suits his own convenience & wishes. Mr. Main[,] in his own report in the enclosed papers[,] admits 'that as far as the Half Pay officers are concerned it has reduced this Establishment to a place of [*sic*] instruction in the Marine Engine', but the officers who are at the College are chiefly those on Half Pay[,] and it may therefore be said that the object of a Naval College for instruction of Naval officers is not carried out. I know from officers of Rank who have been at the College that there is little doing[,] and I think it assumes more the character of a Club than a College.

My object in bringing the subject before the Board is for consideration, & whether the Royal N[aval] College should not be placed on a proper basis for imparting general instruction, to naval officers who may wish it. Their early entry into the Naval Service and their constant employment deprives them of all means which other persons have of obtaining any knowledge of general leisure [*sic*], by attending the Instruction of a public college, and even when they may attain Rank and retire on H[alf] Pay for a time[,] there is still a difficulty in obtaining that knowledge. It appears to me the Admiralty should in some measure provide [for] this want, and that the Naval College should be made one in reality and not in name. It is not possible[,] or is it required[,] to make Naval officers professors, or to require them to dive into the depths of scientific knowledge. it [*sic*] is impossible, but there is no reason why a general knowledge of those subjects should not be imparted to them. at [*sic*] present they are more ignorant of them than many of the Boys in their own ships who[,] thro the means of a public estab[lishmen]t[,][2] have gone thro a certain course of scientific instruction.

[1]To this paper is appended a Milne note, holograph, 1858: 'The origin of this Enquiry was to place the Naval College on some proper basis. When I was a young Commander on Half Pay, I attended the Edinburgh College for several winters and derived the greatest benefit from doing so. The lectures were on subjects more or less connected with General Service[,] and having experienced the great advantage from the study and Instruction I then received, I am most anxious to give my Brother officers of the Navy the means of gaining knowledge by placing the Naval College on a practical basis.'

[2]Greenwich.

I would therefore submit whether some inquiry should not be made on what system the Naval College should be placed. I would be inclined to recommend a course of 3 Months lectures on each of the following subjects[:]
1. Chemistry
2. Natural Philosophy, embracing Mechanics, Hydraulics, Hydrostatics, Optics, Electricity &c
3. Astronomy (Practical) & Fortification
4. Gunnery & the Steam Engine
5. Geology
Some of these subjects should be taught on alternate Days, but all should be taught by daily public lectures of one hour's duration each, and the College Lecture Room should be open to all Naval Officers who might think proper to attend. Those residing in the College should be expected to study the respective subjects for examination at the close of the Course of Lectures.
If some such system was adopted[,] I believe it would be productive of much good to the N[aval] Service, but much will depend on the Ability and Zeal of the Lecturers[,] and I think it may be found necessary to make some changes in the present Estab[lishmen]t.
The first question is should there be some enquiry by Profr Woolley or others to see what course should be adopted.

[**614**] *Milne Minute on Inspection and Preparation for Battle of H.M. Ships*

Admiralty
16 December 1857

The enclosed inspection sheet was introduced into the service in 1849,[1] and ought to be sent to the Admiralty every six months[,] also at the periods of time mentioned in the Note at the head of it.[2] These regulations[,] however[,] are scarcely ever acted on, and ships come to England after having served on Foreign Stations that have never been inspected since they were commissioned, and having been sometimes 2 to 3 years under a Commander in Chief. In this case, the *Brilliant* was inspected by the Comdr in Chief at Sheerness in June 1856 and her next inspection was at Sheerness in Nov 1857, altho she was in company with the

[1]For an example of this sheet, see no. [**205**], above.
[2]When newly fitted out, arriving at or departure from a Foreign station, and on receiving orders to pay off.

Comdr in Chief of the N.A. & W India station in Sep 57, but this is by no means a solitary case.
The Inspection of HM Ships is an important duty and ought not to be neglected, and the rules for these inspections are somewhat ambiguous. I would submit that the Heading of the Inspection Sheet should be altered . . . and that the attention of Comdr in Chief be called to the subject[,] as my Lords have observed a want of attention to this responsible duty.
There are no returns on officers of either the *Duke of Wellington* & [*sic*] *Royal Albert* and I have no doubt many others[.]

[**615**] *Walker Memorandum Respecting Engineers for the Navy* [*Excerpt*]

[Somerset House
January 1858]

With this improved class of persons [Walker hoped to attract], mess arrangements on board ship may be altered[,] so as to bring them in contact with young officers whose social position is higher than their own, and thus not only remove one ground of objection already referred to on the part of Parents to their sons entering this Branch of the Naval Service, but would have the effect of improving their general bearing as officers and giving them juster ideas of the service and their position in it.

[**616**] *Milne Minute on Engineers for the Navy*

Admiralty
30 January [1858]

The duties of an Engineer when he first enters the service must always be to work at the Engines[,] and to put his hand to <u>anything</u> in the Engine room that may be required. he [*sic*] must have '*tow voil*' [*sic*] and 'Engineers Tools' in his hands[,] and he must be a working man. I see serious evil in making him a gentleman so far as relates to work. The evil will be great if he is to be considered in <u>any other light</u>. The Engineers of all private steam vessels are working men, & brought up as working men, and I have great apprehension of the difficulties which will arise if the Engineers of the Navy are to be raised in position, and[,] except in the <u>higher</u> grade[,] I have always looked upon it as a mistake their having been given the Rank they now hold[.] much better to have given them higher pay than to have given gold lace and Epaulettes[,] which appears to be incompatible with their position.

[**617**] *Milne Draft Instructions to Committee on Naval Education*

Admiralty
10 February 1858

My Lords being of opinion that it might prove advantageous to the Naval Service if a more regular course of Instruction on general, scientific, as well as professional subjects was given at the Naval College at Portsmouth, instead of the system now followed at that Establishment, have nominated Rear Admiral James Hope, the Revd G. Fisher of Greenwich Hospital[,] and the Revd Dr. Woolley of Portsmouth Dock Yard to make enquiry into this subject.
1st[:] Into the system and course of Instruction now given at the College[,] and how far it affords the means of general scientific and professional Instruction to naval officers.
2d, Whether the Naval College might not be rendered more generally and practically useful as a place of Instruction to Naval officers by a change in the existing system, my Lords having in view,
1. The Introduction of a regular daily course of Instruction by means of lectures on the following subjects.
Chemistry
Natural Philosophy &c &c
Geology
Astronomy & Fortification
Steam Engine &c
The Lectures on Chemistry & Geology to be combined and Instruction given by one Person,
Natural Philosophy by one person[,] and to give Instruction in the higher branches of Mathematics.
Practical Astronomy & Fortification by one person, or uniting the Practical Astronomy with the Natural Philosophy lectures if thought more advisable[.]
Steam & Steam Engine [*sic*] by one person.
2. Whether the course of Instruction could be limited to a three month course of Lectures and there to recommend [*sic*][.]
3. In directing attention to arrangements of the foregoing description which are altogether different from the present system at the College, my Lords have had in view the peculiar position in which Naval officers are placed, Their [*sic*] early age of entry into the Naval service, and

the many years of continuous employment afloat without having the opportunity of obtaining any knowledge of those various scientific subjects now generally taught in the various establishments in England, and it is with the view of affording the means to N[aval] Officers of attaining this knowledge[,] that their Lordships have appointed (the persons already named) to make enquiry at the N[aval] College[,] and to report their opinion whether any and what improvements can be made, having in mind that whilst the means of attaining the higher branches of Mathematical knowledge should be open to those who wish to devote themselves to this subject, the means of general scientific Instruction should be open to all who may wish to benefit by any improved arrangement.

I would submit to the Board that Rear Ad Hope be requested to undertake this enquiry[,] assisted by Mr Fisher & Mr Woolley[,] and that all the papers should be sent to Rear Ad Hope which have [been] called for from the N[aval] College[,] and that the Enquiry should be made as soon as these gentlemen can meet at Ports[mouth].

Inform the respective parties and Admiral Sir G. Seymour

[**618**] *Pakington to Milne*

Private
27 February 1858

Dear Admiral Milne

We are deeply impressed with the importance of making the Board of Admiralty as effective as possible, and you, and your services there have been so valuable, and your experience is so great, that I much hope I may be able to induce you to remain in your present position.

I trust you will be willing to accede to this proposal, and I may add that it will be as satisfactory to Lord Derby, as it shall be to me, to hear that you have consented.

[**619**] *Pakington Memorandum on the State of the Navy*[1]

Admiralty
March 1858

Confidential

Memorandum on State of Royal Navy. – March 1858

In describing the present naval resources of this country, it will be convenient to refer to them under the heads of –

1. The comparative strength of the Navies of England and France.
2. The system which has prevailed in this country, of paying off and re-commissioning ships.
3. The resources of England for manning her fleets, either permanently or in case of emergency.

England now has in commission 9 line-of battle ships, carrying 855 guns, and having an aggregate steam power of 5,000.

France has in commission 8 line-of-battle ships, carrying 750 guns, with an aggregate steam power of 6,550.

In harbour commission, England has 5 ships, with 494 guns, and 2,350 horse power.

France has 13 ships, with 1,158 guns, and 8,850 horse power.

In modern line-of-battle ships, therefore, of fairly equal power, England has in commission, or harbour commission, only 14, with 1,349 guns, while France has 21, with 1,908 guns.

But we also [have] 9 block ships, which would be useful for some purposes, as was found during the Russian war, although they would not be able to compete with the heavier ships of the present day. These 9 ships carry 540 guns, and have 2,800 horse power.

To make the comparison of the two Navies complete, the number of ships of the same class not in commission should be mentioned.

England has in steam ordinary, in various states of advancement, 13 ships carrying 1,187 guns, and 6,800 horse power; in course of alteration for steam, 5 ships, with 450 guns, and 2,200 horse power; building, 10 ships, with 1,019 guns, and 7,400 horse power.

France has in ordinary, or in course of transformation, 9 ships, with 874 guns, and 5,000 horse power; building, 7 ships, with 630 guns, and 5,750 horse power.

[1]Milne wrote on the back of Pakington's memorandum, 'Answer to the Queen's questions', but it appears that Pakington first submitted it to the Cabinet, and that the Queen and Albert then posed the questions quoted in Milne's memorandum [**622**] to the rest of the Board. Lord Louvaine's response [**627**] refers to 'the Memorandum of 2 April 1858', suggesting the date it was brought to the Board's notice.

The general results of the comparison, excluding altogether our old and comparatively useless block ships, is that, either afloat or building –

England has 42 ships, with 4,005 guns, and 23,750 horse power.

France has 37 ships, with 3,412 guns, and 26,150 horse power.

But it will be observed that we are now building 10 heavy ships, with 1,019 guns, against 7 French ships, with 630 guns; and of these 10 English ships, 5 will be ready for launching during the present year.

Considering the immense importance to England of maintaining her naval superiority, this comparison, especially of the ships immediately available, cannot be considered satisfactory.

But England appears to be advancing more rapidly than France in the construction of screw ships of the line, and although our numerical superiority at present is very small (exclusive of ships building, only two) and the steam power applied to the French ships is greater than to ours, the English ships greatly exceed the French in the number of their guns; and while the French have only 6 ships (afloat and building) which carry 100 guns and upwards, we have 14 of that class.

The superiority of the English over the French navy is greater in frigates and small vessels than it is in line-of-battle ships; though they have more first class frigates in commission than we have.

France has in commission 13 frigates, carrying 635 guns, and 14 sloops and corvettes, carrying 228 guns; 27 ships and 863 guns; about half of these only are steamers.

England has in commission 17 frigates, carrying 615 guns, and 21 sloops and corvettes, carrying 351 guns; 38 ships carrying 966 guns – of these 38 ships, 25 are steamers.

England has also 18 steam frigates and sloops in ordinary, and 8 steam frigates building, all of the latter of the first class, and 2 of them will be launched in June, and 54 sailing frigates in ordinary, 19 of them of the first class.

France has 7 steam frigates of the first class, and 6 steam corvettes now in course of building, and 10 sailing frigates, most of them of the first class.

It is true that the labour of our Dockyards has been of late directed from new ships in course of building, and devoted to the repair and preparation of ships in ordinary, which it has been found necessary to bring forward.

But it does not appear therefore that our permanent dockyard establishments are too small.

The question of what those establishments ought to be is not an easy one at this moment to decide. The present amount of Dockyard work is exceptional.

A considerable number of powerful ships were prematurely and unwisely paid off in 1857, and within a year it was found necessary again to prepare them for service. Great expense and great additional labour in the Dockyards have been thus created, and this labour has caused a temporary difficulty.

But the permanent establishment of artificers and labourers for 1857, was greater than at any former period,[1] except the two immediately preceding years (10,850): and the number proposed by the late Government (12,190), in their estimates for 1858–9, is altogether without precedent.

It is easier to postpone increase of establishments than to reduce them when they have been increased, and although the great size of modern ships, and the additional labour caused by the general application of steam to Her Majesty's ships[,] forbid the hope that we can return to the low Dockyard establishments of former days, it remains to be proved that the establishment of last year is insufficient for the present requirements of this country under ordinary circumstances.

The practice which has long prevailed in the British Royal Navy, of commissioning ships for only three years, is one which appears to be attended with serious disadvantages, and therefore, requires consideration. The opinion of experienced Naval Officers seems to be unanimous in condemning this practice.

The evils which arise from it are mainly two: –

1. Great waste of money.

2. Great injury to discipline.

1. Waste of money. – It has been well said that the period for which a ship ought to be commissioned is the duration, whatever that may be, of the life of the weakest part.

There is no part of a ship which will not endure for five years. To fit a ship out at the end of five years costs no more than at the end of three years, because the rule of the Navy is never to put any stores into a ship when re-commissioned which cannot be warranted for three years, and it is, therefore, customary to put new stores of all kinds, even masts, into all ships when refitted, great waste of course ensues [*sic*].

But the direct money loss of these premature refittings is very great.

The mean cost of all the refittings of the '*Queen*,' 116 guns, and the '*Rodney*,' 90 guns, from 1833 to 1851 was £22,673. In these days of steam it would probably be much higher.

[1]Pakington was wrong on this point; the dockyard establishment reached 14,000 during the latter years of the Napoleonic Wars.

If one of these ships was to be re-commissioned three times in nine years it would cost £68,019. If only twice in nine years, the cost would be £45,346, thus saving £22,673 in nine years, or about £2,500 per annum on each ship.

This saving would vary with the size of each ship; but on the whole of our ships in commission would amount to a very large annual sum.

2. Injury to discipline. – This appears self-evident.

It is well known that no ship can be brought into perfect order [in] under a year. Some Officers say, that for larger ships a longer time is necessary.

But supposing a year to be required, it is clear than only one-third of the force which costs so much can be in effective order at any one time.[1]

On the other side, the argument in favour of paying off and re-commissioning every three years, is that an extended time would bear hardly upon Officers, by diminishing frequency of employment, and those opportunities of practicing their profession, which Naval Officers so eagerly and honourably desire.

This result would, no doubt, be matter for regret; and it must be admitted that this result would ensue, unless it were averted by adopting a system of dividing each period of commission between two Captains.

How far such a system is advisable requires consideration, especially as it seems now to be the subject of much division of opinion amongst professional men.

But the evils which arise from the present short periods are great and obvious, and it is submitted that, for the good of the Naval Service, they ought to be forthwith corrected; and it is further submitted that such correction should be effected either by the adoption of periods of four year single commands, or, periods of five years with divided commands.

The resources of England for manning her fleets, either permanently or in case of emergency, is the subject which remains to be considered, and is, as it has long been, a question of much anxiety.

Our present position in this respect is not satisfactory. We have at this moment two of Her Majesty's finest men-of-war of their respective classes, the '*Marlborough*,' at Portsmouth, and the '*Euryalus*,' at Plymouth, unable to obtain men, and shipping them so slowly that their

[1]Pakington's mathematical skills seem to have been deficient: ⅔ of the ships would have been 'in effective order' at any one time, assuming his premises to have been correct.

Captains expect weeks, if not months, before their complements will be complete.

We cannot hope to see the French system[1] adopted in this country.

If we ever do attain anything like it, we must be content to do so by slow degrees.

Nor is it probable that our press-gang will ever again be tolerated.

On the other hand, let it be our care that England is never again reduced to such straits for manning her ships as she was during the late war.[2]

We shipped butchers' boys and cabmen to fight the Russians, and no harm happened; but to adopt such a course in a struggle with France could only be disastrous.

To what then are we to trust? What changes should be made?

In the first place, it must be admitted that although our present position is not satisfactory, it is materially better than it ever was before. Two great improvements of system have been adopted in the last few years.

In the year 1852, this most important question – 'How to man the Navy?' attracted the attention of the Duke of Northumberland, then First Lord of the Admiralty, and his Board, and his Grace appointed a Committee of experienced and able Naval Officers to consider the subject.

This Committee presented their Report a few weeks after the Duke left office, and amongst much other valuable matter, made two most important recommendations: –

1. To establish a system of 'continuous service,' i.e., to enlist men for ten years at a higher rate of pay.

2. To adopt the principle of a Marine Militia, by voluntary enrolment for five years, the men to have a period to training on board ship every year, and to be liable to permanent service in case of national emergency.

Both of these recommendations were subsequently adopted, and both have been attended with great success. There are now in the Navy about 21,000 continuous service men and boys.

Last year there were 24,000, till the late Government, pressed for economy by the House of Commons, unfortunately shook this new system, and diminished this valuable portion of our force, by offering discharge to all who liked to accept it, and 3,000 took advantage of the offer.

[1]Of maritime conscription.

[2]Milne wrote in the margin of this copy: 'What is the remedy'.

Of these continuous service men, 5,200, are scattered about the home ports in different vessels; the rest are on foreign stations.

The Naval Volunteers amount now to 5,800, of which 4,600 have been drilled, and they are steadily increasing.

The Coast-guard Force has also been increased in number, and could furnish at this time, if necessary, about 5,000 effective seamen.

These two bodies of men (Coast Guard and Volunteers), together with such continuous service men as may be within reach, form, in fact, our Naval Reserve; and by resorting to this reserve, we should now be able, in the event of sudden hostilities, to equip a fleet of 20 line-of-battle ships (including block ships), and a proportionate number of frigates, within a very short time; we are assured within a fortnight.

Looking to the future, we ought at all times to be prepared with an effective Channel Squadron; this Squadron should be strong enough to afford combined exercise and practice for officers and men during the summer, to furnish ships for any special service which might be required, and to send out the customary reliefs without the humiliating exhibition of helpless delay which is no[w] afforded by the '*Marlborough*' and '*Euryalus*.'

It is further desirable that the block ships should be superseded as Coast-guard ships by more effective vessels.

And the continuous service men should be increased as quickly as possible to an extent nearly, if not quite, equal to the whole effective strength of the Navy.

The amount of that effective strength must, of course, depend each year on the pleasure of Parliament, and must vary, from time to time, according to the state of our foreign relations; but it ought never to be reduced below an amount which will be sufficient for the maintenance of an effective Home Squadron in addition to the requirements of our foreign stations.

There is reason to hope that this rule may be acted upon in the present year.

There is now a very large Naval force in China; and it is hoped that the state of affairs in that country may allow the force to be so far reduced with prudence and safety, as to allow a Channel Squadron to be completed, by the aid of continuous service and other seamen, who are now serving in the China Fleet.

If this arrangement can be effected, we shall have at once placed our Naval defences and resources at home in a greatly improved position, without the necessity of requiring a grant of increased estimates from Parliament.

[**620**] *Milne to Pakington*

Admiralty, Private
28 March 1858

Dear Sir John Pakington

I herewith enclose papers numbered 1, 2, 3 &c with reference to the Conversation of yesterday afternoon about Men & ships.[1]

No. 1. Is a list of ships ordered home to be paid off[.] none will be in England before the middle of May and the last may arrive in August. The disposable men from these ships will not be available before August to Sept and October. so [*sic*] soon as these ships are paid off and men become available, you will have to consider what ships on Foreign Stations require to be relieved. See No 2 [*sic*]. some [*sic*] of these ships have already been in Commission nearly 4 years, and at this very time, ships ought to be commissioned to relieve them, but if small vessels were brought forward for this purpose, all the men which [*sic*] are now being picked up on shore would go to them, and the *Euryalus* and *Marlborough* would get none, as these men will not go to any large ship when they can get a small one.

You asked if the men[,] when they came home and were paid off[,] could not be put into large ships for the Channel Squadron[.] no doubt it [*sic*] could, but it would be taking away the only men that [*sic*] could be made available for commissioning small vessels to relieve those in No. 2 Sheet.

No 3 Is [*sic*] a list of the ships in Commission at Home for Channel service[,] to which I have added the *Brunswick*[,] expected next month, but the smaller vessels[,] marked x[,] must be kept ready to send on any special service that may be required[,] and the Home Ports should not be left without some such vessels.

You alluded to the great question of obtaining Seamen on any Emergency. This is the one great and difficult question, and with the exception of the Coast Guard, Marines in Barracks, and Coast Volunteers there is nothing in the shape of a reserve – and the Coast Guard and Coast Volunteers are only in course of being formed.

The Seamen of Great Britain are limited to the wants of the wants of the Naval and Merchant service, there is no Surplus. If the Mercantile Navy is by any cause suddenly increased, Seaman cannot be obtained[:] they do not exist, and the Merchant Navy does not train any Boys to become Seamen. formerly [*sic*] every ship was bound to have a certain

[1]Milne did not preserve copies of these lists with his copy of this memorandum. The text, however, gives a clear indication of his perspective.

number of apprentices. This law no longer exists, therefore[,] when men are wanted for the merchant service, high wages are given and the men are at once drawn from the Royal Navy. This leads to desertion.

In Nova Scotia & New Brunswick a large number of ships are built[,] but no Seamen are imported to man them. The consequence is the men from the Royal Navy are bribed and drugged by whole sale [*sic*] and carried off by [the] dozens[.] at Constantinople during the war the same took place, and high wages are regularly offered at Portsmouth and men from our Navy are shipped off for America.

If we had a war tomorrow where are we to get men [*sic*][?] There is no law to compel men to come to the Navy, except the Press Gang[.] it is no use offering high wages[,] for the Merchant must have them and outbids you, and in fact the country[,] whose safety depends on its Navy[,] has not any means whatever of getting men to man its ships except by recruiting in the sea Ports[,] and asking men as a favour to come & serve.

This is the case at this moment of peace[,] when you want to man one ship of the line and one Frigate[,] and your Desertions are now really great, because the Baltic & American & Fishery fleets of Merchant ships are fitting out and must have men at any price. I hope I have not bored you by this note. It is a serious state of things, but where is the remedy?[1]

[**621**] *Milne Draft Circular on Shipboard Punishments*[2]

Admiralty
16 April 1858

My Lords Commissioners of the Admiralty direct that when any subordinate officer shall continue to misconduct himself[,] after having been punished in accordance with the Custom of the Service by the Captain of the ship, the said Captain is to represent the conduct of such officer to the Commander in Chief or senior officer of the Station or Squadron, who

[1]The question was subsequently turned over to a Royal Commission on Manning appointed by the government in June 1858 in response to a motion by Sir Charles Napier. See Taylor, 'Manning the Royal Navy,' pt. 2, pp. 48–9. For the Commission's findings, see 'Report of the Commissioners appointed to inquire into the best means of Manning the Navy; with Minutes of Evidence and Appendix', *Parliamentary Papers*, 1859, vol. VI, p. 1.

[2]Several drafts of the subsequent circular, No. 323 (19 May 1858), embodying these proposals, with additions to clarify, are contained in ADM1/5698, Box 1. The regulations applied to Midshipmen, Cadets, Masters Assistants, Clerks and Clerks Assistants. The circular as promulgated contained further instructions to proper procedures.

will order a Court of Enquiry consisting of not less than two Captains or Commanders to investigate the complaint, and to hear what the party complained of may have to offer in explanation, and my Lords empower the said Court of Enquiry to deprive the Subordinate officer of either one or more months time of service as the case may require, but never to exceed 12 months. The Sentence to be confirmed by the Commander in Chief or Senior Officer who ordered the Enquiry, and to report the same to the Lords C[ommissioners] of the Admiralty. Captains are to grant to each subordinate officer the usual form of Certificate of Service for the whole period of time he may have served in the ship, but to certify thereon any deduction of time of which he may have been deprived by any C[ourt] of Enquiry held in accordance with the above order[.]

[**622**] *Milne Memorandum on the State of the Navy*[1]

Admiralty
April–May 1858

No 1[:] What are the duties which would be required of the Navy at the outbreak of a war with France[?]
The commencement of Hostilities[,] with France having a Fleet nearly equal to that of this country, and having the perfect command of ready means of manning her Fleet, would require the utmost energy and exertion on the part of the Government, to prevent serious losses, if not disaster to the Country. It would therefore become necessary to Equip with all possible haste.
1. A Channel Fleet for Home defence[.]
2. A North Sea Squadron[.]
3. A Squadron for the Irish & Bristol Channels[.]
4. Squadrons for the Blockade of the Ports of Cherbourgh and Brest[,] and to act offensively on the Coast of France.
5. to [*sic*] send reinforcements to the Channel Islands and Heligoland[.]
6. To send a Squadron to the Mediterranean to reinforce the Ships on that Station[,] and to convey Troops[,] Stores and Provisions to Gibraltar[,] Malta & Corfu.

[1]At the top Milne added: 'Three Questions put by the Queen to the Members of the Board of Adm[iral]ty Early 1858. See my reply enclosed.' He subsequently noted in the margin: 'These Papers were drawn up by each Member of the Board of Admi[ral]ty in answer to 3 questions put to each Member by the Queen thro the Prime Minister in 1858'. This memorandum was subsequently printed, a copy of which may be found in the William Fanshawe Martin papers, Add Mss. 41410. Certain portions of Milne's original draft – in particular appendices detailing British naval strength in previous wars – were not included in the printed version, nor are they reproduced here.

The first and most important point, must be the Home defence, and to prevent any attempt on the part of the Enemy to land Troops. for [*sic*] this purpose[,] the Channel Fleet must as soon as possible put to sea, and the Cherbourgh and Brest Squadrons should proceed to watch those ports, and to act offensively on the Coast of France, so as to keep the attention of the Enemy to the defence of their own Shores, and to the idea of attempts being made not only to destroy their trade, but to attack and burn their Mercantile and other Ports. Having this in view the Hydr[ographic] Of[fice] of the Admiralty should prepare charts of the Coast of France with all requisite information of their respective defences.

The Squadron in the North Sea should be employed for the defence of the mouth of the River[s] Thames and Humber[,] from whence the Buoys should be immediately removed, and the Squadron in the Irish and Bristol Channels should especially protect the Coal Ports of Wales.

The Home Trade[,] as well as Ships arriving from abroad[,] should receive early protection to prevent any difficulties which might arise from the non arrival of Cotton and other articles of raw material which might affect our Manufacturing districts.

After having made these necessary arrangements for Home Defence, the attention of the Government will be required for the defence and safety of our Colonies,

1. Bermuda,
2. The West Indies,
3. Nova Scotia, Newfoundland, New Brunswick,
4. The Canadas,
5. The Cape of Good Hope and Mauritius,
6. The Coast of Africa, Ascension & St. Helena,
7. India, Ceylon, especially Trincomalee Harbour,
8. Singapore & Hong Kong,
9. Australia & New Zealand,
10. The Brazil Station & Falkland Islands,
11. The Pacific Station & Vancouver Island,
12. The defence of the Coaling Stations and the arrangement requisite to be made for the vast supply of Coal required to be kept up all over the world for the use of HM Ships.

It is obvious that the usual Squadrons maintained during peace on these various Stations must be speedily reinforced by ships from England, but the various British Settlements spread over the surface of the Globe cannot be defended by the Navy alone, it is practically impossible[,] and the question arises for the decision of the Government, how far these colonies are to protect themselves, and how far the Military

Departments are prepared to construct and Arm [*sic*] Forts, and find Artillerymen to defend their principal Harbours[,] & this must be especially considered with reference to those colonies where we have naval Arsenals, thus in the Medn., North America, Bermuda, The [*sic*] Cape, and especially Trincomalee, which any interprising [*sic*] Enemy would immediately seize, then thus secure a Base for future operations in the Indian Seas. I have drawn up the accompanying abstracts A and B of the Estimated Naval force which I consider would be necessary for Home and Colonial defence, to meet the Emergency of War with France, but our extensive colonial stations[,] even when thus reinforced by ships from Home[,] will be open to attacks from Flying Squadrons of the Enemy, concentrated for any Special Operations on a particular point unknown to the officers in Command of HM Ships[,] who may be at some distant point of his [*sic*] station. no [*sic*] previous arrangement or foresight on the part of the Home Authorities can prevent this, all that can be done is to furnish a sufficient force of ships to meet any Emergency which may arise[,] and on all occasions to act offensively against the Enemy.

The Abstract C. Is [*sic*] a statement of the Coal required for the use of the Home and Foreign Squadrons[,] reduced to the mere expenditure of 2 days steaming for each ship in a week[,] which may be assumed at [*sic*: 'as'] not an excessive average, and looking at this vast service alone, I have great doubts in my own mind how far it will be practicable to keep the ships supplied, with any certainty, to enable them to act as steam vessels[,] when none stow more than from 5 to 9 days Coal . . .

Abstract A.

Ships and Men required for Home Defence and Medn.

Places &c	Ships of the Line	Frigates	Sloops	Gun Vessels	Men
average men	850	400	220	60	
Channel Fleet	10	12	20	60	21,300
North Sea Squad.	3	7	10	–	7,500
Irish & Bristol Ch.	4	8	10	–	8,800
Cherbourgh & Brest	10	12	15	–	16,600
Channel Islands	–	–	–	–	–
Medn Squadron	8	8	10	–	12,200
Totals	35	47	65	60	66,400
A Reserve to be fitted out	10	10	20	–	

The above number is a rough average[,] but it is not far from what may be required during actual warfare, and for which it is most essential should [*sic*] be rapidly obtained.

Abstract B. Ships and Men required in case of War for Foreign Stations

Places	Ships of the Line	Frigates	Sloops	Gun Vessels	Men
average men	850	400	220	60	–
Bermuda	–	3	4	10	2,680
West Indies	10	12	15	–	16,600
Nova Scotia &c	–	–	–	–	–
Canadas	–	–	–	–	–
Cape & Mauritius	6	6	10	–	9,700
Africa &c	–	6	12	8	5,520
India & Ceylon	12	15	20	–	20,600
Singapore & China	–	8	10	–	5,400
Australia &c	–	8	10	–	5,400
Brazil &c	–	6	8	–	4,160
Pacific &c	2	6	6	–	5,420
Total Abroad	30	70	95	18	75,400
Total at Home	35	47	65	60	66,400
Grand Total	65	117	160	78	141,800

This estimate is based on the experience of former operations, since which our Colonies and Commerce has [*sic*] largely increased, and at present[,] altho superior in our number of ships to France, we have not a Naval Force adequate to such Extended Operations.

Abstract C. Average Quantity of Coal required,
At Home[:]

No Ships &c	No	Average Horse Power	The Total Horse Power	Coals required
Ships Line	35	650	22,750	
Frigates	47	450	21,150	
Sloops	65	300	19,500	
G Vessels	60	100	6000	
[total]			69,400 =	6940 Tons per day
Steaming 2 days in a week				13,800 "
at that rate in the Month				55,520
In three Months				166,560
One Years Store				666,240 = £666,240 at 20s./per ton

Note. The Expenditure of Coal per day in Steam vessels is about 1/10th of the horse power
Abroad[:]

No Ships &c	No	Average Horse Power	The Total Horse Power	Coals required
Ships Line	30	650	19,500	
Frigates	70	450	31,500	
Sloops	95	300	28,500	
G Vessels	18	100	1,800	
[total]			81,300 =	8130 Tons per day
Steaming 2 days in a week =				16,260
at that rate in the Month				75,040
In three Months				225,120
One Years Store				900,480 = £2,200,000 at 45s/ per ton

No 2[:] Has England prepared a Fleet of Ships of war, as superior to those prepared by France as the duties they have to perform are more multifarious, more extended and more important[?]
The following return contains[,] as near as public document will give, the relative Naval forces of England and France.

Screw Vessels	England	France
Ships of the Line	35	32
Block Ships	9	–
Frigates	21	6 & 15 Converting
Mortar Frigates	3	–
Floating Batteries	8	5
Corvettes & Sloops	57	17 Corvettes
Gun Vessels	27	80 Sloops and gun vessels
Gun Boats	157	28
Mortar Vessels	–	5
Paddle Vessels		
Frigates	16	20
Sloops	44	9

Independent of the Force of Screw and Paddle Vessels, England has a superiority in Sailing Ships of the Line and Frigates, and also in the number of Screw Ships of these respective classes at present under construction. The preponderance of Naval Force is therefore in favour of England, but the change of system in the Naval Service caused by the introduction of Screw propulsion, has no doubt been detrimental to the interests of Great Britain, as it has enabled France to commence a new Steam Fleet, nearly on Equal [*sic*] terms with this country.

It is absolutely essential to the interests of Great Britain to maintain the command of the Sea, and it is therefore necessary to advance our Ship building with every reasonable expedition [*sic*], and to continue to construct Ships of the Line and powerful Frigates, as our present force in this respect is not adequate to the wants of a great maritime nation with extensive Colonies to protect, or to meet the combined Naval Force of any two nations which might unite against this Country.

The time has not yet arrived when Great Britain can alter or change her policy in Ship building, altho I believe it is not far distant when changes will be made in Naval Armaments & Ships, caused by the new features of modern warfare.

The Introduction [*sic*] of firing concussion shells from Horizontal [trajectory] Guns has rendered it almost impossible for Ships as at present constructed to withstand the fire of this description of shell, and I have reason to believe that had these shells been more extensively used from Fort Constantine at the attack on Sebastopol, every ship opposed to that Fort would have been burnt. But the new mode of firing Molten Iron[,] so vastly more destructive than either Red Hot Shot or Shells, will prevent our present Ships from attacking any Fort which has the means of firing this terrific and fearful missile, which at once sets fire to wood or any other inflammable material. It therefore comes to this, that for the purpose of attacking Shore Defences[,] our larger ships of War will be totally unfit, they will inevitably be destroyed whenever Molten Iron is used, and with more certainty than those bomb proof vessels which attacked Gibraltar were destroyed with the Red Hot Shot fired from that Fortress at the memorable Siege of that place which commenced in the year 1799.

Naval operations will therefore in course of time become limited to naval Actions between the respective Fleets, Forts and Shore Defences and will be hereafter attended by Guns & Mortars as well as Rockets of Long Range, placed in the smaller class of Vessels, which will present a small object of attack to the Guns of the Enemy.

Should these views be correct, and time alone can decide the question, The [*sic*] Introduction of Iron Cased Ships will become general, and the Board of Admiralty have already ordered Experiments to be made on various kinds of Iron & Steel to test the merits of each description as best suited for this purpose.

But to maintain Naval position of this Country[,] no time should be lost in keeping up a considerably superior Force in Ships to that of France, and thus maintain the superiority afloat which has heretofore enabled England to maintain the command of the Sea.

No 3[:] What are the resources of England in point of Seamen, and to what Extent are those resources organized and available in case of War[?]

Before considering these two questions[,] it appears to be necessary to State [*sic*] the number of Seamen who are now employed in British Ships, and the means which were adopted during former War's [*sic*] to obtain men for the Navy.

The number of Seamen employed in British Merchant Ships on the 31th Decr. 1857 was as follows.

Masters – 19,328

British Seamen – 162,012, Including 23,974 Boys & apprentices but excluding 14,375 Foreign Seamen[.]

During no one period of the year is more than about one fourth of this force in England at the Sametime [*sic*][,] and about one fourth of the Whole [*sic*] number are men who would be free from the Impress. Accordingly, there are only about 30,000 to 35,000 Seamen available in England at onetime [*sic*].

In regard to the means formerly adopted for obtaining men for the Navy.

1. A proclamation was issued recalling all seamen from Foreign Service.

2. Men were entered by Voluntary Enlistment, and bounties were paid to Volunteers, when these means failed and Ships were detained for want of Men, An Order in Council was obtained by which impress warrants were issued and men were taken by force.

3. An Act of Parliament was passed, calling upon each Sea Port and also the Counties to furnish a certain fixed number of Quota men for the Service of the Fleet[,] and Large bounties were offered by the principal Towns and Counties in addition to the bounty paid by the Government.

4. The Sea Fencibles were established and the Fishermen and sea faring population on the Coast were enrolled for Local defence.

Such were the various measures adopted by Government during previous War's [*sic*] for the purpose of obtaining men for the Fleet; there was no organized system, no special arrangements, but every seafaring man was considered liable to serve for the defence of the Country, and when his services were not voluntarily given by the acceptance of a bounty[,] he was liable to the impress and could be taken by force, and this compulsory measure was in former times the only means of ensuring a supply of men for the Naval Service.

The Question now put is, 'To what Extent are the resources of England in regard to Seamen organized and available in case of war.'

No compulsory system has been organized, or made available to bring forward the Seamen of England in case of war.

It appears necessary however to review the steps that have from time to time been taken to obtain seamen for the Fleet in case of any sudden Armament. Since 1812[,] various proposals and suggestions have been made for this purpose, and Lord Melville[,] when First Lord of the Admir[a]lty[,] endeavoured to form a registration of Seamen with the view of their being called out when required but [his attempt] failed.

In 1835, the Act of Parliament 5&6 William 4th Chap XIX was passed[,] which first established a registration of British Seamen and[,] as stated by Sir J[ames] Graham in the H[ouse] of C[ommons,] 'The measure would be the first step towards that more perfect system which would accomplish the important object which he had anxiously in view, the speedy and total abolition of impressment . . .'

In the same year another act [*sic*][,] 5&6 Wm 4 Chap XXIV, was passed for improving and conferring benefits on the Seamen serving in the Royal Navy, by limiting their <u>time</u> of Service to five year's [*sic*] and extending bounties.

In 1844[,] the Act of 7&8 Vic, Chap 112 was passed[,] extending and regulating the Registration of British Seamen, and[,] in the words of the Act[,] it is affirmed that [']the prosperity, Strength and Safety of this United Kingdom, and Her Majesty's Dominions, do greatly depend on a large, constant and ready supply of Seamen.'

The Board of Admiralty[,] having in view the necessity for adopting some measure which should provide a more permanent system for the Entry and Service of men in the Royal Navy[,] appointed early in 1852 a Committee of the most experienced Naval officers to consider the numerous proposals for Manning the Navy. This Committee[,] after very full investigation[,] reported as follows,

1. That a more permanent character should be given to the Naval Service, and that Seamen should be entered for 10 year's [*sic*] continuous service[,] with increased rates of Pay and earlier pensions.

2. That the Fishermen and Seafaring population should be voluntarily enrolled as a body of Coast Volunteers.

3. That Seamen should be permitted to leave the Naval Service at the expiration of ten and fifteen years with pensions, to go into the Merchant Service[,] and thus to form a reserve to be called out in case of war.

4. That 10000 Seamen[,] exclusive of officers[,] should be maintained for the defence of the Home Ports and independent of any Channel Squadron.

But the Committee[,] after very full enquiry and consideration, could not recommend any plan by which Seamen could be obtained for the rapid manning of the Fleet during war, 'That any Ballot in the Seafaring population could not be relied on for adequately manning the Royal Navy in case of any sudden emergency'[,] but recommended 'That every means should be resorted to with due economy for the formation of Naval reserves on the preferable mode of a voluntary principle'[.]

Again[,] the Committee state 'If[,] however[,] the measures for establishing a Reserve force which we recommend with the offer of ample Bounties, should still be found insufficient to meet the exigencies of a protracted war, and that the public feeling be repugnant to the use of the Means [*sic*][,] of the efficiency of which in all former wars or Armaments, our Naval Annals afford ample proof, but which lately have been more generally considered at variance with the spirit of the British Institutions [*sic*], we are not aware of any effectual substitute[,] unless by maintaining of much larger numbers of Seamen than would be required for the ordinary wants of the Naval Service in time of peace.'

So soon as the report of this Committee was received, the Board of Admiralty immediately adopted certain of the recommendations[,] and the Act 16th&17th Vic[,] Chap LXIX was passed, by which,

1. Seamen were to be enlisted for 10 years continuous service.
2. The Bounty clauses of 5&6 Will 4 Chap XXIV were altered[.]
3. Power was taken [*sic*] to call out seafaring men by Proclamation either during peace or war, by Classes, or age, or by Register Ticket[.]
4. The Coast Volunteers were also established & enrolled[,] . . . to consist of 10,000 men[.]

Considerable benefits and advantages were also conferred on the Seamen of the Fleet, by numerous regulations which had been introduced into the Service during a period of ten or twelve years.

In September 1853[,] the Board of Trade brought to the notice of the Admi[ra]lty that the act of 16th&17th Vic Chap 131[,] by which the owners of British Merchant Vessels, might employ any number of Foreign 'Seamen in British Ships, had rendered valueless the Registration Ticket, which every British Seaman was bound to have, and that the continuance of the registration System was a constant source of annoyance to the Seamen, and consequently proved a frequent cause of falsehood and immorality, as well as an inducement to seek employment under a Foreign Flag.' The Registration Ticket was consequently done away with, and thus fell to the ground the registration of Seamen[,] a measure introduced in 1835, and the only practical instrument on which to found any organized system for manning the Fleet, for I must express my decided conviction that no measure which may be based on the principle of Voluntary Enlistment for the purpose of obtaining Seamen for the Fleet, will ever give confidence to the Government, or will ever be the means of meeting the wants of a great or pressing Emergency. The only practical measure which can be efficient must be founded on the knowledge of the residence or position of each individual Seaman liable to serve, and this cannot be done without Registration.

In regard to reserves of Men[,] the Board of Admiralty adopted every measure which could lead to this object,

1. By allowing men to retire from the Service with Pensions after 10 or 15 years service.
2. By the transfer of the Coast Guard from the Board of Customs, and [by] rendering that Service more numerous as well as more efficient.
3. By enrolling the Coast Volunteers from the Seafaring population on the Coast[,] of whom 6000 have already been enrolled.
4. By retaining in reserve the Long Service Naval Pensioners[.]

These various measures are progressing in a favorable [*sic*] manner, but even when completed to the full number's [*sic*] intended[,] the measure is merely a make shift [*sic*], altho ships may no doubt be manned on an emergency as a substitute for more efficient mean's [*sic*][,] but the real great question and the most important one in which the safety of this Country is involved is, 'How are Seamen to be obtained in case of war'[?] we require in the first month at least 30,000 men, and the wants of the Country during a protracted war will require that number to be increased to at least 100,000 men. The whole Merchant Service does not produce 175,000 men[,] and never more than 30,000 to 35,000 [are] in England at onetime [*sic*][.] moreover the former registration of Seamen belonging to the Merchant Service did not include the Seafaring population of the Country, Fishermen, Boatmen, Barge Men &c[,] that in number must exceed 100,000 men[,] and any measure adopted for manning the Navy ought to include these men.

The question then really is, What [*sic*] are the measures which ought to be taken to procure men for the Fleet[?]

The sources from which Men are to be drawn are the Seamen and the Seafaring population of the Country, and to obtain these by any organized system[,] I am of opinion they must be registered, and some boon held out to them in order that they should enrol themselves for the Service of the State in case of War, but with power of calling them out when their Services are required.

As this subject is to form the Enquiry [*sic*] by a Royal Commission[,] it is perhaps unnecessary to enter into details.
The Registration Ticket to Seamen was a total failure[:] it drove our men to hail as Americans[,] and the Ticket had to be given up[,] and no Seaman <u>can</u> be Compelled to serve in the Navy[.] Bounty of £10 was given during the Crimean War and after the Italian Armament, causing discontent to our own men in HM Ships. So we have only the Naval reserves to look to[,] & half if no[t] more are [at any time] absent from this Country[.]

[**623**] *Drummond Memorandum on the State of the Navy*

Admiralty
May 1858

<u>Most Confidential</u>
Memorandum

The remarks contained in the Memorandum submitted for consideration[1] point out the necessity of immediate attention to the present state of the defence of Great Britain:

1st. What are the duties which would be required of the Navy of Great Britain at the outbreak of war with France?

The first steps to take would be to organize and equip a powerful fleet for the protection of our own shores, and to reinforce our squadrons on foreign stations.

At Home[:]
We should require –
A Channel Fleet;
A Squadron on the Irish Coasts, and west coast of Scotland;
A North Sea fleet;
The reinforcement of our garrisons at Alderney and the Channel Islands
Abroad[:]
An <u>immediate</u> reinforcement of the Mediterranean squadron, and the provisioning and coaling of Gibraltar, Malta, and Corfu.
We should then consider –
Bermuda,
Canada,
Mauritius,
The West Indies,

[1]Pakington's memorandum of March 1858, [**619**].

The East Indies and Ceylon,
China,
New South Wales,
Pacific,
Brazil,
The Islands of St. Helena and Ascension

Our extensive Colonies would in war prove a weakness. They must be considered after our home defences are in a measure provided for; and it becomes a question to what extent the Colonies could be independent, and provide towards their own defence, by raising men and fortifying their harbours.

We should also require to consider our several coaling stations abroad, and the protection necessary to keep them available.

These several duties would require the entire strength of the Navy to be put forward in order to carry them into execution.

In estimating our necessary requirements, we may be guided, to a certain extent, by what we had during the great war, although, from the introduction of steam, there will be many more demands upon our resources.

For home defences, Channel and Mediterranean fleet, we should require in ships: –

30 Sail of the line,
40 Frigates,
100 Sloops and small vessels.
with [*sic*] a reserve of one-third to be brought forward.

To reinforce our foreign stations, and employ there: – Ships.

30 Sail of the line,
60 Frigates,
100 Sloops and small vessels.

In order to man these fleets, we should require a number of at least 135,000 men; but before we consider how these men are to be procured on an emergency of war, it would be well to ask this question, Have [*sic*] we a sufficient number of ships or are we building them?

As to the number of ships[,] I consider we are deficient, both in ships of the line and frigates, particularly in the latter. I am also of opinion that we have not advanced sufficiently within the last three years towards making up the required number of ships, and that in comparison with the Navy of France and that of Russia, we are now in a backwards state, both as regards construction of ships and powerful engines.

We will now consider –

2ndly, What are the resources of England in point of seamen, and how [are they to be] organized and available in case of war?

Nobody, who has given any attention to the subject of manning our fleet, can deny that we are at present totally without resources sufficient to enable us to meet an enemy, such as France would be; and when we consider that we must depend chiefly upon our Navy, for the defence of Great Britain, as well as of our numerous colonies and possessions abroad, this subject requires very serious attention.

Seamen, fit to man our fleet, and uphold the honour of our nation, cannot be picked up at hazard, or at a moment's notice; they require to be well-trained, and accustomed to the duties of a ship of war.

The present vote for the Navy is as follows –

52,000 officers and men, including 15,000 marines;

7,000 coast guard;

6,000 Royal Naval coast volunteers;

To these numbers may be added about 5,000 available pensioners; making as a grand total,

70,000.

These, then, are the resources of England in point of seamen and marines; our total reserves would be called up immediately; and instead of enabling us to equip fleets such as would be necessary to cope with France, they barely exceed half the number estimated as absolutely requisite, and would scarcely afford sufficient means for the defence of our own shores; indeed, this would only be the case, if we had the entire number voted, actually at home, whereas we have about 20,000 men, including 6,000 marines, and the men and officers in the ordinary and reserve harbour ships; our available force, therefore, at home, including our reserves, is reduced to a total of about 35,000 men.

Much has been said against the present system of the Coast Guard. I do not think it perfect – it may be improved; but it must be borne in mind that whereas, in 1852, we had but a small reserve, we have, by the adoption of continuous-service men, the employment afloat of a considerable portion of the vote for Coast Guard, and the organization of Naval Coast Volunteers, made a step in the right direction towards a permanent Navy and reserve: but this is not sufficient. It is quite evident that the demands upon the Navy, even during peace, are far beyond what the present numbers voted will permit our attending to [*sic*]. Even in our inland war, going on for a year in India, the services of our seamen have been called for. In China, what was intended to have been accomplished by soldiers, has been chiefly accomplished by sailors and marines; and at home we have been for upwards of a year deprived of any naval force whatever, beyond a few advanced ships, only half manned.

We require, therefore, to have at once a Permanent Navy of 60,000.
30,000 continuous service men and boys.
5,000 entry of merchant seamen.
5,000 to include officers, and ratings of servants and others.
20,000 marines, of whom 5,000 should be Marine Artillery.

As our ships are now armed with heavy guns throwing shell, it would be of the greatest advantage to be able to embark practiced and good gunners from the Marine Artillery, on the first outbreak of a war.

A Navy thus constituted would enable us to have always ready home defences.

We will now consider the Reserves.

I would increase the Coast Guard to 10,000 men, training a portion in ships at sea, during the summer months. The Naval Coast Volunteers should at once be increased to 15,000, and might, if thought requisite, be raised to 20,000 on the outbreak of war.

I am of opinion that, with judicious management and some slight addition of officers as staff, this force will not only prove to be most useful for our home defences, but that it will supply our Navy partially with volunteers.

Now comes the question of how our mercantile marine is to be made available. Impressment, according to the present laws, still exists. During the great war, a large proportion of our seamen was thus procured; can it be resorted to in the event of war? I think not. Yet we have not fewer than 170,000 men employed in the merchant-service. It would appear that, of this number, after deduction of the foreigners and men protected from impressment, we have not more than 80,000 men available, and of this number about one fourth, or rather more, may be found in the United Kingdom at any one time. Surely the country has a right to command the services of a portion of this number in the event of an emergency such as war; and I think that immediate steps should be taken to ensure the power of doing this.

The Report of the Manning Committee in 1853 suggested many alterations and improvements for the Navy, some of which are now producing a good effect; but, upon the subject of making the mercantile service available as a reserve, it settled no plan on which instructions could be framed: on the contrary, it pointed out that the ballot could not be relied upon; that the registration of seamen had failed; [and] that bounties, as formerly given, would not do enough to secure a sufficient supply of seamen. It is therefore the more necessary that Parliament should decide this question without further delay.

In considering the present state of the Navy, it is well to remember that, within a very few years, we have created a Steam navy, and that other countries have done, and are now doing, the same. It may be added, that both France and Russia are making rapid strides to go beyond us in the building and arming of ships.[1] In the power of manning their fleets at the outbreak of war, they are already superior to us in their organization and reserves.[2]

These are facts which ought not be lost sight of, and more particularly as regards the state of our home defences, and power to resist the invasion of a neighbour such as France.

We are employed in making a harbour and fortress at Alderney, also at Portland; for what? Not to fall into the hands of an enemy on the first outbreak of a war; yet this not only may happen, but must inevitably be the case, if we do not adopt the only means which is in our power to prevent such a catastrophe and national disgrace.

We require to keep in commission during peace such a permanent Channel fleet as would be sufficient to resist any surprise from an enemy, and which would form the nucleus of a fleet for war; and also to have our reserves of ships in such an efficient and forward state as would enable us to send to sea powerful fleets.

I would most earnestly recommend that this step should be taken at once, not waiting for a more convenient time, or until our forces can be reduced on foreign stations. We are at this moment undefended, and not in the position a first-rate Power ought to be.

The present state of our arsenals, both for the building of ships, and the repairs of ships and engines, requires attention.

We must recollect that to create and to keep in repair powerful steam-fleets, it is requisite to have our establishments on a great scale: we must be prepared to add largely to the several departments, if we are to keep our place among nations. When we look at what has been accomplished during the last twenty years at Toulon and Cherbourg, and contrast our works at Portsmouth and Plymouth, we cannot but acknowledge that we have not advanced in the improvements towards the deepening of our natural harbours, and the creation of docks for large ships, so fast as is required.

[1]This claim, like most such, was hyperbolic. France and Russia were indeed making rapid strides in building and arming ships, but neither power, especially Russia, was bent on surpassing the Royal Navy. At best, Louis Napoleon was seeking a technological advantage that he must have realised was ephemeral. See Theodore Ropp, *The Development of a Modern Navy: French Naval Policy 1871–1904*, ed. Stephen Roberts (Annapolis, 1987), pp. 9–10; J. R. Hill (ed.), *The Oxford Illustrated History of the Royal Navy* (Oxford, 1995), pp. 163–4, 188–9; Andrew Lambert, *Battleships in Transition: The Creation of the Steam Battlefleet 1815–1860* (London, 1984), pp. 97–111, 113–14.

[2]So alarmists routinely claimed. The performance of both French and Russian navies during the Crimean War strongly suggests otherwise.

There are many details into which I need not enter. I have confined myself to the principles. I consider the importance of this subject is such as must call for the serious attention of the Government.

I feel confident the natural protection of our islands, namely, a fully manned and well-trained fleet, cannot be dispensed with.

The placing of our Navy upon such a permanent footing during peace as will enable us to be prepared for the emergency of war, is also indispensable; and I conclude with a recommendation that this course should be adopted immediately.

[**624**] *Milne Minute on Proposed Alterations in the Terms of Continuous Service*[1]

Admiralty
17 May 1858

There can be no doubt that one of the most important measures connected with the Naval Service is the manning of our ships, and to organize this is [the] duty of the Board. Admiral Martin has[,] with this view[,] put forward certain proposals amending Circular No 121 of June 1853[,] which was framed to carry out the recommendations of the Manning Committee of 1852, and first established [*sic*] the Continuous Service System. The Board of Admiralty[,] in framing that Circular[,] had to consider the <u>various periods</u> of time the Seamen had served in the Navy, and to arrange their Entry [*sic*] into the Continuous Service[,] that all men might derive the benefit of that regulation. This led to the Clauses 1,2,3,4,5 & 6 at page 5 of the Circular.[2] These were necessary at the time to induce men to come forward for general service. It is now proposed to abrogate all these clauses except No 1, and that no man will be received for Continuous service unless he enters for 10 Years at once. I think this will prove a failure, and I would recommend that Clauses 2 and 3 be retained in

[1]The proposal originated with First Naval Lord William Fanshawe Martin.

[2]The advertised rates of pay extended to: 1. All men who volunteered for ten years' continuous general service. 2. Those men signed on for a single commission and then volunteered for continuous service. The rates of pay for the latter status were to commence from the date of their volunteering. 3. Those men then serving who volunteered for not less than seven years of continuous service. 4. Men who had already served ten years or more from the age of eighteen upwards, who volunteered for seven years, or for long enough to attain twenty years' service. 5. Men who have served sixteen or more years, who signed up for long enough to attain twenty-one years' service. 6. Men who had completed one engagement under any of the foregoing clauses were entitled to the higher rates of pay for continuous service men upon re-enlisting under specified conditions, but only if they re-enlisted as continuous service men.

principle, especially No 3. It will induce men who are serving to enter for 7 years, by allowing part of their previous service to count for pension.

The number of men who can be continuous service [*sic*] is 26,000[,] and we now require 4,700 to complete this number. This should be done as soon as possible[,] and by retaining clauses 2 & 3 it will materially aid in this object.

I doubt the expediency of promulgating any new regulation limiting the age of future entry to 25 years of age, but in any order given for now completing the Continuous Service[,] I see no reason why the limit should not be restricted to 30 years.

<u>Short Service Pensioners</u>

I consider these positions should only be allowed to men whose ships are being paid off, and on no account should men serving abroad[,] and who may have completed 10 or 15 year's [*sic*][,] be allowed to Volunteer for this reserve Pension and draw the <u>Pension and Pay</u>. almost [*sic*] every man who may may [*sic*] have completed the time would no doubt accept the offer, but the object of this Pension was to get men into a <u>reserve at Home</u>, and[,] if <u>called</u> out[,] he would be allowed to draw Pension & Pay of his rating, but if he voluntarily returns to the <u>Service</u> then he forfeits the pension, therefore to give it <u>to men</u> on Foreign Stations when serving would be a dangerous precedent[.]

It is also <u>unadvisable</u> to allow any more men to take the pension at present. the [*sic*] Coast Guard and Coast Guard ships have already drawn nearly 3000 men out of the Navy since 1856, and to make a further demand from our Vote of about 25000 men would be inexpedient when Seamen are much wanted[,] more especially trained men. for [*sic*] this reason[,] I think the regulation of Volunteers for this reserve should be limited to ships paying off and not extended to Foreign Stations. When you get an excess in the Vote [then] allow men to withdraw.

In regard to the doing away with the Entry of 2d C[lass] Boys[,] I think it a measure which seriously effects [*sic*] the Naval Service and could not work advantageously; if Ad Martin has those views on this subject, the experiment might be tried in two or three ships, of different rates.

Looking at this whole question[,] and the fact that the late war has prevented the Circular [*sic*] No 121 from being fairly worked out, I think it would be better to leave it as it is for at least another year, but to issue an order to enter continuous service men as the Board may decide[,] by excluding the Clauses 2 to 6 inclusive or retaining No 2 and 3. I am afraid any new Circular would cause inconvenience and unsettle the men's minds.[1]

[625] *Board Minute on Proposed Alterations in the Terms of Continuous Service*

Admiralty
[May 1858]

My Lords have considered the views submitted in the enclosed minutes with respect to new regulations as to entry for continuous service, & are of opinion that it is not desirable to adopt new regulations until the Commission appointed to consider the Manning of the Navy, shall have made a report. But my Lords are of opinion that no time ought to be lost in strengthening the Naval Force of the Country by the entry of Seamen for Continuous Service . . .

[626] *Saunders Dundas Memorandum on the State of the Navy*

Admiralty
June 1858

Most Confidential
Memorandum for Sir John Pakington

The Memorandum on the state of the Navy, on which the opinions of the Board have been required, contains a clear and forcible statement of matters which should occupy the serious attention of the Admiralty. The questions raised within it are of a nature to render it impossible that they can be indefinitely postponed with safety, until the time has arrived at which the prospect of a war with France might be no longer doubtful; and sooner or later they may force themselves on the notice of the country.

There is nothing new, however, in the details presented to us, and nothing which has not already suggested itself. It must, nevertheless, be admitted that there is also nothing in the practical arrangements of the Board, or in the present condition of the Naval service, which can furnish satisfactory answers to such questions.

Some explanation of these startling deficiencies is to be found in the fact that time will be necessary for the creation of a Steam Navy, and

[1]Saunders Dundas also composed a minute opposing the proposed changes. See ADM1/5698, Box 1.

the financial questions connected with the preparation of Naval means are altogether beyond the control of the Board of Admiralty. The expenditure necessary, also, to place the British dominions, at home and abroad, in a condition of absolute security against France would be enormous.

The means of procuring seamen are likewise defective and the number which would be required to equip and distribute the forces requisite to give security to the Colonies, and to protect the trade in all parts of the world, is such that it seems hopeless to expect they could be suddenly supplied without interruption to commerce, to an extent which would be almost more injurious than any casual losses which might be inflicted by an enemy on distant stations at the first commencement of a war. Under any circumstances, the power to secure their services is beyond the control of the Board of Admiralty, unless we are to suppose that impressment could again be successfully enforced. In the face of the documents attached to the Memorandum,[1] it must be needless to discuss the past history of impressment, or the present practicability of such a measure, and little practical good can arise at all, except from a careful scrutiny of the means which actually exist, and of the manner in which they can be best improved and made available.

The first question, as truly stated, is to consider what are the duties which would be required of the Navy at the outbreak of a war with France? These duties may be conveniently divided under two distinct heads, viz.: –

1. The Protection of the British Channel[2] and the Shores of Great Britain and Ireland[,] And [*sic*]

2. The protection of trade and Colonies in distant parts of the world.

If the first of these two objects could be secured, and if proper garrisons could be maintained in our most important possession abroad, there would be, comparatively, little risk of surprise, or of any vital blow upon distant stations at the beginning of a war; but it should be carefully observed, that in the case of war with France, the measures necessary for the defence of our possessions in the Mediterranean can scarcely be separated from those which would be required for the absolute protection of the shores of the United Kingdom.

In the event of a threatened attack upon England, nothing is more probable than that the first aggressive attempts on the part of France might be upon Minorca, Malta, Corfu, or other important positions in the Mediterranean. Such attempts would necessarily compel us to de-

[1]Not included in this edition.

[2]Scotsman Saunders Dundas seems to have scorned the traditional name.

tach from the ports in England a considerable portion of the naval force which might have been provided for the more immediate protection of this country, and it will always be in the power of France to transfer her forces rapidly from one point of attack to another. An armament at Toulon might seriously threaten Minorca or Malta; but the whole military force, and the seamen, could be transferred to the ports on the western or northern shores of France in less time than would be required for us to protect our possessions in the Mediterranean, if not already prepared at the commencement of a war. The troops destined for a descent upon England or the Channel Islands would not necessarily be identical with those collected at Toulon, but those at Toulon would be available to replace others in the interior, which might be thrown suddenly into the northern ports. A few days would suffice to transfer a considerable number of seamen. It must be evident, therefore, that a sufficient naval force in the Mediterranean before the actual commencement of a war would be indispensable, in addition to the force that might be required for the protection of the Channel and the coasts of England.

An increase of

8 Sail of the Line
6 Large frigates
10 Sloops or small vessels

would be but a small addition to the present force in the Mediterranean if war were imminent, but such an addition would at once withdraw from the home ports a larger squadron than is at all likely to be established in the Channel in the existing state of our finances, and, under these circumstances, it seems vain to expect that satisfactory answers can be afforded by the Admiralty to the questions which have been proposed for our consideration. It is, nevertheless, right and necessary that these questions should be carefully studied, and that there should be some clear understanding between the several Departments of the Government.

In judging the amount of naval force which would at once be required by this country, and having clearly determined that it should combine security to the shores of England, and effectual protection to Ireland, with the maintenance of our possessions in the Mediterranean, it becomes necessary to determine the proper amount of force for the home station in addition to that specified for the Mediterranean.

Looking to the contingency of a sudden attempt, with a view to a landing upon our shores, it may be remembered that no attempt could be altogether sudden if it were to involve the necessity of collecting a large force either at Cherbourg or at any other one of the principal ports of France. The recent experience of an embarkation at Baljik has demonstrated that time and means are necessary for such an undertaking, and no landing, with a view to positive invasion of England, could be attempted without some security for the communications afterwards by sea with the invading army. It is true that great risks might be incurred for such an object, but with the warning which the mere collection of such a force at any one port must necessarily convey, it can scarcely be doubted that a much smaller force would be enough to frustrate the attempt.

Other means, however, might be adopted. In the summer season, the distances extending between all the various ports from Dunquerque to Brest, or even to L'Orient and the Loire, are not too great to prevent the possibility of suddenly combining the movements of several squadrons and a numerous flotilla, destined to rendezvous at a particular point in the Channel. In settled weather, by matured arrangements, and with the aid of steam and of the telegraph, a single day and a summer's night might be sufficient to unite them with tolerable punctuality. Against such an effort great precaution would be required, and the preparation of an adequate force, to be stationed near each of the principal ports of France, would be indispensable.

To be safe in England, the Navy afloat should be in a condition not merely to wait in anxious expectation of an attack, but boldly to court engagement, as formerly, at the entrances of the ports of France. It is not to be denied that the preparations of this country are inadequate for the purpose. We have neither ships afloat, nor troops on shore; we have neither men nor officers for the rapid equipment of a powerful Navy. The works at Alderney are incomplete, and the Channel Islands are imperfectly defended; while it is impossible to overrate their importance as affecting the command of the British Channel.

There are still other contingencies to be considered. The efforts of France might be mainly directed to obtain complete command of the Mediterranean, and, possibly, to an attempt on Gibraltar. Her operations in the British Channel might be limited to desultory attacks on particular ports, for the double purpose of disturbing our arsenals, and occupying the continued attention of the naval forces in England, and on the coasts of Ireland and Scotland. There is no point, therefore, which could safely be left unguarded. Our squadrons would require to be distributed; and if weak at most points they might be strong at none, unless time were to be afforded for concentration by failure in the general arrangements of the enemy. To counteract these efforts, the only safe course must to be to assume the offensive; and instead of feebly guarding the most important positions on our coasts, our Navy should be prepared to enforce, effectually, a strict blockade of the ports of the enemy.

Under every view of the probable course of hostilities, it is plain that, in addition to the wants of the Mediterranean, a very considerable naval force would be required on the Home stations.

The subjoined list contains an outline of the number and description of vessels which might be necessary. The distribution is arbitrary, but it will be enough to show that the greatest force which has ever been maintained in the Channel, during peace, would be insufficient to provide for the necessities of a sudden war with France. The numbers specified are far from being excessive; and if Russia were to be joined to France, a still further increase would be necessary in the North Sea

Portsmouth Station:
- 6 Sail of the Line,
- 3 Large frigates,
- 2 Small ditto,
- 8 Sloops and small vessels,
- 15 Gun-boats, &c.

Devonport Station:
- 6 Sail of the line,
- 3 Large frigates,
- 2 Small ditto,
- 8 Sloops and small vessels,
- 15 Gun-boats.

Sheerness Station to the Tweed:
- 4 Sail of the line,
- 3 Large frigates,
- 2 Small ditto,
- 10 Sloops,
- 30 Gun-vessels, or gun-boats and tenders.

Leith and Cromarty:
- 2 Sail of the line,
- 2 Large frigates,
- 2 Small ditto,
- 12 Gun-vessels or boats.

Ireland

Cork:
- 2 Sail of the line,
- 2 Large frigates,
- 4 Sloops,
- 6 Small vessels,

6 Gun-boats.

Bantry and the Shannon

2 Sail of the line,
2 Large frigates,
2 Sloops,
6 Gun-boats.

North of Ireland:

1 Frigate,
3 Sloops.

Milford, Holyhead, and Dublin:

2 Sail of the line,
1 Large frigate,
2 Small frigates,
6 Gun-vessels.

Clyde and Mersey:

2 Large frigates,
2 Small frigates,
4 Sloops,
6 Gun-vessels or boats.

Channel Islands:

2 Large frigates,
4 Small frigates or sloops,
12 Gun-vessels (Alderney),
15 Gun-boats (Jersey).

Mediterranean:

12 Sail of the line,
6 Large frigates,
4 Small frigates,
10 Sloops,
20 Gun-vessels and tenders.

In the above estimate of force there can be no intention to convey the idea that, under all the circumstances of war, it will be requisite to maintain at every port or station the precise number of vessels which have been assigned to each. On the contrary, the ships specified would be so dispersed, for the express purpose of being able to assemble a certain amount of force, at short notice, upon any one particular point. The ships from Cork and Bantry, for instance, joined to those from Devonport and Milford, might be united off Ushant; and with the aid of the telegraph, others might also be detached from the eastward in support. In the same manner, the ships at Sheerness could give support to the Humber or to Leith, and others might be detached from the westward, according to the known force of the enemy at Cherbourg, or in the western ports. In general it is more than probable that a force at Portland, in connection with a powerful squadron in the Channel Islands, would present the most effectual check to the sudden movement and combination of the enemy's squadrons from the ports of Brest, Cherbourg, and St. Malo, and a force in the Downs should be at hand to watch the motions of vessels from Dunquerque and other eastern ports of France.

If it should at all appear that the ships and vessels enumerated would be more than sufficient for the duties which would be required, it should be remembered that detachments from home might be unavoidable for Nova Scotia, or the St. Lawrence, or for Bermuda and the West Indies; and the forces now stated present a total of 24 sail of the line, 35 frigates, and 39 sloops, in addition to smaller steam-vessels, or gun-vessels and gun-boats. To these must be added the force in the Mediterranean, consisting of not less than 12 sail of the line, 10 frigates and 10 sloops, with 20 gun-vessels and tenders; and it will be observed, that nothing has been said specially of Lisbon, Cadiz, or Gibraltar.

Before entering into the requirements for other more distant stations, it may be well to observe, in the first instance, that if it should be impossible to provide for the manning and the armament of the ships which would be wanted for active operations in the Channel and Mediterranean, it can be of little avail to discuss the requirements for other parts of the world. For the effectual defence of this country the reserves of seamen and the force of marines should be at all times enough for the rapid equipment of the fleet already enumerated. There can be no difficulty in arriving at a correct estimate of the numbers of officers, seamen, marines, and boys required for the purpose, according to the complements at present allowed, and if satisfactory arrangements could be made for the equipment of such a force, the squadrons in other parts of the world might safely be left to be dealt with from other sources, according to the exigencies of the moment and the gradual development of the war.

It is necessary, however, to form some estimate of the strength of the squadrons to be required for these other stations, and to study the peculiar wants of each of them. The following may accordingly be assumed as giving a moderate account of the forces which might probably be indispensable upon each station within a twelvemonth after the first declaration of a war; and it should never be forgotten that a decidedly weak squadron upon a distant station must present a positive inducement to a surprise.

West Indies and North America:
- 6 Sail of the line,
- 6 Large frigates,
- 4 Small frigates,
- 10 Sloops,
- 10 Small vessels and tenders,
- 20 Gun-boats at Bermuda.

Cape of Good Hope and Coasts of Africa:
- 2 Sail of the line,
- 3 Large frigates,
- 4 Small frigates,
- 10 Sloops,
- 6 Gun-boats or small steamers and tenders.

The Brazils:
- 2 Sail of the line,
- 3 Frigates,
- 6 Sloops,
- 4 Small vessels.

East Indies:
- 4 Sail of the line,
- 6 Large frigates,
- 10 Smaller frigates,
- 15 Sloops,
- 10 Small steam or gun-vessels,
- 20 Gun-boats (in China),
- 4 Hospital and receiving ships.

Australia and New Zealand:
- 3 Large frigates,
- 3 Small frigates,
- 6 Sloops,
- 6 Small vessels.

The Pacific:
- 4 Sail of the line,
- 6 Large frigates,
- 6 Small frigates,
- 6 Sloops,
- 8 Small vessels and tenders,
- 2 Store-ships.

Having thus stated the number of ships and vessels proposed for each of the foregoing stations, it may be proper to consider briefly the circumstances which might require special attention upon each station.

Commencing with North America and the West Indies, it may be noticed that the command would be too extensive to be placed entirely under the control of a single flag officer during war; and in all probability it would require to be divided, or two Rear-Admirals might be placed under one Commander-in-Chief, whose head-quarters should be at Bermuda. The security of Newfoundland and Nova Scotia, the protection of the coal fields at Cape Breton and at Pictou, with the free navigation of the St. Lawrence, would be objects of paramount importance, and would give ample occupation for one flag officer, with an effective squadron. It cannot be necessary to dwell on the importance of Bermuda; and when the extensive interests involved in the security of our West India possessions are fully considered, it will probably appear that the forces estimated for this station might be insufficient if other forces from England could not be sent readily in pursuit of squadrons which might be detached from France.

The next station is that of the Cape of Good Hope; and within its limits are comprised the Colony of Sierra Leone, the Islands of Ascension and St. Helena, the very important and valuable possession of the Mauritius [*sic*], in addition to the Coasts of the Cape Colony. The suppression of the slave trade on the coasts of Africa may be fairly excluded from this estimate. It may be doubted whether all our efforts for that one object have been successful during peace, as they would be altogether unavailing if war were to be extended over the Atlantic [*sic*]; but the coaling stations on the route to the East Indies could in no case be prudently neglected.

The naval station at Simon's Bay, and the capital of the colony at Table Bay, would be wholly defenceless in the absence of an adequate naval force.

The Island of Mauritius, if strongly fortified, might be defended by a proper garrison; but with a mixed population, and partly of French extraction, the countenance and control of a British naval force could scarcely be dispensed with in the presence of an enemy's squadron. For all these reasons it will be evident that the force proposed for the protection of such varied and important interests can in no sense be regarded as excessive.

On the Brazil Station there are no important interests beyond the general protection of the trade; but a force would be required, and it should watch the movements of an enemy proceeding to the Pacific, and the Falkland Islands ought not to be neglected. They might even be important if the theatre of war were to be extended to the Pacific, and especially in the event of a union between France and Russian or in doubtful relations with the United States of America.

Next in order may be noticed the extensive station included within the limits of the East India command. Some slight protection to the territories of the East India Company might be afforded by the Indian Navy, but it would be altogether unsafe to trust only to that defence. The naval station at Trincomalee is unhappily ill fortified, and is exposed to an attack even by a small squadron. Singapore, in connection with China, is scarcely less important; and there are other possessions in the Straits of Malacca which ought not to be negligently exposed. The frequent visits of French Squadrons to New Caledonia and other Islands of the Eastern Archipelago should be enough to point out that, in the event of war, Great Britain cannot afford to be indifferent to their movements; and it must be unnecessary, in this short notice, to advert either to Hong Kong, and our trade in China, or to the extensive territories of Australia and New Zealand.

If, in addition to the Indian Navy, it were possible to create and to foster a Colonial Navy in those now populous countries, it would afford not only the best security against the inroads of French squadrons, but the best counterpoise to the undoubted efforts of Russia in the Amour [*sic*] and in Kamchatka. The subject is altogether a large one, and it will be enough to allude to it to point out that here also, as upon other stations, the force suggested would be small in proportion to the extent of the station, and the important interests requiring to be protected.

In the Pacific, our squadrons would require to be dispersed over a large extent of ocean; powerful squadrons of [the] enemy's frigates might be expected, and our interests everywhere would need protection. Our possessions in the Hudson's Bay territory, and at Vancouver's Island, and the trade connected with them, are gradually growing into importance, to say nothing of the trade in Chile and in Peru or Mexico, and in the widely-scattered islands of the Pacific. The general tendency to encroachment, on the part of the United States, could hardly fail to complicate the difficulties of our position in the event of war with France; and squadrons sufficient to command respect, would be necessary to maintain our position.

The foregoing statements have been intended to show, that after the full development of the war, a force would be required which would amount, with officers and men, collectively, to, viz., –

54 sail of the line, at 800 each	43,200
54 large frigates, at 500 each	26,500
47 small frigates, at 300 each	14,100
92 sloops, average 140 each	11,880
136 steam or gun-vessels [*sic*], at 90 each	12,240

97 gun-boats, at 50 each	4,750
Total	112,670

It is almost needless to observe that this estimate can only be approximate, but the total numbers will be found to be less than the numbers borne in the fleet in 1805, or in any subsequent year, to the close of the war in 1814. Between 1792, at the outbreak of the Revolutionary War, and 1795, the total force of the Navy was increased from 17,361 to 99,608, actually borne.

When the large increase of population in our colonies, and the proportionate increase of trade in all parts of the world, are taken into account, it will be evident that there can be no exaggeration in the estimate as now stated. On the contrary, it should be remarked, that no account has been taken of the number which would be required for indispensable harbour service, in addition to the complements of the fleet at sea.

It is plain, however, that it would be ruinous during peace to burden the finances of the country with the maintenance of reserves, either of men or officers, equal to the equipment of a force which has rarely been maintained, except at the periods referred to, and towards the close of a very protracted war; but it is not less certain that the sudden commencement of a similar war in the present state of the Navy of France, is a contingency which cannot be lightly disregarded, and it will not be too much to assert that means should be at the disposal of the Government to equip rapidly the force enumerated for the Home Stations and for the Mediterranean.

In addition to the ships at present employed at sea upon these stations, the numbers specified would entail the necessity for a further rapid increase of force at the outbreak of a war, which would amount to nearly 60,000 officers and men. The numbers now borne in the whole service afloat do not exceed a total of 46,000 officers and men, exclusive of the Marines in barracks, but not excepting the Harbour service afloat. Of this total, about 25,000 men, in round numbers, may be stated to be seamen, stokers, and artificers, exclusive of officers, marines, and boys. In the same proportion it would follow that the reserves of seamen, stokers, and artificers, should amount habitually to 30,000 or 32,000, with about 7,000 marines in barracks fit for embarkation.

In the foregoing estimate it has been thought less necessary to consider the actual strength of the French Navy at the present time, than to determine the amount of British force upon each station which would be required, if only a portion of that Navy were to be collected upon particular points. It cannot be too often observed, that the necessity for distribution, and the requirements for guarding our colonies and trade in all parts of the world, and under great variety of circumstances, render it impossible to judge of our actual strength by a mere numerical comparison with the ships in each class of the French Navy. The security of Great Britain, and her possessions abroad, must clearly depend upon her power to meet attacks upon every station upon which a French force might happen to be concentrated; and it is in this point of view only that the second question proposed for the consideration of the Board can be properly dealt with. It becomes necessary, therefore, to inquire, 1st, What [*sic*] is the total strength of the French Navy? And [*sic*], 2ndly, What [*sic*] is the total amount of force which could be safely detached from the coasts of France, for hostilities against the foreign possessions or the foreign trade of Great Britain?

The latest information of which we are in possession would give the total strength of the Steam navy of France to consist of, viz.: –

24 Sail of screw ships of the line,
15 Ditto ditto ditto building,
6 Screw frigates afloat,
15 Ditto converting,
20 Paddle-wheel frigates afloat,
8 Screw corvettes afloat,
6 Ditto building and converting,
9 Paddle-wheel corvettes afloat,

making a total of 39 sail of the line, 41 screw and paddle frigates, and 24 corvettes.

Transports and other experimental vessels are supposed to be preparing, of which our information is more or less imperfect; but a short time may, perhaps, suffice to place the whole of this steam force in a condition to put to sea. For purposes of aggression, the number of ships will hardly appear enough to enable France to undertake hostilities against England simultaneously in the Channel and in the Mediterranean, and to detach at the same time any considerable amount of force to distant stations. It would, nevertheless, be more than enough to render it necessary that the British fleet on the Home stations and Mediterranean should be in force sufficient to guard against unexpected attacks of formidable squadrons; and it is so far satisfactory to believe that the total British force of steam-ships which are actually afloat, or are likely to be launched and serviceable in the ports of England in the course of the present year, may be stated to be, viz.: –

23 Screw-ships of the line afloat,
6 Ditto ditto building and completing,
9 Block-ships afloat and equipped,
4 Screw-frigates in commission,
8 Large screw-frigates afloat,
2 Ditto ditto building and completing,
4 Small screw-frigates refitting,
3 Mortar-frigates,
4 Large screw-corvettes afloat,
5 Ditto ditto building and completing,
5 Small screw-corvettes afloat,
6 Ditto ditto refitting,
5 Ditto ditto building and completing,
1 Gun-vessel building and completing,
4 Ditto afloat,
9 Ditto refitting,
84 Gun-boats, 60 horse-power, afloat and on slips,
17 Gun-boats, 40 horse-power, afloat and on slips,
7 Gun-boats, 20 horsepower, afloat and on slips,

making a total of 38 sail of the line, 18 frigates, 3 mortar-frigates, 25 corvettes, 14 gun-vessels, [and] 108 gun-boats.

To these may be added 6 paddle-frigates and 16 paddle-sloops, exclusive of the existing squadrons in commission in the Channel and in the Mediterranean, which ought reasonably to be taken into account in a comparison with the total force of the Navy in France. Of the paddle-sloops enumerated[,] a large proportion at the present moment require to be repaired and refitted; but it is believed that the present strength of the dockyards should be enough to overtake [*sic*] the work which would be required if exertions were necessary, and close attention is paid to this subject.

In reference to that portion of the Memorandum which adverts to the supposed rapid progress in the building of ships in France, as compared with this country, there can be no question that great efforts appear to have been made in France, as well in the building of ships as in the construction of steam-machinery; but when the known difficulties experienced in England in the construction and repairs [*sic*] of steam-engines are dispassionately considered, there seems to be no reason to suppose that it will not be in the power of this country to compare with the French Navy. Too much stress may, perhaps, have been laid upon the comparative strength of each service in ships of the line; and if there may be one point more than another which may require attention, it must be to consider the classes of ships-of-war upon which it will be most expedient to expend the resources of this country. Opinions are gradually gaining ground, not only that the sizes of our ships of the line are becoming excessive, but that the uses in general to which such ships can be applied in future wars in the Atlantic are altogether questionable; and it would almost appear as if each country judged it proper to persevere in the construction of ships of the line solely because the practice was continued by the other. It is, at least, deserving of remark that in the former wars of England with other Navies the heaviest guns were those carried in general on the lower decks of ships of the line, and, practically, the force of ships in every class might have been estimated as superior, not alone because the number of their guns was greater, but also because their calibre was generally the largest in ships of the larger classes. The exact reverse may nearly be stated to be the case in the armaments of the present day, and in general the weight and calibre of the guns are greater in proportion in ships of the smaller classes.

The '*Diadem*' may be instanced as one of the most powerful frigates of the present day. Her armament is heavier than in most ships of the line, and her guns are the same as those which can be carried by some of the smaller gun-boats. The complements of all ships are calculated according to the number and description of their guns, and an equal number of guns of the same weight and calibre embarked in gun-boats would ensure the presence of a much greater number of men when collected for any service at a particular point.

It cannot be necessary in a short notice to do more than allude to the disadvantages of heavy draught of water, and the cost of timber and other material of the largest dimensions, which are ever difficult to procure for the construction of the heaviest ships of the line.

The advantages to be obtained by the power of distributing force upon every station, as contrasted with the necessity for concentrating large complements of men in large ships, which can seldom be brought into use, are not less deserving of attention, more especially when the difficulties of procuring seamen are deliberately considered.

The time has certainly arrived at which it will be proper for this country to be guided by her own real interests, and not to be fettered by the defective practice of other countries; and this subject will probably be found to be of much greater importance than the question of continuing ships in commission for shorter or longer periods. Nobody can dispute that it must be disadvantageous to disperse a well-organized crew in a perfect state of discipline; but in the many accidents of service in all parts of the globe it will generally be found impossible to adopt absolute rules, or to prescribe any uniform practice. Unexpected defects in a ship's hull, injuries to boilers, and the exceptional wear and tear of engines, as well as of sails and rigging, are all casualties to which the Naval service must be constantly liable; and even if dockyards were at hand upon every station[,] it would still be important to consider the natural feelings of officers and men when debarred from intercourse with their nearest relations, and possibly compelled to associate with disagreeable companions in the confined society of a ship. Nothing in the duties of the Army will furnish an exact comparison with the services of seamen under such circumstances; and the very nature of their profession is such as to engender the love of variety and the desire for change. Great caution must therefore be exercised in prescribing absolute rules upon such a subject; but, in general, it seems probable that a period not exceeding four years' service will be found to be the most economical for ships of most classes. The wear and tear of ships of the line, with boilers and rigging in good condition at the outset, may, perhaps, be extended to five years with economy; but the circumstances and services of the crew should never be overlooked, or the climate disregarded. The real cure for many of the evils arising from short periods of commission is to be found in the more complete development of the general system of continuous service for seamen in the Navy, or, in other words, in the formation of a standing Navy; and it is in the proper consideration of this subject that we must look for the only answers which can be given to the third question proposed in the Memorandum.

A close calculation of the complements of the ships and vessels mentioned as ready, or capable of being got ready, in the ports of England in the course of the present year, would give a total of precisely 38,000 officers and men, which would require to be added to the present estimates for the Navy if this fleet were to be equipped for service. Of this number about 24,000 would be seamen and artificers.

Assuming, then, that the defects of the ships can be overtaken [*sic*] by the Dockyard Establishments, it is still evident that the Admiralty have no power to command the services of an adequate number of seamen. It is also by no means irrelevant to observe that the restrictions on the entry of subordinate officers into the service during several years past have so greatly reduced the total numbers that there is even a large deficiency in the existing complements of the ships now in commission. These restrictions have been in accordance with the expressed wishes of the House of Commons in discussions upon the Navy Estimates, but at this moment there are neither mates, midshipmen, second masters or masters-assistant available for any increase of force.

With respect to seamen, the total numbers available in the coast-guard service may be stated to be 5,500. To these may be added about 2,500 effective seamen employed in harbour-service, which could be quickly replaced by pensioners if necessary. Boys in considerable numbers might, no doubt, be rapidly collected from the shore; but in the Marines, with the numbers now in China, the total effective force available for embarkation at home does not exceed 4,000 officers and men. This reduced number may be regarded as altogether exceptional, but there still remains a deficiency of not less than 16,000 seamen which would be urgently and immediately required in the event of war.

The recommendations of the Manning Committee of 1852, contemplated the habitual maintenance at home of a body of not less than 10,000 seamen in reserve, in addition to the resources of the coast-guard service, and of the coast volunteers, which latter force must be considered at present as experimental.

The pressing necessities of the late Russian war, and the more recent interruptions occasioned by hostilities in China and India, have hitherto prevented the recommendations of that Committee from being systematically carried out to the full extent which might have been practicable under other circumstances. Time and steady system will both be necessary for that purpose, and as a Commission from the Crown has been appointed once more to consider the best means of manning the Navy, it seems needless to dwell further upon this part of the subject. An opportunity, perhaps, is now afforded of effecting much good; and it is greatly to be desired that the Report of this Commission may be such as to command the attention of Parliament and of the country, and to set at rest the undoubted difficulties of the whole question.

At present, the steady increase of the numbers of seamen borne for continuous service, and a still further extension of the Coast Guard service, with a more complete organization and training of a force of Coast volunteers, not limited merely to home service, appear to be the only prospective resources.

[**627**] *Lord Louvaine Memorandum on the State of the Navy*

Admiralty
June 1858

Most Confidential

Remarks on the Memorandum dated April 2, 1858

No doubt can exist in the mind of any person who has carefully examined into the present state of our maritime forces, that they are in such a condition as to warrant serious apprehensions. That they are by no means commensurate with the task allotted to them is clear, when it is remembered that, for the prosecution of operations in China; for the support of our Indian Empire; for the suppression of the Slave Trade; and for many other purposes, requiring the dissemination of the British Navy over the whole surface of the globe; and more important than all these, for the defence of the shores of England, but 59,380 men were voted by Parliament, including seamen, marines, and coast-guard.

As regards the latter object, viz., the safety of the shores of Great Britain, it is evident that the number voted is no measure of the force really available to that end. In fact, at the present moment (besides 7,380 men voted for the coast-guard), the whole force at home, either on board the ships in ordinary, or fitting out, including every man employed in any capacity in Her Majesty's naval service, does not amount to 10,000 men. In this calculation, the coast volunteers are not included, for they are certainly not to be reckoned upon for real or prolonged service at present. Therefore the numbers I have mentioned comprise the entire available resources of the country in case of a sudden attack; for, in such an emergency, our fleets abroad are of as little use as if they belonged to another nation. The duties these will have to perform are already too great for their powers; the Admiralty is daily besieged with applications for additional assistance in all parts of the world; and the hope that their services will be hereafter less urgently required, derives no probability from the present aspect of the political horizon.

It may, I think, be taken for granted that, as in military, so in naval operations, the rule holds good, that success will attend that Power which can soonest, and with most certainty, concentrate its forces upon the vital point of its enemy. Thus, the possession of the Channel being our vital point, a successful concentration of the fleet of any hostile Power in its waters is a contingency against which it should be our first object to guard. In order to secure this point, a Channel fleet is absolutely necessary, as a permanent establishment, to be composed of vessels at least equivalent to ten sail of the line, and this fleet should be maintained in addition to the forces required for foreign purposes.

Though it would be presumptuous in a non-professional person to pretend to lay down the position it should generally occupy, it would probably be thought advisable that it should never be more distant than the Tagus; and that, for the purposes of discipline and instruction, it should be kept, as much as possible, at sea.

Such a fleet would require a complement of about 10,000 men; in addition 5,000 more should be borne, in readiness at the different ports to man the ships required to relieve those on foreign stations whose time was completed. This would occasion but small additional expense, compared to that of our present system, under which a large number of men are kept in pay, doing no real duty, during the time (often very protracted) which is required to complete the crews of the ships newly commissioned. For instance, the '*Marlborough*' has been four months in an inefficient state, but all the while bearing on her books a large number of men receiving pay from the dates of their entry.

If to the force as above recommended, amounting to 15,000 men, the present coast-guard were to be kept in a state of practical efficiency for service afloat, England might consider herself safe against an unexpected attack, the only species of danger from which she has much to fear. There have, however, been indications already of the necessity of great care and vigilance to prevent the men composing this force from considering their position in light of a mere comfortable retirement, and becoming entirely averse and unfit to return to the sea service.

The advantage may here be suggested of bringing together at convenient seasons the ships manned by the coast-guard afloat, for exercise at sea, and of including annually in their complements a portion of the coast-guard ashore for the same purpose.

These conclusions will, probably, meet with little criticism or objection; but the methods by which they are to be carried into effect are neither so easy to determine, nor so certain of acceptance.

I entirely disagree with the views of the writer of the Memorandum submitted for perusal, as to the utility of impressment, considered as a means of manning the Navy. Barbarous and illegal as was the process by which, in too many instances, it was carried into execution, there is no doubt that, to a great extent, it proved effectual in maintaining the Navy of this country in a condition which enabled it to meet and overcome every enemy in every action in which the antagonists were fairly matched. The cases alluded to, in which defeats took place during the late American war, were not of this character.

All foreign Navies, that of the United States excepted, are manned by what is, in point of fact, a regulated system of impressment. France, especially, has organized her forces so well, that she can at any time, within the space of a few weeks, put on board her ships from 40,000 to 70,000 in addition to her ordinary levy. And to meet this immense power on an emergency, England has to depend on outbidding the offers of the merchant-service in the labour-market – a task difficult and dangerous on many accounts, and likely to become more so, since the chance of prize-money from the capture of vessels engaged in private commerce has been taken away.

I need not dwell at great length on this part of the question, only remarking that it acquires additional importance when it is remembered that navies no longer require the same complement of skilled seamen as of old, to enable them to keep the sea and engage in battle. The largest ships will henceforth be fought under steam, requiring little more nautical knowledge on the part of their crews than is necessary to give them the means of fighting their guns. And this change in the conditions of naval warfare confers a terrible superiority on such nations as can, by a regularly organized system of compulsory service, put forth their strength at any moment, over those who need a longer preparation to fit them for the conflict.

The Royal Commission [on Manning] just appointed will doubtless throw much light on this most difficult subject, and it would be presumptuous in me to attempt to anticipate their judgment and recommendations. But it may be permitted to me to express my belief that, in order to make any service popular, the first necessity is to show a strict and equitable adherence to promises made and advantages held out; that in such matters the good faith of Government should not be liable even to a suspicion; and that the changes made should be as few and gradual as possible – a point which, I think, has hardly received sufficient attention of late years.

Larger pensions for wounds, if not for good service, might be advisable; the employment of seamen in every capacity in which their services may be available in the different departments of the public offices; a relaxation of the rules of the Royal Hospitals, as regards the families of pensioners; some privileges in regard of the operation of the Poor Law – these are all points which might produce a greater inclination to enter the naval service. I am inclined to believe, however, that the best and safest resource will be found in the early enrolment and training of boys, which might be greatly increased, while their treatment, once entered, might possibly be improved. Additional regiments of Marines should be raised; the service is most popular,[1] and when not required afloat they are as useful on shore as other regiments. Upon the first outbreak of a war, when a supply of sailors is most difficult to obtain, an increase in the complement of Marines borne in the ships then in commission would liberate a large number of seamen for distribution among ships brought forward to meet the emergency.

If the liability of every man to be called upon to bear arms in the defence of his country be ever again enforced by the revival of the ballot for the Militia, another means of recruiting the ranks of the Navy

[1]Louvaine did not provide the source of this information.

may be found in allowing the men drawn in the seaboard towns and counties their option to serve afloat for the same period as for that which they are liable on shore, when it is probable than many would prefer the former service.

I have purposely omitted to make any suggestions upon that portion of the Memorandum which refers to the numbers and stations of our naval forces abroad, whether during such intervals of peace as may be vouchsafed to us hereafter, or in the event of a war. This would appear to be a task better left to the professional members of the Board of Admiralty; and I have therefore confined my observations to points which are within the capacity of one who has not more than the usual means of information requisite to form a judgment upon them.

It is evident, however, that in the event of a war[,] this country must not reckon upon the immunity from attack which her insular position formerly secured to her; whilst, at the same time, the temptations to assail her possessions abroad are incalculably increased. If the command of the Mediterranean was reckoned indispensable to the maintenance of her prestige formerly, how much more is it so now, when it constitutes the high road to the empire of India, now become an integral part of Her Majesty's dominions? To assert this will be no easy task against the greatly increasing power of France, whilst that of America is ready to attack our colonies, now raised to unexampled prosperity and riches, but still as dependent for protection as ever upon the mother country, which is thus drained of the forces so urgently required for her own protection. Surely these great and wealthy communities ought to contribute something towards their own defence, and so become an invaluable assistance, instead of a positive encumbrance to her.

But even their help will not relieve England from the necessity of exertions as great as those required to bring to a successful termination the war of 1815. The danger will be greater and more immediate, and the struggle fiercer; for the preparations of her enemies have been better calculated, more carefully planned, and more perseveringly carried out.

It were well that Englishmen could be brought to consider that if these preparations are to be met upon anything like an equality, past outlay may be looked upon as no guide for future expenditure, and that, at whatever the cost superiority is to be secured, that cost must be incurred, under the penalty of ruin. It is, in fact, not a question which addresses itself to the Admiralty especially; it is one whose tremendous import must be felt by everyone, whatever his station, who claims a right to the name of Englishman.

In conclusion, I would record my conviction, that the solution of the questions proposed in the Memorandum is daily and hourly becoming more vitally indispensable; that a great change has taken place in the relative position of England and the surrounding nations, and that even if at present superior to them individually and severally, the time may be, and probably is, fast approaching, when, by the union or one or more of them, she may be compelled to enter upon a struggle, not for victory, not for the supremacy so long enjoyed by her, but for existence, and that moment will be hastened or deferred in exact proportion to the wisdom which is to dictate the measures henceforward to be pursued, for the purpose of securing the efficiency of her naval power.

[**628**] *Milne Memorandum on the Proposed Shipbuilding Programme for 1858–59*[1]

[Admiralty
*c.*June–July 1858]

On Surveyors programme 1858–59
The report of the Surveyor of the Navy in transmitting the programme of new works for ship building requires the very serious attention of the Board, for it is evident that unless steps are taken to increase our Ships of the Line and large Frigates[,] our naval force will be inadequate to cope with the Navy of France. Our Ships of the Line and Frigates of a few years back were small vessels in comparison with the ships now required to carry large and heavy machinery[,] as well as armament and coal. Thus Ships of the Line were formerly 2600 Tons[;] now they are 3900. The Eighty Gun ships were 2200 tons[,] are now 3300. The Fifty Gun Frigates were 1500 Tons[,] now 2600. The Forty Six Gun Frigates 1060 Tons[,] now 1900. The same increase of Tonnage has been given to smaller vessels of all classes. again [*sic*][,] in the repairs of these larger Ships, a much greater amount of work has to be performed than to the old class of ships. The removal of Machinery and Boilers from Steam Vessels has also caused a larger amount of Dock Yard Work, and the immense increase in the number of small vessels, Gun Boats & Floating Batteries, which were created for the Russian war and are now

[1]An incomplete draft of this memorandum on the Surveyor's proposed programme for 1858–59 can also be found in MLN/142/2. Milne seems to have suggested in the initial version that the Board consider reducing the numbers of classes and of smaller vessels, to cut down on repairs and thus facilitate the construction of new larger ships. That suggestion, however, is only implied in the draft printed here. The memorandum was prompted by a long paper by Surveyor Baldwin Wake Walker, which is preserved in ADM1/5698, Box 1.

thrown upon the Dock Yards[,] has added largely to the work of these Establishments. It is therefore evident, that whatever may have been done in former year's [*sic*] by the Established [*sic*] number of workmen in the Yards in building new ships and the repairs of others, that the same number of men will be found totally inadequate to meet the present wants of the Service. The Surveyor has pointed out, how much the building of new ships has gotten in arrears during the last 12 months, by the men being withdrawn for the repair of Ships and he strongly urges on the Board that steps should be taken on this subject.

I would most strongly urge on the Board to consider the present strength of the Navy and the number of Ships which should be constructed of each class. Some such steps appear to me to be necessary, so as to place the Naval force on some more definite footing than at present. Our new ships should be hastened by every means possible.

[**629**] *Fanshawe Martin Memorandum on the State of the Navy*

Admiralty
[*c*.1 July 1858]

Most Confidential

The Memorandum[1] is full of well-grounded solicitude, and of warning[,] which it would be perverse and willful to disregard.

Her Majesty desires to be informed 'what duties would be required of the Navy at the breaking out of a war with France.'

The duties of the highest importance would be, to give security to these islands and to our commerce in the seas around them[,] to maintain an ascendancy in the Mediterranean; to protect our colonies and distant trade; and to send military reinforcements, stores, provisions, and coals to our foreign stations.

To be equal to these four services, of what should our Navy consist, and how should our ships be disposed of when the emergency has arisen?

We stand in the very presence of the great maritime power of France, with her well-arranged resources for the speedy equipment of a prodigious fleet.

But the military means of the two nations must also be compared, even when determining what should be the amount of our naval strength. The Navy of France is backed by an army numerically vastly superior to our own, and should she crush resistance at sea, her army would

[1]Pakington's Memorandum of March 1858, [**619**].

come into immediate conflict with the unprepared inhabitants of this country. Yet, the existence of France would not be endangered by the destruction of her Navy, nor would it, if she were engaged with England alone, entail upon her the dreadful calamity of an invasion.

For a great object, France may, therefore, prudently fight without a reserve; but for England to do so, would be to hazard her national existence upon the result of a single naval action.

To guard against this fearful risk, we should, on the breaking out of a war, have at sea, for home defence, a force at least equal to the whole fleet she can oppose to it [*sic*]; and we ought to have ready for sea a reserve of one-fourth of that amount.

Whether this should be distributed or not, and, if distributed, in what portions, must, of course, depend upon the attitude the enemy assumed, and upon the degree to which his ships were united or dispersed.

No land force in England, however great, would diminish her entire dependence upon naval superiority. It is as indispensable that she should command the Channel as [to] prevent an invasion.

A long continued blockade of our ports would make it impossible to collect our revenue, whilst our expenses would be enormous; it would throw millions out of employment, who could not be controlled; it would produce a famine, since our supplies would be cut off; and, in fact, it would be equivalent to a national bankruptcy and a social convulsion.

To command the Mediterranean is also of vital importance. Should we not remain paramount there, France would immediately seize Minorca, capture the Ionian garrisons, and destroy our merchant shipping within the Straits. Already having Algiers, she would make it impossible for us to send a bag of bread or a soldier to Malta without a convoy strong enough to fight her fleet.

If her ships could quit and enter the Mediterranean at pleasure, Toulon would become, with regard to her aggressive power upon us, as important as the ports she has adjacent to our shores. She could either unite her southern squadron with the squadrons in the north, or use it to destroy our trade and attack our colonies.[1]

If France continue mistress of the Mediterranean [*sic*], Malta and its troops must fall into her hands, and our overland transit to India would be cut off.

She would thus have the means of operating against our Indian Empire, with all the prestige of success [*sic*], and with comparative

[1]Fanshawe Martin seems resolutely to have ignored the question of where the French might obtain the coal needed for such wide-ranging operations.

rapidity and cheapness of action. Probably, it were better to abandon India, than to fight for it, on such terms; even if we could still keep open our communications by the Cape of Good Hope. But expulsion from the Mediterranean will be an evidence that we have lost the command of the seas; which, to an island unequal to sustaining its population, means far more than a severance from foreign possessions.

It is necessary to consider the doom of England under such altered conditions, that the exceeding importance of a Naval supremacy in the Channel, and in the Mediterranean, may be justly estimated.

On both stations, our fleet should be greater than that of France by at least one-fourth; as England cannot dispense with a reserve to redress a defeat, or any other great disaster at sea.

The necessity for guarding our colonies and foreign trade is acknowledged, even by those who argue that the apprehension of an invasion of this country is unfounded and imaginary. It is admitted that the fidelity of our possessions depends upon the protection and prosperity derived from their connexion with us; and that the existence of a vast number of our manufacturing countrymen depends upon the unchecked admission of raw material, and upon exporting, without hindrance, the produce of their manufactories.

How, then, shall the colonies and distant trade be defended?

France, requiring no protection from ships, has her whole Navy available for aggression.

For us to reinforce each station to an extent that would defy attack, is obviously impossible.

Shall we then by dispersing, among all the foreign stations, the ships we have disposable after securing our shores, give to every station, what must be an insufficient addition, and expose each in succession to an overwhelming force?

The best universal protection to the colonies would be, to hold one or two strong squadrons, at Scilly or in Bantry Bay, ready to follow any force that might elude the vigilance of our blockading or Channel squadrons.

Rather than distribute these squadrons over the world, in ignorance of where the blow should fall, it would be better to keep them concentrated and in hand, and thus deter the enemy from venturing on distant enterprises.

Unless, therefore, circumstances unmistakably marked a colony as being an object of attack, our foreign stations should not be greatly reinforced.

There is another strong argument in favour of this arrangement. By whatever amount we reinforce squadrons abroad, by so much should we increase the difficulty and expense of providing for them; since forty or fifty thousand more men, and their ships, so scattered, would entail a prodigious scheme of arrangement, and a vast expenditure for their supplies and stores. This additional tax upon our means of transport, would be avoided by the more simple expedient of keeping a squadron in Bantry Bay or at the Scilly Islands.

Our American and West Indian stations might be exceptions, for we can conduct no great war on the seas without imminent risk of a collision with the United States.

Angry questions of blockade and search would inevitably be forced upon us. Ships and stores would be prepared for our enemy by American merchants, and armed vessels would sail direct from the United States to act against us, under the belligerent flag.

Unless, then, the people of that country should show a more friendly feeling for us than they have yet exhibited, it would be right to calculate upon a rupture with them following very speedily on a rupture with France.

To reinforce our foreign garrisons, and to supply our different stations, is the fourth matter that would require immediate attention, on the breaking out of a war.

Each station should be so provided, that, if attacked, a relieving squadron would find all that would be needful for its replenishment; or, if it arrived in quest of an enemy, whose object had been miscalculated, all requisites would be found for a continuance of the pursuit.

Even if the enemy's large ships should be kept in port by our blockades, yet many of their small cruizers would get to sea, and cut off those supplies, if not accompanied by ships of war.

The transport and convoy service will, therefore, absorb a considerable amount of merchant tonnage and of naval force.

By the foregoing estimate of the duties of the Navy during a French war, and a French war only, it appears that England should have in the Channel and Mediterranean, a force one-fourth greater than that of France; and that, in addition to the ships she now has in different parts of the world, she would have to provide a larger squadron on the American coast, the requisite convoys, and a squadron to succour, from home, any colony that might be attacked. For all these services, England would need a fleet nearly twice as large as that possessed by France. Our positive force may very properly vary with hers, but the proportion of two to one, whilst our relative necessities remain what they are, must not be much diminished.

To conduct a war with vigour, our land defences should be so strengthened that the Navy may be released from the immediate and constant guardianship of our home ports, and be employed in blockading and aggressive operations. Our arsenals and great commercial ports cannot now defend themselves against a fleet that might evade our squadrons, and by some stratagem induce them to take a false line of pursuit; nor can they give protection from a powerful force to disabled ships. This incessant dependence upon the Navy would forbid enterprises which otherwise might be properly undertaken: for to whatever extent the Navy is required for defence, by so much less is it available for attack.

There can be no doubt of the importance of Alderney, since the fortifications and harbour have been constructed. But, as providing for its defence in due time is a military measure, it should not be left without a sufficient garrison, nor be allowed to add to the pressing calls upon the Navy on the breaking out of a French war.

The Scilly Islands and Bear Haven are positions as necessary to be held as Alderney. They should be so fortified as to be beyond the risk of capture, and to be a protection [*sic*] to our shipping. During a French war, each should be the head-quarters of a squadron.

The French ports must, of course, be watched or attacked by squadrons assigned to that duty; but it would be the business of the small ships from Alderney, Scilly, and Bear Haven to guard our trade in the entrance of both the Channels [English and Irish], and to prevent the enemy's Mediterranean fleet from passing, unnoticed, into either of them.

This might be effected by so arranging look-out ships, that a constant signal communication might be kept up between Bear Haven[,] Scilly, and Alderney, where there would be powerful divisions ready to move in any direction.

No other arrangement would keep us so well informed of all that might enter the Channels, or afford so much confidence and protection to our trade and shores. With a view to this scheme, the projected submarine telegraph between England and Alderney should be continued to Scilly and Bear Haven.

That our ships abroad may be free to act offensively, there should be no undefended dockyards, arsenals, and stores in the Colonies. Such places would be objects for attack, or rather for capture, if left by the Navy, and, therefore, they virtually represent the blockade of the ships, which cannot quit them [*sic*].

As each of these might be the basis of naval operations, and a resort for repairs, it is the province of the naval authorities to point out that they should be secured, at least, from falling an easy prey. A scheme for colonial defence should, at once, be devised, and the less the Colonies require from this country, under ordinary circumstances, and for immediate defence, the greater will be the power of giving protection to each, and, therefore, to all, from the concentrated means of succour which will exist at home.

The appended Tables contrast the ships of the French Navy with those of England, and show decidedly that the second question in the Memorandum submitted by Her Majesty cannot be satisfactorily answered; for England has not 'prepared a fleet as superior to that of France, as the duties are more multifarious, more extended, and more important.'

However, the dockyard establishments are now working on a system that is termed 'task and job,' in order that the greatest industry may be called forth to repair our ships, and to increase their number. But our real deficiency is greater than that which is exhibited by the Tables; for the force of a fleet depends not only upon its strength numerically, but on its discipline and aptitude for work.

The high order of the large squadron kept up by France [*sic*] shows the value she attaches to having well-disciplined ships, and that we must be prepared to meet a thoroughly instructed and practiced enemy.

Such may be the task of our home force, without any notice, and upon the successful performance of it this country depends.

Nothing, however, can qualify ships to grapple with others in high efficiency but the constant practice of their crews.

In this respect, also, an effort must at once be made to improve our condition; for, if it be neglected, we may some day unexpectedly find the Channel in possession of a French squadron.

It is hoped that the Channel squadron now forming, and a scrupulous attention to the selection of Admirals and Captains, will give us a force of the character that is so greatly wanted.

It is undeniable that a ship has usually spent a third of her time in bringing her discipline to perfection, but this will no longer be the case, when the service of the men is continuous.

That system will involve the necessity, or rather combine the advantage, of keeping a few hundred men in the home ports, ready to relieve those on foreign stations. These men will join newly-commissioned ships, as perfect crews; and the periodical disorganization that has attended the discharge of ship's companies from the service, and the dilatory collection of others, are evils which will no longer be exhibited.

The third question of the Memorandum relates to the manning of the fleet.

Continuous service, and an arrangement for supplying the vacancies among the men, by youths brought up in school-ships, will give a command of men [*sic*] for as large a peace establishment as may be desired; and by carrying into effect the intention of giving short-service pensions, and with the coast guard and coast volunteers, a considerable reserve of seamen will, after a few years, be at [our] command.

How the men of the commercial marine may be rendered promptly available, will be considered by the Commission Her Majesty has been pleased to appoint.

There are always between 20,000 or 30,000 merchant seamen in England; and the greater part of these would, of course, be thrown out of employment if the ships could not proceed to sea.

Many of them would probably enter the Navy; but, if all did, they would be inadequate to our wants; which, for home defences, for squadrons to succour colonies, and for convoy and transport services, cannot be estimated at less than 80,000 men in addition to our peace establishment. At present, besides the men voted for active service afloat, we have 5,000 marines on shore, 7,000 men in the coast-guard, 6,000 naval coast volunteers, and about 3,000 or 4,000 pensioners fit to serve: 21,000 in all.

These would not man the necessary number of ships of the line; and the frigates, sloops, and gunboats would require as many more, even for home defence.

By the law they cannot be compelled to go more than 100 leagues from England, and we may not be able to persuade them to go a greater distance, as it is notorious that many have been tempted to join the force by the protection thereby enjoyed against impressment, and the chance of being taken from their homes. But including them, the men we have professedly at our disposal, are insufficient for our first necessities, even after exhausting our nominal reserve; and there are no organized means for obtaining a future supply.

Till some satisfactory plan for manning the Navy, in the event of a sudden armament, shall be devised, there can be no safety but in keeping in commission a much larger force than would be necessary were there an ample and well-arranged reserve.

There is one portion of our available force which, at present, does not appear to be organized in such a way that a great amount of benefit could be derived from it.

The portion of the Coast-Guard [*sic*] which serves afloat is constantly becoming less and less efficient and, in a few years, will be almost worthless for immediate actions.

It is neither a school for officers nor for men; but it places both under conditions the most likely to destroy their professional worth.

The men are also possessed with a feeling that they are not required to go to sea, unless there should be 'an emergency.'

All these evils, and some others, may be redressed by employing the same men in gun-boats, and other vessels, on the coast of Great Britain and Ireland, and by combining them in squadrons for practice.

It is true that, with a Channel squadron, and the gun-boat flotillas, we should probably have 10,000 or 15,000 men for home defence, and a sudden and treacherous blow could not be averted by other means. No timely succour could be obtained from the ships on foreign stations; and, since the coasts of England must be defended, at the risk of all else being sacrificed, if it be incompatible with our means to be strong both at home and abroad, it would be more prudent to concentrate our ships than to scatter them over the world. Probably such a concentration would not only free us from the risk of a sudden attack at home, but also from the danger of an attack being made elsewhere; for to strike England suddenly, in the expectation of striking her fatally, is very tempting, and therefore, very probable; to strike her at an extremity, and thus to warn and rouse her, is less probable, because far less tempting.

There appear to be no measures in progress commensurate with the need for the military defence of our principal stations abroad.

We are bound to acknowledge that, as regards the ships, the men, and its defences, this country is not in the state which it ought to be.

But it has been shown that our dockyards are in full activity, and that measures are in progress to secure, for future years, the men that will be wanted under ordinary circumstances, and to improve the efficiency of those now serving.

Good as this may be for the time to come, it does not rescue us from present danger; for, France is armed and we are not.

Abstract of the British Navy. – July 1, 1858

	Commission		Harbour Commission		In Ordinary		Building		Total	
Class	Steam	Sailing	Steam	Sailing	Steam	Sailing	Steam	Sailing	Steam	Sailing
Ships of the Line	10	5	4	6	16	26	13	–	43*	37
Block-ships	–	–	9	–	–	–	–	–	9	–
Frigates	17	9	1	1	20	56	5	–	43	66
Corvettes and Sloops	62	15	–	2	30	37	12	–	104	54
Gun-vessels	16	–	–	–	12	–	–	–	28	–
Gun-boats	53	–	–	–	108	–	–	–	161	–
Despatch-vessels	2	–	–	–	1	–	–	–	3	–
Floating Batteries	1	–	–	–	7	–	–	–	8	–
Tenders &c	4	12	27	–	4	3	–	–	35	15
Troop and Store ships, Surveying Vessels &c	11	8	–	–	4	2	–	–	15	10
Yachts	5	–	–	–	–	–	–	–	5	–
Mortar-vessels	–	–	–	–	–	45	–	–	–	45
Mortar-floats	–	–	–	–	–	40	–	–	–	40
[Totals]	181	49	41	9	202	209	30	–	454	267
									721	

Screw Ships of the Line[:]

	Afloat	Building or Converting	Total
Good ships	21	10	31
Inferior Ships	9	3	12
[Total]	30	13	43

*Fanshawe Martin noted in handwriting in the margin ‘30 built & afloat.’

Abstract of the French Navy. – July 1, 1858

Class	Commission		Harbour Commission		In Ordinary		Building		Total	
	Steam	Sailing	Steam	Sailing	Steam	Sailing	Steam	Sailing	Steam	Sailing
Ships of the Line	8	1	19	–	4	11	7	–	38*	12
Frigates	6	6	29	–	2	22	4	9	41	37
Corvettes	8	7	10	–	–	5	3	2	21	14
Gun-boats	13	–	15	–	–	–	–	–	28	–
Small Vessels	68	42	16	–	1	15	10	2	95	59
Transports	12	19	8	–	–	7	6	–	26	26
Floating Batteries	–	–	5	–	–	–	2	–	7	–
Mortar Vessels	–	–	–	–	–	–	3	–	3	–
[Totals]	115	75	102	–	7	60	35	13	259	149
									408	

*Fanshawe Martin noted in handwriting in the margin '31 [steam] ships of the line built.'

[Steam Ships of the Line]

	Number	Guns	Horse-power
Built for Screw – [total] 8	1	130	1,200
	6	90	900
	1	90	800
Building – 7	4	90	900
	2	90	800
	1	90	650
Converting to Screw – 4	1	114	600
	2	90	600
	1	80	450
Converted to Screw – 19	2	114	600
	1	114	140[*sic*]
	5	90	650
	3	90	500
	4	80	650
	4	80	450
Total	38		

[**630**] *Corry Memorandum on the State of the Navy*

Admiralty
29 July 1858

Confidential
Memorandum on the Relative State of the English and French Naval Forces

I think it my duty to direct attention to some considerations which occur to me on a subject which I believe has yet to be decided, viz., whether the increased rate of expenditure authorized on 'Task and Job' shall terminate next month, or be continued to the end of the financial year – by which latter alternative alone can the scheme of 'New Work' be executed, which was proposed by the Surveyor, and which was sanctioned by the Board shortly after we came into office.

This is the immediate question to be determined; but it forms only a comparatively insignificant part of one of far wider scope, which, in my opinion, has been too long neglected. I mean whether our superiority over France can be maintained at the present rate of building ships and providing their engines, or whether, in order to maintain such superiority, it may not be necessary, for some years to come, to appropriate much larger sums to those purposes.

The question appears to me to be by far the most important that could claim the attention of the Admiralty, or that of the Government; inasmuch as the naval supremacy of England is the keystone of her prosperity and power. Our system of manning the navy may be inferior to that of France; our reserves of seamen may be inferior; our dockyards may not possess the same amount of accommodation; but I have such confidence in the naval resources of England, that I believe these, and other such difficulties, might be overcome on the occurrence of a great emergency requiring us to have recourse to extraordinary measures, and to put forth all our naval strength. But there is one difficulty which would be insuperable, and that would be to make good any considerable deficiency in the number of our ships, especially of the larger classes, during even the first year of a war, when months, or perhaps weeks, might be decisive of our destiny.

I wish, in making these observations, to invite more particular attention to the great falling off in the number of our <u>effective</u> line-of-battle ships, as I think it is a subject on which, for many years, the most erroneous opinions have been prevalent.

The experiences not only of the long peace, but even of the short war which succeeded it, were alike calculated to mislead public opinion in this respect.

During the peace – from 1816 to 1854 – when, perhaps, we never had twenty sail of the line in commission at any one time, people not unnaturally began to ask what was the use of maintaining in Ordinary some fifty or sixty line-of-battle ships and as many frigates, in addition to those in commission, and of building ships at great cost, of which some afterwards were broken up without ever having been at sea. But they forget, in the long enjoyment of peace, that the main object of a navy is to meet the exigencies of war, and that if ships, sufficient for this, be not maintained in reserve during peace, in accordance with the traditional policy which has prevailed in England for centuries, it would be too late to think of providing them when war might render their services necessary. In like manner, the inferences drawn from the Russian war, gave rise to most mistaken conclusions on this subject. It is a common belief that the country was called on to make a great naval effort on that occasion; whereas in reality our naval force was small in comparison with what was required in former wars, when our wealth and resources were far less than they now are, and small in comparison to what would be again required of us if France were again to become our enemy. This is a contingency of which we ought never to forget the possibility; more especially as we may be sure that, however cordial may be our existing relations with that country, the extent of the naval organization, which she is sacrificing so much to complete, can have reference to England alone, because her navy is already far more than strong enough to crush that of any other nation.

During the Russian War the greatest number of line-of-battleships in commission was 33, and the greatest number of seamen and marines borne was 67,971. In the year 1760, during the Seven Years' War, the number of line-of-battle ships in commission was 113, and of seamen and marines borne 86,626. Towards the end of the American war, in 1782, the line-of-battle ships in commission were 126, and the seamen and marines borne 105,443. In 1799 the line-of-battleships in commission were 120, and the seamen and marines borne 120,409, and in 1809 the line-of-battle ships in commission were 113, and the seamen and marines 144,387. These figures must be sufficient to shew how erroneous is the belief that the Russian war imposed upon us the necessity for a great naval effort, and although it is true that any given number of ships of the line represent at present a much greater force than the same number in former times, yet the true criterion of the actual force of ships employed is the number of seamen and marines required to work their guns, and it will appear from the above comparison that our naval force in the last war, was only as 67 to 86 in 1760, to 105 in 1783, to 120 in 1799, and to 144 in 1809 – so small, in comparison to the force employed in former times, was that which we thought it such an effort to assemble in the Russian War.

The question which I now wish to propose is this – Whether, in the event of another great maritime war, the present strength of our line-of-battle would be sufficient, or even nearly sufficient, to maintain our naval supremacy; and, if we must answer this question in the negative, I repeat it will be too late if we defer until the outbreak, or even the near approach, of such a war the preparation of the means which would be required to meet its exigencies.

Tupinier,[1] a great authority on naval subjects in France, somewhere observes 'on n'improvise rien en marine.' We tried it in the last war. We attempted to 'improvise' a fleet of gunboats and of mortarboats, and we succeeded in time for a review at Portsmouth (after the war was over), but for the destruction of Sweaborg and Cronstadt 'too late.'

If this was the result in the case of vessels of the smaller classes, and which could therefore be built in a comparatively short space of time, what would be our position, if on the outbreak of a war with France –

[1]Jean Marguerite, Baron Tupunier, who published two works on naval matters, *Considérations sur la Marine et sur son Budget* (Paris, 1841) and *Rapport sur le matériel de la Marine, presènte a M. le Vice-Amiral de Rosamel, Ministre Secrétaire d'Etat au departement de la Marine* (Paris, 1838).

possibly with France in alliance with some other Naval Power – we should have to sit down and calculate how many ships of the line we should require for the very safety of our coasts, in the Channel, and in the North Sea; how many to ensure the command of the Mediterranean (now become the key to the command of India also); how many in those other seas where British interests, commercial and territorial, would be in danger? – what, I repeat, would be our position if we found at our disposal some twenty or thirty ships of the line less than the number required? Yet this is the position in which, if we may judge from past experience, we should be unquestionably placed; unless indeed our former armaments were extravagantly large (– which, however, no one will, I think, pretend to argue, who remembers how critical History [*sic*] has shown our position to have been at various times, notwithstanding the magnitude of those armaments –) or unless the enemies we might be called on to encounter are now neither so formidable nor so attentive to the development of their naval resources as in former times. This, the facts to which I am about to direct attention will, as regards at least our most formidable rival, sufficiently disprove.

I am well aware that an opinion prevails among some Naval men, that line-of-battle ships will in future wars be superseded by vessels of smaller classes. The preponderance, however, of argument appear to me greatly in favour of those who entertain a contrary opinion; and I appeal to those, who think that line-of-battle ships may be dispensed with, whether, if the responsibility of the defence of our shores rested with them, they would feel quite at ease if they heard there were in the Channel some thirty steam-ships of the line belonging to an enemy, while we had but half the number, supported by smaller vessels, to oppose them?

I cannot but think that we should incur the greatest danger, if – so long as other nations maintain large fleets of line-of-battle ships – we alone were to adopt a different policy, on the faith of what is after all but a mere speculative opinion unsubstantiated by any actual experiences of war.

It is true, indeed, that in the recent operations in the Baltic and the Black Sea the most effective service was performed by gunboats and other small vessels; but it should be borne in mind that the late war was altogether exceptional in its character. We were then in alliance with a Naval Power second only to ourselves; there were no enemies' fleets to meet us on the seas; our commerce and our shores, as well as the distant parts of our Empire, were as secure as if peace had remained uninterrupted, and moreover line-of-battleships could do but little against batteries, generally unapproachable except by vessels of light draught of water. I am confident, however, that if we should again be at war with a nation having such a fleet of steam line-of-battleships as France now possesses, – and still more, such as France will possess before two years are over, – our naval supremacy would be in the greatest jeopardy, unless in the mean time, we provide a much larger force of this class of ships than we are now providing, and restore the relative proportions between the line-of-battle of England and France which existed in former times.

I have long thought that the number of line-of-battle ships, which, in the event of a great maritime war, England would require for her defence, has been much under-estimated. Even before so many of our old sailing line-of-battle ships had been rendered useless for purposes of war by the successful application of the screw-propeller, our line of battle had been reduced to 61 ships, as compared to 129, of which it consisted in the year 1792, and a much larger number at the Peace in 1815. So long ago as the year 1688, the English navy comprised 101 line-of-battle ships, and in the great wars which have occurred during the last 100 years, we had actually in commission, as I have already shown, – in 1760, 120; in 1783, 126; in 1799, 120; and in 1809, 113. At present our line-of-battle consists of 30 effective ships, with 13 'building' and 'converting,' which, at the present rate of expenditure in the dockyards, cannot be completed until four years from the present time.

From this computation I have, as a matter of course, excluded the block-ships, inasmuch as they have no pretension to be classed as line-of-battle ships. In size they are inferior to a second-class frigate of the present day; their want of speed would exclude them from the operations of a steam-fleet, and only four of their number can be considered as sea-going ships. The remaining five, which were fitted as supports only to the floating-batteries in the late war, are jury-rigged, and of such small power that they would not be safe in bad weather off a lee-shore. In addition to this, they are all so old and defective that they must cease to be serviceable in a few years. I have also excluded our old sailing line-of-battle ships, to which I will presently more particularly advert, and no one, I think, will argue that they can be considered effective men-of-war.

Such vessels as the '*Ganges*' and the '*Indus*' may answer well enough as floating houses for our Admirals on distant stations in time of peace; but in time of war a squadron of sailing ships would not be safe without a squadron of steam ships to protect it, and to the operations of the latter it could prove nothing but an encumbrance.

The number, therefore, of our effective line-of-battle ships is now reduced to thirty, with thirteen building and converting; and whatever may be the individual superiority in force of modern ships, I maintain that numbers so reduced could not possibly be distributed over the different stations, so as to meet the exigencies of a maritime war.

It must also be borne in mind that this great diminution has been the result, not of a policy well considered and deliberately determined on, but of an accident, – the introduction of the screw-propeller, which rendered nearly two-thirds of our old line-of-battle ships absolutely useless – and of that absence of all adherence to policy, which has long prevailed in respect to the building of ships of war.

Every authority has, on the contrary, been in favour of maintaining the strength of our line-of-battle ships. The Finance Committee, which sat in 1827, recognized the necessity of maintaining it; Sir George Cockburn, whose experience as a naval officer, as well as a naval administrator, entitles his opinion to the greatest weight, insisted that it should be at least double that of any other nation; and Sir James Graham stated, in 1833, that the strength of our line-of-battle, which then consisted of eighty ships, had been reduced to a smaller number than at any period since the Revolution of 1688; and that he considered it necessary to check any further reduction, which could alone be effected by adhering to the rule of building, or executing work, equal to three line-of-battle ships, as a maintaining rate, every year.

The policy of successive Boards of Admiralty has professedly been based upon this principle; yet I find, on referring to the programmes since 1833, as executed, that the work on ships of the line has amounted, on the average, to only 1 4/8ths per annum (or one ship and three-quarters), being a deficiency of one ship and a quarter for every year. Even during the latter part of this period, when it had become necessary not only to <u>maintain</u> the navy, but, in consequence of the substitution of steam for sailing ships, in a great measure to <u>recreate</u> it, the same want of adherence to system has prevailed, and the new work, executed on line-of-battle ships, has actually been less than what was laid down as necessary merely to maintain the old sailing navy.

During the last ten years, that is, since the first line-of-battle ships with the screw-propeller were commenced, the work executed has been equal to only twenty-five ships of the line, or two and a-half a-year, being half a ship less a-year than what was previously considered necessary <u>as a mere maintaining rate</u>. The quantity of work, proposed by the Surveyor and provided for in the programmes for these ten years, was equal to thirty-seven ships of the line, or, in other words, if the programmes had been carried out, we should now have possessed forty-two screw line-of-battle ships, instead of thirty, the actual number.

But the strength of our line-of-battle has of late years been reduced not only positively, but also relatively, as compared with that of France.

In 1840 we had 77 effective ships, and 12 building; total, 89. France had 21, and 25 building; total, 46.

In 1854, England had 11 screw ships of the line; France 7. In 1858, England has 30, France 30, and by the end of next year, at the present rates of building in the two countries, France will have 40 screw ships of the line, England only 36.

To France, a great naval disaster would be little more than an ambition frustrated: to England, it would be little less than ruin. France, with the exception of a few insignificant possessions, has not a colony to defend except one within two days' sail of her greatest naval arsenal. England, on the other hand, has empires in the antipodes, and colonies in almost every sea. France has a languishing commerce, on which her prosperity comparatively but little depends; while England has a commerce, the interruption of which, for any lengthened time, would be almost tantamount to a national bankruptcy. Nevertheless we look on with folded arms at the rapid strides which France is making towards the organization of a navy with which she may dispute with us the mastery of the seas, and even wrest it from us; and we grudge the additional expenditure which would secure to us that superiority which, for upwards of two centuries, we have maintained, and to which, under Providence, we have been indebted for our greatness, our wealth, perhaps even for our independence as a nation.

During the last six years France has added twenty-nine sail of the line to her steam fleet. This effort she has been enabled to accomplish in consequence of nearly the whole of her sailing navy having consisted of vessels of comparatively modern construction, and of great stowage, and consequently well adapted for conversion for the screw.

Our navy, on the other hand, consisted principally of old ships, built at a time when the several classes of line-of-battle ships were more than one-third smaller than they are now constructed. Moreover, in many instances, they were in such bad repair that it would have cost as much to convert them as to build new ships, to which in every respect they would have been greatly inferior.

In 1848, when line-of-battle ships were first built for the screw, we had, as I have already stated, sixty-one sailing ships of the line. Of these, five have been converted into block-ships, seven[1] into screw ships of the line, and six more have been recommended by the Surveyor for conversion. Of the remainder[,] none are considered to be in a sufficiently good state of repair to render them fit for conversion to

[1]Corry's footnote: 'the other converted ships were taken in hand before they were launched, and are therefore not included in the sixty-one ships afloat in 1848.'

screw line-of-battle ships; and if the remaining forty-three had been burnt by an incendiary they could not have been more effectually lost to the country, for every practical purpose of war, than they have been rendered unavailable as line-of-battle ships by the agency of steam. Supposing, a few years since, a calamity to have occurred such as I have imagined, – namely, the destruction by fire of any number of our line-of-battle ships, – the consternation which it would have created in the public mind may be readily imagined. Those, who clamour the loudest for economy, would have readily admitted the necessity of restoring the Navy to its former condition, however costly might have been the expense. Now, however, when we are called upon to re-build a navy, – not of sailing ships at the rate of some £1000 per gun, but of steam-ships at the rate of some £2000, including the cost of their engines; – now, when, concurrently with this, we have to reconstruct the dockyards in order to provide for the increased size of our ships, to build factories for the repair of their boilers and machinery, together with other numerous expenses incidental to a steam fleet – it is gravely asked why the estimates should be higher than at former times. Notwithstanding that the introduction of the screw-propeller has rendered many of our line-of-battle ships absolutely useless for purposes of war, our ship-building is expected to go on the same as if no extraordinary effort was required to supply their place.

Ten years ago, before the strength of our line-of-battle was thus impaired, I believe there was not a single well-informed and reflecting officer of the French navy, who was not convinced how hopeless it was for France to expect to become our rival on the seas. I write it advisedly, however, when I say that I believe that it would now be difficult to find a single French officer who does not think that France is our equal. France, already our match as respects the number and force of her line-of-battle ships, could, in the event of war, without serious danger to any of her material interests, concentrate nearly the whole of her most powerful ships upon any given point of attack she might choose to select, while England would be under the necessity of dispersing her fleet over almost every sea. Such at least are the grounds on which the more intelligent officers of the French Navy found their expectation, in the event of a war with England, of achieving a maritime superiority for their country.

The manner in which our line-of-battle ships were distributed among the different stations during the last four great maritime wars, as well as in the Russian War, will be explained by the subjoined tabular statement.

SHIPS OF THE LINE IN COMMISSION

Seven Years' War, 1760.

East Indies	19
West Indies	29
Mediterranean	11
Convoys	8
At Home	34
" " fitting	6
Harbour Service, not fully manned	6
Total	113

Number of Seamen and Marines borne, 86,626.

American War, 1783.

East Indies	19
North America and West Indies	52
Mediterranean	1
Convoy	1
Unappropriated	1
At Home	38
" " fitting	12
Paying off	2
Total	126

Number of Seamen and Marines borne, in 1782, 105,443; in 1783, 65,677.

French Revolutionary War, 1799.

East Indies	6
Cape of Good Hope	6
North America and West Indies	13
Mediterranean	58
Particular Service	1
Convoy	1
At Home	35
Total	120

Number of Seamen and Marines borne, 120,409.

War With France, 1809

East Indies	3
Cape of Good Hope	2
North America and West Indies	8
South America	4
Mediterranean	26
Baltic	22
Portugal	4
Off Cherbourg	2

Off Texel and Scheld [*sic*]	6
At Home	31
Convoys	5
Total	113

Number of Seamen and Marines borne, 144,387.

War with Russia, 1856.

East Indies	1
West Coast of America	1
North America and West Indies	4
Mediterranean	4
Baltic	14
Unappropriated and fitting	2
At Home	7
Steam	19
Sailing	14
[total]	33

Exclusive of 6 Block Ships

Number of Seamen and Marines borne, 67,791.

Such was the manner in which our line-of-battle ships were dispersed in former wars; and as, in the event of war, our possessions in distant seas, as well as our own shores, would be in the same want of protection in the present, as in former times, it is obvious, I imagine, that a similar dispersion would again be necessary. Thus a fleet of thirty sail of the line, or even forty, – which at the present rate of building we may expect to possess some four years hence – would be so frittered away on various stations, that our weak and scattered squadrons would be unable to resist the force which France could concentrate for the purpose of overpowering them.

Such was the consideration which was the basis of Sir George Cockburn's maxim, – that the Navy of England should be double that of any other nation. It must be remembered, moreover, that now, when the movements of a fleet can be executed with so much punctuality and dispatch, the geographical position of France confers on her a power of concentration, as regards the two capital stations – the Channel and the Mediterranean – which England unfortunately fails to possess. For instance, if it were the object of France to attack us in the Channel, the Toulon division of her fleet might arrive at Brest before we could possibly obtain any certain knowledge of its destination. Again, if an attack on Malta or the Ionian Islands, or a descent upon Egypt were meditated, the Brest division might in like manner be ordered round to Toulon; and our fleet in the Mediterranean, before we had any possibility of reinforcing it, might be overpowered by numbers. I would further remark, that, in my opinion, obvious reasons exist for thinking that steam has generally given far greater facilities for attack than for defence. If such be the case, the application of the screw-propeller is anything but a reason for dispensing with that relative superiority over the Navy of France, which in former times Great Britain considered it necessary to maintain.

Hitherto I have adverted only to the relative state of the progress and preparation of the Navies of England and France as regards steam line-of-battle-ships. We have recently, however, had the opportunity of obtaining the most accurate information with respect to the general efforts which France is making for the development of her Steam navy; this information being derived, not from the pen of an alarmist, but one, the general tendency of whose observations, considered apart from the facts he has brought to our notice, is rather calculated to allay, than to increase, apprehensions on the subject.

Shortly after the present Government came into office, I requested Lord Cowley,[1] with Lord Malmesbury's[2] sanction, to endeavour to obtain some precise information with reference to a report, transmitted by one of our Consuls in France, that ten additional sets of engines had been ordered for ships of the line. With this object, Colonel Claremont[3] was directed by Lord Cowley to visit the principal dock-yards and factories of France, in which steam-engines are constructed for the Imperial navy. Colonel Claremont, in his report, describes what he saw and heard in these establishments. Thus it appears, from the information he has given us, coupled with authentic information obtained by the Admiralty, that the aggregate horse-power of the engines of the French Navy, now in course of construction, is 20,500;[4] whereas for the English Navy it is only 11,250. Colonel Claremont says, the French do not seem at all pressed about these orders. This he explains, by observing, that 'they expect it will take from fifteen to eighteen months to complete them,' a statement which exactly corresponds with information previously received at the Admiralty, to the effect that the greater part of these preparations will be completed by the end of next year.

[1]Henry Richard Charles Wellesley, first Earl Cowley, K.C.B. (1804–84). British Ambassador to France, 1852–67.

[2]James Howard Harris, third Earl of Malmesbury (1807–89). Secretary of State for Foreign Affairs, 1852, 1858–59; Lord Privy Seal, 1866–68, 1874–76.

[3]Edward Stopford Claremont, C.B. Her Majesty's Military Commissioner at Paris.

[4]Corry's footnote: 'That is the amount of which we have precise information, but we have reason for believing that the actual amount is considerably more.'

Colonel Claremont adds, – in language certainly not intended to create alarm; – 'Nothing I have seen proves a greater degree of activity than is necessary to carry out the openly-avowed intention of the French to convert all their sailing ships, that are fit for it, into steam-ships, so as to have a fleet consisting of 150 steam ships and seventy-two transports,'[1] 'At present,' he adds, 'they have twenty-six[2] screw line-of-battle ships afloat, and twelve building and converting; they have afloat sixteen screw frigates, and fifteen screw steam frigates building and converting, and they have nineteen paddle-wheel frigates, – in all fifty steam frigates: with corvettes, avisos, and gunboats they will more than attain to [*sic*] the figure of 150, which they have fixed on; and although no extraordinary exertions are used to obtain this result, yet it is evident that they are slowly but surely taking great pains to make their Navy very efficient, and it must rest with the Government to decide whether that will be an entirely safe state of things as regards England, and whether we are and shall be able still to maintain our superiority.'[3]

Colonel Claremont further states; – 'They were laying down (at Toulon) the first timbers of an iron-sided frigate (*Fregate blindees*) to be called "*La Gloire*," and these timbers appear to me quite as large and heavy as those of a three decker. There are to be two of these frigates built here, and four others in other ports. They are to have thirty-six heavy guns, most of them rifled 50-pounders, which will throw an 80-pound hollow shot; their engines will be of 800 or 900 horse-power, and they will be cased with wrought iron.'

A Government order, it appears, had been received at Havre for four engines, which Colonel Claremont had no doubt were intended for these frigates. The Director, however, either could not or would not inform him for what vessels they were designed. These six iron-sided frigates are in addition to those before enumerated, and will, if the experiment should prove successful, be as formidable, at least, as any ships of the line.

I have before stated, that the aggregate horse-power of the engines, now in course of construction for the French Navy, is 20,500, the cost of which, at the price per horse-power in England, would be £1,271,000, and of this Colonel Claremont states that 11,450 horse-power has been

[1]Corry's footnote: 'Captain Cracroft informed me to day that France will have transports for more than 80,000 men and 10,000 horses ready by next year, and that what struck him the most in the French Dockyards was the efforts that were being made to convert the old sailing frigates into steam transports. (August 2.)'

[2]Corry's footnote: 'Colonel Claremont omits four recently completed; the actual number is thirty afloat, and ten building and converting.'

[3]Corry's footnote: 'If we hesitate to act, I think I can answer the question.'

ordered by the Government for the present year. This fact was correctly stated by General Allard in the sitting of the Corps Legislatif on the 20th of April last.

The total amount of the horse-power of the engines in course of construction for the English Navy is only 11,250; of this only 2,100 has been ordered for this year, and the sum to be taken in the estimates for 1858–9 is only £200,000 for new engines and previous liabilities.

The general comparative recapitulation of the progress of the steam Navies of England and France is as follows. France has thirty steam-ships of the line, – England has also thirty. At the present rate of building in the two countries, by the end of next year France will have forty, England thirty-six. France, moreover, will have, in addition to these, six iron-sided frigates, the completion of which may be anticipated at an early period; engines for four of them having been apparently already ordered. France has steam engines in course of construction for her Navy of 20,500; England of 11,250. Engines of 11,450 horse-power have been ordered for the French Navy this year; for the English Navy of 2,100 horse-power only. If the relative state of the preparations of the two countries were generally known, I am satisfied that the voice of public opinion would be irresistibly pronounced in favour of maintaining, at whatever cost, the naval superiority of England.

Under these circumstances, it appears to me to be absolutely necessary that immediate steps should be taken towards the accomplishment of this all-important object. The remedy, therefore, which I would propose is as follows:–

We have at present thirteen line-of-battle ships, 'building' and 'converting,' seven ordered to be built, of which the frames have been in part provided, and we have six old three-deckers recommended by the Surveyor to be reduced to two-deckers, and converted for the screw. That is to say we have twenty-six line-of-battle ships 'building,' 'ordered to be built,' 'converting,' and 'convertible' to steam ships. These, with the thirty already built, would give us fifty-six steam line-of-battle ships as compared with forty French steam line-of-battle ships, and six iron-sided frigates – equal to forty-six sail of the line – which would be a small preponderance as compared with the relative proportions of the two navies ten years ago, and at former times; and small also with reference to the relative naval exigencies of the two countries.[1]

[1]Corry's footnote: 'From intelligence recently received at the Admiralty, there can be little doubt of the determination of the French to convert all their sailing ships so as to have a fleet of fifty-screw [*sic*] ships of the line in the course of a few years, with a proportionate number of frigates and smaller vessels.'

The French line of battle will be completed to forty sail of the line by the end of next year. The iron-sided frigates will probably be completed by the end of the following year, or, at the latest, during the course of the year 1861.[1] Thus, I think it absolutely necessary to the future safety of the country, that the whole of our ships of the line, which I have before enumerated,[2] should be completed by the same time, or as soon after as possible; nor do I find that there will be any difficulty in effecting this by the end of the financial year 1861–62.

I have gone carefully into this question with the Surveyor of the Navy, and his two Chief Assistants in the Ship-building and Engineer Departments. From the communications which I have held with them, it appears that, with the existing establishment of artificers, and at the present rate of expenditure, – assuming that 'task and job' be continued to the end of the present year, – twelve of the thirteen steam line-of-battle ships, now building and converting, can be finished by the time I have specified.[3] To complete, by the same time, the six line-of-battle ships recommended for conversion, and the eight remaining line-of-battle ships (namely one building and seven ordered to be built) the entry of additional artificers would be required, as well as the necessary provision of shipbuilding materials and machinery. The estimate for this extra work is as follows:

Labour and materials to convert 6 sailing ships to screw ships	£150,000
Cost of engines, 6 of 500 horse-power	180,000
Total	£330,000
Labour and materials to build 8 screw ships as proposed	£837,960
Cost of engines, 8 of 800 horse-power	384,960
Total	£1,222,920
Grand Total	£1,552,920

This additional amount, according to what I propose, would be distributed over the three and a half years intervening between the time when arrangements might be made for the commencement of the work, and the end of the financial year 1861–1862.

[1]As of 1859 France had 32 completed steam line-of-battle ships. The first of the ironclad frigates, *la Gloire*, was indeed completed in August 1860, close to the latest date that Corry suggested, but none of the follow-up vessels were finished before 1862. See *Conway's All the World's Fighting Ships, 1860–1905* (London, 1979), pp. 284–6.

[2]Corry's footnote:

Building and converting	13
Ordered to be built	7
Proposed to be converted	6
Total	26

[3]Corry's footnote: 'The end of the financial year 1861–62.'

I propose that measures be at once taken for commencing the conversion of the six sailing line-of-battle ships. For want, however, of sufficient dock accommodation, four only can actually be taken in hand this year. The cost of the work, which might be executed on them before the 31st of next March, is estimated by the Surveyor at £50,000.

The same amount would be required to meet the installments on their engines, which would come in course of payment during the year, so that the total extra cost on account of these ships, chargeable to the financial year 1858–59, in excess of the vote, would be £100,000, to which there would remain to be added another £100,000 for 'task and job' to the end of the year, and £50,000 additional for steam engines, which ought to progress *pari passu* with the work executed in the Shipwright Department – making a total excess of £250,000. The balance to be provided to complete the six additional ships, proposed to be converted, would be £230,000, – which, together with £1,222,920, required for the eight line-of-battle ships to be built, would be £1,452,920 – to be distributed over the financial years 1859–60, 1860–61, and 1861–62 – being for each year an additional charge of £484,300.

By this arrangement we should have a fleet of fifty-six steam line-of-battle ships by the beginning of the year 1862, as compared with the forty-six steam line-of-battle ships and iron-sided frigates which the French will have ready before that period; and it would remain, in the mean time, to consider what ulterior measures would be necessary in order to complete the Steam Navy to its proper strength.

I purposely abstain from making any suggestion as to building iron-sided frigates, in imitation of the French, inasmuch as we shall not be in a position to entertain the question until the experiments on the '*Alfred*' are brought to a conclusion.[1] On this subject I will only observe, that if it be decided to build any of these vessels, their cost will exceed that of ships of the line; the estimate for the hull and machinery of an iron-sided frigate being no less than about £200,000.

In submitting these proposals for consideration, I beg to observe, that no one can be more fully convinced than myself how important it is to the country, as well as to the Government, that wise economy should be practiced in the administration of the various Departments of the State. The maintenance, however, of the Navy on its proper footing is of such paramount importance, that it should yield to no other consideration than a dire financial necessity. If steam navies are too expensive for us; if we are too poor to maintain our position as the greatest Naval Power,

[1]On the *Alfred* trials, see Andrew Lambert, *Warrior: Restoring the World's First Ironclad* (London, 1987), p. 17.

we have no alternative but, like Spain, to submit to our destiny with the best grace we may. But, on the other hand, if we are really the most wealthy and most prosperous nation of the world; if our naval resources, our mechanical skill, and our means of producing the material elements of a Steam Navy, are unequalled, surely we ought not to allow ourselves to be outstripped by a Power immeasurably our inferior in all these respects, – a Power which seems to have learnt from us that lesson which we appear to have forgotten, namely that the nation which commands the sea commands also the world. One circumstance I would point out, and the reflection which it suggests is a consolatory one, that if the steam-engine, as applied to the Navy, has added greatly to the national expenditure, it has also added, as applied to other purposes, immeasurably more to the national wealth.

If, instead of thus proposing an addition to the Naval Estimates, I had recommended that half a million should be taken off their amount, I am well aware how much more palatable would have been my advice. But, having given the subject my best consideration, I feel satisfied that we shall incur the greatest danger, unless we resort, and that without delay, to some such measures as I have suggested. The greatest Military Power of the world is within sight of our own shores, and surely it cannot be safe for us to allow her to become our equal on the seas. The fact is an indisputable one that France, – who started a few years ago far behind us in the race for superiority, – has already almost overtaken us, and will, in a few years, unless we increase our efforts, have passed us by.

I am hardly sanguine enough to hope that any advice of mine will carry with it sufficient weight to induce the Government to adopt the measures I have recommended. At all events, however, it will be some satisfaction to me to have unburdened my mind on a subject, the importance of which cannot be over-rated, and which I have anxiously considered, and having placed on record my deliberate conviction with respect to a question, on the practical solution of which may depend, and that at no distant day, the safety of the Queen's Dominions.

[**631**] *Draft Board Minute on Baldwin Walker's Proposed Increase of Naval Force*

Admiralty
29 July 1858

My Lords having taken into their serious consideration the statements contained in the submission of the Surveyor of the Navy, dated 27 July,

on the respective state and condition of the English and French Navies, having also duly considered the effect of postponing the carrying out of the Surveyor's proposal to convert the
Trafalgar,
Neptune,
Royal George,
Waterloo,
Royal William
& *Queen*, Sailing Line of Battle Ships, into Screw Two-deckers of 90 guns, and of deferring the completion of the programme of Works for the present year until after the requisite funds shall have been voted in the Session of 1859, deem it necessary to place on record the deep sense they entertain of the importance of the facts stated with regard to the present equality of the French Navy with that of Great Britain, and the certain superiority which France will in a few months have obtained, that this Board would incur the most serious responsibility if they delayed to call the attention of H.M. Govt to this unprecedented condition of the British Navy as compared with that of France, irrespective of those of other countries in Europe.

They consider, therefore, that no time should be lost in giving the necessary authority to the Surveyor of the Navy to make the required additions to the Dockyard Establishments.[1]

[**632**] *Lyons to Pakington*[2]

Private
2 September 1858

My dear Sir John Pakington

You have been so very kind and considerate towards me that I feel encouraged to write you upon a matter I have so much at heart that I really believe my early restoration to health will materially depend upon a satisfactory solution of it. The request I venture to make of you is that if it should be in contemplation to revise the Order of the Bath[,] you will do me the honour to allow me to have a little conversation with you before anything is determined upon. I will not trouble you with particulars now, as it may be more convenient for you to have them

[1]The subsequent minute by Fanshawe Martin reads: 'Write to Treasury in accordance with this Minute, sending copy of Surveyor's submission. WM 29-7-58.' Baldwin Walker's proposed scheme was revisited in November 1858, when the Board began contemplating the following year's Navy Estimates. See below, nos [**644–7**].

[2]Lyons sent this copy to Milne, with a covering letter.

when the time approaches for taking them into consideration, but I will, with your permission[,] just mention that I believe I should have no difficulty whatever in proving to you that at more than one critical moment in the winter of 1854–1855[,] the expedition would have come to a disastrous end if I had not been able to reassure Lord Raglan by convincing him, documents in hand, that with Captain Milne in London and Mr Cleeve[1] on the spot[,] the difficulties would in all human probability be overcome. They were overcome, Thank God, & yet those two remarkable men are placed in the same categorie [*sic*] as Mr Filder[,] who was the principal cause of those difficulties. This could hardly have happened if I had been in England at the last distribution of the Bath, and when you know the story, I am sure that you will feel that I should fall in my own esteem as well as yours if I were not to come forward now in this quiet way & give you the opportunity of doing justice to the claim of Captain Milne, Mr. Cleeve & one or two other officers . . .

My suggestion would naturally be that Milne should have K.C.B. & Mr. Cleeve C.B.

[**633**] *Milne to Pakington*[2]

Pitfour, Aberdeenshire
10 September 1858

Dear Sir John Pakington

The personal repugnance which naval officers have of speaking of self has heretofore prevented me from addressing myself to you[,] and I still feel somewhat diffident in doing so now, as it is at variance with my own character and conduct [in] this life, but this may be carried too far and to ones own prejudice. The *Gazette* of Tuesday last[,] I observe[,] has advanced the Acc[ountan]t G[enera]l[3] and the late Compt[rolle]r of Victualling[4] to the honour of the K.C.B. this [*sic*] mark of royal favour, imposes a duty on me, and I therefore feel assured you will not be offended if I mention to you that I was recommended to Her Majesty for the honour by Sir C Wood at the period of the late change of Govt[,] and that recommendation met with Her Majestys high approval. This recommendation of Sir C Woods [*sic*]

[1]Frederick Cleeve, C.B. (d. 1905). Passed Clerk, 1840; Paymaster, 1848; Paymaster (Res.), 1865; Paymaster (Ret.), 1865; Lyons' Secretary on HMS *Agamemnon*.

[2]This copy was preserved by Milne.

[3]Richard M. Bromley.

[4]Thomas T. Grant.

was not sought for by myself, it was[,] as he told me[,] the unanimous opinion of the Board of Admiralty. it [*sic*] was founded on services rendered to the Admiralty for a period of more than ten years, on special services rendered during the war when[,] for the first fifteen months of that period, I conducted the vast Transport Service and when[,] on two or three occasions[,] I was specially sent for by the Cabinet of the day to carry out[,] with the utmost dispatch[,] the movement of French and Sardinian Troops to the Crimea[,] and which led to the future success of that expedition. I could even point out that the operations in the Black Sea were successfully carried out by my personal communications with the officers in Command of the Naval and Transport services, and I could enlarge on many other subjects connected with that Expedition in which I bore a peculiar [*sic*] part. I can also state that my services at the Admiralty were considered so necessary during the Commencement of the war, that I was refused service afloat when I applied to go to the Baltic with Sir C Napier, and in the succeeding year [when] I was offered the appointment of Captain of the Fleet. I merely mention these circumstances to shew that I was not unworthy of having been recommended by the First Lord of the Admiralty for the mark of Royal Favour[,] and I can state to you, that my brother officers in the service have over and over again expressed their extreme surprise that no mark or recognition of my services had been conferred upon me. You may ask [']but why have you not been *Gazetted*['?] because Sir C Wood has resigned office, and he had no power to carry matters further, but he told me[,] after reading to me Her Majestys high approval, for those were the very words, that he would leave a written memo of the circumstances with his successor in order that the requisite measures might be taken. These are the facts[.]

I have never once alluded to the subject to you[,] because I considered it indelicate to do so[,] and because I felt assured you would carry out the recommendation after it had received H Majestys approval[,] at the proper time.

I have waited for some months under the expectation and[,] as you alluded to the Order of the Bath before my leaving the *Diadem*[,] I mentioned the circumstances to your private secretary, but he stated he had never heard of my case[,] and that the Memo might have been lost with some other paper's [*sic*]. I requested him to mention the facts to you. I wrote him last week and asked him if he had done so, but I have not received any answer. Duty to myself[,] to my family[,] and to my own Character [*sic*] requires that I should make this explanation to you as the First Lord, and I think you will feel that I have done what is right and proper in now addressing myself to you, and to request that you will see that fair and impartial justice is done me. I ask no more than that my name may be *Gazetted* and to bear [the] date when you first came into office[,] for I think you must participate [*sic*] in my feelings that I ought not to be *Gazetted* with a date junior to the Acc[ountan]t General and late Compt[rolle]r of Vict[uallin]g who[,] I may say[,] served under me as a member of the Board only a few years, and I may add that the late Compt[rolle]r of V[ictualling] has over and over again expressed to me, that the largest Transport service in which the country was ever engaged could not have been carried on if I had not taken [it] into my own hands.

I am sorry to have entailed [*sic*] so long a letter upon you, but I could not make it shorter.

[**634**] *Pakington to Milne*

Westwood Park, Droitwich, Private
16 September 1858

My dear Admiral Milne

I have this morning received your letter of 10th Inst and I am very glad you have written to me so openly & frankly on the subject of your desire to receive the honour of Civil K.C.B.

There is evidently some misunderstanding as to what took place on this subject at the time of the late change of Government[.]

I have no recollection of having heard or had a word on the subject of your aspiring to this honour or of Sir C Wood's intention to recommend you for it, until I heard from Murray[1] after the conversation on board the *Diadem* to which you refer.

Sir C Wood may have mentioned it to me (amongst many other matters) and I have forgotten it [*sic*][,] or he may have left a written memo & I have lost it, but I do not believe he did either.

But even if he did, the question remains, & with greater force than you seem to suppose, why did not Sir C Wood carry his intentions into effect? You say he had no power, having resigned. I think you will find, on enquiry, that this is a mistake . . . [2]

[1]Herbert Harley Murray, Pakington's Private Secretary.

[2]Pakington went on at considerable length, the gist of argument being that he and Prime Minister Lord Derby saw no reason for them to reward Milne for his service to previous Governments. This view is quoted in a Milne memorandum of a conversation with Pakington, of 6 November 1858: 'Lord Derby and myself consider it is not for us to reward you for services to us since Feb last[,] nor for services during the war[,] nor for services under another Government. Sir C Wood should be called upon by you to state officially if he recommended you to the Queen and if he did so[,] we ought to carry out the Queen's approval.'

[**635**] *Wood to Pakington*[1]

Hickleton, Private
25 September 1858

Dear Pakington

You must go beyond the words of your last letter before you can come to a just judgment in Milne's Case. His service was under 3 or 4 First Lords, Graham[,] the D of Northumberland[,] Baring and[,] I think[,] Lord Auckland. He had done well under all and finished under me by excellent service during the war. If I had recommended any civilians for War Service I should have recommended Milne. You have recommended Bromley. Now Bromley had been CBd for his Treasury service[;] his K.C.B. therefore must be set down to his service at the Admiralty[.] Now in my opinion his 3 or 4 years as Acc[ountan]t G[enera]l are by no means equal to Milnes 10 years. If you had not recommended Bromley, Milne might have waited. When service has been rendered under several Governments, it must fall to one Government to reward it. You have done so in the case of Bromley. You cannot say that he has rendered under you such service as to merit [the] K.C.B. Therefore you rewarded him either for War service under Graham and me or for general service. In either case[,] Milnes services are greater than Bromleys and you will forgive me for saying that Milne is not fairly treated, so far as regards the case between Milne and Bromley.

With regard to myself[,] it is not unusual for a Chief to reward by recommending a man who goes out with him. If Milne had gone out I should have recommended him, as you have kept him I did not think it right to recommend[,] after our resignation[,] one of your men. That I had no indisposition to reward Milne[,] my writing to the Queen is proof, and I am sorry that you should suppose that my abstaining from taking the formal step of recommending was to throw any burden upon you. at [*sic*] any rate I did not leave myself open to the more usual

[1]This copy is in Milne's hand. Milne's papers also contain an extensive correspondence between Milne and Wood on the matter. The cover letter which Wood wrote to Milne along with this letter (26 September 1858) is misfiled in Milne's papers under MLN/166/2:

Private

Dear Admiral Milne

I received yesterday the enclosed letter from Sir J. Pakington, & I also enclose a copy of my answer. as [*sic*] his letter is marked private you must keep its contents to yourself[,] but I think it is necessary that your shd know how the matter stands.

I cannot for the life of me understand Pakingtons view of the case, but I have done my best to put it right.

Send me them back.

complaint against people going out that they grasp at all patronage. Recommendations for honours is [*sic*] usually considered a piece of patronage and not a disagreeable duty . . . I intended and endeavoured to leave as much to you, not of trouble[,] but of what is considered patronage as could fairly be expected[,] and I believe that I left you more than is usual.

The Main Question (as the Speaker would say) concerns Milne. You have[,] for what seemed to you good reasons[,] recommended Bromley, for past service under others or during the war. You have not recommended [one who] stands in the same relative position as Bromley[,] and whose service and claims are[,] I think[,] far stronger. I think that he has reason to feel hurt.

Forgive me for writing plainly[,] perhaps strongly[,] but it is better that I should say what I believe to be the truth. Milne is not a political friend of mine or the party. I made my first acquaintance with him at the Admiralty[,] where I learned to appreciate his services. I have now a strong personal regard for him, produced by the constant and friendly intercourse of three years, but my estimate of his services has not been influenced by this feeling.

[**636**] *Milne Minute on Gunnery Captains*

Admiralty
14 October 1858

In August last the question of having a new Rating of 'Captain of Guns' was mentioned[,] and the enclosed letters were written to Capt Hewlett[1] of the *Excellent* on the subject. I have now seen for the first time a letter to the Board from Sir T. Maitland, Chairman of the Gunnery Committee on the same subject, pressing very strongly the necessity of having properly qualified men as Captains of Guns sent into HM Ships when first commissioned. I entirely agree as to this necessity. The question is how it is to be done[?] at present[,] the *Excellent* supplies the following number of qualified Gunners Mates and Seamen Gunners to ships when Commissnd[:] Ships of the Line[,] 29 to 17[;] Frigates[,] 14 to 6[;] Sloops 3. It is therefore obvious that[,] as each class of ship will require the following number of qualified Captains of Guns to be sent to them when commissioned[,] viz. Ships of the Line 70 to 120[,]

[1]Richard Strode Hewlett, C.B. (*c*.1810–75). Entered, *c*.1822; Lt, 1837; Cmdr, 1845; Capt., 1850; Rear-Adm. (Ret.), 1870; Vice-Adm. (Ret.), 1873. The enclosures to which Milne referred are missing from ADM1/5698, part II.

Frigates 30 to 60[,] Sloops 5 to 30[,] independent of the men required for the magazines and shell Rooms, that the *Excellent* Estab[lishmen]t will not be able to give [*sic*: 'supply'] these Captains of Guns, and it must also be mentioned that the Establishment of the *Excellent* is falling off[,] and unless some steps are taken[,] this valuable Gunnery Estab[lishmen]t will fall to the Ground [*sic*], some early steps are therefore absolutely necessary.

To obtain Captains of Guns, all HM Ships in Commission should qualify Seamen for this rating, but some encouragement and benefit . . . must be held out to them.

I would therefore submit that all Able or Leading Seamen[,] as well as Petty Officers[,] who can pass the Examination for a Captain of a Gun as laid down in the regulations by Cap Hewlett[,] should be allowed 1d per Day in addn to his pay, but the number in each ship should not be allowed to exceed the number of Guns mounted or in the [official gunnery] Establishment of the ship[.] That all such men should bear a small grenade [patch] on the Arm.

I would further submit that the present regulations in regard to the men in the *Excellent*[,] which allows 2d per day to men with 1 C[lass] Certificates and 1d per day to men with 2d Class[,] should cease and[,] instead[,] that the following regulation be established[:] Those men who take 1 C[lass] Certificates to have 3d per day[;] 2d C[lass ditto] to have 2d [per day;] 3d C[lass] or Captains of Guns to have 1d [per day.]

If the Board concur in the necessity for some change in the gunnery system[,] Capt Hewlett might be called on for an opinion, as to this proposal.[1]

[**637**] *Milne Memorandum on Dockyard Policing Arrangements*

Admiralty, Confidential
16 October 1858

Write to the Super[inten]d[en]ts of the Dock & V[ictualling] Yards to report[,] for the information of their Lordships[,] what are the regulations in force respecting the awards paid to the Police of the Yards on the discovery of stolen property from the Yards, and whether any portion on the value of such Stores are [*sic*] paid to the men[,] either

[1]ADM1/5698, Box 2 also contains minutes by Fanshawe Martin (opposed), and Saunders Dundas, who thought the matter part of a larger question of how 'to place the system of gunnery instruction & training in the service upon a proper fitting,' but who was 'decidedly averse to incurring further expense in the form of encouragement until the whole subject received the consideration which it undoubtedly requires'.

individually or collectively, or [*sic*] on the conviction of the offenders. My Lords have to draw the serious attention of the Superintendents to the number of cases in which metal and other Stores have been stolen from the Govt Estab[lishmen]t[s][,] and in a late case to no less than ten casks of metal having been recovered from the vicinity of one of the D[ock] Yards to a house in London [*sic*], and to the necessity of measures being adopted to check the plunder which appears to be carried on. The Sup[inten]d[en]ts are to report their opinion whether any steps can be taken for a more vigilant exercise of supervision over the workshops, and the men employed, and what other measures they can recommend to be adopted[,] and if[,] in their opinion[,] the men of the Police Force are of a proper description for the exercise of the duties entrusted to them.

[**638**] *Abstract of Returns from the Dock and Victualling Yards respecting the Police Force*

Somerset House
[1858]

What awards to Police, on the Discovery of Property; & Conviction[?]
Deptford: No rewards, there having been no conviction since yard re-opened in 1844. Recommends a small reward to Police giving such information as leads to &c.
Woolwich: No awards whatever are paid.
Chatham: No award but twice in the last 17 years. Recommends a small reward.
Sheerness: No award made, but note is made of name of Policeman making discovery &c.
Portsmouth: According to Act of Parliament, half the amount of Fines is paid to the Policeman informing, but no other payment is made.
Devonport: According to Act of P[arliamen]t, in case of conviction & fine, half amount of fine is paid to Policeman informing &c. If the offender is imprisoned, Admiralty grant reward not exceeding £10 on prosecution conviction, & 15/ on summary conviction. This applies to all persons in or out of yard.
Pembroke: No awards of any kind. Only one case on record where a conviction has been obtained on the information of Dockyard Police!
Royal Clarence: No awards paid.
Royal William: Half fines, according to Act of Parlt as above, & a few cases of special gratuity from Admiralty, but no other rewards.

Suggestions for increased vigilance &c.[:]
Deptford: No suggestions for improvement.
Woolwich: No suggestions for improvement.
Chatham: Out of 52 detections, 24 have been afloat, suggests further means to stop [depredations] afloat, for which at present they [i.e. the thieves] use a Boat.
Sheerness: Thinks that the County Police should be more watchful in detecting Receivers of stolen goods who live outside the Yards.
No suggestion for increased vigilance in Yards.
Portsmouth: Government property is considered 'fair game', and is received at nearly all the Marine Store Dealers. Thefts in the Yard might be lessened in number, by doing away with small workshops & cabins, so that the men at work may be easier seen [*sic*].
Considers that the greater proportion of robberies are made afloat.
Devonport: Believes that the majority of Thefts to be from ships in Commission. Suggests Capt. Williams's Harbour Police (see enclosure to Devonport Letter).[1]
No suggestions for increased vigilance in Yard.
Pembroke: Cannot prevent robberies or detect them! In the absence of an increased Police Force, can only suggest that Inspectors more frequently visit the Workshops.
Royal Clarence: No increased vigilance necessary.
Royal William: No suggestions for increased vigilance.

Report on Present State of Police Force.
Deptford: Metropolitan Police do duty so well, that no alteration is called for.
Woolwich: Metropolitan Police do their duty perfectly, and are most efficient from being often changed.
Chatham: Selected from Laboring Classes, not of the neighbourhood. Since force was established 25 years ago, only 28 men discharged for misconduct.
Sheerness: Steady respectable men, most correct in performing their duties, and against whom there has never been a complaint.
Portsmouth: Cannot vouch for the honesty of all the men & considers their pay bad. Difference between Serjeant's & Men's pay (11/6 a week) not sufficient. Suggests appointment of 3 Metropolitan Police as Sub-Superintendents at £150 a year. Recommends Water Police. Thinks present powers of the Dockyard Police not clearly defined or effective.

[1]Not preserved in ADM1/5723.

Devonport: Cannot suggest anything, except that the Metropolitan Police should do the duty, and be frequently changed.
Pembroke: Men are very steady, and the best that can be got! but [*sic*] lack the activity and energy of London Police.
Royal Clarence: Does not think that any other class of men would do the duty better. Suggests increasing pay of Serjeants for same reasons as Sup[erinten]d[en]t at Portsmouth.
Royal William: Men are active, respectable, and fit for their duty.

[639] *Haddington to Milne*

25 October 1858

My dear Admiral Milne

I venture to enclose a letter from the mother of a youth who is desirous of entering the service as clerk assistant, a class I believe under your control & patronage[.]

I have reason to know a great deal about the family. The mother is a widow & is reduced to great distress & is[,] of course[,] doing all she can to provide for her children.

Can I hope that you will be disposed to enquire into this case, & if the lad is duly qualified, to sanction his appointment[?]

At any rate for old acquaintance sake you will forgive this intrusion . . . .

[640] *Drummond to Milne*

[?Admiralty]
27 October 1858

My dear Milne

I have been so much out of doors, and moving about that I have never put pen to paper since I heard from you, and first let me tell you all I recollect in the matter referred to by you. I cannot say what Sir C Wood told Sir John Pakington relative to you[,] as I was not present, but from a conversation I had with Sir Charles Wood[,] I was always under the impression that he had named to Sir J[ohn] P[akington] your claims for the KCB[,] and that it was only a question of time & opportunity for you to receive it. There was no written memo left to my knowledge on the subject [*sic*] . . . Write me a line of news if any. the [*sic*] question of the cadets I hope will not fall thro'. I think we are a majority. When is Sir John to be in town again?

[**641**] *Milne to Solicitor-General*

27 October [1858]

What are the Acts of Parliament which relate to Embezzlement of Government Stores from the Dock Yards[,] and what are the rewards ordered to be paid to the Informer's [*sic*] or to the Police or others on Conviction[?]

[**642**] *Haddington to Milne*

30 October 1858

My dear Admiral Milne

I thank you very much for the kindness of your letter & the friendly readiness you express to attend, duty permitting, to any wishes I may express . . .

[**643**] *Pakington to Milne*

Westwood Park, Droitwich, Private
14 November 1858

My dear Milne

As I am sure the enclosed letters[1] will be satisfactory to you, I will not delay sending them to you.

You will see that you were under some mistake [*sic*] with regard to Sir Chas Wood's correspondence[,] inasmuch as it was not directly with the Queen, as you supposed.

This[,] however[,] is immaterial both as to the substance and as to the effect.

Lord Derby's note, which I have just received, will show you that he regards the question as I do, and I hardly need add that I shall, as soon as possible, take the necessary steps for conferring upon you an honour which I believe, with Sir Chas Wood, to be thoroughly well deserved and in which, upon private grounds, it will be gratifying to me to have had some share.

[1]Not preserved in Milne's papers.

[**644**] *Fanshawe Martin Minute on Baldwin Walker's Proposed Increase of Naval Force*[1]

[Admiralty
November 1858]

Whatever may be the number of each class requisite at some future period, the amount of Ships of the Line of France leaves us no choice but to increase our force of that class without loss of time.

The policy for this year is clearly indicated, however[,] it may be modified in years to come. We shall not be safe until our absolute naval means greatly exceed those of France. We must remember, that a combination against us is highly probable, that we have many remote dependencies to defend, that the force of France is concentrated, and that our existence depends upon success. My opinion is that the Surveyor's recommendation for this year should be adopted, but, that the armament of the Line of Battle Ships which he proposes to alter, should be different from that which has hitherto been placed on board such ships:–
Their upper decks should certainly be armed with more guns of the greatest power and range, and the two foremost and two aftermost guns on each deck, should be replaced by single guns of the same sort as those here recommended for the upper decks, if it can be done without a great sacrifice of the elevation, depression, and training of the guns.

The Two Decked ships which are to be built should have their main decks entirely armed with guns of the greatest power.

If the armament of ships of the Line be not improved, they may under very probable circumstances fall to Frigates better armed than they will be for effective distant fire.

It has been asserted and it may be insisted upon that Ships of the Line would always be accompanied by Frigates. If they be not safe without escort, certainly the [number of] Frigates must be added to simultaneously with Ships of the Line. But the necessity will vanish, if the Ships of the Line be properly armed.

The Surveyor in his submission says 'as regards Frigates, we should not have in the event of War an available force equal to that of France, inasmuch as a large number of this class of ships would be required to protect our extensive commerce and possessions.'

[1]'Opinion of Board on proposed increase of Naval Force.' Baldwin Walker's Proposal was dated 27 July 1858. Martin's memorandum, like that following by Saunders Dundas, [**645**], is undated. Both Milne's and Corry's opinions were composed in November, about the time that the Board would first have begun considering the Navy Estimates to be presented to Parliament early the following year. I have thus assumed that both of the undated Minutes date to roughly the same period.

The question[,] then[,] as to armament of Ships of the Line, enters largely into the consideration as to the urgency for Frigates; and if the arming of the former Class be not improved, our immediate efforts should be as much directed to Frigates, as to Ships of the Line.

An additional reason for giving some of the new guns to Ships of the Line is, that they may possibly have to deal with iron-plated ships, and to such an encounter their present hollow shot guns are quite unequal. My assent[,] therefore[,] to the Surveyor's proposition, is conditional upon an improved armament being given to the Ships of the Line he proposes to alter, as well as those he proposes to build. The requisite alteration and construction of ships, is a most serious matter, involving probably many millions of money. I am strongly impressed, that the Surveyor should call for the opinions of all the principal Shipwright Officers upon the adaptability of each Sailing Ship in their respective Ordinaries, for conversion to a Screw Ship.

With respect to each Ship they propose to alter, the Shipwright Officers should report if they would lengthen her by the bow, by the stern[,] or amidships, and whether they would cut her down by removing either one or two decks. In each case, they should state the probable cost of the alteration and the value of the ship when altered.

The Surveyor should also require the Shipwright officers to report upon each Sailing Ship in their respective Ordinaries which they do not propose to convert, and to state fully why it is not desirable to convert her.

Upon a subject so important[,] we should assure ourselves that no good suggestion shall remain unheard. When the professional opinions have been obtained and considered by the Surveyor, it may be determined what portion of the strength of the Yards may be employed to carry them into effect with regard to Screw Frigates to be converted from Sailing Frigates, & with regard to Screw Frigates to be converted from Ships of the Line.

[**645**] *Saunders Dundas Minute on Baldwin Walker's Proposed Increase of Naval Force*

[Admiralty
November 1858]

I have read the papers submitted to the Board[,] in which the Surveyor urges upon the notice of the Government the necessity for keeping pace in the building of ships of the Line with the progress of other countries in Europe in construction of ships of the same class. The importance of increasing the number of Frigates is also considered by him as scarcely less important.

In both these suggestions I concur to the full extent of believing it to be absolutely necessary that the progress in building ships of war should be more rapid than has been the case for the last few years, & that a large increase is necessary for this purpose in the Dock Yard Establishments, but the particular classes of ships on which it will be most desirable to expend money & materials must depend greatly[,] in my opinion[,] upon the armaments which it may be proposed to place on board. It should be remembered that in all former wars in the Atlantic in which the Navies of Europe have been engaged[,] the Ships of the Line were always those which carried the heaviest armament as well as the greatest number of guns, & I cannot avoid entertaining doubts as to the Policy of largely increasing the number of Ships of the Line unless the armament of such ships is to continue superior to that of the largest Frigates. If the latter class of ships is to carry heavy 95 Cwt Guns on the broadsides, while the ships of the line are to be armed on the Lower Decks with guns of no greater power than 68 pdr. hollow shot guns[,] I cannot think that Pivot Guns on the Upper Decks of the Ships of the Line will be sufficient, & more especially in weather when the Lower deck Ports can be fought only with difficulty & when a Squadron of fast frigates might chuse [*sic*] its own distance from [*sic*: 'against'] an equal number of ships of the line consisting only of sailing ships converted into steam ships. For these reasons[,] & looking especially also to the diminished number of Frigates now in the service[,] I am of opinion that more attention should be paid to the construction of such ships than appears to be contemplated in the general plan proposed by the Surveyor. Other reasons connected with the power of raising more men for our ships & the distribution of force of [*sic*: 'on'] distant stations combine also to make me attach quite as much & perhaps more importance to the construction of heavy Frigates with heavy armament in preference to lending the whole strength of the Dock Yards to the conversion of old ships of the Line with less powerful armament. If new ships of the line of more modern form & from entirely new designs are in contemplation[,] it may then certainly be possible to construct such ships to carry fewer guns with heavier shot & longer ranges, but otherwise the construction of Frigates should at least keep pace with the construction of Ships of the Line.

[**646**] *Milne Minute on Baldwin Walker's Proposed Increase of Naval Force*

Admiralty
17 November 1858

There can be but one opinion on this paper, that we must by every mean's [*sic*] in our power keep our Navy superior to that of France. To do so[,] it is essentially necessary that we should increase the number of our Ships of the Line and Frigates. The present Estab[lishmen]t of Workmen in our Yards is not sufficient to meet this emergency[,] and it is therefore necessary that an increase should take place[.] this increase of Workmen must lead to an increase in the Store of Timber[,] which[,] altho now larger than during the last 30 years and equal to 72000 loads, will not meet the requirements of an increased number of Workmen.

In the final decision on this important paper the following points will require consideration.

1. Are ships of the line to be built, if so would it be expedient to give them heavier guns to cope with heavily armed frigates[?]
2. Should they be 3 Deckers or 2 Deckers[?]
3. If Frigates are to be built[,] what are to be the Classes of Frigates and what armament[?]
4. Would it be expedient to build more of the *Arrogant* and *Tribune* Class[?]
5. In regard to the vessels of the smaller classes[,] it appears to be requisite to consider what class of vessel is to be built[,] as we now have far too many of <u>different descriptions</u>. Classification is much required.

In regard to the Naval force of the Country, we must bear in mind that our extensive colonies require almost 2/3ds of our Naval Force[,] whilst France[,] with few colonies[,] has her Force at Home, and it is therefore most important that our Home resources both in Ships & Men should be increased.

[**647**] *Corry Minute on Baldwin Walker's Proposed Increase of Naval Force*

Admiralty
22 November [1858]

The necessity for a great and immediate effort for the maintenance of the superiority of our naval forces over those of France can no longer be a matter of opinion – we know from information derived from sources of unquestionable authenticity that, at the present rates of expenditure in the two countries on the building and conversion of Screw Line of Battleships and Frigates, the Navy of France would, before long, be actually superior to the Navy of England in ships of those classes which would be decisive of the fate of a naval war. It may be a subject for debate, whether, with reference to financial considerations, the increased expenditure necessary to the organization of a steam fleet sufficient to secure our superiority over France ought, under existing circumstances, to be incurred, but, when it is remembered that the alternatives are to submit to the cost, or lose our superiority, I cannot doubt the answer that would be given to such a question.

I assume, therefore, that the necessity for increased estimates will be admitted[,] and that it need only be considered whether the sum proposed by the Surveyor over and above the Vote for the current year is unnecessarily large, and whether he proposes to apply it in the most advantageous manner.

With reference to the first point, I concur without hesitation, with the Surveyor. There is a difference of only £12000 a year between what he now proposes, as an addition to the estimate for this year for the building and conversion of Line of Battleships, and what I proposed in the Paper which I drew up on this subject a few months ago.

My proposal was to raise the number of Screw Line of Battleships to 56, in three years, at an additional cost of £484,000 a year.

The Surveyor proposes to raise them to the same number in two years[,] at the additional cost of £496,000 a year, that is to say to effect the same object at a less expense [*sic*] and in a shorter time.

He contemplates this saving in time and expense by the conversion of four old sailing ships – the *Nelson*, *Rodney*, *Prince Regent*, and *Albion* in addition to the six recommended by him for immediate conversion in his submission of last July, but of which, for want of sufficient dock accommodation, four only could then be taken in hand. The remaining two, with the four above specified, together with the *Royal Frederick* and the *Irresistible*, new ships, not yet launched, and always intended to be completed as screw vessels, constitute the eight conversions now proposed by the Surveyor, so that the additional conversions recommended are only four – and not eight as might be inferred by the wording of his submission.

It appears from a document furnished to me by the Surveyor last July . . . that the six ships then recommended for conversion would exhaust the whole of those which were considered in a sufficiently good state of repair, or to have sufficient capacity, to render conversion advisable, but I find that the four additional ships now proposed to be converted have proved, on examination, to be sounder than was anticipated, and[,] as they are all vessels of sufficient capacity, I agree with the Surveyor in thinking that, although any extensive conversion of old and inferior ships would be a waste of public money, the additional conversions may be carried out with advantage to the extent now recommended by him. One of the arguments advanced by the Surveyor in favour of converting these ships is the difficulty of procuring the necessary quantity of timber for building, within the time specified, the required number of new ships, and there is no subject which appears to me more deserving of the serious attention of the Admiralty than this. It is estimated in the Department of the Storekeeper General that the greatest quantity of shipbuilding timber that could by possibility be obtained from all parts of the world in one year would be 35000 loads, and that, to obtain this, it would be necessary to exhaust all the sources of supply in England, Italy, Africa, the East Indies, Cuba, and elsewhere.

The estimated annual expenditure of shipbuilding timber with the existing establishment of 4000 shipwrights is 25000 loads. The addition of 1500 shipwrights to the present Establishment now proposed by the Surveyor would raise the estimated annual expenditure to 33000 loads, and[,] as the necessity of working from time to time on task and job would occasionally arise, it may be assumed that the actual expenditure of shipbuilding timber with an establishment of 5500 Shipwrights would be at least 35000 loads, or, in other words, that no matter what the emergency might be (as, for instance, on the occurrence of war) it would be impossible to provide for any further addition to the work executed in the Dockyards, at least without exhausting the store of timber, which although unusually large at present (41000 loads)[,] is only equal to the proper establishment, that is to say two years expenditure, at an annual expenditure of 35000 loads. I believe that this difficulty might in some measure be met by the substitution, to a greater extent, of iron for wood in the construction of ships of war, as, for instance, of iron for wooden beams which are much used in the merchant service, but, besides this, every effort should be made to open additional markets, more especially as we have reason to believe that some of those from which we are now drawing supplies are becoming rapidly exhausted.

To return from this digression to the Surveyor's submission, I agree with him in thinking that a considerable addition to our force of screw frigates is hardly less necessary than to that of our ships of the line, more especially as so many of the latter will consist of old sailing ships converted to screw[,] which will be unequal to the heavy armament necessary to enable them to cope with ships armed with guns of the longest ranges, without the assistance of frigates.

When it is considered that, as appears from a Table annexed to the Surveyor's submission, we had upwards to 200 frigates during the course of the last great naval war, and upwards of 300 at its close in 1815, that[,] as at present we possess but 18 screw, and 19 Paddlewheel frigates, and that the cost of a heavy frigate, with her engines, may be estimated at about £150,000, I do not think that the Surveyor's proposal to appropriate £200,000 a year to the construction of frigates in addition to the present expenditure can be looked upon as extravagant.

There remains the consideration of a question which is only glanced at by the Surveyor in the concluding paragraph of his submission, as one for future discussion, but which I am strongly impressed with the conviction demands [*sic*] the immediate attention of the Admiralty, and is in some degree at least, already ripe for decision.

I allude to the question of building a certain number of iron-coated frigates[,] of which six are now in progress in France, of which two are more than half completed.

I concur with the Surveyor in the opinion that at present no prudent man would consider it safe to risk upon the performance of ships of this novel character the naval supremacy of Gt Britain, but, on the other hand, if experiments go to prove that iron plates of the proper thickness and construction, on wood, are a complete protection against ordinary guns, & penetrable only by a description of shot not now in use in any Navy, I do not think it would be prudent to shut our eyes to the enormous advantage ships thus defended would have over wooden ships[,] which might be sunk by a single broadside from guns of the description now in ordinary use.

With reference to the recent experiments on the *Alfred*, Captain Hewlett of the *Excellent* states in his report, 'the experiments tend to show the immense advantage ships clothed with wrought iron have over those not so protected. It puts a vessel with a few heavy guns more than on a par with the heaviest three-deckers, supposing that she has more speed, and, under such circumstances the issue of an action could not long remain doubtful.'

In the experiments against the *Erebus*, iron Floating Battery, the iron failed to afford under certain circumstances the necessary protection, but Captain Hewlett remarks, with reference to this comparative failure, 'From the above trials it appears that iron Floating Batteries are very inferior in power of resistance against shot [compared] to vessels built of wood and coated with iron.'

This view of the case is further confirmed by subsequent experiments against the *Meteor*, wooden Floating Battery coated with iron. Captain Hewlett says 'In no case throughout the trials on the *Meteor* did it appear that the damage, inboard [*sic*], would have caused any inconvenience to the men working the guns. Even the wrought iron shot, although doing considerable injury to the plates, did not penetrate at 40 yards, nor cause damage of consequence inboard.'

Under these circumstances[,] I am strongly of opinion that a portion of the Votes for next year should be appropriated to, at least, two wooden frigates to be coated with iron, in order to guard, in some degree, against the advantage France would have over use from the exclusive possession of this formidable arm.

[**648**] *Thorne*[1] *to Milne*

HMS *St. Vincent*, Portsmouth, Private
6 December 1858

My dear Admiral

I have great pleasure in replying (seriatim), to the queries contained in your note of the 30th ulto, on the following points connected with the present system of Paymasters duties, since they have been made Accountant Officers, in addition to their former proper duties.

You state, it has been said, and the opinion gains ground that the Paymasters cannot in justice to themselves, or to the Crown, discharge both duties, viz. give attention to the provisions and stores, and also to the Cash Accounts. You ask my opinion.

I think both duties can be faithfully discharged by the Paymaster, if an efficient Staff be afforded, and the duties properly divided with the Assistant Paymaster – the Paymaster of course giving a general superintendence, and bearing all the responsibility to the Crown. The Cash disbursements to be always made by the Paymaster.

1. Can the Paymaster discharge both duties in a Brig or Sloop?

1. Most assuredly.

2. Can he do so in a Frigate?

2. Yes – for the Cash Account will not absorb more of his time, but there will be ample leisure for due attention being given to the care, and the expenditure of the provisions, Clothing &c.

3. Can he do so in a Ship of the Line?

[1]Edward Thorne (d. 1863). Passed Clerk, 1815; Paymaster; 1829; Paymaster-in-Chief, 1862. Serving in *St Vincent*, Guardship of the Ordinary at Portsmouth.

3. Yes – provided the Staff be efficient.
4. In a Flag Ship on a Foreign Station?
4. Now here I opine that the duties might, and ought to be separated, for the Paymaster cannot give up the necessary time to the Cash disbursements, without neglecting his other onerous duties, or personally superintending the Provisions and Clothing, in his charge – especially when provisions and Fresh Meat have to be purchased for the Fleet. Again, it is more than probable that the Cash required by other ships in the Fleet would have to be procured by the Paymaster of the Flag Ship, on a Foreign Station. His time would thus be occupied on shore in procuring Cash for the Bills required, consequently he cannot give due attention to the joint duties of the Paymaster and Accountant.
5. In a Flag Ship at the Home Port?
5. Yes – provided he has an efficient Assistant and Staff.
6. Ought the Ship's Steward to be raised to the rank of Warrant Officers [*sic*]?
6. Decidedly not – for if you make Officers of them, they will be above their business, and hesitate to perform the menial duties of the Steward['s] Room.
The objection to create [*sic*] a new Rank of Officers is also too manifest, especially when their Services are not permanently required, except in Seagoing Ships.

[**649**] *Milne Minute for the Board on Naval Cadets' Certificates*

Admiralty
2 January 1859

It is absolutely necessary that a Certificate[,] as per enclosed[,] should be given to each cadet on leaving the *Illustrious* Training Ship[,] in order that he may be aware of the times at which he is to pass the examinations for Midn &c &c. The changes which have been made in the time of Service of the Cadets, and the Changes which are again to be made[,] renders such a Certificate necessary. One copy should be given to the Cadet, one retained in the Training Ship and one sent to [the] Admiralty as a record.
I would submit that the Commission Board should make [print] this & that it should be printed on good thick paper and in a proper official form.

Certificate of Service of Naval Cadets discharged from H.M.S. Training Ship at Ports[mou]th

1. Name of Cadet –
2. Date of his passing into the Service at the R.N. College –
3. Age at that date –
4. Date of entry on board the Training Ship –
5. Date of discharge from the Training Ship –
6. Time allowed him to count for sea service & from what date –
7. Date at which he should pass his examination for Midshipman under the X Clause of Circular 288, provided he has served eighteen months –
8. Date at which he should pass his intermediate examination under XII Clause of the Circular 288[,] provided he has served eighteen months from his last examination –
9. Date at which he should pass his examination for the Rank of Lieutenant[,] provided he has served two years from the date of his passing his intermediate examination –

Sec[ond] Form to come in here[:]
Date at which he passed the following examinations

	Examination	Date of Passing	Signature of Captain
For Midn under Clause 6 & 7			
Intermediate under Clause No 8			
For Lieut. in Seamanship			

Note[:]
This Certificate is to be given to each Cadet on his discharge from the Training Ship[,] and is to be produced [*sic*] to the Captain of the ship in which the Cadet is serving[,] in order that the requisite examinations may take place at the proper periods[,] and a notation is to be made when the respective examinations under Clauses 7, 8, & 9 have been passed. This certificate is also to be produced when passing for the Rank of Lieutenant.[1]

[1]The subsequent form, copies of which are enclosed in ADM1/5716, Box 1, closely follows Milne's draft, 'Date of Birth' becoming no 2, an easier way to determine dates at which exams should be taken.

[**650**] *Milne Draft Board Minute on Policing the Dockyards*

Admiralty
6 February 1859

My Lords having under consideration the Establishment of a water police in conjunction with the Police of the Dock Yard for the purpose of preventing depredations on board HM Ships &c, my Lords send you [the Dockyard Superintendent] a copy of their Solicitors opinion[,] and you are to report for their information what number of men you consider this force should consist of and the regulations which[,] in your opinion[,] should be established to carry out the proper protection to [*sic*] the ships & stores in the Harbour.[1]

[**651**] *Milne Questionnaire on the Quality of Coal Supplied to the Royal Navy*[2]

Admiralty
7 February 1859

Write to the Captains of the Steam Reserves at Ports[mouth], Devonp[or]t & Sheerness, say that my Lords wish to have a full report on the question of Coal used in HM Ships[,] and they are to afford[,] after full Enquiry with the most experienced Engineers[,] such information as they may consider will enable their Lordships to draw satisfactory conclusions in regard to the Nr [North] Country & Welch [*sic*] Coal, & Patent Fuel..

1. What description of Coal is preferred for use in the Naval Service – North Country, Welch, or Patent Fuel[?]

2. What are the relative advantages of these kinds of Coal when in use[?]

[1]The legal opinion was that any two Lords of the Admiralty could 'make deputy any person or persons including any of the Dock Yard Police by Warrant to act afloat in searching and detaining boats and other craft suspected improperly to contain Naval Stores,' based on an Act of 39&40 George III.

[2]This request followed a report of December 1858, forwarded by Walker in early January 1859, stating the apparent superiority of Welsh coal. The latter suggested that careful experiments be carried out at sea; Milne's minute was evidently the first step toward so doing. See 'Account of the quantity of coal purchased by the Government for the Navy, 1857 to 1859, distinguishing Welsh from Hartley coal', *Parliamentary Papers*, 1860, vol. XLII, p. 261, and 'Account of the quantity of steam coal annually purchased by the Navy, and supplied to each depot abroad, with the cost, Showing also how obtained, and arrangements for payment, 1855 to 1859', *Parliamentary Papers*, 1860, XLII, p. 263.

3. What are their disadvantages, in regard to use in HM Ships[?]
4. What is considered the relative expenditure of the different kind[s] of Coal under the same circumstances[?]
5. What are the advantages or disadvantages of each kind of Coal in regard to stowage in HM Ships[?]
6. Which is the best description of Coal for retaining in store aboard to prevent deterioration[?]
7. Whether No[rth] Country & Welch Coal should be used separate or mixed[?]
8. Whether it is considered the usual Furnaces now fitted are adapted for burning all descriptions of Coal[?]
9. Whether it is considered from the experience of Engineers or other's [*sic*][,] any of the Coals which are from time to time delivered for use in HM Ships are unfit for the service[,] if so state the names of these Coals, & cause of their unfitness.

[**652**] *Milne to Lyster*[1]

Admiralty, Confidential
12 February 1859

Dear Cap Lyster

I write you perfectly in confidence[,] so say nothing to any one nor take any notice, but we hear from very good authority, that in some of the Yards much rascality is going on in the sale of Old Stores[.]
1. New Articles are mixed up with the Old Lots[.]
2. When Lots are taken away[,] new articles are thrown into the Carts or Boats and covered over with the Old Lots.
3. Purchasers take away ½ Lots & return another day for the remainder[,] and then get away [with] other articles.
4. Information is privately given to purchasers by men in the Yard what are the Lots having new articles.

Some of these facts have already been proved to our satisfaction[,] and on the very best authority[,] but not in your Yard. I want you[,] therefore[,] to be on your guard and to look about you in the Store Houses &c before and after Sales, and I think the following will be of use[:]
1. No lottery of Old Stores to take place in the same place where new articles are kept.

[1]Henry Lyster (*c.*1799–1864). Entered, 1811; Lt, 1824; Cmdr, 1841; Capt., 1845; Rear-Adm., 1863; Capt.-Superintendent, Royal William Victualling Yard, Plymouth.

2. The Room where all Articles are to be exposed for sale to be entirely independent of the General Stores.
3. A Clerk or some responsible person to attend the making up of the Lots[,] and the Lots to be clearly marked.
4. Deliveries of Lots to be made by a clerk[,] a Police man always to be present[,] & Lots opened.
No Second Entry to be allowed for half Lots if it can be avoided, but[,] if necessary[,] men to be checked at the gate.

I think it right to point out all this to you, so you can quietly go into the question as you may see fit[,] without causing suspicion[.]

[**653**] *Milne to Dockyard Superintendents and Solicitor General*

Admiralty
14 March 1859

Write to the Superintendants [*sic*] of Chatham, Sheerness, Pembroke and Royal Clarence and ask with reference to former letter on the subject of Police in October last, Why [*sic*] half the amount of any Fines inflicted on men for having govt. property in their possession are not given to the Police[,] in accordance with the Act of Parl?
Solicitor[:]
Look over the enclosed papers.[1] The system at the different Yards in paying rewards to the Police appear's [*sic*] to be different at the respective yards [*sic*][,] and the Superintendants [*sic*] do not appear to be aware under what Acts, they are acting. If you observe this difference[,] it would be as well if you were to frame some general Regulations[,] and send either [*sic*] copies of the Acts of Parliament or give a precis of the various Acts[,] and to say what fines should be inflicted.

[**654**] *Graham to Milne*

Grosvenor Place, London, Private
19 March 1859

My dear Sir Alexander[2]

You have always been a kind Friend [*sic*] to my Cousin, Keith Stewart. He is short Four [*sic*] months of Sea Time for his effective Flag [*sic*]. He is most anxious to have an opportunity of completing the

[1]The abstract of policies at the different dockyards for rewarding informants [**638**], above.

[2]Milne was gazetted with the K.C.B. on 20 December 1858.

full Time: and I should be sorry to see him placed on the retired List, considering the services of his Father[1] both at the Board and afloat. I enclose a letter,[2] in which he details to me his own services. I forward it to you for your own perusal, that you may judge of his personal claims. Can any thing be done for him, when Capt Eyres,[3] having completed his Sea-Time, gives up the command of the *St Vincent* at Portsmouth?

I believe that applications will be made to Sir John Pakington in Keith's behalf [*sic*]. I cannot so interfere: but if you can edge in a good word for him, I shall be obliged.

[**655**] *Milne Memorandum on the 1859–60 Shipbuilding Programme*

[Admiralty
Spring 1859?]

This programme of 1859–60 is satisfactory[,] as it appears the following will be launched in 59 or before April 1860,

Ships of Line	6
Frigates	4
Sloops	8
Smaller Do.	3

Independent of the conversion of 4 Sail of the Line and four heavy Frigates. There is one question[,] however[,] which ought to have consideration [*sic*] by the Board[,] which is that we have no class of Vessel between the 51 Gun Frigate and the 21 & 17 Gun Corvette[,] except those enormous ships like *Mersey*, *Ariadne* &c.

I am of opinion a ship of about 36 Guns would be a useful [?service] class and that the construction of a class of ship of this description[,] between *Tribune* of 31 Guns and 1570 Tons and 300 HP, and the *Arrogant* of 47 Guns, 1872 T[ons] and 360 HP should be considered. Such a class of ship would be a great addl [*sic*: 'addition'] to our force[,] and they would be powerful ships for Foreign Stations. They should have fair speed and good Stowage [*sic*], but if we are to go on and insist on high speed as the necessity for every ship[,] it is obvious this cannot be obtained without high power by Engines of large size[,] requiring space and large Stowage of Coal[,] which must detract from the other advantages which every ship ought to possess.

[1]Admiral Sir George Stewart, eighth Earl of Galloway, Kt. (1768–1834).
[2]Presumably returned to Graham.
[3]Henry Eyres, C.B. (*c.*1806–60). Entered, 1818; Lt, 1827; Cmdr, 1837; Capt., 1841.

We also require a Class of Ship for Admirals Flag Ships on Foreign Stations. This is absolutely necessary, our present large Frigates are crowded with officers[;] they have but little for stowage of the requisite stores[.] add to this state of things the Admiral[,] His Secy[,] His Flag Lt. & Clerks[,] a Secre[tar]ys Office and a Captains Cabin [&] Stewards Berths[.] Where are they to go[?] The ship must either be [encumbered] with Cabins as far as the Main Mast[,] or a Poop of sufficient dimensions must be built on the Ship. It is no use blinking the question[.] Something ought to be done to place the Admirals on Foreign Stations in a proper position[.]

[**656**] *Milne to Codrington*[1]

Admiralty
16 April 1859

Write the Comdr in Chief at Malta[,] and State my Lords would wish to know whether a Contract could be entered into at Malta for the Supply of White Sennett[2] Hats made of <u>Malta Straw</u> and[,] if so[,] at what price per 100. It has been stated they can be obtained for about 2 shillings each. The Comdr in Chief is to order 100 to be made . . . fixing a good pattern in Shape and workmanship[.][3]

[**657**] *Milne Memorandum on Coaling Facilities at Home and Abroad*

Admiralty
24 May 1859

Coal Depots
The enclosed paper[4] points out the various positions at which Coal Depots are established at Home & Abroad[,] and the Quantity of Coal in Government Stores. it [*sic*] also points out the various places at which the Admiralty has <u>agreements</u> or <u>local contracts</u>, for the Supply of Coal to HM Ships on demand. These various arrangements are sufficient to meet the requirements of the Service during a period of Peace, but it is now necessary to consider what steps should be adopted in case of war. If that

[1]Henry John Codrington, Rear-Adm. Superintendent, Malta Dockyard.

[2]Sinnet or Sennit; plaited leaves or other fibres used in hatmaking.

[3]Milne envisioned furnishing these to ships' crews, presumably as an ancillary to the uniform allowance that had been established two years earlier.

[4]Not preserved in ADM1/5716, pt II.

war should be with a Maritime country[,] then I think there can be no doubt, that that country would declare Coal to be a contraband of war, and if the Merchants of any neutral state were to supply us with Coal[,] or even if a Coal Depot was allowed to be kept on shore or afloat, it would be considered a breach of neutrality. If this view is correct, our Coal Depots or stations would be limited to our own shores or colonial stations, and all existing agreements or contracts at Foreign Ports would fall to the ground. Our ships therefore could not obtain Coal at Lisbon, Madeira, Fayal[,][1] Cape de Verdes[,] Rio [de] Janeiro, Fernando Po, Luanda,[2] Havanah [*sic*], and indeed at any Foreign Port.

In some of our Coal arrangements[,] supplies are obtained from the Contract Steam Packet Companies, but these also fail us in case of War, for altho the enemy may not interfere with the Mail Service, so long as that service adhered [*sic*] to noninterference [*sic*], yet if the Depots supplied us with Coal, then the Enemy might consider their so acting as aiding & assisting in war operations. If these views are correct[,] it must be obvious that our ships of war will be much crippled for want of coal and single ships, [*sic*] must resort to our own stores wherever they may be.

Squadron's [*sic*] must be supplied on their respective cruizing grounds by Colliers[,] either sailing or screw[,] and these vessels will have to proceed to the nearest Depot to complete their cargoes, be it England, Gib[ralta]r, Malta or else where [*sic*]. This[,] again[,] will render it necessary largely to increase our Stock of Coal abroad. before [*sic*] going further[,] I submit these remarks for the consideration of the Board. The question is a most important one, and a decision is necessary. a [*sic*] Fleet of Screw Colliers would be required.[3]

[**658**] *Legal Opinion on the Question of Coaling in Neutral Countries during Wartime*[4]

Doctors' Commons
10 June 1859

. . . The Lords of the Admiralty request the opinion of Her Majesty's Advocate, her Majesty's Attorney and Solicitor General, the Admiralty Advocate, and the Admiralty Counsel upon the following points. –

[1]Westernmost of the Azores.

[2]Angola.

[3]MLN/142/3 [4]: contains a draft copy of the questions posed by Milne.

[4]The opening portion of this paper virtually duplicated Milne's 24 May Memorandum on the subject, [**657**].

In case of this Country being at War, and while at war;
1st. Would it be a breach of neutrality to obtain Coal in a Neutral Port for Her Majesty's Ships of War, before or after the Enemy should declare Coal to be Contraband of War, if the Coal be purchased in the market of a Neutral State.
2nd[.] Would it be a breach of Neutrality if coals [*sic*] were obtained for Her Majesty's Ships of War from a Neutral Government Store[,] after or before Coals were declared by the Enemy Contraband of War.
3rd[.] Would it be so if the Admiralty had a store on shore, within a Neutral State, or a Ship as a Depot within the Ports [*sic*] or Waters of a Neutral State, for the supply of Coals to Her Majesty's Ships of War, after or before Coals were declared by the Enemy Contraband of War; the Coals stored in such Ship or Store being by the Admiralty obtained in, and sent from Her Majesty's Dominions?
Opinion

In answering these three questions, we assume that Great Britain has become a Belligerent, and that Her Enemy has declared Coal destined for her use, to be Contraband of War. –

The questions appear to us to relate solely to the procuring of Coal by Her Majesty's Ships in Neutral Ports, excluding all question as to the hostile capture on the high seas, of Coals destined for the use of Her Majesty's Ships, a point upon which our opinion does not appear to be required.

Subject to these observations, we are of opinion[:]
First. that [*sic*] Neutral Powers might permit Her Majesty's Ships to purchase Coals in their markets from private individuals, without thereby absolutely and necessarily committing a breach of neutrality. – at the same time we must observe that Her Majesty's Government would not be entitled to insist upon either the grant or continuance of any such permission; It [*sic*] would clearly be competent to any Neutral Power, either *ab initio* or at any period *durante bello*, to restrict or prohibit absolutely the export of this Article. There are not wanting modern Precedents for such conduct on the part of Neutrals. Her Majesty has herself exercised, especially in 1825, during the contest between Greece and Turkey, this undoubted right of every independent State, as to Arms, Ammunition, &c. See Royal Proclamation Windsor 1825. – And indeed it is obvious that[,] under many conceivable circumstances[,] Neutral Powers might find themselves obliged to prevent Her Majesty's Ships from regularly supplying themselves with Coal in their Ports.
Secondly. We are of opinion that this question must be answered in the affirmative, so far as regards the grant or permission to an Enemy by a Neutral Power to obtain from the Government Stores, Coals

which have been declared by either Belligerent Contraband of War. Such grant or permission would, under those circumstances, be a breach of Neutrality.

With regard to such grant or permission before Coals have been declared by either Belligerent, Contraband of War, we are not prepared to say that such a grant or permission would, under all circumstances, necessarily amount to a clear breach of Neutrality. At the same time, a state of circumstances is easily conceivable in which such grant or permission would seriously compromise the position of the Neutral; and which would clearly justify Him [*sic*] in restricting, or in absolutely withdrawing such grant or permission.

Thirdly – We are of opinion that the case suggested, so far as it relates to shipment of coals from a Store or Coal Ship of Her Majesty's Government, in a Neutral Port before they have been declared by either Belligerent, Contraband of War, falls within the principle of our answer to the first question.

With respect to such a shipment of Coals from a Store or Coal Ship of Her Majesty's Government in a Neutral Port; after they had been declared Contraband of War by either Belligerent, we are of opinion that a Neutral Power would be clearly justified in limiting or withdrawing, '*durante bello*', a grant or permission made '*alio intente, et durante face*'; and we are further of opinion that the continuance of such grant or permission might under many conceivable circumstances, amount '*jure gentium*', to a breach of Neutrality.

It will result from the views which we have expressed, that Her Majesty's Government may, in the event of its being a Belligerent, not improbably find itself unable to obtain any regular supplies of Coal for Steam Ships of War in Neutral Ports; and may be (as it were) left to its own resources in this respect.[1]

[**659**] *Summary of the Hope Committee's Report on the Royal Naval College*[2]

[Portsmouth?]
June 1859

We shall conclude our Inquiry by a summary of its results:

1st[.] We are of opinion that the Instructions of their Lordships as respects Mates, so long as they resorted to the College, – Marine

[1]The opinion was signed by J. D. Harding, FitzRoy Kelly, H. M. Cairns, Robert Phillimore, and W. Atherton.

[2]The paper is labelled: 'Revision of R Naval College'.

Officers educating for the Artillery, – and gentlemen preparing for their special duties as Naval Instructors, have been fully realized, – and that as respects the Half-Pay Officers and Engineers, they have been realized to as great an Extent [*sic*] as could reasonably be expected, under the circumstances of their more advanced age.

2ndly. We recommend very strongly the re-establishment of a class of students analogous to the Mates, to be drawn from the young Lieutenants and Commanders who[,] with the Marine Officers educating for the Artillery and the Gentlemen preparing for Naval Instructors[,] should be considered the primary Object [*sic*] of the Institution, and . . . viewing the means for improvement which the College would afford to officers on Half-pay of a more advanced Age as a most valuable adjunct to it. – We further recommend that every facility should be afforded to them not inconsistent with its primary object.

3dly. As respects the 1st Class of students[,] we are not prepared to recommend any change of the Mode [*sic*] in which the Instruction is at present conveyed, considering it the best which can be adopted; but as respects the Half-pay officers, we consider that the Mode of Instruction by Lectures is the subject of a fair Experiment, and that for that purpose a competent Lecturer should be added to the Establishment.

4thly. That we are not prepared to recommend any immediate change in the period of residence at the College, but we are of opinion, that when the success of imparting Instruction by means of Lectures has been proved, it may again come under consideration with advantage.

5thly. We recommend the appointment of a Committee triennially, to report to their Lordships the state and Progress of Education in the Navy.[1]

[**660**] *Hope's Report on the Royal Naval College*

[Portsmouth?], Confidential
June 1859

I shall now furnish a summary of the recommendations contained in the foregoing summary.

[1]In June 1859 Milne appended a note to this summary and Hope's own confidential report which follows, which reads:

Royal Naval College[:]

The original papers of this subject are with these returns.

1. The original proposal for a revision of the College by Ad Milne[.]

2. The Report of the Committee for revision of the Naval College by Ad. Hope[.]

3. The time has not arrived for carrying out the new system[,] as it depends on any changes of the Professors of the College[.]

1st[.] That of the Midshipmen obtaining their 1st Class Certificates, those passing with full numbers shall be promoted immediately, and those not so passing shall be promoted within six months of the day on which they pass, according to their respective degrees of proficiency, and that every 3rd Class Certificate shall carry with it a dis-qualification for promotion for six months except in the case of Board promotions for Service.

2ndly[.] That a permanent Board of Examiners for Seamanship be established at Portsmouth, whose certificate shall be indispensable to promotion by merit.

3rdly[.] That Lieutenants promoted by merit shall be employed immediately[,] and after three years service at sea shall be appointed to the *Excellent*, in order to compete for the College after six months service in that ship[,] and that the unsuccessful candidates for the College be allowed to complete their course as Gunnery Lieutenants in that ship.

4thly[.] That all Lieutenants with three years sea service as mates or Lieutenants and under 25 years of age, be allowed to compete for the College[,] and that the unsuccessful candidates receive appointments to the *Excellent* if there are vacancies for them.

5thly. That a Commanders Commission be given yearly to the first at the final examination at the College[,] and professional inducements be held out to the other students who shall obtain a high and fixed [*sic*] standard of proficiency.

6thly[.] That the Officer promoted by merit from the College be privileged to continue his studies for one year at Cambridge on full pay[,] and that the reward of professional employment be held out as the result of high place in the examination for Mathematical honours [*sic*].

7thly[.] That every encouragement be held out to the younger Captains and Commanders on Half pay to join the class of College Students by a full participation in the advantages of Residence[,] and of the Rewards held out to them[,] and that increased means of improvement be afforded to those who may not feel disposed to follow this Course[,] by the establishment of lectures on Chemistry, Geology, and Natural Philosophy and by instruction in Steam, Fortification and the use of Instruments.

8thly[.] That the first at the final yearly examination of the Marine Artillery Officers be attached to the division at Chatham for the purpose of going through the course of practical engineering at the School there.

9thly[.] That the question of the mode in which the College may be rendered more useful to the Officers of the Surveying Service be considered.

I shall now conclude by expressing the very strong conviction I entertain that had not their Lordships been led to undertake the consideration of this question, the very general feeling which prevails as to its importance must have eventually forced it on their notice[,] and that the regard I bear to the honour[*sic*][,] no less than the welfare[,] of the Service leads me to hope that it will be dealt with in that large & liberal spirit, which alone is worthy of the leading maritime nation of the world.

[**661**] *Milne Memorandum on Captains' Rates of Pay*

Admiralty
20 June 1859

The present system of paying the Captains of HM Ships under the Order in Council of the 30th of January 1856[,] having been considered injurious to those Captains in the 2d or 3d Class who command Ships of the Line, and who are thereby unable to bear the expenses to which they are subject, It [*sic*] is considered advisable to reestablish the Rates of Pay according to the rates of the ships[,] as established by the Order in Council of 11th Augt. 1854[,] with the exception of the Pay to be drawn by Captains in command of Ships below the Fourth rate[,] which it is recommended [*sic*] should be increased from £399.19.7 per Annum to £450.3.4. Adopting this regulation the following changes will taken [*sic*] place[:]

2d Class[:]

7 Captains now in the 2d Class pay of £574.17.6 will be increased to £701.2.1[.]

6 Captains will be increased to £600.14.7[.]

1 Captains [*sic*] will be reduced from £574.17.6 to £500.

12 Captains will be reduced from £574.17.6 to £450.3.4.

3d Class[:]

3 Captains will be increased from £459.3.4 to £701.2.1[.]

5 Captains from ditto to £600.14.7.

9 Captains from Ditto [*sic*] to £500.7.1[.]

This great change will again cause great inconvenience to officers[,] and it is a question for the very serious consideration of the Board whether the proposed change is really necessary.

Secondly[:] If [*sic*] it is determined to revert to the Order in Council of 1854, Then [*sic*] how is it to be carried out[?]

If done at <u>once thro</u> all the grades[,] some officers will gain[,] some will lose.

If made prospective from a fixed date, then it will take between 4 & 5 years before it can come into force.
As soon as the Board determine on the course to be adopted, An [*sic*] estimate must be made by the Acc[ountan]t G[enera]l and reference made to the Treasury for sanction to [*sic*] the add[itiona]l expense.

[**662**] *Bowles to Milne*

Portsmouth
24 June 1859

My dear Milne,

It has not, as I am sure you will believe, from any want of interest or regard that I have not written sooner, but it was useless to plague you with enquiries while the changes were going on, and[,] in my opinion[,] I ought rather to congratulate than console with you on your name not appearing in the new Board.[1] You have been shut up in London full as long as was good for your health, and have gained as much experience in the Civil branches of your profession as will be necessary for your future career, which I am confident will be equally honourable to yourself, and useful to your country.

Times are, I fear, approaching when your services will be again called for, and if you can get a few months of air and exercise first[,] it will be so much the better.

My sister joins in very kind regards to Lady Milne and yourself . . .

[**663**] *Ridley*[2] *to Milne*

Portsmouth Dockyard
25 June 1859

My dear Milne

I have just seen your nephew[,] Mr Justice Home[,][3] and he tells me that you are really going out. I am very sorry for it, for I have had much experience of your way of doing business[,] & have always felt sure of a satisfactory solution of any D[ock] Yard difficulty in your department when ever [*sic*] I could communicate with you. You have always been so early & certain in taking notice of any communication

[1]Lord Derby's Ministry fell from power on 18 June, to be replaced by Lord Palmerston's Liberal government.
[2]Presumably one of the clerks in the Portsmouth Dockyard office establishment.
[3]David Milne-Home (1838–1901).

I have made to you[,] that I shall feel quite at a loss when you are gone. . . .

[**664**] *Milne to Saunders Dundas*[1]

Admiralty
25 June 1859

My dear Dundas,

I am getting more than anxious about this very important question of Depots of Coal all over the World. I have, as you are aware, brought this subject before the Board on several occasions, and it has been submitted from the Storekeeper General of the Navy to know what supplies are to be sent to the different Foreign Stations; the large number of Ships which have been commissioned, renders it necessary that some steps should be taken; the Stores at Gibraltar and Malta have been largely increased, and so far as the present wants of the Mediterranean Fleet is [*sic*] concerned, their is no difficulty at these two places, but no arrangements have been made for any other Ports except Corfu. If Ships are sent to Alexandria, there is no coal Depot there, although we may obtain some moderate supply from the P. and O. Company. The movement of Ships is regulated by the Cabinet, and is entirely unknown to myself as a Member of the Board, or to the Storekeeper General; therefore it is impossible to make arrangements for coal, for such movements. Thus at Naples, Leghorn, Genoa, &c &c, we have no coal; the Captains of Ships must therefore purchase in the market, when they require supplies, but most likely there will be none to purchase; the only other course which the Admiralty can adopt, is for three or four Screw Colliers to be attached to the Mediterranean Fleet, to draw supplies from Malta; this ought to be done.

But there is a much larger question for consideration. – Are we to prepare for War? If so, Coal Depots should be at once established all over the World, where our ships are now employed, and where they are likely to require supplies. The Members of this Board are entirely ignorant of the intentions of the Government, and therefore this becomes a Cabinet Question. – If war should be declared, our Foreign Stations will not be found ready for war operations; although we keep in store, about one year's supply for the casual wants of the Service, that small store would be found totally inefficient [*sic*: 'insufficient']. What is to be done? My own opinion on this subject should be at once

[1]Saunders Dundas remained at the Board as First Naval Lord until his death in 1861.

submitted to the new First Lord; I therefore write to you as the Senior Naval Lord, with whom rests the Service afloat, that you may take such steps as the emergency may demand. –

The expenditure of Coal by our Ships, is <u>one tenth</u> of the Horse Power of the Engines. This is a fair average. Thus, in the Mediterranean[,] by the return of the 1st June, the Horse Power of the Mediterranean Fleet was 12,830, or equal to an expenditure of 1,283 Tons per day, and say Steam is used two days in each week, the expenditure of Coal would be equal to 2566 Tons per week; but taking it at one half of this, the monthly expenditure would be about 5000 Tons a Month [*sic*] or 60,000 in the year, equal to about £100,000. –

If War should be suddenly declared, we would require large supplies at the Cape, Ascension, Trincomalee, Hong Kong, Jamaica, Barbadoes, Antigua &c. In fact, no less a sum than £250,000 would have to be <u>at once</u> laid out, in the shipment of about 100,000 Tons of Coal abroad.

The question is a momentous one, and one for the serious consideration of the Government; and it all centres in this; Is [*sic*] the Admiralty to keep up a supply of coal on all Foreign Stations, equal to the contingencies of a War? If not, then when War may be declared, our Fleets will be crippled for want of coals.

Pray see to this . . .

You already know the decision of the Law Officers of the Crown on the question of Coal in Neutral Ports, this opinion has been sent to the Secretary of State for Foreign Affairs.

[**665**] *Bell*[1] *to Milne*

Admiralty
30 June 1859

My dear Sir Alexander

I feel much gratified by your expression of approval of the way in which I have done my duty with you, during the last 7 years; I can only say that, as regards myself personally, I very deeply regret that I am no longer (for the present at least) to be officially associated with one for whom I have so high esteem, and who has invariably treated me with so much consideration and kindness, and I know that I speak the opinion of all the best men in the office when I say that your departure from Head Quarters is looked upon not only as a source of

[1]Robert Bell, Admiralty Clerk.

great personal regret to themselves, but as a real and serious national loss.

I do sincerely hope that our intercourse may not cease with the official relationship as Master and secretary, and again assure you that it will be a real pleasure to me to be of any service, great or small to you.

With best regards to Lady Milne, and hopes that the relaxation from official care[s] will quite restore you to health.

[**666**] *Milne Draft Memorandum on Proposal to Establish a Naval Reserve*

[August 1859]

This proposal of Sir F. Barings[1] is one of the most important which has ever been submitted to the Board[.] it grapples with a difficult subject which heretofore has engaged the attention of every Board of Admiralty[,] but without any practical result or any attempt to develop a plan[.] No one can doubt the absolute necessity for a Naval Reserve[,] and if Sir F. Barings plan can be carried out it will be the first step towards the defence of the country and the Manning of the Navy[.] Without wishing in the least to raise any difficulties or objections to the proposal[,] I have ventured to express some opinion on the outline now put forward with the view of giving every assistance to carry out so desirable a proposal.

In the first place[,] what are the benefits and advantages which a seaman once entered in the Navy obtains & looks forward to[?]

1. Pay, with advantage of Allotments &c, Extra Pay &c.
2. Hospital treatment when sick[.]
3. Prizemoney [*sic*]. Africa & Brazils[.][2]
4. Pension for Injury or Long servitude
5. Serving as a Pensioner & having Pay & Pension[.]
6. Greenwich Hospital as a Retirement[.]

With such advantages held out in the Naval Service[,] few men will leave it voluntarily, but a number of men will be obliged to seek other employment for want of Ships of War, and the Govt must hold out

[1]It is not clear why Milne made reference to Baring. The measure – 'A Bill for the Establishment of a Reserve Volunteer Force of Seamen, and for the Government of the Same' – was brought in by Admiralty Secretary Lord Clarence Paget and Civil Lord Samuel Whitbread, and the Royal Commission on Manning neither included nor examined Baring.

[2]Prize money was paid for capture of slavers.

some benefit to the seaman who is to serve in the Coasting Trade for the benefit of the Country. It is proposed to give him £6 pr. annum.

I think this will not be sufficient but he should be allowed to look forward to prospective advantages [*sic*] –

1. I think we ought to look up on [*sic*] these men as a part of the Navy in Reserve[.]

2. To allow time served in the Reserve[,] say 5 years[,] to count as 3 Year's [*sic*] for Pension and Greenwich Hospital[.]

Suppose we obtain men to enter under such conditions[?]

1. They will[,] of course[,] be registered at the Registration office in a Separate Ledger as Naval Reserve[,] and divided into 4 or 6 Divisions.

[2.] Granted Govt Stamped Certificates [of Service.]

[3.] To be mustered and paid at the present Coast Guard Station or Custom House where the party may then be serving[,] and his Certificate signed[.]

[4.] The owner of the Vessel should be forced to allow him to attend the muster[.]

[5.] The owner should not be allowed to refuse the Services of a seaman of the Naval Reserve if he offers[,] but need not take more than 3 out of 5 in the Crew [*sic*].

[6.] [To be required to serve] When called out by Proclamation.

[7.] Owner to give notice to the Adm[iral]ty of all reserve seamen serving on board.

[**667**] *Milne to Somerset*[1]

Inveresk, Musselburgh
22 September 1859

My dear Sir

When I had the honour of waiting upon you at the Admiralty in June last, I mentioned with reference to your offer of active employment that[,] after some weeks relaxation in the Country[,] I would write to you on the subject[.] I now beg leave to offer my services of Active Employment and I hope it may be in your power to accede to my request[,] and[,] after so many years of service as a Member of the Board of Admiralty[,] I trust it may not be thought irregular on my part in expressing a wish to be considered as a candidate for the Command of the North American and West India Station[,] with which I am intimately acquainted from having been there in Command of ships for

[1]Fragment of a draft preserved among Milne's papers.

a period of five years, from 1836 to 1841[,] and a further wish for that appointment is that my Father[,] the Ad Sir D Milne[,] held that command from 1817 to 1819 when I first entered the N[aval] Service . . .

[**668**] *Somerset to Milne*

Admiralty
23 September 1859

Dear Sir Alexander Milne

I have received your note and shall be happy to consider you a candidate for employment; but in regard to the special command to which you allude[,] I cannot do more than give your application a fair consideration with that [*sic*] of others who have also claims to be employed[.]

[**669**] *Saunders Dundas to Milne*

Admiralty
24 September 1859

My dear Milne

The same post which brought me your letter brought one also from George Courtenay[1] in rather a complaining tone at having been frequently passed over, & asking for the N. American command. Seeing nothing in your own letter to keep it back, & thinking it as well that you should be as early in the field as any others I gave it at once to Moore[2] for delivery to the Duke, & of course in due time I conclude that he will consider your wish.

I have myself written recently to H[ousto]n Stewart to ascertain his wishes, &[,] as I find he will be [only] too happy to keep Mrs Stewart at Bermuda until after the Winter[,] there will be no occasion to select a successor before November. It will also be desirable to man up the ships for China before fitting out a new Flag Ship for the West Indies, & therefore every thing must remain in abeyance for the present.

[1]George William Conway Courtenay (1795–1863). Entered, 1805; Lt, 1813; Cmdr, 1823; Capt., 1828; Rear-Adm., 1854.

[2]Capt. John Moore, C.B., Somerset's private secretary.

You will have been interested in Mr McClintocks[1] return. I reckon that Lady Franklin must have received at least £6000 more Pay [*sic*] than was ever due.[2]

[**670**] *Somerset to Milne*

Admiralty
10 October 1859

Dear Admiral Milne

As you told me that you were anxious for employment, I have submitted your name to Her Majesty as a successor to Sir Houston Stewart in that important command.

Her Majesty had graciously approved. A ship will be commissioned in November and your flag can be hoisted in December next.

I hope this will be agreeable to you . . .

[**671**] *Milne to Somerset*

[*c*.12 October 1859]

My dear Sir

I have the honour [*sic*] to acknowledge your note of the 9th [*sic*][,] acquainting me with your having submitted my Name to Her Majesty for the Command of the N. American & W India Station. I beg to express my sincere thanks to you for the confidence you have reposed in me[,] and I trust I will discharge the Import[ant] duties of that extensive command in such a manner as to [?permit] the approval of the Lords of the Admiralty (of your selection)[.]

I will take an early opportunity of waiting on your Grace and expressing my thanks in person . . .

[1]Sir Leopold McClintock, Kt., K.C.B. (1818–1907). Entered, 1831; Lt, 1845; Cmdr, 1851; Capt., 1854; Rear-Adm., 1871; Vice-Adm., 1877; Adm., 1884. McClintock commanded an expedition financed by Lady Franklin in 1857, after the Navy had abandoned the search for her husband.

[2]In May 1859 McClintock found a cairn containing a paper which recorded the fate of the expedition from 1845 to 25 April 1848; Franklin himself had died on 11 June 1847.

[672] *Pakington to Milne*

17 November 1859

My dear Sir A. Milne

I was not aware, till Lady Pakington received an application from a young Naval cousin of hers, a few days since, that you had been appointed to succeed Houston Stewart in the North America Command.

I expected & wished that you might have that appointment, and now it is confirmed. I must write a line as an old Colleague & Friend, to offer you my congratulations & good wishes.

I am glad & [*sic*] hear that Lady Milne will go with you.

I suppose you will sail soon, & I heartily wish you all honour & success during your period of command[,] and that you may return more valuable than ever as a Lord of the Admiralty!

LIST OF DOCUMENTS

35. Milne to David Milne, 17 March 1828, MLN/169/2
36. Milne to David Milne, 19 April 1828, MLN/169/2
37. Milne to David Milne, 23 August 1828, MLN/169/2
38. Milne to David Milne, 24 March 1829, MLN/169/2
39. Milne to David Milne, 18 June 1829, MLN/169/2
40. Milne to David Milne, 10 July 1829, MLN/169/2
41. Milne to David Milne, 4 December 1829, MLN/169/2
42. Milne to David Milne, 2 May 1830, MLN/169/2
43. Milne to David Milne, 12 May 1830, MLN/169/2
44. Milne to David Milne, 21 May 1830, MLN/169/2
45. Milne to David Milne, 30 May 1830, MLN/169/2
46. Milne to David Milne, 21 December 1836, MLN/169/2
47. Milne to David Milne, 1 January 1837, MLN/169/2
48. Milne to David Milne, *c.*20 January 1837, MLN/169/2
49. Milne to David Milne, 9 February 1837, MLN/169/2
50. Milne to David Milne, 1 March 1837, MLN/169/2
51. Milne to David Milne, 22 March 1837, MLN/169/2
52. Milne to David Milne, 24 April 1837, MLN/169/3
53. Declaration of Capture of *Arrogante*, 23 November 1837, MLN/101/12
54. Declaration of Capture of *Matilda*, 4 December 1837, MLN/101/12
55. Milne to Jauncey: Prize Instructions, [5 December 1837], MLN/101/12
56. Milne to Peyton, 10 December 1837, MLN/101/12
57. Milne to David Milne, 31 January–17 February 1838, MLN/169/3
58. Milne to the Governor of Santa Marta, Colombia, 7 March 1838, MLN/101/12
59. Leith to Milne, 2 April 1838, MLN/102/6
60. Milne to Leith, [*c.*12] April 1838, MLN/101/12
61. Leith to Milne, 15 April 1838, MLN/102/6
62. Milne to David Milne, 15 April 1838, MLN/102/1
63. Milne to Leith, [June 1838], MLN/101/12
64. Paget to Milne, 29 August 1838, MLN/102/1
65. Milne to Wood, 16 September 1838, MLN/101/12
66. Douglas to Milne, 16 September 1838, MLN/102/6
67. Milne to David Milne, November 1838, MLN/169/3
68. Milne to David Milne, 30 January 1839, MLN/169/3
69. Milne to Douglas, 2 April 1839, MLN/101/12
70. Adam to Milne, 13 August 1839, MLN/102/1
71. Milne to David Milne, 6–12 November 1839, MLN/169/3

72. Milne to Douglas, 27 December 1839, MLN/101/15
73. Thomas Harvey to Milne, 15 February 1840, MLN/102/6
74. Declaration of Capture of *Mercedita,* 13 April 1840, MLN/101/15
75. Milne to Woodman: Prize Instructions, 13 April 1840, MLN/101/15
76. Milne to Douglas, 22 April 1840, MLN/101/15
77. Milne to Douglas, 7 May 1840, MLN/101/15
78. Milne to Thomas Harvey, 23 May 1840, MLN/101/15
79. Milne to Prescott, 7 June 1840, MLN/101/15
80. Prescott to Milne, 10 June 1840, MLN/102/2
81. Milne to the Governor of St Pierre's and Miquelon, 20 June 1840, MLN/101/15
82. Milne to the Officers of HMS *Crocodile*, [July 1840], MLN/101/15
83. Bishop Spencer to the Officers of HMS *Crocodile*, [July 1840], MLN/101/15
84. The Captains of the *Binicos*, *Sometre*, *Alcide*, and *Frainida* to Milne, 30 July 1840, MLN/102/3
85. Milne to the Captains of the *Binicos*, *Sometre*, *Alcide*, and *Frainida*, 30 July 1840, MLN/102/3
86. Milne Report on the Newfoundland Fisheries, 7 June–13 August 1840, MLN/101/15
87. Milne to Prescott, 6 October 1840, MLN/101/15
88. Prescott to Milne, 9 October 1840, MLN/102/2
89. Milne to Harvey, 19 October 1840, MLN/101/15
90. Thomas Harvey to Milne, 6 November 1840, MLN/102/2
91. Milne to Axholm, 27 December 1840, MLN/101/15
92. Barrow to Thomas Harvey, 29 December 1840, MLN/102/2
93. Milne to David Milne, 31 December 1840, MLN/169/3
94. Minto to Milne, 3 January 1841, MLN/169/3
95. Milne to Axholm, 26 January 1841, MLN/101/15
96. Declaration of Capture of *Secundo Rosario*, [27 January 1841], MLN/101/15
97. Milne to Gordon: Prize Instructions, 28 January 1841, MLN/101/15
98. Milne to Leith, 5 February 1841, MLN/101/15
99. Milne to John Harvey, 5 April 1841, MLN/101/15
100. Milne to FitzRoy, 28 April 1841, MLN/101/15
101. Milne to FitzRoy, 20 July 1841, MLN/101/15
102. Milne Report on the Gulf of St Lawrence Fisheries, 2 October 1841, MLN/101/15
103. Adam to Milne, 22 October 1841, MLN/102/6

104. Adam to Milne, 22 October 1841, MLN/102/6
105. Milne to David Milne, 14 November 1841, MLN/169/3
106. Milne to Sir David Milne, 15 November 1841, MLN/102/1
107. Milne to Moore, 17 November 1841, MLN/101/15
108. Milne to David Milne, 17 November 1841, MLN/169/3
109. Milne to David Milne, 1 December 1841, MLN/169/3
110. Milne to David Milne, 6 December 1841, MLN/169/3
111. Gage to Milne, 20 March [1842], MLN/102/4
112. Barrow to Sir David Milne, 21 April 1842, MLN/102/8
113. Barrow to Sir David Milne, 23 April 1842, MLN/102/8
114. Milne to Barrow, 27 April 1842, MLN/101/18
115. Milne to David Milne, 7 May 1842, MLN/169/3
116. Milne to David Milne, 10 June 1842, MLN/169/3
117. Milne to Sir David Milne, 21 June 1842, MLN/101/18
118. Milne to David Milne, 1–9 July 1842, MLN/169/3
119. Milne to Sir David Milne, 27 July 1842, MLN/101/18
120. Milne to David Milne, 14 November 1842, MLN/169/3
121. Hamilton to Milne, 12 January 1843, MLN/102/4
122. Gage to Milne, 16 January 1843, MLN/102/4
123. Milne to David Milne, 22 January 1843, MLN/169/3
124. Milne to Jean Milne, 23 September 1843, MLN/169/3
125. Sir David Milne to Milne, 16 November 1843, MLN/102/4
126. Milne to Bowles, 17 November 1843, MLN/101/18
127. Milne to David Milne, 18 November 1843, MLN/169/4
128. Milne to David Milne, 17 December 1843, MLN/169/4
129. Milne to Sir David Milne, 29 May 1844, MLN/101/18
130. Milne to David Milne, 4 July 1844, MLN/169/4
131. Sir David Milne to Milne, 6 July 1844, MLN/102/4
132. Milne to David Milne, 27 July–10 August 1844, MLN/169/4
133. Milne to Lord Howard de Walden, 21 August 1844, MLN/101/18
134. Milne to David Milne, 3 September 1844, MLN/169/4
135. Milne to Herbert, 1 October 1844, MLN/101/19
136. Milne to Sir David Milne, 12 October 1844, MLN/101/19
137. Bowles to Milne, 13 October 1844, MLN/102/4
138. Milne to David Milne, 13 October 1844, MLN/169/4
139. Milne to Rowley, 14 October 1844, MLN/101/19
140. Milne to Meek, 28 November 1844, MLN/101/19
141. Milne to Admiralty Secretary, 21 December 1844, MLN/101/19
142. Milne to Briggs, 23 December 1844, MLN/101/19
143. Bowles to Milne, 29 December 1844, MLN/165/1
144. Milne to Sir David Milne, 31 December 1844, MLN/101/19
145. Milne to Sir David Milne, 5 January 1845, MLN/101/19

208. Milne Memorandum on Proposals to Reduce the Grog Ration, [1849], MLN/153/5
209. Milne Proposal on Reporting Courts Martial Verdicts, [1849], MLN/153/5 [21]
210. Milne Report on HMS *Plumper*, [1849], MLN/148/1 [2]
211. Milne to Napier, 6 April 1849, Add Mss 40041, fol. 217
212. Napier to Milne, 12 April 1849, Add Mss 40041, fols. 217–18
213. Ellenborough to Milne, 26 April 1849, MLN/102/5
214. Milne to Baring, 2 July 1849, MLN/165/1
215. Napier to Milne, 13 December 1849, Add Mss 40041, fol. 228
216. Milne to Napier, 20 January 1850, Add Mss 40041, fol. 228
217. Milne Draft Paper on Naval Measures to be taken in Case of War, [*c*.1850], MLN/142/1 [1]
218. James W. D. Dundas Memorandum on the State of the Flag List, 14 August 1850, MLN/152/7 [1]
219. Bowles Memorandum on the State of the Flag List, 4 February 1846, MLN/152/7 [1]
220. Bowles Memorandum on Promotion by Selection, March 1846, MLN/152/7 [1]
221. Bowles to Milne, 17 November 1850, MLN/152/7 [2]
222. Milne Paper on Promotion, Retirement, and the Flag List, [1850], MLN/152/7 [3, part II]
223. Milne Proposal to Establish an Admiralty Library, 26 June 1851, ADM1/5614
224. Milne Proposal on Instruction and Examination of Officers in Steam Engineering, September 1851, ADM1/5610
225. Milne Draft Circular for the Education and Examination of Officers in Steam Engineering, 20 October 1851, ADM1/5610
226. Board Minutes on Milne's Draft Circular for the Education and Examination of Officers in Steam Engineering, [October 1851], ADM1/5610
227. Milne Memorandum on Education and Examination of Officers in Steam Engineering, [October 1851], ADM1/5610
228. Milne Paper on Coaling Steamships, 3 November 1851, ADM7/617, Case 136
229. Baring to Milne, [November 1851], MLN/165/1
230. Milne to Baring on French Naval Preparations, December 1851, MLN/156/4 [26]
231. Milne to Baring, 4 February 1852, MLN/166/7
232. Cockburn to Milne, 26 February 1852, MLN/165/2
233. Ogle to Milne, 29 February 1852, MLN/165/9

283. Milne to Napier, 12 March 1854, Add Mss 40024, fol. 55
284. Milne to Newcastle, 14 March 1854, ADM1/5632
285. Cunard to Milne, 15 March 1854, MLN/156/3 [2]
286. Graham to Milne, 16 March 1854, MLN/165/4
287. Milne to Newcastle, 17 March [1854], Ne C10,351
288. Milne to Newcastle, 20 March 1854, Ne C10,352
289. Milne to Newcastle, 21 March 1854, Ne C10,353
290. Newcastle to Milne, 23 March 1854, MLN/165/1
291. Milne to Newcastle, 24 March [1854], Ne C10,354/2
292. Napier to Milne, 24 March 1854, MLN/166/2
293. Milne to Newcastle, 27 March 1854, Ne C10,355
294. Houston Stewart to Milne, 30 March 1854, MLN/156/4 [5]
295. Napier to Milne, 1 April 1854, MLN/166/2
296. Cunard to Milne, 5 April 1854, MLN/156/3 [3]
297. Napier to Milne, 5 April 1854, MLN/166/2
298. Milne Draft Orders to Christie, 6 April 1854, MLN/156/4 [1]
299. Houston Stewart to Milne, 7 April 1854, MLN/156/4 [6]
300. Cunard to Grant, 8 April 1854, MLN/156/3 [4]
301. Draft instructions for Belcher, [8 April 1854], ADM1/5632
302. Cunard to Milne, *c.*10 April 1854, MLN/156/3 [5]
303. Hastings to Milne, 8 April [1854], MLN/156/4 [8/2]
304. Napier to Milne, 9 April 1854, MLN/166/2
305. Hastings to Milne, 11 April 1854, MLN/156/4 [10]
306. Hastings to Milne, 11April [1854], MLN/156/4 [11]
307. Milne to Napier, 13 April 1854, Add Mss 40024, fols. 137–8
308. Graham to Milne, 20 April 1854, MLN/156/4 [12]
309. Cunard to Milne, 24 April 1854, MLN/156/3 [6]
310. Milne to Newcastle, 27 April 1854, Ne C10,358
311. Milne to Newcastle, 27 April 1854, Ne C10,357
312. Cunard to Milne, 1 May 1854, MLN/156/3 [7]
313. Milne to Napier, 2 May 1854, Add Mss 40024, fols. 170–71
314. Cunard to Milne, 4 May 1854, MLN/156/3 [8]
315. Milne to Graham, 10 May 1854, Ne C10,359/1
316. Milne to Newcastle, [10 May 1854], Ne C10,359/2
317. Milne to Newcastle, [11 May 1854], Ne C10,360/2
318. Cunard to Milne, 19 May 1854, MLN/156/3 [9]
319. Milne to Newcastle, 20 May [1854], Ne C10,361
320. Christie to Milne, 24 May 1854, MLN/156/1 [1]
321. Milne to Napier, 30 May 1854, Add Mss 40024, fols. 226–9
322. Graham to Milne, [*c.*1] June 1854, MLN/165/4
323. Milne Draft Board Minute to Newcastle, 5 June 1854, MLN/156/4 [2]

364. Milne to Christie, 29 July 1854, MLN/169/6
365. Milne to Boxer, 29 July 1854, MLN/169/6
366. Milne to Mundy, 31 July 1854, MLN/169/6
367. Milne to Grant, 1 August 1854, MLN/169/6
368. Milne to Michael Seymour, 1 August 1854, MLN/169/6
369. Milne to Grant, 4 August 1854, MLN/169/6
370. Milne to Grant and Austin, 5 August 1854, MLN/169/6
371. Milne to Boxer, 8 August 1854, MLN/169/6
372. Milne to Napier, 8 August 1854, Add Mss 40025, fols. 161–2
373. Milne to Houston Stewart, 9 August 1854, MLN/169/6
374. Christie to Milne, 10 August 1854, MLN/156/1 [6]
375. Mundy to Milne, 11 August 1854, MLN/156/4 [16]
376. Milne to the General Screw Steamship Company, 11 August 1854, MLN/169/6
377. Milne to Cunard, 11 August 1854, MLN/169/6
378. Mundy to Milne, 14 August 1854, MLN/156/4 [17]
379. Milne to the P&O Company, 15 August 1854, MLN/169/6
380. Milne to Horse Guards, 15 August 1854, MLN/169/6
381. Milne to Napier, 15 August 1854, Add Mss 40025, fols. 208–9
382. Milne to Newcastle, 17 August 1854, Ne C10,363/1
383. Milne to Houston Stewart, 18 August 1854, MLN/169/7
384. Christie to Milne, 19 August 1854, MLN/156/1 [7]
385. Milne to Newcastle, 21 August [1854], Ne C10,364
386. Milne to Napier, 22 August 1854, Add Mss 40025, fol. 255–6
387. Milne to Napier, 27 August 1854, Add Mss 40025, fol. 275–6
388. Milne to Grant, 9 September 1854, MLN/169/7
389. Milne to Grant, 11 September 1854, MLN/169/7
390. Milne to Grant, 13 September 1854, MLN/169/7
391. Milne to Grant, 16 September 1854, MLN/169/7
392. Milne to Boxer, 16 September [1854], MLN/169/7
393. Graham to Milne, 21 September 1854, MLN/165/4
394. Christie to Milne, 27 September 1854, MLN/156/1 [8]
395. Graham to Milne, 5 October 1854, MLN/165/4
396. Mundy to Milne, 13 October 1854, MLN/156/4 [7]
397. Milne to Newcastle, 23 October [1854], Ne C10,365
398. Milne to Boxer, 23 October 1854, MLN/169/7
399. Milne to Napier, 24 October 1854, Add Mss 40026, fol. 214
400. Milne to the British Consul at Marseilles, 24 October 1854, MLN/169/7
401. Milne Draft Instructions to the Hudson's Bay Company, 27 October 1854, MLN/159/1 [7]
402. Christie to Milne, 28 October 1854, MLN/156/1 [9]

403. Milne to Newcastle, 1 November [1854], Ne C10,366
404. Milne to Newcastle, 2 November 1854, Ne C10,367
405. Milne to James W. D. Dundas, 3 November 1854, MLN/156/4 [8]
406. Milne to Boxer, 3 November 1854, MLN/169/7
407. Milne to Newcastle, 5 November 1854, Ne C10,368
408. Ramsay to Roberts, 9 November 1854, Ne C10,369
409. Milne to Graham, 11 November 1854, MLN/156/6 [1][f]
410. Milne to Graham, 11 November [1854], MLN/156/6 [1][b]
411. Cunard to Milne, 11 November 1854, MLN/156/3 [10]
412. Milne to Cunard, 11 November [1854], MLN/169/7
413. Milne to Allen, 11 November [1854], MLN/169/7
414. Milne to Chappell, 11 November [1854], MLN/169/7
415. Milne to Ellis, 11 November 1854, MLN/169/7
416. Milne to [?Graham], 11 November [1854], MLN/156/6 [1] [a]
417. Milne to Boxer, 13 November 1854, MLN/169/7
418. Milne to James W. D. Dundas, 14 November 1854, MLN/169/7
419. Milne to [?Graham], 14 November [1854], MLN/156/6 [1][c]
420. Graham to Milne, 14 November 1854, MLN/165/4
421. Cunard to Milne, 15 November 1854, MLN/156/3 [11]
422. Milne to Ellis, 17 November 1854, MLN/169/7
423. Milne to Graham, 17 November 1854, Ne C10,370/1, 2
424. Milne to Bevis, 18 November [1854], MLN/169/7
425. Milne to Laird, 18 November [1854], MLN/169/7
426. Milne to Newcastle, 18 November [1854], MLN/169/7
427. Milne to Austin, 18 November 1854, MLN/169/7
428. Milne to Cunard, [18 November 1854], MLN/169/7
429. Milne to Christie, 18 November 1854, MLN/169/7
430. Milne to Houston Stewart, 18 November [1854], MLN/169/7
431. Milne to Horse Guards, 20 November [1854], MLN/169/7
432. Milne to Graham, *c.*21 November 1854, Ne C10261/2
433. Milne to James W. D. Dundas, [21 November 1854], MLN/156/ [9]
434. Milne to Newcastle, 21 November 1854, MLN/156/ [9]
435. Christie to Milne, 23 November 1854, MLN/156/1 [10]
436. Milne to Boxer, 26 November 1854, MLN/169/7
437. Milne to Craigie, 27 November [1854], MLN/169/7
438. Milne to Craigie, 28 November [1854], MLN/169/7
439. Milne to Houston Stewart, 29 November [1854], MLN/169/7
440. Newcastle to Milne, 1 December 1854, MLN/165/1
441. Milne to Bevis, 1 December [1854], MLN/169/7
442. Milne to Newcastle, [4 December 1854], Ne C10,371

443. Milne to Austin, 4 December [1854], MLN/169/8
444. Milne to Grant, 4 December [1854], MLN/169/8
445. Milne to Grant, 5 December [1854], MLN/169/8
446. Milne to Newcastle, 5 December [1854], MLN/169/8
447. Milne to Horse Guards, 6 December 1854, MLN/169/8
448. Milne to Boxer, 8 December 1854, MLN/169/8
449. Milne to Christie, 8 December 1854, MLN/169/8
450. Milne to Houston Stewart, 8 December 1854, MLN/169/8
451. Milne to Grant, 9 December 1854, MLN/169/8
452. Milne to Newcastle, 12 December 1854, Ne C10,372
453. Milne to Graham, 14 December 1854, MLN/156/4 [10]
454. Milne to Christie, 15 December 1854, MLN/169/8
455. Milne to James W. D. Dundas, 15 December 1854, MLN/169/8
456. Craigie to Milne, 15 December 1854, MLN/156/4 [18]
457. Milne to Christie, 18 December 1854, MLN/169/8
458. Milne to Houston Stewart, 18 December 1854, MLN/169/8
459. Boys to Milne, 22 December [1854], MLN/156/1 [11/2]
460. Milne to Mundy, 22 December [1854], Ne C10,373
461. Christie to Milne, 1 January 1855, MLN/156/1 [11/4]
462. Milne to Christie, 4 January 1855, MLN/169/8
463. Milne to the P&O Company, 5 January 1855, MLN/169/8
464. Christie to Milne, 8 January 1855, MLN/156/1 [11/1]
465. Milne to Neatheson and Company, 8 January 1855, MLN/169/8
466. Milne to Newcastle, 8 January 1855, MLN/156/4 [11]
467. Milne to Christie, 15 January 1855, MLN/169/9
468. Stirling to Milne, 17 January 1855, MLN/166/2
469. Milne to William Fanshawe Martin, 18 January [1855], MLN/169/9
470. Milne to West India Company, 18 January [1855], MLN/169/9
471. Christie to Milne, 19 January 1855, MLN/156/1 [12]
472. Milne to Stopford, 19 January 1855, MLN/169/9
473. Milne to Grant, 22 January [1855], MLN/169/9
474. Milne to Newcastle, 22 January [1855], MLN/169/9
475. Christie to Milne, 22 January 1855, MLN/156/1 [11/3]
476. Milne to Frederick Grey, 25 January 1855, MLN/169/9
477. Milne to Stirling, 29 January 1855, MLN/169/9
478. Milne to Houston Stewart, 29 January 1855, MLN/169/9
479. Milne to Newcastle, 31 January 1855, Ne C10,376
480. Milne to Lyons, 2 February 1855, MLN/156/4 [12]
481. Christie to Milne, 2 February 1855, MLN/156/1 [13]
482. Milne to Stopford, 2 February [1855], MLN/169/9
483. Christie to Milne, 5 February 1855, MLN/156/1 [14]

525. Milne to Wood, 15 June 1855, Add Mss 49532, fol. 103
526. Michael Seymour to Milne, 7 July 1855, MLN/165/11
527. Milne Memorandum on Commanders' Memorial, 19 July 1855, ADM1/5659
528. Milne Draft Circular on Acting Masters, 20 July 1855, ADM1/5660
529. Milne to Wood, 27 July 1855, Add Mss 49532, fol. 127
530. Milne to Fremantle, 28 July 1855, MLN/169/10
531. Milne to Tatham, 2 August [1855], MLN/169/10
532. Lyons to Milne, 18 [August] 1855, MLN/165/8
533. Milne to Fremantle, *c.*1 September 1855, MLN/169/10
534. Milne to Grant, 8 September 1855, MLN/169/10
535. Fremantle to Lyons, 17 September 1855, MLN/165/8
536. Lyons to Milne, 18 [September] 1855, MLN/165/8
537. Milne to Lyons, 18 September [1855], MLN/169/10
538. Milne to Fisher, 29 October [1855], MLN/169/10
539. Milne to Fremantle, 29 October 1855, MLN/169/10
540. Milne to Fremantle, Grey, and Stopford, 2 November [1855], MLN/169/10
541. Milne Minute on Proposed Alterations in Transporting Ordnance Stores, 2 November [1855], MLN/169/10
542. Milne to Saunders Dundas, 5 November 1855, MLN/169/10
543. Milne to Lyons, 6 November 1855, MLN/169/10
544. Milne to Maitland, 12 November 1855, MLN/169/10
545. Milne to Cochrane, 13 November 1855, MLN/169/10
546. Milne Instructions to the Transport Department, 15 November [1855], MLN/169/10
547. Milne to Sartorius, 16 November 1855, MLN/169/10
548. Milne to Austin, 17 November 1855, MLN/169/10
549. Milne Draft Instructions for Maitland, 10 December [1855], MLN/169/11
550. Milne Memorandum on Chaplains' Pay, 23 December 1855, MLN/169/11
551. Milne to Frederick Grey, 27 December [1855], MLN/169/11
552. Milne to Gibbons, 2 January 1856, MLN/169/11
553. Milne to Frederick Grey and Fremantle, 15 January 1856, MLN/169/11
554. Milne to Austin, *c.*1 February 1856, MLN/169/11
555. Milne to Tulloch, 7 February 1856, MLN/169/11
556. Tulloch to Milne, 8 February 1856, MLN/166/2
557. Milne Instructions to Superintendents of Transports, 15 February [1856], MLN/169/11

GENERAL INDEX

SHIP INDEX

In instances in which two ships bear the same name, the launch date of each appears in parentheses.

NAVY RECORDS SOCIETY
(FOUNDED 1893)

The Navy Records Society was established for the purpose of printing unpublished manuscripts and rare works of naval interest. Membership of the Society is open to all who are interested in naval history, and any person wishing to become a member should apply to the Hon. Secretary, Professor A. D. Lambert, Department of War Studies, King's College London, Strand, London WC2R 2LS, United Kingdom. The annual subscription is £30, which entitles the member to receive one free copy of each work issued by the Society in that year, and to buy earlier issues at reduced prices.

A list of works, available to members only, is shown below; very few copies are left of those marked with an asterisk. Volumes out of print are indicated by **OP**. Prices for works in print are available on application to Mrs Annette Gould, 5 Goodwood Close, Midhurst, West Sussex GU29 9JG, United Kingdom, to whom all enquiries concerning works in print should be sent. Those marked 'TS', 'SP' and 'A' are published for the Society by Temple Smith, Scolar Press and Ashgate, and are available to non-members from the Ashgate Publishing Group, Gower House, Croft Road, Aldershot, Hampshire GU11 3HR. Those marked 'A & U' are published by George Allen & Unwin, and are available to non-members only through bookshops.

Vol. 1. *State papers relating to the Defeat of the Spanish Armada, Anno 1588*, Vol. I, ed. Professor J. K. Laughton. TS.

Vol. 2. *State papers relating to the Defeat of the Spanish Armada, Anno 1588*, Vol. II, ed. Professor J. K. Laughton. TS.

Vol. 3. *Letters of Lord Hood, 1781–1783*, ed. D. Hannay. **OP**.

Vol. 4. *Index to James's Naval History*, by C. G. Toogood, ed. by the Hon. T. A. Brassey. **OP**.

Vol. 5. *Life of Captain Stephen Martin, 1666–1740*, ed. Sir Clements R. Markham. **OP**.

Vol. 6. *Journal of Rear Admiral Bartholomew James, 1752–1828*, ed. Professor J. K. Laughton & Cdr. J. Y. F. Sullivan. **OP**.

Vol. 7. *Hollond's Discourses of the Navy, 1638 and 1659*, ed. J. R. Tanner. **OP**.

Vol. 8. *Naval Accounts and Inventories in the Reign of Henry VII*, ed. M. Oppenheim. **OP**.

Vol. 9. *Journal of Sir George Rooke*, ed. O. Browning. **OP**.

Vol. 10. *Letters and Papers relating to the War with France 1512–1513*, ed. M. Alfred Spont. **OP**.

Vol. 11. *Papers relating to the Spanish War 1585–1587*, ed. Julian S. Corbett. TS.

Vol. 12. *Journals and Letters of Admiral of the Fleet Sir Thomas Byam Martin, 1773–1854*, Vol. II (see No. 24), ed. Admiral Sir R. Vesey Hamilton. **OP**.

Vol. 13. *Papers relating to the First Dutch War, 1652–1654*, Vol. I, ed. Dr S. R. Gardiner. **OP**.

Vol. 14. *Papers relating to the Blockade of Brest, 1803–1805*, Vol. I, ed. J. Leyland. **OP**.

Vol. 15. *History of the Russian Fleet during the Reign of Peter the Great, by a Contemporary Englishman*, ed. Admiral Sir Cyprian Bridge. **OP**.

Vol. 16. *Logs of the Great Sea Fights, 1794–1805*, Vol. I, ed. Vice Admiral Sir T. Sturges Jackson. **OP**.

Vol. 17. *Papers relating to the First Dutch War, 1652–1654*, ed. Dr S. R. Gardiner. **OP**.

*Vol. 18. *Logs of the Great Sea Fights*, Vol. II, ed. Vice Admiral Sir T. Sturges Jackson.

Vol. 19. *Journals and Letters of Admiral of the Fleet Sir Thomas Byam Martin*, Vol. II (see No. 24), ed. Admiral Sir R. Vesey Hamilton. **OP**.

Vol. 20. *The Naval Miscellany*, Vol. I, ed. Professor J. K. Laughton.

Vol. 21. *Papers relating to the Blockade of Brest, 1803–1805*, Vol. II, ed. J. Leyland. **OP**.

Vol. 22. *The Naval Tracts of Sir William Monson*, Vol. I, ed. M. Oppenheim. **OP**.

Vol. 23. *The Naval Tracts of Sir William Monson*, Vol. II, ed. M. Oppenheim. **OP**.

Vol. 24. *The Journals and Letters of Admiral of the Fleet Sir Thomas Byam Martin*, Vol. I, ed. Admiral Sir R. Vesey Hamilton. **OP**.

Vol. 25. *Nelson and the Neapolitan Jacobins*, ed. H. C. Gutteridge. **OP**.

Vol. 26. *A Descriptive Catalogue of the Naval MSS in the Pepysian Library*, Vol. I, ed. J. R. Tanner. **OP**.

Vol. 27. *A Descriptive Catalogue of the Naval MSS in the Pepysian Library*, Vol. II, ed. J. R. Tanner. **OP**.

Vol. 28. *The Correspondence of Admiral John Markham, 1801–1807*, ed. Sir Clements R. Markham. **OP**.

Vol. 29. *Fighting Instructions, 1530–1816*, ed. Julian S. Corbett. **OP**.

Vol. 30. *Papers relating to the First Dutch War, 1652–1654*, Vol. III, ed. Dr S. R. Gardiner & C. T. Atkinson. **OP**.

Vol. 31. *The Recollections of Commander James Anthony Gardner, 1775–1814*, ed. Admiral Sir R. Vesey Hamilton & Professor J. K. Laughton.

Vol. 32. *Letters and Papers of Charles, Lord Barham, 1758–1813*, ed. Professor Sir John Laughton.

Vol. 33. *Naval Songs and Ballads*, ed. Professor C. H. Firth. **OP**.

Vol. 34. *Views of the Battles of the Third Dutch War*, ed. by Julian S. Corbett. **OP**.

Vol. 35. *Signals and Instructions, 1776–1794*, ed. Julian S. Corbett. **OP**.

Vol. 36. *A Descriptive Catalogue of the Naval MSS in the Pepysian Library*, Vol III, ed. J. R. Tanner. **OP**.

Vol. 37. *Papers relating to the First Dutch War, 1652–1654*, Vol. IV, ed. C. T. Atkinson. **OP**.

Vol. 38. *Letters and Papers of Charles, Lord Barham, 1758–1813*, Vol. II, ed. Professor Sir John Laughton. **OP**.

Vol. 39. *Letters and Papers of Charles, Lord Barham, 1758–1813*, Vol. III, ed. Professor Sir John Laughton. **OP**.

Vol. 40. *The Naval Miscellany*, Vol. II, ed. Professor Sir John Laughton.

*Vol. 41. *Papers relating to the First Dutch War, 1652–1654*, Vol. V, ed. C. T. Atkinson.

Vol. 42. *Papers relating to the Loss of Minorca in 1756*, ed. Captain H. W. Richmond, R.N. **OP**.

*Vol. 43. *The Naval Tracts of Sir William Monson*, Vol. III, ed. M. Oppenheim.

Vol. 44. *The Old Scots Navy 1689–1710*, ed. James Grant. **OP**.

Vol. 45. *The Naval Tracts of Sir William Monson*, Vol. IV, ed. M. Oppenheim.

Vol. 46. *The Private Papers of George, 2nd Earl Spencer*, Vol. I, ed. Julian S. Corbett. **OP**.

Vol. 47. *The Naval Tracts of Sir William Monson*, Vol. V, ed. M. Oppenheim.

Vol. 48. *The Private Papers of George, 2nd Earl Spencer*, Vol. II, ed. Julian S. Corbett. **OP**.

Vol. 49. *Documents relating to Law and Custom of the Sea*, Vol. I, ed. R. G. Marsden. **OP**.

*Vol. 50. *Documents relating to Law and Custom of the Sea*, Vol. II, ed. R. G. Marsden.

Vol. 51. *Autobiography of Phineas Pett*, ed. W. G. Perrin. **OP**.

Vol. 52. *The Life of Admiral Sir John Leake*, Vol. I, ed. Geoffrey Callender.

Vol. 53. *The Life of Admiral Sir John Leake*, Vol. II, ed. Geoffrey Callender.

Vol. 54. *The Life and Works of Sir Henry Mainwaring*, Vol. I, ed. G. E. Manwaring.

Vol. 55. *The Letters of Lord St Vincent, 1801–1804*, Vol. I, ed. D. B. Smith. **OP**.

Vol. 56. *The Life and Works of Sir Henry Mainwaring*, Vol. II, ed. G. E. Manwaring & W. G. Perrin. **OP**.

Vol. 57. *A Descriptive Catalogue of the Naval MSS in the Pepysian Library*, Vol. IV, ed. Dr J. R. Tanner. **OP**.

Vol. 58. *The Private Papers of George, 2nd Earl Spencer*, Vol. III, ed. Rear Admiral H. W. Richmond. **OP**.

Vol. 59. *The Private Papers of George, 2nd Earl Spencer*, Vol. IV, ed. Rear Admiral H. W. Richmond. **OP**.

Vol. 60. *Samuel Pepys's Naval Minutes*, ed. Dr J. R. Tanner.

Vol. 61. *The Letters of Lord St Vincent, 1801–1804*, Vol. II, ed. D. B. Smith. **OP**.

Vol. 62. *Letters and Papers of Admiral Viscount Keith*, Vol. I, ed. W. G. Perrin. **OP**.

Vol. 63. *The Naval Miscellany*, Vol. III, ed. W. G. Perrin. **OP**.

Vol. 64. *The Journal of the 1st Earl of Sandwich*, ed. R. C. Anderson. **OP**.

*Vol. 65. *Boteler's Dialogues*, ed. W. G. Perrin.

Vol. 66. *Papers relating to the First Dutch War, 1652–1654*, Vol. VI (with index), ed. C. T. Atkinson.

*Vol. 67. *The Byng Papers*, Vol. I, ed. W. C. B. Tunstall.

*Vol. 68. *The Byng Papers*, Vol. II, ed. W. C. B. Tunstall.

Vol. 69. *The Private Papers of John, Earl of Sandwich*, Vol. I, ed. G. R. Barnes & Lt. Cdr. J. H. Owen, R.N. Corrigenda to *Papers relating to the First Dutch War, 1652–1654, Vols I–VI*, ed. Captain A. C. Dewar, R.N. **OP**.

Vol. 70. *The Byng Papers*, Vol. III, ed. W. C. B. Tunstall.

Vol. 71. *The Private Papers of John, Earl of Sandwich*, Vol. II, ed. G. R. Barnes & Lt. Cdr. J. H. Owen, R.N. **OP**.

Vol. 72. *Piracy in the Levant, 1827–1828*, ed. Lt. Cdr. C. G. Pitcairn Jones, R.N. **OP**.

Vol. 73. *The Tangier Papers of Samuel Pepys*, ed. Edwin Chappell.

Vol. 74. *The Tomlinson Papers*, ed. J. G. Bullocke.

Vol. 75. *The Private Papers of John, Earl of Sandwich*, Vol. III, ed. G. R. Barnes & Cdr. J. H. Owen, R.N. **OP**.

Vol. 76. *The Letters of Robert Blake*, ed. the Rev. J. R. Powell. **OP**.

*Vol. 77. *Letters and Papers of Admiral the Hon. Samuel Barrington*, Vol. I, ed. D. Bonner-Smith.

Vol. 78. *The Private Papers of John, Earl of Sandwich*, Vol. IV, ed. G. R. Barnes & Cdr. J. H. Owen, R.N. **OP**.

*Vol. 79. *The Journals of Sir Thomas Allin, 1660–1678*, Vol. I *1660–1666*, ed. R. C. Anderson.

Vol. 80. *The Journals of Sir Thomas Allin, 1660–1678*, Vol. II *1667–1678*, ed. R. C. Anderson.

Vol. 81. *Letters and Papers of Admiral the Hon. Samuel Barrington*, Vol. II, ed. D. Bonner-Smith. **OP**.

Vol. 82. *Captain Boteler's Recollections, 1808–1830*, ed. D. Bonner-Smith. **OP**.

Vol. 83. *Russian War, 1854. Baltic and Black Sea: Official Correspondence*, ed. D. Bonner-Smith & Captain A. C. Dewar, R.N. **OP**.

Vol. 84. *Russian War, 1855. Baltic: Official Correspondence*, ed. D. Bonner-Smith. **OP**.

Vol. 85. *Russian War, 1855. Black Sea: Official Correspondence*, ed. Captain A.C. Dewar, R.N. **OP**.

Vol. 86. *Journals and Narratives of the Third Dutch War*, ed. R. C. Anderson. **OP**.

Vol. 87. *The Naval Brigades in the Indian Mutiny, 1857–1858*, ed. Cdr. W. B. Rowbotham, R.N. **OP**.

Vol. 88. *Patee Byng's Journal*, ed. J. L. Cranmer-Byng. **OP**.

*Vol. 89. *The Sergison Papers, 1688–1702*, ed. Cdr. R. D. Merriman, R.I.N.

Vol. 90. *The Keith Papers*, Vol. II, ed. Christopher Lloyd. **OP**.

Vol. 91. *Five Naval Journals, 1789–1817*, ed. Rear Admiral H. G. Thursfield. **OP**.

Vol. 92. *The Naval Miscellany*, Vol. IV, ed. Christopher Lloyd. **OP**.

Vol. 93. *Sir William Dillon's Narrative of Professional Adventures, 1790–1839*, Vol. I *1790–1802*, ed. Professor Michael Lewis. **OP**.

Vol. 94. *The Walker Expedition to Quebec, 1711*, ed. Professor Gerald S. Graham. **OP**.

Vol. 95. *The Second China War, 1856–1860*, ed. D. Bonner-Smith & E. W. R. Lumby. **OP**.

Vol. 96. *The Keith Papers, 1803–1815*, Vol. III, ed. Professor Christopher Lloyd.

Vol. 97. *Sir William Dillon's Narrative of Professional Adventures, 1790–1839*, Vol. II *1802–1839*, ed. Professor Michael Lewis. **OP**.

Vol. 98. *The Private Correspondence of Admiral Lord Collingwood*, ed. Professor Edward Hughes. **OP**.

Vol. 99. *The Vernon Papers, 1739–1745*, ed. B. McL. Ranft. **OP**.

Vol. 100. *Nelson's Letters to his Wife and Other Documents*, ed. Lt. Cdr. G. P. B. Naish, R.N.V.R. **OP**.
Vol. 101. *A Memoir of James Trevenen, 1760–1790*, ed. Professor Christopher Lloyd & R. C. Anderson. **OP**.
Vol. 102. *The Papers of Admiral Sir John Fisher*, Vol. I, ed. Lt. Cdr. P. K. Kemp, R.N. **OP**.
Vol. 103. *Queen Anne's Navy*, ed. Cdr. R. D. Merriman, R.I.N. **OP**.
Vol. 104. *The Navy and South America, 1807–1823*, ed. Professor Gerald S. Graham & Professor R. A. Humphreys.
Vol. 105. *Documents relating to the Civil War, 1642–1648*, ed. The Rev. J. R. Powell & E. K. Timings. **OP**.
Vol. 106. *The Papers of Admiral Sir John Fisher*, Vol. II, ed. Lt. Cdr. P. K. Kemp, R.N. **OP**.
Vol. 107. *The Health of Seamen*, ed. Professor Christopher Lloyd.
Vol. 108. *The Jellicoe Papers*, Vol. I *1893–1916*, ed. A. Temple Patterson.
Vol. 109. *Documents relating to Anson's Voyage round the World, 1740–1744*, ed. Dr Glyndwr Williams. **OP**.
Vol. 110. *The Saumarez Papers: The Baltic, 1808–1812*, ed. A. N. Ryan. **OP**.
Vol. 111. *The Jellicoe Papers*, Vol. II *1916–1925*, ed. Professor A. Temple Patterson.
Vol. 112. *The Rupert and Monck Letterbook, 1666*, ed. The Rev. J. R. Powell & E. K. Timings.
Vol. 113. *Documents relating to the Royal Naval Air Service*, Vol. I (1908–1918), ed. Captain S. W. Roskill, R.N.
*Vol. 114. *The Siege and Capture of Havana, 1762*, ed. Professor David Syrett.
Vol. 115. *Policy and Operations in the Mediterranean, 1912–1914*, ed. E. W. R. Lumby. **OP**.
Vol. 116. *The Jacobean Commissions of Enquiry, 1608 and 1618*, ed. Dr A. P. McGowan.
Vol. 117. *The Keyes Papers*, Vol. I *1914–1918*, ed. Professor Paul Halpern.
Vol. 118. *The Royal Navy and North America: The Warren Papers, 1736–1752*, ed. Dr Julian Gwyn. **OP**.
Vol. 119. *The Manning of the Royal Navy: Selected Public Pamphlets, 1693–1873*, ed. Professor John Bromley.
Vol. 120. *Naval Administration, 1715–1750*, ed. Professor D. A. Baugh.
Vol. 121. *The Keyes Papers*, Vol. II *1919–1938*, ed. Professor Paul Halpern.

Vol. 122. *The Keyes Papers*, Vol. III *1939–1945*, ed. Professor Paul Halpern.

Vol. 123. *The Navy of the Lancastrian Kings: Accounts and Inventories of William Soper, Keeper of the King's Ships, 1422–1427*, ed. Dr Susan Rose.

Vol. 124. *The Pollen Papers: the Privately Circulated Printed Works of Arthur Hungerford Pollen, 1901–1916*, ed. Professor Jon T. Sumida. A. & U.

Vol. 125. *The Naval Miscellany*, Vol. V, ed. Dr N. A. M. Rodger. A & U.

Vol. 126. *The Royal Navy in the Mediterranean, 1915–1918*, ed. Professor Paul Halpern. TS.

Vol. 127. *The Expedition of Sir John Norris and Sir Francis Drake to Spain and Portugal, 1589*, ed. Professor R. B. Wernham. TS.

Vol. 128. *The Beatty Papers*, Vol. I *1902–1918*, ed. Professor B. McL. Ranft. SP.

Vol. 129. *The Hawke Papers: A Selection, 1743–1771*, ed. Dr R. F. Mackay. SP.

Vol. 130. *Anglo-American Naval Relations, 1917–1919*, ed. Michael Simpson. SP.

Vol. 131. *British Naval Documents, 1204–1960*, ed. Professor John B. Hattendorf, Dr Roger Knight, Alan Pearsall, Dr Nicholas Rodger & Professor Geoffrey Till. SP.

Vol. 132. *The Beatty Papers*, Vol. II *1916–1927*, ed. Professor B. McL. Ranft. SP

Vol. 133. *Samuel Pepys and the Second Dutch War*, transcribed by Professor William Matthews & Dr Charles Knighton; ed. Robert Latham. SP.

Vol. 134. *The Somerville Papers*, ed. Michael Simpson, with the assistance of John Somerville. SP.

Vol. 135. *The Royal Navy in the River Plate, 1806–1807*, ed. John D. Grainger. SP.

Vol. 136. *The Collective Naval Defence of the Empire, 1900–1940*, ed. Nicholas Tracy. A.

Vol. 137. *The Defeat of the Enemy Attack on Shipping, 1939–1945*, ed. Eric Grove. A.

Vol. 138. *Shipboard Life and Organisation, 1731–1815*, ed. Brian Lavery. A.

Vol. 139. *The Battle of the Atlantic and Signals Intelligence: U-boat Situations and Trends, 1941–1945*, ed. Professor David Syrett. A.

Vol. 140. *The Cunningham Papers*, Vol. I: *The Mediterranean Fleet, 1939–1942*, ed. Michael Simpson. A.

Vol. 141. *The Channel Fleet and the Blockade of Brest, 1793–1801*, ed. Roger Morriss. A.

Vol. 142. *The Submarine Service, 1900–1918*, ed. Nicholas Lambert. A.

Vol. 143. *Letters and Papers of Professor Sir John Knox Laughton (1830–1915)*, ed. Andrew Lambert. A.

Vol. 144. *The Battle of the Atlantic and Signals Intelligence: U-Boat Tracking Papers 1941–1947*, ed. Professor David Syrett. A.

Vol. 145. *The Maritime Blockade of Germany in the Great War: The Northern Patrol, 1914–1918*, ed. John D. Grainger. A.

Vol. 146. *The Naval Miscellany: Volume VI*, ed. Michael Duffy. A.

Occasional Publications:

Vol. 1. *The Commissioned Sea Officers of the Royal Navy, 1660–1815*, ed. Professor David Syrett & Professor R. L. DiNardo. SP.

Vol. 2. *The Anthony Roll of Henry VIII's Navy*, ed. C. S. Knighton and D. M. Loades. A.